Public Health
and
Preventive
Medicine
in
Canada

C. P. Shah
third edition

Public Health and Preventive Medicine in Canada

Chandrakant P. Shah, MD, DCH, MRCP (Glas), FRCPC, SM (Hyg), FACPM, FAAP

Professor
Department of Preventive Medicine and Biostatistics,
Department of Health Administration, Department of Paediatrics, and
Department of Family and Community Medicine; Faculty of Medicine,
and
Faculty of Social Work,
University of Toronto
and
Active Staff, The Hospital for Sick Children, Toronto

with

Sunil S. Shah, BSc (Hons), MHSc

with

Rajiv R. Shah, B.A.

PRINTED BY THE UNIVERSITY OF TORONTO PRESS

ISBN 0-9694044-2-5

Canadian Cataloguing in Publication Data

Shah, Chandrakant P. (Chandrakant Padamshi), 1936-
    Public health and preventive medicine in Canada

3rd ed.
Includes bibliographical references and index.
ISBN 0-9694044-2-5

1. Public Health - Canada 2. Medical care -
Canada 3. Medicine, Preventive - Canada.
I. Shah, Sunil S. (Sunil Steven), 1969-
II. Shah, Rajiv R., 1971-   . III Title.

RA449.S53   1994   362.1'0971   C94-930924-9

Printed for Dr. C. P. Shah by the University of Toronto Press in support of
the University's Scholarly Publishing Programme.

CONTRIBUTING AUTHOR

**Marilyn L. James MD, FRCPC,
AAFP(BE), MPH, MHP, FAFPHM, FRACMA,**

Associate Medical Officer of Health
Hamilton Wenworth County Health Department

FOREWORD

Canadian Health Sciences students need a Canadian textbook of public health and preventive medicine, and Dr. Shah has produced a promising one. International textbooks are fine - often excellent - for methods and general principles, but are understandably lacking in material about Canadians and their health services. It is important to have this material placed in a Canadian context: things like the Lalonde report, multicultural and aboriginal health, provincial variations and our distinctive health insurance system.

This books offers a comprehensive treatment of the speciality perhaps too comprehensive in a few places, but this thoroughness will make it useful as a reference work as well as a textbook. The book treats some topics peculiar to public heath which are not well handled in traditional epidemiology texts (e.g., assessment of health status), and recognizes recent developments in health policy.

This book continues Dr. Shah's earlier work in strengthening the speciality of Community Health through promoting undergraduate and postgraduate education. We owe him our thanks. I think that the book will be useful to students and teachers in Community Health Sciences; we must hit Dr. Shah hard with feedback to make the next edition even better.

Robert A. Spasoff, MD, FRCPC
Professor
Department of Epidemiology and Community Medicine
Faculty of Medicine
University of Ottawa

February 1994

PREFACE TO THIRD EDITION

The diverse nature of the content of public health and preventive medicine has made it difficult to integrate and write a concise textbook for undergraduate students in health sciences who intend to practise their professions in Canada or students interested in an overview of Canadian health and the health-care system. While a number of individuals have written texts on different aspects of this topic, none has been written for Canadian undergraduates. As someone who, for the past 20 years, has been intimately involved in teaching undergraduate, graduate and postgraduate students in different health sciences disciplines and who has been involved with the licensing examination and the development of educational objectives in community health for different disciplines, I had felt the necessity for such a book. The enthusiastic response which the first two editions received from students and teachers across the country is the testimony to my original belief.

This book reviews public health and preventive medicine for those preparing for the Qualifying Examination of the Medical Council of Canada (LMCC). It may also be used by foreign physicians preparing for the Evaluating Examination for Graduates of Foreign Medical Schools of the Medical Council of Canada. There are some deliberate omissions in this book as far as detail is concerned as excellent textbooks on subjects such as biostatistics and epidemiology are available. In other instances, details are omitted because of different legislation in different Canadian jurisdictions. However, general principles are covered. Anyone desiring to study a particular topic in greater depth is advised to consult one of several comprehensive textbooks of community medicine that are available.

In preparation for the third edition, a number of collegues, teachers and students were ask to provide comments on improving this book, and I am happy to say that their input was very constructive. While I have tried my best, I am sure there are still shortcomings, one of which is difficult to rectify. Many students have pointed out that data on health status and health-care delivery are not up to date. The usual sources from which data are obtained have a lag time of approximately five years. In the third edition, most chapters have been updated and the book has been reorganized and expanded. In the last few years considerable new information has become available in Canada on health status, health promotion, environmental health and health services. Similarly, many provinces have reviewed their health-care systems and have charted new courses. To reflect this new reality a number of chapters have been added. I would like to add a word of caution to new readers. The first two chapters of the book are dense and synoptic in nature and are not intended to replace any standard text book on the subjects covered. A detailed index lists the relevant page numbers for quick reference and Appendix I outlines educational objectives.

I am indebted to many individuals across the country for their support and comments. While this list does not include everyone who has made contributions, I would like to offer thanks to: Drs. R. Jin, T. Ostbye, D. Raphael, L. Panaro, G.

Liss, E. Vayda, R. Deber, M. Chipman, and R. Spasoff. Special thanks to Dr. Marilyn James for her contribution to many chapters and for researching material, and to my son Rajiv for helping with preparing summaries and checking references for manuscripts. I am indebted to Mrs. A. Poley and Mr. O. Prowse for their efforts in editing and Mr. D. Alland, Mr. A. Shortell and Ms. B. Rose from the University of Toronto Press for the helpful suggestions for the lay-out of the book. I thank Drs. K. Glasgow and B. Warashawsky for the arduous task of proof-reading the material. The typing, with endless revisions, was done by Ms. S. Tomlinson, and formatting, graphics and the production of camera-ready copy was done by Mr. D. Hore and my son Sunil, all of whom deserves special thanks for their efforts and deligence. Finally, I thank my wife for her patience during the process.

C.P. Shah
University of Toronto
Toronto, Ontario
February 1994

Dedicated to my mother-in-law and my mother and my wife

The late Mrs. Samjuben J. Parekh
and
Mrs. Surajben P. Shah
and
Dr. Sudha C. Shah

CONTENTS

Part 1: Health and Disease

CHAPTER ONE
Concepts, Determinants and Promotion of Health

CHAPTER TWO
Measurement and Investigation

CHAPTER FIVE
Health Status and Consequences

CHAPTER SIX
Health of Special Groups

CHAPTER SEVEN
Chronic Diseases and Injuries

CHAPTER EIGHT
Communicable Diseases

CHAPTER NINE
Environmental Health

CHAPTER TEN
Occupational Health and Disease

CHAPTER ELEVEN
Periodic Health Examinations

Part 3: Canada's Health-Care System

CHAPTER TWELVE
Evolution of National Health Insurance

CHAPTER THIRTEEN
Federal and Provincial Health Organizations

CHAPTER FOURTEEN
Local Health Services

CHAPTER FIFTEEN
Resources and Expenditures

CHAPTER SIXTEEN
Emerging Issues in Health Care Delivery

CHAPTER SEVENTEEN
Regulation of Health Professionals

Appendices and Index

Part 1

Health and Disease

CHAPTER ONE
Concepts, Determinants and Promotion of Health

Many diseases have been contained or almost eradicated in Canada with the advent of better living conditions, the availability of antibiotics, new technology and the universality of health care. Mortality in the population has been drastically reduced and life span has increased. Chronic diseases, however, have emerged as an important health concern. With these transitions, our concepts of health and disease have changed. The focus of health care is shifting towards disease prevention, health promotion and "caring" rather than "curing." In this chapter we describe modern concepts of health and disease or illness, the determinants of health and disease in the population and newer approaches towards the promotion and maintenance of health of the population.

1.   CONCEPTS OF HEALTH AND DISEASE

1.1.   CONTEMPORARY DEFINITIONS OF HEALTH

Health is multidimensional: it is not merely the presence or absence of disease but also has social, psychological and cultural determinants and consequences. In 1948, the World Health Organization (WHO) was the first to acknowledge the multidimensional nature of health. The WHO defined **health** as: *"A complete state of physical, mental and social well-being and not merely the absence of illness."*[1]

More recently, the WHO has developed a new definition of health which recognizes the inextricable links between an individual and her/his environment. This is a **"socio-ecological"** definition. As such, **health** is defined as: *"The ability to identify and to realize aspirations, to satisfy needs, and to change or cope with the environment. Health is therefore a resource for everyday life, not the objective of living. Health is a positive concept emphasizing social and personal resources, as well as physical capacities."*[2] Measures of health need to incorporate these distinct dimensions of human experience and determinants of health are more than biological. Health, therefore, involves more than just the integrity of the body; it encompasses social and political concerns and the relationship of individuals to the environment in which they live. From this perspective, health is not just the responsibility of the traditional "health" sector, but of all sectors, institutions and organizations that may influence the well-being of individuals and communities. Furthermore, the "new" definition of health provides the foundation for the developing concept of "health promotion" which was defined in the First International Conference on Health Promotion, held in Ottawa in 1986. (The conference declaration has been known as the "Ottawa Charter for Health Promotion.") Its simple summary definition of **health promotion** is: *"The process of enabling people to increase control over, and to improve, their health."* Health promotion efforts thus attempt to increase the degree of control which individuals and communities have over their health and the determinants of health.

1.2.   CONCEPTS OF DISEASE AND ITS CONSEQUENCES

The strength of the current "broad" definition of health is that it includes psychosocial as well as biophysical dimensions. "**Disease**" refers to abnormal, medically defined changes in the structure or functioning of the human body, while "**illness**" (or "**sickness**") refers to the individual's experience or subjective perception of lack of physical and/or mental well-being and consequent inability to function normally in social roles.

Disease and illness have their consequences; a useful systemic taxonomy was developed by Wood[3] for the WHO. He defines three concepts which refer to distinct and important dimensions of human experience in the context of disease. **Impairment** is defined as "any loss or abnormality of psychological, physiological or anatomical structure or function." **Disability** is "any restriction or lack of ability to perform an activity in a manner or within the range considered normal for a human being." **Handicap** is defined as "the disadvantage for a given individual, arising out of impairment and disability, that limits or prevents the fulfilment of a role that is normal (depending on age, sex and social and cultural factors) for that individual as determined by society." Consequently, "impairment" refers to changes in the individual's body, "disability" to changes in what the individual can and cannot do, and "handicap" to changes in their relationship with the physical and social environment. According to Wood, handicap can only be truly understood through sociologic enquiry. These concepts are linked dynamically in the following way:

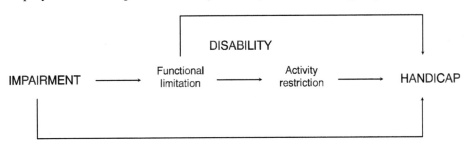

The relationships between impairment, disability and handicap are not necessarily direct. Disability and/or handicap may result from impairment and handicap may be the outcome of disability, but this is not necessarily the case. Nor is there any necessary relationship between the severity of impairment and disability and the extent of handicap experienced. For example, a recent study of people with multiple sclerosis found that the psychosocial handicaps they experienced were not related to the severity of the underlying disease.[4] Similarly, a study of individuals with chronic respiratory disease found that clinical measures of lung function were not good predictors of disability and that there was considerable variation in the extent of handicap associated with a given level of disability.[5] This highlights the fact that these relationships are mediated by social, cultural and other factors.

The conceptual distinctions made in this scheme are important in that they point to the many ways in which the well-being of people with various kinds of disorders may be maximized. Clinical medicine has as its focus the limitation of impairment, rehabilitation is concerned with limiting disability and maximizing independent functioning, and social welfare mechanisms modify the disadvantage experienced by people with impairments and disabilities. For many persons with chronic and disabling disorders, minimizing the social impact of their disease is the primary route to improving the well-being of both patient and family.

Illness behaviour can be defined as any activity undertaken by individuals who perceive they have a potential health problem for the purpose of defining their state of health and discovering and undertaking an appropriate remedy. The study of illness behaviour addresses the following question: in the presence of signs and symptoms, what will a person do, and why? This often, but not always, involves the use of medical care. The significance of illness behaviour is that it determines the volume of professional services used as they are currently provided by the health-care system. There is a wealth of evidence to show that the majority of signs and symptoms people experience are not brought to the attention of a medical professional but are dealt with in alternative ways. This phenomenon is known as the "clinical iceberg" and means that there is always a gap between the need and demand for medical care.

The clinical iceberg is important for two reasons. First, many people tolerate symptoms which may be painful or otherwise distressing but which may well respond to medical treatment. Secondly, it means that cases of a particular disorder which eventually present for medical treatment may not be representative of cases of the disorder in the population as a whole. Here, it is crucial to distinguish between factors related to the onset of the illness and factors related to the seeking of medical care. Numerous factors have been shown to be related to illness behaviour. Level of medical knowledge, the perception of the costs and benefits associated with a medical consultation and the influence of lay-referral networks are of some significance. However, one of the most important factors is **cultural variation in perception of illness**.

People of differing cultural backgrounds interpret signs and symptoms in different ways. What may be regarded as part of the normal pattern of everyday life by one cultural group may indicate illness to another. It is also the case that there are cultural differences in ways of managing health problems of various kinds. Some cultural groups have highly developed systems of ethno-medicine; traditional and professional healers may be consulted according to the nature of the problem and whether or not it is recognized by scientific medicine. **Culture** is likely to play an important role in the formation and expression of health beliefs. The beliefs about health and illness held by individuals and groups are now seen as being very important with respect to the seeking of medical care, patient-practitioner communication, patient responses to consultation and the degree of patient compliance with medical advice.

Compliance is the extent to which an individual follows the advice given to them by a health-care provider or health educator. Compliance is a major factor in determining the success or failure of treatment regimens and/or lifestyle change directed toward improving health. Whether the individual will follow the advice depends upon many factors including the nature of the health problem, the type, length and the cost of the regimen, the make up of an individual, and the pattern of communication between the provider and the individual. Although the compliance with therapeutic regimens of individual depends upon the severity, duration and outcome of a disease, it not always predictable. However, in lifestyle changes such as smoking cessation, which require major effort and where the benefits are not immediate, the compliance rates are lower. Similarly, patients with psychiatric illness have very low compliance rates. Compliance is improved when the provider does not maintain a condescending attitude towards clients, does not use professional jargon while explaining the need for treatment, and provides enough time to clients for queries. There are some general assumptions about the rate of adherence to a treatment regimen among the patient population. The **Rule of One-Third** states that about one-third will totally comply with treatment, one-third will comply partially and the remaining third will not comply. Models that explain or predict the likelihood of compliance with **health education** efforts will be described later in this chapter under "Health Promotion Stratagies - Education."

1.3.   THEORIES OF DISEASE CAUSATION

Just as definitions of health have changed over time, so have theories regarding the nature and causes of disease. Recently the role ascribed to social and psychological factors in the causal processes leading to disease has received increasing attention. Underlying much of what constitutes medical practice is the **Biomechanical/Biomedical Model**. This has its roots in the Cartesian revolution of the eighteenth century in which mind and body were seen as separate entities, the body being a physical entity which was activated by mental processes. According to this view, the body is akin to a machine which can be corrected when things go wrong by procedures designed to repair damage or restore the functioning of its component parts. These procedures involve neutralizing the specific agents causing disease or modifying the pathological processes responsible for disease. Thus the model focuses on the causes and treatment of ill health and disease in terms of biological cause and effect. This approach largely ignores the part played by social, psychological and economic factors in disease onset and recovery. Even in a specialty such as psychiatry, the biomedical model has prevailed in explaining abnormal behaviour. Genetic abnormalities and problems with the biochemistry or physical structure of the brain are some of the popular explanations from the biomedical perspective.

The Biomechanical/Biomedical model is fully compatible with the **Germ Theory of Disease** which emerged at the end of the 19th century. Although the idea that disease was caused by a transmissible agent had been around since the 16th century, it was verified only during the latter half of the 19th century. The work of Pasteur and Koch showed that these agents were living organisms which enter the body via food, water or air. From this theory emerged the **Doctrine of Specific Etiology:** the idea that each disease has a single and specific cause. The Germ Theory of Disease seems to suggest that the mere introduction of an organism into a community is sufficient to cause disease. This is clearly not the case; we are exposed to a wide variety of organisms yet rarely succumb to disease. Consequently, it is incorrect to designate an organism or other noxious agent as **the** cause of disease. From an epidemiologic point of view, such an agent is a "necessary but not sufficient" cause, since suitable conditions, with respect to the host and the environment, must be present for disease to develop.[6,7] The **epidemiological triangle** portrays the interaction between agent, host and environment. The **agent** may be chemical (e.g., lead), biological (e.g., bacteria), or physical (e.g., violence). **Host** factors may be genetic or acquired and influence susceptibility to disease, while **environmental** factors may be biologic, social or physical and affect exposure and susceptibility. From this point of view, all diseases are multifactorial and can be prevented by procedures which modify either the host or the environment.

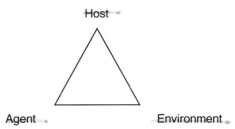

Often, in chronic degenerative disorders such as heart disease, no single agent can be identified. In order to explain disorders of this type MacMahon and Pugh introduced the idea of a **web of causation**.[8] Here, diseases such as heart disease develop through the interactions of many factors which form complex, interweaving chains. These factors may be biophysical, social or psychological and may promote or inhibit the development of the disease in question. For example, some of the factors implicated in heart disease are diet, smoking, physical inactivity, stress, Type A personality, obesity, cholesterol levels, hypertension and diabetes. Some of these factors have also been associated with the onset of other disorders such as cancer.

More recently, the **theory of general susceptibility** has been developed to explain why some social groups are more vulnerable to disease in general. For example, single, divorced and widowed men have consistently higher mortality rates than married men. One explanation for these differences is that marital status is associated with a wide variety of psychological and lifestyle factors, some of which are related to the risk of disease and death. There is also an accumulating body of research which shows that a lack of social support or close social and emotional ties increases vulnerability to disease and death. This work is a direct challenge to the doctrine of specific etiology. In this susceptibility theory, non-specific social and psychological factors are associated with a variety of health outcomes.

2.   DETERMINANTS OF HEALTH

Traditionally, providers of health care working in hospitals, such as medical practitioners and nurses, have been concerned primarily with the diagnosis and treatment of existing disease in individuals. Thus, the Biomedical Model has been pre-eminent. It has been widely believed that the quantity and quality of services available to individuals from such health-care providers are the chief factors in determining the health of the population. Furthermore, significant changes in health outcomes (such as decreasing morbidity and mortality rates) have been generally attributed to improvements in medical care. More recently, however, as previously explained, this view has been challenged and gradually replaced by the more comprehensive concepts of health. The inspiration for a broader view of the factors influencing health status has come from two main sources.

First, critical assessment of the recent history of disease has revealed that major infectious diseases such as tuberculosis and cholera, which were the leading causes of death in western societies at the turn of the century, began to decline in importance long before the introduction of effective therapy. Improvements in sanitation and general living conditions were much more important than medical intervention in reducing mortality due to these scourges. Secondly, evaluation of the factors underlying today's major causes of death and disability has been illuminating. For example, motor vehicle accidents, the major cause of death and potential-years-of-life-lost in young adults, are largely the result of self-imposed risks and lifestyle habits. Mortality caused by accidents cannot be reduced by traditional forms of medical treatment, but rather by changes in behaviour, such as increased caution, sobriety, and use of seat belts. Therefore, a concept of health must include other factors in addition to traditional curative medicine.

A Canadian example of a more comprehensive view of the determinants of health is the **Health Field Concept** put forward in 1974 by Marc Lalonde, then Minister of Health, in "A New Perspective on the Health of Canadians."[9] The Lalonde document outlined four elements which interact to determine the health of Canadians: **Human Biology**, **Environment**, **Lifestyle** and the **Health Care Organization**. More recently, the fields have been modified to incorporate psychosocial factors such as gender and ethnicity. The fields are described below.

2.1. HUMAN BIOLOGY

Human Biology encompasses those aspects of health (both mental and physical) which are determined by the organic structure and physiological functioning of the human body. The **genetic make up** of the individual determines the likelihood of inherited disorders and the predisposition to later acquired diseases. The individual's constitution is also a determinant of **susceptibility to risk factors** arising from certain lifestyles and environments. "Environmental sensitivity," for example, is one health condition that is little understood, although it is increasingly recognized as important. Changes in the human body due to **maturation** and **aging** are also important factors that can interact with the other three Health Field elements in determining the individual's state of health. The human biology element has many facets, only a few of which are adequately understood. The medical and allied sciences have made great progress in understanding the complex process of the human body and mind, but much remains to be elucidated.

2.2. THE ENVIRONMENT

The environment, as described in the Lalonde document Health Field concept, includes all factors external to the human body which may affect health. These factors are broadly categorized here as being of the "physical" environment. More recently the concept of environment has expanded and includes the "psychosocial" environment. Individuals often have little or no control over the presence of environmental risk factors or risk conditions but, depending on the factors, may be able to exercise some control over the degree of exposure.

2.2.1. The Physical Environment

Factors in the physical environment include the quality of air, water and soil; the safety of food, drugs and other products which humans consume or are exposed to; the physical handling and disposal of waste; and the control of excessive noise. The physical environment can affect human health directly by exposure to potentially hazardous agents such as chemicals or radiation, or indirectly by, for example, global warming, which is predicted to result in diminishing food production.   A major challenge is the development of methods of economic production which sustain a healthy environment ("sustainable development") as a legacy for our children's future.

The physical environment is not only outdoors but also indoors, including important issues such as the ergonomics of workplaces and indoor air quality (e.g., so-called "sick building syndrome").

2.2.2. The Psychosocial Environment

The psychosocial environment also contributes to health and ill-health. Social and physical environments—as are manifested in the places where people live and work, their education, and their income and social supports—have a major impact on people's health. In attempting to identify the role of social and psychological factors in disease onset, researchers have either adopted an historical perspective investigating changes in the health of modern populations over time, or have focused on specific factors which predispose an individual to illness. The best example of the former is provided by the work of McKeown[10] who showed by careful historical analysis that the massive decline in mortality from infectious disease during the 18th and 19th centuries was not due to any specific medical interventions but was the product of social and environmental progress.   In particular, improvements in agricultural production led to better diets and a population more resistant to infectious disease. In addition, improvements in sanitation and the development of clean water supplies reduced the exposure of the population to infectious organisms. By the time medicine had developed specific therapies for diseases such as tuberculosis, for example, 90% of the decline in mortality from that disease had already occurred and was due to improvement in social environments.

Studies on contemporary populations have looked at factors such as bereavement, social mobility, migration, cultural change, income, unemployment and hazards involved in the organization of work. A systematic approach to social factors and illness is to be found in research on stressful life events and health. The assumption is that life changes, particularly those involving some form of loss, are stressful and work via a variety of mechanisms to render an individual vulnerable to health problems. Such events have been found to be related to the onset of psychiatric disorders such as depression[11] and a range of physical illnesses. However, whether or not life stress does lead to some form of illness seems to depend on the presence of one or more mediating factors. The personality characteristics of individuals, their coping styles and the presence of social support are the main variables which have been shown to have some influence on the response to life stress. This is a complex area conceptually and methodologically, but current research does indicate that an individual's social circumstances frequently exert a significant influence over health status.

A recent Ontario report on the determinants of health, from the Premier's Council on Health, Well-Being and Social Justice, cites a number of studies which conclude that both societal inequalities in income and **powerlessness**, or lack of perceived control, contribute to ill-health in a community.[12] Data from Organization for Economic Cooperation and Development (OECD) countries indicate the lowest infant mortality and highest life expectancy occurs where there are the least income inequalities. The study by Marmot et al. in the United Kingdom (UK) identified a strong association between the incidence of heart disease and the lack of decision-making latitude in the workplace. Finally, the UK Whitehall study demonstrated a clear relationship between one's place in the social hierarchy (as determined by position in the civil service) and mortality risk.

Inequities may be horizontal, in which there is unequal distribution of resources, or vertical, whereby those with a disadvantage do not have resources to reduce differentials. Some social groups have markedly better health than others, with lower death rates and less illness and disability. It is for this reason that such inequities have recently been identified by the Federal Government and the Government of Ontario as a major health policy issue.

Socioeconomic status is the variable most commonly used in the analysis of inequities in health. All industrialized nations have some system for classifying their populations into socioeconomic strata or groups. Such systems may be based on **occupation, education** or **income**, or some combination of all three. There are, of course, a number of other important variables which are related to health and mortality. Differences in health can also be connected to geographic location, gender, race or ethnic origin and employment status.

In Canada, until recently, relatively little data existed which documented the links between health and socioeconomic status. Data showing provincial differences in health are more readily available. Nevertheless, the analysis of mortality data and data obtained from the Canada Health Survey provides evidence of the poorer health status of lower socioeconomic groups.[13] In addition, Wilkins and Adams[14] have used composite health indicators to show that overall life expectancy, years of life free of disability and quality-adjusted-life-years are directly related to income. Data from other countries have shown a clear inverse relationship between socioeconomic status and a wide range of health indicators, including acute and chronic illness rates, days of restricted activity, psychiatric symptoms, high blood pressure, height, obesity, low birth weight, prematurity, ability to conceive and self-perceived health.[15] Moreover, there is evidence to show that these differences have widened over the past four decades in spite of universal access to health care in many developed countries.

Explaining Socioeconomic Differences in Health

A number of explanations have been advanced to account for the association between socioeconomic status and health. The **artefact explanation** claims that such differences are not real but a product of our attempts to measure complex social entities such as socioeconomic status and health with inadequate instruments. However, the evidence concerning health inequities is overwhelming. Systematic gradients exist whether we use objective or subjective measures of health and whether socioeconomic status is measured by income, education or occupation.

The **theory of natural and social selection** argues that inequities in health are created and maintained by a process of social mobility whereby healthy individuals move up the socioeconomic scale and less healthy individuals move down. Some studies confirm that conditions such as schizophrenia and chronic bronchitis often lead to a downward occupational drift, with the affected individual ending up in low paid, unskilled manual labour or unemployment. Other studies have shown that healthy women were more likely to be upwardly mobile at marriage, marrying men from a socioeconomic group higher than that in which they were born, while less healthy women tended to be downwardly mobile. While these studies indicate that health **can** influence socioeconomic status it is unlikely that this theory can fully account for the extent of the differences in health observed.

The **materialist explanation** suggests that inequities in health have their origins in material deprivation. That is, groups at the lower end of the socioeconomic scale lack adequate financial and other resources to maintain their physical and psychological well-being and to protect themselves from hazardous physical or social environments. Most of the evidence tending to support this theory has focused on differences in income and wealth, working conditions, the quality of housing and the nature of communities in which people live. The lower socioeconomic groups are frequently disadvantaged in terms of all four. Evidence from numerous studies has demonstrated an inverse relationship between material deprivation and health. For example, differences in the health of children from different socioeconomic groups has been linked to poor quality housing and hazardous domestic environments. Overcrowding, damp conditions and inadequate heating all have an impact on health and are associated with increased rates of respiratory illness and deaths from accidents in the home. As well, men from lower socioeconomic groups often work in more hazardous environments and this is reflected in data on deaths from accidents at work, or deaths from occupationally related disease.

Cultural or behavioural theories attempt to explain inequities in health with reference to differences in knowledge, attitudes and behaviours. Individuals in lower socioeconomic groups are thought to be less healthy because they consume health-damaging substances such as tobacco and alcohol at higher rates, have diets which are high in sugars and fats and low in fibre, are less likely to take exercise regularly and make less use of preventive health services. This explanation is valid to the extent that lifestyles and consumption patterns are related to socioeconomic status and, in turn, are associated with the onset of conditions such as heart disease or cancer.

Clearly, the implications of the materialist and cultural explanations of inequities in health are radically different. The materialist theory suggests that widespread social change is necessary to ensure that all individuals have equal opportunities for maintaining and improving their health. This involves a fundamental redistribution of resources in society to ensure that all have access to those goods and services necessary to produce health. The cultural theory is narrower in its implications and suggests that the remedy lies in health education to change health damaging attitudes and behaviours. The problem with this approach is that it assumes such attitudes and behaviours are freely chosen, rather than environmentally induced, and it carries with it a tendency to **blame the victim** for situations over which they have relatively little control. As some have pointed out, cultural and behavioural patterns deleterious to health are rooted in the material conditions of life of people in the lowest socioeconomic groups. Efforts to change attitudes and behaviours are likely to fail if these material conditions are not addressed at the same time. This is embodied in the socio-ecological approach to health promotion which regards social change as a prerequisite for changes at the individual level.[16] Health-related behaviour does not occur independent of the influence of the surrounding physical and social environment. A final factor which may contribute to differences in health status is **inequality in access to and use of medical services.** There is evidence from a number of jurisdictions in Canada that low income groups use family practitioner services less in relation to need than their high income counterparts. Differences in the quality of care have also been observed; patient-practitioner communication is one area in which the lower socioeconomic groups are particularly disadvantaged.

2.3.   LIFESTYLE, BEHAVIOURS AND RISK FACTORS

Lifestyle consists of aspects of individuals' behaviour and surroundings over which they may exercise control, although recognition of the importance of the social and physical environmental context in this concept is increasing. A recent definition of lifestyle which incorporates elements of social as well as individual responsibility is that: "healthy lifestyles comprise patterns of health-related behaviour, values and attitudes adapted by groups of individuals in response to their social, cultural and economic environment."[17] Decisions made by individuals which result in favourable or adverse consequences for health are many and may play an important role in today's major health problems.

Risk continuum: A useful conceptualization of the health effects of a lifestyle factor is that of the **degree of risk** posed by the health-related behaviour. Figure 1.1 shows the "risk continuum" which is derived from alcohol consumption, an example of a substance abuse lifestyle factor.[18] The level of risk indicates the most appropriate strategies, such as "health promotion" or "health recovery" programs. For individuals at minimal or no risk, further enhancement of health is appropriate as well as avoidance of risk. With alcohol consumption, less than 14 drinks per week is generally defined as low risk to health, and of course no consumption means no risk. For individuals at low to moderate levels of risk, reduction of risk is appropriate. Such persons may be consuming 15 to 34 drinks per week and, at the upper end of this range, be experiencing problems such as impaired driving. Early (medical/social) intervention may be necessary. Higher levels of consump-

Figure 1.1: Risk Continuum

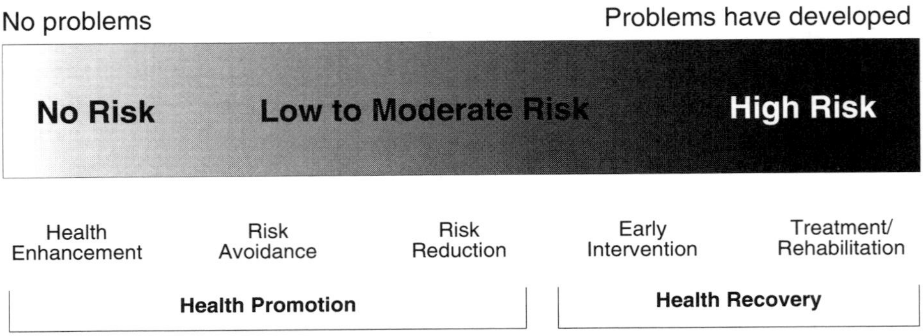

No problems   Problems have developed

No Risk	Low to Moderate Risk	High Risk

Health Enhancement	Risk Avoidance	Risk Reduction	Early Intervention	Treatment/ Rehabilitation

Health Promotion	**Health Recovery**

Reproduced from: The Ontario Ministry of Health: A framework for the response to alcohol and drug problems in Ontario, 1988.

tion are usually associated with significant health problems requiring treatment and rehabilitation ("health recovery").

2.4.   HEALTH CARE ORGANIZATION

The Health Care Organization is what is traditionally defined as the health care system. It includes medical and dental practice, nursing, hospitals, chronic care facilities, rehabilitation, drugs, public health services, and health services provided by allied health professionals such as chiropractic, podiatric and optometric services. The Canadian health-care system is examined in detail in chapters 12 to 18.

3.   APPROACHES TO ACHIEVING HEALTH

Previous sections have described a shift in the concept of health from a predominantly biomedical one to a multi-dimensional concept. Interacting components of many aspects of life may affect health and are viewed as a resource for living. We now move on to a discussion of the implications in terms of prevention of disease and of the attainment of health.

3.1.   TRADITIONAL MODEL OF PREVENTION

Traditionally, there have been three approaches to disease prevention; primary, secondary and tertiary. **Primary prevention** is aimed at preventing disease before it occurs, thereby reducing the incidence of disease. Examples include immunization programs, dietary recommendations, avoidance of taking up smoking and the use of seat belts and other protective devices. **Secondary prevention** involves the early detection of disease in an asymptomatic period before it progresses and the treatment which may occur as a result of screening. **Tertiary prevention** attempts to reduce complications by treatment and rehabilitation, which are carried out primarily by the existing health-care system.

Recommendations regarding many primary and secondary preventive measures in relation to medical practitioner management of the individual patient are incorporated in the Periodic Health Examination, which is fully described in chapter 11. The remainder of this chapter concentrates on population health and emphasizes approaches that are more appropriate for the community. **Population health** is variously defined as the study of the determinants of health and disease, health status, and the degree to which health care affects the health of the community.

3.2.   HEALTH PROMOTION: EPP'S FRAMEWORK

The traditional model of prevention has commonly employed the modification of human biology, the environment (e.g., clean water supply) or the organization of health care services (e.g., mass screening for phenylketonuria). However, the paradigm shift in understanding the determinants of disease in the Lalonde Health Field Concept implies that in order to have additional impact on the health of Canadians, non-traditional approaches to prevention will have to be developed. They should aim at changing unhealthy lifestyles and environments. These approaches are embodied in the concept of **health promotion**, which first gained legitimacy in the Lalonde document. A newly emerged concept is the use of different communication techniques to enhance health or to encourage the maintenance of an existing healthy lifestyle.

The *Declaration of Alma Ata on Primary Health Care*[19] in 1978 set the stage internationally for numerous initiatives in health promotion. Notable was *Targets for Health for All by 2000,*[20] adopted by the European Region of the WHO. This document proposed improvements in health, specified the locus of action, and provided tools to monitor progress towards health goals. The United States began to develop health goals based on health promotion and disease prevention with the publication of *Healthy People*,[21] the Surgeon General's Report on Health Promotion and Disease Prevention. This report was followed by the development of 226 specific objectives with target dates for achievement and, more recently, by a mid-course review.

Within Canada, the concepts of Health Promotion are serving as a basis for a reformulation of national and provincial health policies. At a national level, the Honourable Jake Epp, then Minister of National Health & Welfare, released *Achieving Health for All: A Framework for Health Promotion*[22] in 1986. Subsequently, Health and Welfare Canada, the European Region of the WHO and the Canadian Public Health Association endorsed the *Ottawa Charter for Health Promotion*.[2] This provides a clear vision of current Health Promotion concepts and calls on all concerned bodies to join forces to introduce strategies for Health Promotion in line with the moral and social values that underlie the Charter. In Ontario, three recent government reports[23-25] strongly endorsed the principles of Health Promotion and made specific recommendations designed to incorporate these into government health policy. The Quebec government has undertaken a major health planning project, *Objectif: Santé*,[26] which incorporates principles of Health Promotion in selecting specific health improvement objectives.

The 1986 discussion paper *Achieving Health For All: A Framework For Health Promotion*[22] outlined three major challenges which are not being addressed adequately by current health policies and practices. The first problem is that disadvantaged groups have significantly lower life expectancy, poorer health and a higher prevalence of disability than the average Canadian (chapter six); secondly, various forms of preventable diseases and injuries continue to undermine the health and quality of life of many Canadians; and thirdly, many thousands of Canadians suffer from chronic disease, disability, or various forms of emotional stress, and lack adequate community support to help them cope and live meaningful, productive and dignified lives. The Epp document calls for a "health promotion" approach to these three problems. The document refers to the WHO's definition of **health promotion** (i.e., "the process of enabling people to increase control over, and to improve, their health"). It outlines three *mechanisms* intrinsic to health promotion; *self care*, or the decisions and actions individuals take in the interest of their own health; *mutual aid*, or the actions people take to help each other cope; and *healthy environments*, or the creation of conditions and surroundings conducive to health. Implementation requires three *strategies*: *fostering public participation*; *strengthening community health services*; and *coordinating healthy public policies*. This approach integrates ideas from several arenas: public health, health education and public policy. It expands the use of the term "health promotion" to one which complements and strengthens the existing system of health care. The differences between the concepts of Disease Prevention and Health Promotion are indicated in table 1.1. The table also highlights the complementary nature of these approaches, which means they can be utilized in combination.[27]

Table 1.1: Disease Prevention vs. Health Promotion Approach

Health Promotion	Disease Prevention
Health = positive and multidimensional concept	Health = absence of disease
Participatory model of health	Medical model
Aimed at the population in its total environment	Aimed mainly at high-risk group in the population
Concerns a network of issues	Concerns a specific pathology
Diverse and complementary strategies	One-shot strategy
Facilitating and enabling approaches	Directive and persuasive strategies
Incentive measures are offered to the population	Directive measures are enforced in target groups
Changes in man's status and his environment are sought by the program	Program focusing mostly on individuals and groups of subjects
Non-professional organizations, civic groups, local, municipal, regional and national governments are necessary for achieving the goal of health promotion	Preventive programs are the affair of professional groups from health disciplines

Source: Stachenko S and Jenicek M. Conceptual Differences Between Prevention and Health Promotion: Research Implications for Community Health Programs. *Can J Publ Health* 81:53-59, 1990. Reprinted with the permission of the author and the journal.

3.3.   HEALTH PROMOTION STRATEGIES

A number of strategies have been developed or adapted for the promotion of health. Many of them are aimed at influencing healthy behaviours, and determinants of health which influence these behaviours.   Methods which involve changes in lifestyle may include any of a number of approaches which may be directed at an individual or community level. Health promotion approaches in general, as articulated in the Ottawa Charter,[2] involve **advocacy** for health, the **enabling** of people to achieve the conditions necessary for reaching their full potential for health, and **mediation** by health professionals between differing groups in society in the interests of health. Specific strategies include: **education, communication, legislation, fiscal measures, community organizational change, community development** and **local community action**.[28] Legislation and fiscal measures may affect policy which has traditionally not fallen under the purview of health, a strategy called **healthy public policy**. Communication and education in conjunction with some other approaches (such as community organization) may be directed to whole populations. This strategy is called **community-wide prevention**. Fincham has provided an excellent Canadian review of the theory, strategies and outcomes of community-based health promotion programs discussed below.[29]

3.3.1. Health Education

Persons who have already adopted unhealthy lifestyles often find it difficult to change their lifestyles even if this is desired. Health education can be defined as any combination of learning experiences designed to facilitate voluntary actions conducive to health. The aim of health education is to encourage people to positively modify their lifestyles while also encouraging them to resist reverting to former bad habits. It is increasingly recognized that social influences affect behaviour. Without reinforcement from change in social norms, health education is less effective in producing a change in behaviour.

A number of theoretical views of behaviour change underpin the types of programs developed in health education. A unifying concept is that proposed by Green, where behaviour is a result of predisposing, reinforcing and enabling factors.[30] **Predisposing factors** comprise knowledge (for example, the health consequences of smoking), attitudes, beliefs and values. Fishbein and Aizen[31] have identified that the intention to change behaviour is also a strong predictor. **Reinforcing factors** (such as those provided by the social context of family, society, or health professionals) involve reward or feedback for the discontinuation or adoption of behaviour. **Enabling factors** include skills such as smoking cessation techniques as well as the availability of reasonably priced, low fat foods in the supermarket to support dietary change.

An influential theory of **social learning** propounded by Bandura[32] is constructed from a number of related concepts which need to be addressed in lifestyle education. There is a strong correlation between social learning principles and some health-related actions. The essential concept is of **reciprocal determinism**, which is recognition that the social environment influences behaviour, which in turn has an effect on the environment. Behaviour is the result of personal and environmental factors. The importance of the social environment as the context for learning has been developed in the **social influences model**.

Apart from components of behavioural capability (the acquisition of skills and knowledge), reinforcements, and supportive social environments, there are other components of social learning theory. These are: a) observation (such as with role models); b) expectations of positive results from behaviour change (as provided by **peer-assisted learning**); c) expectancies (such as better appearance following loss of weight which may be a more potent motivator than the expected health benefits); d) perceptions of an individual's situation (e.g., in relation to birth control education such as what the implications of pregnancy might be); and e) emotional factors which may pose barriers to behaviour change(such as anxiety associated with the anticipation of giving up a lifestyle habit).

Self-efficacy and self-control are components of behaviour change which are increasingly being incorporated into health education for sustained behaviour change. **Self-efficacy** refers to the cognitive state that one feels when one is confident that one can achieve a behaviour change. This may be reached by the achievement of short-term goals. **Self-control** relates to decision-making capacities for healthy choices and self-monitoring, such as those utilized in guided self-management programs for smoking cessation.

An important model, the **Health Belief Model**[33] which attempts to explain the factors influencing compliance (see figure 1.2). This model suggests that behaviours undertaken by individuals in order to remain healthy, including the use of preventive services, are a function of a set of interacting beliefs. In order to be motivated to take action to avoid illness, an individual must be in a state of readiness to take action and must believe that the action will have positive consequences. In order to be ready to act, the individual needs to feel susceptible to the disease in question and to believe that it would have some significant impact on his/her life. Beliefs about the benefits of the action in question involve consideration of barriers to action such as time, cost and inconvenience.

Current formulations of the model include the role of cues and modifying factors. Cues consist of specific events which act as a stimulus to preventive health behaviours. Modifying factors consist of sociodemographic variables such as age, sex and race; sociopsychological variables such as personality and peer group pressure; and other variables such as knowledge of, and prior experience with, the disease. All of these factors influence the individual's perception of susceptibility to disease and seriousness, as well as perception of the benefits of health-related actions. This model has provided the foundation for many health education and awareness programs. One of the implications of this model is that these programs need to be carefully targeted at specific social and cultural groups and need to be based on a detailed understanding of their health beliefs.

More recently a **Stages of Change Model** has provided a useful framework to understand how changes of lifestyle behaviour can be facilitated.[34] In studies of cigarette smokers, four different stages were identified: Stage 1 has a Precontemplation stage where the individual was unaware of a behaviour-related health problem; Stage 2 has a Contemplation stage when change was considered; Stage 3 has an Action stage where initial attempts at change were made; Stage 4 has Maintenance, or long-term change. Individuals may move through these stages non-linearly. Barriers to change at each stage, and facilitative processes, have been identified in figure 1.3.

Evaluation of most health education programs has provided mixed results, although more recent evidence indicates some level of effectiveness for skills training for young people in relation to prevention of smoking (in particular, peer-led approaches).[28] There are indications that education applied to prevention of alcohol abuse in drinking establishments, by server-intervention education programs (which train servers to recognize and take action to reduce the occurrence of intoxication), has some effectiveness.

Figure 1.2: Health Belief Model

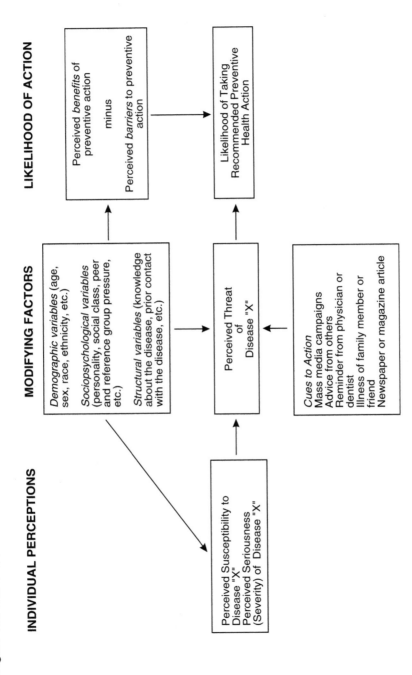

Reproduced with the permission of the publisher, from Becker MH, Haefner DP and Kasl SV, et al. Selected Psychosocial Models and Correlates of Individual Health-Related Behaviours. *Medical Care* 15:27-46, 1977.

3.3.2. Communication/Behaviour Change

Communication of information is an empowering strategy to promote health. The use of mass media is potentially an important tool for influencing awareness, knowledge, attitudes and behaviour. The classic study which revealed the potential of mass media to affect behaviour in relation to cardiovascular risk factors on a community-wide basis was the Standford Five Community Study, which was a community trial.[35] In the control city (which was comparable on a sociodemographic basis to the experimental community) prevalence of risk factors increased during the period of the study, while in the community given an intensive mass media approach over two years there was a reduction in risk behaviours. A review of mass communication programs directed at alcohol abuse in Canada indicates that although attitudes and knowledge levels are affected, behaviour change is infrequently affected. **Several** studies were cited where behaviour change **was** influenced.[28] Mass media is a modality that assists in setting and framing the public agenda and is probably most effectively used in conjunction with other health promotion measures.

3.3.3. Social Marketing

Social Marketing is a health promotion modality which utilizes the principles of commercial marketing to promote social change. It influences the acceptability of a social idea by a target group. Key concepts are the "marketing mix" of four variables: product, price, place and promotion. The **product** may be "good health," for example.[36] The **price**, a concept which is based on exchange theory, represents what consumers must give up if they accept the health promoter's offer. The **place** concerns the distribution channels used to reach the consumer; for example, distribution of leaflets on Acquired Immune Deficiency Syndrome (AIDS) through clinics serving the population at risk for sexually transmitted diseases. **Promotion** is the way in which the product is promoted to the customer; examples are advertising or personal "selling." Social marketing is a planned activity involving target group analysis based partly on demographics and segmentation of the market for specific messages and channels. Increased effectiveness of social marketing for non-responsive persons may be achieved by increasing the focus in the messages provided on the actual actions involved in a behaviour, the target of the action, or the context and time of the behaviour.[37]

3.3.4. Healthy Public Policy

Healthy public policy has an impact on health and is one of the major strategies for achieving health. Examples of healthy public policy include extensive legislative restrictions on smoking in public places, public transit facilities and workplaces. Seat belt legislation is another prime example despite the fact that although earlier models of cars had seat belts available and the general public was somewhat aware of their benefit in case of accidents, usage was poor. Compliance improved when a fine was imposed by legislation if passengers were found not wearing seat belts. Rising health costs and the economic burden of motor vehicle accidents appeared

Figure 1.3: The Stages of Change Model

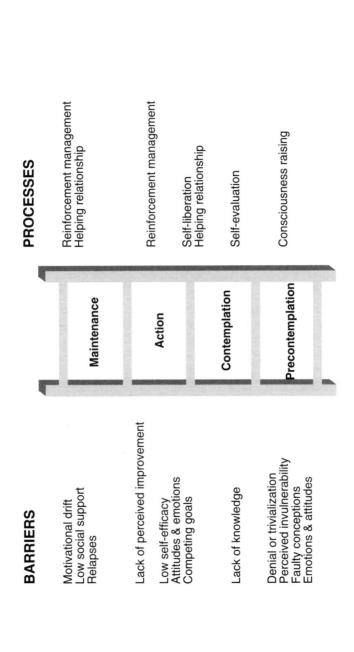

PROCESSES

Maintenance
Reinforcement management
Helping relationship

Action
Reinforcement management
Self-liberation
Helping relationship

Contemplation
Self-evaluation

Precontemplation
Consciousness raising

BARRIERS

Motivational drift
Low social support
Relapses

Lack of perceived improvement

Low self-efficacy
Attitudes & emotions
Competing goals

Lack of knowledge

Denial or trivialization
Perceived invulnerability
Faulty conceptions
Emotions & attitudes

Source: Reproduced with the permission of the publisher, from Skinner HA. Early Identification of Addictive Behaviours Using a Computerized Lifestyle Assessment. In: *Addictive Behaviours Across the Lifespan: Prevention, Treatment and Policy Issues*. Baer JS, Marlatt GA and McMahon GE, eds. Newbury Park, California: Sage Publications, 1993.

to be a determining factor in the introduction of this legislation, especially since other countries had achieved positive results. While seat belt usage in Ontario increased to 71% with early and strict enforcement of the legislation in 1976, adherence had declined to 36% in 1978 as a result of less stringent enforcement by authorities.[38] This was an indication that part of the public was still unwilling to accept responsibility for its own health unless some immediate payment was involved, pecuniary or otherwise. With stricter enforcement of the law again, seat belt usage in Ontario climbed back to 80.9% in 1991.

Thus, despite the fact that people are aware of certain risk-taking behaviour and the associated health hazards, many persons are resistant to change. Various adverse behaviour patterns are made to appear more desirable and attractive by the use of sophisticated advertising techniques by industry. The implementation of legal deterrents to individual behaviours such as seat belt legislation, anti-smoking by-laws, or older legal drinking age is an approach to overcoming these barriers to change. Government control is also mediated by tax and pricing policies with the objective of reducing accessibility of certain "luxury" commodities (such as cigarettes and alcohol) to the public by raising prices. The effectiveness of these policies depends on the amount of the individual's disposable income. Programs based on personal motivation and behavioural change take much longer and involve a smaller percentage of the participating public. Yet the latter process must not be ignored, since it is important to make individuals responsible for their own health and the health-care system, in addition to depending solely on the external imposition of rules and regulations.

The Epp document differs from the Lalonde report, which mainly advocated healthy lifestyles and a safe environment. Epp's document probably better reflects current thinking at the international level, which has a broader perspective on health promotion and recommends **healthy public policies** for achieving good health for all. Healthy public policies espouse the concept that responsibility for improving health lies beyond traditional health policies such as having universal health insurance. They promote the view that social policies favouring affordable housing, public transportation, and income maintenance will have more impact on the health of the Canadian population than the infusion of additional resources in the health-care sector. Due to the intersectoral and multi-sectoral nature of factors determining health, what is needed to achieve health for all is the implementation of a good set of healthy public policies in which health becomes incorporated into the agenda of government departments and private agencies that would normally not consider health a priority.

3.3.5. Community Organization and Community Development

The Epp document regards enhanced public participation as one of its major strategies. The nature and extent of public participation can be conceptualized along a spectrum of increasing community capacity to organize around issues of community concern. **Community efficacy** represents the state of community confidence necessary to bring about desired social change.[39] Mechanisms include lobbying, coalition-building and political action. **Community development** refers to the process of community members identifying issues and problems affecting their community, and developing and acquiring, as necessary, the planning skills and capacity to bring about the implementation of change. Health-care organizations, such as public health departments, may facilitate this community-initiated and directed process.

Community organization also involves the identification of problems within a community and the mobilizing of resources for change.[40] The process is, however, driven to some extent by the goals and strategies established by the health sector, and it assists the community to achieve the change. Three elements of community organization have been identified: a) **social planning**, which implies the rational solution of problems using the existing power structure; b) **community locality development**, or the development of a community for an organized approach to a given problem; and c) **social action**, which implies a shift in power structures in the community. Organizing occurs when interest is focused on a concern by the development of leadership, commitment, bargaining, protest, education and persuasion. This may result in changes within administrative structures themselves or "inter-organizing"—the development of joint structures for community problem-solving.

3.3.6. Community-wide Prevention

Recognition of the prevalence of multiple preventable factors in communities and the potential application of multiple preventive and promotion modalities has been debated. The debate has resulted in the emergence of the community-wide approach to complement, or replace, a high risk approach where attention has been focused on specific risk factors or special high risk groups. For example, the Canadian Heart Health Initiative has commenced pilot projects in a number of provinces which are population-based, multifactorial approaches incorporating combinations of elements of communication-behaviour change, community organization and social marketing.[41] Other programs such as the Heartbeat Wales Project, the Minnesota Heart Health Program and the Pawtucket Program are using selections of the various approaches discussed above. Evidence supporting the effectiveness of community-wide prevention was provided initially by the North Karelia Project in Finland, which showed a reduction in cardiovascular mortality subsequent to the introduction of a community-wide prevention program, and the Stanford Five-City Project in which cardiovascular risk decreased after five years of this type of program.[42]

3.3.7. Innovation-Diffusion Theory

Complementary theories have developed to explain the process by which health promotion innovations spread in communities and to identify the most effective ways to encourage people to adopt a different behaviour.[29] Roger's Theory of Diffusion conceptualizes a population as comprised of "innovators, early adapters, an early majority, a late majority" and those who "resist" most efforts for change. Community leaders tend to be early adapters and can be effective as project advisors. Other characteristics of an innovation that will affect its adoption are whether it is simple, workable, reversible, flexible, advantageous, cost-effective, low risk and compatible with value systems. Elder has applied concepts of behaviour modification (i.e., positive and negative consequences) in a Behavioural Community Psychology theory.[29] The area of diffusion of innovation is currently one of the main arms of health promotion research.

4.   SUMMARY

This chapter outlines the concepts of health and disease, determinants of health, and approaches to achieving health.

Health has been defined in various ways; the WHO defines it as "the ability to identify and to realize the aspirations, to satisfy needs, and to change or cope with the environment. Health is therefore a resource for everyday life, not the objective of living. Health is a positive concept emphasizing social and personal resources, as well as physical capacities."

Impairment is defined as "any loss or abnormality of psychosocial, physiological or anatomical structure or function." Disability is "any restriction or lack of ability to perform an activity in a manner or within the range considered normal for a human being," and handicap is defined as "the disadvantage for a given individual arising out of impairment and disabilty, that limits or prevents the fulfillment of a role that is normal for that individual."

Illness behaviour can be defined as any activity undertaken by individuals who perceive they have a potential health problem for the purpose of defining their state of health and discovering and undertaking an appropriate remedy. Illness behaviour depends on many factors, one of which is cultural background.

There are several theories of disease causation. First, the Biomechanical/ Biomedical Model holds that the body is akin to a machine which can be corrected when things go wrong by procedures designed to repair damage or restore the functioning of its component parts. Second, the Germ Theory of Disease states that a living organism enters the body via food, water or air and hence each disease has a single and specific cause. Lastly, and most recently, the theory of General Susceptibility has emerged. In this theory, broad, non-specific social and psychological factors are seen to be associated with a variety of health outcomes.

The determinants of health include: (i) the individual's human biology—those aspects of health both mental and physical which arise out of the basic biology of humans or are due to the organic make-up of the individual; (ii) the individual's physical and psychosocial environment—factors in the physical environment include food, drug, air and water quality, and waste disposal; (iii) lifestyle, behaviour and modifiable risk factors (i.e., aspects of an individual's behaviour and surroundings over which he or she has some control; and (iv) health-care organization (i.e., the health-care system).

Approaches to acheiving health include: (i) prevention, and (ii) health promotion strategies.

(i) Prevention: there are three levels—primary, secondary and tertiary. Primary prevention is aimed at preventing disease before it occurs. Secondary prevention involves early detection of disease in an asymptomatic period before it progresses and the treatment which may occur as a result of screening. Finally, tertiary prevention attempts to reduce complications by treatment and rehabilitation.

(ii) Health Promotion Strategies: a number of strategies have been developed or adapted for the promotion of health. These include education, communication/ behaviour change, social marketing, healthy public policy (including fiscal measures and legislation), community development and organization, community-wide prevention, and diffusion of innovations.

5.   REFERENCES

1. *Health Indicators.* Culyer AJ, ed. Oxford: Martin Robertson, 1983.
2. *Ottawa Charter for Health Promotion.* Health and Welfare Canada, Canadian Public Health Association and WHO. Ottawa, 1986.
3. Wood P. The Language of Disablement: A Glossary Relating to Disease and its Consequences. *Int J Rehab Med* 2(2):86-92, 1980.
4. Harper AC, Harper DA, Chambers LW, Cino PM and Singer J. An Epidemiological Description of Physical, Social and Psychological Problems in Multiple Sclerosis. *J Chronic Dis* 39(4):305-310, 1986.
5. Williams SJ and Bury MR. Impairment, Disability and Handicap in Chronic Respiratory Illness. *Soc Sci Med* 29(5):609-616, 1989.
6. Mausner J and Kramer S. *Epidemiology: An Introductory Text.* Philadelphia: WB Saunders, 1985.
7. Rothman KJ. *Modern Epidemiology.* Toronto: Little, Brown and Co., 1986.
8. MacMahon B and Pugh T. *Epidemiological Principles and Methods.* Boston: Little, Brown and Co., 1970.
9. Lalonde M. *A New Perspective on the Health of Canadians.* Ministry of Supply and Services, Canada. Ottawa, 1975.
10. McKeown T, Record RG and Turner RD. An Interpretation of Decline Mortality in England and Wales during the Twentieth Century. *Popul Studies* 29(3):391-422, 1975.
11. Brown G and Harris T. *The Social Origins of Depression.* London: Tavistock, 1979.
12. *Nurturing Health. A Framework for the Determinants of Health.* Premier's Council on Health, Equity and Social Justice. Healthy Public Policy Committee. Toronto, 1991.
13. Manga P. Equality in Access and Inequalities in Health Status. In: *Health and Canadian Society.* Coburn D, D'Arcy C, Torrance G and New P, eds. Markham, Ontario: Fitzhenry and Whiteside, 1987.
14. Wilkins R and Adams O. *Healthfulness of Life.* Institute for Research on Public Policy. Montreal, 1983.
15. MacIntyre S. The Patterning of Health by Social Position in Contemporary Britain: Directions for Sociological Research. *Soc Sci Med* 23(4):393-415, 1986.

16. *Health Inequalities in the City of Toronto 1991.* City of Toronto: Department of Public Health, Community Health Information Section. Toronto, 1991.

17. Conway J. With Gun and Camera in Darkest Ontario: Searching For The Elusive Health Lifestyle Concept. *Public Health and Epidemiology Reports Ont* 3(16):268-269, 1992.

18. *A Framework for the Response to Alcohol and Drug Problems in Ontario.* Ministry of Health, Government of Ontario, Toronto, 1988.

19. *International Conference on Primary Health Care. Alma Ata, U.S.S.R., 1978.* Geneva: WHO, 1978.

20. *Targets for Health for All by the Year 2000.* Copenhagen: WHO Regional Office for Europe, 1984.

21. *Healthy People: The Surgeon General's Report on Health Promotion and Disease Prevention.* U.S. Department of Health, Education and Welfare, Washington DC, 1979.

22. Epp J. *Achieving Health For All: A Framework for Health Promotion.* Ministry of Supply and Services, Canada, Ottawa, 1986.

23. *Health for All Ontario.* Report of the Panel on Health Goals for Ontario, chaired by Spasoff, RA. Ministry of Health, Government of Ontario, Toronto, 1987.

24. *Health Promotion Matters in Ontario: A Report of the Minister's Advisory Group on Health Promotion,* chaired by Podborski S. Ministry of Health, Government of Ontario, Toronto, 1987.

25. *Toward a Shared Direction for Health in Ontario.* Report of the Ontario Health Review Panel, chaired by Evans J. Ministry of Health, Government of Ontario, Toronto, 1987.

26. *Objectif Santé.* Comite d'Etude sur la Promotion de la Santé. Direction Generale des Publications Gouvernementales. Gouvernement de Quebec, Quebec, 1984.

27. Stachenko S and Jenicek M. Conceptual Differences Between Prevention and Health Promotion: Research Implications for Community Health Programs. *Can J Public Health* 81(1):53-59, 1990.

28. Noack H and McQueen D. Health Promotion Indicators. *Health Promot* 3(1):1-125, 1988.

29. Fincham S. Community Health Promotion Programs. *Soc Sci Med* 35(3):239-249, 1992.

30. Green LW and Kreuter MW. *Health Promotion Planning; An Educational and Environmental Approach,* 2nd ed, Toronto: Mayfield Publishing Company, 1991.

31. Fishbain M and Aizen I. *Beliefs, Attitudes, Intentions and Behaviours: Introduction to Theaory and Research.* Reading, Mass: Addison-Wesley Press, 1975.

32. Bandura A. *Social Learning Theory.* New York: General Learning Press, 1971.

33. Becker MH, Drachman RH and Kirscht JP. A New Approach to Explaining Sick-Role Behaviour in Low-Income Populations. *Am J Public Health* 64(3):205-216, 1974.

34. DiClemente C, Prochaska JO, Fairhurst SK, et al. The Process of Smoking Cessation: An Analysis of Precontemplation, Contemplation, and Preparation Stages of Change. *J Consult Clin Psychol* 59(2):295-304, 1991.

35. Shea S and Basch CA. Review of Five Major Community-Based Cardiovascular Disease Prevention Programs. Part 1: Rationale, Design and Theoretical Framework. *Am J Health Promot* 4(3):203-213, 1990.

36. Hastings G and Haywood A. Social Marketing and Communication in Health Promotion. *Health Promot Int* 6(2):135-145, 1991.

37. McDonald PA. Framework for Using Social Marketing with Non-Responsive High Risk Populations. *Public Health and Epidemiology Reports Ont* 3(7):105-109. Ontario Ministry of Health. Ontario, 1992

38. Robertson LS. The Seat Belt Use Law in Ontario - Effects on Actual Use. *Can J Public Health* 69(2):154-157, 1978.

39. Wallerstein N. Powerlessness, Empowerment, and Health Implications for Health Promotion Programs. *Am J Health Promot* 6(3):197-205, 1992.

40. Bracht N and Tsouros A. Principles and Strategies of Effective Community Participation. *Health Promot Int* 5(3):199-208, 1990.

41. The Canadian Heart Health Initiative. Health and Welfare Canada, Ottawa. Insert in *Health Promot* 30(4):2-19, 1992.

42. Shea S and Basch C. A Review of Five Major Community-Based Disease Prevention Programs. Part II: Intervention Strategies, Evaluation Methods, and Results. *Am J Health Promot* 4(4): 279-287, 1990.

CHAPTER TWO
Measurement and Investigation

As indicated in the previous chapter, concepts of health and disease are changing and are multidimensional. For measurement of health, both quantitative and qualitative data are used. The science of epidemiology has been widely used for quantitative approaches to studying the health of populations. This chapter provides an overview of the principles of epidemiology and some basics of statistics. The reader is referred to standard epidemiology texts for an in-depth treatment of this subject.[1-3]

1. EPIDEMIOLOGICAL STUDIES

Epidemiology is "the study of the distribution and the determinants of health-related states and events (such as diseases) in specified populations, and the application of this study to the control of health problems."[4] The distribution of disease is studied in terms of person, place and time. **Personal** attributes include age, sex, race and ethnicity. **Place** factors include location of residence, work and school, and they can involve comparisons between urban and rural, north and south, and among different countries. **Time** factors describe the occurrence of health events per specified unit of time and trends over different periods of time. The determinants of diseases may be studied in terms of at-risk (demographic) groups, lifestyle factors (e.g., diet, smoking), occupation and environment (physical, psychosocial, political and economic).

The science of epidemiology has been well recognized in recent years for investigating epidemics and identifying new health problems in populations. Examples include: (i) "unusual" infectious diseases (e.g., AIDS, Lyme disease, Legionnaire disease, toxic shock syndrome); (ii) exposures to environmental and occupational hazards (e.g., ozone pollution, pesticides and asbestos); and (iii) diseases for which no agent has yet been identified (e.g., Reye syndrome, Kawasaki disease). Epidemiologists use certain basic methodologies, such as studies, in order to identify and evaluate the causal or contributing factors to disease, its distribution and possible means of treatment.

1.1. DESCRIPTIVE STUDIES

An epidemiologic descriptive study, as expected, describes the occurrence of disease or other phenomena in terms of person, place and time. For example, a study of children in the care of child welfare agencies revealed that 400 per 1000 such children were disabled. One cannot make any causal attribution from descriptive studies; they may, however, generate hypotheses which may be investigated by further study. In this example, one may hypothesize that disabled children are more likely to come into care than the non-disabled. This hypothesis may be tested in an analytic study.

1.2. ANALYTIC STUDIES

In these studies, a hypothesis is tested to find out if there is an association between a given disease, health state or other dependent variable (outcome), and possible causative factors.[2] Analytic studies are of two types: observational and experimental.

1.2.1. Observational Studies
There are three types of observational studies:

Cross-sectional or Prevalence Study
In this type of study, one examines the relationship between diseases or other health-related factors and other variables of interest as they exist in a defined population at one particular time.[4] The population is divided into those with and without the disease, and then various characteristics of the two groups are examined. One can also subdivide the total population by different variables such as age or sex and look for disease in these groups. A *cross-sectional study* reveals the prevalence of disease, disability, and risk factors in a given population at one point in time. **Prevalence rates** are calculated by dividing the number of individuals who have an attribute or disease at a particular time by the population at a risk of having the attribute or disease at the same point in time. Most data obtained in surveys, including census data, report prevalence rates. Prevalence rates are usually expressed per 1000 population.

Retrospective Study
Retrospective studies "test etiological hypotheses in which inferences about exposure to the putative causal factor(s) are derived from data relating to characteristics of the persons under study or to events or experiences in their past".[4] "Retrospective" means looking back in time; hence, a retrospective study begins after the disease has already appeared. Usually it takes the form of a **case-control study**, in which persons with the disease of interest (**cases**) are compared to similar persons without the disease (**controls**) who have had similar opportunity

for exposure to the presumed (putative) causal factor. Investigators collect data by examining medical and other relevant records, and by interviewing cases and controls. If the presumed factor (variable) is present in cases significantly more frequently than in controls, then an association exists between this variable and the disease. This association is expressed by the **odds ratio**, the ratio of the odds in favour of exposure (to the variable) among cases to the odds of exposure among non-cases.[4] (For derivation of the odds ratio formula see chapter 3, section 1.1.2 Lifestyle, Behaviours and Risk Factors.)

Retrospective studies are less costly and time-consuming than prospective studies (discussed below), but they may suffer from recall bias; that is, persons who have, or had, a disease may be more prone to recalling, or believing, that they were exposed to a possible causal factor, compared to those who are free of disease. Retrospective studies may also show a spurious (untrue) association between a factor and a health outcome because of unrecognized **confoundings**. A confounding factor is associated with both the exposure factor under study and the occurrence of the health outcome.

An example of a retrospective study is an investigation by Denson et al.[5] into the relationship between smoking mothers and hyperactive children. The cases were the mothers of 20 hyperkinetic (hyperactive) children. The mothers of 20 children with dyslexia (reading disabilities) and the mothers of 20 children brought to the emergency room as a result of minor accidents comprised two control groups. Controls were matched to cases by age, sex and socioeconomic status, so that there was no significant difference between the groups on these variables. The use of matched controls permits a study to attain significance with relatively few subjects. Study results indicated that the mothers of hyperkinetic children smoked much more (23 cigarettes/day on average) than the mothers of children in the two control groups, who smoked six and eight cigarettes a day on average respectively. Mothers' ages and the birth weights of their babies were not significantly different among the three groups. This does not prove that maternal smoking causes the hyperkinetic syndrome, but the association in this study and others should stimulate more research into a possible mechanism.

Prospective or Cohort Study

This type of study may be considered an organized observation of a natural experiment. A **cohort** is a group of persons with a common characteristic (e.g., year of birth, residence, occupation or exposure to a suspected cause of disease) that may be followed over time by study investigators. Hence cohort studies are also considered **prospective** (forward looking in time). (Some cohort studies are called "retrospective" if the whole period of observation is in the past but the cohort's outcomes are still analyzed from the beginning to the end of the period; i.e., forward in direction.) From a defined population free of the disease under study, a cohort who becomes exposed to the hypothesized causal factor is chosen along with a "control cohort" who ideally has the same characteristics except that it is not exposed to this factor. Both groups are followed for a certain period of time (e.g., 5, 10, or 20 years) and the observed occurrence of disease or other outcomes in the two cohorts are compared.

Prospective studies provide an estimate of the **incidence rate**, the rate at which new disease or other events in a defined population occur over a certain time period. The rates numerator consists of the number of new events (e.g., new cases of a disease diagnosed or reported) over a given time period, and its denominator is the number of persons in the population in which the cases occurred.[2] Prospective studies can also provide an estimate of **attributable risk**, the rate of a health outcome attributable to the hypothesized risk factor for this outcome. Attributable risk is calculated by subtracting the incidence rate in non-exposed persons from the rate in the exposed. Finally, prospective studies can furnish an estimate of **relative risk**, the ratio of the incidence of a health outcome (disease or death) among the exposed to that among the unexposed.

Incidence density can also be calculated from prospective studies and is defined as the number of new cases that occur per unit of population-time (for example, person-years at risk). At times, it is difficult to follow a cohort who is exposed to an agent for an extended period of time. In such cases, the length of time each person is exposed is added up and used as a denominator for the calculation of incidence density (i.e., the number of new cases divided by the person-years at risk). An example would be expressing the incidence rate of lung cancer in terms of 1000 person-years exposed to smoking.

Prospective studies have the great advantage that possible causes of disease are identified before the disease appears, thus reducing the possibility of many sources of **bias** (systematic error in making inferences and making and recording observations). However, they are expensive and not useful for studying rare diseases, and it takes many years before results can be analyzed. Uncontrolled confounding factors may also lead to a spurious association between the exposure factor and the health outcomes under study. Table 2.1 summarizes the advantages and disadvantages of case-control and cohort studies.

A classical cohort study is one which was carried out in Framingham, Massachusetts, and is used here to show the different concepts outlined above.[6] Of the total 10,000 men and women in Framingham, 5209 randomly selected individuals were recruited into the study and followed for several years. Health habit history, physical examination and appropriate laboratory investigations were recorded initially and at two-year intervals. The investigator was interested in studying the effect of high-density lipoprotein (HDL) cholesterol levels on coronary heart disease (CHD). (High levels of HDL cholesterol are known to have a protective effect for CHD.) He found that the incidence of CHD in men was 176.5/1000 when HDL cholesterol levels were less than 25 mg/mL, whereas it was 25/1000 when HDL cholesterol levels were between 65 and 74 mg/mL. From these data, one can conclude that the *attributable risk* of low levels of HDL cholesterol compared to high levels is 151.5/1000 (176.5/1000-25/1000). The *relative risk* for developing CHD with lower HDL cholesterol levels compared to higher levels is 7.1 (176.5/1000 divided by 25/1000).

Table 2.1: Comparison of Cohort and Case-Control Studies

	Cohort Study	Case-Control Study
Advantages	Yields incidence rates, relative risk, and attributable risk.	Small numbers
	Lack of bias	Quick to do
	Can get natural history of disease	Suitable for rare diseases
	Can study many diseases	Cheap
		Can study many factors
Disadvantages	Large numbers	Recall bias
	Long follow-up	Yields only an estimate of relative risk
	Attrition	Problems in control group selection
	Costly	Does not yield incidence rate
	Changes over time	Incomplete recall
	Locked into factor under investigation	Locked into disease

1.2.2. Experimental Studies

Experimental studies are those in which conditions are under the direct control of the investigator, and they are conducted like laboratory experiments. In a **therapeutic trial**, a group of people with a disease is randomized into two or more groups. It is expected that randomization will ensure equal distribution of all major characteristics, such as age, sex, and socioeconomic status. One group is subjected to the intervention being evaluated, usually a treatment, while the other group(s) (controls) is given either an inactive treatment (placebo) or current standard treatment. When subjects are blinded to their treatment status, this procedure is called a **single-blind** trial. The effectiveness of the treatment can only be evaluated when there is a comparison group because the health status of individuals or groups changes constantly. Outcomes for both groups ideally are assessed by an individual who does not know to which group each patient belongs, thus reducing the possibility of bias in the observer. Trials where neither patient nor observer knows the group assignment are called **double-blind randomized** clinical trials. If the health outcomes in the treatment group are statistically significantly better than those in the control group, then the treatment is considered to have been effective in this trial.

Although many clinical trials evaluate new drugs or operations, alternative forms of health care delivery can also be studied in this way. For example, Shah et al. examined the attitudes of parents whose children were sent home rather than kept in hospital after minor surgery.[7] Children scheduled to have surgery were randomly assigned to two groups: 1) the experimental group, whose members were discharged by eight hours after surgery and were provided with home care and 2) the control group, whose members were kept in hospital for the usual one to three days. The groups were similar in age, sex, socioeconomic status and type of surgery. After the children had recovered from surgery, the parents were asked about their child's symptoms and their satisfaction with the treatment. Parents were also asked about their preference for care (i.e., whether they would prefer their children to be hospitalized for minor surgery or prefer them to be at home on the same day as surgery). There were 116 children in each group. Most parents of the control children (66.4%) preferred hospitalization, but the parents of experimental subjects favoured home care (78.4%). Thus, it appears that such home care is well accepted by those who have experienced it.

Although trials can yield reliable and valid results, there are many situations in which trials cannot be carried out on humans. If a treatment is believed to be superior, it would not be ethical to deprive patients in the control group of the treatment. If we wish to test a factor thought to cause or predispose a person toward a disease, ethical considerations forbid deliberately exposing humans.

If we wish to study the effect of removing an environmental factor thought to cause disease (for example, some kinds of air pollutant), a comparison study of two communities which already have different levels of the pollutant would be much cheaper and faster than a trial in which the pollutant levels were lowered and levels of disease tracked over time. **Community trials** of preventive health interventions are delivered programmatically to whole populations. One community is given an intervention (mass regimen) while another serves as a control. This methodology, for example, was used to evaluate the effects of naturally fluoridated water supplies on the prevalence of dental caries. There are intrinsic reasons why community trials are likely to produce more equivocal results than randomized clinical trials. Community trials are **quasi-experimental** since allocation of the intervention is not randomized among individuals in the communities. It is particularly difficult to control for **contamination** which occurs when the comparison communities also receive some of the intervention, and **confounding** is also a concern. Frequently the outcomes observed are risk behaviour changes in the population, which are intermediate rather than "final" outcome data. Community trials have provided evidence for the effectiveness of community-wide approaches to cardiovascular disease prevention.

Recently, a new type of research technique has appeared in the literature, termed **meta-analysis**.[8] Meta-analyses are "studies of studies," synthesizing the results of many studies. Initially, a thorough search for all relevant studies, published and unpublished, is required; the studies are critically reviewed and their results combined statistically. Usually meta-analysis is applied to clinical trial data but it may be applied to other analytic studies as well. By pooling the data from many sources, meta-analysis can reduce the alpha and beta errors described later in this chapter. Its purposes include: (i) increasing statistical power for outcome assessment and subgroup evaluation; (ii) resolving uncertainty; (iii) improving estimates of effect by increasing sample size; and (iv) providing answers to questions not posed by the original trials. In recent years, the number of clinical trials has multiplied, and several trials of the same treatment may be published serially, often over a span of 10 years or more. At what point should one stop doing more trials? Lau and his colleagues have described a method of using meta-analysis in which the results of clinical trials are accumulated as they are published. This procedure is called **cumulative meta-analysis** which could be used to identify a significant difference between an existing treatment and an experimental one as information from such trials accrue. Such ongoing analyses may help investigators to decide whether continued study of a problem is needed.[9, 10]

1.2.3. Causal Associations

The types of studies outlined in the previous sections are undertaken, frequently in a step-wise fashion, with the overall objective of identifying and establishing associations between exposure to a factor (or factors) and disease or ill-health. Each type of study has its strengths and limitations. *Descriptive studies* serve to generate hypotheses about potential risk factors. *Prevalence studies* can identify potential risk factors in a specific population which can be further investigated by *case-control studies*. By comparing rates of exposure in cases of disease with those free of the disease, case control studies indirectly give an estimate of relative risk. *Cohort studies* are far more costly and time-consuming as subjects are followed over time. However, in cohort studies the relative risk of disease following exposure to a putative risk factor, as well as absolute risk, can be accurately determined. Finally, randomized *experimental (clinical) trials* give the highest calibre information on the effect of a factor, or its removal, on individuals. Community intervention studies, although only quasi-experimental, provide this information for communities. Before concluding that an exposure is causally responsible for a disease (i.e., that there is **causal association**), the following criteria established by Bradford Hill should be satisfied:[11]

- **Experimental evidence:** Is there experimental or quasi-experimental evidence that removal of the putative causative factor results in reduction of disease incidence?
- **Consistency of the association:** Do the findings of studies of the same and different design in different populations demonstrate the same association?
- **Strength of the association:** How large is the relative risk of the outcome in relation to exposure?
- **Dose-response:** Does the severity of the likelihood of the outcome increase as the amount, intensity or duration of the exposure increases?

- **Temporal relationship:** Did the exposure occur before the onset of the disease?
- **Plausibility:** Is the association plausible, given the existing basic science and clinical knowledge about the disease?
- **Coherence:** Does the association make sense in terms of the theory and knowledge about the disease process?
- **Specificity:** Is the association specific for a particular disease or group of diseases? (In practise, however, this often is not satisfied.)
- **Analogy:** Do other established associations provide a model for this type of relationship?

2. INVESTIGATION OF DISEASE IN POPULATIONS

The above section provided an overview of different epidemiological methods in studying health and disease in the population. The following section describes several situations in which these methods are applied to investigate disease in populations.

2.1. OUTBREAKS OF INFECTIOUS DISEASES

An **outbreak** of disease is the occurrence of new cases clearly in excess of the baseline, or normally expected, frequency of the disease in a defined community or institutional population over a given time period. An **epidemic** has a synonymous definition, although in common parlance an "outbreak" usually means an epidemic that is localized, of acute onset and/or relatively short in duration. Recent notable examples of outbreaks—some would say "epidemics"—include the cases of lethal meningococcal disease in adolescents and young adults in five provinces of Canada during 1991 and early 1992. Less noticeable are the outbreaks of diseases of moderate morbidity for the general population but of more severe morbidity for those already compromised in health, such as influenza among nursing home residents or viral gastroenteritis among infants and children in day care. The investigation of an infectious disease outbreak requires particular epidemiological methods that establish the cause, risk factors and modes of transmission of the disease. The control of the outbreak can then be achieved by removing or neutralizing the agent, strengthening the resistance of the "hosts" (persons susceptible to the disease), and interrupting the means of transmission in the environment. Thus, the **agent-host-environment** triad (mentioned in chapter one) is utilized. In addition, the outbreak control response must incorporate appropriate communication and sensitivity to public perceptions of risk, which may differ from "expert" opinions.

2.1.1. Verification of Existence of an Outbreak

As mentioned above, defining that an outbreak exists requires knowledge of the baseline "normally expected" or "usual" frequency of cases of the disease in the specified population. Depending on the type of disease and population, the expected frequency may be a certain number per week or month, or none at all. In addition, in the early stages of an outbreak, the specific diagnosis of the disease or causative agent is usually not yet known, so the most prominent clinical symptoms are used to identify a possible or suspected "case." For example, a nursing home might initially define an outbreak as "three or more residents having diarrhea and vomiting within a 72-hour period," since one or two may be considered within the expected frequency.

Once an outbreak is suspected, investigators (usually from local public health departments) must first ascertain the history of symptoms and signs of the affected persons, so that an initial **case definition** can be formulated from the most common symptoms and/or signs. Included in the case definition is the likely date of onset of illness of the first case (for example, "any person having onset on or since a specified date, of vomiting, fever >38.5° and bloody stools"). Laboratory confirmation of the clinical diagnosis is sought as soon as possible—e.g., culture or serology—and results, when available, can define a case more precisely

After a "case" is defined, the extent of the outbreak should be determined by active surveillance—that is, active efforts to identify all those who may have been exposed to the infectious agent (population at risk) and who may have illness fitting the case definition. In a community outbreak, this may involve contacting hospital emergency rooms, physicians' offices and local schools. Typical epidemiologic information recorded include: personal characteristics (age, sex, etc.); location (residence, school or worksite); details about the illness (date and time of onset, major symptoms); laboratory tests and treatment (if any); immunization status (if relevant); and close contacts with other persons. A **line listing** is typically made of all suspected and confirmed cases.

2.1.2. Implementation of Initial Control Measures

Depending on the symptoms, the suspected agent, the population at risk and the location, initial control measures will be adopted. These may include: isolation of residents in a facility; augmented hand washing and cleaning; cohort nursing (which involves utilizing the same nursing staff for cases for the duration of the outbreak); exclusion of symptomatic staff; immunization (e.g., for influenza or measles); prophylactic medication for those exposed or at risk (e.g., rifampin for bacterial meningitis); or withdrawal of contaminated food from distribution.

Outbreaks of *nosocomial infections* (i.e., those acquired during stay in a health-care facility), require the convening of an *outbreak management team* to coordinate the efforts of many departments—such as housekeeping, maintenance, dietary, nursing and medical staff—in instituting investigation and control measures.

2.1.3. Data Collection and Analysis

As described above, information about the cases—demographic, epidemiologic and laboratory—is gathered and organized in a manner ready for analysis. Telephone and in-person interviews, and sometimes formal questionnaires, may be needed to obtain complete information from cases, family members, health-care providers, and so on.

Analysis of these data is required for investigators to explain the outbreak on the basis of an hypothesis about the causative agent, risk factors and modes of transmission or propagation of the outbreak. The hypothesis may be tested, if time and resources permit, by analytic epidemiology such as case-control studies. Commonly, an epidemic curve is constructed, usually as a frequency histogram with the number of cases plotted on the vertical axis and their dates or times of onset along the horizontal axis. The location (geographic or institutional) of cases may be depicted as a spot map. Attack rates are often also calculated. The use of these methods are described in the following paragraphs.

The investigation and control of **communicable diseases** (infectious diseases that are contagious) requires knowledge of the spectrum of infectious diseases and the relevant terminology. The spectrum of infectious disease is illustrated by the following schematic diagram:

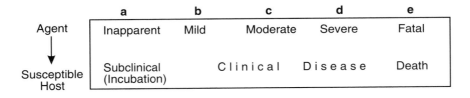

Investigators can determine the severity and pathogenicity of the offending organism by calculating several rates. The **attack rate** is the total number of people who developed clinical disease divided by the population at risk, usually expressed as a percentage. Using the above schematic diagram, the attack rate can be derived by (b+c+d+e)/(population at risk). The **secondary attack rate** is the number of cases among contacts occurring within the accepted incubation period following exposure to a primary case, in relation to the total exposed contacts; the denominator may be restricted to susceptible contacts when determinable.[3] The **pathogenicity rate** describes the power of an organism to produce clinical disease in those who are infected; this is expressed as (b+c+d+e)/(a+b+c+d+e). **Virulence** describes the severity of disease produced by the organism in a given host and is numerically expressed as a ratio of the number of cases of severe and fatal infection to the total number clinically infected, or (d+e)/(b+c+d+e). **Case fatality rate** is the proportion of persons contracting a disease who die of that disease, namely e/(b+c+d+e).

A **reservoir** of infection is a person, animal or inanimate object in which infectious agents can live and multiply for extended periods of time. **Transmission** of such agents occurs by various means through the environment or from one host (human or animal) to another. **Direct** transmission involves the transfer of infectious agents directly from one host to another. **Indirect** transmission can occur through a vehicle, vector or the air. In **vehicle**-borne transmission, organisms are spread via inanimate materials, objects or media (e.g., toys, clothes, milk, food). **Vector**-borne transmission may be mechanical (e.g., simple carriage of agents by animals) or biological (e.g., organisms multiplying inside insect vectors and, in cyclopropagative transmission, continuing the life cycle). Malaria is an example of the latter kind of transmission of parasites from their mosquito vectors to human hosts. **Airborne** transmission may occur via droplet nuclei or dust particles.

A **carrier** is defined as an individual who harbours a specific infectious agent in the absence of overt clinical disease. A carrier state may be of long or short duration, and it may serve as a potential source of infection.

The **communicable period** is the time during which an infectious agent may be transferred from an infected person or vector to another person. **Generation time** is the interval between the entry of infection into the host and its maximal infectivity. **Incubation period** is the time interval between invasion by an infectious agent and the appearance of the first symptom of the disease. Often generation time is equivalent to the incubation period. **Infectiousness** reflects the ease of disease transmission.

The **epidemic curve** (mentioned previously) can visually indicate whether the epidemic (outbreak) has a common (or "point") source or whether it is propagated. In a **common source epidemic**, cases become ill because of exposure to a single (common) source of infection; the exposure may be of long or short duration. A **point source** outbreak is of short duration, with the number of cases rising and falling acutely due to short-term exposure to the infectious source; for example, food poisoning in a group of persons eating the same item(s) at a church picnic. Hence the epidemic curve would show a single, sharp "peak." A **propagated epidemic** may begin with only a few exposed persons but is maintained by person-to-person transmission. The epidemic curve will generally show a series of peaks. Influenza or measles provide good examples of propagated epidemics.

2.1.4. Specific Control Measures

Depending on the cause of the outbreak that is determined and the mode of transmission, specific control measures (such as immunization or specific improvements in the processes of food preparation) may be implemented. Readers are advised to refer to standard textbooks of epidemiology and infection control for details regarding the investigation and control of outbreaks.

2.2.   CLUSTERS OF DISEASE

One of the most frequent problems faced by local health units or a provincial department of health is the concern of local residents and practising physicians about apparently excessive numbers of health problems or diseases in their community.   For example, residents may express concern about an apparent excess number of cancer deaths or birth defects in their community.   The excess number of cases is often referred to as a cluster.   Caldwell[12] defines a **cluster** as a number of like or similar things occurring together in time and space.   The definition could apply to any disease or health event with a local, regional, or national pattern of incidence, or even groups of cases linked by shared exposure or activities, interpersonal or occupational.   This definition includes the notion of disease aggregation and its etiology.   In common usage in epidemiology, "cluster" is used for noninfectious diseases, while "epidemic" and "outbreak" refer to infectious disease.

The first step in investigation is to identify the type of disease cluster: (i) clustering of possibly related diseases within the same person;   (ii) clustering within families or other interpersonal networks;   (iii) clustering in time (i.e., cases of the same disease within a short time period);   (iv) clustering in space (i.e., within close geographic proximity);   or (v) clustering in both time and space.

Next, one determines the population at risk of exposure to the putative causal agent of the disease (e.g., a suspected environmental carcinogen).   A similar but non-exposed group is defined as a reference population (control group) for comparison.   A "case" definition is formulated and cases, both new and existing, are actively ascertained in both the exposed and the reference populations within a standard time frame for observation.   By means of statistical tests, the observed number of cases in the population at risk can be compared to the "expected" number in the reference population.

If one does find a statistically significant excess of cases (a "true cluster"), then appropriate epidemiological studies are needed to assess the degree of exposure to the suspected causal factor (e.g., a chemical or physical agent) and to test the hypothesis that this agent is indeed a cause of, or significant risk factor for, the disease in question.

2.3.   ASYMPTOMATIC DISEASE

Prior to the development of symptoms, or physical signs noticeable to health professionals, diseases may exist in affected persons without their knowledge (asymptomatic disease).   Diabetes, hypertension and cancer (such as breast cancer or cancer of the uterine cervix) fall into this category.   The commonly used method for detecting asymptomatic disease in a population is screening.   **Screening** is defined as "the presumptive identification of unrecognized disease or defect by the application of tests, examinations or other procedures which can be applied rapidly.[1,13] Thus, the goal of a screening program is early detection—identifying which persons in the community probably have a disease and which probably do not. Examples of screening procedures are mammography for breast cancer and pap tests for cervical cancer in the female.

2.3.1. Types of Screening

There are three types of screening (mass, selective, and multiphasic) which are usually carried out in the community.

Mass screening for tuberculosis by chest x-ray, for example, is done in many developing countries where the disease is still highly prevalent. It is not performed en masse in developed countries where the prevalence is low. However, mass screening of women for cervical cancer by the Papanicolaou smear is generally accepted in developed countries.

Selective screening is performed on selected subgroups of a population at increased risk of developing certain diseases. Tay-Sachs disease (which is transmitted by a recessive gene and causes mental retardation and early death among infants), is quite common among French Canadians in some parts of Quebec. Thus, screening for carriers coupled with genetic counselling may be worthwhile in this population. Periodic examinations of blood and urine lead levels among occupationally exposed persons is another form of selective screening.

Multiphasic screening programs include a medical history, physical examination and various measurements and investigations. The objective is to detect as many disease states as possible with one screening intervention. Screening of this nature is done by large organizations, especially US organizations (such as Kaiser Permanente and the Health Insurance Plan of New York) which operate prepaid group health plans.

2.3.2. Characteristics of Screening

Screening tests, however, are not diagnostic tests. Persons with positive or questionable results must be referred for diagnostic evaluation and if indicated, treatment. For screening to fulfil its intended purpose, there should be adequate, effective, and accessible methods of diagnosis and treatment for screened individuals found abnormal. When one performs a screening test on an apparently healthy population, there are a number of possible outcomes (figure 2.1). The positive or negative results may not reflect the presence or absence of disease.

Screening tests are evaluated in terms of their validity, reliability and yield. The **validity** of a screening test is measured by the frequency with which the result of the test is confirmed by an accurate diagnostic method and is often expressed in terms of its sensitivity and specificity. **Sensitivity** is the proportion (percentage) of truly diseased persons identified as diseased by a test. **Specificity** is the proportion (percentage) of truly non-diseased persons who are so identified by the test (table 2.2).

Figure 2.1: Mass Screening

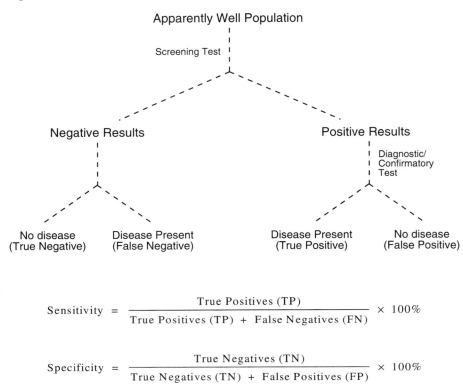

$$\text{Sensitivity} = \frac{\text{True Positives (TP)}}{\text{True Positives (TP) + False Negatives (FN)}} \times 100\%$$

$$\text{Specificity} = \frac{\text{True Negatives (TN)}}{\text{True Negatives (TN) + False Positives (FP)}} \times 100\%$$

Tests with low sensitivity and specificity (i.e., low percentages of correctly identifying those who have and do not have the disease, respectively) are poor screening tests. To have high sensitivity, screening tests must produce few false negative results; for high specificity, few false positive results should arise. A screening test is never 100% sensitive and specific. High sensitivity is gained at the expense of specificity and vice versa. Thus, raising test sensitivity will result in loss of specificity and the appearance of false positives.

Positive predictive value is measured as the proportion of true positives in all test positives (i.e., the proportion of cases who truly have the disease among those with positive tests). The predictive value of a positive test tends to be higher when the disease is more prevalent (table 2.3). The **negative predictive value** is the test's ability to identify all those who truly don't have the disease among all those who tested negative.   The predictive value of a negative test decreases with increasing disease prevalence.

Table 2.2: Result of a Hypothetical Screening Test

Disease Present

		YES	NO
Result of Test	**POSITIVE**	True positive	False positive
	NEGATIVE	False negative	True negative

$$\text{Positve Predictive Value} = \frac{\text{True Positives (TP)}}{\text{True Positives (TP) + False Positives (FP)}} \times 100\%$$

$$\text{Negative Predictive Value} = \frac{\text{True Negatives (TN)}}{\text{True Negatvies (TN) + False Negatives (FN)}} \times 100\%$$

The **reliability** of a screening test refers to its ability to produce consistent results when applied to different populations or repeatedly to the same individual. The **yield** from a screening test is the amount of previously unrecognized disease detected in the population; it depends on the sensitivity of the screening test as well as the prevalence of unrecognized disease in a population. For example, the yield from the Papanicolaou smear is very low among virgins but is much higher among sexually active females.

2.3.3. Criteria for the Population Based Screening Program

As new tests or procedures emerge for screening for a disease, there are pressures on health professionals and the health-care system to adopt and institutionalize them. Then, however, screening can only be justified if the following criteria are met:[14]

1. Diseases for which screening is used should be important health problems. When there is an extremely low incidence of a disease in a population, the cost and effort of mass screening may be prohibitive. Epidemiological studies to deter-

Table 2.3: Predictive Values of a Positive Test with 99% Sensitivity and 95% Specificity at Three Levels of Prevalence

Item	Level of Prevalence		
	1 Per cent	10 Per cent	20 Per cent
a) No. in population	1000	1000	1000
b) Diseased	10	100	200
c) Not Diseased	990	900	800
d) True Positive (b x 0.99)	10	99	198
e) False Positive (c x 1-0.95)	50	45	40
f) Total Positive (d + e)	60	144	238
g) Predictive Value of a Positive Test (d/f)	17%	69%	83%

mine the incidence and prevalence of various diseases in a community may be necessary before embarking on any large scale screening operations.

2. Facilities for diagnosis and treatment should be available since lack of follow-up negates any possible benefit of the screening test.

3. Effective noncontroversial treatment for patients with confirmed disease should be available.

4. Screening tests should have high sensitivity and specificity; screening must be safe, rapidly applied, (usually) given by well-trained technicians and acceptable to the screened population. While chest radiographs or a blood test may not bother most individuals, the discomfort produced by sigmoidoscopy may be unacceptable.

5. The natural history of the disease (i.e., the precursor, asymptomatic, and symptomatic stages) should be thoroughly understood. If controlled studies have demonstrated that the natural history of the disease is not favourably altered by earlier detection and treatment, then screening for that particular disease should not be instituted. For example, periodic screening by chest x-rays for lung cancer does not improve the prognosis of the disease. Primary prevention methods such as cessation or prevention of smoking are more effective than chest x-ray screening in controlling lung cancer.

6. Prior agreement or policy must stipulate what action will be taken for borderline results in order to avoid the problem of over-diagnosis of disease.

7. Comparing the costs and efficiency of various screening methods for a disease are essential for achieving maximum benefit for minimum cost.

8. It is important to compare control and screened groups at regular intervals to establish whether the screening procedure and subsequent investigations have any greater effect than just regular observation of the control groups. In one study, it was demonstrated that systematic, regular examination of a control group of individuals appeared to exert a similar effect on the blood pressure, glucose tolerance, and cholesterol level compared to the screened group.

9. Compliance with screening recommendations is essential. There may be no benefit in screening without compliance with effective treatment.

10. If instituted, screening programs should be a continuing process rather than having "one time only."

Beyond these accepted criteria, one should make other considerations before instituting a province-wide or country-wide program:[15]

• Are the screening program requirements for time, money, and costs appropriate for the community ?
• Are other equally worthy procedures and efforts being given equal consideration or are existing resources being redirected unnecessarily?
• Does the procedure create new medical risks, and how are these assessed in relation to the procedure?
• Does the procedure place additional strain on health-care resources in a disproportionate manner to the magnitude of the health problem being studied?
• What are the limitations of using screening assessments as a widespread diagnostic tool in relation to other diagnostic approaches?
• Are there specific ethical or moral issues raised by the program?
• How will the objectives of the screening program be communicated to the various groups?

3. RELEVANT STATISTICAL CONCEPTS

Statistics are frequently used in studying the health and disease of populations. Statistics deal with the collection, classification, description, analysis, interpretation and presentation of data and are the backbone of all epidemiologic research. A brief summary is provided here; more detailed discussion is available in standard statistical textbooks[16] and in a short review.[17] A population can consist of individuals, events, observations or any other grouping. Data can be derived from an entire population or from a sample.

A **sample** is a selected part of the population and may be randomly selected, systematically selected, stratified selected, cluster selected or non-random (convenience) in nature. The sampling strategy will influence the amount of bias.

Data collected can be either grouped or ungrouped, qualitative or quantitative. Data can be discrete (e.g., a finite number such as 2 or 3, but not 2.5) or continuous (where an unlimited number of possible values can exist as in measurements with decimal points).

Health data consist of sets of numerical information about anything related to health. They are the basic scientific tools with which we study health and disease, but, like any tools, they must be of suitable quality to do the job expected. First, data must be **reliable**—when the same group of people is measured more than once, similar values must be obtained. Second, data must be **valid**—it must relate to the problem studied. For example, we expect hospital admissions to provide a valid assessment of the incidence of third-degree (very severe) burns, but not to measure the incidence of diabetes, since many patients with diabetes are not hospitalized. Thus, **validity** reflects an expression of the degree to which a measurement measures what it purports to measure. Also, data in the health field must have sufficient resolution to give the answers being sought; like a microscopist, the epidemiologist may need to see one part of the problem in great detail. For example, a report of a slight increase in the national incidence of tuberculosis would not indicate where the cases were or in what groups of people they occurred. No action could be taken until these details were known utilizing epidemiologic and statistical techniques. Third, data must be **precise** - the measuring instrument defines how "sharply" it can provide a value. For example, a measurement of four decimal places is more precise than two decimal places. Of course, very precise data may be neither valid nor reliable.

Measures of **central tendency** describe the middle, or most commonly occurring, observed values in a series and include the mean, median and mode.

The **mean** is the sum of all values in a series divided by the actual number of observations in a series. It can be calculated by:

$$\bar{x} = \sum \frac{x_i}{n}$$

Figure 2.2: Distribution Curves

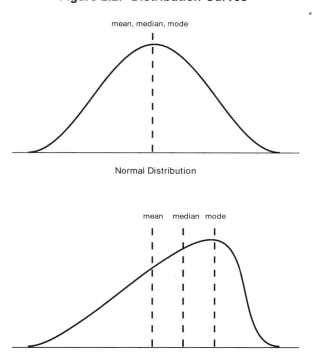

mean, median, mode

Normal Distribution

mean   median mode

Distribution Skewed to the Left

The **median** is obtained by ranking the data and choosing the value that divides the series into two equal groups so that there are as many observations above as there are below the median value.   The **mode** is the most frequently observed value in a series of observations.

The **distribution** of observations may be normal (Gaussian) or skewed (figure 2.2). If a group of observations is normally distributed, the mean, median and mode have the same value. If the distribution is skewed, then the mode and median move to the direction of the skew. The *mean* is not easily affected and thus is considered the best measure of **central tendency**.

The variability of observations can be measured by the range, variance, and standard deviation.

The **range** is the difference between the lowest and highest observation in the distribution.   For example, if a series of five observations of systolic blood pressure are 140, 160, 150, 120 and 110 mm Hg, the range is 50 mm Hg; this is the difference in value between the high of 160 mm Hg and the low of 110 mm Hg.

The **variance** is the sum of the squared deviations from the mean divided by the number of observations in the series minus 1. It is obtained by using the formula:

$$s^2 = \frac{\sum (x - \bar{x})^2}{n-1}$$

The **standard deviation** is the positive square root of the variance:

$$s = \sqrt{\frac{\sum (x - \bar{x})^2}{n-1}}$$

A theoretical normal distribution has as its mean an observation named mu (μ). The range of observations between one standard deviation below and above the mean covers 68% of all observations. This range covers the 16th percentile to the 84th percentile. The range between two standard deviations below and above the mean covers 95% of all observations. This range extends from the 2.5th percentile to the 97.5th percentile. The range between three standard deviations above and below the mean covers 99% of all observations.

Data may also be represented pictorially by way of pie charts (circles), Venn diagrams, histograms and bar graphs.

Epidemiologists use tests of statistical significance to evaluate results obtained in their investigations. Tests of statistical significance evaluate the chance of results as extreme as those observed being the results of random variation (i.e., due to chance rather than the factor hypothesized to cause the outcomes measured).

Tests of statistical significance include the X^2 (**chi-square**) test and the **t-test**. Another method used to assess significance is the calculation of 95% confidence intervals around a given measure.

The use of 95% **confidence intervals** is becoming increasingly popular in the literature. The upper and lower limits define the range of probability at a 5% significance level. If the mean of a set of systolic blood pressures is 130 mm Hg, and the 95% confidence limits are 120 mm Hg and 140 mm Hg, then the inference is that 19 times out of 20 the true mean lies somewhere in the range between 120 and 140 mm Hg.

Depending upon the data set, an appropriate statistical test is chosen and applied. Using statistical tables, a conclusion regarding statistical significance may be made. These are usually found in the back of most statistics texts.

The **null hypothesis** states that there is, in fact, no real difference between the groups being compared, and that the differences seen are due to chance. Thus, a p-value of 0.05 or less allows one to reject the null hypothesis and select the alternative hypothesis (i.e., that there is, in fact, a difference between the groups being compared). It must be pointed out that at a p-value less than 0.05 there is still a small chance that random variation may be responsible for the observed difference.

Table 2.4: Type I and Type II Error Probabilities

Truth

		Treatment Benefits (H$_1$)	No Benefit (H$_0$)
Result from the Study	**POSITIVE**	**True positive** Correctly reject H$_0$ p= 1 - β	**False positive** Type I Error Incorrectly reject H$_0$ p= α
	NEGATIVE	**False negative** Type II Error Incorrectly do not reject H$_0$ p= β	**True negative** Correctly do not reject H$_0$ p= 1 - α

Table 2.4 indicates the type of errors that can occur in the interpretation of data. The truth, or gold standard, is whether the intervention confers benefit or not. A **Type I or alpha error** is the incorrect rejection of a null hypothesis or asserting that there is a difference between treatments when in fact there is not. Thus, in a situation of p=0.05, there is a 5% chance, or 1 out of 20 chance, of rejecting a null hypothesis which should not be rejected.

A **Type II or beta error** occurs when the null hypothesis is not rejected when it should be or when there is a failure to recognize a difference in the result of an intervention when it is actually present.

The chance of a Type II error occurring is used to determine the power of a study, which is 1 minus beta. The power of a study is the probability that a difference will be detected when there is indeed a difference.

The levels of acceptable error are set by the investigator. In general, an alpha level of 5% and beta level of 20% (power 80%) are acceptable. After setting the desired alpha and beta levels, one can calculate the sample size required for a study. If the expected difference and the sample size are small, the risk of missing a genuine difference is large. If the expected difference and the sample size are large, the risk is small.

Another technique used in data analysis is **multivariate analysis**. This method concurrently controls for many factors in order to remove confounding effects. A **confounding variable** or factor can account for some or all of the association between the exposure factor under study and an observed outcome. (For example, the apparent association between alcohol consumption and the occurrence of chronic bronchitis is best explained by the known association of cigarette smoking with both of these phenomena. Smoking is thus the confounding factor.) Multivariate analysis can be performed in different ways, depending on whether the data are collected retrospectively or prospectively. It may also be used to develop prediction models.

Figure 2.3: Scatter Diagram Showing Correlation Coefficient

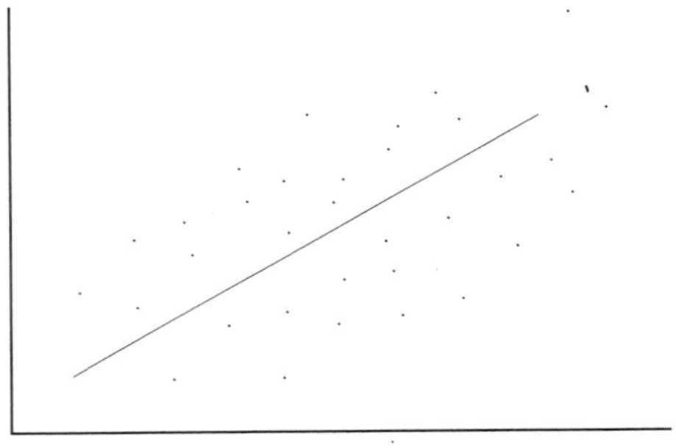

The **correlation coefficient,** or r value, is yet another method of data analysis. This method involves the plotting of quantitative data on a scatter diagram and an r value is calculated (figure 2.3).

A high value (e.g., r=0.9) indicates a high correlation between the variables under study. It does not imply causality.

4.   SUMMARY

This chapter examined the data quality, epidemiologic studies, investigation of diseases in populations and some relevant statistical concepts. Health data consist of sets of numerical information about anything related to health and is assembled from many sources. These data must meet three criteria: they must be reliable, valid and must have sufficient resolution.

Epidemiologic studies are a commonly used method for data collection and analysis. Epidemiology is the study of the distribution (which is studied in terms of person, place and time) and the determinants of disease, health related states and events in populations. Epidemiology can be applied to control of health problems. There are two types of epidemiological studies: descriptive and analytical.

A **descriptive study** investigates the occurrence of a phenomenon in relation to person, time and place. Causal associations should not be drawn from the results of a descriptive study; however, the results may lend themselves to an hypothesis for investigation of a causal association or relationship.

In **analytic studies**, an hypothesis is tested to find out if there is an association between a given disease, health state or other dependent variable, and possible causative factors. There are two types of analytic studies: observational and experimental.

Observational studies include: (1) *cross sectional or prevalence studies*—such studies examine the relationship between diseases and other variables of interest as they exist in a defined population at **one** particular time. The population is divided into those with and without the disease and then various characteristics of the two groups are examined. This study reveals the prevalence of disease, disability, and risk factors in a given population at one point in time; (2) *retrospective studies*—these studies are used to test etiologic hypotheses in which inferences about exposure to the putative causal factor or factors are derived from data relating to characteristics of the persons under study or to events or experiences in their past. The study takes the form of a case-control study in which patients (cases) with the disease are compared with similar people without the disease (controls) who have also had the opportunity for exposure. Hence, a retrospective study begins after the disease has appeared; (3) *prospective or cohort studies*—in these studies a cohort (a group of people with common characteristics) is identified, and the initial characteristics and health status are compared to those of a control cohort (chosen on the same basis as the original cohort, except for exposure to the suspected cause of disease), and both groups are followed for a certain time period to observe for evidence of disease or other outcomes. These studies yield incidence rates, attributable risk, relative risk, and incidence density.

Experimental studies are those in which conditions are under the direct control of the investigator, and they are conducted like laboratory experiments. These studies include randomized clinical trials or therapeutic trials and community trials. In a therapeutic trial, subjects with a disease are randomized into two or more groups. One group is subjected to the intervention which is being evaluated—usually a treatment—while the other group (control) is given either an inactive treatment (placebo) or current standard treatment. Subjects are usually blinded to the treatment status and this procedure is called a single-blind trial. Trials where neither patient nor observer knows the group assignment are called double-blind randomized clinical trials. If the final outcomes show a statistically significant difference between the study group and the controls, then the results obtained are usually attributed to the treatment. The community trial is used when a comparison study of two communities is desired in order to see what effects a variable has on the health of the community. One community is given an intervention while another serves as a control.

For a cause-effect relationship (i.e., to establish causal association), the following criteria must be met: experimental evidence, consistency of association, strength of association, dose-response, correct temporal relationship, plausibility, coherence, specificity, and analogy.

The stages in the investigation for an infectious disease include: verification of the existence of an outbreak, implementation of initial control measures, analysis and specific control measures.

The commonly used method for detecting asymptomatic disease is screening. In order to screen for a disease, a number of criteria must be met. There are various types of screening which can be carried out within a community; two examples are mass screening and selective screening. Screening tests are evaluated in terms of their validity, reliability, and yield. The validity of a screening test is measured by the frequency with which the result of the test is confirmed by an accurate diagnostic method and is often expressed in terms of its sensitivity and specificity. The sensitivity of a test is the proportion of truly diseased who are identified as diseased by a test. Specificity is the proportion of truly non-diseased persons who are so identified by the test. Tests with low sensitivity and low specificity are poor screening tests. However, a screening test is never 100% sensitive or specific. High sensitivity is gained at the expense of specificity and vice versa. The reliability of a screening test refers to its ability to produce consistent results when applied to various screened populations or even repeatedly on the same individual. The yield from a screening test is the amount of unrecognized disease that is detected in the population, and thus it will depend on the sensitivity of the screening test as well as the prevalence of unrecognized disease in a population.

Statistics deal with the collection, classification, description, analysis, interpretation and presentation of data, and they are the backbone of all epidemiological research.

5. REFERENCES

1. Mausner J and Kramer S. *Epidemiology: An Introductory Text,* 2nd ed. Philadelphia: WB Saunders, 1985.
2. Hennekens C, Buring J and Mayrent S, eds. *Epidemiology in Medicine,* 1st ed. Boston: Little, Brown and Co, 1987.
3. Sackett D, Haynes R and Tugwell P. *Clinical Epidemiology: A Basic Sciences for Clinical Medicine.* 2nd ed, Toronto: Little, Brown and Co., 1991.
4. Last J. *A Dictionary of Epidemiology,* 2nd ed. New York: Oxford University Press, 1988.
5. Denson R, Nanson J and McWatters M. Hyperkinesis and Maternal Smoking. *Can Psychol Assoc J* 20(3):183-187, 1975.
6. Castel W. Epidemiology of Coronary Heart Disease: The Framingham Study. *Am J Med* 76(2A):11-12, 1984.
7. Shah C, Robinson G, Kinnis C and Davenport H. Day Care Surgery for Children: A Controlled Study of Medical Complications and Parental Attitudes. *Med Care* 10(5):437-50, 1972.
8. Sacks H, Berrier J, Reitman D, Ancona-Berk V and Chalmers T. Meta-analysis of Randomized Controlled Trials. *N Engl J Med* 316(8):450-455, 1987.
9. Lau J, Antman E, Jimenez-Silva J, Kupelnick B, Mosteller F and Chalmers T. Cumulative Meta-Analysis of Therapeutic Trials for Myocardial Infarction. *N Engl J Med* 327(4):241-247, 1992.
10. Kassirer J. Clinical Trials and Meta-Analysis—What Do They Do For Us? *N Engl J Med* 327(4):273-274, 1992.
11. Bradford Hill A. *The Principles of Medical Statistics,* 9th ed. London: The Lancet LTD, 1971.
12. Caldwell G. Time-Space Cancer Clusters. *Health Environ Digest* 3(5):4-5, 1989.
13. Whitby L. Screening For Disease - Definitions and Criteria. *Lancet* 2(3):819-821, 1974.
14. Glausnov I, Dowd J, Jaksic E, et al. Repetitive Health Examination as an Intervention Measure. *Bull WHO* 49(4):423-432, 1973.
15. Task Force on the Use and Provision of Medical Services. *1989-1990 Annual Report.* Government of Ontario and Ontario Medical Association. Toronto, 1990.
16. Glantz S. *Primer of Biostatistics,* 2nd ed. New York: McGraw-Hill Inc, 1987.
17. Leaverton P. *A Review of Biostatistics. A Program for Self-Instruction,* 4th ed. Boston: Little, Brown and Co., 1986.

Part 2

Health of Canadians

CHAPTER THREE
Health Indicators and Data Sources

The rational planning and evaluation of services to meet the health-care needs of a population must be based on data concerning the health status of that population and how it is evolving. As government involvement in the provision of health care has increased, interest in the measurement of health and demand for data on the health of the population for which governments are responsible has increased. A number of contemporary trends have reinforced and consolidated that interest. These include: changes in the demography of the population; patterns of disease and illness and medical practice; disenchantment with technology; and the increasing costs of health care.

The measurement of health dates back to the mid-19th century when governments first began to collect information on death and the causes of death. These mortality statistics continue to be a major source of information about health. However, data on mortality are useful only in developing countries where death rates remain high. In industrialized countries where death rates are much lower, mortality statistics and associated measures such as life expectancy are no longer adequate as indicators of health. They do not take into consideration illness that does not result in death nor the often profound disability and distress which may accompany such illness. In accordance with contemporary concerns about the quality of life, this broader definition has made the measurement of health more complex. We must now take into account the physical, psychological and social status of the individual.

1.   HEALTH INDICATORS

Health indicators are qualitative and quantitative statistical indices which describe the health of a population. A useful hierarchy of community health indicators, which addresses health in its broad sense and which has been utilized in the Canada and Quebec Health Surveys, considers health on three main levels: **determinants**, **health status** and **consequences,** with each of these levels incorporating biological, psychological and social elements.[1] **Determinants** are factors which are not health problems per se but are believed to be related to the development of disease.   **Health status** is viewed in the framework as health problems which are "concrete, medical conditions of individuals or groups"[2] or pathology.   **Consequences** are the effects of health problems on the individual, such as in disability; on the health-care system, such as hospitalization; and on society in general, including the economic burden.   The following section provides specific definitions and methodologies for deriving some representative common health indicators.   A comprehensive description of health indicators for Canada is presented in the subsequent two chapters.   It is important to note that there is no ideal taxonomy of indicators. The framework utilized is only a guide to a useful way of organizing information on many aspects of health.   Additionally, there is a paucity of indicators for some aspects which theoretically are considered important and for which further research is needed.   Ease of access is a health indicator which may in itself only be an indirect, proxy measure for the underlying concept.

Usually, health data take into account the population where the events have occurred.   Hence in most situations, one needs a numerator, i.e., the occurrence of an event under observation, and a denominator, i.e., size of population where the event occurred.   As ill health events are relatively rare, they are expressed in terms of per 100, 1,000, 10,000, or 100,000 population.   For example, the smoking prevalence for a given population may be expressed as 40% whereas death rates are expressed as 7 deaths per 1000 people per year.   A rare event like lung cancer in males is expressed as 55 per 100,000 population per year.   Similarly, use of hospital days is expressed as 112 days per 1,000 population.

The commonly used means of data expression are ratio, proportion and rate.   A **ratio** is an expression of the relationship between two items that are usually independent of each other.   If there are six males and 12 females, then the ratio of males to females is 1:2.

A **proportion** is the relationship of a part to its whole expressed as a percentage.   If there are 25 ill persons out of 100 persons, then the proportion of ill persons is 25%.

A **rate** is an expression of the probability of an occurrence of an event in a defined population at risk during a specific time period.

In the following sections, commonly used health indicators are defined and in some instances their derivations are explained.   More detailed information on the subject is provided in the book *Demographic and Health Indicators*.[3]   Other commonly used indicators for disease, disability and risk factors are **incidence** and **prevalence rates**, and **attributable** and **relative risk**, which have been described earlier in the section on cross-sectional and prospective studies.

1.1. DETERMINANTS

1.1.1. Environment

As discussed in chapter one, the environment encompasses both the physical and psychosocial milieu to which the population is exposed.

Physical Environment

Canadians may be exposed to toxic substances or other environmental hazards from a variety of sources, including food, water, air, soil, and consumer products. Federal, provincial and municipal health and environment ministries and agencies have programs for monitoring levels of contamination and other environmental hazards, and for risk assessment of exposures. Risk assessment is the qualitative and quantitative determination of the risk to human health posed by an environmental agent.[4] There are several ways in which the environment is monitored in relation to quality and degree of contamination.

Health risk assessment of **food chemical contaminants** is a scientific, multi-step process usually carried out by the Health Protection Branch, Health Canada. Similar approaches are used in addressing potential health threats from other sources. Health risk assessment consists of the following steps:

(i) *Determination of the toxicity of the chemical contaminant*, (i.e., its capacity to cause harm), enables scientists to establish a quantity of the chemical that humans can consume on a daily basis, for a lifetime, with reasonable assurance that their health will not be threatened. This quantity is called the **tolerable daily intake or TDI**.

TDIs for humans are usually based on studies carried out on laboratory animals. In these studies, researchers establish a level of exposure to the chemical at which no adverse effects are observed in the animals. This level is then divided by a safety factor to derive the TDI. Depending on the extent of the laboratory studies and the adverse effects that the substance can cause, the safety factor may range from 100 to several thousand or more.

(ii) *Determination of the **probable daily intake, or the PDI**, of the chemical contaminant* is necessary to determine which foods, if any, can contribute more of the contaminant than others. To do this, scientists must first identify all foods that may contain the substance being evaluated, keeping in mind that the chemical may occur naturally in some foods.

Food intake is the factor that contributes to dietary exposure to a specified chemical contaminant. Collecting valid data is extremely difficult since food consumption habits vary greatly based on such factors as gender, age, location, cultural background and socioeconomic status. Both average and high consumption rates must be taken into account, as well as the potential exposure of specific sub-groups in the population (such as children or the elderly). Finally, consideration must be given to other potential sources of exposure, such as air and water, in order to arrive at a realistic estimate of probable daily intake.

(iii) If the probable daily intake of the contaminant under review exceeds the tolerable daily intake then risk management options are considered.

Identification of potential contamination of nutritional sources includes the **monitoring of breast milk** for contaminants such as dioxins and PCBs (polychlorinated biphenyls) and the levels of these contaminants in fish, and animals in local environments where subsistence fishing and hunting is practised by the First Nations Peoples.

In Canada, **water quality** should conform to accepted guidelines, such as the Guidelines for Canadian Drinking Water Quality. These are designed to ensure that the water is free from pathogenic organisms, harmful chemicals, radioactive matter and should be palatable. **Maximum acceptable concentrations (MACs)** for a wide range of chemicals, esthetic objectives and microbiologic characteristics for water have been defined.

The microbiologic assessment of drinking water generally involves assessment for coliform organisms as a marker of fecal contamination. More recently, in recreational water, the presence of *Escherichia coli* at specified levels is regarded as an indicator of fecal contamination. Although viruses have been implicated in water-borne disease outbreaks, no specific virologic standard applies. The turbidity of water is assessed both for esthetic purposes and because turbidity can interfere with the detection methods for bacteriologic quality and with the disinfection process.

MACs are also applicable in assessing individual **air contaminants**. The air quality index, whereby the levels of six contaminants of concern, namely ozone, oxides of nitrogen and sulphur, carbon monoxide, lead and total sulphur particles, is also utilized as a summary index for monitoring air quality.

Industrial engineers use several methods for setting standards for the exposure limits to hazardous substances in the work environment. When legislation recognizes these limits these constitute legal standards. Where levels are not defined, the acceptable code of practice is usually set on a 40-hour work week (i.e., eight hours a day). They rely on **threshold limit values** (TLVs). These TLVs are usually known as time weighted averages (TWAs). These values are determined by the American Conference of Governmental Industrial Hygienists (ACGIH), and the assumption is that a small percentage of workers will suffer adverse effects as a result of exposure at the TLV-TWA levels set. These values are published annually. A revision of the values is undertaken if the scientific literature provides justification.

An example of another type of environmental indicator is the motor traffic accident mortality rate which is the mean annual number of motor vehicle accident deaths during a given period per total population at mid-period multiplied by 100,000.

Psychosocial Environment
Indicators of the psychosocial environment incorporate demographic indicators, such as the age and sex of the population, and population growth rate, both of

which are discussed in the next chapter. Definitions of natality and fertility rates and life expectancy, which are also demographic indicators, are given below:

Crude Birth Rate: The annual number of live births per 1,000 population.

General Fertility Rate: The annual number of live births per 1,000 women in the age group 15-49 years. This is a more refined measure of fertility than the crude birth rate.

Total Fertility Rate: The average number of children that would be born alive to a woman during her lifetime if she were to pass through all her childbearing years conforming to the age-specific fertility rates of a given year.

Life Expectancy at Birth: This is the average number of years a newborn baby is expected to live if current mortality trends continue. Generally speaking, it is an indication of the intrinsic health of a population, or the integrated result of the interaction of many determinants of health and disease in the population.

Indicators of the social environment also include demographic indicators that have slightly more emphasis on the social content. **Sociodemographic** indicators include ethnicity, language, family size, proportion of single-parent families, proportion of low birth weight infants (births of infants weighing less than 2,500 gms), and proportion of elderly persons (the health of the elderly is discussed in chapter six). **Socioeconomic indicators** include educational levels, literacy, unemployment rates and income distribution.

1.1.2. Lifestyle, Behaviours and Risk Factors

These determinants are measured in many ways. Common indicators, for example, might include the following: the proportion of the population who are smokers, who are obese, who consume 14 or more alcoholic drinks per week or who wear seat belts. The risk of adverse health outcomes for individuals may be measured by either relative risk or odds ratio (defined in chapter two).   To calculate these risk measures, data on the number of persons who have the disease or do not have it and those who were exposed to the suspected causal or risk factor or not exposed are arranged in a two-by-two table in the following manner.

	DISEASE (cases)	NO DISEASE (control)
POSITIVE	a	b
NEGATIVE	c	d

(Exposure)

The relative risk of those exposed having the disease, compared to the unexposed is:

$$\left(\frac{a}{a+b}\right) \div \left(\frac{c}{c+d}\right)$$

The **odds ratio** (OR) of a case (i.e., a diseased person) having been exposed, compared to a control (non-diseased), is **a** x **d/b** x **c.** One can see that for rare diseases, i.e., where the values of **a** and **c** are small, the formula for RR approximates **(a/b)/(c/d)**, which equals **a** x **d/b** x **c.** In such a scenario, the OR (derived from a case-control study) is a suitable estimator of the RR (derived from the more costly cohort study). For details, readers are advised to consult a standard epidemiological textbook. The indicator described below (PAR) and its derivations indicate the degree to which a lifestyle, behaviour or risk factor is contributing to disease in the population, and what the potential impact of eliminating the factor could be.

Attributable Fraction or **Population Attributable Risk (PAR)** is a measure of the amount of disease associated with an exposure within a population.[4] This can be derived by subtracting the incidence rate in the unexposed groups from the incidence rate in the total population and dividing by the incidence rate in the total population. This indicator provides an estimate of the proportion of cases which may be ascribed to the factor in question. PAR can also be calculated directly from the relative risk and the prevalence of exposure to the risk factor in the population.[5] For details, readers are advised to consult a standard epidemiological textbook.

1.1.3. Indicators of Human Biology

These determinants of health include age and sex. Put simply, women, men, children and the elderly have different potentials for health and ill-health. Due to the interaction with social and economic conditions, age/sex has been incorporated under social environment determinants.[2] Other indicators of human biology, however, are poorly developed, and genetic inheritance, where known, is currently the best example of this type of indicator. The Human Genome Project offers the potential for complete knowledge of the human gene and the identification of an individual's genetic make up. Mass screening programs for phenylketonuria (PKU) are well-established, and screening occurs for Tay-Sachs disease and the sickle cell trait and is anticipated for cystic fibrosis. Many ethical issues are raised by the prospect of mass genetic screening for diseases and abuse of the technology, as it may stigmatize the individuals.[6] The implications of genetic screening will likely emerge as a public health concern.

Indicators of contact with the *health system* are discussed later in this chapter.

1.2. HEALTH STATUS

Health status indicators include **subjective** assessments, such as the inclusion of questions concerning the perception of one's own health or the proportion of persons reporting one or more health problems in surveys. **Objective** indicators of health status include mortality, hospital morbidity, and non-hospital morbidity from records of consultation. Morbidity is generally measured in terms of incidence and prevalence rates of the diseases, and also in terms of hospital morbidity. The derivation of incidence and prevalence rate has been described in chapter two. Hospital morbidity is generally measured in terms of hospital separation rates. The latter is made up of the number of individuals who are either discharged from hospital or have died divided by the number of people in the population. Some objective indicators of community health status are indicated below, and their derivations are summarized in table 3.1.

Infant Mortality Rate
The annual number of deaths in children less than one year of age per 1000 live births in the same year. The infant mortality rate is another useful indicator of the level of health in a community and is commonly used for comparing health among different nations.

Crude Death Rate
The annual number of deaths per 1000 population.

Perinatal Mortality Rate
The annual number of stillbirths (gestation 20 weeks or more) and early neonatal deaths (up to first seven days of life) per 1000 total births. Perinatal mortality usually reflects standards of perinatal care, maternal nutrition, and obstetric and pediatric care.

Neonatal Mortality Rate
The annual number of deaths in a year of children under 28 days of age per 1000 live births in the same year.

Maternal Mortality Rate
The annual number of maternal deaths from puerperal causes within 42 days of delivery per 100,000 live births in the same year.

Age and Sex-specific Death Rate
The annual number of deaths in a particular age and sex group per 1000 population of that sub-group.

Standardized Death Rates
As risk of dying varies widely by age (i.e., older people are at a greater risk of dying than younger ones), the annual frequency of deaths in a population depends on its age composition. Hence comparing two populations' crude death rates may give a false impression. For example, the crude death rate in the native population of Canada is 5.5/1000 compared with 7.2/1000 for the entire Canadian population. However, 43% of the native population is under 15 years of age compared with only 23% for the Canadian population. The basic principle of standardization is to introduce a standard population with a fixed age and sex structure. For example,

an age-standardized mortality rate is the overall death rate that a population would have if it had the standard age structure. Age-standardized rates are sometimes called age-adjusted rates because the standardization is an actuarial way of adjusting the crude rate to remove the effect of any difference between actual age structure in the population and the standard age structure. There are two approaches to standardization:

Direct Method[7] When age-specific mortality rates are available for the study population, the age-standardized mortality rate (SRATE) is obtained by calculating the weighted average of these age-specific rates, using the number of persons in the respective age groups in the standard population as the weights. The method of calculating the standardized rates is given below to enhance the readers' understanding of the concepts involved. It is expressed in notation as:

$$ SRATE = \frac{Pi \times mi}{Pi} $$

where **SRATE** is the age-standardized mortality rate, **mi** is the age-specific mortality rate in the study population for persons in age group **i**, and **Pi** is the number of persons in the age group in the standard population. Comparisons of different standardized rates are valid only if they are based on the same standard population. However, there is no single standard population acceptable for all purposes. The most commonly used standard populations for international comparison are the world standard population (a hypothetical model). For Canada, the 1971 population of Canada is used as the standard.   This is done to permit comparisons to national statistics compiled by Statistics Canada, since that is their choice of standard population. For the above example, when we apply native Indian age-sex specific death rates to the reference population (in this case the Canadian population) and recalculate the death rate, we obtain the standardized rate. In this instance, it is 10.5 per 1000 population, which is much higher than the earlier crude death rates we had obtained for the Indian or Canadian populations. Thus, **age-standardized rates** are the annual number of deaths per 1000 population which would be observed in the population if it had the same age composition as a reference (or standard) population. This is referred to as the **direct** method of standardization.

Indirect Method Indirect standardization is a comparison of observed deaths in a study population and the number of deaths that would be expected if the population had the same mortality rate as the standard population; it is therefore a ratio rather than a standardized rate. The most commonly used ratio is the standardized mortality ratio (**SMR**):

$$ SMR = \frac{mi \times pi}{Mi \times pi} $$

Table 3.1: Derivations of Commonly Used Health Status Indicators

$$\text{Incidence rate} = \frac{\text{number of new cases of disease in a time interval}}{\text{population at risk}} \times 1000$$

$$\text{Prevalence rate} = \frac{\text{number of existing cases of disease at a point}}{\text{total population}} \times 1000$$

$$\text{Hospital morbidity rate} = \frac{\text{total no. of hospital separations in a year}}{\text{total population at midyear}} \times 1000$$

$$\text{Perinatal mortality rate} = \frac{\text{annual no. of still births} + \text{live births dying under 7 days}}{\text{total births (still and live)}} \times 1000$$

$$\text{Neonatal mortality rate} = \frac{\text{annual no. of deaths of children under 28 days}}{\text{annual live births}} \times 1000$$

$$\text{Maternal mortality rate} = \frac{\text{annual no. of deaths from puerpual causes per year}}{\text{annual live births}} \times 1000$$

$$\text{Infant mortality rate} = \frac{\text{annual no. of deaths under one year of age}}{\text{annual live births}} \times 1000$$

$$\text{Crude death rate} = \frac{\text{annual no. of deaths}}{\text{total population}} \times 1000$$

$$\text{Age and sex - specific death rate} = \frac{\text{annual no. of deaths in a specific subgroup}}{\text{total population in that subgroup}} \times 1000$$

$$\text{Standardized mortality ratio (SMR)} = \frac{\text{total observed deaths}}{\text{expected deaths}} \times 100$$

$$\text{Proportionate mortality ratio (PMR)} = \frac{\text{deaths from a specific cause}}{\text{total deaths}} \times 100$$

$$\text{Case fatality rate} = \frac{\text{number of deaths from a specific disease}}{\text{total no. of cases of that disease}} \times 100$$

SMR is the standardized mortality ratio, **mi** is the age-specific mortality rate in the study population for persons in age group **i**, and **pi** is the number of persons in age group **i** in the study population, **Mi** is the age-specific mortality rate in the standard population. When comparing the mortality or morbidity of a region with that of another, **SRATE** is preferable to **SMR** because the former is calculated by applying the age-specific mortality rates of each region to only one standard population distribution. On the other hand, if the comparison is made between a region and the province, then the use of **SMR** is preferred because the denominators of **SMRs** (i.e., the expected number of deaths in regions) are all based on one set of age-specific mortality rates, i.e., the provincial experience. Hence the **standardized mortality ratio (SMR)** is the ratio of observed deaths to expected deaths per 100 population. This ratio is frequently used in occupational health studies and the expected number of deaths is obtained from the comparison population (usually a larger population such as the national one). For example, if the mortality rate in industry X is 200 per 1000 persons, and the national mortality rate is 150 per 1000 persons, then the **SMR** is 133.

Potential-Years-of-Life-Lost (PYLL)
This estimates the total years of life lost before age 75 for persons diseased between birth and the 75th year of life. It shows the burden of premature deaths by different causes and the cost in terms of person-years lost to society.

Proportionate Mortality Ratio (PMR)
The ratio of deaths from a specific cause to the total number of deaths.

Case-Fatality Rate
The number of deaths from a specific disease per total number of cases of that disease.

1.3.   CONSEQUENCES

Indicators of the consequences of health problems include: the economic burden, which incorporates direct and indirect costs of ill-health; indicators for the economic evaluation of health programs relating effectiveness to costs; rate of hospitalization; disability, data for this indicator being largely derived from surveys; and prescription drug use, which is also an indicator of the consequences of ill-health, although not well developed as a methodology.

Economic Burden of Ill Health
Economics relates to the utilization of society's resources. Resources utilized for one purpose are unavailable for another, a concept known as **opportunity cost**. The economic burden of ill health has become increasingly prominent in recent years. This section looks at the meaning and precision of measurement of this concept.

The costs of ill health are measured in terms of **direct** and **indirect** costs. Estimates of direct costs attempt to measure the expenditure for prevention and treatment of disease. They include: i) personal health care, which consists of hospital costs, non-hospital medical care costs, and other costs (such as dental care, prescribed drugs); ii) publicly funded health-care costs; iii) education; and iv) research. Estimates of indirect costs measure the loss of productive services due to morbidity and mortality. They include financial loss due to premature death or loss of workdays due to temporary or permanent disability. For example, the number of person-years of productive work lost because of automobile accidents is an indirect cost, or indirect burden, of ill health. Usually, data limitations, conceptual problems, and imperfections limit the scope and accuracy of these estimates.

Gross National Product
On an aggregate basis, the proportion of the **Gross National Product** (GNP) or the **Gross Domestic Product** (GDP) spent on health expenditure and the **per capita** expenditure, or the average amount spent per person, on health by government are indicators of the burden of ill health. The GNP is a measure of all the goods and services produced by a country and is a measure of productivity. The GDP includes all resources available to the country irrespective of whether earned by local production or foreign investment in the country. It is useful for international comparisons. The per capita measure has limitations based on what is included and the lack of adjustment for demographics characteristics of the population.

Economic Evaluation of Health Programs
Health programs may be evaluated in terms of their effects on morbidity and mortality (**health outcomes**), changes in behaviour (**impact**), and from an economic perspective (i.e., in terms of utilization of resources, an example of **process**). A number of indicators are used in the economic evaluation of programs. These economic indicators, which may be factors in choosing between competing programs, are derived from different types of economic analysis.

Community Effectiveness
For these analyses, direct and indirect costs are measured as described above and expressed in dollar terms, related to the effectiveness of programs. The differences in the analyses lie in how the effects of a program are conceptualized and measured. The effectiveness (i.e., whether desired outcomes are achieved) of an intervention under ideal conditions, such as in a randomized control trial, is called its **efficacy**. However, the efficacy of an intervention is only one component of the analysis of its usefulness as applied in the community, called **community effectiveness**, which includes other indicators. These are **coverage** and **compliance**. Coverage is the proportion of the target or at-risk population reached by the program. Is it directed to, accessible to and available to those who would maximally benefit? Compliance deals with provider and consumer compliance.

Provider compliance indicates the degree to which health care providers cooperate with providing the program and all its elements. Consumer compliance indicates the degree to which those who need the intervention use it. This can be expressed in the following relationship:

$$\frac{\text{Community}}{\text{Effectiveness}} = \text{efficacy} \times \text{coverage} \times \frac{\text{provider}}{\text{compliance}} \times \frac{\text{consumer}}{\text{compliance}}$$

Quality of Life

The concept of quality of life has been used increasingly in the health sector in the assessment of the benefit of a procedure, drug or services provided, as it is realized that the major objective is to improve the quality of life and not merely to increase longevity by these interventions. Torrance et al.[8] describe the **health-related quality of life** which measures a broad array of physical, social, and emotional functions which are accrued by the intervention; for example, a) sensory function (speech, sight, hearing); b) mobility and physical function; c) emotional function; d) cognitive function; e) self-care function regarding activities of daily living; and f) the level of pain and discomfort. In quantitative terms, one approach to measuring quality of life is the **quality adjusted life year (QALY)**. A QALY is the modification of the actual anticipated duration of survival by the expected level of functioning and quality of life for that period as measured by health-care providers.

An important economic concept is that of efficiency. A program is **efficient** if it achieves desired results with a minimum of inputs. Inputs, or resources utilized, are usually calculated in dollar terms, and effectiveness is quantitated in the same manner. There are three approaches to evaluating the relative efficiency of health programs. These are described below:

Cost-Effectiveness Analysis[9] The effects of programs are expressed in health-related terms, such as years of life gained. The ratio of the effects to the costs are compared between programs. For example, if programs A and B cost the same, but A results in an extension of life, A is considered more cost-effective.

Cost-Benefit Analysis The effects of programs are expressed in health-related terms and then converted to dollar terms. For example, years of life gained are translated to dollars that could be earned during this period for a person of working age.   The ratio of the benefits to costs are compared for different programs.

Cost-Utility Analysis The effects of programs incorporate a component indicating the social value of a program which may be estimated according to a number of techniques including standard gamble and time-trade-off methods. Readers are referred to the article by Laupacis et al. for further details.[10]

Hospital Separation Rate
The number of hospital separations (discharges and deaths) recorded in the year per 1000 population. It reflects the frequency with which hospital care is sought, and is influenced by a number of factors such as the availability of care and insurance coverage.

Hospital Days of Care
The total number of days of care for all hospitals per 1000 population in a year. This rate may also be expressed for certain diseases to allow comparisons.

Disability Days
Days spent in bed, days during which the individual has to abandon his or her principal activity or days when activities restricted for health reasons are considered disability days. These are quantified as the annual rate of disability days per 1000 population.

2. SOURCES OF HEALTH DATA

As indicated earlier, Canadians collect large sets of data related to health and health care. However, these data are scattered and often hidden in governmental and non-governmental publications. The following are some of the common data sources in Canada. Data can be existing or may be obtained by surveys.

2.1. SURVEYS

A health survey is usually conducted by interview and/or examination of a sample of the population. It can also be conducted with a self-administered questionnaire, by telephone, mail, or in some other way. It can be done regularly and repeatedly, or as needed to investigate a special problem (e.g., blood-lead levels of children living near lead smelters in Toronto). Health surveys directed at a selected or representative sample of the population do not follow individuals through time or produce retrospective or prospective studies for testing associations (e.g., cause and disease, treatment and result). However, they are useful for surveillance of levels of illness, impairment, disability and many related social factors in people who do not necessarily access the health-care system. Although simple in concept, surveys pose a number of methodological problems. Respondents have been shown to forget even major events. If the questionnaire is neither designed properly nor presented conscientiously, it may give ambiguous or misleading results. If interviewers are not adequately trained, they can easily influence the quality of responses. Missing data are also a problem.

In 1978 and 1979, the Canada Health Survey was conducted by Health and Welfare Canada and Statistics Canada.[11] This survey of over 12,000 households focused on risk factors, perceived health status and consequences of ill health. Both interviews and self-administered questionnaires were used, and a subset of the same population underwent a limited physical examination and laboratory testing. Plans to repeat the survey annually have been postponed in the interest of fiscal restraint, but the first year of the survey provided much valuable information, some of which is quoted in later chapters of this book.

In 1983-84, Statistics Canada, as part of its Labour Force Survey (LFS), carried out the Canadian Health and Disability Survey.[12] The definitions used for disability and handicap were those developed by the World Health Organization and were defined in a previous chapter. The sample of disabled persons among adults aged 15 and over was identified by administering a screening questionnaire to five-sixths of the LFS sample; those identified as disabled by the screening questions were then interviewed. For children, the parent or caretaker answered the questions. Approximately 65,800 households were surveyed consisting of 126,698 adults and 59,195 children.

Statistics Canada has recently provided an excellent overview of population-based health surveys undertaken in Canada from 1985 to 1991 briefly reviewing the populations sampled, the types of information collected and the reports generated.[13] Apart from those surveys described in this section, recent surveys of significance are the Canada Health Promotion Survey,[2] Canada Fitness Survey,[14] Canada Student Health Survey,[15,16] General Social Survey,[17] the National Alcohol and Other Drug Surveys[18] and the Canadian Heart Health Surveys.[19] Provincial governments and local health departments are also carrying out health-related surveys.[20,21] Surveys usually provide prevalence rates of risk factors, disease, disability and utilization of health services, and can also be used to explore relationships among these factors.

Recently the federal government has established a National Health Information Council (NHIC) to formulate plans on the need for data for the health sector.[22] In the fall of 1991, the NHIC recommended that an ongoing national survey of population health be conducted. This recommendation was based on the knowledge of the economic and fiscal pressures on the health care system and the requirement for information to improve the quality of health in Canada, as well as the effectiveness and efficiency of health services. The survey will be done by Statistics Canada in 1994 and will be bi-annual. The objectives of this National Population Health Survey (NPHS)[23] are to: a) aid in the development of public policies designed to improve health, by providing measures of the level, trend and distribution of the health status of the population; b) provide data for analytic studies that will assist in understanding the determinants of health; c) collect data on the economic, social, demographic, occupational and environmental correlates of health; d) increase the understanding of the relationship between health and the use of health services, not only in the traditional sense, but also in areas such as home care, self-medication and self-care; e) provide longitudinal data that will reflect the dynamics of the processes of health and illness, as well as cross-sectional variables; f) provide the provinces and territories and other clients with a health survey capacity which would permit them to cost-effectively supplement the content or the sample; g) allow the possibility of linking survey results to administrative data sources for statistical analysis. There are a variety of important sources of administrative data, such as vital statistics data, environmental variables, community variables and health service utilization.

The NPHS will begin data collection in January 1994. A sample of approximately 22,000 households will be selected covering persons of all ages residing in Canada and will be stratified by the provinces and territories. The sampling frame will be such that it will retain reliability of data at the national, provincial and sub-provincial levels. The data will be collected in four major areas: i) measures of health status such as health problems, measures of mental health, and measures of functional limitations; ii) determinants of health such as family history, behavioural, lifestyle, economic and social factors; iii) utilization of health services such as medical and preventive services and iv) socio-demographic information, particularly that related to economic situations such as age, sex, educational attainment, income, ethnicity, marital status and labour force characteristics.

2.2.   ADMINISTRATIVE DATA

Perhaps the most uniformly recorded and reliable health data are administrative (e.g., rates of hospital admission, treatments and discharge diagnoses). Administrative and professional bodies demand these data for use in the planning and evaluation of medical care. Administrative data for hospitalizations in most provinces are summarized yearly and entered into a central provincial file, such as the Hospital Medical Records Institute (HMRI). At present, the main function of HMRI is to prepare easily audited reports for hospitals to use in quality control and planning, but the data may also be used for research. Data are also gathered by all provincial health insurance plans, Workers' Compensation Boards, and dental health plans. In general, administrative data are more useful in studying health care rather than the distribution and causes of disease.

2.3.   REGISTRIES

Disease registries for certain chronic diseases, especially cancer, are another important source of data, particularly if they are population-based. In all provinces, reports are sent by private practitioners, clinics and pathology departments, and each patient's name and clinical information are entered in a central registry. The completeness of the registry is checked by searching for notations of cancer on death certificates. If the registry is complete, the name of any person who died of cancer should already be entered in the registry records, as cancer is usually detected well before death.   A 95% agreement between death certificates and registry is the goal in most provinces.   If registries are well kept, they can provide incidence and prevalence data.   There are other registries, including one for handicapped children in British Columbia and the Canadian National Institute for the Blind.[24] *Chronic Diseases in Canada,* which is published by Health Canada, has provided information on disease registries in Canada.[25]

2.4.   REPORTS

Reports are another source of health data.   There are five types:

(i) Medical Officers of Health, practising physicians and others in the health field report unusual occurrences or apparent **increases in disease rates** to provincial or federal agencies responsible for surveillance.

(ii) Many infectious diseases (e.g., measles, chicken pox) and sexually transmitted diseases are reportable - that is, the law requires that they be reported to the local health authority.   This usually provides the data for incidence rates of infectious diseases. The list of **reportable diseases** in a province is available from the provincial health department/ministry.   A more detailed description of communicable diseases can be found in texts such as *Control of Communicable Diseases in Man* by A. S. Benenson. In Ontario, there are over 60 reportable diseases. These include diseases ranging from AIDS to yersinosis. As of 1990, the Ontario Ministry of Health required municipal public health departments to record all reportable diseases of which they were notified, on a central computer system. The system, which is called the Reportable Disease Information System, provides an up-to-date, province-wide reportable disease data base.   Appendix 1 gives the list of reportable diseases in Ontario. Cancer is also reportable by law in a number of provinces. It must be stressed that under-reporting frequently occurs and so official figures are always lower than the actual incidence of disease.

(iii) Case studies and clinical surveys of a specific disease appear frequently in medical journals.   Selected case reports and "notifiable disease" data are published weekly by Health Canada in the *Canadian Communicable Disease Report.* Such data may be useful in following trends and spotting new epidemics. However, it is difficult to calculate incidence and prevalence rates from these reports, because the precise number of cases and the population base from which they come is unknown. *Chronic Diseases in Canada* provides information on trends in chronic diseases.

(iv) Another source of reports is the provincial Workers' Compensation Board. In each province, notification of industrial accidents and diseases is required to facilitate claim processing and preventive activities.   These data can provide incidence information on industrial accidents and diseases.

(v) *Health Reports* is a quarterly publication of the Canadian Centre for Health Information, Statistics Canada, which was started in 1989. The purpose of this serial is to give readers convenient access to essential health data. The general and disease-specific trends in risk factors, morbidity, mortality, and disabilities are provided. Canadian hospital statistics are also provided in every issue as are listings of other available data. This serial is an excellent source of current health statistics.

2.5.   VITAL STATISTICS

The record of the basic events of the human life cycle—birth, marriage and death—is appropriately called vital statistics. Throughout history, governments have kept some kind of register of their citizens. As early as 1608, an "Ordinance" in Quebec required the clergy to register births, marriages and deaths in each parish. By 1667, this registration was required in duplicate, and one copy was forwarded to the "Judge Royal". In early 18th century England, John Graunt systematized record-keeping, and since then, vital statistics have been the most reliable and consistently recorded data source in the health field.

2.5.1. Birth Certificate
Figure 3.1 is an abridged facsimile of a Statement of Live Birth in Ontario. In Canada, the parents are responsible for filing the certificate with the municipal clerk. Note the relatively limited health information on the birth certificate. There is no medical history of the mother, nor description of the birth itself. Another form, Notice of Live Birth or Stillbirth, must be filled out by the attending physicians and filed with the provincial registrar. This form provides no information about the father, but does record the gestation period and the presence of congenital deformities.

2.5.2. Death Certificate
This must be signed by a licensed physician and includes cause of death, person's name, birth date, sex and place of residence and of death. Figure 3.2 focuses on the part which lists the causes of death. As can be seen, there are three distinct sections for the cause of death. The first, immediate cause of death, is recorded on the first line. For example, an elderly person dying of pneumonia and nothing else will have pneumonia recorded there. The second entity is called 'antecedent causes', which means that there may be a condition or disease which gave rise to the immediate cause of death. For example, an immediate cause of death in women could be metastatic or secondary cancer of the lung. However, if the condition giving rise to this was cancer of the breast, then one would enter cancer of the breast on the second line. The third entity is "any other significant conditions" contributing to death but not directly causing it. For example on the death certificate of a person who died of uremia as a result of chronic nephritis and

Figure 3.1: Birth Certificate, Province of Ontario

Province of Ontario (Canada)   Office of the Registrar-General   *(Abridged)*

Child	1.		2. Sex of Child
Last Name			
Given Names			
Date of Birth	3. Month (by name) day year of birth	4. Please state if mother is: Married, widowed, divorced or single (the term "common law" or "separated" not to be used)	
Place of Birth	5. Name of hospital (If not in hospital give exact location where birth occurred.)		
	Borough, city, town, village, township (by name).	Regional municipality, county or district	

PARENTS	FATHER	MOTHER
Name	6. Surname of child's father	10. Maiden name (before marriage)
	All given names	All given names
Birthplace	7. City, town, or other place of birth (by name)	11. City, town, or other place of birth (by name)
	Province (or country if outside Canada)	Province (or country if outside Canada)
Birthdate	8. Month (by name), day, year of birth	Age (at time of this birth)	12. Month (by name), day, year of birth	Age (at time of this birth)
Usual Residence of Mother	14. Complete street address. If rural, give exact location and Post Office or Rural Route address.	
	Borough, city, town, village, township (by name); Regional Municipality, county or district; Province (or Country)	
Mailing Address of Mother	15. Complete mailing address (if different from 14). If rural give Post Office or rural route address.	

OTHER	16. Duration of pregnancy (in completed weeks)	17. Number of children ever born to this mother (including this birth)	Number liveborn	Number stillborn (after 20 weeks pregnancy)
BIRTH PARTICULARS	18. Weight of child at birth ___ ___ or ___ lbs oz grams	19. Kind of birth State whether single, twin, or triplet	20. If twin or triplet, whether this child was born 1st, 2nd, or 3rd.	

ATTENDANT	21. Name of attending physician (or other attendant)	☐ Physician ☐ Nurse
	Complete mailing address	☐ Other

Figure 3.2: Death Certificate

CAUSE OF DEATH

Part One

Immediate cause of death

(a) _____

due to, or as a consequence of

Antecedent causes, if any, giving
rise to the immediate cause (a)
above, stating the underlying
cause last

(b) _____

due to, or as a consequence of

(c) _____

Part Two

Other significant conditions
contributing to the death but not
causally related to the immediate
cause (a) above

_____

_____

also having chronic bronchitis, uremia should be listed as the immediate cause of death (line a), chronic nephritis should be listed as the antecedent cause of death (line b), and chronic bronchitis should be listed in part 2 as another significant condition. When both the immediate cause of death and the antecedent cause are recorded on the death certificate, then, for cause-specific mortality, the underlying cause is the one which is used for data analysis. Other significant conditions may also be recorded separately.

The current system for recording cause of death information has been described as unreliable.[26] Problems exist in the ambiguity of the WHO instructions and disease definitions to be used by the physician or coroner when filling out a death certificate. A recent critique suggests the need for modifications that are tested for validity before implementation.

Some causes of death require notification of death to the coroner (or medical examiner). In such cases, a physician must not sign the death certificate. These causes include situations where there is reasonable cause to suspect that the person died by violent means, undue negligence or in an unexplained manner. Other causes include a death in a correctional institution, police custody, maternally related situations (e.g., abortion), after anesthesia, in homes for the aged, in work places, and a death associated with involuntary residence in an institution. Each province has its own statute governing the causes to be notified to the coroner.

Birth and death data usually provide the fertility rate, infant mortality rate, crude death rate, life expectancy at birth, potential years of life lost and all other mortality rates described earlier.

2.6.   CONSUMPTION DATA

Various production and consumption data can be related to health. The most obvious of these is food. Tonnage of food produced or imported each year are adjusted to current levels of supplies to produce a "disappearance" figure: the amount of foodstuffs that need to be replaced each year. We know in general the proportion of various foodstuffs which is actually eaten by humans, so the average per capita consumption of meat, for example, can be calculated for any year. Although useful for following long-term historical trends, compared with dietary inventories of the type collected in surveys carried out by Nutrition Canada, such data are not very reliable, as they tell us little about the habits of any individual. In the same way, annual production of cigarettes or litres of alcohol can be immediately related to long-term trends in health. More indirectly, data on industrial processes involving hazardous substances, such as asbestos or those emitting pollutants (e.g., sulphur dioxide from the pulp and paper industry) may be related to levels of health.

3.   RECORD LINKAGE

A wide variety of health data (vital statistics, registries, surveys and reports) is collected about each individual and recorded in many places. Many people feel that if this data were collected in one place, a very useful profile of social, biological and personal data could be constructed. Relationships between possible causes of disease (industrial exposure, levels of pollution, social conditions, family history) and the individual's history of disease would yield much more precise information than the other sources of data we have described. The Canadian system of "geocoding" social and demographic information according to the postal code, and the existence of a centralized agency, Statistics Canada (the ultimate collector and publisher of a great volume and variety of data), sets the stage for this record linkage. The 1991 Task Force on Health Information advised that the capacity for linkage of different data elements was critical to fulfilling the potential of the development of systems for health data.[27]

Approaches to record linkage include integrating health records at the level of the individual patient from different sources and over time. Record linkage can be achieved by the allocation of personal identifiers, possibly on a lifetime basis, a strategy which has been considered at the provincial level. However, these likely would not be portable between provinces. Linkage can also be achieved, with varying degrees of accuracy, by matching based on probabilities of linking personal identifying data in two or more data banks. These include the surname, maiden name (if applicable), first name, date of birth, place of birth and any other identifiers such as the social insurance number if available. A record is strongly matched when a high number of similarities is obtained. If matched, records for individuals in the two data banks may be merged. The qualifier to this is that the data must be of good quality and be sufficiently detailed.

The idea of record linkage has been met with widespread resistance because many feel that the creation of a central data-bank would place too much personal information under the control of a single agency and that the potential for abuse is serious. Indeed, it is easy to imagine the interest such data would have for employers, industrial spies, credit companies and mail vendors, among many others.

4.   SUMMARY

This chapter dealt with health indicators and sources of health data. Health indicators are qualitative and quantitative statistical indices which indicate the health of a population. Health data are examined on three dimensions, namely **determinants**, **health status** and **consequences,** with each level incorporating biological, psychological and social elements.

Determinants are factors which are not health problems per se but are believed to be related to the development of disease. The determinants of health include the environment, lifestyle factors, behaviour and risk factors, human biology and the health-care system. The environment encompasses both the physical aspects and the psychosocial milieu to which the population is exposed and experiences.

With respect to the physical environment, Canadians may be exposed to toxic substances or other environmental hazards from a variety of sources, including food, water, air, soil and consumer products. Risk assessment is the qualitative and quantitative determination of the risk to human health posed by an environmental agent. Indicators of the psychosocial environment incorporate demographic indicators, such as the age and sex of the population and population growth rate. Indicators of the social environment also include sociodemographic variables (such as ethnicity, language and family size) and socioeconomic variables (which include education level, literacy, unemployment rates and income distribution).

Lifestyle factors, behaviours and risk factors are measured in many ways. One such way is by the proportion of the population who are smokers, who are obese or who wear seat belts. The population attributable risk (PAR) indicates the degree to which lifestyle, behaviour or risk factors contribute to disease in the population, and what the potential impact of eliminating the factor could be.

The determinant of human biology includes age and sex. Men, women, children and the elderly have different potentials for health and ill health. Another indicator is genetic inheritance.

Health status is viewed in the framework as health problems which are concrete, medical conditions of individuals or groups, or pathology. Health status indicators include **subjective** assessments (such as the inclusion of questions concerning the perception of one's own health) and **objective** indicators (such as mortality, hospital morbidity and non-hospital morbidity).

Consequences are the effects of health problems on the individual (such as disability), on the health-care system (such as hospitalization), and on society in general, including the economic burden. Indicators of the consequences of health problems include: the economic burden (incorporating direct and indirect costs of ill health), indicators for the economic evaluation of health programs relating effectiveness to costs; rate of hospitalization; disability and prescription drug use.

There are several data sources in Canada. These consist of surveys, administrative data, registries, reports, vital statistics, consumption data and record linkage.

(i) Surveys usually provide prevalence rates for risk factors, disease, disability and utilization of health services, and can also be used to explore relationships among these factors. Recent surveys of interest include: Canada Health Survey, Canada Fitness Survey, Canada Student Health Survey, General Social Survey, National Alcohol and Other Drug Surveys and the Canadian Heart Health Survey. (ii) The most uniformly recorded and reliable health data are administrative. Administrative and professional bodies demand this data for use in the planning and evaluation of medical care. Administrative data are more useful in studying health care rather than the distribution and cause of disease. (iii) Disease registries for certain chronic diseases are important sources of data. Registries can provide incidence and prevalence data. (iv) Reports are another source of health data and examples of available reports are: Health Reports, Workers' Compensation Boards and Canadian Communicable Diseases Report. (v) The events of the human life cycle—birth, marriage, death—are called vital statistics. Birth and death data usually provide the fertility rate, infant mortality rate, crude death rate, life expectancy at birth and all other mortality rates.

5. REFERENCES

1.   *User's Guide to 40 Community Health Indicators.* Health and Welfare Canada. Community Health Division, Health Services and Promotion Branch in collaboration with the National Health Information

Council and Health Information Division, Policy, Planning, and Information Branch. Ottawa, Canada, 1992.

2. Government of Canada. *Canada's Health Promotion Survey: Technical Report 1985*. Ministry of Supply and Services, Canada, Ottawa, 1990.

3. Peron Y and Strohmenger C, eds. *Demographic and Health Indicators*. Ministry of Supply and Services, Canada, Ottawa, 1985.

4. *Determining the Human Health Risks of Environmental Chemicals. Resource Manual*. Environmental Protection Office. Department of Public Health, City of Toronto, Toronto, 1991.

5. Montano L. Population Attributable Risk: A Tool in Public Health. *Public Health and Epidemiology Reports Ont* 3(2):25-26, 1992.

6. Markel H. The Stigma of Disease: Implications of Genetic Screening. *Am J Med* 93(2):209-215, 1992.

7. Wong CH. Measuring Population Mortality and Morbidity Using Rates, Ratios and Confidence Intervals. *Public Health and Epidemiology Reports Ont* 3(9):140-142, 1992.

8. Torrance G, Markham B, Rosenbloom D and Gafni A. *Risk-Benefit and Quality of Life Analyses of Prescription Drugs*. Health and Welfare Canada, Ottawa, 1990.

9. Hull R, Hirsch J, Sackett D and Stoddart G. Cost-Effectiveness of Clinical Diagnosis, Venography, and Non-Invasive Testing in Patients with Symptomatic Deep-Vein Thrombosis. *N Engl J Med* 304(26):1561-1567, 1981.

10. Laupacis A, Feeny D, Detsky AS and Tugwell PX. How Attractive Does a New Technology Have to be to Warrant Adoption and Utilization? Tentative Guidelines for Using Clinical and Economic Evaluations. *Can Med Assoc J* 146(4):473-481, 1992.

11. Government of Canada. *The Health of Canadians: Report of the Canada Health Survey*. Ministry of Supplies and Services, Canada, Ottawa, 1981.

12. Government of Canada. *Report of the Canadian Health and Disability Survey 1983-84*. Ministry of Supply and Services, Canada, Ottawa, 1986.

13. Adams O, Ramsay T and Millar W. Overview of Selected Health Surveys in Canada, 1985 to 1991. *Health Reports* 4(1):25-52, 1992.

14. Government of Canada. *Canada Fitness Survey, 1983*. Ministry of Supply and Services, Canada, Ottawa, 1985.

15. King AJC, Robertson A, Warren W, Fuller K and Stroudt WP. *Summary Report, Canada Health Knowledge Survey: 9-, 12- and 15-Year-Olds, 1982-83*. Health and Welfare Canada, Ottawa, 1984.

16. King AJC, Warren WK, Robertson A, et al. *Canada Health Attitudes and Behaviours Survey: 9-, 12- and 15-Year-Olds, 1984-85*. Health and Welfare Canada, Ottawa, 1986.

17. McKie C and Thompson K, eds. *Canadian Social Trends*. Ministry of Supply and Services, Canada and Thompson Educational Publishing, Toronto, 1990.

18. Government of Canada. *National Alcohol and Other Drugs Survey 1989*. Ministry of Supply and Services, Canada, Ottawa, 1990.

19. Canada Heart Health Surveys Research Group. The Federal-Provincial Canadian Heart Health Intitiative. *Can Med Assoc J* 146(11):1915-1916, 1992.

20. Government of Ontario. *Ontario Health Survey: Information Manual*. Ontario Ministry of Health, Toronto, 1990.

21. Government of Saskatchewan. *A Study of the Unmet Needs of Off-Reserve Indians and Metis Elderly in Saskatchewan*. Senior Citizens Provincial Council, Saskatoon, 1988.

22. National Health Information Council. *Health Information for Canada 1991, Report of the Task Force on Health Information*. Health and Welfare Canada, Ottawa, 1991.

23. National Population Health Survey Project Team, Statistics Canada. Introduction to Statistics Canada's 1994 National Population Health Survey. *Public Health and Epidemiology Reports Ont* 3(13):206-209, 1992.

24. Registration of Chronic Disease. *Chronic Dis Can* 6(4):72-82, 1986.

25. Special Diseases Registries Issue, Part A and B. *Chronic Dis Can* 9(3):50-63, 1988, and 9(4):66-76, 1988

26. Lindahl BI, Glattre E, Lahti R, et al. The WHO Principles for Registering Causes of Death - Suggestions for Improvement. *J Clin Epidemiol* 43(5):467-474, 1990.

27. Lussier R and Bray DF. Towards a Better Use of Records for Statistical Purposes. *Health Reports* 3(3):259-268, 1991.

Appendix 1: List of Reportable Diseases in Ontario, 1991

Acquired Immunodeficiency Syndrome
Amebiasis
Anthrax
Botulism
Brucellosis
Campylobacter enteritis
Chancroid
Chickenpox (Varicella)
Chlamydia trachomatis infections
Cholera
Cytomegalovirus infection, congenital
Diphtheria
Encephalitis, including:
    Primary, viral
    Post-infectious
    Vaccine-related
    Subacute sclerosing panencephalitis
    Unspecified
Food poisoning, all causes
Gastroenteritis, institutional outbreaks
Giardiasis, except asymptomatic cases
Gonorrhoea
Haemophilus influenzae b disease, invasive
Hemorrhagic fevers, including:
    Ebola virus disease
    Marburg virus disease
    Other viral causes
Hepatitis, viral
    Hepatitis A
    Hepatitis B
    Hepatitis C
    Hepatitis D (Delta hepatitis)
Herpes, neonatal infection
Influenza
Lassa Fever

Legionellosis
Leprosy
Listeriosis
Lyme Disease
Malaria
Measles
Meningitis, acute
    i. bacterial
    ii. viral
    iii. other
Meningococal disease, invasive
Mumps
Ophthalmia neonatorum
Pratyphoid Fever
Pertussis (Whooping Cough)
Plague
Poliomyelitis, acute
Psittacosis/Ornithosis
Q Fever
Rabies
Rubella
Rubella, congential syndrome
Salmonellosis
Shigellosis
Syphilis
Tetanus
Toxic Shock-like Syndrome
Trichinosis
Tuberculosis
Tularemia
Typhoid Fever
Verotoxin-producing E. coli
Yellow Fever
Yersiniosis

CHAPTER FOUR
Determinants of Health and Disease

The Health Field Concept explained in chapter one and the Health Indicators outlined in chapter three are used here as a conceptual base to describe health and disease in the Canadian population. In this chapter, a broad view of health is adopted as a framework for consideration of the many aspects of life in Canada which interact to produce health and ill health. The next chapter will describe the measurable outcomes of the interaction of these determinants of health.

1. HUMAN BIOLOGY

The genetic potential of the individual has an impact on health in many complex and poorly understood ways. There are, however, a few well-explained situations. Mutant genes, within the Canadian gene pool, lead to congenital malformations and genetic disorders within the population. The high prevalence of the gene for Tay-Sachs disease in the French Canadian population is an example. Familial aggregations of autosomal recessive and dominant conditions, some diseases of multifactorial origin, and other inherited conditions are prevalent in Canadian (Old Colony) Mennonites who are descended from a small number of founding families and whose conservative members practise endogamy.[1] The diseases include: insulin-dependent diabetes mellitus, auto-immune diseases, and Tourette's syndrome, which were described initially in Mennonites living in a sub-district of Alberta. Clusters of malformations, inborn errors of metabolism and other inherited disorders were found in Mennonite families in rural areas of three other western provinces and southern Ontario. In Quebec, the incidence of Sickle Cell Haemoglobinopathy (HbS) is estimated at nine cases per 100,000, occurring mainly in the black population and those of Central American ancestry.[2] Nova Scotia has an indigenous black population which is genetically predisposed to carriage or expression of the gene for Sickle Cell Anemia. Age and sex are important determinants of health; due to their interaction with social and economic factors, they are discussed in the next section dealing with demography, sociodemography and socioeconomic indicators.

2.   THE ENVIRONMENT

2.1.   THE PSYCHOSOCIAL ENVIRONMENT

Demography is the study of populations, especially with reference to size, density, fertility, mortality, growth, age distribution, migration and vital statistics. Sociodemographic and socioeconomic indicators represent the interaction of these factors with social and economic conditions. The two major sources of data in this section are the 1991 Census of Canada[3] for age, sex, marital status, household composition and population figures, and the User's Guide to 40 Community Health Indicators,[4] the latter being a valuable source of references for definitions and data on determinants of health for Canada. The framework for categorizing community health indicators in the User's Guide provided the basis, with some exceptions, for the organization of this chapter as well as the subsequent chapter on Health Status and Consequences. Data obtained from sources apart from the two indicated are specifically referenced.

2.1.1. Demography
On June 4, 1991, Canada's population was 27,296,860 of which 49.3% were male; 41.8% of the population were single, 50.0% married, 4.9% widowed and 3.3% were divorced. Of the total population, 20.9%, 67.5% and 11.6% were in the age groups 0-14 years, 15-64 years, and 65 years and over, respectively. In the age group 65 and over, 58.0% of the population was female. In 1996, the projected Canadian population will be 28,849,100, of which 49.2% will be male. It is projected that in 1996, the population 65 years and older will constitute 12.2 % of the total population.[5] In the age group 65 years and over, 59% of the population will be female.

Population distributions by age and sex from 1901-1991 (figure 4.1) indicate that the population has more than doubled since 1941. The ratio of males to females has remained roughly constant, but there has been a definite change in the age distribution. In 1901, there were proportionately more children 0-14 years of age compared with the present. This was because of early age at marriage and large family size, as is the case in most developing countries. These factors are reflected in the **total fertility rate** (TFR) expressed as births per 1000 women between the ages of 15 and 49 years. In 1941, compared with earlier years, there were proportionately fewer children aged 0-14 years. This was largely due to postponed childbirth during the Great Depression and World War II, which is reflected in low fertility rates during this period. In the late 1940s, births increased during what is popularly described as the postwar "baby boom", and by 1961, there were proportionately more children 0-14 years of age. Generally birth and fertility rates have been declining since the baby boom, and the effect on the population's age distribution may be traced by a closer examination of figure 4.1.

Figure 4.1: Populations Pyramids, 1901-1991, Canada

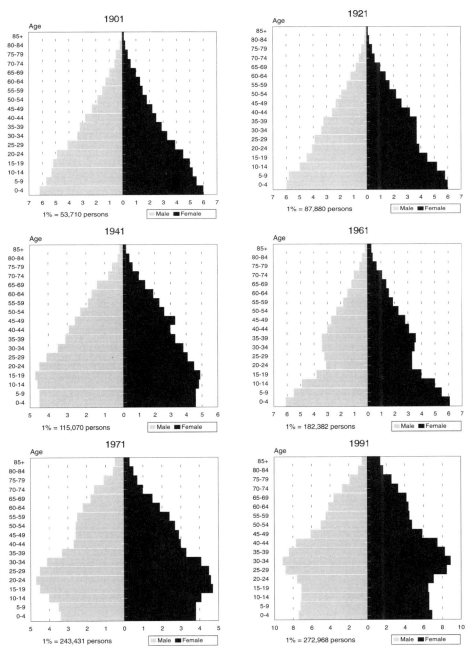

Source: Statistics Canada

Since 1972 the TFR has remained below the level of 2.1, which is the replacement level needed for maintenance of the population at a steady state.[6] Due to increased industrialization, level of education, and availability of contraception, family size fell gradually during the early part of the century.

With the availability of better contraception, more liberal abortion laws, and more women participating in the labour force, the proportion of children in the 0-14 year age group decreased in 1971 and that in the 15-29 year age group increased. The decrease in the proportion of young children in the population is reflected in the decreased demand for pediatricians and pediatric units in general hospitals. A temporary increase in this proportion, predicted to occur when the "baby boomers" grew up and produced families, has not happened.

The lone-parent status of families, particularly families headed by single females, often denotes disadvantage to children as many of them live below the poverty line. The effects of poverty on the health of children is described in chapter six. In 1990, there were 12.9% **lone-parent families** whereas in 1980 there were 11.3%.[7] As described subsequently in chapter six, single parent families frequently live in poverty.

Population **growth** is the sum of **natural increase** and **net migration**. Natural increase is the difference between the number of births and number of deaths. In 1992, for example, the crude birth rate was 15.1 births per 1000 population and the crude death rate was 7.2 deaths per 1000 population. Thus, the rate of natural increase was 7.9 per 1000 population.[8] Net migration is the difference between immigration and emigration. Immigration has always been an important source of population growth in Canada. During the period 1986-91, Canada's population increased by 6.5%. More than half of the recent increase was due to net migration, which accounted for 61% of growth in 1990 (natural increase accounting for the remainder).[9,10] For the year ending April 30, 1991, there were 221,798 immigrants coming to Canada while 39,201 Canadians emigrated.

Geographic distributions also have an impact on the health status of a population. While approximately three-quarters of the population live within 320 kilometres of the United States border, the remaining population is spread over a vast land mass. Providing health-care services to a widely dispersed population in northern Canada has been an historical challenge.

Life Expectancy

Life expectancy at birth in Canada increased significantly between 1941 and 1990 from 63.0 to 73.7 years for males, and from 66.3 to 80.6 years for females. The chief reason is the significant decline in infant mortality, from 61 deaths per 1000 live births in 1941 to 6.8 in 1990. Life expectancy has increased significantly more for females than for males, such that the gap between the two has broadened from 3.3 years in 1941 to 6.9 years in 1990. This is due to a decline in death rates among women at all ages over a longer period than for males. This increasing difference between the sexes appears to be levelling off.

The sex differential in death rates may be partly attributed to differences in lifestyle, such as smoking, drinking, and occupation. Males have traditionally experienced higher mortality from ischemic heart disease, respiratory diseases and lung cancer, as well as motor vehicle and other accidents, all of which are related to lifestyle. The influence of biologic factors seems to be important since infant males have higher mortality rates as well.

Life expectancy has traditionally been the index of health most commonly used for international comparisons, as data for it are readily available. According to the Canada Yearbook 1991,[11] between 1983 to 1985 Canada ranked second among industrialized nations for both female and male life expectancy; life expectancy differences between Canada and Japan, the highest ranking nation in this respect, were 0.35 years for females and 1.6 years for males.

Life expectancy at birth is also related to social positioning and degree of economic well being of the population. Life expectancy at birth for Status Indians is 6-10 years lower than the rest of Canadians. Life expectancy of Status Indians in 1981 was at a level which was attained by the rest of Canadians in 1941.

2.1.2. Sociodemographic Indicators

Aging
An important demographic change with far-reaching implications is the rise in the proportion of the population over 65 years of age, largely through increased longevity and a decreased proportion of children in the population. The significance of this change for health care lies in the fact that in 1991, the elderly, who comprise 11% of the population, accounted for 40% of all patient days in general hospitals, allied special hospitals, and mental hospitals. The number of the population over 65 years of age in 1991 grew by 17.5% between 1986 and 1991, and the population in the 75 and over age group grew by 21.7%. The highest median age ever recorded in Canada was 33.5, in 1991. Aging is discussed in more detail in chapter six.

Immigrant Population
The composition of the Canadian population is changing in relation to ethnicity and is expected to continue changing as more immigrants are allowed into Canada in order to offset the decreasing Canadian fertility rate. Approximately one in six Canadians or 15% (3.9 million) are immigrants, and from 1981 to 1986, 63.5% of immigrants were born in a developing nation.[12] During the same period, 43% of all immigrants to Canada were from Asian countries, although they made up 18% of the total population of immigrants living in Canada. By 1986, 30% of the total foreign-born population in Canada consisted of immigrants from developing nations, indicating a relative decline in European immigration.[13]

Ethnicity

In 1991, 9.4 million Canadians (37.5%) reported having at least one ethnic origin other than French or British, 6.2 million (24.9%) of whom had neither French nor British background.[14] Other than British or French, the most frequently reported ethnic origins (either single origin or multiple origins) are, in descending order: German, Italian, Ukranian, Dutch, aboriginal, Polish, Scandinavian, Chinese, Jewish, South Asian, black, Portuguese, Hungarian, Greek, Yugoslav, and Spanish. Members of visible minorities make up 6.3% of the population (1.6 million), and almost half of these live in Ontario, with the largest groups being Chinese, black and South Asian. People in a visible minority comprised 17% of the 3.4 million residents of Toronto in 1986, compared to 6% in Canada as a whole.[15]

Language

Given the ethnic diversity described above, it is not surprising that 3.5 million people reported a mother tongue other than French or English.[9] Neither English nor French is spoken in 5.9% of Canadian homes, and 1.2% (291,000) of the population is unable to conduct conversations in either official languages. The eight most common mother tongues in Canada reported in the 1991 Census were: English (for 16,516,180 persons); French (for 6,505,565); Italian (449,660); Chinese (444,945); and German (424,640); followed by Portuguese, Polish, Ukranian and Spanish. Nearly three-quarters of a million people cited two languages as their "mother tongue."

Family Environments

Over the past 20 years, the impact of family abuse and violence on the health of individual family members has been recognized. There are three principal types of family violence: wife battering, child abuse and elder abuse. Abuse is threatening or intolerable behaviour which may involve physical violence and threats. Wife battering constitutes 76% of reported family violence; however, there is significant under reporting. The Violence Against Women Survey conducted by Statistics Canada reported that 51% of Canadian women have experienced violence since the age of 16. One in 10 said that they had been assaulted at least once in the 12 months prior to the survey. Nearly one attack in five (18%) was violent enough to physically injure the woman, of these 28% necessitated medical attention. Almost one-third (29%) of those who had ever been married or lived common-law reported being assaulted by their partner. Thus 2.6 million Canadian women have been the victim of wife assault. The methods of assault include: pushed, grabbed, or shoved (25%); threatened (19%); slapped (15%); something thrown (11%); kicked, bit, hit (11%); beaten up (9%); sexually assaulted (8%); choked (7%); hit with something (6%); gun or knife used (5%). Violence was reported more or less evenly across every socioeconomic group.[16] A 1986 survey of Canadian men over 18 indicated that 18% of married or cohabiting men had committed at least one violent act against their partners.[17] In 1988, 15% of all homicide victims in Canada were women murdered by their male partners.

Child abuse consists of neglect, physical, emotional and sexual abuse. Each year, there are approximately 8,000 cases of physical abuse and 80,000 cases of emotional neglect in Canada.[18] The incidence of sexual abuse is unknown but may be as high as one of every two girls and one of every three boys, if all forms of inappropriate sexual behaviour towards children are included.[19] Most cases of sexual abuse occur between the ages of 2 and 6, when children are most trusting and, therefore, most vulnerable to exploitation. Another distinct peak occurs between the ages of 12 and 16, corresponding to pubertal development. **Elder abuse** includes emotional, financial, physical neglect and maltreatment, including questionable institutionalization. It is estimated that approximately 100,000 elderly Canadians (approximately 1 of 30 over the age of 65) may be abused annually.[19]

2.1.3. Socioeconomic Indicators

The "composition" of the population in terms of educational, income and employment characteristics influences health status. The proportion of the population 15 and over, with less than nine years of education is one indicator of socioeconomic status. In 1986, 17.3% of Canadians had quit school before the ninth grade. A related indicator which is unavailable for Canada, but which has been determined for Quebec, is the proportion of live births to mothers with less than nine years of formal education. This proportion is positively correlated with an increased incidence of premature births. In 1990, 4.4% of live births in Quebec were to mothers who had less than nine years of education. Age of the mother at the birth of an infant influences the number of low birth weight infants, prematurity and perinatal morbidity. In 1989, 5.9% of Canadian births were to mothers aged less than 20 and 8.3% were born to mothers aged 35 and over. There is an increased risk for infants in both age groups.

Thirty-eight per cent of the population in Canada, in 1992, have **literacy limitations,** in that they cannot read or write (7%), are able only to read and write simple words (9%), or are able only to read and write simple sentences (22%).[20] These limitations may affect health directly in terms of the inappropriate use of medication, inability to communicate effectively with health-care workers, or difficulty in following instructions (including safety instructions at work). Unhealthy lifestyles, due to limited access to health information, has an effect on their health status. This latter concept has been termed **health literacy**.

Income is another major socioeconomic indicator. The proportions of the population living below the low-income cutoff points indicate poverty levels. Statistics Canada low-income cutoff points have been based on a survey of family expenditures and are adjusted annually in line with the consumer price index. A family that spends more than 56.2% of income on the basic needs of accommodation, food and clothing falls below the cutoff. These levels are adjusted for family size and location. In 1985, 15.9% of Canadian families were living in poverty whereas in 1991 13.2% of the families lived below the poverty line. This figure excludes the residents of the Yukon Territory, Northwest Territories and Indian reserves. The average family income in Canada in 1990 was $51,342. **Unemployment rates** in Canada are high, increasing from 7.4% in 1981 to over 11% in 1993.

The proportion of welfare recipients indicates those who cannot adequately meet their needs nor those of their dependants because of their inability to find work, the loss of a spouse who is the main support of the family, illness, disability, or other reasons. These payments fall below the previously described low-income cutoff points set by Statistics Canada. For Canada as a whole, 6.0% of the population was receiving welfare in March 1990.

Living alone may be associated with social isolation and possibly with lower socioeconomic status and a higher incidence of suicide. In 1991 in Canada, **23%** of all private households, comprising over 2.3 million persons, were occupied by single persons. The extended survival of elderly women and the breakdown of families are major contributing causes.

Although homeless men and women do not have illnesses which differ from the general population, it is associated with increased health risks. The homeless are twice as likely to suffer from arthritis or rheumatism, five times as likely to contract emphysema or chronic bronchitis, three times as likely to experience asthma and six times as likely to have epileptic attacks.[21] Many homeless persons are ex-patients of mental health institutions, runaway teenagers, women and children escaping from domestic violence, the elderly, alcoholics and natives.

There are three recognized types of homelessness: **chronically homeless** people live on the streets in the daytime and seek shelter at night, often have alcohol, drug or solvent abuse problems and are either current or former psychiatric patients; **periodically homeless** people have left home for a length of time and, often include native people who have left their reserve, runways from home, and battered women and their children; **temporarily homeless** people due to crisis or hospitalization, include the working poor who are waiting for public housing since they can no longer afford their own home.[22] In Metropolitan Toronto from July 1987 to June 1988, there were 25,000 different individuals or families admitted to the Hostel Operations Unit of Metro Toronto Community Services. Most (57.2%) were lone males older than 25, and a further 21.7% were lone males who were less than 25 years of age.

The social environment includes the **working environment**. The significance of safety in the work environment is illustrated by the fact that a work injury resulting in lost time occurred, on average, every 51 seconds in Canada in 1988.[23] In Ontario alone, there were 293 work-related fatalities in 1988.[24] The number and characteristics of work-related health problems are changing as working environments change. Since World War II, a gradual shift of the labour force has occurred from goods-producing jobs in manufacturing, construction and primary industries to less hazardous service-producing jobs such as finance, amusement and business services. The increased participation of women in the work force, generally in the service sector, has led to new concerns about the safety of the working environment for the pregnant mother and fetus.

It is apparent from the preceding discussion that both demographic and socio-economic determinants strongly affect the overall health status of a population, particularly health problems concentrated in certain gender, age, ethnic, or income subgroups. It follows that demographic and socioeconomic determinants are essential considerations for the effective planning of health care.

2.1.4. The Physical Environment

The environment has been widely discussed in the media in the past two decades, usually in regard to the pollution of air and water from industrial and domestic sources. A federal report which gives a good overview of environment and health in Canada[25] indicated that in 1990, 97% of Canadians surveyed were concerned about the effect of environmental pollution. Environmental health problems range from acute poisoning to chronic irritation to cancer and genetic damage. Though the negative impact of the environment on health has been widely publicized, it must not be forgotten that there are elements in the environment which have a directly beneficial effect on health, such as the protection against dental caries enjoyed by the 37% of Canadians whose local water supply is "naturally" fluoridated.

Specific information on many of the environmental indicators defined as determinants of health in chapter three is presented in chapter nine which deals with environmental health. Several examples of environmental indicators are as follows: a) The National Dioxin Sampling Program undertaken by the Ministry of Fisheries and Oceans has detected levels of dioxins in rivers which have resulted in closures of shellfish harvesting in the immediate vicinity of pulp mills to prevent further contamination. b) Monitoring of the presence of Polychlorinated biphenyls (PCBs) in the breast milk of Canadian women by Health Canada has shown a dramatic reduction in recent years. c) Recent increases have been detected in the incidence of melanotic and non-melanotic skin cancers which are related to the decrease in thickness of the ozone layer (an environmental indicator), resulting in greater exposure to ultraviolet radiation.

Agricultural Risks At least two million Canadians are involved in activities related to agriculture or live on family farms. There are concerns about health and safety issues in modern, competitive agriculture, which is largely dependent on mechanization and the use of pesticides, herbicides, fertilizers, fungicides and efficient feeding techniques.[26] Grain workers and swine and poultry producers are at significant risk for respiratory disorders, the latter as a result of intensive feeding techniques and confinement of poultry. Disabling injuries from trauma are likely severely underestimated as they are poorly studied in Canada. Occupational exposure to chemicals such as solvents and fungicides have been linked with neuro-degenerative disease in case reports; however, no population-based studies to estimate agricultural risks have been undertaken.

The environment is perhaps the most encompassing of the four elements in the health field concept. Through it, we see how environmentalists lobbying for control of pollution, consumer advocates working for better quality of food and other products, and union leaders negotiating for safer working conditions, all have a role in improving the health of Canadians.

3.   LIFESTYLE AND BEHAVIOURAL RISK FACTORS

The Lalonde Report placed great emphasis on lifestyle elements and the personal behaviour of Canadians as a major factor in determining their health. The following discussion shows that this emphasis was not misplaced. Much of our knowledge about Canadian behaviour comes from the Canada Health Survey of 1978-79, and Canada's Health Promotion Survey of 1985 and 1990 (cited extensively in this section, unless specified).[27,28] The more recent information on cardiovascular risk factors on a national basis has been derived from the Canada Heart Health Survey:[29] a series of population-based surveys, consisting of a probability sample of 26,293 men and women aged 18-74, undertaken by nine provincial departments of health and Health and Welfare Canada between 1986 and 1990.

3.1.   SUBSTANCE ABUSE

Substance abuse refers to the problems associated with the use of alcohol and tobacco, overuse of tranquillizers and sedatives and use of illicit drugs such as cannabis, cocaine, heroin and LSD. The most commonly used drugs are alcohol and tobacco. The Risk Continuum framework for assessing the health risks of substance abuse has been described in chapter one.

3.1.1. Tobacco
Large decreases in tobacco consumption in Canada have been recorded recently. From 1980-1990, Statistics Canada reported a 35% decline in tobacco consumption as measured by cigarettes smoked by people 15 and over. In 1989 alone, overall tobacco consumption fell by 6.8% mainly as a result of decreased cigarette consumption.[30,31]

According to Statistics Canada, over the last two decades the proportion of Canadians who smoke has decreased from 41% of the population aged 15 and over in 1966 to 26% in 1990 (about 5.4 million people). However, the smoking rates of males and females have converged, as more women have taken up smoking while male smokers have declined. The Heart Health Survey[29] reported that approximately 30% of males and 28% of females aged 18 and older smoke cigarettes daily. Seventeen per cent of males and 9% of females smoke more than 25 cigarettes per day. For the age group 18-24, 33% of males are regular smokers as are 32% of females. Men in the 25-44 age group are more likely to smoke regularly (35%) than women (34%), although this gap has narrowed over time. Sex differences in smoking behaviour are most apparent among those over age 45. In the 45-64 year range, 31.5% of men and 22% of women are regular smokers. Among adults over age 65, 16% of men and 12% of women smoke regularly.

A 1991 survey of Ontario students reported that 21.5% of females and 21.9% of males smoked.[32] This was a downward trend from 34.7% overall in 1979. Another trend noted was that first use of tobacco prior to grade nine had decreased from 89% to 69% between 1977 and 1991. In 1991, 6.1% of grade seven students smoked. High school students are not representative, however, of all youth. It is reported that 92% of street youth smoke daily.[33]

3.1.2. Alcohol
The 1989 National Alcohol and Other Drugs Survey[34] reported that 78% of Canadians over the age of 15 years are "drinkers" (i.e., consumed alcoholic beverages at least once in the 12 months prior to the survey). Another 16% of the population reported they are former drinkers, having consumed alcohol at some time earlier in their lives, while 7% reported that they have never consumed an alcoholic beverage. A "drink" in this survey was defined as: one bottle of beer, one glass of draft, one glass of wine, one wine cooler, or one straight or mixed drink with 44 mL (1.5 oz) of hard liquor. The number of drinks consumed by current drinkers aged 15 years and over in the week preceding the survey was: 1-7 drinks for 38% of current drinkers, 8-14 drinks for 9%, 15 or more drinks for 6%, and no drinks for 47%. The average current drinker consumed 3.7 drinks per week in 1989 compared with 5.1 in 1985. The trend indicates that fewer adults are drinking, and those who are drinking, are consuming less. Statistics Canada reported that the Social Survey in 1991 confirmed this trend with 55% of the population surveyed reporting that they were current drinkers (consumed alcohol at least once a month) compared to 65% in the 1978 Social Survey. Males consume disproportionately more alcohol at all ages than females.

After the age of 20 years, there is an inverse relationship between age and the prevalence of alcohol consumption. Drinking is more likely to occur among those in the work force, those with higher incomes and those with higher education. It has been estimated that 7% of the total drinking population consumes 40% of all alcohol sold. This amounts to an average of 68 litres of absolute alcohol per year for each individual within this heavy drinking group. This is equivalent to 2280 bottles of beer, *plus* 77 bottles of table wine, *plus* 76 bottles (780 mL) of spirits per person, per year.

The per capita consumption of alcohol for Canadian adults increased steadily from 7.1 litres (of absolute alcohol) in 1958 to a little more than 11 litres during a plateau from 1975 to 1981.[35] Since 1981, per capita consumption has declined to approximately 10 litres of absolute alcohol per year in Canada (half of this is consumed as beer).

Alcohol remains an important factor in health problems such as cirrhosis, motor vehicle accidents, family violence and violent deaths. There has, however, been a decline in persons charged with impaired driving offences in Canada beginning in 1984-85.

Repeated surveys of Ontario students in different grades have shown a significant reduction of alcohol use in both sexes from 76.3% to 66.2% between 1977 and 1989 with a sharp decline occurring after 1979. There does, however, appear to be a concentration of problem drinking among those who report heavy use (particularly for males). This group has increased frequency of drinking, drinking to intoxication, and drinking resulting in police contact or medical attention. Again, students are not representative of all members of this age group, as a 95% prevalence of drinking has been reported in street youth, 6% of whom drink daily.[29]

3.1.3. Drugs

The National Alcohol and Other Drugs Survey of 1990 indicated that cannabis (marijuana or hashish) is the most commonly used illicit drug in Canada; 23.2% of Canadians have used it at least once during their lives, and 6.5% are current users, i.e., those who have used it in the previous 12 months. Almost one half (48.6%) of current users of cannabis use it less than once per month, 24.8% use it between 1-3 times a month, and 22.4% use it once a week or more. Use of cannabis is twice as common among men (8.9%) as it is for women (4.1%). The highest rate of current use is among respondents 20-24 years of age (23.7%).

Cocaine or crack has been used by 3.5% of adult Canadians at some time in their lives, and 1.4% are current users. The highest rate of current users for cocaine is among respondents 25-34 years of age. Approximately 4.9% of men and 1.8% of women of that age had used cocaine or crack during the year preceding the survey. LSD, speed, or heroin have been used by 4.1% of adult Canadians at some time in their lives. Less than one-half per cent (0.4%) of Canadians report using these substances during the year preceding the survey. A very small proportion of Canadians (1.3%) had injected themselves with drugs using needles shared with someone else. This implies that approximately 235,000 Canadians shared a needle on at least one occasion. The Ontario Student Drug Use Survey found a reduction in the use of illicit drugs. Cannabis use, for example, declined from 31.7% of high school students in the late 1970s to 11.7% in 1991.

A less widely perceived problem is the overuse and the inappropriate use of over-the-counter and prescribed medications. The Canada Health Survey found that 48% of Canadians take some type of medication in any given 48- hour period, but only 60% do so on the advice of a physician. The National Alcohol and Other Drug Survey indicated the proportion of Canadians using the following prescription drugs 30 days prior to the survey were: 5% used narcotics such as codeine, morphine or demerol, 3.6% used sleeping pills, 3.1% used tranquillizers and 2% used antidepressant drugs. Generally, usage rates were higher among women than men. Senior citizens are highly medicated, each taking on average 15 prescriptions per year in Canada, whereas seniors in Nova Scotia each took an average of over 24 prescriptions per year.

3.2.   NUTRITION

Nutrition is fundamental to maintaining good health and to preventing disease and reducing its severity.   The best information available is that gathered by Nutrition Canada in a national survey of physical health and nutritional intake,[36] which was reported in 1973.   Although national data on nutrition have been limited since this survey, the apparent nutrient intakes of Canadians from 1953 to 1986 have been analyzed according to Family Food Expenditure Surveys conducted biannually by Statistics Canada.[37] The trends were similar to another indirect indicator of nutritional status, apparent per capita domestic (food) disappearance.   Significant nutritional deficits were identified.   Households in the lowest income decile consumed on average 467 calories less than the average, with the result that 11.4% of these households had protein intakes below the Recommended Nutrient Intakes for Canadians.   Those on social assistance also had a consumption pattern similar to those in the lowest income decile households.

The proportion of calories from fat (average 40%) and carbohydrates (average 47%) did not vary with income.   This proportion is much higher than that recommended by National Nutritional Guidelines.   Single-parent households had substantially less adequate apparent protein intake than average.   Senior households appeared to be less vulnerable to protein or calorie deficiency when income status was controlled.   Compared with the recommended levels, the diet of seniors was inadequate in micro-nutrient intake, particularly for folate, thiamine, iron, calcium, riboflavin, niacin and vitamin C.   Seniors in lower income brackets had a lower intake of micro-nutrients compared with those in higher income.

The Canada Health Promotion Survey (1990)[28] determined the proportion of over- and underweight adults by measuring the Body Mass Index (BMI).   The BMI is calculated as the weight in kilograms divided by the square of the height in metres.   This survey found that 51% of the Canadians aged 20 and over had a BMI in the range of 20 to 25 (acceptable weight), 11% had a BMI less than 20 (underweight), 16% had a BMI of 25-27 (possibly overweight), and 22% had a BMI over 27 (overweight).   Young women in particular were more likely to be underweight (28% of women aged 20 to 24).   Men, particularly middle-aged (45-54 years), are more likely to be overweight (35%).   Over 50% of Canadians want to change their weight, primarily through weight loss.   About 68% of women at an acceptable weight want to lose weight as do 22% of women in the underweight category.   Losing weight in the future is seen by 10% of Canadians as the most important action to improve health.

There are indications that the proportion of overweight Canadians has risen. The General Social Survey in 1991 estimated that 23% of the population aged 20 to 64 were overweight, compared to 17% in 1985. The Canada Heart Health Survey in 1992 indicated that the prevalence of obesity, as defined by a BMI ≥ 27, was 35% in men and 27% in women. Abdominal obesity was also higher in males and increased with age and with BMI.[29]

A concern relevant to nutrition for immigrants to Canada is the cultural lack of familiarity with the types of food available in Canada and a lack of domestic skill in preparing a varied diet using available foods. Although single male Ethiopian refugees were found to have generally adequate nutrient intakes, their diets in Canada[38] were found to be lacking in variety and in fruits and vegetables other than large quantities of orange juice. Refugees more skilled in preparing available food felt more satisfied with their eating habits, and had higher BMI (although overall BMIs and arm circumference measures for the group were lower than Canadian and American standards).

3.2.1. Plasma Lipids and Lipoproteins

It is well known that high blood cholesterol levels and other lipoprotein disorders are associated with increased risk for cardiovascular disease. Forty-eight per cent of male and 43% of female participants aged 18 to 74 (in the Canada Heart Health Survey) had total plasma cholesterol levels greater than 5.2 mmol/L. Lower levels have been advised by a number of authorities. Eighteen per cent of males and 16% of females had levels of total cholesterol in the high risk category of > 6.2 mmol/L. Serum cholesterol levels in males rose with age up to the age of 45 to 64, whereas levels were stable in younger females and increased dramatically at age 45-54. Eight per cent (of both sexes) had high density lipoprotein levels (HDL) in the high risk category below 0.9 mmol/L. Fifteen per cent (of both sexes) had levels of low density lipoprotein (LDL) above the high risk level of 2.3 mmol/L and the same percentage had high risk triglyceride levels above 1.3 mmol/L.

3.3.   USE OF PROTECTIVE DEVICES

Seat Belts

Motor vehicle accidents are a leading cause of death and injury in Canada, especially in young adults. The established role of seat belts in reducing fatalities has been well publicized, yet according to a 1988 national survey only 79% of Canadian drivers wear them all or most of the time. Quebec has the highest rate of seat belt use at 86%, while Prince Edward Island has the lowest at 50%.[39] There are regional variations within provinces. A survey in Ontario in 1991 indicated an overall usage rate for those over 16 years of age of 80.9%, which had increased significantly from 69.6% in a 1984 survey. A rate, however, of only 73.5% was reported for Northern Ontario.[40] Also worrisome is the fact that the lowest rates of seat belt use occur among impaired drivers and young drivers, the two groups who have the highest accident rates. The use of infant restraints has increased (to 93.3% in the 1991 Ontario survey) as had the use of toddler restraints, up from

79% in 1984 to 88% in 1991. The prevalence of correct use of restraints, increased to 20.9% for toddlers and 38.5% for infants. These low percentages clearly suggest the need for further safety education about correct usage of child restraints. The most common misuse of child seats was not securing the tether strap.

Bicycle Helmets
Wearing bicycle helmets has been demonstrated to be effective in preventing serious head injury and death.[41] Prevalence rates of bicycle helmet use by cyclists in Ottawa increased threefold from 10.7% in 1988 to 32.2% in 1991, the highest rate, with greatest increase for commuters (44.6% in 1991).[42] However, only one-quarter of elementary school children, 17% of secondary school students and 20.2% of post-secondary students wore helmets in 1991.

3.4.   PHYSICAL ACTIVITY AND FITNESS

Canada's Health Promotion Survey[28] reported frequency of exercise by Canadians over the age of 15 in three categories: (i) *regular* (3 or more times weekly); (ii) *occasional* (1-2 times weekly); and (iii) *sedentary* (never exercise or exercise less than once per week). Twenty-two per cent of respondents exercised regularly, 50% exercised occasionally, and 26% were sedentary. Daily physical activity decreases with age to middle adulthood and then increases after age 44 for both men and women. Canadians most likely to engage in daily exercise in their leisure time are men aged 65 and older. Active use of leisure time becomes more common as education, income and occupational status increase in all age groups and in both sexes. Too much leisure time is still claimed by TV, magazines, radio and other activities of a sometimes educational but sedentary nature. Ninety-six per cent of the population watches TV, and approximately one-third of Canadians over 14 years of age watches 15 or more hours per week. However, there is some evidence that more leisure time is being devoted to exercise. A 1985 survey showed that 82% of adults reported participating in a sport or exercise activity in the previous week compared with 35% in a similar survey in 1972. The proportion of the population who report being physically "very active" has increased in the General Social Survey (Statistics Canada) from 27% in 1985 to 32% in 1991.

3.5.   SEXUAL PRACTICES

While there are no large scale studies on human sexuality in Canada, the acquired immune deficiency syndrome (AIDS) epidemic has generated more interest in this field. The recent reports, AIDS in Canada - Knowledge, Behaviour, and Attitudes of Adults,[43] and the Canada Youth and AIDS Study,[44] have provided the necessary information about sexuality. Many of today's adolescents are beginning their sexual experiences by the age of 14. Nearly one-half of the grade

11 respondents have had sexual intercourse. Although fewer younger students had sexual intercourse, the percentages are still high: 26% of grade nine respondents (more males than females), and at least 12% of males and 8% of females in grade seven. Approximately 75% of college and university students and about 85% of early school-leavers reported having had sexual intercourse at least once in their lifetime. Eighty-six per cent of adult Canadians have had sexual intercourse with a member of the opposite sex. About 1% of both males and females reported a homosexual orientation. Most sexual acts reported are vaginal intercourse among heterosexual couples, 28% of males and 24% of females reported having oral sex often; 2% of men also reported having anal sex often.

Thirty-five per cent of men and 14% of women reported that they had two or more sexual partners in the past five years. About one-quarter of all men and 7% of women have had three or more partners, and about 15% of the men and 3% of the women reported six or more partners. Aside from gender, the only factors affecting the number of sexual partners were marital status and age (single and younger tending to have more partners). Education and other socioeconomic measures had no effect.

Among respondents with two or more partners in the previous five years, 6% of men and 2% of women reported that they had "had sex without using a condom with someone (they) thought might be a carrier of the AIDS virus" and 41% of the men and 27% of the women reported that they had "had sex without using a condom with someone (they) did not know very well." Changes in behaviour to avoid contracting AIDS were reported by 54% of the men and 41% of the women. Of these, 70% said they had reduced the number of partners; about 90% said they were "more cautious"; 60% had started to use condoms or used them more often; and about 40% said that they had, on at least one occasion, not had sex because of fear of exposure to AIDS. Condoms were "never" used by 44% of the men respondents with two or more partners, 24% used them "sometimes" or "seldom," 13% "almost every time," and 19% "every time" they had sex. Among the women, 62% reported never using a condom, and only 12% used them every time.

3.6.   PREVENTIVE HEALTH PRACTICES

Recent Measures to Improve Health
In 1990, the Health Promotion Survey reported that 49% of Canadians had made at least one change to improve their health in the year prior to the survey. More women (52%) than men (46%) reported doing something to improve their health. The most frequent measure taken by the men (42%) and women (33%) to improve their health was to increase the amount they exercise. Only 12% reported attempts to improve eating habits, which is of concern considering the prevalence of diets not in accordance with current nutrition recommendations. Nine per cent of Canadians had attempted to lose weight recently. In terms of substance abuse,

only 2% of all adult Canadians had recently reduced the amount smoked and only 1% were attempting to reduce alcohol use in the year preceeding the survey.

Screening for Blood Pressure

Canada's Health Promotion Survey[28] examined certain preventive health practices among Canadians. With regard to screening for hypertension, 78% of all Canadians reported that they had their blood pressure checked within the 12 months preceding the survey. For both sexes the frequency of blood pressure monitoring increases with age. Men under age 45 were the least likely to have had their blood pressure checked during the six preceding months. Across all ages women were more likely than men to have their blood pressure checked regularly. Frequency of blood pressure monitoring was affected by education, stress, body weight, personal beliefs about diet, attitudes toward hypertension as a public health issue, and perceived need for information on hypertension. The majority of the population understood the importance of blood pressure screening in the absence of overt disease; only 17% believed it important only if there is a problem. Of the total population, 10% wanted more information on high blood pressure. The Canada Heart Health Survey indicated that 16% of men and 13% of women had diastolic blood pressures ≥ 90 mm Hg.[29]

Screening for Cervical Cancer

Regarding female preventive health practices, the survey found that more than half of all women have regular Pap smears. Seventy per cent of adult women reported having had a Pap smear within the three years of the survey (in accordance with the recommended screening guidelines) and 18% of the women had never had a Pap smear. These women were most likely to be under 19 years of age or 65 and over. The Ontario Health Survey[45] reported that 32% of females aged 16 to 19 did not know whether they had ever had a Pap test, which is disturbing in view of the early onset of sexual activities previously discussed. About three quarters of women aged 20 to 34 had a Pap smear in the previous year. These rates declined with age; less than half of the women aged 55 to 64 years old were having Pap smears.

Screening for Breast Cancer

Breast examination is frequently done by doctors but less frequently by women themselves. Of all adult women, 65% have had their breasts examined by a doctor or nurse during the year prior to the survey. Unfortunately, examination was more frequent among younger women and declined with age even though the risk of breast cancer, in fact, increases with age. Breast examination was most frequent in women aged 20 to 24 (71.9%), declining to 56.9% and 49.7% in women aged 55-64, and 65 and over respectively. Seventy-three per cent of all women reported having been shown how to do breast self-examination, yet only 27% of all women examine their own breasts every month.

In women aged 50 to 69, for whom routine screening mammography is recommended every two years, 55% reported ever having had a mammogram, and only 40% had had one within a two-year period prior to the survey.

Dental Hygiene
The vast majority of Canadians (97%) brush their teeth at least once a day and 79% brush their teeth twice a day. This preventive practice is more widespread among women, younger Canadians and those with a higher education and income.

4.   HEALTH-CARE ORGANIZATION

This health field element is the subject of later chapters in this book, and will not be discussed in detail here. The major feature is the availability of universal health insurance for all Canadians, which has significantly contributed to increasing the access to health care within the population.

5.   SUMMARY

This chapter dealt with the determinants of health and disease in the Canadian population. The determinants of health include: human biology, environment (psychosocial and physical), lifestyle and behavioural and risk factors, and health-care organizations.

The genetic potential of the individual is a major aspect of human biology and has an impact on health.

Demography is the study of populations, especially with reference to size, density, fertility, mortality, growth, age distribution and migration. Sociodemographic and socioeconomic indicators represent the interaction of demography with social and economic conditions. In June of 1991, Canada's population was 27.3 million. Population distributions by age and sex from 1941-91 indicate that the population has more than doubled since 1941. The ratio of males to females has remained roughly constant, but there has been a definite change in the age distribution. With the availability of better contraception, more liberal abortion laws, and more women participating in the labour force, the proportion of children in the 0-14 year age group decreased since 1971, and at the same time there was an increase in the 65 year and over age group.

Geographic distributions also have an impact on the health status of a population. Three-quarters of the population live within 320 kilometres of the US border, the remaining population is spread over a vast land mass. Providing health-care services to this widely dispersed population in the northern areas of Canada is a definite challenge.

Life expectancy at birth in Canada has increased significantly between 1941 and 1990. The chief reason for the increase is the significant decline in infant mortality. Life expectancy has increased significantly more for females than for males. The life expectancy today for males is 73.7 years and for females it is 80.6 years.

Sociodemographic indicators include: aging, immigrant population, language and family environments. An important demographic change is the rise in the proportion of the population over 65 years of age. The composition of the Canadian population is changing in relation to ethnicity and is expected to continue changing as more immigrants are allowed into Canada in order to offset the declining Canadian fertility rate. As an example of Canada's ethnic diversity, 3.5 million people reported a mother tongue other than French or English. Family violence plays a role on the health of the individual family members. Family violence, which is prevalent among Canadians, takes the form of child abuse, wife battering and elder abuse.

The composition of the population in terms of education, income and employment characteristics influences health. The proportion of the population 15 and over with less than nine years of education is an indicator of socioeconomic status. Thirty-eight per cent of the population in Canada in 1992 had literacy limitations. These limitations may affect health directly in terms of the inappropriate use of medicines, failure to communicate effectively with health-care workers, and difficulty in following instructions.

Income is another major socio-economic indicator. A family that spends 56.2% of its income on the basic needs of accommodation, food and clothing is defined as living in poverty. In 1990 13.2% of Canadian families were living in poverty. Unemployment rates in Canada are high, increasing from 7.4% in 1981 to over 11% in 1993.

Homelessness is associated with many health risks. Many homeless persons are ex-patients of mental health institutions, runaway teenagers, alcoholics or aboriginal peoples.

Environmentally caused health problems include: acute poisoning, chronic irritation, cancer and genetic damage.

Occupational hazards can also affect the health of an individual. For example, grain workers and swine and poultry producers have been found to be at a significant risk for respiratory disorders. As well, occupational exposure to chemicals such as solvents and fungicides has been linked with neurodegenerative disorders.

The lifestyle of Canadians is a major factor in determining their health. Substance abuse, nutrition, use of protective devices, activity and fitness, sexual practices and preventive health practices are behaviours and risk factors that affect the health of an individual.

Substance abuse refers to the problems associated with the use of alcohol and tobacco, overuse of tranquillizers and sedatives and use of illicit drugs. In the last two decades, the proportion of Canadians who smoke has decreased. However, the smoking rates of males and females have converged, as the number of male smokers has been declining. Large decreases in tobacco consumption in Canada have been recorded recently. In the last decade, there has been a 35% decline in tobacco consumption. With respect to alcohol, trends indicate that fewer adults are drinking, more have stopped drinking, and those who are drinking are consuming less. Alcohol remains an important factor in health problems such as cirrhosis, and in motor vehicle accidents, family violence and violent deaths. The National Alcohol and Other Drugs Survey indicated that cannabis is the most commonly used illicit drug in Canada. However, the Ontario Student Drug Use Survey found a reduction in use of illicit drugs.

Nutrition is fundamental to good health and in the prevention or reduction in severity of disease. Households with low incomes consumed on average 467 calories less than the average, with the result that 11.4% had protein intakes below the Recommended Nutrient Intakes. Fifty-one per cent of Canadians have an acceptable weight (according to the BMI), 11.0% are underweight, 16.0% are potentially overweight and 22.0% are overweight. Young women tend to be mostly in the underweight group, whereas middle-aged men constitute a large proportion of the overweight group.

Seat belts and bicycle helmets are examples of protective devices. Even though the established role of seat belts in the reduction of fatalities has been well publicized, only 79% of Canadian drivers wear them all or most of the time. The effectiveness of wearing bicycle helmets in the prevention of serious head injury and death has been demonstrated.

Frequency of exercise is categorized into three groups: regular, occasional, and sedentary. Twenty-two per cent exercised regularly, 50% exercised occasionally and 26% were sedentary. The proportion of individuals who carry out regular exercise decreases with increasing age.

Many of today's adolescents are beginning their sexual experiences by the age of 14. Thirty-five per cent of men and 14% of women reported having two or more sexual partners in the past five years. Factors affecting the number of sexual partners were an individual's marital status and age. Education and socioeconomic status had no effect.

Canada's Health Promotion Survey examined certain preventive health practices among Canadians. Fifty-seven per cent of people reported that they had had their blood pressure checked within the last six months. Frequency of blood pressure monitoring is affected by education, stress, body weight, personal beliefs about diet, attitudes towards hypertension and perceived need for information on hypertension. The survey also found that more than half of all women have regular Pap smears. However, breast-self examination by women is done less frequently.

Health-care organization is also a determinant of health. The major feature is the availability of universal health insurance for all Canadians which has significantly contributed to reducing the inequities in access to health care within the population.

6.   REFERENCES

1. Jaworski M, Severini A, Mansour G, et al. Genetic Conditions Among Canadian Mennonites: Evidence for a Founder Effect Among the Old Colony (Chortitza) Mennonites. *Clin Invest Med* 12(2):127-141, 1989.
2. Yorke D, Mitchell J, Clow C, et al. Newborn Screening for Sickle Cell and Other Haemoglobinopathies. *Clin Invest Med* 15(4):376-383, 1992.
3. *1991 Census of Canada. The Nation Series.* Statistics Canada. Ministry of Industry, Science and Technology, Ottawa, 1992, pp 6-57.
4. *Users' Guide to 40 Community Health Indicators.* Health and Welfare Canada. Community Health Division, Health Services and Promotion Branch in collaboration with the National Health Information Council and Health Information Division, Policy Planning and Information Branch. Canada, 1992.
5. Statistics Canada. Population Projections for Canada and the Provinces. Ministry of Industry, Trade and Commerce, Ottawa, 1979, p 453.
6. Statistics Canada. *Health Reports* 1(2):211-223, 1989.
7. Satistics Canada, 1991 Census. Ottawa, *The Daily* April 13, 1993.
8. Statistics Canada. Quarterly Demographic Statistics. Ministry of Industry, Science and Technology 6(2):1-18, 1992.
9. Statistics Canada. Getting Bigger Faster. *Canadian Social Trends* (Insert) Summer 1992.
10. *Current Demographic Analysis: Report on the Demographic Situation in Canada 1988.* Ministry of Supply and Services, Canada, Ottawa, 1990.
11. *Canada Year Book 1990.* Ministry of Supply and Services, Canada, Ottawa, 1989, pp 3-18.
12. *Multicultural Canada: A Graphic Overview.* Government of Canada. Policy Research, Multiculturalism Sector, Multiculturalism & Citizenship Canada. Minister of Supply and Services Canada. Ottawa, 1989.
13. Statistics Canada. Changing Faces: Visible Minorities in Toronto. *Can Soc Trend* Winter 1991, pp 26-28.
14. Samuel J. Third World Immigration and Multiculturalism. In: *Ethnic Demography: Canadian Immigrant, Racial and Cultural Variations.* Halli SS, Trovato F and Driedger L, eds. Ottawa: Carleton University Press, 1990, pp 383-398.
15. Simmons A. 'New Wave' Immigrants: Origin and Characteristics. In: *Ethnic Demography: Canadian Immigrant, Racial and Cultural Variations.* Halli SS, Trovato F and Driedger L, eds. Ottawa: Carleton University Press, 1990, pp 141-160.
16. Statistics Canada, The Violence Against Women Survey. Ottawa, *The Daily* November 18, 1993.
17. *Canadian Social Trends.* Ministry of Supply and Services Canada. McKie C and Thompson K, eds. Ottawa: Thompson Educational Publishing, Inc., 1990, pp 170-172.
18. Robinson SC. Child Abuse - The Obstetric Responsibility. *Bull Soc Obstet Gynacol Can* 2(2):1-2, 1981.
19. *Family violence: A Review of Theoretical and Clinical Literature.* Health and Welfare Canada, Ministry of Supply and Services, Canada, Ottawa, 1989, p 36.
20. Canadian Public Health Association. *Health Digest* 16(2):8, Summer 1992.
21. Ambrosio E, Baker D, Crowe C and Hardill K. *The Street Health Report: A Study of the Health Status and Barriers to Health Care of Homeless Women and Men in the City of Toronto.* City of Toronto Public Health Department, 1992.

22. Begin P. *Homelessness in Canada*. Ministry of Supply and Services, Canada, Ottawa, 1992.

23. *Work Injuries 1986-1988*. Ministry of Supply and Services, Canada, Ottawa, 1989.

24. *Workers' Compensation Board Annual Report 1988: Statistical Supplement. Toronto*: Workers' Compensation Board, 1989.

25. *A Vital Link. Health and the Environment in Canada*. Health and Welfare Canada. Published under the authority of the Minister of National Health and Welfare. Ministry of Supply and Services. Canada Communication Group - Publishing. Ottawa, 1992.

26. Zedja J, Semchuk K, McDuffie H and Dosman J. A Need for Population-Based Studies of Health and Safety Risks in Canadian Agriculture. *Can Med Assoc J* 145(7):773-775, 1991.

27. Rootman I, Warren R, Stephens T and Peters L, eds. *Canada's Health Promotion Survey - Technical Report*. Health and Welfare Canada. Ministry of Supply and Services, Canada, Ottawa, 1988.

28. Stephens T and Fowler-Grahman D, eds. Health and Welfare Canada. Canada's Health Promotion Survey 1990: Technical Report. Ministry of Supply and Services, Canada, Ottawa, 1993.

29. Canadian Heart Health Surveys Group. Canadian Heart Health Surveys: A Profile of Cardiovascular Risk. *Can Med Assoc J* Suppl 146(11):1969-2029, 1993.

30. Trends in Canadian Tobacco Consumption, 1980-89. *Can Med Assoc J* 143(9):905-906, 1990.

31. Kaiserman MJ. Tobacco Production, Sales and Consumption in Canada, 1991. *Chronic Dis Can* 13(4):68-71, 1992.

32. *The Ontario Student Drug Use Survey. Trends Between 1977 and 1991*. Addiction Research Foundation. Toronto, Ontario, 1991.

33. Addiction Research Foundation. *Drugs in Ontario*. Toronto, Ontario, 1991, pp 1-47.

34. *National Alcohol and Other Drugs Survey*. Health and Welfare Canada, Ottawa, 1990.

35. Mao Y, Johnson R and Semencins R. Liver Cirrhosis Mortality and Per Capita Alcohol Consumption in Canada. *Can J Public Health* 83(1):80-81, 1992.

36. The Federal-Provincial Canadian Heart Health Initiative. *Nutrition Canada National Survey*. Ottawa: Information Canada, 1973, pp 1-121.

37. Apparent Nutrient Intakes of Canadians: Continuing Nutritional Challenges for Public Health Professionals. *Can J Public Health* 82(6):374-380, 1991.

38. McIsaac J, Tucker K, Gray-Donald K and Stafford-Smith B. Nutritional Status of Single Male Government-sponsored Refugees from Ethiopia. *Can J Public Health* 82(6):381-384, 1991.

39. *Road Safety Annual Report 1988*. Ministry of Supply and Services, Canada, Ottawa, 1989.

40. Ministry of Health of Ontario. The 1991 Ontario Ministry of Transportation and Communications Seat Belt Survey: Some Interesting Findings. *Public Health and Epidemiology Reports Ont* 3(11):168-174, 1992.

41. Thompson R, Rivara F and Thompson D. A Case-Control Study of the Effectiveness of Bicycle Safety Helmets. *N Engl J Med* 320(21):1361-1367, 1989.

42. Cushman R, Pless R, Hope D and Jenkins B. Trends in Bicycle Helmet use in Ottawa from 1988 to 1991. *Can Med Assoc J* 146(9):1582-1585, 1992.

43. Ornstein M. *AIDS in Canada: Knowledge, Behaviour and Attitudes of Adults*. Toronto: University of Toronto Press, 1989.

44. King AJC, Beazley RP, Warren WK, et al. *Canada Youth and AIDS Study*. Kingston: Queen's University, 1988.

45. Ministry of Health Ontario. Premiers Council on Health, Well-Being and Social Justice. *Ontario Health Survey 1990. Highlights.*

CHAPTER FIVE
Health Status
and Consequences

The previous chapter examined aspects of Canadian life which impact on our health. But how does one identify health status and assess its relative significance? The two health status indicators, namely mortality and morbidity, and the ensuing disability and economic burden, are the most commonly used measures of health in Canada. Much information is available on death in Canada, but morbidity, which encompasses all other health outcomes, is more difficult to assess. Several different approaches to the assessment of morbidity will be outlined in this chapter. Other outcomes, such as human suffering or quality of life, are of no less importance but as the methodologies for their measurement are difficult and evolving, they are not used extensively in assessment of health and planning of health-care.

1. HEALTH STATUS

1.1. SELF-ASSESSED

The most fundamental health outcome is the perception of well-being by the individual. This may or may not lead to other outcomes such as limitation of usual activities, consultation with a health professional, hospitalization, or death. Canada's Health Promotion Survey[1] (1990) asked individuals 15 years and over: "In general, compared to other persons your age would you say your health is ... excellent, very good, good, fair or poor?" Similarly it also asked questions related to long-term activity limitations, and level of happiness. The highlights of the study were:

- Nearly nine out of 10 Canadians (88%) assessed their health to be good, very good or excellent, compared with the health of others their age.
- Just over one in 10 people (12%) reported either fair or poor health.
- Older Canadians were more likely to report poorer health. Below age 45, fewer than one in 10 people reported that they were in fair or poor health; this number reaches nearly one in four (26%) in the 65 and over age group.

- Upper-income Canadians enjoy better health. In the highest household income quintile, 74% reported very good or excellent health status, compared to 37% in the lowest income quintile.
- Non-smokers were more likely to report excellent health than smokers (28% compared with 22%).
- Obese Canadian adults were more likely to report fair or poor health than persons in the normal weight range (14% compared with 9%).
- Just under four million adult Canadians (15%) reported having some form of a long-term activity limitation that restricted their ability to perform activities at work, around the home or at leisure. Those with a long-term activity limitation were nearly four times as likely (81%) to report poor health status as those without a limitation (19%).
- The majority of Canadians (88%) reported experiencing some level of stress in their lives. One in 10 people (12%) reported that their lives are "very stressful," whereas almost one in two (48%) reported "somewhat stressful."

Subjective Morbidity
Few data are available on this subject, but the Canada Health Survey has afforded us a look at Canadian perceptions.[2] Inquiries were made about all health problems at the time of the survey, and more than half of the respondents identified one or more health problems. Fewer than half of the problems reported did not induce the individuals to limit their activity, visit a health professional, or treat themselves with a commercial remedy. A Quebec survey[3] identified health problems in private households as a proportion of the total population in private households. The leading health problem, arthritis and rheumatism was reported by 10.6% of households, followed by mental problems (8.8%), headaches (8.3%), skin diseases and allergies (7.7%) and backaches (7.2%). Although some of this subjective morbidity may be trivial in nature it is worthy of examination to learn more about the relationship between perceived ill health and the pursuit of health-care, and the potential role of health education in this process.

In 1967, Robert Kohn estimated the health of a standardized population of 100,000 Canadians based on the following outcomes: i) individuals perceiving themselves to have at least one health problem or disability; ii) whether individuals consulted health professionals or were admitted to hospital for these problems; and iii) the number of deaths. It is possible to create similar estimates based on information from the Canada Health Survey and other recent sources. Figure 5.1 illustrates these estimates, which give a glimpse of the health of an average group of Canadians on an average day. It is notable that the figures do not differ significantly from those of Kohn 25 years earlier.[4] With the exception of death, these outcomes do not necessarily reflect disease; healthy people may feel ill, see a doctor, and even be admitted to hospital. All of these outcomes do, however, have consequences for health-care and its planning.

**Figure 5.1:   Health of a Population of 100,000 Canadians
on an Average Day**

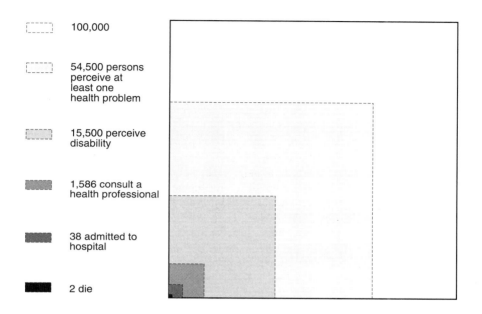

100,000

54,500 persons
perceive at
least one
health problem

15,500 perceive
disability

1,586 consult a
health professional

38 admitted to
hospital

2 die

Source: Adapted from R. Kohn, *Royal Commission on Health Services: The Health of Canadian
People*, Ottawa, 1967.

1.2.   OBJECTIVE INDICATORS

1.2.1. Mortality

The crude mortality rate in Canada was 7.2 deaths per 1000 population per year in
1991.   This number is important, but much more information is gained by
examining mortality in more detail.   Mortality may be expressed in terms of life
expectancy, age- and sex-specific death rates, causes of death by age and sex, and
potential-years-of-life-lost.   Most of these terms have been explained in chapter
three.   Each yields different useful information about Canadian health.   Life
expectancies for the Canadian population were discussed in chapter four.

Trends in Age- and Sex-Specific Death Rates (1951-1991)

Figure 5.2 illustrates age-specific mortality rates for both sexes for the years 1951
to 1991. Below the age of one year, there has been a steady decline in mortality
rates throughout this period which appears to be continuing.   In 1991, the infant
mortality rate per 1000 live births was 6.4 (6.9 for males and 5.9 for females).
Internationally, among the developed countries, three—Japan, Sweden, and Den-

mark—had the lowest infant mortality rates (5.0, 6.1, and 6.2) while Portugal, Greece and the United States had the highest rates (14.2, 11.7 and 10.0, respectively). The majority of these deaths occur during or shortly after delivery due to congenital anomalies and conditions specific to the perinatal period, such as hypoxia or placental anomalies. After the first week of life (the post-neonatal period) most infant deaths are due to congenital anomalies, sudden infant death syndrome, respiratory tract infections, or accidents. There is room for improvement in infant mortality, as the success of Japan shows.

From one to 14 years of age, mortality rates continue to decline slowly to very low levels. More than half of these deaths are due to motor vehicle and other accidents, and are potentially preventable.

In the 15 to 24 year age group, a very serious trend developed in the late 1960s and early 1970s with a sharp increase in death rates, especially among young men. The gap between male and female rates widened so that the mortality among males was about 3 times that for females. In this age group, the most significant causes of death are motor vehicle and other accidents, and suicide.

Recently, a significant drop in the death rate for this age group occurred, especially for males. This was due mainly to a decrease in mortality from motor vehicle accidents, which may have been a result of the introduction of lower speed limits and increased seat belt usage. In spite of this favourable trend, most of the deaths in this age group must be regarded as preventable, and there is much room for improvement.

For the age group 25-44, mortality rates were relatively stable throughout the 1960s and early 1970s, with a slight decline. Male rates in this and the next age group, 45-64 years, remain about double the female rates. The excess male mortality at these ages is largely due to accidents, ischemic heart disease, suicide, and cancer of the lung, each of which is determined to some extent by lifestyle.

In the 45-64 year age group, female rates have been slowly declining for several decades. Male rates, on the other hand were relatively stable until the mid-1970s and have fallen since. This is, in part, due to the decline in mortality from ischemic heart disease, the leading cause of death in men at these ages.

Beyond age 65, there remains a wide gap between male and female death rates, although both rates now appear to be on the decline. The major causes of death for both men and women are ischemic heart disease, cerebrovascular disease, and respiratory illness.

Causes of Death by Age and Sex

As listed in figure 5.3, the leading causes of death ranked by number of deaths are neoplasms, coronary heart disease, respiratory diseases and accidents for men; for women, neoplasms, cardiovascular disease, stroke, and respiratory disease. Based on current knowledge of the etiology of these health problems, many of these deaths could be prevented or delayed by lifestyle modifications. When Canadian mortality is examined from this point of view, it becomes clear why the Lalonde report placed emphasis on the lifestyle element of the health field concept.

**Figure 5.2: Trends in Age-Sex Specific Mortality Rates
per 1000 Population in Canada, 1951-1991**

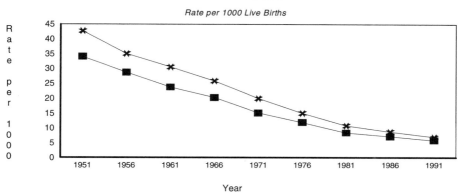

Infant Mortality Rate

Rate per 1000 Live Births

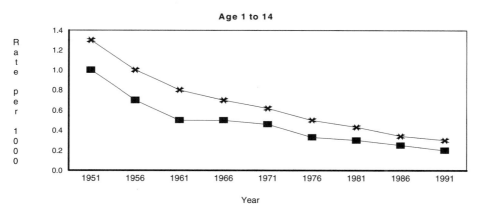

Age 1 to 14

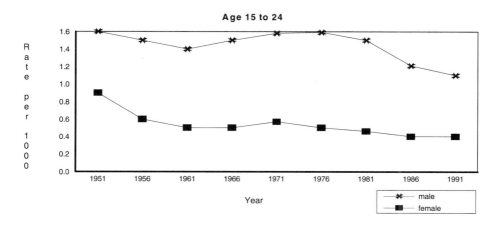

Age 15 to 24

**Figure 5.2:   Trends in Age-Sex Specific Mortality Rates
per 1000 Population in Canada, 1951-1991** *(con't)*

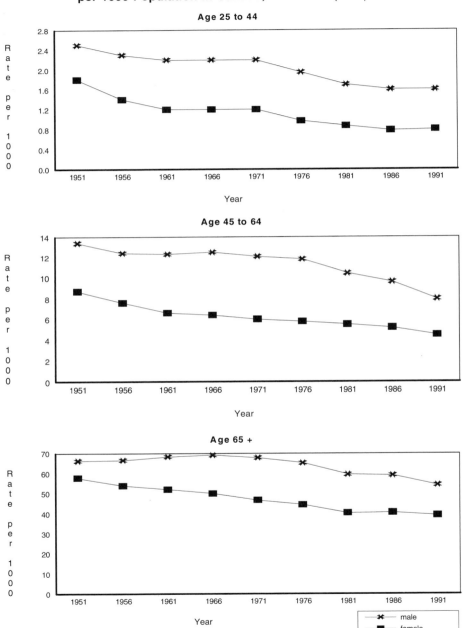

Source: Adapted from Health Field Indicators, H&W, 1986 and Statistics Canada

Figure 5.3: Leading Causes of Death by Sex, Canada, 1991.

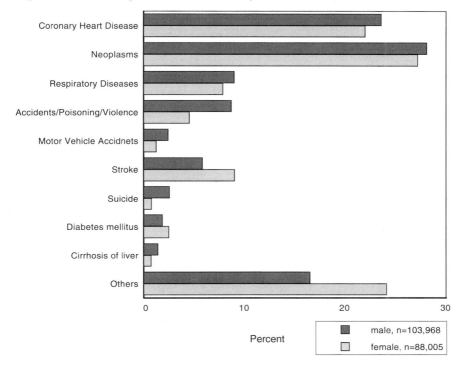

Source: Causes of Death, Health Reports, 4(1), 1992

Figure 5.4 provides a broad overview of the prevailing causes of death by sex and age group in Canada in **1991.** It demonstrates the relative contribution of our lifestyle to mortality up to middle age and emphasizes differences in causes of death between males and females. Highlights of this figure are as follows:

(1) In children, perinatal disorders and congenital anomalies account for a significant proportion to total mortality because of the concentration of deaths in infancy. Accidents, however, account for one-sixth of deaths of boys aged up to 14, but only about one-tenth of deaths among girls up to 14 years old. Accidents and suicides together comprise three quarters of the deaths of young men ages 15 to 24, and over one-half of young female deaths in the same age group.

(2) In the age-group 25-44, accidents, suicide, cancer and heart disease are important causes of death for both sexes. Over the last decade, AIDS has become one of the major causes of death amongst males.

(3) In mid-life, the leading causes of death are cancer and coronary heart disease. Cancer takes a particularly large toll among women, accounting for 52% of deaths

Figure 5.4: Causes of Death by Age and Sex, Canada, 1991

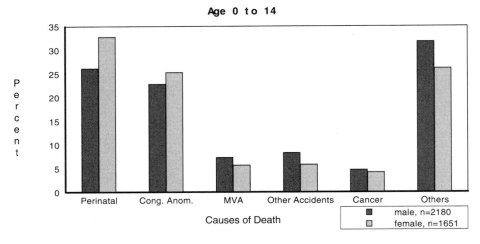

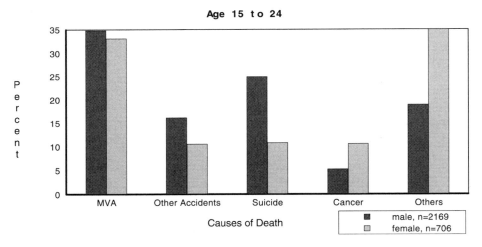

between ages 45 and 64 years.   Coronary heart disease and cancer are each responsible for approximately 24% of deaths among men in this age group.

(4) At older ages, coronary heart disease and cancer continue to be the leading causes of death, but the proportion of deaths due to coronary heart disease increases, especially among women, while the relative importance of cancer declines.   Stroke becomes a significant cause of death after age 70.   In men, chronic obstructive lung disease (chronic bronchitis, emphysema and asthma) becomes relatively more important.

Figure 5.4: Causes of Death by Age and Sex, Canada, 1991 *(con't)*

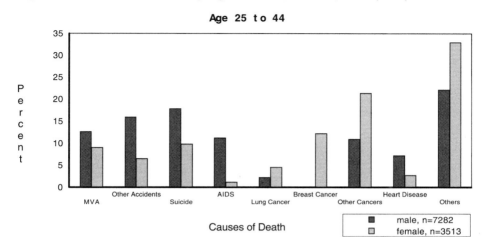

Age 25 to 44

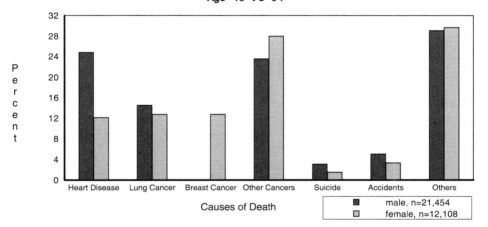

A comparison of the 1981 and 1991 deaths reveals changes in the relative importance of leading causes of death: coronary heart disease has decreased in relative importance to 23% in 1991 from 29% in 1981 for all ages and both sexes combined. In addition:

- the proportion of deaths due to cancer has increased in all but the youngest age groups; it was 27% in 1991 compared with 24% in 1981 for all ages and both sexes combined;
- among cancer deaths, lung cancer increased in relative importance slightly in men (from 32% to 33%) and more dramatically among women (from 12% to

Figure 5.4: Causes of Death by Age and Sex, Canada, 1991 *(con't)*

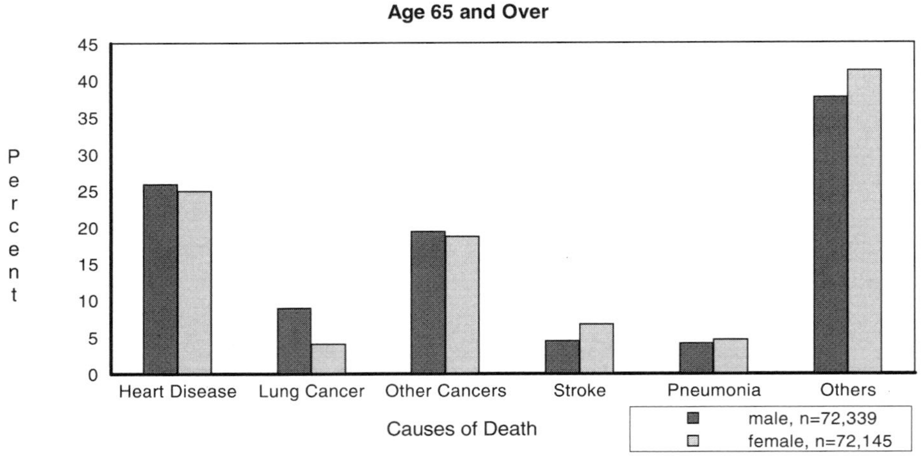

Age 65 and Over

Source: Causes of Death, 1991. Statistics Canada no. 84-208, 1993

19%); lung cancer now ranks second in a wider age range among women: from ages 25 to 74 years in 1991, compared with 40 to 64 years in 1981;
• motor vehicle accidents have decreased in relative importance overall (from 3% of all deaths to 2%).
• AIDS has become one of the leading causes of death among males aged 25-44 years.

Potential-Years-of-Life-Lost (PYLL)
For any cause of death, the potential-years-of-life-lost is calculated by totalling the years of life remaining until age 75 for each person who dies of that cause between birth and age 75, within a given time period, using the midpoint of a five-year interval. Thus, a person who dies at age 21 would contribute 54 years to the total. This indicator has the main effect of assessing premature mortality, which may be useful for setting priorities for prevention. The first four causes listed in figure 5.5 are responsible for approximately 50% of PYLL. Immediately apparent is the importance of motor vehicle accidents, coronary heart disease, suicide and cancer. Males lose approximately three times as many years as females for these causes of premature mortality.

Cancer
Reporting cancer cases to provincial cancer registries is voluntary but results in a valuable database for the investigation of potential causes of malignancies through

Figure 5.5:   Potential-Years-of-Life-Lost (PYLL) per 100,000 Person-Years, by Leading Causes of Death, Canada, 1990

Expected Life Span of 75

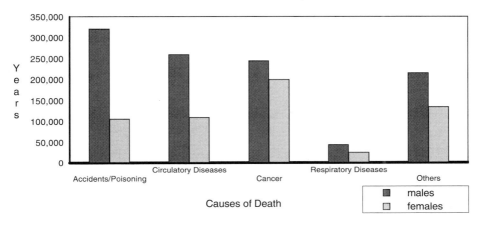

Source: Chronic Diseases in Canada, 13(6), 111, 1992.

case-control studies, and allows the long-term evaluation of the effect of new therapies, early detection programs, and changes in environmental and lifestyle factors. It was estimated that in 1993, 116,200 new cases of cancer (excluding non-melanoma skin cancer) would be diagnosed in Canada, with the number of new cases increasing by about 3,000 per year.[5] Deaths from cancer in 1993 were estimated at 59,700. Prostate and lung cancer in males and breast cancer and lung cancer in females are the most frequent cancers, in terms of incidence and deaths, followed by colorectal cancer. Table 5.1 illustrate the frequency of the sites of cancer.

1.2.2. Morbidity

Mortality, though of great importance, is clearly only one part of the health status of a population. Morbidity, which includes all health outcomes other than death, is difficult to quantify due to a paucity of accurate information. No single source of information reflects all morbidity, but by looking at several sources, an appreciation of the nature and extent of morbidity may be gained and trends may be detected. It is also important to remember that in examining a particular health problem, some aspects of morbidity may be more relevant than others. Time off work may be a better reflection of morbidity associated with the common cold than hospital admission rates, which might more appropriately be used to assess the morbidity of bleeding duodenal ulcer. Each of the sources of information described in this section is of value in assessing some aspect of morbidity.

Table 5.1:   Per cent Distribution of Estimated New Cases and Deaths for Major Cancer Sites, Canada, 1993

Site	Males: Incidence	Males: Mortality	Females: Incidence	Females: Mortality
Lung	21	34	12	20
Breast	-	-	30	20
Prostate	21	12	-	-
Colorectal	14	10	14	11
Leukemia & lymphoma	9	9	8	9
Bladder	6	3	2	2
Uterus & cervix	-	-	7	4
Stomach	3	4	2	3
Kidney	3	3	3	2
Pancreas	2	4	3	5
Ovary	-	-	4	5
Oral	4	2	2	1
All others	17	19	13	18

Source: National Cancer Institute of Canada: *Canadian Cancer Statistics 1993*, Toronto, Canada, 1993 .

Communicable Diseases

As described in chapter three, selected diseases in Canada are reported to central authorities on a voluntary or mandatory basis.   These centralized reports constitute an important source of information on morbidity.   The Canadian Communicable Disease Surveillance System disease-specific case definitions are used for federal surveillance.[6]   Provinces may provide annual summaries of reportable disease experience incorporating time trends.[7]   The following examples will serve to illustrate the type and value of the data available.   Most of the communicable diseases for which reporting is mandatory are reasonably well-controlled, and appear in the population with low frequency, which is not true for the major sexually transmitted diseases (STDs).   Data from Health Canada indicating the incidence of vaccine-preventable and sexually transmitted diseases in Canada in 1988 is shown in table 5.2.

Table 5.2:   Crude Rates in Canada (Per 100,000 Persons) of Vaccine-Preventable Disease and T.B. in 1988.

Disease Category	Crude Rate per 100,000 Population
Vaccine Preventable Diseases	
Diphtheria	0.00
Whooping cough	4.30
Tetanus	0.00
Measles	2.30
Rubella	2.20
Mumps	2.50
Poliomyeletis	0.00
Tuberculosis	7.80
Sexually Transmitted Diseases and Hepatitis	
Syphilis	6.10
AIDS	3.10
Gonorrhea	80.00
Chlamydia (Quebec)	295.10
Hepatitis A and B	18.00

Source: National Cancer Institute of Canada: *Canadian Cancer Statistics 1993*, Toronto, Canada, 1993 .

Occupational Injuries and Illness
Since the advent of widespread financial compensation for injuries and illness in the working environment, a quasi-voluntary reporting system has developed. Figure 5.6 illustrates the incidence of occupational injuries and diseases from the Ontario Workers' Compensation Board records, 1991.[8]   There was a total of 155,475 work-related-lost-time claims reported for the year 1991, of which 96.2% were related to injuries.   The most common injuries were strains and sprains (which accounted for about half), and contusions and wounds.   Occupational diseases are infrequent compared with injuries. The most common diseases were tenosynovitis, chemical burns, welder's flash, poisoning and dermatitis.   The permanent disabilities related to occupational exposure were chronic back problems, strains and hearing loss. Despite safety programs to reduce work injuries and increasing awareness of occupational illness, the incidence of these important health problems has changed little.

Figure 5.6:   Percentage Distribution of Occupational Injuries as Causes of Temporary Disability Among Workers, Ontario, 1992

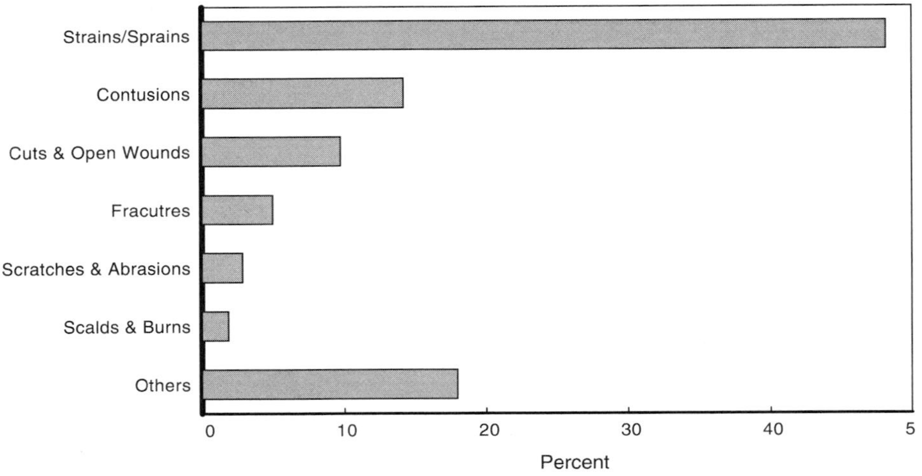

Source: Annual Report, 1992, Ontario Workers' Compensation Board, Statistical Supplement

Causes of Hospitalization

General Hospitals Hospitalization may vary according to availability of beds and local medical practice. Though hospitalization data omit important information about morbidity in outpatients, it does reflect the magnitude of serious illness and use of vital resources. Figure 5.7 indicates the pattern of major causes of hospitalization in general hospitals in Canada (in 1985-86) in descending order of importance. Expressing hospitalization in terms of patient-days inflates the importance of illness requiring longer hospital stays; conversely, using separations emphasizes shorter stays, such as for obstetrical admissions. In 1986-87, short-term hospitalization totalled 1.3 patient days per person per year and long-term 0.8 days, amounting to 2.1 days in total. For residential care facilities, the figure was 3.2 days, resulting in 5.2 days for all institutional days per person per year.[9] In 1987-8, Canadians spent over 51.5 million days in general hospitals[10] (about two days per person per year). Females use more hospital days than males, but much of this excess is due to obstetrical admissions and the health-care utilization by the preponderance of elderly females. The five leading causes of hospitalization shown in figure 5.7 were also represented in the list of common causes of death. Mental illness, with low mortality, accounted for the second highest total number of hospital days in 1985-6.[11] For the same period obstetric admissions also accounted for a significant proportion of hospitalizations, almost half a million. Delivery without complication is not true morbidity but must be considered in planning for hospital services.

Figure 5.7: Leading Causes of Discharges and Number of Days in General Hospitals, 1985-1986, Canada

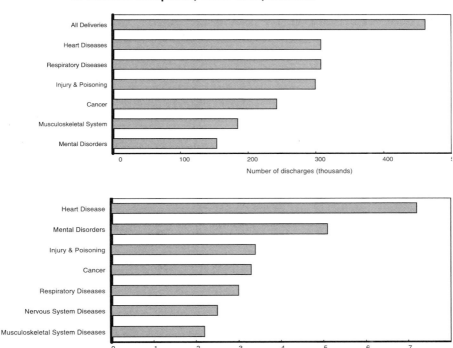

Source: Health Reports 2(1), 40-41, 1990.

Mental Hospitals   Figure 5.7 shows the significant contribution of mental illness to patient days even in general hospitals. When all institutions that provide psychiatric care are taken into account, including special mental hospitals and psychiatric units in general hospitals, the tremendous hospital morbidity associated with mental illness is apparent. In 1988-89, these institutions provided 13.7 million patient days of care for the 192,126 cases of mental disorder in which the patient was either discharged or died. Since 1978 there has been a slight shift in the hospitalization of mental disorder cases towards treatment in general hospitals (from 78% in 1979 to 82% of separations in 1988-89).[12] The average length of stay in psychiatric hospitals decreased (from 332 to 259 days), while that of psychiatric patients in general hospitals rose (from 20 to 32 days). Table 5.3 illustrates the separations and days of care secondary to mental disorders in both general and psychiatric hospitals. Functional psychosis includes schizophrenia, affective psychoses, paranoid state, other non-organic psychoses and child psychoses. The general clinical disorders includes neuroses, personality disorders, sexual devia-

Table 5.3: Separations and Days of Care in General and Psychiatric Hospitals, 1985-1986, Canada

Type of Mental Disorder	Separations (%) n=178,308	Days of Care (%) n=11,266,162
General clinical disorders	38	15
Functional psychosis	36	47
Alcohol and drug problems	19	6
Organic psychotic conditions	7	21
Mental retardation	1	13
Total	**100**	**100**

Source: Health Reports, 2(1), 41, 1990.

tions and disorders, adjustment reaction, conduct disorders and depressive disorders. The leading cause of separations and hospital days of care used are functional psychoses and organic psychotic conditions.

Dental Morbidity
Dental illness is considered separately in this chapter to emphasize its significance. Little mortality but a great deal of morbidity is associated with dental disease. The recent Health Promotion Survey mentioned earlier indicated that overall, 84% of Canadian adults reported having one or more or their natural teeth. This proportion was fairly consistent throughout all provinces, with the exception of Quebec, where 73% of the population were dentate. The proportion of toothless persons increased with age; 35% of 55-64 years old and 50% of the population over the age of 65 years are toothless. This measure may be said to reflect dental disability, and is useful in planning dental care.

As there is no large scale reporting by dental health professionals and hospitalization is infrequent, the only information on dental morbidity comes from studies and surveys.[13-15] Dental caries and periodontal disease were assessed by means of indices based on a dental examination. The index for caries, for example, was the DMFT (decayed, missing, filled teeth) score which identifies the number of teeth involved with caries. The rate of dental caries in elementary school children in Canada, and particularly in Ontario, shows a steady long-term decline which appears to be continuing.[16] The Canadian average of DMFT at age 13 is 3.1. Ontario has the lowest (1.7), British Columbia (2.9) and Alberta (3.1) are in the middle, while Quebec (4.2) and Atlantic Provinces (5.5) have the highest DMFT index in 13-year-old children. When compared with children from other developed nations with regards to DMFT index, Canadian children rated very favourably.

2.   CONSEQUENCES

The consequences of illness are personal disability, impairment or handicap as well as the utilization of health-care resources in the management of the condition, and the economic burden to the community.

2.1.   DISABILITY

Disability has been defined in various ways by those who have quantified it as a measure of morbidity (see chapters one and three). All definitions include the notion of the inability to carry on usual functions of living and working. All attempts subdivide disability by degree of severity. Sources of disability information include surveys, disability pension plans, and records of time lost from work due to ill health. Data from two different surveys will serve as examples.

The Canada Health Survey examined both short-term and long-term disability. Short-term disability was based on the individual's experience during the previous two weeks; disability days were recorded if the individual was unable to do things he or she would normally do for all or most of the day. Total annual short-term disability days per person were 19.9 for females and 12.5 for males. The average was 15.7; 5.3 of those days were for bed-disability. A strong relationship with age was observed with those over 65 years of age accounting for 35 annual disability days per person.

The Health and Activity Limitation Survey,[17] using the international definition of disability and handicap, found that over 4.1 million Canadians or 15.5% of the population reported some level of disability. Disability rates increased with age (table 5.4). Two thirds of disabled persons aged 15 and over reported more than one type of disability. The prevalence of multiple disabilities increased with age; of the disabled population aged 15 to 34, 46% reported having more than one disability, increasing to 76.0% in the population aged 65 and over. In the age group over 15, 60% of all disability problems identified in the survey related to mobility or agility, 16% related to hearing and 8.6% related to eyesight.

Table 5.4: Disability Rates in the Canadian Population, 1991

	Population with Disabilities	
	Number	Disability Rate (%)
Both Sexes	4,184,685	15.50
0 - 14 yrs	389,355	7.00
15 - 64 yrs	2,346,455	12.90
65 and over	1,448,875	46.30
Females	2,217,640	16.20
0 - 14 yrs	156,365	5.70
15 - 64 yrs	1,182,145	12.90
65 and over	879,130	48.40
Males	1,967,045	14.80
0 - 14 yrs	232,990	8.10
15 - 64 yrs	1,164,310	12.80
65 and over	569,745	43.40

Source: The Daily, October 13, 1992, Statistics Canada.

2.2. PHYSICIANS' SERVICES

Since the advent of government health insurance in Canada, it has been possible to acquire information about the kinds and numbers of illnesses treated by physicians outside hospitals. National data are unavailable, and provincial comparisons are difficult due to differences in reporting, but an example of data from the Saskatchewan Health Care Commission for 1990-91 is shown in table 5.5. These data indicate that the largest number of services were related to health check ups, respiratory, cardiovascular, urinary conditions and diabetes. In Canada overall, for all physician's services whether inside hospitals or in the community, 10.6% were for well-patient care, followed by respiratory diseases (9.1%), cardiovascular diseases (8.9%) and nervous system and sense organ diseases (8.2%).

2.3. PRESCRIPTION DRUG USE

The prevalence of drug use from a population perspective is a relatively new area of investigation. Large scale data are available from Saskatchewan and are reported here.[18]

Table 5.5:   Utilization of Physician's Services by Common Medical Conditions, Saskatchewan, 1990-91

Conditions	Number of Services (thousands)
General medical examination	579
Acute upper respiratory infection (except influenza)	539
Hypertension	282
Diseases of genitourinary tract	247
Otitis media	247
Ischemic heart disease	228
Bronchitis	216
Diabetes mellitus	187
Asthma	186
Arthritis	175
Hay fever	166
Chronic sinusitis and other respiratory symptoms	158
Neurosis	155
Others	9,567
Total	**12,922**

Source: Annual Statistical Report, 1990-91, Saskatchewan Health, Government of Saskatchewan, 1992.

- In 1990-91, 94% of Saskatchewan's total population were eligible to receive benefits under the Prescription Drug Plan. Certain classes of individuals such as those on social assistance or residing in special-care homes, were exempted from the deductive program.
- There were 5.6 million prescriptions processed during the fiscal 12-month period.
- An average of 13.1 prescriptions were dispensed to each active beneficiary exempted from the deductible program. An average 7.6 prescriptions were dispensed to each active beneficiary under the deductible program.
- An average of 16.1 prescriptions were dispensed to each family unit exempt from the deductible program. An average of 12.8 prescriptions were dispensed to each family unit under the deductible program.
- The average drug cost of a prescription was $16.59.
- Two-thirds of the population were prescribed at least one drug during 1989.[19]

• The average number of prescriptions per patient was 8.2, with females receiving notably more prescriptions than males, particularly for cardiovascular drugs and sedatives/antidepressants.
• Amoxicillin was the most commonly prescribed drug overall.
• Benzodiazepines were still being prescribed on a long-term basis.

2.4.   USE OF DENTAL CARE SERVICES

The recent Health Promotion Survey indicated that three out of four Canadians aged 15 and over (75%) visited a dentist in the past 12 months. This proportion fluctuates from 80% in Ontario to 58% in Newfoundland. Whereas the highest proportion of Canadians reporting a dental visit is in the 15 to 19 year age group (81%), rates were at their lowest in the 20 to 24 age group (67%). The rates then slightly increased to the 35 to 44 year age group and levelled off. With few exceptions, these trends were fairly consistent from one province to another. There is a positive association between income and dental visits; 69% of very poor Canadians went to a dentist in the past 12 months compared with 86% of rich people. The common reasons for visits to a dentist by Canadians aged 15 and over were for check up or cleaning purposes, tooth filling or extraction and to have crown or bridge work done in order to replace, repair or maintain missing or damaged teeth and for periodontal treatment.

2.5.   ECONOMIC BURDEN

The total burden of ill health for Canada in 1986, defined as that created by illness, disability and premature death on individuals and on Canadian society, was estimated to be in the order of $97 billion, of which $50 billion were direct costs and $47 billion were indirect.[20] This burden is three times the amount of the national annual deficit. The three leading causes of direct expenditure were hospital care costs (17.6%), followed by professional services, which are medical and other health practitioner services (10.3%), and pensions and benefits (7.1%). Drug costs accounted for 3.7% of total direct costs. For indirect costs, premature mortality accounted for 26.3% and chronic disability 19.6%. The remainder of the indirect costs were for short-term disability. Cardiovascular disease, injuries and violence, cancer, and arthritis and related conditions accounted collectively for half of the total costs. Cardiovascular disease was the leading cause of both direct ($5.2 billion) and indirect costs ($11.6 billion), making it the most expensive category overall. Injuries ranked next (total cost of $11 billion) followed by cancer (total cost of $9.1 billion). Overall, chronic conditions were responsible for the major economic burden. Compensable Workers' Claims accounted for just over two and a half billion dollars in expenditure, predominantly for injuries. Figure 5.9 illustrates the economic burden of illness in Canada.

Figure 5.9: Cost of Illness by Disease Category, Canada, 1986.

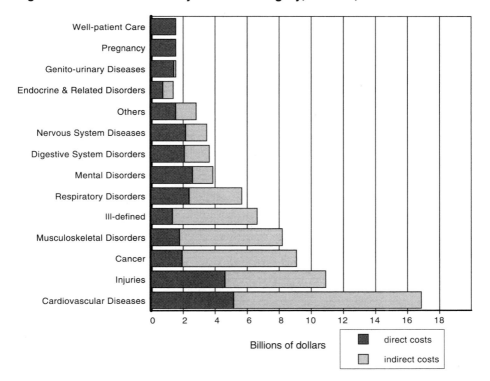

Source: Laboratory Centre for Disease Control, Health and Welfare Canada, 1991.

3.   SUMMARY

The two health status indicators, mortality and morbidity, are the most commonly used measures of health in Canada.

The trend in age- and sex-specific death rates from 1951-1991 indicate that over a 40-year period death rates have been declining at different rates for different age groups. Below the age of one year, there has been a steady decline in mortality rates. In 1991, the infant mortality rate per 1000 live births was 6.4. The majority of these deaths occur due to congenital anomalies, sudden infant death syndrome, and perinatal problems. From 1 to 14 years of age, mortality rates continue to decline slowly. More than half of these deaths are due to motor vehicle and other accidents, and are preventable. In the 15 to 24 year age group, the most significant causes of death include motor vehicle and other accidents, and suicide. Recently a significant drop in the death rate for this age group occurred, especially for males. For the 25-44 year age group, mortality rates have recently begun to decline slightly. Male rates in this age group and in the 45-64 year age group remain about double the female rates, being largely due to accidents, ischemic heart disease, suicide, cancer of the lung and AIDS (particularly for age group 25-44). In the 45-64 year age group, both male and female mortality rates are on the decline. Although there is a wide gap between male and female death rates beyond the age of 65, both rates now appear to be on the decline. The major causes of death for both men and women are ischemic heart disease cerebrovascular disease, and respiratory illness.

The leading causes of death for men ranked by number of deaths include neoplasm, coronary heart disease, respiratory diseases and accidents. For women, the leading causes are neoplasm, cardiovascular disease, stroke and respiratory disease. Many of these deaths could be prevented or delayed by lifestyle modifications. Lung cancer in males and breast cancer in females are the most frequent cancers, both in terms of incidence and deaths. However, lung cancer is expected to exceed breast cancer as the leading cause of death in women by the end of the century.

No single source of information reflects all morbidity. There are several sources of information which are of use in assessing some aspect of overall morbidity. (i) Centralized reports of communicable diseases indicated that the crude rate for vaccine-preventable diseases are low except for tuberculosis. However, the crude rate for sexually transmitted diseases and hepatitis are high. Specifically, chlamydia and gonorrhea have the highest crude rate. (ii) The most common injuries causing temporary disability as a result of workplace accident were strains and sprains, followed by contusions. Occupational diseases are infrequent compared with injuries. (iii) The main causes of hospitalization include heart disease, mental disorders, injury and poisoning, cancer and respiratory diseases. Canadians spent 51.5 million days in general hospitals. As a result of obstetrical admissions and longer longevity, females have a higher use of hospital days than males. (iv) There is a great deal of morbidity associated with dental disease. Dental caries in elementary school children has been declining steadily.

The consequences of illness are disability, impairment or handicap as well as the utilization of health-care resources and the economic burden to the community. Over 4.1 million Canadians, or 15.5% of the population, reported some level of disability, with females having a slightly higher rate than males. The prevalence of multiple disabilities increases with age, with loss of mobility or agility being the largest form of disability, followed by hearing and eyesight problems. The largest number of services rendered by physicians to their patients were related to routine check ups, respiratory, cardiovascular, or urinary conditions and diabetes. The total burden of ill health for Canada in 1986 was estimated to be approximately $97 billion, of which $50 billion was direct costs and $47 billion was indirect costs. Health-care costs, professional services, and pensions and benefits constitute the three leading causes of direct expenditures. Premature mortality, chronic disability and short-term disability primarily account for the indirect expenditures. Cardiovascular disease is the leading cause of both direct and indirect costs.

4.   REFERENCES

1. Stephens T and Fowler Graham D, eds. Health and Welfare Canada. *Canada's Health Promotion Survey: Technical Report 1990*. Ministry of Supply and Services, Canada, Ottawa, 1993.
2. *The Health of Canadians: Report of the Canada Health Survey*. Ministry of Supply and Services, Canada, Ottawa, 1981.
3. *User's Guide to 40 Community Health Indicators, 1992*. Community Health Division, Health Services and Promotion Branch, Health and Welfare Canada in collaboration with the National Health Information Council and the Health Information Division, Policy, Planning and Information Branch, Health and Welfare Canada. Ministry of Supply and Services, Canada, Ottawa, 1992.
4. Kohn R. *Royal Commission on Health Services: The Health of the Canadian People*. Ottawa: Queen's Printer and Controller of Stationery, 1967.
5. Statistics Canada, Health and Welfare Canada, Provincial Cancer Registries, National Cancer Institute of Canada. *Canadian Cancer Statistics 1992*. Toronto: National Cancer Institute of Canada, 1992.
6. Health and Welfare Canada. Canadian Communicable Disease Surveillance System: Disease-Specific Case Definitions and Surveillance Methods. *Can Dis Wkly Rep* 17(Suppl3):35-36, 1991.
7. Public Health Branch. Mandatory Health Programs and Services. *Communicable Disease Control. Summary of Reportable Diseases 1990*. Ministry of Health, Government of Ontario, Toronto, 1991.
8. The Workers' Compensation Board of Ontario. *Statistical Supplement to the 1991 Annual Report*. Communications Branch. Toronto, 1992.
9. Canadian Centre for Health Information. Statistics Canada. *Health Indicators*. Table 117, U-2. Ottawa, 1991.
10. Gagnon M and Mix P. Hospital Statistics - Preliminary Annual Hospital Statistics 1987-88 and List of Canadian Hospitals 1988. *Health Reports* 1(1):113-117, 1989.
11. Riley R and Richman A. The Treatment of Mental Disorders in Hospitals. *Health Reports* 2(1):37-56, 1990.
12. Data Releases. Mental Disorder Separations, 1988-89. *Health Reports* 3(2):101, 1991.
13. Public Health Branch. *Dental Health Indices 1987/88 Survey*. Ontario Ministry of Health, Toronto, May 1990.
14. Payette M, Brodeur JM, Lepage Y and Plante E. *Enquete Santé Dentaire Quebec, 1989-90*. Montreal: Department de santé commuataire, Hopital Saint-Luc, 1991, pp 1-258.
15. Gray H and Gunther D. *A Comprehensive Review of Dental Caries Experience Shown by Grade 7 Students in the Provincial Health Units of British Columbia, 1987*. Victoria: Dental Health Branch, Minister of Health, Government of British Columbia, 1987.
16. Johnston D, Grainger R and Ryan R. The Decline of Dental Caries in Ontario School Children. *J Can Dent Assoc* 52(5):411-417, 1986.
17. *The 1991 Health and Activity Limitation Survey - Highlights*. Statistics Canada. Catalogue 11-001E. Ottawa, 1992.
18. *Annual Statistical Report 1990-1991*. Saskatchewan Health Prescription Drug Services Branch. Regina, 1992, p 4.
19. Quinn K, Baker M and Evans B. A Population-wide Profile of Prescription Drug Use in Saskatchewen, 1989. *Can Med Assoc J* 146(12):2177-2186, 1992.
20. Health and Welfare Canada. Economic Burden of Illness in Canada, 1986. *Chronic Dis Can* Suppl 12(3):1-37, 1991.

CHAPTER SIX
Health of
Special Groups

The previous two chapters outlined the determinants of health, health status and consequences in the Canadian population as a whole. This chapter will examine the health of certain segments of the population: **Aboriginal Peoples**, the **elderly**, **poor children**, and the **disabled**. Some possible means of improving their health will be examined. The health of each of these groups reflects the influence of the determinants of health. For the first three, the determinants are *race*, *age* and *psychosocial factors*. The fourth, the disabled, has been chosen because it indicates how the determinants of health frequently interact and compound further the inequities in health that this subgroup experiences relative to the rest of the population. Preexisting inequities in the health of the disabled are increased by differences in income and education.

1. THE HEALTH OF ABORIGINAL PEOPLE

The Aboriginal Peoples, also known as the First Nations Peoples or Native Canadians, are categorized by the census into four groups; Status Indians, Non-Status Indians, Metis, and Inuit. The term Aboriginal People, in this chapter, is used only to designate Status and Non-Status Indians. The term "Status Indian" has specific legal connotations, and is described later in the chapter.

At the time of the arrival of European settlers, Aboriginal Peoples were described as tall, slim, full of vigour and healthy. With colonization, Aboriginal Peoples were subjugated and stripped of their land, religion, culture, language and autonomy. They were restricted in terms of where they could live, who could be called Indian, and whether they could vote or not in the Canadian Confederation. Over four centuries, colonization took its toll on the physical, mental, emotional and spiritual health of the Aboriginal communities. The present day determinants of health reflect these injustices.

1.1.   DETERMINANTS

Much of the data on health determinants and status are derived from publications of the Medical Services Branch of Health Canada[1,2] *Health Status of Canadian Indians and Inuit 1990.*[1]

According to the Census categorization,[3] Status Indians are defined as Aboriginal Peoples registered under the Indian Act. Most of this chapter will deal with Status Indians as abundant data are available on this population; some information, however, will be presented on off-reserve Aboriginal Peoples. Although information is lacking, it is believed that their health status is actually worse than the health status of on-reserve groups. This may be due to the additional stresses of the urban environment, particularly a very high unemployment rate (28%)[4] racial discrimination and lack of a social support network.

1.1.1. The Psychosocial Environment

Prior to the arrival of the Europeans in the 16th century, approximately 222,000 Aboriginal Peoples lived in Canada. War, famine, diseases and epidemics (such as smallpox and cholera), introduced by the European settlers, took a great toll from the 17th to 19th centuries. By the time of Confederation, there remained roughly only 102,000 Aboriginal Peoples.[5] By 1941, estimates of the Aboriginal population fluctuated between 100,000 and 122,000, representing approximately 1.1% of the total Canadian population. Since then, the Aboriginal population has grown and by 1988, there were approximately 443,884 Status Indians, representing 1.7% of the total population. The population growth of Aboriginal Peoples is due only to natural increase. While the crude birth rate per 1000 population declined from 44.3 in 1965 to 29.3 in 1988, it is almost double the Canadian rate. Similarly, Aboriginal death rates have declined, but they are still higher than the rates for other Canadians.

Of the 443,884 Status Indians in Canada in 1988, 31.2% were in the age group 0 to 14 years, 64.3% in the 15 to 64 year age group, and 4.4% in the age group 65 years and over. Although the proportion in the youngest age group had declined slightly since 1986, the predominance of younger Aboriginals is in contrast to the total Canadian population. The ratio of males to females was 0.975 in 1986. Of the total Aboriginal population in 1988, 23% lived in Ontario, 10% in Quebec, 4% in the Atlantic Region, and 60% lived in the four western provinces. However, when viewed as a percentage of the total provincial or territorial population, Aboriginal Peoples constituted 18% of the Northwest Territories and 21.7% in the Yukon Territories. Approximately 62% of Status Indians lived on reserves (also known as the First Nations Communities), the proportion of the off-reserve Status Indians increasing from 29% in 1985 to 38% in 1988. There are 2,284 reserves in the country with 65% of the Aboriginal population living in either rural or remote locations. The average Aboriginal income was only two-thirds that of the non-Aboriginal average. About half of the adult Aboriginal population is in the labour force; most of them in low paying service industry jobs. In 1986, life expectancy at birth for Aboriginal males was 63.8 years and 71.0 years for females, while it was 73 years for Canadian males, and 79.7 years for females, between 1985 and 1987.

In 1986, the off-reserve Aboriginal Peoples (which includes both Status and Non-Status Indians) accounted for at least half of all Canada's Aboriginal population; one-third of these people lived in families in a small number of larger cities.[6] Overall, off-reserve Aboriginal Peoples have lower levels of education, higher levels of unemployment and lower incomes than other Canadians. Forty-five per cent were aged 19 and under; only 8% were over 55. Mobility was common, 61% of the off-reserve population older than age five having moved within the previous five years.

1.1.2. The Physical Environment
In 1984, almost half (47%) of Aboriginal housing on reserves failed to meet basic standards. Over one-third (36%) were seriously overcrowded, and 38% lacked some or all basic amenities such as running water, indoor toilets, baths or showers.[7] There were few recreational facilities for children or adults. There are correlations between metal contaminants such as lead, aluminum, and cadmium in the environment and their elevated levels in hair samples of Aboriginal adults and children in Alberta; a control community had lower levels in hair samples.

1.1.3. Lifestyle and Behavioural Risk Factors

Alcohol, Smoking and Substance Abuse
While no useful national trend data are available for **alcohol** use among Aboriginal Peoples, the 1984 report by the Federation of Saskatchewan Indian Nations on alcohol and drug abuse provides some suggestive information. Alcohol use among both adults and adolescents was widespread, with 84% of adults and 74% of adolescents reporting use in the past year. While these levels are not very different from those reported for the general Canadian population (see chapter four), it was estimated that alcohol *abuse* levels were between 35% and 40% for the adult population and between 10% and 15% for Aboriginal adolescents. The prevalent drinking patterns for Aboriginal adults were periodic, high-volume drinking (binge drinking) and problem drinking (trouble with the law, fighting, and/or family problems while drinking).[8] An Ontario Needs Assessment Survey of Aboriginal children and youth also indicated a high prevalence of alcohol abuse. Ten percent of children in grades three to eight reported drinking enough to get "high" at least once in the past year, while 53% of youth in grades seven to 13 reported the same.[9] For the latter group, this is about double that of non-Aboriginal youths in Ontario and New Brunswick.

Some data indicate that **smoking** is quite prevalent among adults (66%) and school children (51.4% in 1986 for Cree Indian in Quebec).[10,11] The male rate is higher than the female. A 1988 survey indicated that 48.2% of Aboriginal mothers smoked during and after pregnancy. There were regional variations: 61.7%

smoked during pregnancy in Quebec and 29.6% in the Pacific Region. While no specific country-wide data are available, **gasoline** and **glue sniffing** appear to be common among Aboriginal teenagers.[12] Two surveys in the mid 1980s, one large sample on Manitoba reserves and a smaller high school sample from a Quebec Indian reserve, indicated prevalence of continued use of solvents of 6% and 9%, respectively. Twenty per cent of the Manitoba youth and 15% of the Quebec youth reported solvents abuse.

Nutrition
Data from Nutrition Canada 1972 indicate that Aboriginal Peoples were at high risk for deficiency of nutrients such as iron, vitamins, and protein.[13] Prevalence of obesity is marked in females aged 30 and over (more than 70%), and among males aged 40 and over, about 40% are obese. Overall physical activity levels among Aboriginal Peoples is low, but not dissimilar to that for the general Canadian population.

Breast-feeding Overall, 60.7% of the 3,453 infants (84.3% Aboriginal) born in areas served by the Medical Services Branch were breast-fed at birth, declining to 42.0% at three months and 31.1% at six months. Rates were lowest for mothers under 18 and for infants of low birth weight. This has an added relevance as many of the northern Aboriginal communities have no potable water supply and the price of baby formula or milk is very high.

1.1.4 Health-Care Organizations
The federal government is responsible for the health-care of Aboriginal Peoples on reserves, and the provincial government for those off the reserves. Two-thirds of Aboriginal Peoples live in rural or remote areas, and health services are less than optimal for them. Primary care in remote areas is provided by either nurses or community health workers supplemented by infrequent visits from physicians. Admission rates for general and mental hospitals, usually located at great distances from the communities themselves, are high compared with other Canadian rates.[14,15] With the exception of immunization, public health programs and rehabilitation services are nonexistent. Part of the problem stems from jurisdictional boundaries within the federal government, and between federal and provincial governments. Geographic isolation also makes it difficult to provide appropriate services to northern communities. The priorities set by Aboriginal Peoples are frequently at variance with those developed by the government, and hence there are inappropriate strategies for prioritizing and delivering health programs.

1.2.   HEALTH STATUS AND CONSEQUENCES

1.2.1. Mortality
In the past 10 to 20 years, there has been substantial decline in Aboriginal mortality; the gap in mortality, however, between the Aboriginal and general Canadian population remains wide.

Infant Mortality From 1984 to 1988, the average Aboriginal infant mortality rate was 17.1 per 1,000 compared with the 7.8 per 1,000 Canadian average.

Crude and Adjusted Mortality Rates The crude death rate for the Aboriginal population in 1988 was 5.4 per 1000 population, compared with a crude death rate for all Canadians of 7.3 per 1000 population. Due to the high proportion of young people in the Aboriginal population, age-standardized death rates are more useful for comparison purposes. In 1988, the Aboriginal mortality rate, standardized to the 1986 Canadian population, was 10.0 per 1,000 (1.4 times the Canadian rate).

Age-Specific Death Rates As seen in figure 6.1, age-specific Aboriginal death rates were much higher than the Canadian rates, except in the age group 80 years and over.[15]

Causes of Death Between 1986 and 1988, the four leading causes of death in order of decreasing frequency were injury and poisoning, diseases of the circulatory system, neoplasms, and diseases of the respiratory system, whereas for Canada as a whole, the four leading causes of death were circulatory diseases, neoplasms, injuries and poisoning, and respiratory diseases. The age-standardized death rate due to injury and poisoning was four times higher in Aboriginal Peoples than in all Canadians. The age-specific Aboriginal suicide rate for the 15 to 24 year age group was five to six times higher than that of other Canadian youth. The Aboriginal death rates due to circulatory diseases are not too different from Canadians overall, especially for those over 65. Recently, however, the cardio-vascular mortality rate has been declining more slowly than that of Canadians overall, and now slightly exceeds the national average.

Potential-Years-of-Life-Lost (PYLL) In 1983, the PYLL up to the age of 75 among Aboriginal Peoples was approximately 46,400 years of which 30,000 were con-tributed by males. The ratio of the Aboriginal to the Canadian PYLL was 2.2. Among specific causes of PYLL, the ratio ranged from 0.37 for cancer to 3.9 for accidents, injury and poisoning.[16]

1.2.2. Morbidity

Perceived Morbidity A Recent National Survey by Statistics Canada indicated that 58% of those asked reported their health as excellent or very good, 29% as good and 13% as fair or poor.[17]

Infectious Diseases Aboriginal Peoples have a high incidence of gastroenteritis, diphtheria, rheumatic fever, respiratory problems and infectious hepatitis. Data from the Pacific Region in 1983 to 1984 indicated that infectious and parasitic diseases were responsible for 3.4% of all Aboriginal hospitalization and 10.2% of hospitalization of infants less than one year old. Botulism, sometimes fatal, occurs in Aboriginal (and more frequently, Inuit) communities due to ingestion of

**Figure 6.1: Age-Specific Death Rates: Indian Death Rates
as a Percentage of Canadian, 1986**

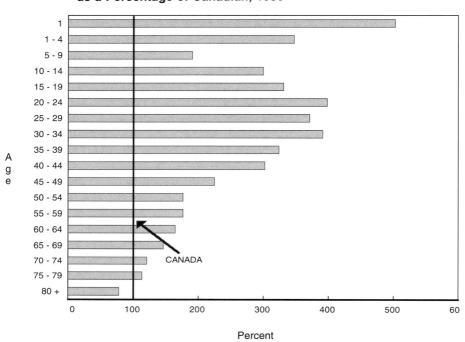

Source: Health Status of Canadian Indians and Inuits, 1990, Health and Welfare Canada, Ottawa, 1991.

fermented marine mammal meat, raw or parboiled fish or salmon eggs. The incidence of meningitis among Aboriginal Peoples and Inuit in the Northwest Territories is 7% in the first eight years of life, some 200 times that of the general population.[18] The incidence of pneumonia among Aboriginal children is about 8.3 times higher than the general population.[19]

Chronic Conditions Thirty one per cent of the Aboriginal population aged 15 and over were told by their health-care professionals that they had a chronic health problem. In order of frequency the common problems mentioned were: arthritis and rheumatism, high blood pressure, bronchitis, heart problems and diabetes.[20] Chronic conditions among Aboriginal children were primarily chronic otitis media and psychomotor developmental delay. The incidence rates of all these conditions far exceeded the Canadian norms. The presence of diabetes was reported by 6% of Aboriginal adults compared with 2% of Canadian adults aged 15 and over. The average age of onset of diabetes is about 43 years. Both new and reactivated tuberculosis are also of concern; rates for all age groups far exceed the

Canadian average, although the overall incidence in Aboriginal Peoples is declining. In 1983, the rate in the five to 14 year age group was 27.1 times higher among Aboriginals than among other Canadians. The age-standardized rate for all Aboriginal Peoples was 132.9 per 100,000, 14 times that of the Canadians. Other indicators, such as dental caries and nutritional disorders, are also higher than in the general population.

Disability In Northwestern Ontario, Shah et al.[21] found the disability rate among Aboriginal Peoples for age groups 0 to 14, 15 to 34, 35 to 64 and over 65 years to be 13.3%, 31.4%, 50.3%, and 79.2%, respectively. These rates are almost double the corresponding rates for the rest of the Canadian population (chapter five). The major disabilities for people 15 years and over were in the areas of mobility, agility, and hearing.

1.3.   FUTURE DIRECTIONS

One of the major solutions proposed by Aboriginal Peoples is to gain control over their health, social and educational programs. Another proposed solution proposed is to settle the unresolved and disputed land claims and to have their rightful place as the original people of this land recognized in Canadian society.[22,23] Empowerment of Aboriginal communities is essential for improvement of their health. To achieve this end, recent amendments to the Constitutional Act 1982, were proposed as part of the Charlottetown Accord (1992), by which Aboriginal communities would be considered one of four levels of government in Canada. Unfortunately, all amendments to the Constitution proposed at that time were rejected. The government of Canada is also in the midst of transferring control of health services from the federal bureaucracy to the local level of Aboriginal Government or Band Councils. Through a planned process to transfer control to local Bands, the health services will become more responsive to the needs of Aboriginal communities.

2.   THE HEALTH OF THE ELDERLY

The number of seniors and their proportion in the population of Canada continues to grow. The increases in the number of the very elderly, those aged over 85, is especially large. Seniors are a heterogeneous group, each generation having a different social history. This section identifies some characteristics relevant to the health of the elderly. Many stereotypical notions about seniors and the so-called limitations of advanced age need to be abandoned. For example, even though disability increases with age, aging and poor health are not synonymous. This concept is discussed in the sections on biological determinants and subjective morbidity.

2.1. DETERMINANTS

2.1.1. Psychosocial
Information in this and the next section is derived from the 1991 Census, *Canada's Seniors*, and *The Active Health Report on Seniors*, which are fully referenced at the end of the chapter. The conventional definition of the elderly is persons aged 65 years and over. On June 4, 1991, there were 3,169,970 Canadians who were 65 years or older,[24] constituting approximately 11.6% of the population. It is estimated that by 2021, the elderly will number 7.5 million. It is predicted that by the year 2020, people over the age of 65 will constitute greater than 15% of the population. This increase is attributed to an increase in average life expectancy, the aging of the baby boomers, and the projected decline in fertility.[25] For convenience, the elderly are subdivided into three subgroups, 65 to 74 years, 75 to 84, and over 85. These subgroups are also referred to as the young elderly, middle elderly, and old elderly. Life expectancy in 1988 at age 65 was 19 years for women and 15 years for men.

Another striking trend is the expanding population of **elderly women**. In 1991, there were 1.2 times more women than men in the 65 to 84 year age group; the ratio was 2.3:1 for those aged 85 and over. The female proportion of the population over the age of 65 has increased from 49% in 1951 to 57% in 1991 and is projected to be approximately 60% in 2001. This is explained by the increased longevity of women on average, and the gain in female life expectancy relative to males. The aging population may also be subdivided by marital status and sex. Approximately 57.4% of elderly women are single, whereas 77% of elderly men are married. Widows constitute 50% of the elderly female population, whereas widowers are only 13% of elderly men. Widows account for a greater proportion of the elderly because women tend to marry older males and then outlive them.

The **income** of the elderly has increased substantially over the last few years, narrowing the gap between the elderly and the rest of the population. Currently the elderly are heavily dependent on public pension and income security plans which comprise their single largest source of income. In 1987, these plans constituted 66% of the total income of households headed by elderly women and 48% of the income of those headed by elderly men.[26] Sixty-four per cent of seniors own their own home, frequently mortgage-free; therefore, income is not the only relevant indicator of socioeconomic status for the elderly. Older Canadians are more likely to be of British origin (55% of those over 80 are of British origin compared with 39% under 65). A sizeable proportion (11%), however, speak neither English nor French at home.

Seniors may be stereotyped as being passive and dependent; however, the majority are "well elderly" who remain healthy into their 80s or even 90s, needing only minimal assistance. Many seniors are active and contribute to the community. For example 15% of the elderly provide baby-sitting services to friends and family not of the same household. Eighty per cent of women over 80 and 50% of men do their own housework. Living situations for the elderly range from full independence in the community, to community living with support from family and community services, to long-term institutionalization.[27] For the demographic reasons cited above, the living situation of elderly women, 34% of whom live alone, frequently differs from men, 14% of whom live alone. Surveys show that, above all else, seniors value independence and fear admission to a nursing home. Chapter 16 describes community-based, long-term care arrangements which can maximize independent life in the community. Some provinces have developed this arrangement, and preliminary findings indicate that this is the way of the future. The average age for entry into long-term care institutions is 82 in Canada, but there is a tendency for over-institutionalization. Eight per cent of elderly Canadians live in institutions, where some custody or care is provided, compared with 5% in the US. This proportion of elderly in institutions is actually higher due to the elderly occupying acute hospital beds while awaiting transfer to long-term care facilities.

2.1.2. Physical Environment

With advancing age, there is increasing prevalence of visual, auditory and loco-motive disability in the elderly, predisposing them to falls and injuries that may have serious consequences. There is less ability to tolerate hazards in the physical environment, for example, loose rugs in the home or poor roadside lighting. Wandering and forgetfulness associated with dementia may exacerbate these hazards.

The potential role of aluminum in drinking water and tea in the development of Alzheimer's Disease (AD) has not been substantiated, although there is some evidence supporting this hypothesis. Further studies are needed to clarify if aluminum or other environmental factors contribute to the pathogenesis of AD and to determine whether the elderly are at risk from exposure to the levels found in treated water and tea.[28]

2.1.3. Biology of Aging

Aging is a lifelong process, encompassing a series of transitions from birth to death. Reaching the age of 65 does not therefore herald old age. Although functional disability appears to accompany aging, it is not clear how much is intrinsic to the aging process and whether death is always the result of a disease process. This is the prevalent biomedical model. The degree of handicap also depends on society's response. **Successful aging** has been defined in terms of retaining the ability to function independently, remaining mobile and undertaking all the activities of daily living (e.g., dressing, bathing, using stairs, getting in and out of bed, and eating). In addition to age itself and measures of physical and mental health status, two major social predictors of successful aging have been identified: not having one's spouse die and not entering a nursing home. These indicate the interaction of biological and psychosocial factors.[29]

There is biological controversy about the process of aging. On one hand, the organism can be viewed as having a preprogrammed life span after which natural death occurs (due possibly to a general decline in withstanding external stressors). As increasing proportions of the population age to the natural limit of about 85, survival will tend to "rectangularize" at the "biological wall."[30] This is known as rectangularization of the mortality curve. According to this scenario[31] the onset of chronic disease may be postponed, thus compressing the period of disability, a concept known as "**compressed disability**."[32] On the other hand, it is argued that life expectancies can increase almost indefinitely. Some studies[33-35] argue that the average period of decreased vigour will probably increase if life expectancy increases indefinitely. They also suggest that chronic diseases will occupy a larger proportion of the life span. There may be a **biological basis for the female health advantage**, surpassing lifestyle and environmental influences, that is related to the genes in the X chromosome.[36]

Other biological factors, such as differences in physiology and the metabolism of drugs related to aging, are important. Doses of medication not geared to the elderly can result in **adverse drug effects**, which are responsible for a significant proportion of hospitalizations.

2.1.4. Lifestyle and Behavioural Risk Factors

Alcohol, Smoking and Drug Use Among people 65 years and over, 65.9% of males and 45.7% of females are current drinkers. Of the current drinkers 31.9% of men and 10.7% of women drink more than three times a week.[37] Less than 20% of the elderly smoke regularly. Twelve per cent of the elderly use tranquillizers and 21% use sleeping pills.

Nutrition The majority of the population aged 65 years and over have diets deficient in nutrients such as protein, iron, calcium and thiamine. The mean intake for all nutrients is not related to living arrangements; for example, whether an elderly person was living alone or with a family. Many elderly are malnourished,[38] probably due to low income or psychosocial and motivational factors.

Exercise and Other Activities Many able-bodied seniors exercise regularly; this proportion increased from 50% to 60% between 1976 and 1981. In the period of a month, over 50% of those aged 65 or more travel outside their neighbourhood, attend entertainments and/or participate in group activities.

2.2. HEALTH STATUS

2.2.1. Mortality

The common causes of death for both sexes in the age group over 65 are cancer, coronary artery disease, stroke and pneumonia. Mortality rates for elderly women started to decrease in Canada in the middle of this century; male rates did not drop until recently.[39] It is postulated that the trend for women may have been due to a decline in infectious disease and cardiovascular mortality. However, for males, the negative impact of lifestyle behaviours may have outweighed the decline in infectious disease mortality.

2.2.2. Morbidity

Self-Assessed Morbidity About three-quarters of those aged 65 to 74 considered their health "good" or "excellent" as reported in Canada's Health Promotion Survey. Fifty-seven per cent of those aged over 75 had the same perception. More seniors over age 65 (70%) found life "not stressful" than did adults under 55 (48%). There was a differential in terms of income with fewer poor elderly considering themselves in good health. Statistics Canada reports that, in the General Social Surveys of 1985 and 1990, 90% of those older than 55 years reported being "happy", or "very happy and satisfied" with their lives, and two-thirds to three-quarters reported "good" or "excellent health." Those with activity limitations due to poor health, were more likely to report unhappiness. The leading health problems in the elderly are arthritis and rheumatism (reported by 63% of elderly women and 46% of men), hypertension (33% of women and 43% of men), limb and joint disease, respiratory and heart disease (each about 25% of seniors) and diabetes (9%).[40]

Objective Morbidity The prevalence of dementia in the elderly has consistantly been found to be between 2.5% to 5% for severe dementing illnesses, and 4.3% to 12.7% for mild dementing illnesses.[41] The prevalence increases almost exponentially with age, from between 12.1% to 22% for those over 80 years of age to almost half of those over 90 years. The ongoing Canadian Study of Health and Aging should provide a better estimate of the actual population prevalence of dementia and potential risk factors. Dementing illness is most frequently Alzheimer's disease (60% to 80%). Diagnosis must include disordered judgement and behavioural manifestations of unstable emotionality, in addition to forgetful-ness. Dementia is a strong predictor of institutionalization as 50% of institution-alized elderly suffer from advanced cognitive impairment.

Gait disorders may result in falls and subsequent injury. In elderly women, the most common injury is a fracture of the neck of the femur.

2.3.   CONSEQUENCES

2.3.1. Disability

In the Canada Health Survey, the overall disability rate for the elderly was 46.0%, which increased to 80% for the very elderly, who are more likely to have severe disability. In the 1990 Health and Activity Limitation Survey for Canada (HALS), the proportion of disabled seniors 65 and over with mild disability was 35.1%, those with moderate disability was 32.5% and those with severe disability was 32.4%. About 85% of disabled seniors lived at home, although this decreased to 53.9% for those 85 and over. Of those reporting disability, approximately three-quarters report more than one disability. The major types of disability reported were in mobility, agility, vision and hearing. Annual disability days for the Canadian elderly were 35 per person; 30 for males and 39 for females.

In the Canadian population aged 60 and over, 20.3% of males and 26.6% females were edentulous in both jaws. Further, approximately 77% of the elderly had not seen a dentist in the preceding year.[42] A study of the oral health status of adults in Ontario[43] confirmed some assumptions about seniors' dental health. Almost 30% of seniors (the proportion increasing with age) reported that they avoid eating with other people because of a dental problem, avoid laughing or smiling, are embarrassed with the appearance of their teeth or condition of their mouth, or avoid conversation with others. The dental health of those seniors living in institutions was poorer; 25% of those in collective living centres required dental treatment urgently and 75% required preventive dental services.

2.3.2. Health-Care Utilization

The five leading causes of patient days in hospitals for males over age 65 were diseases of the heart, stroke, chronic obstructive lung disease, pneumonia, and benign prostate disease.[44] For females the five leading causes were diseases of the heart, stroke, fracture of lower limb, arthropathies and related disorders, and diabetes mellitus. The average length of stay in hospital for males who had a stroke was 53.7 days, and for females was 76.8 days. For diseases of the heart, the average length of stay was 17.6 days for males and 25.8 days for females.

Although the elderly are major consumers of health-care, a large proportion of them are healthy. The young elderly enjoy good health and psychological, physical and financial independence. Fewer than 2% of this group are in long-term care facilities. The middle and old elderly are more likely to be increasingly dependent due to the onset of disease and disability. In this group, 15% are in long term care facilities at any one time.

Hospital use rises dramatically with age. The old elderly use approximately 10 times more hospital days than any other age group under 60. Roos et al. analyzed Manitoba data for utilization of health services.[45] They found that the elderly make only 1.7 more physician visits per year than the 25 to 44 year age group and only 0.9 more visits than the 45 to 64 year age group. An analysis of hospital use in a Manitoba cohort study showed that 42% of the elderly were never admitted to hospital. However, 2% of the elderly population used 20% of total hospital days with most of this is in the last year prior to death. Ontario data show that in 1982 to 1983, senior citizens constituted 10% of the population and consumed 40% of acute care hospital days.[46]

As previously indicated one view of aging is that as life expectancy increases to a finite limit many more people will die of old age. With the improved health status of Canadians, individuals will be healthier for a longer period, subsequently develop chronic conditions and disabilities later in life and therefore be disabled for only short periods of time prior to death. Thus, it has been postulated that there will be a concentration of morbidity and disability in the older age groups. The alternative theory which postulates an ever-increasing life expectancy and period of diminished vigour, with chronic diseases occupying more of the life span, would result in a dramatically increased need for health-care services. Canadian data appear to support this second theory. This theory has major fiscal implications, and prevention of chronic diseases can be shown to significantly decrease health-care expenditures by the elderly.

Ethical Considerations in the Care of the Elderly It is a physician's responsibility to be certain that a patient understands the implications of a health-related decision. Options for care must be presented and the results of each option must be made clear. For an incompetent elderly patient, reliance has to be placed on a surrogate such as the next of kin. In situations where prior wishes are unknown, the principle of beneficence must apply. The decision may be made in consultation with the surrogate and other professionals. 'Do not resuscitate' (DNR) orders should be contemplated where the patient has explicitly expressed such wishes. In other situations, the guidelines on resuscitation and on informal decision making established by the Canadian Hospital Association, Canadian Medical Association and the Canadian Nurses Association should be followed. Some patients express their wishes in the form of 'living wills' (advance directives), and these wishes should be followed.

2.4.   THE FUTURE

Most jurisdictions in Canada have recognized the need for improved geriatric services. Many have planned for the expected increase in the number of elderly people by increasing funding for gerontology programs. Some jurisdictions are looking at innovative ways of program delivery, which are discussed in chapter 16. Canada has the advantage of being able to draw on the experience of other countries. Health promotion for the elderly is becoming an important approach to the development and maintenance of optimum levels of functioning as aging occurs. These approaches may incorporate physical activity, social support, awareness of adverse responses to medication in the elderly, nutrition counselling and programs to prevent falls. Future cohorts of the elderly will not be the same as current ones, as they will be better prepared for retirement. They will also have a louder political voice. The proliferation of private pension plans and the increase in the number of women entering the work force will decrease the reliance of the elderly on government transfer payments.

3.   THE HEALTH OF POOR CHILDREN

3.1.   DETERMINANTS

3.1.1. Psychosocial, Physical and Lifestyle

In 1990, the majority of the 5.6 million boys and girls under age 15 in Canada lived in comfortable socioeconomic conditions. A large minority, however, comprising one in six children in Canada (17%) was identified by Statistics Canada as living in poverty.[47] This compares unfavourably with Scandinavian countries where the rate of childhood poverty is 5.4%. Evidence of the plight of these children can be seen in the numbers relying on food banks and in the recognition by some agencies of the necessity of providing breakfast to many schoolchildren. The prevalence of children from low income families is un-equally distributed across the provinces, ranging from the highest in Saskatch-ewan (22.6% in 1988) to the lowest in Ontario (11.9%).[48] The almost million children born into or living in poverty in Canada face both short-term and long-term social, educational and health disadvantages. The poverty threshold levels used by Statistics Canada are Low Income Cut-offs (LICOs), which are based on a subsistence concept of poverty and calculated on expenditure patterns. Accord-ingly, a family is considered poor if it had to spend 56.2% or more of its income (adjusted for family size) on food, clothing and shelter. The poverty line for rural areas is generally lower than for urban areas because of the higher cost of accommodation in the latter. More recently, Statistics Canada has adopted a relative income approach[49] whereby poverty is defined in the context of the prevailing standards of living. The new Low Income Measures (LIMs) have been set at an income level of less than 50% of the median family income in Canada, adjusted for family size. Using 1990 income distribution data, this poverty level is $28,081 for a family of four living in a city.[50]

Several groups are at particular risk for poverty. Statistics Canada data show that in 1988, approximately 58% of families headed by **single mothers** in Canada lived below the poverty line. In Metropolitan Toronto, the average income for a female single parent in 1983 was $8,771, if under age 35, and $14,813 if over age 35. In comparison, two-parent families with one child had an average income of $33,988. **Immigrants** are another group at risk for poverty. In 1985, the poverty rate among children of immigrants in the Ottawa-Carleton region was 72.2% for

Vietnamese, 48.6% for Arabs, 37.4% for Chinese, and 27.0% for Greeks. Aboriginal Peoples are also at high risk for poverty. In 1986, 50% of the Aboriginal adult population was in the labour force, and the average Aboriginal income was two-thirds that of the non-Aboriginal. In spite of these statistics, poverty is not overtly visible in Canadian society; we do not see starving children with kwashiorkor or marasmus. In developed countries, the toll of poverty is subtle and its impact is largely unrecognized. Nevertheless, it is harmful, particularly to the health of children.

Association Between Poverty and Health
The influence of poverty on child health is mediated by a complex interaction of causes and events which are probably cumulative. Although it is clear that poverty places children at risk for adverse health outcomes, the exact mechanisms are not well elucidated.[51] A number of possible mechanisms exist for this association (see chapter one). Maslow[52] proposed the concept of hierarchy of needs in human beings. He identifies basic needs as food, clothing and shelter. In western societies, basic needs depend on disposable income, and the lack of parental income contributes to the burden of ill health in children. For example, unsafe, crowded housing could lead to an increase in both accidental injuries and communicable diseases. Low quality "junk food" can lead to nutritional disorders. Lack of money for transportation and child care can affect utilization of medical care, and lack of money for medicine can affect treatment. Parents may be required to spend much of their time working for their income, and the resulting inadequate parental supervision may lead to ill health (i.e., injuries and neglected health problems). Lack of income may also generate stress-related disorders in both parents and children. Among the impoverished, there is a higher prevalence of health-damaging behaviours such as smoking, which is often related to coping with stressful circumstances in the absence of social support. In a recent study, children in disadvantaged households were three times more likely to be exposed to a family environment in which both parents smoked.[11] Poverty can be conceived of as a socioenvironmental risk condition or a living situation which makes it difficult to achieve a healthy family lifestyle and which increases susceptibility to ill health.[53]

Another theory is that certain **parental characteristics**—including age, marital status, health status, educational and cultural backgrounds and personality—may predispose children to both poverty and ill health. This explanation assumes that lack of parental skills, time, dedication, or knowledge can adversely affect the health and development of children. Chamberlin refers to "the family balancing act" which incorporates the concept of goodness of fit between the psychological adequacy of the parent in coping capacity and resources, the environmental stresses and support (or lack therefore), and the characteristics of the child.[54] Poverty and ill health are not causally related in this explanation.

Poverty and ill health are clearly associated with one another but may be a consequence of other circumstances. For example, chronically ill parents may be poor and, as a result of ill health, have less time and energy for proper parenting. Psychiatric illness and personality disorders (e.g., substance abuse) may result in poverty and inadequate parenting. Single parents may not be able both to earn a living and care for children adequately. Parents of very large families, or families having one or more ill or disabled children, may have trouble coping financially and emotionally. Adolescent parents tend to be poor and lack the maturity required for parenting. Parents with less formal education or a cultural background different from the mainstream may not have adequate knowledge of child health-care or the health-care system. One danger of an uncritical application of this explanation is stereotyping. We must not assume that all chronically ill, young, or single parents are inadequate parents.

Evidence is accumulating that position on the social hierarchy and the perceived powerlessness which accompanies relative low income, where wide disparities exist between rich and poor in society, are independent risk factors for poor health of families.[55] In a comparison of countries belonging to the Organization for Economic Cooperation and Development (OECD), those with the greatest equity in after-tax income have the lowest infant mortality rates and longest life expectancies.

3.1.2. Access to Medical Care

Lower consumption of medical care by the poor may also contribute significantly to the negative impact of poverty on health. Canadian studies have shown conflicting results on this issue because of differing definitions of benefits and services, differing population units (families compared with per capita) and lack of controls for confounding factors such as age and sex.[56] Manga found that the per capita cost of medical services in Ontario did not vary significantly with income. Low income families had a greater number of physician visits, but less costly services were provided per visit, and a greater proportion of visits were hospital rather than office-based. Looking specifically at children, Manga found that, except for the lowest income group, benefits and average cost of services increased with increasing income.

3.2. HEALTH STATUS

3.2.1. Mortality

The following sections present available Canadian evidence comparing the health status of poor children with other children. For mortality, four major studies are used, Wigle and Mao[57] (for 1971 data), Dougherty[58] (1981), Wilkins[59,60] (1986) and a Canadian Institute of Child Health (CICH) profile.[14] In these studies, data from Canadian urban census tracts were grouped according to median household income. Income levels were divided into quintiles; level 1 being the highest and level five the lowest. Mortality rates were compared among these quintiles.

Infant Mortality

The effects of poverty on mortality begin before birth and may predate conception. The association between poverty and health-damaging behaviours has been
previously addressed. **Low birth weight** (LBW) is the single most important
cause of infant mortality, especially in the neonatal period (0 to 28 days). A record
linkage study of births in eight Canadian provinces found that early neonatal
mortality (in the first week of life) was inversely related to birth weight, with 75%
of early neonatal deaths attributable to LBW.[61] Nutritional status at the time of
conception, poor weight gain during pregnancy with insufficient intake of calories
and protein, drug use, alcohol use, and smoking during pregnancy are among the
many causes of LBW.[62] In a controlled study, dietary enhancement in low income
mothers in Montreal led to a 50% reduction in LBW in the second-born. Indian
and Inuit mothers in Northern Canada may lack adequate nutrition due to the high
cost of staples such as milk. Babies born to women who smoke are, on average,
200 gm lighter, and at higher risk of LBW than those born to non-smokers. The
rate of LBW in 1986 in the poorest income quintile was 1.4 times that in the
richest quintile. Mothers with little education are twice as likely to have a LBW
infant than those with a university education. Because the incidence of LBW is
inversely related to social class, and since infants of the same weight tend to have
the same neonatal mortality rate regardless of social class,[63,64] the effects of
poverty on neonatal mortality are mediated through LBW.[65,66]

This does not apply however to the post-neonatal period, where infants of the
same weight have a higher mortality rate in the lower socioeconomic groups.[67] In
Canada, the 1986 male infant mortality rate was 2.0 times higher in families in the
lowest income groups than in those with the highest income quintile; the female
infant mortality rate was 1.6 times higher in poor families (1.9 times in 1971). The
mortality rate for children in families with the lowest income level was higher for
all major causes of death in infancy, including pneumonia, respiratory distress
syndrome, immaturity, difficult labour/birth injury, and congenital anomalies of
the nervous system and circulatory system. In 1986, it was estimated that at birth,
males in the highest income level have a life expectancy 5.6 years longer than
those at the lowest income level, and affluent females have a 1.8 year longer life
expectancy than poor females. Wigle and Mao have stated that eliminating this
differential would increase life expectancy more than the prevention of all cancer
deaths.

Mortality Rate in 1 to 14 Year Age Group

Overall mortality was higher in 1971 and in 1986 for poor children than for those
who are not poor. Total mortality in boys aged 1 to 14 years was 2.0 times higher
in the lowest income level than in the highest. The mortality rate for girls who
were poor was 1.5 times higher in both 1971 and 1986.

(i) Accidents and Violent Deaths   Accidents are the major cause of death in
children in developed countries, and children from the lowest income class are at

substantially greater risk. Dougherty found that the mortality rate in Montreal from motor vehicle accidents (pedestrian) for girls aged 1 to 14 years was nearly six times higher for the lowest income level than for the highest and was slightly greater in girls than boys. The incidence of drowning was increased by 3.4 times for poor boys while there was no difference for the girls. Overcrowding and lack of safe play areas contribute to higher mortality among the poor.

(ii) Suicide and homicide rates   Suicide and homicide rates are 2.6 times higher among poor males, and 4.1 times higher among poor females in the age group 1 to 14 when compared with their wealthier counterparts. In the age group 15 to 19, the suicide rate for poor males is 1.9 times higher and homicide 3.4 times higher than for the highest income group.

(iii) Infections   Children from low income families are also at greater risk for acquiring infectious diseases. In the 1 to 14 year age group, the death rate in 1981 from respiratory diseases (of which pneumonia is a major contributor) was 2.0 times higher in boys from low income families than those from high income families, and 6.1 times higher for poor girls.

(iv) Malignancies   In 1981, the risk of mortality from cancer in Canadian children aged 1 to 14 years was 2.0 times higher for girls in the lowest income group than for those in the highest income group. For low income boys, the risk was 2.3 times greater. The bad outcome for poor children may be due to such factors as more advanced disease at the time of diagnosis, inadequate access to care, poor compliance with therapy or poor nutrition.

3.2.2. Morbidity

General measures of health status are usually directly related to social class; the higher the social class of the children, the better their health is. The National Health Interview Survey in the US found that low income children had lower parental ratings of general health and slightly more restricted activity days, more bed disability days and a higher rate of school absenteeism.[68] In the Ontario Child Health Study, Cadman et al.[69] found that the prevalence rates of chronic health problems per 1000 children who were below the poverty line was 237, compared with 183 per 1000 children above the poverty line.

Nutritional Disorders   Low income children are at greater risk for nutritional disorders. The US National Health and Nutrition Examination Survey found that poor children were most likely to develop iron deficiency anemia.[70] Iron deficiency anemia was found in 25% of 218 infants from 10 to 14 months of age whose mothers lived in the five poorest districts of Montreal.[71] Low income mothers have a tendency to discontinue breast-feeding early on and switch to using cow's milk (which is known to cause occult intestinal bleeding and possibly contribute to iron deficiency anemia in the infant). A follow-up evaluation of infants, whose iron status and treatment were known, demonstrated lowered scores on mental and developmental tests at five years of age, raising the issue of whether iron deficiency anemia, even if treated, causes irreversible defects.[72]

Height, weight and head circumference have been found to vary inversely with social class at different ages in many countries, including Canada.[73] The differences between the lower and higher classes in western countries are in the order of 0.5 kg for weight, 2 cm for height and 1 cm for head circumference at age seven. However, around adolescence, low income women tend to become more obese than high income women, and the difference is maintained into adulthood.[74]

Dental Caries Two surveys of randomly selected 13- and 14-year-olds in Alberta[75] and Quebec[76] found that dental caries, as measured by the decayed/missing/filled teeth (DMFT) index, varied inversely with social class. The ratio of filled teeth (F) to the DMFT index, which reflects the amount of dental care received, was directly related to social class. The social class gradient was largest in Quebec, with an F/DMFT ratio of 65.1% for the highest socioeconomic group and only 17.4% for the lowest.

3.3.   CONSEQUENCES

Disability
The rate of childhood disability in 1986 was more than twice as high among children from poor families compared with affluent ones. Seven per cent of children from the poorest quintile had some degree of disability, compared with 3.5% from the richest. The differences between income quintiles were even more pronounced when only severe disability was considered, in which case the rate was 2.7 times higher among the poor compared with the rich.

A landmark study, the Ontario Child Health Study (OCHS): Children at Risk[77] provides a good insight on the effect of poverty on mental health of children. The OCHS was a cross-sectional, province-wide survey of the mental and physical health of a randomly selected sample of more than 3,000 children aged 4 to 16 years. In this study, the authors tried to assess the impact of social assistance, subsidized housing, and living in a one-parent family on (i) the prevalence of psychiatric disorders, (ii) the proportion of children perceived to need professional help, and (iii) the proportion of children with poor school performance.

For children living on social assistance, compared with those not on social assistance, the risk of developing a psychiatric disorder was 2.8 times higher (31.2% compared with 18.8%). Similarly the risk for children living in one-parent families was 1.7 times higher (21.7% compared with 14.2%) than for two-parent families, and for children living in subsidized housing, the risk was 2.6 times higher than those in non-subsidized houseing (30.4% compared with 14.2%). All these relative odds were highly significant (p<0.001). The relative odds for children in each category needing professional help (i.e., children on social assistance, in subsidized housing, and from one-parent families) were significantly higher compared with their counterparts. The proportion of girls (but not boys) with poor school performance was significantly higher in all three categories.

3.4. HEALTHY PUBLIC POLICY

Canada ratified the UN Convention on the Rights of The Child, which established the essential standards for healthy child development, on December 11, 1991, and has taken a number of national initiatives to foster these goals. An all-party resolution had been previously passed to eliminate child poverty by the year 2000. The new initiatives include the federal government's Brighter Futures Program; the implementation of a child benefit, which consolidated Family Allowances, the Child Tax Credit and the Dependent Child Tax Credit into a single monthly payment and includes an additional amount for low income working families; Canada's Action Plan for Children, which will provide the framework for addressing long-term needs of children; and the Child Development Initiative, which is a five-year partnership with the provinces to ensure ongoing funding of prevention, protection and promotion programs through community action and partnerships. There was some concern that support for additional day care places was not included. Another concern expressed by child advocates has been with respect to the recent parliamentary committee report indicating that the present definition of poverty inflates the number of poor children in this country and needs to be re-examined. Despite this, the plight of poor children is still on the political agenda.

4.   THE HEALTH OF THE DISABLED

The World Health Organization defines disability as "any restriction or lack ... of ability to perform an activity in the manner or within the range considered normal for a human being." This definition applies to individuals whose conditions have existed for more than six months and whose limitations were not completely eliminated by the use of a technical aid. Disability is distinguished from impairment and handicap (see chapter one). There are seven categories of disabilities:[78]

(i) Mobility: limited ability to work, move from room to room, carry an object for 10m, or stand for long periods.
(ii) Agility: limited ability to bend, dress or undress oneself, get in and out of bed, cut toenails, use fingers to grasp or handle objects, reach or cut one's own food.

(iii) Sight: limited ability to read ordinary newsprint or see someone from 4m even when wearing glasses.

(iv) Hearing: limited ability to hear what is being said in a conversation with one other person or two or more persons, even when wearing a hearing aid.

(v) Speaking: limited ability to speak and be understood.

(vi) Other: limited because of a learning disability, an emotional or psychiatric disability or developmental delay.

(vii) Unknown: limited, but nature of limitation not specified.

4.1. PROFILE OF THE DISABLED

Most of the statistical information in this section is derived from the Health and Activity Limitation Survey for Canada (HALS)[78-80] and the Statistical Profile of Disabled Persons in Ontario[81] for that province. In 1986, 3.3 million or 13.2% of Canadians had some level of disability. While this had grown to 15.5% of the population in 1991 (4.2 million), most of the increase was due to mild disability. One reason for this was a change in survey methodology which incorporated more learning disabilities. An analysis of disability by sex and age has been given in table 5.4. As the rate of disability in the population increases with age, these data support the hypothesis that disability increases proportionally with age.   The disability rate for females in 1991 was 16.2%, slightly higher than the male rate of 14.8%. The higher female rate reflects the longer life span of women. In 1992, Nova Scotia, Manitoba and New Brunswick recorded the highest disability rates, at 21.3%, 17.7% and 17.6%, respectively.   The lowest rates were recorded in Newfoundland (10%), the Yukon (11.1%) and the Northwest Territories (12.6%). In 1986, of the 3.3 million Canadians with disabilities, 86,505 were of Aboriginal ancestry; 14,990 lived on-reserve while 71,515 resided off-reserve.

In 1991, 7% or 389,355 of children under age 15 years, were disabled. The majority of the disabilities for children of all ages were mild although long-term health conditions such as asthma and cerebral palsy were reported for more than half of the disabilities. Apart from these health conditions, speech difficulties were the most common disability in those aged 0 to 9 years, hearing difficulties the next most common and occurred slightly more frequently in the older age groups, and vision difficulties was the least common sensory disability. Psychiatric conditions as a cause of disability were most frequent in the 5 to 9 year age group.

Education
Disabled respondents to the HALS tended to have less formal education than the non-disabled, as disabilities often interfered with their education.   Among the disabled, mildly disabled individuals were more likely to have attained a higher level of education than those with moderate or severe disabilities. Nearly half (45%) of severely disabled respondents had eight years of education or less, compared with 25% of those who were mildly disabled. Twenty-one per cent of

respondents said that their education was interrupted for lengthy periods of time causing them to change schools or alter courses. Six per cent claimed that they started school later than most non-disabled children. The more severe the disability, the greater effect it had on an individual (e.g., in beginning school, changing schools, changing course of study). Of the disabled children between the ages of 5 to 14 years in 1991 in Canada, almost 30% attended a special school or special classes within regular schools. Disabled Aboriginal persons aged 15 to 64 residing off-reserve tended to have a higher level of education than their counterparts residing on-reserve. On the reserves, 65% reported having zero to eight years of education, 22% reported having some secondary education and 13% reported having post-secondary education.

Income

Disabled Ontarians from age 15 to 64 (inclusive) had gross incomes 46% lower than non-disabled Ontarians of the same age group. However, the income of disabled seniors was only 18% lower than those of their non-disabled counterparts. Disabled Aboriginal adults living on-reserve tended to have lower incomes than either those living off-reserve or disabled non-Aboriginal adults. In 1986, a total of 80% of disabled Aboriginal adults (on-reserve) had either no income or a total income of $10,000 or less. The income of disabled Aboriginal adults living off-reserve resembled that of non-Aboriginal disabled adults; 59% and 57%, respectively, had either no income or a total income of $10,000 or less. The most common sources of additional income reported by the disabled under 65 years were the Canada Pension Plan (CPP) (45%) and Workers' Compensation (32%). For those over 65, the Veterans' Disability Pension provided 35% of the disabled peoples income, CPP provided 32% and Workers' Compensation contributed 25%.

Forty eight per cent of the 2.3 million disabled persons aged 15 to 64 in Canada in 1989, who were living in private households, were employed compared with 72.9% of the non-disabled. Of those working, over half reported a work limitation due to their disability.

Living Situation

Nine per cent of disabled women and 6% of disabled men live in institutions. Of those living in the community, many report difficulty in moving outside of their neighbourhood, especially for long distance travel, and 5% reported using special facilities such as access ramps where provided. Three-quarters of women with slight to moderate disabilities were able to prepare meals for themselves, compared with only half of those severely disabled. In relation to personal care, such as feeding, the proportion of the severely disabled requiring assistance was 24%, compared with 1% of those mildly disabled.

Causes of Disability

There are a number of causes of disabilities, and age plays an important role in determining the cause. The nature of the disability in the adult population aged 15 and older were as follows; the most common disabilities were in mobility, agility, hearing, speaking and seeing. The medical conditions that most frequently cause disability are diseases of the musculoskeletal system (connective tissue, arthritis and rheumatism) and hearing disorders. Among children, the major causes of disability were due to developmental delay, and hearing or vision problems. For individuals over 50 and the non-institutionalized, a disease is reported as the most common cause of disability. On the other hand, those under 50 were usually born with their disability or cited accidents as the major cause of their disability. It should be noted that male respondents (more so than females) reported that their disability was the result of a disease or accident. For example, in Ontario, 21% of disabled males cited accidents as a cause, compared with 14% of females; 36% of disabled males cited disease as a cause, compared with 25% of females. For the disabled living in institutions,[82] 45% reported disease as the main cause; for 30%, aging, or the effects of stroke, were reported as the cause of their disability. For those aged 15 to 34 living in institutions, mental retardation, diseases of the nervous system and diseases of the sense organs were reported as the main causes of their disability. However, those 55 years and over, diseases of the musculoskeletal system and connective tissue were cited as the main causes.

Approximately 4% (or 8,700) of disabled children between the ages of five and 14 had a diagnosis of cerebral palsy; 2,000 were diagnosed as having spina bifida; 3,400 as having muscular dystrophy; and approximately 35,500 had hearing impairments.

4.2.   HEALTH STATUS AND CONSEQUENCES

Degree of Disability

In 1986, forty-five per cent of the disabled population indicated that they had a mild disability, 32% a moderate disability, and 23% a severe disability. Slightly less than 66% of the disabled population cited restricted mobility as the most frequent disability, followed by limitations in agility. Aboriginal Peoples also reported limited mobility as the most frequent disability. Forty-three per cent of the disabled persons between the ages of 15 to 34 reported a mobility disability, compared with 75% of disabled seniors 65 and over in the 1986 HALS. Eighteen per cent of the disabled population (552,580 persons) aged 15 years and older reported a visual disability, and 973,830 individuals 15 and older reported a hearing disability. In the general Canadian population, 66% of the disabled population aged 15 and older reported having more than one type of disability, with the prevalence of multiple disabilities increasing with age. In addition, over 75% of off-reserve disabled Aboriginals reported having only one or two disabilities, compared with about 65% of those living on-reserve.

Substance Abuse

It is sometimes assumed that adults with severe physical disabilities are suscepti-ble to alcohol and drug abuse due to low self-esteem, social isolation and other problems as a result of their physical conditions. However, a recent survey of wheelchair-bound college students found that the rate of alcohol and illicit drug use was similar to the general college population. Approximately 20% of disabled students are considered "problem users" of drugs and alcohol. Another survey administered to disabled university students found 40% of them drinking alcohol one or more times a week and 14% smoke marijuana one or more times a week. Once again, however, these rates are similar to the general college population.[83] As with young adults in general, drug usage among disabled college students is correlated with a previous history of drug usage.

Nutrition

Disabled children are at risk for malnutrition. This risk is attributable either directly or indirectly to several factors: physical disability and/or cognitive delay, altered nutrient requirements caused by their medical condition and/or drugs used to treat their medical condition. Severe developmentally handicapped children are significantly below their expected weight. Gouge and Ekvall found that one-third of handicapped children were below the third percentile for weight. This is primarily a result of eating dysfunctions which affect a notable portion of disabled children.[84]

Health-care Utilization

Eighty-two per cent of those severely disabled had visited a medical practitioner in the preceding three months, for 50% this had been on three or more occasions. Eight per cent of severely disabled females and 10% of such males had been hospitalized three or more times in the preceding year.

4.3.   THE FUTURE

As indicated in chapter one, the impairments and handicaps related to disability are mediated by the social context of the disabled person. Societal attitudes towards the disabled, and the degree of modification of the physical, working, educational and other aspects of the psychosocial environment to accommodate the disabled, have great impact on the quality of life a disabled person experi-ences. The disabled consumer movement has emerged in recent years to have an impact in the political arena to enhance the quality of life of the disabled.[85] An example of response has been the increased incorporation of access ramps and toilet facilities for the disabled in public buildings. Some long-term care facilities have recognized that they are in fact "home" for the institutionalized disabled, with consequent changes in how they see themselves as institutions. With the growth in the elderly segment of the population and the survival of many seriously injured who have major disabilities (particularly neurological damage) the movement will likely gain momentum in bringing about needed changes in the sociopolitical context of disability and health organizations.

5.   SUMMARY

This chapter examined the health of certain groups in the Canadian population in terms of the determinants of their health, health indicators and consequences. The groups considered include Aboriginal Peoples, the elderly, poor children and the disabled.

Aboriginal Peoples include Status Indians, Non-Status Indians, Metis and Inuit. However, this chapter only considered the health of Status and Non-Status Indians. In 1988, there were 443 884 Status Indians in Canada, of which 31.2% were in the age group of 0 to 14 years, 64.3% in 15 to 64 year group and 4.4% in the age group 65 and over. The high proportion of young people in the Aboriginal populations is quite different from the Canadian population. The life expectancy for males is 63.8 years and for females 71.0 years, which is significantly shorter than for the general Canadian population.

Approximately 62% of Status Indians live on reserves. Their incomes are approximately two-thirds that of the non-Aboriginal average. Most of their employment is in the service industry and is low paying. In 1984, almost half of Aboriginal housing failed to meet basic standards. Alcohol abuse levels have been estimated at between 35% and 40% for the adult Aboriginal populations and between 10% and 15% for Aboriginal adolescents. Smoking is also quite prevalent amongst school children and adults. Aboriginals are at a high risk for being obese and deficient in nutrients such as iron, vitamins, and protein.

The federal government is responsible for the health-care of Aboriginal Peoples on reserves, and the provincial government for those off the reserves. Since two-thirds of Aboriginal Peoples live in rural or remote areas, health services are less than optimal. On many remote reserves, primary care is provided by nurses or community health workers.

In the last 20 years there has been a substantial improvement in Aboriginal mortality, however, the gap in mortality between Aboriginals and the general Canadian population is still wide. In 1988, the Aboriginal mortality rate standardized to the Canadian population was 10 per 1000, which is 1.4 times the Canadian rate. The four leading causes of death in order for the Aboriginal population were: injury and poisoning, diseases of the circulatory system, neoplasm, and diseases of the respiratory system. Aboriginals have a high incidence of gastroenteritis, diphtheria, rheumatic fever, respiratory problems and infectious hepatitis. Hospitalization rates for Aboriginals are high compared with Canadian rates. Furthermore, the disability rates are almost double the corresponding rates for the rest of the Canadian population. The major disabilities for Aboriginal Peoples 15 years and over were in the areas of mobility, agility, and hearing.

One of the major solutions proposed by Aboriginal Peoples to improve their health status is to gain control over their health, social and educational programs. Another solution proposed is to settle the unresolved land claims and have their rightful place in Canadian society recognized.

The conventional definition of the elderly is persons aged 65 years and over. The number of seniors and the proportion of seniors in the population continues to grow with a tendency towards an increasing proportion of the very elderly (aged over 85). In June 1991, the elderly accounted for 11.6% of the population. It is estimated that by 2021, 15% of the population will be elderly. It is also interesting to note that in 1991 there were 1.2 times the number of 65- to 84- year-old women than men in the same age group. The income of the elderly has increased substantially over the last few years with the result of narrowing the gap between the elderly and the rest of the population. The elderly are dependent on public pension and income security plans for their income. Many elderly people are predisposed to falls and injuries due to their increased rate of visual, auditory and locomotive disabilities. As well, they have low tolerance levels to the presence of hazards in the physical environment. Successful aging has been defined in terms of retaining the ability to function independently, remaining mobile and undertaking all the activities of daily living. The predictors of successful aging include: a surviving spouse, having not entered a nursing home and the age of the individual. Over 50% of the elderly drink alcohol, while less than 20% smoke regularly. Many elderly are malnourished. The majority of the population aged 65 years and over have diets which are deficient in nutrients such as protein, iron, calcium and thiamin.

Mortality rates for elderly women are lower than those for males. The leading health problems in the elderly include: arthritis, rheumatism, hypertension, limb and joint disease, respiratory and heart disease, and diabetes. Alzheimer's Disease represents the most frequent dementing illness in the elderly population. The overall disability rate for the elderly was 45%, increasing to 80% for the very elderly. The major types of disability reported in the elderly were in mobility, agility, vision and hearing. Hospital usage by the elderly rises dramatically with age. The old elderly use approximately 10 times more hospital days than any other age group under 60.

It has now been recognized that there is a need for improved geriatric services. Health promotion for the elderly is becoming an important approach to the development and maintenance of optimum levels of functioning as aging occurs. These approaches include physical activity, social support, nutrition counseling and programs to prevent falls.

A family that spends over 56.2% of their income on the basic needs of accommodation, food and clothing lives in poverty. In 1990, one in six children (17%) in Canada were living in poverty. Several groups are at particular risk for poverty, and they include single mothers, immigrants, and Aboriginal Peoples. These children face both short-term and long-term social, educational, and health disadvantages. It is well documented that poor children have poor health. However, the exact mechanisms of how poverty affects health is not clear.

The effects of poverty on mortality begin before birth and may predate conception. Low birth weight is the single most important cause of infant mortality and is inversely related to social class. Hence the effects of poverty on neonatal mortality are mediated through low birth weight. Overall mortality in the 1-14 year age group was higher in 1986 for poor children than for those who were not poor. Accident was the major cause of death in children. Children from low income families are also at a greater risk for infectious diseases, chronic health problems, dental caries and nutritional disorders. Height, weight, and head circumference have been found to vary inversely with social class at different ages. The rate of childhood disability in 1986 was over twice as high among children from poor families compared with rich families. Children whose parents were living on social assistance had a 2.8 times higher chance of developing a psychiatric disorder.

The federal government has taken on new initiatives to address the problems of children living in poverty. They include the Brighter Futures Program and the implementation of a child benefit which consolidated Family Allowances, the Child Tax Credit and the Dependent Child Tax Credit into a single monthly payment with an additional amount for low income working families.

The WHO defines disability as "any restriction or lack ... of ability to perform an activity in the manner or within the range considered normal for a human being." Seven categories of disabilities have been identified: mobility, agility, sight, hearing, speaking, other, and unknown. In 1991, 15.5% of the population or 4.2 million Canadians had some level of disability. Mobility is cited as the most frequent disability, followed by agility as the next most frequent type. In 1991, 7% of children under the age of 15 were disabled. Disabled individuals tended to have less formal education than non-disabled individuals, as disabilities often interfered with their education. Disabled Ontarians from age 15-64 had gross incomes that were 46% lower than non-disabled Ontarians, within the same age group.

There are a number of causes of disability, and age plays an important role in determining the cause. Medical conditions leading to disability most often are diseases of the musculoskeletal system and hearing disorders. Among children, the major causes of disability were developmental delay and hearing or vision problems. For individuals over 50, diseases were the leading cause of the disability, whereas for under 50, accidents was the major cause of the disability.

Disabled children are at a risk for malnutrition. This risk is due to: physical disability and/or cognitive delay, altered nutrient requirements caused by their medical condition and/or drugs used to treat the medical condition. The disabled consumer movement has emerged in recent years to have an impact on the political arena to enhance the quality of life of the disabled.

6.   REFERENCES

1. *Health Status of Canadian Indians and Inuit 1990*. Medical Services Branch, Minister of National Health and Welfare, Ottawa, 1991.
2. Bobet E. *Inequalities in Health: A Comparison of Indian and Canadian Mortality Trends. Demographics and Statistics*. Planning and Information Coordination. Program Transfer, Policy and Planning. Medical Services Branch, Health and Welfare Canada, Ottawa, 1990.
3. Canada's Native People. *1981 Census of Canada*. Ministry of Supply and Services, Canada, Ottawa, 1984.
4. Shah CP and Dubeski G. First Nations Peoples in Urban Settings: Health Issues. In: *Health and Cultures: Exploring the Relationships*. Masi R, Mensah L, McLeod KA and Oakville K, eds. Oakville, Ontario: Mosaic Press, 1993, pp 71-93.
5. Siggner AJ. The Socio-Demographic Conditions of Registered Indians. Statistics Canada. *Canadian Social Trends* 1(1):1-9, 1986.
6. Statistics Canada. Canada's Off-Reserve Aboriginal Population. *Canadian Social Trends* 23(1):2-7, 1991.
7. *Indian Conditions: A Survey*. Minister of Indian Affairs and Northern Development, Ottawa, 1980.
8. *Alcohol and Drug Abuse among Treaty Indians in Saskatchewan: Needs Assessment and Recommendations for Change*. Federation of Saskatchewan Indian Nations and Health and Welfare Canada, Saskatoon, 1984.
9. *Brief to the Standing Committee on Health and Welfare, Hearings Concerning Resources Required to Address Substance Abuse*. Union of Ontario Indians. Ottawa, June, 1987 [unpublished].
10. McIntyre L and Shah CP. Prevalence of Hypertension, Obesity, and Smoking in Three Indian Communities in Northwestern Ontario. *Can Med Assoc J* 134(4):345-349, 1986.
11. Millar WJ and Hunter L. The Relationship Between Socioeconomic Status and Household Smoking Patterns in Canada. *Am J Health Promot* 5(1):36-43, 1990.
12. *Health Status of Canadian Indians and Inuit: Update 1987*. Medical Services Branch, Minister of National Health and Welfare, Ottawa, 1988.
13. *Nutrition Canada: National Survey*. Information Canada, Ottawa, 1973, pp 63-75.
14. Avard D and Harvey L, eds. The Health of Canada's Children: A CICH Profile. Canadian Institute of Child Health. Ottawa, Ontario, 1989, pp 105-107.
15. Postl B and Moffat M. The Health of Canada's Native People: An Overview. *Can Fam Phys* 34(11):2413-2419, 1988.
16. Layne N. Potential Years of Life Lost Amongst Canadian Indians, 1978 and 1983. *Chronic Dis Can* 7(1):7-8, 1986.
17. Language, Tradition, Health, Lifestyle and Social Isues. Statistics Canada. no. 89-533, 1993, pp 108-117.
18. *Report of the Subcommittee on Indian Health Care to the Health Services Review Committee*. Chairman, Postl BD. University of Manitoba, Winnipeg, Manitoba. May, 1985.
19. Evers SE and Rand CG. Morbidity in Canadian Indian and Non-Indian Children in the Second Year. *Can J Public Health* 74(3):191-194, 1983.
20. 1991 Aboriginal People Survey. Statistics Canada. Ottawa, *The Daily* June 29, 1993, pp 3-6.
21. Shah CP, Park IR and Casson I. *Prevalence of Disabilities in Two Native Communities in the Sioux Lookout Zone of Northwestern Ontario*. Presented at the Canadian Association of Physical Anthropology. Vancouver, November, 1989.
22. Scott-McKay-Bain Health Panel (Ont.), *From Here to There: Achieving Health for All in the Sioux Lookout Zone*. Bacon J, ed. Toronto, 1989.
23. *Special Committee on Indian Self-Government*. House of Commons. Issue No. 40. Ottawa, 1983.
24. *1991 Census Canada. The Nation Series*. Statistics Canada. Ministry of Industry, Science and Technology, Canada, Ottawa, 1992.
25. *Population Projections for Canada and the Provinces 1989-2011*. Statistics Canada. Department of Supply, Canada, Ottawa, 1992.
26. Gautier P. Canada's Seniors. Statistics Canada. *Can Soc Trends* 22(2):16-20, 1991.

27. *Canada's Seniors. A Dynamic Force.* Government of Canada. Ministry of Supply and Services, Canada, Ottawa, 1988.

28. Jaiyeola A. Alzheimer's Disease and Aluminum: How Strong is the Evidence? Why Drinking Water? *Public Health and Epidemiology Reports Ont* 4(12):112-114, 1991.

29. Roos P and Havens B. Predictors of Successful Aging: A Twelve Year Study of Manitoba Elderly. *Am J Public Health* 81(1):63-68, 1991.

30. Barer ML, Evans RG, Hertzman C and Lomas J. Aging and Health Care Utilization: New Evidence on Old Fallacies. *Soc Sci Med* 24(10):851-862, 1987.

31. Fries JF. Aging, Natural Death and the Compression of Morbidity. *N Engl J Med* 303(3):130-135, 1980.

32. *Health Care for the Elderly: Today's Challenges Tomorrow's Options.* Report of the CMA Committee on the Health Care of the Elderly. Ottawa: Canadian Medical Association, 1987, p 7.

33. Ableson J, Paddon P and Stohmenger C, eds. *Perspectives on Health.* Statistics Canada, Queens Printer, Ottawa, 1983.

34. Manton KG. Changing Concepts of Morbidity and Mortality in the Elderly Population. *Milbank Mem Fund Q* 60(2):183-244, 1982.

35. Schneider EL and Brody JA. Aging, Natural Death and the Compression of Morbidity: Another View. *N Engl J Med* 309(14):854-856, 1983.

36. Wylie CM. Health-Related Contrasts Between Older Men and Women. In: *Recent Advances in Geriatric Medicine. Number Three.* Isaacs B, ed. Melbourne: Churchill Livingstone, 1985.

37. Health and Welfare Canada (1990), *National Alcohol and Other Drugs Survey (1989): Highlights Report.* Eliany M, Giesbrecht N, Nelson M, Wellman B and Wortly S, eds. Ministry of Supply and Services, Canada, Ottawa, 1990.

38. Posner BM. *Nutrition and the Elderly: Policy Development, Program Planning, and Evaluation.* Lexington, Massachusetts. Health, 1979.

39. Health and Welfare Canada. Mortality of the Elderly in Canada. *Chronic Dis Can* 11(1):1-3, 1990.

40. Health and Welfare Canada and Statistics Canada. *The Health of Canadians: Report of the Canada Health Survey.* Ministry of Supply and Services, Canada, Ottawa, 1981.

41. Canadian Task Force on The Periodic Health Examination. Periodic Health Examination, 1991 Update: 1. Screening for Cognitive Impairment in the Elderly. *Can Med Assoc J* 144(4):425-431, 1991.

42. Locker D, Leake JL, Lee J, Main PJ, Hicks T and Hamilton M. Utilization of Dental Services in Four Ontario Communities. *J Can Dent Assoc* 57(9):879-881, 1991.

43. Locker D, Leake JL, Hamilton M, Hicks T, Lee J and Main PJ. Oral Health Status of Older Adults in Four Ontario Communities. *J Can Dent Assoc* 57(9):727-732, 1991.

44. Brancker A. Cancer: Incidence, Hospitalizations and Deaths in Canada. *Health Reports* 1(1):51-67, 1989.

45. Roos NP, Shapiro E and Roos LL. Aging and the Demand for Health Services: Which Aged and Whose Demand? *Gerontologist* 24(1):31-36, 1984.

46. Horne RV. *A New Agenda - Health and Social Service Strategies for Ontario's Seniors*, Toronto: Government of Ontario, 1987.

47. Cregheur A and Devereux MS. Canada's Children. *Canadian Social Trends* 21(1):2-5, 1991.

48. *Children in Poverty : Toward a Better Future.* Standing Senate Committee on Social Affairs, Science and Technology, Ottawa, Ontario, 1991

49. Spector A. Measuring Low Incomes in Canada. *Canadian Social Trends* 25(1):8-9, 1992.

50. Income Distribution by Size in Canada. Statistics Canada. Catalogue 13-207, 1991.

51. Shah CP. The Health of Low-Income Families. *Can Med Assoc J* 137(6):485-490, 1987.

52. Maslow AH. *Toward a Psychology of Being,* 2nd ed. New York: Van Nos Reinhold, 1968.

53. *Health Inequalities in the City of Toronto. 1991.* Community Health Information Section. Department of Public Health, City of Toronto. Toronto, 1991.

54. *Beyond Individual Risk Assessment: Community Wide Approaches to Promoting the Health and Development of Families and Children. Conference Proceedings.* Chamberlin RW, ed. The National Centre for Education in Maternal and Child Health. Washington D.C., 1988

55. *Nurturing Health. A Framework on the Determinants of Health.* Premier's Council on Health Strategy. Toronto, Ontario, 1991.

56. Manga P. *Equality of Access and Inequalities in Health Status: Policy Implications of an Apparent Paradox.* Working paper 86-13. University of Ottawa, Ottawa, 1986.

57. Wigle DT and Mao Y. *Mortality By Income Level in Urban Canada*. Ministry of National Health and Welfare, Ottawa, 1980.
58. Dougherty GE. Social Class and the Occurrence of Traffic Injuries and Deaths in Urban Children. *Can J Public Health* 81(3):204-209, 1990.
59. Wilkins R, Adams O, and Brancker A. Changes in Mortality by Income in Urban Canada from 1971 to 1986. *Health Reports* 1(2):137-74, 1989.
60. Wilkins R and Sherman GJ. Birth Outcomes and Infant Mortality by Income in Urban Canada, 1986. *Health Reports* 3(1):7-31, 1991.
61. Silins J, Semenciw RM, Morrison HI, et al. Risk Factors for Perinatal Mortality in Canada. *Can Med Assoc J* 133(12):1214-1220, 1985.
62. *Preconceptional Health: Principles and Program Strategies*. Ministry of Health Ontario. Public Health Branch. Toronto, Ontario, 1991.
63. *Inequalities in Health: Report of a Research Working Group*. Working Group on Inequalities in Health. Department of Health and Social Services, London, UK, 1980.
64. Higgins A. Nutritional Status and the Outcome of Pregnancy. *J Can Diet Assoc* 37(1):17-35, 1976.
65. Hemminki E and Starfield B. Prevention of Low Birth Weight and Pre-Term Birth. Literature review and suggestions for research policy. *Milbank Mem Fund Q* 56(3):339-361, 1978.
66. Paneth N, Wallenstein S, Kiely JL and Susser M. Social Class Indicators and Mortality in Low Birth Weight Infants. *Am J Epidimiol* 116(2):364-375, 1982.
67. Cohen SE, Sigman M, Parmelee AH and Beckwith L. Perinatal Risk and Developmental Outcome in Preterm Infants. *Semin Perinatol* 6(4):334-339, 1982.
68. Kovar MG. Health Status of U.S. Children and Use of Medical Care. *Public Health Reports* 97(1):3-15, 1982.
69. Cadman D, Boyle MH and Offord DR. Chronic Illness, Function Conditions and Limitations in Ontario Children: Findings of the Ontario Child Health Study. *Can Med Assoc J* 135(7):761-767, 1986.
70. Singer JD. *Diet and Iron Status, a Study of Relationships: United States 1971-74*. DHHS publication number (PHS) 83-1679 (Vital and Health Statistics, ser 11) US Department of Health and Human Services. Hyattsville, MD: National Center for Health Statistics, 1982, pp 1-83.
71. Lehmann F, Gray-Donald K, Mongeon M and Di Tommaso S. Iron Deficiency Anemia in 1-year-old Children of Disadvantaged Families in Montreal. *Can Med Assoc J* 146(9):1571-1577, 1992.
72. Lozoff B, Jimenez E and Wolf AW. Long-Term Developmental Outcome of Infants With Iron Deficiency. *N Engl J Med* 325(10):687-694, 1991
73. Meredith HV. Body Size of Infants and Children Around the World in Relation to Socioeconomic Status. *Adv Child Dev Behav* 18:81-145, 1984.
74. Garn S. Continuities and Changes in Fatness from Infancy Through Adulthood. *Curr Probl Pediatr* 15(2):1-47, 1985.
75. Stamm JW, Lizaire A, Fedori D, et al. Dental Health Status of Alberta School Children. *Can Dent Assoc J* 46(2):98-107, 1980.
76. Stamm JW, Dixter CT and Langlair RP. Principal Dental Health Indices for 13-14 Year Old Quebec Children. *Can Dent Assoc J* 46(2):125-137, 1980.
77. *Ontario Child Health Study: Children at Risk*. Queen's Printer for Ontario, Toronto, 1989, pp 8-13.
78. Hamilton M. The Health and Activity Limitation Survey. *Health Reports* 1(2):175-187, 1989.
79. Hamilton M. The Health and Activity Limitation Survey: Disabled Aboriginal Persons in Canada. *Health Reports* 2(3):279-287, 1990.
80. Statistics Canada. 1991 Health and Activity Limitation Survey. Ottawa, *The Daily* October 13, 1992.
81. S*tatistical Profile of Disabled Persons in Ontario*. Vol. 2. Ministry of Citizenship: Office for Disabled Persons. Queen's Printer for Ontario, Toronto, 1990.
82. Dowler J and Jordan-Simpson D. Canada's Disabled Population in Institutions. *Health Reports* 2(1):27-36, 1990.
83. Substance Abuse among the disabled. *Science News*. 136 : October 7, 1989.
84. Evers S, Munoz MA, Vanderkooy P, et al. Nutritional Rehabilitation of Developmentally Disabled Residencies in a Long-Term Care Facility. *J Am Diet Assoc* 91(4):471-473,1991.
85. Coburn J, D' Arcy, Torrance G and New P. Health and Canadian Society. In: *Sociological Perspectives,* 2nd ed. Markham, Ontario: Fitzhenry and Whiteside, 1987.

CHAPTER SEVEN
Chronic Diseases and Injuries

The major causes of mortality, morbidity and the burden of illness in the Canadian population have been indicated in chapter five. Overall, cardiovascular disease and cancer are the leading contributions to chronic disease, with a significant proportion due to injuries, both unintentional (e.g., motor vehicle accidents) and intentional (e.g., suicide). The economic and personal burden of chronic illness to Canada is substantial. Substance abuse (predominantly smoking and problematic alcohol use) and improper diet are major determinants of chronic illness and are discussed below. Communicable diseases, particularly those for which efficacious vaccines are available, and sexually transmitted diseases are still of major concern and are dealt with in the next chapter.

This chapter presents more detailed information on chronic non-communicable diseases, emphasising current approaches to prevention and control. As many chronic illnesses are preventable and few are curable in the traditional medical model, the roles of primary and secondary prevention, and more recently health promotion, have emerged as increasingly important. The reader is referred to chapter one for the underlying principles of disease prevention and health promotion which provide the framework.

1. LIFESTYLE ISSUES

The major underlying cause of many chronic diseases is substance abuse, in the form of tobacco use, excessive alcohol use, or improper diet. In order to avoid repetitiveness, we incorporated strategies for primary and secondary prevention of major diseases in the sections on substance abuse and diet.

1.1. SUBSTANCE ABUSE

Although much attention focuses on illicit drugs, the major burden of illness caused by substance abuse is due to use/ abuse of **tobacco and alcohol**, which are readily available, socially sanctioned, and promoted widely. These substances are discussed separately, in the context of the burden of illness caused by each, and then together in a framework indicating approaches to their control and to prevention of the consequences of their use/abuse. Strategies for the office practice of individual health professionals are included. A risk continuum framework of the spectrum of problems arising from use/abuse of these substances and the appropriate level of response has been provided in figure 1.1.

1.1.1 Tobacco

Smoking is the single most preventable cause of death in Canada. In 1989, 38,000 Canadians died of smoking-related deaths. The effects of smoking have mush-roomed into major health problems, namely lung cancer, where smoking is responsible for 80% of cases, chronic obstructive lung disease and cardiovascular illness. The population attributable risk (PAR, see chapter three) for smoking in relation to cancer deaths is 29%, for cardiovascular deaths, 17%. Women over 40 who are on the pill and who smoke are at particular risk. Smoking is considered to be the major preventable cause of cancer. Not only is it the major cause of lung cancer, it also contributes to the incidence of a number of other cancers. The age-standardized mortality rates per 100,000 for lung cancer have increased from 40 for males and six for females in 1970 to 58 for males and 20 for females in 1990. The overall cancer death rates of male smokers are double those of non-smokers. Female deaths, while much lower in number than males, have risen proportion-ately at a greater rate than for males within the last 15 years, paralleling the increase in female smoking. The overall cancer death rate of female smokers is 30% greater (and rising) than that of non-smokers. Smoking is the major preventable cause of low birth weight which, in turn, is the major risk factor of infant mortality in Canada. Infants born to women who smoke, on average, weigh 200 gms less than those of non-smoking mothers.

Smoking also affects the mortality rates for chronic obstructive pulmonary disease (COPD), which includes bronchitis, emphysema, and asthma. Smoking is not only a hazard to those who smoke. The Report of the Working Group on Passive Smoking stated that there is strong evidence of an association between residential and workplace exposure to environmental tobacco smoke and respira-tory illness.[1] Studies have demonstrated an elevated risk of lung cancer in the partners of smokers. In terms of economic burden, the costs to society attributable to tobacco use (for premature mortality, hospitalization, physician services and fires) were estimated at $7.1 billion in 1982.[2] The costs in terms of quality of life and disability-free life expectancy are additional.

Smoking has been well-entrenched in our society as a symbol of sophistication and even liberation for females. Smoking was also widely promoted by govern-ments in North America during the Second World War, and likely this promotion greatly expanded the prevalence of smoking. Recent Canadian surveys estimate the percentage of male and female regular smokers to be 29% and 28% respec-tively. Of the Canadian population who are regular cigarette smokers, 13% of these smoke more than 25 cigarettes per day. An additional 5% smoke occasionally or are pipe or cigar smokers. For those under 45, males and females had equal prevalence of regular smoking. For those over 45, males were more frequently regular smokers. The age group with the highest proportion of female smokers was 25 to 34 (34%), with similar percentages for the age groups 15 to 24 and 35 to 44. For males, the prevalence of smoking was highest also in the 25 to 34 year age group (35%).

Brief Interventions for Smoking Cessation by Health Professionals
Studies have provided evidence that health-care providers, including physicians and non-physicians, can be effective in motivating patients to quit smoking by using brief interventions of smoking cessation messages reinforced on multiple occasions.[3] Cessation techniques developed by the National Institutes of Health[4] and by the Canadian Council on Smoking and Health (*Guide Your Patients to a Smoke Free Future*[5]) can be utilized and incorporated into office procedures. The manual for the latter technique (available from the Canadian Council on Smoking and Health) lists the following steps: (a) select an office smoking cessation coordinator; (b) create a smoke-free office; (c) identify all smoking patients; (d) develop patient smoking cessation plans; and (e) provide follow up support.

In the late 1980s incidence and mortality rates for lung cancer in males began to plateau, likely reflecting the fall in tobacco consumption in men which began in the 1960s. Only well-designed health promotion strategies aimed at preventing the uptake of smoking by impressionable youth, as well as cessation in older smokers, can continue the reversal of trends in smoking prevalence. Recent findings on passive smoking have had an impact on public policies. With increased awareness of adverse effects of passive smoking in closed environments some cities have passed legislation banning smoking in the workplace. Similarly, the federal government has also banned smoking in all federal buildings and air flights operating in Canada. These strategies are aspects of a comprehensive approach to tobacco use prevention which includes multiple strategies directed at multiple sites and on an intersectoral basis (discussed under the section on health promotion, below).

1.1.2. Alcohol
There are various diseases and/or injuries associated with alcohol consumption such as cirrhosis, suicide, breast cancer, respiratory cancer, motor vehicle and other accidents. In social terms, an estimated 1.8% of all deaths are directly attributable to alcohol abuse and an estimated 10.5% of all deaths are alcohol-related.[6] Mortality from cirrhosis of the liver has increased since the postwar period, coincident with rising levels of alcohol consumption.[7] Although cirrhosis itself can be caused by several factors other than alcohol, the alcohol-related component is responsible for most of the increased death rate in Canada. In 1985, there were 18,000 alcohol-related deaths, or 40 per 100,000 population. The death rate is 2.5 times higher for males than females.

While mortality and potential-years-life-lost (PYLL) to society are of concern, morbidity is an even greater problem. In industry, for instance, losses from reduced productivity and absenteeism due to alcohol abuse are calculated to be in the region of one million dollars daily. In addition, alcohol gives rise to family and social problems. Alcoholism is also one of the leading causes of hospitalization in mental institutions. Overall costs related to alcohol abuse, i.e., health care, law enforcement, social welfare and reduced productivity, in Canada in 1981 were estimated to be $5.25 billion, of which $2 billion was for health care. The cost of law enforcement related to alcohol consumption has been estimated to be $62.5 million.[8]

Along the spectrum of risk there are two defined groups of drinkers in whom problems most often appear. These two groups consist of "problem drinkers" and those who are "alcohol dependent."[6] **Problem drinking** does not always progress to alcohol dependence but is still associated with considerable medical and social consequences. **Alcohol dependence** is physical and psychological. It is characterized by a pattern of alcohol tolerance and symptoms, and progressive loss of control despite obvious harm and social complications. Although the most severe alcohol-related consequences occur in those with alcohol dependence, problem drinking accounts for a larger proportion of alcohol-related illness because it is more prevalent. The prevalence of problem drinkers in family practice settings among patients is estimated to be between 10% and 15%.[6] Problem drinkers consult their physicians twice as often as non-problem drinkers. The use of other psychoactive substances is more likely in a problem drinker or alcohol-dependent person. There are approximately 502,700 Canadians who are alcohol dependent. Five times more men than women are alcohol dependent. Men are at highest risk of becoming alcohol dependant when they are between 35 to 64 years of age, while women are at greatest risk between 45 and 64 years of age. Cirrhosis eventually develops in 5% to 10% of alcohol-dependent men; women, however, appear more susceptible to cirrhosis. Problem drinkers and alcohol-dependent people have higher rates of other diseases and injuries including suicide, cancer and accidents.

Early Detection and Brief Interventions by Health Professionals:

The physician is in a good position to identify problem drinking and alcohol dependence quickly and offer early intervention for those drinking at levels that increase their risks for medical and psychosocial consequences.[9] Good evidence exists for the effectiveness of brief intervention programs for those at an early stage of problem drinking. Efficient approaches include behavioural self-control training (involving goal setting and self-monitoring), controlling the rate of consumption and learning substitutes for drinking behaviour. A potential problem can be identified by asking the patient a few structured questions such as those in the Michigan Alcoholism Screening Test (MAST)[10] or the CAGE questionnaire.[11] Problem drinkers and alcohol-dependent people can visit their physician to have their problem diagnosed and treated appropriately. Many motivated problem drinkers and alcohol-dependent people who want to quit drinking are also being assisted by self-help groups such as Alcoholics Anonymous.

1.2.   HEALTH PROMOTION IN RELATION TO SUBSTANCE ABUSE

It is salutory to note that the majority of Canadians, in fact, have no personal problem with the use of alcohol or other drugs, including tobacco, but there remains the enormous economic burden to society in general and the suffering of those close to the people affected.   It is the goal of federal, provincial and municipal governments to reduce this burden and achieve a substance abuse free environment for all citizens.   While a plethora of information has entered the public arena, it is necessary to restructure the environment to ensure that healthy choices in relation to substance use are the easier choices and are supported by changes in community norms.

The Health Promotion approach provides a framework for drawing together different methods for enhancing, maintaining or regaining the various physical, psychological and social dimensions of health.   It uses a number of policies, services and programs designed to enhance the healthfulness of individuals and their environments, not just the physical but also the social, cultural, and economic environments.[12] The supportiveness of environments is provided by policies and programs that help people to help themselves and build on their strengths. **Effective health promotion programs** should be: a) **comprehensive**, dealing with all environments in which individuals work, live and play, based on the social influences model of health promotion; b) **coordinated** as part of a larger framework, coalition, or partnership working towards the same goal; and c) **participatory**, so that the people involved in behaviour change are actively involved in identifying the problems and designing the programs. Swarbrick's *Model Program for Substance Abuse Prevention* gives a good guide to community participation at all levels of planning for a community program to combat substance abuse.[13]

In order to reduce community influences that encourage drinking and smoking, the following strategies, incorporating education, policies and environmental support, have become established in a number of settings and are being increasingly adopted elsewhere. In the **community at large,** the availability of alcohol and tobacco can be reduced by federal, provincial, and municipal regulatory action. The Tobacco Products Control Act (1988) which was struck down initially but reversed recently by the Supreme Court of Canada is a federal attempt to phase out advertising and promotion of tobacco products, and to regulate warning labels on cigarette packets. This was expected to have reduced the cigarettes consumption. Measures to reduce smoking in minors include enforcement of fines for cigarette sales to minors and supervised use, or outright banning of cigarette vending machines.[14] The recent federal legislation has raised the minimum legal age of persons to whom tobacco products can be sold, from 16 years old to 18 years old; has restricted the location of cigarette vending machines to bars, taverns and similar beverage rooms; and has increased the penalty for selling tobacco to young persons from $100 to a maximum of up to $50,000 for repeated offences. There is an inverse relationship between cigarette smoking in the young and real cigarette prices, which can be controlled by taxation policies. Canadian tobacco taxes used to be the highest, second only to Norway in magnitude. However, with the recent reduction of the federal and provincial taxes the price of cigarettes in most provinces have significantly dropped to half of its original price. This is a retrogressive step in the fight against tobacco use and will have a negative impact on its consumption.

It is established that increases in accessibility to alcohol facilitate a higher rate of consumption, and the converse is also true. Evidence indicates a positive relationship between per capita consumption and alcohol-related diseases. It is known that alcohol consumption is related to its price. In fact, the volume of beer which cost 7% of the average weekly salary in 1944 now costs only 1.5%. This is reflected by the sales of alcoholic beverages which have risen in recent years by as much as 20% to 40%. Measures to counter the widespread availability of alcohol include restricting the availability of alcohol by local licensing provisions for the number and location of outlets, their hours of opening and whether these are enforced; for pricing policies (using taxation); and for drinking ages. For the prevention of alcohol abuse, a number of specific strategies have been directed towards reducing drinking and driving in the community at large and in licensed premises. Integrated drinking and driving plans include licensed premises policies and server training programs; in the latter staff in licensed establishments undergo training to understand the effects of alcohol, to identify persons becoming intoxicated and to take steps to modify the drinking behaviour or other action. Other modalities are designated driver programs and drinking/driving countermeasures. Visible enforcement of blood alcohol concentration (BAC) limits by police spot checks can increase drivers perceived risk of apprehension.

Media campaigns such as "Break Free" (part of the national program to reduce tobacco use,[2] and "Really Me"[15] (part of Canada's Drug Strategy) campaigns have been conducted by the Health Promotion Directorate of the federal government. These health promotion approaches increase substance abuse awareness and reinforce other activities conducted by other partners such as the provinces. "Magnet events," which are events such as youth concerts that appeal to certain segments of the community, in which drug-free messages are displayed, also raise awareness about substance abuse.

School-based policies on alcohol, drugs and smoking can complement integrated education and prevention programs that incorporate quit smoking programs and drug education curricula. Peer-assisted learning is an approach to smoking prevention that utilizes the influence of peers. In post-secondary schools, server intervention, designated driver programs and education programs should also be implemented along with campus policies. In the **home setting,** parents should be encouraged to discuss alcohol and smoking issues and values with children. Educational material supporting smoke-free homes and self-help smoking cessation kits can be introduced into the home. Parents can be educated about quitting smoking and alcohol use. **Workplaces** provide further sites for health promotion policies such as alcohol and smoke-free policies, health programs, quit smoking programs run by trained staff and drinking-driving countermeasure programs. Finally, **the health-care setting** itself can be a useful role model by adopting smoke-free workplace policies, and providing education and smoking cessation support. Early detection and intervention programs for alcohol abuse are the responsibility of health-care providers.

National programs for substance abuse have espoused the principles of health promotion. The objectives are to reduce tobacco use in Canada, protect the health and rights of non-smokers, prevent smoking in the young (especially), and smoking cessation. Canada's Drug Strategy initiative incorporates the concept that reduction of supply through law enforcement is not sufficient and that long-term community-based efforts are needed to control substance abuse. Alcohol is a widely available drug in our community but social norms to support its appropriate use, rather than its abuse, are appearing.

1.3.   DIET

Chapter four, Determinants of Health and Disease, provided information on nutritional status of Canadians. Diet, particularly fat intake, is a major factor in the development of many chronic diseases, including the two leading killers, cardiovascular disease and cancer. Nutrition is also a factor in osteoporosis, chronic liver disease and dental health. Obesity is a risk factor for diabetes and synergistic with other risks for cardiovascular disease (CVD). The following information on dietary risk factors is derived from the Heart Health Surveys.[16] Obesity (BMI over 25 for men and 27 for women), which is associated with an increased risk for CVD, is found in 35% of adult men and 27% of women in Canada. The obese proportion of the population increases with age. There is also cause for concern about the prevalence of underweight people, particularly young women, which can be associated with health problems. In a survey in Ontario, 14 per cent of females between ages 20 to 64 were underweight, this proportion rising to 21% of women aged 20 to 34.[17]

Serum lipids are another risk factor for cardiovascular disease. The majority of CVD deaths occur among people with moderately elevated blood cholesterol (5.2 to 6.2 mmol/L or 200 to 240 mg/dL). A high LDL (low density lipoprotein fraction) is associated with increased risk as are high triglyceride levels. Almost half of adult Canadians (48% of males and 43% of females) fall into the range for elevated cholesterol, while 18% of males and 16% of women have blood cholesterol levels above 6.2 mmol/L (240 mg/dL). For Canadians, 15% had LDL above 4.1 mmol/L, 15% had triglyceride levels above 2.3 mmol/L and 8% had HDL-cholesterol levels below 0.9 mmol/L. These cut off points for lipid levels have been established by the Canadian Consensus Conference on Cholesterol.

Dietary factors are regarded as a major cause of cancer.[18]   International correlations between fat intake and breast cancer have suggested a positive association, as for other cancers such as colorectal and cancer of the prostate. Migrant studies have been supportive. High dietary fat intake has been shown in a number of studies, including a large cohort study, to increase the risk for colorectal cancer. However, following a recent publication from the same cohort study, there was no support for a positive association between dietary fat and breast cancer (Nurses' Health Study).[19] In light of this large study (the second cohort study not supporting the association), the contribution of dietary fat to breast cancer must now be regarded as modest or equivocal.   Eleven out of 16 case-control studies indicate an association and three cohort studies report relative risks ranging from 1.35 (for premenopausal breast cancer) to 1.7.   The evidence for and against this association is well discussed by Howe.[20]

Obesity is strongly associated with endometrial cancer and increases the risk of breast cancer in post-menopausal women; however, increasing evidence suggests that obesity is protective against breast cancer in pre-menopausal women. There is inconsistent evidence that dietary fibre is protective for colorectal cancer. There was a complete lack of protective effect of fibre for breast cancer in the Nurses' Health Study though there is good evidence that cruciferous vegetable consumption is protective. Only 16% of females and 10% of males (overall 13% of Ontarians) were meeting the recommendation from the National Guidelines for Nutrition that no more than 30% of calories in the diet should be derived from fat.[21]

National Guidelines for nutrition have been published by Health and Welfare Canada in the report called **Nutrition Recommendations,**[21] which recommends that the Canadian diet should provide:

- energy consistent with the maintenance of body weight within the recommended range;
- essential nutrients in amounts recommended;
- no more than 30% of energy as fat (33 g/1,000 kcal or 39 g/5,000 kJ) and no more than 10% as saturated fat (11 g/1,000 kcal or 13 g/5,000 kJ);
- no more than 55% of energy as carbohydrate (138 g/1,000 kcal or 165 g/5,000 kJ) from a variety of sources;
- no more than 5% of total energy as alcohol, or two drinks daily, whichever is less;
- no more caffeine than the equivalent of four regular cups of coffee per day;
- a reduction in the sodium content of the Canadian diet; and
- fluoridation of community water supplies containing less than 1 mg/L fluoride to that level.

These dietary guidelines are appropriate for the prevention of colorectal and other dietary-related cancers with two added recommendations. They are: (i) consume a variety of green and yellow vegetables, tubers, citrus fruits, and whole grains and cereals; and (ii) minimize the contamination of foods with carcinogens from any source (e.g., barbecuing).

The Epp framework strategies (creating healthy environments, re-orienting health services and increasing prevention) can be applied to improving diets and reducing the burden of illness which follows, in particular, the excessive intake of saturated fats. In encouraging healthy eating, for example, action should be directed to the **community at large**, involving the media and community organizations in promoting healthy eating campaigns. Healthy food policies in **schools** can be introduced by healthy choices among cafeteria items. Individuals and families can receive educational material to promote healthy eating habits in **home** environments. In **restaurants** and **supermarkets**, labelling the content (especially fat) of grocery and menu items facilitates healthy choices at point-of-purchase. Finally, similar strategies can be implemented in **workplaces** and **health-care settings**.[22] Nutrition action should also include **policy** and **regulatory** changes to agricultural, marketing and trade practices, designed to facilitate more widely-available healthy choices of food.

2.   SPECIFIC DISEASES

2.1.   CARDIOVASCULAR DISEASE

Since the first national mortality statistics were published in 1921, cardiovascular disease (CVD) has been the leading cause of death in Canada, accounting for nearly half of all deaths each year. Although mortality rates from cardiovascular disease have declined in recent times, it still poses a major burden.[23,24] In 1988, 78,383 Canadians died from CVD, 14% more than cancer, the second leading cause of death. CVD is a broad term covering a number of diseases of the circulatory system. The most common forms of CVD are ischemic or coronary heart disease (IHD), particularly acute myocardial infarctions ("heart attacks"), and cerebrovascular disease (CBVD or stroke). Ischemic heart disease and CBVD accounted for over 60,626 deaths, with IHD representing one-quarter of all deaths. Incidence of CVD increases dramatically with age. In the 25 to 44, 45 to 64 and 65 years and over age groups, CVD accounts for 13.5%, 33% and 48% of all deaths respectively. The rates for women are almost half those of men, except for stroke where the rates are approximately equal. The probability of a male aged less than 75 dying from an acute myocardial infarction is 10.2%; for a woman of the same age group 5.3%. This risk increases dramatically for females over 75, less so for males. Premature death from cardiovascular disease (before age 70) is the leading cause of potential life lost (200,000 years).   There is an inverse relationship between socioeconomic class and incidence of CVD. The lower the socioeconomic level, the higher the incidence of cardiovascular disease. A general trend of higher to lower CVD rates from the eastern to western provinces exists. With 77% of all CVD deaths attributable to IHD and CBVD, these two manifestations have been the target of much research in the areas of public policy, screening for risk factors and clinical interventions.

Currently, IHD and CBVD account for approximately 8.5 million days of hospitalization (11.5% of all admissions). It is estimated that almost 10% (20.4 million) of all visits to physicians each year are for cardiovascular disease. As greater numbers of Canadians enter the 55 to 74 year age group it is anticipated that increases in coronary artery bypass grafting (CABG) and related procedures will occur. Currently the rate of CABG and angioplasties is highest in this age group (289/100,000). Prescription drugs for management of cardiovascular disease account for 12.1% of all prescriptions dispensed in Canada. The economic impact is high, comprising 21% ($16.8 billion) of the costs of disease in Canada. Direct costs account for $5.2 billion; indirect costs, largely due to premature mortality and disability, more than double this amount ($11.6 billion). Twenty-six per cent of Canada Pension Plan disability payments were for CVDs, largely IHD. An estimated 13% of the health-care dollar in Ontario is spent on CVD-related health services. With this kind of impact, socially and economically, the burden of CVD deserves much attention from physicians and Canadians in general.

The underlying cause of CVD is atherosclerosis. Factors contributing to atherosclerosis include smoking, high blood pressure, obesity, diabetes, lack of physical activity, high levels of dietary fat, elevated total cholesterol and low density lipoprotein (LDL) cholesterol, and genetic factors. The role of apolipoproteins, especially apoprotein b, in predisposing genetically to cardiovascular disease is currently being elucidated. The prevalence of these risk factors throughout the Canadian population varies among age, sex, social class, regions and cultural groups.

While CVD is still the leading cause of death, there has been an encouraging decline in CVD mortality rates since the mid-1960s (about 2% per year). The 1988 death rates are almost half those in 1969. The CVD age-standardized mortality rates (ASMRs) per 100,000 population (standardized to the 1981 Canadian population) have shown a steady decline. This decline has been more pronounced in men than in women. However, international comparisons indicate that age-standardized mortality rates from cardiovascular disease in some countries, e.g., Japan and France, are more favourable than in Canada, with consequent diminished burdens of premature death. In the mid-1980s, Japan's ASMR for cardiovascular disease deaths was 174/100,000 deaths, and for France, 210/100,000, compared to a rate of 265/100,000 in Canada. (All figures for international comparisons are standardized to 1976 world population). Of the CBVD component (mainly strokes) of cardiovascular disease mortality in Canada, the ASMRs began a steady decline in the 1960s, whereas the ASMRs for IHD gradually rose until the late 1960s; they started a rapid decline in the early 1970s. For males and females together, the ASMRs for IHD per 100,000 were 46 in 1950, 131 in 1960, 235 in 1970, 179 in 1980, and 134 in 1988.[25]

Although age and sex cannot be altered, other CVD risk factors—high blood pressure, obesity, smoking, and serum cholesterol—amenable to preventive health practices. Data on the prevalence of risk factors have been provided by provincial heart health surveys (except in Ontario) carried out from 1986-1990, as part of a federal-provincial Canadian Heart Health Initiative.[16] These surveys found that two-thirds of Canadians (64% of males and 63% of females aged 18 to 74) have at least one major cardiovascular risk factors (i.e., **smoking, hypertension** and a **high blood cholesterol** level). The prevalence of multiple risk factors, which are synergistic in increasing risk, was highest in the 45 to 54 year old males (34%) and the 65 to 74 year old females (37%). Higher prevalence of these risk factors was noted with lower socioeconomic level, and awareness of having a risk factor was lowest for those with the least years of education. Among 16% of men and 13% of women, the diastolic blood pressure was 90 mm Hg or greater, or they were on antihypertensive treatment. Just over one-quarter of this group were unaware that they were hypertensive. Quebec has the highest prevalence of smokers (33%), while British Columbia has the lowest (22%).

2.1.1. Community-Wide Approaches to Heart Health

The decline in cardiovascular mortality in Canada has been attributed, in part, to the reduction in the prevalence of smoking, reduced consumption of dietary fat, improved detection and management of hypertension, as well as improved surgical approaches to treatment of symptomatic heart disease. The current widespread prevalence of risk factors is, however, still of concern. Many Canadians, particularly those over 55, have not been persuaded to adopt a "healthy" lifestyle which includes regular checkups for CVD risk factors, as well as attention to diet, physical exercise and tobacco use reduction. Physicians have played a less than optimal role in risk factor identification and reduction. This situation led to an expressed need for a public health strategy to reduce CVD mortality in Canada.[6]

Regular screening for high blood pressure among adults should become part of the periodic health examination. Readers, however, are advised to refer to a number of recent documents which outline the recommendations and some controversies related to clinical preventive services, particularly in relation to screening for elevated cholesterol.[26-28] Although a relationship has been established between high total cholesterol levels in populations and CVD mortality, cholesterol screening has, in fact, poor test characteristics of sensitivity and specificity, as well as a low predictive value for most individuals. In the Framingham study, the level of cholesterol in the individual did not discriminate between those who would subsequently develop coronary heart disease and those who did not. Additionally, the lack of feasibility and efficiency of mass screening has been presented as a strong counter-argument[29] to the initial recommendation that, as resources permit, determination of lipid risk factors should become part of the periodic health examination for all adult Canadians.[9] The total cost of implementing such a program in the first year, given a prevalence of 53.5% for moderate- and high-risk cholesterol elevations among cardiovascular symptom-free Canadians, was estimated at approximately $500 million. Although these estimates are likely too high, given the prevalence of moderate hypercholesterolemia found in the provincial heart health surveys, it provides an order of magnitude of the costs for laboratory tests and physician visits in a mass screening program. The Ontario Ministry of Health, and the Ontario Medical Association recommended, given the diminishing returns of widespread screening, a high-risk strategy of detection and treatment of those already with cardiovascular symptoms or risk factors, coupled with encouragement of community-wide dietary and lifestyle changes. The Canadian Consensus Conference on Cholesterol recommends screening for blood cholesterol for:

- patients known to have coronary heart disease;
- patients with a family history of hyperlipidemia or early onset of coronary heart disease (heart attack in a parent, grandparent, brother or sister before age 60 years);
- patients with hypertension, diabetes mellitus, renal failure or obesity, especially abdominal obesity;

It should be noted that two large clinical trials have now demonstrated the benefit of drug treatment in reducing total serum cholesterol, or its subfractions, to prevent or delay the onset of coronary heart disease in middle-aged men with very high total cholesterol levels. A note of caution, however: in both single and multiple risk factor reduction trials, cardiovascular mortality has been reduced, but overall mortality has, in fact, been higher in those subjects in whom preventive interventions were given.[30]

Community-based models for primary (and secondary) prevention of heart disease, utilizing many of the health promotion strategies described in chapter one, have been promulgated, following the demonstration of their effectiveness for reducing cardiovascular risk in populations in a number of studies.[31,32] Some limitations in evaluating community effectiveness mentioned in chapter two should be borne in mind. The earliest project was undertaken from 1972-1982 in North Karelia, Finland, which had one of the highest cardiovascular mortality rates in the world. The intervention strategies were based on the Behaviour-Change Model, the Communication-Behaviour Change Model, the Innovation-Diffusion Model and the Community Organization Model, as described in chapter one. In the "experimental" community of North Karelia, efforts were directed towards reducing the cardiovascular risk factors of serum lipids, diet, cigarette smoking and diastolic hypertension. The strategies were awareness-raising by media, educational activities, training for local personnel and active community groups, community organization activities, organization of health services, monitoring feedback, and management activities. The evaluation after 10 years indicated statistically significant declines in males of the prevalence of smoking (28% reduction), hypercholesterolemia (3%) and systolic hypertension (3%). There were nonsignificant declines in women for smoking (14%), and cholesterol (1%) but significant for systolic hypertension (5%). During the study period, between 1974 and 1979, the cardiovascular mortality rate in North Karelia dropped by 24% in comparison to the general Finish population where it declined 12%.

The Stanford Three-City and Five-Community studies have provided information on the effectiveness of intensive mass media campaigns, particularly for the initial Three-City study (1972-1975), where significant positive effects were found on all physiological variables except weight. The expanded Five-City study utilized a fuller range of strategies as indicated above and found a 15% reduction in the logistic risk regression score for all mortality and 16% for cardiovascular mortality.[31,32]

These models have provided the basis for the Heart Health initiative currently undertaken by Health and Welfare Canada in partnership with the provinces.[33] This initiative involves a commitment to the development of a **database** on cardiovascular risk factors (previously described), implementation of **provincial heart health demonstration programs**, and **diffusion** of the findings. The initiatives are being co-ordinated by departments of public health, due to their population-based (rather than high-risk) approach. They recognize the importance of social and other environmental changes that will make healthy choices easier under the rubric of the Epp health promotion framework, the appropriate referral of those detected with risk factors for follow up, and building community-based partnerships. The initiatives are multidisciplinary, intersectoral, and part of broader health promotion programs involving multiple strategies at multiple sites. A "Declaration on Heart Health"[34] issued by the Advisory Board at the International Heart Health Conference in Victoria, British Columbia, in May 1992, was intended to give a sense of urgency to the prevention and control of the most important cause of death in most of the world's countries. The Declaration affirmed that effective, and widely tested methods to prevent cardiovascular disease exist, and called for their translation into action that incorporates Heart Health into daily life. The call to initiate and support prevention directed at the entire population is made to many segments of society: health; education; social science professionals and their associations; government agencies concerned with health, education, trade, commerce and agriculture; the private sector; community health coalitions; voluntary organizations; employers; and the media.

Application of the community-based population-wide approaches, backed by research within the framework of health promotion developed in Canada, can be expected to reduce the prevalence of risk factors for cardiovascular disease. Trends in prevalence of some risk factors, such as smoking, are encouraging. Actions to improve diet by fat reduction and to encourage active lifestyles are important strategies that need more attention.

2.2.   CANCER

In 1991, cancer ranked second overall as a leading cause of death.   Among children, cancer ranked fourth.   Cancer deaths constituted 27% of all deaths for 1991.[35]   In 1992, cancer was the leading cause of PYLL, followed closely by heart disease.   More than one in three Canadians will develop some form of cancer in their lifetime.   Up until the age of 55 years, cancer incidence and mortality is about equal in both males and females, and increases gradually.   After 55 years of age, both male and female rates begin to rise at a faster rate; however, the male rate increases more sharply.   For those born in 1985, the three most likely cancers males will develop over a lifetime are lung (9.0%), prostate (8.5%) and colorectal (6.5%).   For women, they are breast (10%), colorectal (7%) and lung (3.5%).[35] There are higher rates of oropharyngeal, lung and bladder cancer in Quebec (likely related to higher incidence of smoking), stomach cancer in Newfoundland (correlating with more frequent intake of smoked fish) and higher rates of melanoma in B.C. (possibly related to greater sunlight exposure).   The incidence of all cancers increased by 1% per year for men and 0.7% for women between 1981 and 1987.   The mortality rate increased annually by 0.6% among men and 0.5% among women between 1981 and 1989.

In terms of the morbidity burden, cancer was responsible for 5% of the total 3.6 million hospitalizations in 1984-85, and 8% of the total hospital days.   The average length of hospitalization for a cancer patient (18 days) was one week longer than the overall average length of stay.[36] Cancer was the third most costly component of health care in 1986, with $2 billion in direct costs and $7.1 billion in indirect costs contributing to the $9.1 billion total cost.   The amount of indirect costs indicates the enormous burden on society.[37]

A prognostic indicator for cancer is the ratio of deaths to cases.   Overall, excluding non-melanoma skin cancer, the ratio was 51% (from estimated figures for Canada in 1992).   Prognosis for individual cancers varies from **poor** (ratios greater than 66% for lung, stomach, pancreas and brain cancers), to **fair** (ratios 33% to 66% for colorectal, lymphoma, kidney, leukemia, ovarian cancers) to **very good** (ratios less than 33% for breast, prostate, bladder, oral, melanoma, uterus, cervical cancers).   There has been a steady decline in mortality for childhood cancers due to improved treatment of lymphoma and leukemia.   Despite some improvement during the 1970s and 1980s, the relative five-year survival for women after cancer diagnosis in B.C. (1980-1984) was only 54%; and for men, 45%.   Once diagnosed with cancer, chances are about one in two that a person will die from the disease within five years.   Despite the advances and the better outlook for some cancers, the prognosis overall remains unfavourable and emphasis must be on prevention and care rather than cure.

Most common causes of cancer deaths in Canada were outlined in table 5.1 (chapter five).   While a few cancers may be associated with inherited genetic factors (e.g., polyposis of the colon and the inherited form of retinoblastoma), environmental factors such as water and air quality, diet and lifestyle are considered important determinants. The latter two are the most important. Smoking and alcohol are two lifestyle habits which play major roles in a number of non-occupational cancers where multiple factors may be responsible. Variations in cancer rates in immigrants indicate possible environmental effects in the development of some neoplasms. Proportional mortality rates for cancer of the stomach and lung in Ontario show a gradient for different generations for immigrants from the same country. The highest rates are for the immigrants, intermediate for the first generation and lowest for the second generation. Some change in lifestyle, dietary patterns or other environmental exposure may be responsible for the observed shift in rates. Exposures to high concentrations of certain chemicals in the occupational environment are associated with cancer. For example, asbestos and chromite ore inhalation are associated with carcinoma of the lung, and benzidine and beta-naphthylamine with bladder cancer (see chapter ten).

2.2.1. General Framework for Cancer Control

An excellent planning framework for cancer control strategies in Canada has been contributed by Miller (1992)[38] and on the basis of this, specific strategies for leading cancer sites proposed (table 7.1). This framework could also be usefully applied to control of other chronic disease. The steps are the following:

(a) Assessing the current situation: (i) determine the relative importance of cancer to other diseases; (ii) determine the relative importance of different cancer sites; (iii) identify differences between provinces in the range of indicators, as well as differences between Canada and other countries. (Indicators may include: number of cancer cases diagnosed (incidence); number of deaths from cancer; survival; sex-ratio; cumulative incidence to give risk over the age range cumulated; premature mortality; trends); and (iv) determine the availability of resources for cancer control.

(b) Setting objectives for cancer control: (i) reduction in morbidity from cancer; (ii) reduction in mortality from cancer; and (iii) improvement of the quality of life of cancer patients.

(c) Evaluating possible strategies

(d) Setting priorities using quantitative assessments: (i) determine the potential effectiveness of different strategies; (ii) determine the potential cost of different strategies; (iii) determine the cost-effectiveness of all different and competing strategies; (iv) modify the priority for action on the basis of other considerations; and (v) monitor trends in disease to evaluate effectiveness of strategies.

2.2.2. Strategies for Site-Specific Cancer Control

Secondary and tertiary prevention are highly developed for certain cancers. The Pap smear allows cervical cancer to be picked up in the early stages and improves

Table 7.1: Estimates of Potential Effects of Prevention or Early Detection on Cancer Incidence

Cancer Site	Action	Incidence Reduction PAR (a) (%)	Potentially Preventable (%)
Lung	Eliminate smoking	90	60
	Reduce occupational exposure to carcinogens	20	
Colorectal	Reduce fat and increase vegetable consumption	60	77
Breast	Reduce fat and increase vegetable consumption	27	70
	Reduce obesity (postmenopausal women)	12	
	Screen women aged 50 to 69	25 (b)	
Prostate	Reduce fat consumption	20	78
Lymphoma	Reduce exposure to herbicides and pesticides	?	86
Bladder	Eliminate smoking and reduce dietary cholesterol	60	73
	Reduce occupational exposure to carcinogens	27	
Body of the uterus	Reduce obesity	30	82
	Protective effect of oral contraceptives (ages 20-54)	28	
Stomach	Reduce nitrite in cured meats and salt-preserved foods, and increase fruit and vegetable consumption	80	52
Leukemia	Reduce exposure to radiation and benzene	?	70
Oral, etc.	Eliminate smoking and reduce alcohol consumption	80	68
	Increase fruit and vegetable consumption	10	
Pancreas	Eliminate smoking	40	64
	Reduce sugar and increase vegetable consumption	30	
Melanoma of the skin	Reduce unprotected exposure to sunlight	20	77
Kidney	Eliminate smoking	40	67
	Reduce fat consumption	30	
Brain	Reduce occupational exposure to carcinogens	?	70
Ovary	Reduce fat consumption	30	53
	Protective effect of oral contraceptives (ages 20-54)	26	
Cervix	Eliminate smoking	23	62
	Encourage use of barrier contraceptives	?	
	Screen women aged 20 to 69	60	

(a) PAR = Population Attributable Risk. Estimates are for males, except for breast, body of uterus, ovarian and cervical cancer.
(b) Indicates effect is on mortality, not incidence
(?) Signifies no estimate of effect is available

Source: Reproduced from Miller AB, Planning Cancer Control Stategies, Chronic Diseases in Canada 13(1): S36, 1992.

the five-year survival rate for women. Since the etiology of most cancers is unknown, emphasis on secondary and tertiary prevention is more appropriate at the present time. The exception is primary prevention against smoking. Specific strategies for control of individual cancers prioritized in accordance with the framework proposed by Miller are discussed in the following section.

Lung cancer

Based on all the indicators previously described, lung cancer is the number one priority. Ninety per cent of lung cancer in males, and almost the same proportion in females, is related to smoking. Passive exposure to smoke almost certainly increases the risk of lung cancer. The actual risk from exposure to radon in homes is under study, although radon has been identified in less than one per cent of Canadian homes (see chapter nine). Occupational exposures to asbestos and radiation in hard rock mining increase the risk of lung cancer. Proposed methods of early detection (such as sputum cytology, frequent chest X-rays) do not reduce mortality. No more than 10% of cases with the disease are cured; this does not appear likely to improve.

Colorectal Cancer

In terms of incidence and mortality, this cancer ranks second in Canada, although it is the third leading cause of premature cancer mortality. Diet, particularly saturated fat intake, has been linked to increased risk for this cancer. Consumption of fresh fruits and vegetables may have a protective effect. Beer drinking increases the risk of colorectal cancer. Miller suggests that 60% or more of colorectal cancer can be prevented through dietary modification. There is no firm evidence recommending early detection by the fecal occult blood test for the general population. Those with a family history of polyposis should be under clinical surveillance. The five-year survival rate from colorectal cancer in Saskatchewan is 49% in both sexes.

Breast Cancer

Breast cancer is the leading cause of premature mortality from cancer in females. Risk factors which are largely non-preventable and contribute to 17% of breast cancer include the age at first childbirth, parity, age at menarche, age at menopause and whether artificial menopause was performed. Dietary fat makes a modest contribution to breast cancer.[19] Obesity is a risk factor for postmenopausal breast cancer. Prolonged course of estrogens at the time of menopause increases risk of breast cancer. For oral contraceptives, however, an overall cost-benefit analysis indicates that the benefits likely outweigh the risks.

Recommendations for primary prevention of cancer through diet have been given in the preceding sections. Although the dietary association between fat and breast cancer may be more modest than previously postulated, a small but highly prevalent increased risk may have major impact on morbidity on a population basis. Additionally, dietary fat is a risk factor for colorectal cancer and ischemic heart disease, and its reduction in diet is not harmful.   Therefore, prudent population-based approaches to improving nutrition would follow the previously recommended guidelines.   Alcohol has been reported as a risk factor for breast cancer in a number of studies, and sensible use of this drug is encouraged in women.   A little over one-third of women with diagnosed breast cancer die of their disease.

Most studies in women aged over 50 have demonstrated that early detection of breast cancer by mammography every one to three years results in reduction of mortality in women aged 50 to 70.   The cost-effectiveness of screening in this age group compares favourably with other medical procedures.   The effectiveness of screening in those aged 40 to 49 years was investigated by a large randomized controlled trial in the National Breast Screening Study.[39]   In women under 50, there was no benefit in reducing mortality from breast cancer, from screening with yearly mammography and physical examination of the breasts (at least in the first seven years after screening was initiated).   In women aged 50 to 59 years, there was no impact on mortality from breast cancer (at least for seven years) compared with physical examination alone, although more tumours were detected.   Recommendations for mass screening programs, to be undertaken according to provincial policies, were made by a Workshop Group in 1989, cosponsored by Health and Welfare Canada, the Canadian Cancer Society and the NCIC, at the request of the Conference of Federal-Provincial Deputy Ministers.[40]   Screening programs have been established in five provinces: Nova Scotia, Ontario, Saskatchewan, Alberta and British Columbia.   Most direct their programs to women 50 and over; however, the program in B.C. notably includes women 40 to 49.

Prostate Cancer

Prostate cancer is fourth in terms of incidence and deaths. It is not, however, a major cause of premature cancer deaths, ranking ninth in PYLL.   Dietary fat is considered to play some causative role despite inconsistent evidence, and hence, dietary fat reduction can be recommended.   Hormonal treatment reduces symptoms and appears to prolong life.

Early detection of prostate cancer is a controversial subject.   The present available methods of screening are digital rectal examination (DRE), transrectal prostatic ultrasonography (TRUS) and serology for prostate specific antigen (PSA).   The Canadian Task Force on Periodic Health Examinations recommends DRE in men over 40 years of age.

Leukemias

These are a heterogeneous group.   They represent the leading cancers in children. Radiation, occupational exposure to benzene, and viruses (HTLV-I and II) are known causes.   However, it is unlikely that control of currently known causes would prevent more than a fraction of these diseases.

Cancer of the Uterine Cervix

Cancer of the cervix now ranks only 16th for number of cases and deaths in Canada and 14th in terms of premature mortality. This is due to Pap test screening programs. A number of reviews have indicated that screening is effective in reducing incidence and mortality. However, more attention is necessary in relation to the appropriateness of screening and the organizational aspects, particularly quality assurance.[41] Some groups, such as women of the Aboriginal Peoples, have not benefited. Canadian programs lack two of the elements of a screening program considered essential: measures to ensure high coverage and attendance, such as a personal letter of invitation, and identification of individual women in the target population for screening. Current recommendations for the frequency of screening advises that all women aged over 18 who have had sexual intercourse should be encouraged to enter a cervical screening program and be rescreened every three years until age 69. Women over age 69 who have had normal cytology and at least two satisfactory smears in the last nine years can discontinue the program.

Cancer of the cervix is strongly associated with early age at first intercourse and multiple sex partners. There is evidence to suggest that human papilloma virus (HPV) infections of the cervix may cause cervical cancer; however, epidemiological evidence is not as yet confirmatory. Safer sex practices can be recommended in general.

2.3. RESPIRATORY DISEASES

In 1991, respiratory diseases ranked third and fourth among men and women respectively as leading causes of death. The overall respiratory disease death rate per 100,000 population was 67.9 for males and 45.0 for females. There is a J-shaped curve to the age-specific mortality rates for both sexes. In the age group under one year, rates for respiratory disease were 15.3 and 16.1 per 100,000 population for males and females, respectively. In 1987, between the ages of one and 44 years, the respiratory disease death rate was below 3.5 per 100,000 population.[42] After the age of 45, the rates increase dramatically from 13.5 for males and 7.8 for females in the 45 to 54 year age group to 1282.6 for men and 610.4 for women in the 75 years and older age group. The 75 and older age group, although small in number, also had the largest number of deaths caused by respiratory disease (9,398 in total) during 1987.

There has been a substantial decrease in cardiopulmanary disease (COPD) mortality rates in children 0 to 4 years old since 1950-54, when they were 5.43 and 4.47 for males and females respectively. In 1980-84, the infant COPD mortality rates had dropped to 0.56 for males and 0.43 for females. In contrast to this decline, the COPD mortality rates per 100,000 population for people over 65 years of age in 1980-84 were approximately double what the rates were for the same age group in 1950-54.[42] Much of this increase, as in the case of lung cancer rates, can be attributed to the increased number of regular smokers in recent times. In 1985-86, respiratory disease, in total, ranked fifth in hospitalization days and third in hospital separations. COPD is the only leading cause of death which is increasing in incidence.

Important factors influencing respiratory disease mortality rates that have been identified include smoking (active and passive) and indoor-outdoor air pollution (see chapter nine). While smoking is considered to be an important risk factor for frequency and severity of respiratory illness, air pollution levels in a number of Canadian communities have also been found to affect hospital admissions for respiratory diseases.[43] Important particulates are oxidants and oxides of nitrogen.[44] Second-hand smoke also contributes to the level of nitrogen oxides in closed environments.[45] While both pollutants are associated with increased admission rates for upper respiratory infections, bronchitis appears to be related to oxides of nitrogen. Increased respiratory cancer rates have been observed in the city of Hamilton, Ontario, coincident with accelerated steel production over a 30-year period. Furthermore, the numbers affected decreased as residence became more distant from the steel plants.

Pollutants interact, and their combined effect on disease may be either additive or multiplicative (smoking and asbestos combined has a multiplicative effect). To keep individual pollutant levels in the environment within accepted limits is not enough, since the combined effects of such pollutants may be producing disease. Also the permitted limits may not be adhered to throughout the year. Yassi and Friesen[44] remarked that oxidant levels in major Canadian cities were often over the limits in 1988.

Approaches to prevention and cessation of smoking have been discussed above in the section on substance abuse. Health promotion in relation to air pollution has been discussed in chapter nine. More research is needed into pollutants and their effects, alone and combined, on human health. Primary prevention in this area is not as straightforward as it appears.

2.4.   CONGENITAL AND GENETIC DISEASES

Success in the prevention and treatment of childhood infectious diseases has reduced infant mortality rates to a level where congenital anomalies are now the second leading cause of death in infants (30% of all infant deaths). Among 1 to 14 year olds, it is the third leading cause of death (11.5% of all deaths). The most common malformations leading to infant death were due to defects of the heart and circulatory system. Approximately 3% of newborn children have a serious congenital anomaly.[46] Congenital heart defects are the most common congenital anomalies with an incidence rate of 80 to 100 per 10,000 live births. The incidence rate per 10,000 births in Ontario for the most common congenital anomalies were: 11.5 for cleft lip/palate, 9.7 for hypo/epispadias, 8.3 for spina bifida, 6.5 for anencephaly, 4.6 for Down's syndrome, and 4.2 for hydrocephalus.

Etiological factors for malformations include hereditary or familial tendencies, and non to genetic factors such as maternal diabetes mellitus, anticonvulsant drug use during pregnancy, and maternal infection with herpes, syphilis, rubella, toxoplasmosis and cytomegalovirus. Other etiological factors associated with congenital anomalies are nutritional deficiencies,[47] exposure to external environmental agents[48] and those related to personal lifestyles.[49,50]

There are now more than 200 known genetic and metabolic disorders. Many of these can be diagnosed prenatally. Some of these can cause mental retardation, for example, phenylketonuria. Many of these diseases are preventable with proper counselling in susceptible populations. Certain genetic disorders have high frequencies in various ethnic groups which make up part of the Canadian mosaic; thalassemia, for example, occurs once in every 25 Italian births; Tay-Sachs disease affects about one in every 1,000 births to Ashkenazi Jews and phenylketonuria has an incidence of one in 10,000 live Caucasian births. Five per cent of Caucasians are carriers for cystic fibrosis. Selective screening and genetic counselling in susceptible populations is probably the most appropriate form of primary prevention.

A number of prenatal screening methods detect congenital malformations or chromosomal abnormalities.[51] They are chorionic villus sampling, amniocentesis, fetoscopy and ultrasound examination. Chorionic villus sampling provides the earliest available fetal screen at eight to 12 weeks; however, it requires considerable technical skill. Termination of pregnancy at this early stage (first trimester) is much easier for the woman. Amniocentesis, the most widely-used method, is usually done at 15 to 16 weeks; it is associated with a less than 1% risk of miscarriage. Fetoscopy can be used to check for fetal malformations at 17 to 18 weeks, during which one can also obtain a blood sample. The final method is ultrasonography (ultrasound examination). Although this method requires a high level of skill to do well and can only identify structural abnormalities, it offers the dual advantages of being non-invasive and giving immediate results. Neonatal screening for metabolic disorders such as phenylketonuria and hypothyroidism are widely used.

3. INJURY

An estimated one in five Canadians had at least one accident in 1987.[52] Injuries were second only to cardiovascular diseases in total costs to society in 1986, accounting for $11 billion in expenditures, indirect costs contributing $6.4 billion.[37] Pensions and benefits made up over half (57%) of the total direct costs, more than any other category. Motor vehicle accidents accounted for one-third of incidents reported in the 1987 survey, and were responsible for 6.3% of future income lost due to premature mortality in 1986. Sports or leisure activity accidents were the next most frequent (23%) and largely occurred to males aged 15 to 34. These were followed by work-related accidents (21%) and accidents in or around the home (10%), frequently falls. Injuries are classified as non-intentional (previously termed as accidents), and intentional (homicide and suicide, predominantly). Accident rates tend to be higher in the western provinces.

Injuries are the leading cause of death during the first half of the human life span and the second to cancer as a leading cause of PYLL. In terms of economic burden, they are among the top four, with indirect costs as high as for cardiovascular disease. They are the leading cause of death of children aged under five, school-aged children and of young adults. In Canada, six children are killed every day as a result of injury. From the age of one to 24, injury is responsible for 63% of all deaths. The causes in younger children are falls at home—particularly in the living room from couches onto coffee tables and "roughhousing"—poisoning, and motor vehicle accidents as a passenger or pedestrian. For school-aged children bicycle accidents are responsible for 14% of injury-related deaths; three-quarters involve head injury. Falls are an important cause of injury in the elderly, especially fractured neck of femur in elderly women. Thirty-five per cent of deaths in Aboriginals are due to violence. The leading causes of death in Aboriginals are intentional and non-intentional injury, the latter most frequently due to boating accidents, drowning and poisoning. Occupational injuries are responsible for 96% of Workers' Compensation costs. Back complaints represent 15% of these injuries.

An injury surveillance system involving 13 reporting hospitals in 1990, The Children's Hospital Injury Research and Prevention Project (CHIRPP), has been set up in Canada and is obtaining information on the nature and circumstances related to injuries. The deaths from injury are only the tip of the iceberg in relation to their total impact. It is estimated that for every death there are 45 injuries that involve hospital admission, 1,300 visits to the emergency room and an unknown number of untreated injuries. Accidents reported in the General Social Survey in 1988 resulted in personal injury to 79% of victims, hospital care for 45%, activity-loss days for nearly 80% and financial loss for half this proportion. The activity-loss days amounted to 51 million days in 1987, and additional consequences were nine million bed-disability days and two million days in hospital. Nearly two-thirds of work accidents resulted in hospital care; these commonly occurred in those aged 25 to 44. Spine and back injuries comprised 39% of these work injuries. Occupational accidents are described in chapters five and 10.

The following sections give specific details on the major causes of non-intentional injury (motor vehicle accidents), followed by intentional injuries.

3.1. NON-INTENTIONAL INJURY

3.1.1. Motor Vehicle Accidents

The highest percentage of PYLL arises from fatal motor vehicle accidents since mortality from this cause occurs primarily in the young.   Among males and females, in 1987, motor vehicle accidents (MVA) accounted for 31% (3,090) and 28.9% (1,249) of all accidental and violent deaths respectively (9,882 for males and 5,846 for females).[53] The MVA death rate per 100,000 population has declined from 43 to 24 for males and from 15 to 8 for females, in the time period 1966 to 1987 respectively.   The MVA death rates per 100,000 population in 1987 were highest in the 15 to 24 year age group (50.5 for males and 14.6 for females), and the 75 years and older age group (34.0 for males, 16.9 for females).   Accidents including MVA are also a major cause of hospitalization.   Accidents have been the leading cause of hospitalization among people under 45 years of age for at least the last three decades.   In 1985, MVAs accounted for 15% and 11% of accident-related hospital discharges for males and females respectively.[54]   During 1985, motor vehicle accidents ranked second behind falls in accident-related hospital discharges for males, and third behind falls in the adverse effects of therapeutic drugs for females.

Important risk factors for MVA include the mental attitude and condition of the driver, the design and condition of the vehicle, road design and conditions, and seat belt usage.   Primary preventive methods would therefore include environmental as well as individual measures.   Driving while intoxicated is considered a major factor in accidents.   In 1988, 17% of Canadians aged 16 to 69, an estimated three million adult Canadians, reported driving after having two or more drinks in the preceding hour.   This figure represents 24%—about one-quarter—of those who say they are both drinkers and drivers.   Men are three times more likely than women to report driving after drinking (26% compared to 8%).   They also do it more often; 17% of men report having driven after drinking on three or more occasions in the past month, compared to 9% of women.   Younger Canadians are more likely to drive after drinking than are their older counterparts; 23% of those under 35 years have driven after drinking in the past year, compared to 13% of people aged 45 to 54.   The likelihood that single people and those in higher income groups will drive after drinking is also quite high; almost one-quarter of those in each category report having done so.[55]

Drinking has been implicated in a large proportion of fatal road accidents.   Of 747 automobile drivers killed in road accidents in eight provinces during 1985, 79% had a blood alcohol level of above 80 mg/100 mL (i.e., were legally impaired).[56] Most of the drinking and driving occurs at night.   Surveys conducted in Ontario, Quebec, Manitoba and Saskatchewan during 1986/87 found the night-time prevalence of impaired drivers (i.e., blood level over 80 g/100 mL) to be highest in Manitoba (5.3%) and lowest in Quebec and Saskatchewan (3.6%).[57] Drinking while impaired by alcohol, among night-time drivers, is most common in the 25 to 39 year age group (4.1% to 8.5%), except in Quebec where the highest rate is seen in the 40 to 59 year age group. Impaired drivers are over-represented in MVA and are less likely to wear seatbelts. In the 1988 General Social Survey, 42% of current drinkers reported having an accident in the three years prior to the survey compared to 27% of non-drinkers, and there was a direct relationship between the consumption and accident prevalence. There was a 60% higher risk of accidents in males drinking more than seven drinks a week. Roadside testing for blood alcohol levels has had a limited effect on the prevalence of impaired driving. More effort is needed to eliminate drinking and driving.

Non-Intentional Injury Prevention

It is important to recognize that a major attitudinal change is necessary in order to prevent injuries. That is, injuries just don't happen by chance or "accidentally," but in most cases are preventable. There are usually circumstances in which action could be taken in advance to prevent or minimize the extent of damage. A useful framework has been provided by **Haddon** in which non-intentional injuries are conceptualized as resulting from interactions between **host** (person), **agent** or **vector** (e.g., a car), and **environment**. Interventions directed to any factor may reduce the onset or extent of injury sustained. Injury occurs when forces beyond the capability of the organism to withstand are applied. In this model, success of injury prevention depends on the degree of passivity of the measure (therefore requiring minimal effort) and deterrents and incentives. A modification of the Haddon matrix concept for public health to incorporate the concept of behavioural components and health education, affecting predisposing beliefs and attitudes about accidents, safety enabling factors, and reinforcing policies and actions that can be adopted, has been developed by Gielen. Interested readers are advised to review this approach.[58]

Preventive injury interventions are visualized as a two-dimensional matrix in which pre-injury, time of impact and post-injury preventive measures may be taken in relation to the person, agent causing injury or the environment. In the pre-injury phase attention should be directed to the elimination of the source of the energy, reduction of exposure to the energy or reduction of the magnitude of resistance to the energy. Attention directed to the injury phase should reduce the magnitude and duration of exposure and decrease the host's susceptibility to injury. In the post-injury phase, the environment can be altered to reduce the source of the injury in the future and efforts directed to rescue and resuscitation of victims in the short term. For example, in relation to motor vehicle accidents, pre-injury strategies include: appropriate use of car seats and seat belts for all children in cars; teaching children road safety; wearing of bicycle helmets; reduction of vehicular speed especially in areas with schools and in residential sections; and road design. Protection at the time of injury involves the action of the seat belt in restraint and helmets reducing brain damage. Post-injury prevention involves ready access to trauma centres and review of accident sites for future precautions.

The most successful public health measures are also those that are involuntary (e.g., those which reduce ejections in crashes, protect vehicle occupants with inflatable air bag cushions in forward deceleration and remove rigid objects from roadsides). Recently, non-glaring daytime running lights have been recommended to increase vehicle visibility. Seat belt use, which is pre-injury action by the host, is the simplest and most available method of reducing risk in motor vehicle accidents. Legislation enacted in most jurisdictions in Canada has reduced mortality and morbidity due to motor vehicle accidents with a consequent decrease in the economic burden. Recent work suggests that the Selective Traffic Enforcement Program (STEP) is a useful approach to increase seat belt use. The STEP strategy uses a media and law enforcement blitz for several short periods. The result is a long-term gradual increase in the percentage of vehicle occupants using their seat belts. Risk reduction strategies that require voluntary change in behaviour patterns, such as wearing seat belts, need constant reinforcement. Wearing of helmets by motor cyclists is established as a preventive measure, and there is good evidence to support helmet use by bicyclists. Medical practitioner programs promoting the latter have, however, had only limited success in Ontario, and legislation is anticipated for enforcement. A survey indicated that only 12% of children wear bicycle helmets, and this figure is less if they are aged under nine.

Demonstrated effective strategies against injury are seat belt restraints, childproof medicine containers, bars on upper-storey windows, motorcycle helmets and bike helmets, the effectiveness of the latter strategy demonstrated through case-control study. Shoulder seat belts reduce the risk of occupant fatality and serious injury in frontal crashes by 40% to 70%.

3.2. INTENTIONAL INJURY

3.2.1. Suicide
Suicide has accounted for about 2% of all deaths in Canada annually since the late 1970s.[59] Suicide rates have increased rapidly since the early 1960s and are currently higher than they were during the depression fifty years ago. The overall suicide rate per 100,000 Canadians in 1987 was 14.3. Although Alberta's rate was highest in 1986, Quebec had the highest rate (18.3 per 100,000) in 1987.[25,60] Mao et al.[61] note that the male rates have stabilized, while female rates are declining. The male rate is consistently more than double the female rate, and in the 15 to 24 year old age group the male rate is five times the female rate. In 1987, the Canadian suicide rate per 100,000 population for males was 22.4, whereas it was 6.3 for females.[25] The PYLL due to suicide is large as it frequently involves young adults.[62] In 1986, there were 97,613 PYLL for males from suicide, the third leading cause of PYLL. This was a 9.0% increase from 1981, while PYLL decreased for the other two major causes of premature loss of life, cardiovascular disease and motor vehicle accidents. These high young adult male suicide rates only appeared over the last three decades.

People at high risk for suicide include: people with AIDS, Inuit, Status Indians, street youth, psychiatric patients (especially schizophrenics and people with affective disorders), prison inmates, people with a past history of attempted suicide, elderly women, both Canadian-born and Asian women, and the bereaved.[62] A number of social factors have been associated with suicide, namely mobility, disorganization and isolation with disruption of family relationships, lack of purpose in life, no religious affiliation, and particular cultural attitudes and beliefs. Important contributing medical factors are the lack of adequate community and psychiatric services, since it is apparent that many suicidal persons actually contact such services before the act itself.[63] The most frequent sets of predisposing circumstances identified in a survey of suicides in a region of Quebec[64] were psychiatric or psychological problems (60%), problematic circumstances (52%) and physical health problem (12%). In 44% of clients there had been suicidal ideation or attempts; alcohol or other drug addiction ranked second to depression-anxiety in terms of risk. The methods most commonly used in this area were hanging (in almost 30%), use of firearms (most frequently a 12 gauge shotgun or 22 calibre rifle), and poisoning by carbon monoxide (just over 10%) or pharmaceuticals (just under 10%). Drowning occurred in about 7% of cases, mutilation by jumping from a height (5%) and being involved in a collision with a motor vehicle or train (0.4%). A private location was used in over two-thirds of the suicides, and those that occurred in public were usually related to transportation, water or natural areas.

Prevention and Health Promotion

There is some evidence that initiation or improvements in community psychiatric services produce beneficial effects on the rates of suicide. The four major strategies for primary prevention include: public education, reduction in availability and lethality of means, specific education and training programs for healthcare professionals and gatekeepers, and programs aimed at the high-risk groups. A multifactorial strategy for the prevention of suicide was developed in the Quebec and Chaudiere-Appalaches regions in response to high rates of suicide (23 per 100,000) in this area.[64] The primary prevention recommendations involved increasing professional attention to lifestyle problems, particularly alcohol or drug addictions, and to young people with depression. Education programs should aim at reducing the stigma attached to seeking treatment for mental disorders, alcoholism and drug abuse. Crisis intervention facilities should be available. Strategies to prevent actual attempts may involve confiscation of weapons or limiting medications to those who are depressed or expressing suicidal ideation. The likelihood of successful attempts can be addressed by multiple modalities directed towards the physical environment, and legislation to reduce accessibility to firearms, as well other methods which may be utilized.

The media have a central role in shaping public attitudes and in public education. The means for suicide is often related to the availability of lethal substances. Hence, education programs could also aim at such things as discouraging the accumulation of lethal amounts of drugs in household medicine cabinets. Individuals prone to suicide may attempt suicide if their idol or a prominent person is reported to have committed suicide, thus media coverage of suicides should discourage sensationalism. Professional education should include the early warning signs of persons with suicidal tendencies, knowledge about high-risk populations, commonly used means of suicide, methods of intervention and available community resources to deal with the underlying problems. Education should be aimed at physicians, clergy, teachers, personnel of correctional facilities, police and others, as well as mental health professionals. There should be specific programs for the high-risk groups. For example, the elderly may benefit from retirement programs, self-help groups, education of family physicians and public education about the typical personality changes in the suicidal elderly person.[59]

3.2.2. Homicide
From 1986 to 1988, homicide was the third cause of premature life lost due to injury in Canada. One-third of these deaths were related to firearms. The risk of death from a firearm in Canada by suicide, homicide or accident is equivalent to the risk of death from a motor vehicle accident.[65]

While decreases in other causes of violent or accidental death and cancer in children occurred in the mid to late 1980s, homicide of children aged up to 19 increased.[66] Five per cent of all fatal injuries among children are homicides. An excess of male deaths relative to female deaths from homicide occurred in the teen years and continues over the remaining years of life. Firearms were the most frequent instrument of child homicide, being used to kill 228 children from 1981-89. The rising numbers are likely to reflect domestic violence, and while attention to the broad primary causes of tension in families should increase, firearm restrictions would have an immediate impact on child homicide.

Gun Control
About 1,400 firearm related deaths occur each year in Canada. Gun control has been highlighted above as an important potential strategy in prevention of both suicides and homicides. Suicides represent 75% of firearm-related deaths in Canada.[67] The number of suicides using firearms has declined since the introduction of gun control legislation in 1978, and no other methods are suggested. However, the effects of delay or limitation of access to a firearm, until suicidal ideation is passed, for example, has not been well investigated. The epidemiology is simple: all the deaths were caused by the discharge of a firearm. It is estimated that one-quarter of Canadian households own a firearm, in 70% of the households allegedly for hunting. Over 50% of the households had not used a firearm in the previous 12 months and had no-one trained in safe handling. Although protection is often cited as a justification for having a gun, a household member is killed 20 times more often than an intruder.

There is proposed legislation (Bill C-17) to introduce a number of safeguards to prevent the issuance of Firearm Acquisition Certificates (FAC) where there is evidence of risk. A call has also been made for a standard mechanism by which physicians can recommend revocation of a FAC, when indicated, in a more streamlined manner so that this modality can be employed in prevention.[68]

4. SUMMARY

This chapter summarized the current approaches in disease prevention and health promotion in relation to major non-communicable chronic diseases in Canada.

Many chronic illnesses have substance abuse (alcohol and tobacco) and improper diet as their major underlying causes. These illness are preventable, and hence there has been an increasing emphasis on the role of primary and secondary prevention. Chronic illnesses are the cause of the major burden of illness.

Smoking is the number one preventable cause of death in Canada. In 1989, 38,000 Canadians died smoking-related deaths. Smoking is associated with lung cancer, COPD, cardiovascular illness, and low birth weight. Female deaths, while much lower in number than males, have risen proportionately at a greater rate than for males within the last 15 years, paralleling the increase in female smoking. There is good evidence that health-care providers, including physicians and non-physicians, can be effective in motivating patients to quit smoking using brief interventions by incorporating smoking cessation messages which are repeated on multiple occasions and reinforced. As well, well-designed programs of health promotion with strategies aimed at impressionable and susceptible youth populations to prevent the uptake of smoking, as well as cessation in older smokers, can continue the reversal of smoking prevalence.

There are various disease and/or injuries associated with alcohol consumption, such as cirrhosis, suicide, breast cancer, respiratory cancer, and motor vehicle and other accidents. Roughly 1.8% of all deaths are directly attributable to alcohol abuse, and an estimated 10.5% of all deaths are alcohol related. Morbidity problems are of greater concern than mortality and potential-years-of-life-lost. Alcoholism is one of the leading causes of hospitalization in mental institutions. There are two defined groups of drinkers: problem drinkers and alcohol-dependent drinkers. There are about 502,700 Canadians who are alcohol dependent.

Physicians are in a good position to quickly identify alcoholism and offer early intervention for those who are drinking at levels that increase their risks for medical and psychosocial consequences of drinking. Many motivated problem drinkers and alcohol-dependent people who want to quit drinking are also being assisted by self-help groups such as Alcoholics Anonymous. Effective health promotion programs in relation to substance abuse should be comprehensive, coordinated and participatory. School-based policies on alcohol, drugs and smoking can complement integrated education and prevention programs. In the home setting parents should be encouraged to discuss alcohol and smoking issues and values with children.

Diet, particularly fat intake, is a major factor in the development of many chronic diseases including cardiovascular disease and cancer. Poor nutrition is also a factor in osteoporosis, chronic liver disease and dental health. Obesity is a risk factor for diabetes, cardiovascular disease, and endometrial cancer, and increases the risk of breast cancer in post-menopausal women. There is an increasing prevalence of underweight individuals (particularly young women) which makes them susceptible to certain health problems.

National guidelines for nutrition have been published by Health and Welfare Canada. For encouraging healthy eating, action should be directed to: the community at large, schools, homes, restaurants, grocery stores, workplaces and health-care settings.

Cardiovascular disease (CVD) has been the leading cause of death in Canada, accounting for nearly half of all deaths each year. The most common forms of CVD are ischemic or coronary heart disease (IHD) and cerebrovascular disease (stroke or CBVD). In 1988, IHD and CBVD accounted for over 60,266 deaths, with IHD representing one-quarter of all deaths. While CVD is still the leading cause of death, there has been a decline in CVD mortality rates since the mid 1960s. The decline has been attributed in part to the reduction in the prevalence of smoking, reduced consumption of dietary fat, improved detection and management of hypertension as well as improved surgical approaches to the treatment of symptomatic heart disease. An estimated 13% of the health-care dollar in Ontario is spent on some form of CVD-related health service.

The underlying cause of CVD is atherosclerosis. Factors that contribute to atherosclerosis include smoking, high blood pressure, obesity, lack of physical activity, high levels of dietary fat, and increased LDL fraction. Two-thirds of Canadians have at least one of the major cardiovascular risk factors. The incidence of CVD increases dramatically with age. The rates for women are almost half those of men, except for stroke where the rates are approximately equal.

Cardiovascular disease is preventable. Community-based population-wide approaches emphasize augmenting community action, reorienting health services, and enhancing prevention. These are believed to reduce the prevalence of risk factors predisposing individuals to CVD.

Cancer ranked second overall as a leading cause of death. More than one in three Canadians will develop some form of cancer in their lifetime. After the age of 55 years, both male and female cancer rates begin to rise at a faster rate; however, the male rate increases more sharply. Despite advances and the better outlook for some cancers, overall the prognosis is still unfavourable and the emphasis must be on prevention and caring.

Environmental factors (such as water and air quality), and diet and lifestyle are considered to be the most important determinants for cancer. Smoking and alcohol are two lifestyle habits which play major roles in a number of non-occupational cancers where multiple factors may be responsible. Exposures to high concentrations of certain chemicals in the occupational environment is also associated with cancer.

Lung cancer is the number one cancer. Ninety per cent of lung cancer is caused by smoking. Colorectal cancer ranks second in Canada. Diets, particularly those high in saturated fat intake, have been linked with increased risk of colorectal cancer. Breast cancer is the leading cause of premature mortality from cancer in females. In men, prostate cancer is fourth in terms of incidence and deaths. One-third of men with prostatic cancer die of their disease. Leukemias represent the leading cancer in children.

In 1987, respiratory diseases ranked fourth and third among men and women respectively, as leading causes of death. Important factors influencing respiratory disease mortality rates that have been identified include smoking and indoor-outdoor air pollution. Pollutants interact and their combined effect on a disease may be either additive or multiplicative (e.g., smoking and asbestos combined have a multiplicative effect).

Congenital anomalies are now the second leading cause of death in infants. The most common malformations leading to infant death were due to defects of the heart and circulatory system. Etiological factors for malformations include hereditary or familial tendencies, and non-genetic factors such as maternal diabetes type I, maternal infection with TORCH, and anti-convulsant drug use during pregnancy.

Currently there are 200 known genetic and metabolic disorders. Many of these diseases are preventable with proper counselling in susceptible populations. Selective screening and genetic counselling in susceptible populations is probably the most appropriate form of primary prevention.

One in five Canadians had at least one accident in 1987. This caused accidents to be ranked second to cardiovascular diseases in terms of total costs to society; accounting for $11 billion in expenditure. The types of accidents included: motor vehicle, sports or leisure activity, work-related accidents, and those accidents occurring in and around the home. Injuries are distinguished as either non-intentional (also known as accidents) and intentional (homicide and suicide predominantly).

Injuries are the leading cause of death during half the human life span and the second leading cause of PYLL to cancer. Injuries are the leading cause of death for children under five years, school-aged children and young adults. The causes of injury in younger children are due to falling, poisoning, and motor vehicle accidents (MVA).

Important risk factors for MVA include the mental attitude and condition of the driver, the design and condition of the vehicle, road design and conditions, and seat belt usage. Primary preventive methods would therefore include environmental measures in addition to those aimed at the individual. Driving while intoxicated is thought by many to be a major factor in accidents. Most of the drinking and driving occurs at night. This behaviour is most common among the 25 to 39 year age group.

Major attitudinal change is necessary in order to prevent injuries. Pre-injury strategies include: appropriate use of car seats and seat belts for all children in cars, teaching children road safety, wearing bicycle helmets, reduction of vehicular speed in specific areas (e.g., near schools) and road signs. Post-injury prevention involves ready access to trauma centres and review of accident sites for future precautions.

Suicide rates have increased rapidly since the early 1960s. The male rate is consistently more than double the female rate and in the 15 to 24 year old age group, the male rate is five times the female rate. People at high risk for suicide include: people with AIDS, Inuit, Status Indians, street youth, psychiatric patients, prison inmates, people with a past history of attempted suicide, the elderly and Canadian-born and Asian-born women.

There is some evidence that initiation or improvements in community psychiatric services produce beneficial effects on the rates of suicide. The four major strategies for primary prevention include: public education, reduction in availability and lethality of means, specific education and training programs for healthcare professionals and gatekeepers, and programs aimed at the high-risk groups.

5.   REFERENCES

1. Spitzer W, Lawrence V, Dales R et al. Links Between Passive Smoking and Disease: A Best-Evidence Synthesis. A Report of the Working Group on Passive Smoking. *Clin Invest Med* 13(1):17-42, 1990.
2. *Break Free. Directional Paper of the National Program to Reduce Tobacco Use in Canada*. Health and Welfare Canada, Ottawa, 1987.
3. Kottke T, Battista R, DeFriese G and Brekke M. Attributes of Successful Smoking Cessation Interventions in Medical Practice. A Meta-analysis of 39 Controlled Trials. *JAMA* 259(19):2883-2889, 1988.
4. *Smoking, Tobacco, and Cancer Program, National Cancer Institute. How to Help Your Patients Stop Smoking. Trainer's Guide*. U.S. Dept. of Health and Human Services. Public Health Service. National Institutes of Health, Washington, DC, 1992.
5. A Program of The Canadian Council on Smoking and Health. *Guide Your Patients to a Smoke Free Future*. Toronto: Canadian Council on Smoking and Health, 1992.
6. The Periodic Health Examination, 1989 Update. *Can Med Assoc J* 141(3):209-216, 1989.
7. Schmidt W and Popham RE. *Alcohol Problems and their Prevention. A Public Health Perspective*. Toronto: Alcoholism and Drug Addiction Research Foundation, 1978.
8. Health and Welfare Canada (1989), *Alcohol in Canada*. Eliany M, ed. Ministry of Supply and Services, Canada, Ottawa, 1989.
9. Departments of Preventive Medicine and Biostatistics, and Behavioural Science, Division of Community Health, Faculty of Medicine, University of Toronto and the Addiction Research Foundation, Toronto. Preventing Alcohol Problems: The Challenge for Medical Education. Proceedings of a National Conference Niagara-on-the-Lake, Ontario. October 15-17, 1989. *Can Med Assoc J* 143(10):1041-1042, 1990.

10. Selzer ML. The Michigan Alcoholism Screening Test: The Quest for a New Diagnostic Instrument. *Am J Psychiatry* 127(12):1653-1658, 1971.

11. Ewing JA. Detecting Alcoholism: The CAGE Questionnaire. *JAMA* 252(14):1905-1907, 1984.

12. Smythe CL. *Drugs in Ontario: Results of Survey of Users.* London: Addiction Research Foundation of Ontario, 1992, pp 1-47.

13. Swarbrick M. Model Program for Substance Abuse Prevention. Ministry of Health Ontario. *Public Health Epidimiol Reports* 2(21):320-323, 1991.

14. Altman D, Rasenick-Douss L, Foster V and Tye J. Sustained Effects of an Educational Program to Reduce Sales of Cigarettes to Minors. *Am J Public Health* 81(7):891-893, 1991.

15. Health and Welfare Canada. Partners in Canada's Drug Strategy. *Health Promot* 30(2):11-12, Fall 1992.

16. The Federal-Provincial Canadian Heart Health Initiative. Canadian Heart Health Surveys Research Group. *Can Med Assoc J* 146(11):1915-1916, 1992.

17. Ministry of Health Ontario. Premiers Council on Health, Well-Being and Social Justice. *Ontario Health Survey 1990 Highlights.* Toronto: Queens Park, September, 1992, pp 1-51.

18. Miller A. Diet and Cancer - A Review. *Rev Oncol* 3:87-95, 1990.

19. Willett W, Hunter DJ, Stampfer MI, et al. Dietary Fat and Fiber in Relation to Risk of Breast Cancer. An 8 year Follow-up. *JAMA* 268(15):2037-2044, 1992.

20. Howe G. High Fat Diets and Breast Cancer Risk. The Epidemiologic Evidence. *JAMA* 268(15):2080-2081, 1992.

21. Health and Welfare. *Nutrition Recommendations: The Report of the Scientific Review Committee.* Ministry of Supplies, and Services, Canada, Ottawa, 1990.

22. *Ideas for Action on Healthy Eating.* Healthy Lifestyles Promotion Program. Ministry of Health Ontario. Toronto: Queens Printer for Ontario, 1991.

23. Heart and Stroke Foundation of Canada. *Cardiovascular Disease in Canada 1991.* Ottawa, 1991.

24. Nair C, Colbourn H, McLean O and Petrasovits A. Cardiovascular Disease in Canada. *Health Reports* 1(1):1-22, 1989.

25. Statistics Canada. Canadian Centre for Health Information. *Health Indicators. Ottawa,* 1991.

26. Toronto Working Group on Cholesterol Policy. *Detection and Management of Asymptomatic Hypercholesterolemia: A Policy Document by the Toronto Working Group on Cholesterol Policy.* Toronto: Ontario Ministry of Health, 1989.

27. The Expert Panel. The Canadian Consensus Conference on Cholesterol; Final Report. *Can Med Assoc J* 139(2):1-8, 1988.

28. The Expert Panel National Cholesterol Education Program. Report of the National Program Expert Panel on Detection, Evaluation, and Treatment of High Blood Cholesterol in Adults. *Arch Intern Med* 148(1):36-69, 1988.

29. Grover S, Coupal L, Fahkry R and Suissa, S. Screening for Hypercholesterolemia Among Canadians: How Much Will it Cost? *Can Med Assoc J* 144(2):161-168, 1991.

30. Periodic Health Examination, 1993 Update 2: Lowering the Blood Total Cholesterol Level to Prevent Coronary Heart Disease. Canadian Task Force on the Periodic Health Examination. *Can Med Assoc J* 140(4):521-538, 1993.

31. Shea S and Basch C. A Review of Five Major Community-Based Cardiovascular Disease Prevention Programs. Part I: Rationale, Design and Theoretical Framework. *Am J Health Promot* 4(3):203-213, 1990.

32. Shea S and Basch C. A Review of Five Major Community-Based Disease Prevention Programs. Part II: Intervention Strategies, Evaluation Methods, and Results. *Am J Health Promot* 4(4):279-287, 1990.

33. Health and Welfare Canada. Minister of Supply and Services Canada. The Canadian Heart Health Inititiative. A Policy in Action. *Health Promot* 30(4):9,1992.

34. International Heart Health Conference. *Victoria Declaration on Heart Health. Bridging the Gap: Science and Policy in Action.* Health and Welfare Canada, Ottawa, 1992.

35. National Cancer Institute of Canada. *Canadian Cancer Statistics 1990.* Toronto: National Cancer Institute, 1990.

36. Brackner A. Cancer: Incidence, Hospitalizations and Deaths in Canada. *Health Reports* 1(1):51-67, 1989.

37. Economic Burden of Illness in Canada, 1986. *Chronic Dis Can* 12(3):1-37, Suppl, 1991.
38. Miller A. Planning Cancer Control Strategies. Health and Welfare Canada. *Chronic Dis Can* 13(1):1-40, Suppl, 1992.
39. Miller A, Baines C, To T and Wall C. Canadian National Breast Screening Study. 1. Breast Cancer Detection and Death Rates Among Women Aged 40 to 49 years. 2. Canadian National Breast Screening Study. Breast Cancer Detection and Death Rates Among Women Aged 50 to 59 years. *Can Med Assoc J* 147(10):1459-1488, 1992.
40. Workshop Report. Reducing Deaths from Breast Cancer in Canada. *Can Med Assoc J* 141(3):199-201, 1989.
41. Proceedings of the Second National Workshop on Cervical Cancer Screening. Health and Welfare Canada. *Chronic Dis Can* 13(4) Suppl, 1992.
42. Monfreda J, Litven W and Smith E. Chronic Obstructive Pulmonary Disease Mortality in Canada, 1950-1984. *Chronic Dis Can* 7(3):49-52, 1986.
43. Shephard RD. Perspective on Air Pollution: The Canadian Scene. *Can Fam Phys* 21(8):67-73, 1975.
44. Yassi A and Friesen B. Controlling Air Pollution: The Plan to Reduce Nitrogen Oxides (NOx) and Volatile Organic Compounds (VOCs) Emissions in Canada. *Can J Pub Health* 81(1):6-9, 1990.
45. Pengelly D. Inhaled Doses of Contaminants from Ambient Air Pollution, Environmental Tobacco Smoke and Self-Smoking. *Chronic Dis Can* 10(2):28-29, 1989.
46. Lowry R. Common Congenital Anomalies. *Can Fam Phys* 31(5):1033-1037, 1985.
47. Kalter H and Warkang, J. Congenital Malformations Part II. *N Engl J Med* 308(9):491-497, 1983.
48. Kalter H and Warkang J. Congenital Malformations, Etiologic Factors and Their Role in Prevention Part I. *N Engl J Med* 308(8):424-431, 1983.
49. Long S. Does LSD Induce Chromosomal Damage and Malformation? A Review of the Literature. *Teratology* 6:75-90, 1972.
50. Fried P. Marihuana Use by Pregnant Women and Effects on Offspring: An Update. *Neurobehav Toxicol Teratol* 4(4):451-454, 1982.
51. Crawford M. Prenatal Diagnosis of Common Genetic Disorders. *Br Med J* 297(6647):502-507, 1988.
52. Miller W and Adams O. Statistics Canada. *Accidents in Canada*. General Social Survey. Analysis Series. Ottawa, 1991.
53. The Leading Causes of Death at Different Ages, 1987. *Health Reports* 3(1), Suppl 11, 1989.
54. Riley R and Paddon P. Accidents in Canada: Mortality and Hospitalization. *Health Reports* 1(1):23-50, 1989.
55. *National Survey on Drinking and Driving 1988: Overview Report.* Ottawa: Minister of National Health and Welfare, 1989.
56. Donelson AC, Walsh PJ and Haas GC. *Alcohol Use by Persons Fatally Injured in Motor Vehicle Accidents: 1985.* Ottawa: Traffic Injury Research Foundation, 1986.
57. *Road Safety Annual Report 1988.* Ministry of Supply and Services, Canada, Ottawa, 1989.
58. Gielen A. Health Education and Injury Control: Integrating Approaches. Health Educ Q 19(2):203-218, 1992.
59. The Periodic Health Examination, 1990 Update: 2. Early Detection of Depression and Prevention of Suicide. *Can Med Assoc J* 142(11):1233-1238, 1990.
60. McName J and Offord D. Prevention of Suicide. *Can Med Assoc J* 142(11):1223-1230, 1990.
61. Mao Y, Hasselback P, Davies J, Nichol R and Wigle D. Suicide in Canada: An Epidemiological Assessment. *Can J Public Health* 81(4):324-328, 1990.
62. *Suicide in Canada: Report of the National Task Force on Suicide in Canada.* Ottawa: Minister of National Health and Welfare, 1987.
63. Rees WL. *A Short Textbook of Psychiatry.* London: English Universities Press Ltd., 1967, p 114.
64. Bouchard L, Chapdelaine A, Mireault G and Maurice P. Suicides in the Quebec and Chaudiere-Appalaches Regions: A Multifactorial Approach for Suicide Prevention. Health and Welfare Canada. *Chronic Dis Can* 12(6):99-103, 1991.
65. Chapdelaine A, Samson E, Kimberly MD and Viau L. Firearm-Related Injuries in Canada: Issues for Prevention. *Can Med Assoc J* 145(10):1217-1223, 1991.
66. Mark E and Wilkins K. Death Due to Homicide among Canadian Children. Health and Welfare Canada. *Chronic Dis Can* 12(5):81-85, 1991.

67. Kimberly MD, Chapdelaine A, Viau L and Samson E. Prevention of Firearm-Related Injuries in Canada. *Can Med Assoc J* 145(10):1211-1213, 1991.
68. Kane B. MDs Should be Active in Revoking, Restricting Patient's Firearms Acquisition Certificates. *Can Med Assoc J* 146(10):1805-1806, 1992.

CHAPTER EIGHT
Communicable Diseases

Over the last half century, vaccines and antibiotics have reduced the incidence of, and mortality from, many communicable diseases. Despite the widespread availability of most vaccines, localized outbreaks of communicable diseases such as measles, meningitis and tuberculosis still occur in Canada, and they are associated with significant mortality and morbidity. AIDS has emerged as an important public health problem both in relation to its chronicity and prevention. Sexually transmitted diseases in general are a major cause of morbidity, especially among the young. This chapter will focus mainly on these two areas of communicable diseases: vaccine-preventable diseases and sexually transmitted diseases. Chapter two outlined the investigation of communicable disease outbreaks and chapter five provided an overview of the prevalence of certain communicable diseases.

1. VACCINE-PREVENTABLE DISEASES

While vaccine-preventable diseases such as tetanus and diphtheria have been almost eradicated in Canada, sporadic cases and outbreaks of certain infectious diseases, predominantly those formerly more common in childhood, are still being reported. There are also current issues concerning immunization programs for a number of these diseases. While the actual vaccine recommendations are presented in a separate section in this chapter, a brief overview of the recent incidence of vaccine-preventable diseases in Canada, as well as emerging issues relevant to control, are discussed in the following section.

Pertussis
In Canada in 1989 and 1990 there were a large number of outbreaks of pertussis (persistent paroxysmal coughing episodes ending in inspiratory whoop, caused by *Bordetella pertussis*). The severity of the disease has decreased due to widespread vaccination which affords partial protection. However, the disease has a poorer prognosis in infants under one year of age, in whom the case-fatality rate is one in

200. The Laboratory Centre for Disease Control has outlined in its document the management of contacts of sporadic cases and outbreaks of pertussis.[1]

Measles

A major resurgence of vaccine-preventable cases of measles occurred in Canada in the late 1980s and early 1990s. The incidence of measles rose from 2/100,000 in 1981 to 50/100,000 in 1991. There were 10,000 cases of measles in Quebec in 1989 and 6,000 in Ontario in 1991. The cases have largely been in the 10-14 year age group, most of whom had been previously vaccinated. In response, a number of provinces undertook widespread re-vaccination campaigns of school children vaccinated before 1980, or lacking proof of immunity (or of having had measles previously). The resurgence of measles incidence in Canada is largely due to primary vaccine failure: vaccination in the presence of maternal antibody (or before one year of age), improper handling of the vaccine, poor stabilizers in measles vaccine used prior to 1980, or unknown causes. Secondary vaccine failure, or waning, of immunity has not been considered a major factor, because there has not been a steadily increasing attack rate with age. The absence of a law in Quebec mandating immunization (or proof of immunity) prior to entering school has also been considered a contributory factor in the outbreaks in that province. The National Advisory Committee on Immunization (NACI) has provided a strategy for control of measles in Canada.[2]

Rubella

There was a marked increase in the number of cases of rubella in British Columbia, Ontario, and other provinces in the late 1980s.[3] Three hundred and twenty cases were reported in the first four months of 1989. The cases occurred in those of high school age and those aged 20 to 29. Thirty per cent of the cases in B.C. occurred in women of child-bearing age. There was, however, a decline in national cases reported, from 1,384 in 1989 to 402 in 1990. Additionally, only two cases of congenital rubella syndrome (CRS) were reported annually during these two years. It is suspected that serious under-reporting of rubella and lack of identification of CRS is responsible for the apparent decline in rubella in these years and for the lack of CRS reports. Female patients should be warned of the dangers associated with rubella infection in pregnancy.

Influenza

This disease is of continuing concern during the winter months. Influenza A (H3N2) was the predominant serogroup in the 1991-1992 season although some cases of influenza B were reported in infants and young children in southern Ontario. There were 1,347 laboratory-confirmed cases of influenza in all ages in this period.[4] The overall mortality from influenza and pneumococcal infections, which may arise as a complication of influenza, exceeds that of all vaccine-preventable childhood diseases. In Canada, there are from 1,000 to 10,000 excess deaths each year from influenza, predominantly in those over 65. Medicare and hospitalization costs for influenza in Canada are approximately $500 million per year. Influenza immunization programs have been demonstrated to be cost-beneficial. Unfortunately only 10% of those aged over 65 in Canada receive vaccine. It has been shown that if health-care providers recommend vaccination, vaccine uptake by individuals in high-risk groups is improved. Also, increased efforts in organizing influenza programs, particularly in improving provider compliance with national guidelines for immunization, result in massive increases in vaccine uptake.

Meningococcal Disease, Including Meningitis

Bacterial meningitis, a serious inflammation of the coverings of the brain and spinal cord, is usually caused by *Neisseria meningitides* or *Haemophilus influenzae* b (discussed in the next paragraph), and it can result in death or permanent neurological impairment as its most severe consequences. Meningitis can also manifest as overwhelming septicemia and arthritis. The incidence of meningococcal meningitis and disease has varied in Canada from one to three cases per 100,000 people. In the early 1980s the incidence was low. It rose, however, to a peak in 1989, with an incidence of 2/100,000 and then declined in the early 1990s.[5] Small clusters (<10 cases) and unlinked cases of meningococcal meningitis and disease were reported in at least five provinces in 1991-2: Ontario, Quebec, PEI and B.C. in 1991 and in Nova Scotia, Labrador, Ontario, Alberta and Quebec in 1992. The disease primarily affects children, especially those up to one year of age. In recent years, however, the proportion of cases occurring in adolescents and adults has been increasing steadily. Group C has emerged as the most frequent *Neisseria* isolate in the clusters. Despite improved therapeutic management, about 20 people die—mostly infants—from complications every year. The overall case-fatality rate in recent years has been less than 10%, as compared with more than 30% in the 1950s and 1960s.

Haemophilus b Disease

In Canada, with the introduction of the first conjugate vaccine given at the age of 18 months, the incidence of invasive disease, such as meningitis and epiglottis, caused by *Haemophilus influenzae b* was halved after 1987. Previously, invasive disease had occurred in one child in 200 under the age of five. The incidence in the early 1990s was reduced to 27 from 54 per 100,000. Recent introduction of new conjugate vaccines for infants under 18 months, in whom the majority of remaining disease was occurring (at four times the rate of one to four year olds), will further reduce the incidence of the disease. The new conjugate vaccines take advantage of the greater immune response of infants under 12 months to new polysaccharide-protein conjugate antigens compared to those in the first vaccine licensed for children 18 months and older.

Hepatitis B

This is a significant communicable disease. The incidence of reported cases in Canada in 1992 was 13 per 100,000, having more than doubled from five per 100,000 in 1982. Under-reporting likely occurs, and Health Canada estimates the overall annual incidence rate for Canada may be as high as 100 infections per 100,000 people. The peak incidence is in those aged 25-29. There are at least 3,000 reported cases of hepatitis B per year in Canada. Mortality from this disease has increased from 0.5 to 1.5 per million in Canada in the past decade. There are regional variations in reported incidence. B.C. has the highest incidence of hepatitis B, with cases reported rising from 16 in 1980 to 832 in 1992. Awareness is increasing that hepatitis B is a sexually transmitted disease, particularly among young adults. The major modes of spread in Canada are the following: heterosexual transmission (30% of known cases), intravenous drug use (21%), homosexual behaviour (14%), and unknown (25%). Medical and dental occupational transmission accounts for a further 2.8% of cases.

The initial strategy of distribution of hepatitis B vaccine (plasma derived or recombinant) in Canada was to targeted groups: newborns of hepatitis B surface antigen (HBsAg)-positive mothers, household contacts and sexual contacts of HBsAg carriers, sexually promiscuous persons, and people occupationally exposed to blood and body fluids. More recently these programs have been expanded in some provinces to include sexual and household contacts of acute cases, IV drug users, homosexual men and clients of STD clinics who have multiple partners. However, these selective programs fail to provide coverage for the large proportion of patients with hepatitis B with no identifiable risk factor.

An expert consensus has emerged in Canada supporting universal vaccination against hepatitis B.[6] Since 1991 NACI has recommended universal hepatitis B vaccination. The costs, however, have been considered prohibitive by most provincial governments. Additionally the optimum timing of administration of vaccination is problematic. There are arguments for immunization in late childhood or early adolescence for maximum protection against sexual transmission of hepatitis B during adolescence and early adulthood.[7] B.C. was the first province to introduce a universal hepatitis B program for the immunization of grade six students beginning in 1992. Eventually, hepatitis B immunization will be incorporated into the province's routine infant immunization schedule. It is predicted that universal childhood vaccination against hepatitis B would reduce the incidence by 90%; this would be achieved sooner if adolescent vaccination were introduced.

Tuberculosis (TB)

TB is an important chronic infection, especially in at-risk populations such as those with HIV infection, homeless persons, alcohol dependent persons, Aboriginal Peoples, and, in recent years, foreign-born individuals (particularly those from Southeast Asia and Somalia). The incidence of TB in the native population is currently 70 per 100,000. The incidence of TB in Canada in 1989 rose for the first time in 30 years to 7.8 per 100,000, representing 2,035 new active and reactivated

Table 8.1: Vaccine Storage and Handling

1. Expiry dates: check before each use, discard outdated products.

2. Temperature: check temperature routinely, avoid storage of vaccines on refrigerator doors as temperature tends to fluctuate thus inactivating vaccines

3. Transport: use coolers and cold packs to transport vaccines even over short distances

4. Protect: light sensitive products should be stored in boxes and only briefly exposed to light to avoid inactivation.

5. Dilute: with diluent provided, consult manufacturer's direction and use as soon as possible.

6. Inspect: each vial/ampule before administering for colour change, particles or precipitation.

7. Discard: multidose vials which have not been dated at time of first use, inactiviated vaccines which have been inadvertently frozen (Note: live virus vaccines with the exception of OPV may be thawed and used more than once, but not repeatedly).

Source: McIntyre L, Shave D. Update on immunization, drugs and therapeutics for Maritime practioners, 1990;13:(1/2):2. Reproduced with the permission of the authors.

cases.[8] These cases occurred predominantly in Ontario, Saskatchewan and the Northwest Territories. Apart from the difficulties of control in traditional risk groups and HIV-infected persons, the provinces have indicated difficulties in preventing transmission by newly arrived immigrants during the period after arrival prior to requirements for medical examination.[9] Some, in fact, are lost to follow up. Medical practitioners need to be sensitized to the management of TB, particularly as it relates to public health hazards and the possible emergence of multiple-resistant strains in those noncompliant with chemotherapy (a problem present in the US, but not having been identified in Canada as of late 1992).

1.1.   IMMUNIZATION

While the value of immunization in clinical practice is well entrenched, the effectiveness of vaccination in protecting against disease is dependent not only on the efficacy, or performance, of the vaccine under ideal conditions, but also on the degree of coverage achieved (see chapter three). This is dependent on administrative aspects of the vaccination program as well as on consumer and provider compliance, and the maintenance of potency of the vaccine by attention to requirements during transportation and storage. Table 8.1 indicates a number of

Table 8.2.   Immunization Schedules for Children

Infants Beginning Series in Early Infancy

Age	Vaccine
2 months	DPT Polio(1), Hib(2)
4 months	DPT Polio(1), Hib
6 months	DPT Polio(1,3), Hib
after 1st birthday	MMR(4)
18 months	DPT Polio(1), Hib
4-6 years(5)	DPT Polio
10-12 years	Hepatitis B(6), Rubella(7)
14-16 years	Td(8), Polio(IPVonly)(12)

Children 1-6 Years of Age Not Immunized in Early Infancy

Visit	Vaccine
Initial Visit(9,11)	DPT Polio, Hib(11)
1 month after 1st visit	MMR(7)
1 month after 2nd visit	DPT Polio
2 months after 3rd visit	DPT Polio(3)
12 months after 4th visit	DPT Polio
Preschool / 4-6 years(10)	DPT Polio
14-16 years	Td(8), IPV

Unimmunized Children Aged 7 Years and Over, and Adults Not Immunized in Childhood

Visit	Vaccine
Initial Visit(9)	Td(8), Polio(IPV)
1 month after 1st visit	MMR(7)
1 month after 2nd visit	Td(8) Polio(IPV)
12 months after 3rd visit	Td(8), Polio(IPV)
Every 10 years thereafter	Td(8), Polio(IPV)

Footnotes to Table 8.2

1 POLIO: Either OPV or IPV can be used.

2 HIB: The primary series at 2, 4 and 6 months should be completed with the same conjugate Hib vaccine. However, if necessary to change vaccines, the schedule does not have to be restarted.

3 POLIO: The third dose at 6 months of age is optional if OPV has been used.

4 MMR: Should be give given on or, as soon as practicable after the first birthday.

5 MMR: If measles eradication is the goal of the measles immunization program, then a second dose of MMR should be given at school entry.

6 HEPATITIS B VACCINE: If a universal childhood program of hepatitis B vaccination is undertaken, 3 doses of vaccine should be administered at 0, 1 and 6-12 months to children 10-12 years of age.

7 Rubella vaccine is also indiciated for all girls and women of childbearing age who lack proof or immunity. At all medical visits the opportuinity should be taken to check whether girls and women have received rubella vaccine.

8 Diphtheria and Tetanus Toxoid (Td), a combined adsorbed "adult type" preparation for use in persons 7 years of age or more, contains less diphtheria toxoid than preparations given to younger children and is less likely to cause reactions in older persons.

9 Measles, mumps, and rubella vaccines may also be given at the first visit if it is considered likely that a child will not return for further immunization. It has not been shown, however, that full response to all antigens will occur.

10 When the last of the above doses are given before the fourth birthday, consideration should be given to administration of an additional dose at school entry.

11 Children beginning their series at age 12-14 months require one dose followed by a booster dose at age 18 months. Unimmunized children aged 15-19 months require only a single dose. Hib vaccine is not routinely recommended for children aged 5 years and over.

12 Not necessary if OPV previously received.

Source: Adapted from Canadian Immunization Guide, 4th ed., Health Canada, 1993.

steps in vaccine storage and handling that should be undertaken routinely by those involved in vaccine administration.[10]

In recent years, a number of jurisdictions in Canada have instituted legislation for mandatory immunization of young children before school entry. Many of these jurisdictions require those who administer immunizing agents to inform the patient (or parent) of the benefits and material risks of the immunization. Also, there has been a movement at the national level for the establishment of a vaccine compensation fund for those who develop serious side effects of vaccines. Tables 8.2 and 8.3 show the immunization schedules recommended by NACI which have

Table 8.3.   Immunization Schedule for Adults

Vaccine or Toxoid	Indication	Further Doses
BCG	High-risk exposure	None
Diphtheria (adult preparation)	All adults	Every 10 years preferably given combined with tetanus toxoid as Td
Hepatitis B	High-risk exposure	
Influenza	High-risk adults and all persons over 65 years	Every year using current vaccine formulation
Measles	Persons born after 1956: susceptible to measles	None
Meningococcal	High-risk exposure	Unknown
Mumps	Young adults with no history of mumps	None
Pertussis	Not indicated	
Plague	High-risk exposure	
Pneumococcal	Conditions with increased risk of pneumococcal disease	None
Poliomyelitis	Travel to endemic area or other exposure risk	
Rabies (pre-exposure use)	Occupational or other risk	Antibody tested in high risk group every 2 years; if inadequate, booster given
Rubella	Susceptible women of childbearing age and certain male health-care workers.	None
Tetanus	All adults	Every 10 years, preferably as Td
Typhoid	High-risk exposure	Every three years while risk continues
Yellow Fever	Travel to endemic area/required for foreign travel	Every 10 years while risk continues

Source: Canadian Immunization Guide, 4th Ed., Health Canada, 1993.

been adopted by many provinces.[11] The College of Physicians and Surgeons of Ontario in 1990 revised its publication *Immunization: Benefits, Risks, and Reportable Events, A Guide For Ontario Physicians,* and this is **reproduced** in its entirety with the permission of the College.[12] Additional information is included on Meningococcal vaccines, new infant *Haemophilus Influenzae B* conjugate vaccines and recommendations regarding hepatitis B from other sources which are indicated in the text.

1.2   BENEFITS, RISKS AND REPORTABLE EVENTS

The purpose of the following guide is to inform physicians of their responsibilities relating to immunization mandated by amendments to the Health Protection and Promotion Act. This legislation requires those who administer immunizing agents to inform the patient (or parent) of the **benefits** and **material risks** of the immunization, as well as the importance of reporting to a physician certain specific reactions which are called **reportable events**. In general, these reportable events are defined in the legislation and must be reported by physicians to the local medical officer of health. In keeping with the requirements of the legislation, this guide will use the following format in discussing each vaccine: A. Benefits, including information on morbidity and mortality of the disease under consideration; B. Adverse reactions; C. Material risks; D. Reportable events.

While not required by legislation to discuss the adverse reactions of vaccines, they have been included for your information, as it would be wise medical practice to discuss these with your patients. Because of the complexity of the human immune response, no vaccine or other biological substance can ever be considered 100% safe. Anaphylaxis and death are material risks of all vaccines and complex neurological events such as Guillain-Barre syndrome, transverse myelitis, peripheral neuropathy and encephalopathy have been temporally associated with immunization. Fortunately such occurrences are extremely rare.

This guide will cover vaccines against diphtheria, tetanus, pertussis, polio, mumps, and rubella.   Subsequent publications will cover Hemophilus b, polysaccharide vaccines, influenza, hepatitis B, and others. The information in this guide about the Poliomyelitis Vaccine was updated and approved by Council in February 1990. The information about Haemophilus b Conjugate Vaccine and Rabies Vaccine was revised and approved by Council in May 1990.

Diphtheria Toxoid
Benefits Diphtheria most often occurs as membranous nasopharyngitis and/or laryngotracheitis which may lead to airway obstruction. Less commonly the disease manifests as cutaneous or chronic ear infections. Life-threatening complications include heart failure from myocarditis and paralysis from the effects of diphtheria toxin. The case fatality rate is approximately 10%. Diphtheria toxoid prevents disease in most completely immunized individuals and results in milder

illness in the few who get the disease. Immunization does not prevent carriage of toxigenic strains so that it is important to continue routine boosters throughout childhood and adult life in order to prevent disease.

Adverse reactions Slight fever, local pain, redness, and/or swelling at the injection site occasionally occur. Sterile abscesses rarely occur after use of absorbed vaccines containing diphtheria toxoid, most often because of inadvertent subcutaneous rather than intramuscular injection. In children over seven years of age and in adults a reduced dose of diphtheria toxoid must be used in order to minimize adverse reactions.

Material risks Convulsions compatible with simple febrile seizures may rarely occur after diphtheria toxoid in association with high fever. Such convulsions are not associated with brain damage or an increased risk of subsequent epilepsy. Systemic allergic reactions (anaphylaxis, urticaria, bronchospasm laryngospasm, angioneurotic edema) are rare; in children over seven years of age and in adults a reduced dose of diphtheria toxoid must be used in order to minimize adverse reactions.

Reportable events Fever greater than 40.5°C; convulsions; or systemic allergic reactions occurring within 72 hours of vaccination. Other neurologic events occurring within 15 days of vaccination.

Tetanus Toxoid

Benefits Tetanus (lockjaw) is a neurologic disease with severe muscular spasms caused by the neurotoxin produced by *Clostridium tetani* in a contaminated wound. The case fatality rate is approximately 60%. The majority of cases in Canada occur after wounds so trivial that medical attention was not sought. Tetanus toxoid is virtually 100% effective in preventing tetanus in fully immunized individuals. However, because tetanus spores are widely distributed throughout the environment and the bacteria are commonly found in the intestinal tracts of humans and animals, routine boosters every 10 years for life are necessary to maintain protective immunity.

Adverse reactions Slight fever, local pain, redness, and/or swelling at the injection site occasionally occur. Sterile abscesses rarely occur after use of adsorbed vaccines containing tetanus toxoid, most often because of inadvertent subcutaneous rather than intramuscular injection. Severe local reactions, with marked swelling, redness, pain, and tenderness, usually accompanied by fever, malaise, and myalgia may occur in persons who have received an excessive number of boosters of tetanus toxoid.

Material risks Convulsions compatible with simple febrile seizures may rarely occur after tetanus toxoid in association with high fever. Such convulsions are not associated with brain damage or an increased risk of subsequent epilepsy. Systemic allergic reactions (anaphylaxis, urticaria, bronchospasm, laryngospasm, angioneurotic edema) are rare.

Reportable events Fever greater than 40.5°C; convulsions, or systemic allergic reactions occurring within 72 hours of vaccination. Other neurologic events occurring within 15 days of vaccination.

Poliomyelitis Vaccine

Benefits Although most infections with polio virus manifest as asymptomatic or nonspecific febrile illnesses, the infection may lead to paralytic disease or death as a result of damage to lower motor neurons. Two types of vaccine are available, both of which are trivalent formulations containing types 1, 2, and 3 polio virus: the inactivated polio virus vaccine (IPV) which is administered by injection and the live, attenuated oral polio virus vaccine (OPV). Both vaccines prevent paralytic disease in over 95% of recipients.

Adverse reactions No serious side effects of currently available IPV have been documented.

Material risks Because IPV contains trace amounts of streptomycin and neomycin, systemic allergic reactions in individuals sensitive to these antibiotics are possible, but are extremely rare.

The use of OPV has been associated with paralytic disease in both recipients of the vaccine and in their contacts. The risk of such disease is significantly increased in infants with severe immunodeficiency disorders. However, in none of the 14 cases reported in the US between 1973 and 1984 was the diagnosis of immune deficiency known prior to administration of OPV.

To reduce the risk of vaccine-associated paralytic disease in unvaccinated parents or other adult household contacts, administration of one dose of IPV to them at the same time as the child's first dose of IPV is recommended. The adults should then complete their basic immunization. Hand washing following contact such as diaper changing reduces the potential for viral transmission as well. The risk of paralytic disease after receipt of the first dose of OPV is estimated to be one in 9.5 million doses distributed. The risk after subsequent doses is 1% of this rate. The risk of vaccine-associated paralytic disease in contacts is one per 3.2 million doses distributed. These estimates are based on the doses distributed in Canada from 1965-1988.

Reportable events Systemic allergic reactions. Paralytic disease occurring within four weeks of administration of OPV.

Pertussis Vaccine

Benefits Pertussis (whooping cough) is a bacterial infection of the respiratory tract resulting in severe coughing spells (paroxysms), often followed by an inspiratory whoop and vomiting. The paroxysmal stage lasts 2-4 weeks. The total duration of illness in uncomplicated cases is 6-10 weeks. Complications include apneic spells, seizures and pneumonia, encephalopathy and death. Complications are much more common in the first year of life: the frequencies of pneumonia and seizures, and encephalopathy in young infants hospitalized with pertussis are 20% and 0.5%, respectively. At least half of those who develop pertussis encephalopathy sustain permanent brain damage. Pertussis is prevented in over 80% of children who have received at least three doses of vaccine and is milder in vaccinated children who do become ill.

Adverse reactions   Common minor reactions to pertussis vaccine include: fever 30°C - 47%; local redness 2.4 cm - 7%; swelling 2.4 cm - 9%
pain at injection site - 51%; drowsiness - 32%; fretfulness - 53%; anorexia - 21%; vomiting - 6%.

The incidence and height of fever can be significantly reduced by administration of acetaminophen (15 mg/kg/dose) at the time of vaccination and every four hours thereafter as necessary. Fussiness is also significantly reduced. Such treatment has less effect on local reactions. Sterile abscesses may occur at a rate of one per 100,000 doses, most often as the result of inadvertent subcutaneous injection of adsorbed vaccine.

Material risks   Uncommon but severe reactions occurring within 48-72 hours of vaccination include: persistent, inconsolable crying lasting over three hours - 1%; convulsions - one in 1750 doses; hypotonic-hyporesponsive state - one in 1750 cases.

There may be an increased risk of convulsions in a child with a history of previous seizures or with a history of seizures in parents or siblings. Such convulsions almost always occur in association with high fever and do not increase the risk of brain damage or subsequent epilepsy. The incidence of such seizures associated with fever can probably be reduced by the use of prophylactic acetaminophen as discussed above.

Reportable events   Major reactions occurring within 72 hours of vaccination, including: convulsion, hypotonic-hyporesponsive state, fever greater than 40.5°C, persistent crying over three   hours, encephalopathy, and/or systemic allergic reaction.

Measles Vaccine

Benefits   Measles (rubeola) is often a severe disease, frequently complicated by otitis media or bronchopneumonia. Encephalitis occurs in approximately one per 2000 reported cases. Survivors often have permanent brain damage and/or mental retardation. Death occurs in one of every 3000 reported cases. The risk of death and complications is higher for infants and adults than for children and adolescents. Subacute sclerosing panencephalitis (SSPE), a fatal, chronic infection of the brain, is also a complication of measles infection. Prior to widespread use of measles vaccine, virtually all children acquired measles by age 18. The incidence of measles has decreased by over 99% because of routine immunization of infants and children. Moreover SSPE has virtually disappeared from North America. The live, further attenuated measles vaccine (Moratem strain) in current use was licensed in 1968. Measles vaccine is over 95% effective in children vaccinated at 15 months of age or older and is only slightly less effective in infants vaccinated between 12 and 14 months of age.

Adverse reactions   From 5% to 15% of vaccine recipients may develop fever of 39.5°C or greater between 5-10 days after vaccination. Most persons with fever are otherwise asymptomatic. Transient rashes occur in 5% of vaccines.

Material risks As with any agent which may cause fever, the use of measles vaccine may result in a simple, febrile seizure in some children. Such febrile seizures do not increase the probability of subsequent epilepsy or other neurologic disorders.   The incidence of such febrile seizures may be slightly higher in children with a personal history of convulsions or with a history of convulsions in parents or siblings. The benefits of measles vaccine outweigh the risk of febrile seizures in children with a personal or family history of convulsions. Encephalitis and encephalopathy have been reported with a frequency of less than one case per million doses administered, a rate that is lower than the incidence of encephalitis of unknown etiology in the same age group, suggesting that severe neurologic reactions may be only temporally rather than causally related to measles vaccine.

There is no evidence of an enhanced risk of any reactions from administering live measles vaccine to persons already immune to measles, either from natural disease or previous vaccination with live vaccine. Immediate hypersensitivity reactions (bronchospasm, anaphylaxis) have very rarely been reported after vaccination of children who have severe systemic allergic reactions after eating eggs.

Persons with such severe hypersensitivity to eggs should be vaccinated only with extreme caution. Persons who have systemic allergic reactions after topical or systemic use of neomycin should not receive measles vaccine which contains trace amounts of neomycin. Live measles vaccine does not contain penicillin.
Persons with immune deficiency diseases or immunosuppressive therapy should not receive live measles vaccine or any other live, viral vaccine. Patients with leukemia in remission whose chemotherapy has been terminated for at least three months may receive live virus vaccines. Persons infected with human immunodeficiency virus should not receive live vaccines, regardless of the clinical status of their HIV infection. Short-term corticosteroid therapy (two weeks), topical steroid therapy, and intra-articular, bursal, or tendon injections of corticosteroids are not immunosuppressive and do not contraindicate measles vaccination.
Reportable events Atypical measles in a person previously immunized with killed measles vaccine. Seizures, encephalitis, or other neurologic reactions occurring 5-14 days after measles vaccination.

Mumps Vaccine
Benefits Mumps is a common infection of children which may cause fever, headache, and inflammation of the parotid and other salivary glands. It causes aseptic meningitis in 10% of children who get infected. Rarely it can cause encephalitis which usually resolves without sequelae. Mumps can also cause deafness. About one out of every four adolescents or adult men who get mumps develops orchitis, which rarely may cause sterility. Mumps vaccine is a live, attenuated viral vaccine grown in chick embryo cell cultures. It is usually given in combination with measles and rubella vaccines. Because of widespread use of mumps vaccine, which is over 95% effective in preventing disease, the incidence of mumps has decreased dramatically.

Adverse reactions Adverse reactions to live mumps vaccine include parotitis in a very small percentage of recipients. Other reactions are extremely rare. Neurologic complications after mumps vaccination are less frequent than the observed background incidence in normal populations.

Material risks Although no serious reactions have been reported in immunodeficient patients after mumps vaccine, live viral vaccine should not be administered to such individuals. Children who develop systemic allergic reactions after eating eggs should receive mumps vaccine only with extreme caution because of the remote potential risk of hypersensitivity reactions since the vaccine is prepared in chick embryo cell culture.

Reportable events Orchitis, parotitis, and neurologic illness within 21 days of mumps vaccination.

Rubella Vaccine

Benefits Rubella (German measles) is usually a very mild disease in children, with slight fever, rash, and swelling of lymph nodes in the neck which last about three days. Symptoms are more severe in adolescents and adults. Transient polyarthralgia and/or polyarthritis occurs in 15%-25% of adolescent and adult females. Encephalitis and thrombocytopenia are rare complications of rubella.

If a susceptible woman is infected with rubella in the first 12 weeks of gestation, there is a 75% or greater probability of fetal death or serious malformation. The most common congenital malformations involve the eye (cataracts, microphthalmia, glaucoma, chorioretinitis), the heart (patent ductus arteriosus, peripheral pulmonic stenosis, atrial or ventricular septal defects), the ear (sensorineural deafness) and the brain (microcephaly, meningoencephalitis, mental retardation). In addition, most infants with the congenital rubella syndrome have growth retardation. Late complications include juvenile onset diabetes, thyroid insufficiency, and an SSPE-like syndrome.

Rubella vaccine is a live, attenuated viral vaccine grown in human diploid cell cultures. It induces protective antibodies in over 98% of recipients. One dose of vaccine confers long-lasting, probably lifelong, immunity.

Adverse reactions Rash, fever and lymphadenopathy occur in less than 5% of recipients within 10-14 days of vaccination. Polyarthralgia may occur in 15%-20% of adolescent and adult women, approximately 7-21 days postimmunization.

Material risks Polyarthritis is much less common than polyarthralgia after rubella vaccine. Joint symptoms are almost always transient, but chronic arthritis has rarely occurred. Although no serious reactions have been reported in immunodeficient patients after rubella vaccine, live viral vaccine should not be administered to such individuals.

Pregnant women should not receive rubella vaccine, even though the congenital rubella syndrome has not been observed following vaccination of susceptible, pregnant women. There is no risk of transmission of rubella vaccine from a recipient to a household contact so that there is no risk in vaccinating children whose mothers or other household contacts are pregnant.

Reportable events   Chronic arthritis following onset of acute joint symptoms within 21 days of rubella vaccination.   Vaccination of a woman in the first trimester of pregnancy.

Hemophilus b Conjugate Vaccines

Benefits *Haemophilus influenzae* type b is the most common cause of bacterial meningitis and a leading cause of other severe invasive infections in young children. About 60% of affected children have meningitis and 40% have bacteremia, epiglottitis, cellulitis, pneumonia, or septic arthritis. Approximately 1000 cases of meningitis occur annually in Canada, 60%-70% of which occur in children less than 24 months of age. Five per cent of children with meningitis die and 10%-15% have severe neurologic sequelae. Deafness occurs in 15%-20% of survivors and is severe in 3%-7%. The risk of haemophilus meningitis is at least twice as high in children attending full-time group day care as in children cared for at home. The risk is also increased in children with splenic dysfunction (e.g., sickle cell disease, asplenia) or antibody deficiency syndromes and in Inuit children.

Routine immunization of all children is recommended beginning at two months of age.[13] Until data are available, vaccines cannot be considered inter-changeable at doses below 18 months of age. The immunization series should be completed using the vaccine initially chosen. Immunization does not prevent carriage of *H. influenzae* type b so that rifampin prophylaxis should be used in immunized children whenever such prophylaxis is indicated.

Adverse reactions Local redness, induration, and tenderness at the injection site occur in up to 7% of infants. Fever greater than or equal to 39°C occurs in less than 1% and irritability in about 15% of recipients. Rates of local and systemic reactions after the conjugate vaccine were no higher in vaccinated infants than in recipients of placebo. No severe reactions have been reported as a result of more than several million doses of PRP-D vaccine or in clinical trials of the other conjugate vaccines.

Material risks Convulsions compatible with simple febrile seizures may rarely occur after Hemophilus b Conjugate Vaccine in association with high fever. Such convulsions are not associated with brain damage or increased risk of subsequent epilepsy.

Reportable events   Fever greater than 40.5°C; convulsions. Other neurologic events occurring with 72 hours of vaccination. Invasive *H. influenzae* type b disease occurring at any time in a vaccinated child.

Hepatitis B Vaccine

Benefits Most people infected with hepatitis B recover completely. The remain-der constitute a spectrum of chronicity ranging from asymptomatic carrier state, through ongoing debility and liver dysfunction, to cirrhosis and hepato-cellular carcinoma. Rarely the infection causes acute fulminant hepatitis and death within days of onset. Newborns of infected mothers are at greater risk of developing chronic disease.

Two types of vaccine are available. They contain purified forms of hepatitis B surface antigen (HBsAg) which stimulates the production of protective surface antibody (anti-HBs) in the recipient. One vaccine is derived from the plasma of hepatitis B carriers and the other vaccine is produced through recombinant DNA technology. Both are equivalent in their protective efficacy against infection with the hepatitis B virus. Recommendations for hepatitis B vaccination are included in tables 8.2, 8.3. On the basis of evidence now available, NACI no longer recommends booster vaccination in immunocompetent people.[14]

Adverse reactions   Soreness at the site of injection occurs in up to 15% of recipients. Other less frequent reactions include febrile reactions to 38.5°C as well as malaise, fatigue, headache, nausea, myalgia and arthralgia. However, these effects are infrequent and transient, usually resolving within 48 hours following vaccination. Serious neurological disorders including Guillain-Barre syndrome and seizures have been reported in a temporal association with administration of the vaccine. However, no cause and effect relationship has been established, and these events are believed to have occurred by chance alone within large cohorts of vaccine recipients.

Material risks   Systemic allergic reactions including anaphylaxis are possible in the presence of sensitivity to substances used in the manufacture of the vaccines, including formalin, mercury, aluminium and yeast.

Reportable events   Febrile reactions greater than 40.5°C; systemic allergic reactions occurring within 72 hours of vaccination; other neurologic events occurring within 15 days of vaccination.

Rabies Vaccine

Benefits   Rabies is an acute central nervous system disease that is almost invariably fatal. The disease usually lasts two to six days, progressing to paralysis, spasms of the throat muscles on swallowing, delirium, convulsions and death. Human exposure results from the bite of a rabid animal. Infection is also possible via a scratch or when virus-laden saliva is introduced into a fresh break in the skin or onto intact mucous membrane. The disease has an incubation period that is usually two to eight weeks, allowing the opportunity for postexposure prophylaxis.

Human diploid cell rabies vaccine (HDCV) is an inactivated virus vaccine grown in human cell culture. HDCV in combination with Rabies Immune Globulin is highly effective in preventing rabies in exposed individuals. Rabies vaccine is also used for pre-exposure prophylaxis and produces satisfactory antibody titres in virtually all recipients. Pre-exposure immunization does not eliminate the need for prompt postexposure prophylaxis following an exposure but it reduces the postexposure regime.

Postexposure immunization[11] protocols for the administration of postexposure rabies vaccine, and additionally Rabies Immune Globulin (RIG) for passive protection have been developed. (i) The first consideration is whether exposure to saliva, whether by animal bite or contact with an open wound or mucous membrane occurred. (ii) The next consideration is the epidemiology of rabies in the animal species and geographic area involved and whether there is a risk following exposure. (iii) Whether it was likely that the animal was rabid based on the previous information and the behaviour of the animal, e.g., an unprovoked attack, must then be considered. If unlikely, and the animal is a dog or a cat for which adequate arrangements can be made for a 10-day observation period, then it is not necessary to treat the exposed with vaccine unless the animal becomes ill during the observation period. (iv) If the conditions in (iii) are not met and there has been exposure to a potentially rabid animal, HDCV should be administered IM in the deltoid at least on days 0 and 3. If the individual has not been previously administered HDCV (or another rabies vaccine if it gave an acceptable response) these injections are continued on days 7, 14, and 28. Additionally, 20 I.U. of RIG should be infiltrated around the bite and injected into the gluteal region on day 0. (v) If the animal's brain was available for testing and the results not positive for rabies antigen with direct fluorescent antibody response, postexposure prophylaxis can be discontinued.

Adverse reactions About 25% of vaccine recipients may develop local reactions such as pain, redness, swelling or itching at the injection site. Mild systemic reactions such as headache, nausea, abdominal pain, muscle aches and dizziness may occur in about 20% of recipients.

Material risks Acute hypersensitivity reactions, e.g., anaphylaxis or hives, have occurred in about one per 10,000 recipients. Type III hypersensitivity reactions have occurred in about 7% of recipients of booster doses or rabies vaccines and at an overall rate of about nine per 10,000 recipients. These are serum sickness-like reactions characterized by pruritic rash or urticaria, sometimes accompanied by arthralgias, angioedema, fever, nausea, vomiting and malaise. They begin two to 21 days after a dose of vaccine, and last a few days with complete recovery. Two cases of neurologic illness resembling Guillain-Barre syndrome that resolved without sequelae in 12 weeks have been reported, as has one case of a focal subacute central nervous system disorder temporally associated with HDCV vaccine.

Reportable events Systemic allergic reactions occurring within three weeks of vaccination; neurologic events occurring within 15 days of vaccination.

Influenza

Benefits Influenza is an acute illness caused by infection with either Type A or Type B influenza virus. It remains a worldwide epidemic disease and is a cause of significant morbidity and mortality, particularly in high-risk groups. Classic influenzal illness is characterized by sudden onset, fever and nonproductive cough together with headache, muscle aches, nasal obstruction and sore throat. In children, influenza may present as laryngotracheobronchitis (croup).

Complications of the disease in all age groups include pneumonia, either due to the influenza virus itself or a secondary bacterial infection, and worsening of chronic diseases, particularly those affecting the heart and lungs. There is a significant increase in hospitalization and mortality rates in high-risk groups including those over 65 and those with chronic heart and lung diseases. The influenza vaccine is a killed viral vaccine with excellent reliability and potency. It is available as whole virus or "split-virus". The vaccine provides a 30% - 70% reduction in illness in all populations and a reduction of 60% - 87% in deaths in high-risk individuals.

NACI recommended the trivalent influenza vaccine containing A/Texas/36/91 (H1N1)-like strain, an A/Beijing/353/89 (H3N2)-like strain, and a B/Panama/45/90-like strain for the 1992-3 season in Canada.[15]

Adverse reactions The most frequent adverse reactions are local pain and redness at the injection site. These occur in from 25% - 60% of patients. Two types of systemic reactions may also occur. One is fever, muscle aches and systemic symptoms of toxicity beginning six to 12 hours after vaccination and lasting up to two days. Fever and systemic signs occur in the range of 5% - 30%. The other systemic reaction which is extremely rare is an immediate reaction and is presumably allergic in nature. Hives, angioedema, allergic asthma or anaphylaxis may occur. These probably represent reactions to residual egg protein in the vaccine in patients with severe egg allergies. Children 12 years of age or younger should be given the split-virus preparation to reduce the chances of adverse reactions.

Neurologic complications such as the Guillain-Barre syndrome were noted with the 1976 swine influenza vaccine. Subsequent vaccines, however, have not been associated with an increased frequency of this syndrome. A number of adverse incidents affecting the nervous system have been reported following influenza vaccination. These include facial paralysis, encephalitis, demyelinating disease and labyrinthitis. However, a cause and effect relationship has not been proven.

Influenza vaccine is believed to be safe for use in pregnant women without a history of severe egg allergy.

Material risks Immediate reactions which are likely allergic in nature such as hives, asthma, angioedema or anaphylaxis are extremely rare. Individuals with severe allergies to eggs should not be given the vaccine.

Reportable events Immediate reactions such as: hives, angioedema, allergic asthma, anaphylaxis; Guillain-Barre syndrome and other serious neurologic illnesses such as paralysis, encephalitis or demyelinating disease; interference with clearance of warfarin and theophylline.

Meningococcal Vaccine
Benefits General recommendations for the use of meningococcal vaccine for disease prevention are found in the Canadian Immunization Guide, and control of clusters has been discussed in a recent report.[11,16]

Adverse reactions Adverse reactions are uncommon and not severe after a single dose. Immediate wheal and flare reactions occur occasionally, and localized erythema may persist for one to two days. More severe reactions may follow revaccination. The safety of meningococcal vaccines in pregnant women has not been established.

2.   SEXUALLY TRANSMITTED DISEASES

2.1.   INCIDENCE

In general, socioeconomic conditions and changes in lifestyle in North America are likely to have contributed to the observed increase in sexually transmitted diseases (STDs) in Canada. The 1960s brought new affluence, and with it more leisure time, social mobility and general laxity and permissiveness in behaviour. In addition, the ready availability of birth control methods decreased the probability of unwanted pregnancy. The emergence of AIDS as a major cause of death in homosexual males in the 1980s and early 1990s was also related to these changes in social norms. Subsequently, however, HIV infection in users of intravenous drugs, in new immigrants from AIDS-endemic countries, and in sexual partners of these groups, has established the disease in the socioeconomically disadvantaged and their next generation.

Genital chlamydia, gonorrhea and AIDS now account for more than half of the reported cases of all notifiable diseases combined. Despite effective antibiotic therapy, there has been a rise in the incidence of gonorrhea in the past two decades (although a recent downward dip has occurred) and a persistence of syphilis after a rapid decline in the 1940s and 1950s. In 1988, the reported incidence rates for Canada per 100,000 for STDs were: chlamydia (216.8), gonorrhea (80.0); syphilis (6.1); and AIDS (3.1). Syphilis in pregnancy occurred in 17 per 100,000 live births and congenital syphilis in 4.9 per 1,000 live births in Alberta between 1981 and 1988. The incidence of congenital syphilis is related to young maternal age, ethnicity (Aboriginal Peoples), lack of prenatal care and failure of health professionals to repeat non-treponemal tests (VDRL/RPR) in the third trimester. The proportion of penicillin-resistant isolates (PPNG) of *Neisseria gonorrhea* has been increasing in many provinces with consequent treatment implications which are discussed later in this chapter.

Infection with genital *Chlamydia trachomatis* has emerged as the most frequent STD in recent years in Canada, occuring three to five times more frequently than gonorrheal infections, and responsible for over 50,000 reported cases of STD during 1989-90.[17] The rise in the number of reported cases is, in part, related to an increase in awareness of the disease and better diagnostic techniques, resulting in increased reporting. Chlamydial infection became nationally notifiable only in 1990. Some provincial figures are available prior to this. The rate for Quebec in

1989 was 295.1 per 100,000. In Ontario there was a steady rise in the incidence rate of genital chlamydia from 57 in 1985 to 174 cases per 100,000 in 1989. The disease is most prevalent among sexually active adolescents, particularly females aged 15-19 years. Serious long-term consequences for females are pelvic inflammatory disease, ectopic pregnancy and infertility.

AIDS was first identified in Canada in 1979, and its incidence has increased since then. It became a reportable disease in Canada in 1982. The number of cases reported in 1982, 1985, 1988 and 1991 were 29; 360; 1068 and 1184 respectively.[18] The cumulative total of deaths due to AIDS in Canada reached 6,187 of the total (9,083) cases by June 30, 1993.[19] This accounts for 1% of the reported incidence worldwide. Epidemiological evidence indicates that about 50% of HIV carriers will develop AIDS within 10 to 11 years after infection, and it is estimated that 30,000 Canadians have been infected so far. Most AIDS cases were reported from Ontario (39%) Quebec (31%) and British Columbia (19%).

AIDS is caused by the Human Immunodeficiency Virus (HIV) which is transmitted by four routes: (a) sexual contact with an infected partner, (b) via infected blood and blood products, (c) from an infected mother to her unborn child and perinatally, and (d) through needles and syringes shared among intravenous drug abusers. Sexual contact is the most frequent route, both homosexual and heterosexual. Anal and vaginal intercourse pose the greatest risk. Not all individuals exposed to HIV are at risk of HIV infection; the factors influencing this finding are poorly understood. With rare exceptions, most patients have seroconverted by six months after exposure, the majority seroconverting within two to six weeks. Evidence from virus isolation studies indicates that the majority of individuals who are HIV antibody positive have the virus in their lymphocytes. All people with reactive HIV serology must be considered infectious. However, since some infected individuals may not develop the HIV antibody, any person who has been exposed or belongs to a high-risk group should be considered potentially infectious regardless of serologic status.

Of men developing AIDS, nearly 20% are in the 20-29 year age group and 83% reported homosexual or bisexual activity. The number of cases in women, mainly of reproductive age and resulting from heterosexual activity with a person at risk (31%) or with a person from an AIDS endemic country (28%), has grown from 13 in 1983 to 261 in mid-1991. There is a disproportionate number of women affected in Quebec, compared to other provinces, likely linked to immigration. Studies of HIV seroprevalence in child-bearing women in Canada show rates of 6.1/10,000 (Quebec, 1989), 2.8/10,000 (Ontario, 1990) and 2.7/10,000 (B.C. and the Yukon).[20] There were 62 cases of AIDS diagnosed in children under age 15 by August 1991, 80% being the result of perinatal transmission. AIDS is associated with increases in tuberculosis morbidity. Between 2%-5% of all AIDS cases have tuberculosis as well. AIDS has a very high mortality rate (60% of all persons diagnosed with AIDS in Canada have died), with the median length of time between onset of AIDS and death estimated at 10 months. AIDS is becoming one of the major causes of death among males 30-39 years of age in Canada.

2.2.   TRADITIONAL STD PREVENTION

The past and present mainstay of STD services has consisted of attempts to control syphilis, gonorrhea and other sexually transmitted diseases based on secondary prevention involving diagnosis and treatment, and primary or secondary prevention for contacts of the infected. AIDS marks a departure from this model as curative treatment is not available. Representative current treatment schedules for STDs are given in appendix B. Patients with gonorrhea, syphilis and chlamydia may be asymptomatic, making it difficult to control infections and trace contacts. The other problems associated with control are difficulties in the follow up of contacts, poor compliance with treatment regimens by patients and the lack of physician reporting of cases. Contact tracing provided by public health staff is often more effective than that provided by medical practitioners.

2.3   HEALTH PROMOTION IN SEXUAL HEALTH

More recently the concept of **healthy sexuality** has been introduced as a modality of primary prevention.[21] Healthy sexuality is comfort with one's own sexuality, body characteristics and effectiveness in making decisions   among choices relevant to sexuality, such as contraception, pregnancy and prevention of sexually transmitted disease. Developing a positive sexual health status therefore involves a multifaceted approach of health education, self-esteem and decision-making skills for behavioural change, as well as communication of specific knowledge such as methods of birth control (oral contraception and barrier methods) and STD prevention (safer sex techniques).

Education and communication in this area must be innovative and sustain the interest of youth. For example, it has been recognized in a number of surveys on sexual attitudes of Canadian youth that there are a number of barriers to behaviour change towards adoption of safer sex practices. The results of one of these surveys, The Canada Youth and AIDS Survey, have been provided in chapter four. Although young people appear to have adequate knowledge about STDs, they are unlikely to interpret risks personally and will take the view that "it cannot happen to me."[22] Approaches to personalizing the information on AIDS, for example, may be more successful. Having a speaker with AIDS talk to high school students is one approach. Public health units have developed rap videos on safer sex in an attempt to reach youth. Simulation of actual methods of putting condoms on may also enhance personal skill development.

Efforts to provide greater access for communication about sexual health and services with high-risk groups are also being developed. These include: a) more accessible clinics (locating clinics in high schools[23] and providing other user-friendly types of facilities in shopping malls); b) reaching homeless youth in the community through outreach workers employed by health departments; and c) community development. Health promotion strategies are multifaceted; for example, healthy public policy approaches encouraging schools to provide condom machines in washrooms. Furthermore, another important aspect of healthy sexuality are behaviours that are reinforced by creation of healthy social environments in which healthy sexual mores are the community norm. Community development, such as has occurred in gay communities, can result in widespread behaviour change. However, the continued incidence of HIV infection in the 1990s—especially in groups previously largely unaffected—remains a major concern, as are the rising incidence of chlamydia and localized increases in syphilis.

AIDS

Strategies to control AIDS have focused on preventing the spread of HIV infection.[24,25] Strategies to control sexual transmission of the virus include the promotion of behavioural change to limit the number of sexual partners and the use of condoms for safer sex. To prevent transmission by infected blood and blood products, the Red Cross has initiated a policy of requesting members of high-risk groups to refrain from donating blood. Since the fall of 1985, all blood collected by the Canadian Red Cross Society has been screened for HIV antibodies, and further transmission through blood products is highly unlikely. Similarly, all factor VIII concentrate now used by hemophiliacs is heat-treated to inactivate the virus. However, AIDS may still develop in some individuals infected by this route before 1985. Sperm and organ donors are screened for the presence of HIV antibody. Strategies for prevention of spread among drug users involve the establishment of needle-exchange clinics (where clean equipment can be obtained) and the training of IV drug users in disinfecting their equipment using bleach kits.[26] Finally, recommendations have been made for health-care personnel to adopt universal precautions for handling body fluids.

Testing those at risk for HIV has assumed importance largely as a means of reinforcing the need for adopting safer sex behaviour as well as providing clinical information for individual patients about their own HIV status. Guidelines for HIV testing which involve pre-and post-test counselling have been promulgated because it is important that persons being tested understand the disease and the implications of the test.[27] Anonymous testing is being offered to those concerned about confidentiality of results.

The components of health promotion (as established in the Ottawa Charter) have been applied to AIDS in terms of a comprehensive and integrated basis for action in the 1990s.[28] The implementation of **healthy public policy**, interpreted as minimizing structural discrimination against those who are HIV infected, will reduce the alienation of those needing health and social services and increase their contacts. A social **environment supportive** of safer sex practices, such as the use of condoms (and safer injecting drug use), can utilize the principles of social marketing. Development of **personal skills** in safer sexual behaviour can be achieved by applying the communication-education theory, particularly by developing infrastructures for communication to at-risk groups, such as outreach programs and small group sessions. Promotion of the **strengthening of communities** has resulted in action to enhance behaviour change and behavioural norms in at-risk groups. Strategies for the last component of the Ottawa Charter approach, **re-orientation of the health system** emphasizing a community approach, have been indicated throughout the above section.

2.4. GENERAL GUIDELINES FOR THE TREATMENT OF SEXUALLY TRANSMITTED DISEASES[29]

Trends in the common sexually transmitted diseases were described in chapter five. This section will describe general approaches to the treatment of STDs, incorporating two authoritative sources of information. The primary source is the *Canadian Guidelines for the Prevention, Diagnosis, Management and Treatment of Sexually Transmitted Diseases in Neonates, Children, Adolescents and Adults*,[29,30] produced by an interdisciplinary committee of experts from across Canada, under the aegis of the federal Laboratory Centre for Disease Control. This section largely reproduces the 1988 Canadian guidelines, but treatment regimens are updated where indicated in the 1992 (most recent) version.

Multiple STD Infections
The presence of a sexually transmitted infection should alert the clinician to the likelihood of infection with other sexually transmitted organisms, including the AIDS virus (HIV). Attention should be focused on management of disease syndromes, not just on infection by a single organism. A careful and thorough search, using physical examination, serologic tests, smears and cultures, is essential to determine appropriate treatment.

Sexual Abuse
STDs are transmitted primarily by sexual contact. These infections do occur in children and adolescents. The presence of any of the following in **any prepubertal child** (defined as, female: no breast budding; male: no penile or testicular enlargement) **should make consideration of sexual abuse mandatory**: gonorrhea, chlamydial infection (except that acquired perinatally), syphilis (except congenital), genital warts, trichomoniasis, genital herpes infection and bacterial vaginosis. Hospitalization may be indicated until such time as the situation can be clarified. Adequate microbiologic documentation must be obtained by taking appropriate slides and cultures and performing other tests. This information can be obtained from a specialist or an authoritative manual.

Confidentiality
Confidentiality of records and medical services must be assured in both inpatient and outpatient settings.

Sexual History

A careful sexual history should include details of the specific types of sexual activity, sites of sexual contact, sexual orientation, use of condoms, use of birth control, number of partners, previous STDs and STD symptoms in the patient and partner(s). Terminology that is understood by the patient must be used. This is particularly important for the prepubescent child and young adolescent.

Contacts

The source of the STD must be found and treated. This includes sexual contacts and parent(s) of infected neonates, as well as sexual abuse perpetrators. Sexual activity must not be resumed until the patient and partner(s) are adequately treated and have returned for a test of cure.

Compliance

Compliance with treatment protocols may be a significant problem for many individuals. Therefore, treatment for outpatients should be as simple as possible without compromising therapeutic principles. Access to facilities, costs of medication, dosage schedule and perception of the severity of illness all affect compliance.

Education and Counselling

Individuals are often not adequately educated in methods of protecting themselves from infection with an STD or pregnancy. Appropriate education and counselling must be provided and must include information on STDs, including AIDS, and how to have safer sex. Education and counselling should be adjusted to the cognitive and emotional development of the individual patient.

Follow Up

Rigorous followup is necessary for all STDs to determine whether there has been an appropriate clinical and microbiologic response to therapy and whether there is now evidence of infection with a second organism.

Isolation of Hospitalized Patients with STDs

Most hospitalized patients who have an STD are not infectious to their health care providers or other patients. Good hand washing technique on the part of older patients and health-care providers must be stressed. Neonates and infants with gonococcal ophthalmia, disseminated gonococcal disease, disseminated or mucocutaneous herpes simplex or congenital syphilis must be isolated according to accepted infection control protocols.

Reporting of STDs

Many STDs are reportable by law to the local medical officer of health. Local regulations should be consulted regarding the reportability of specific STDs. Reporting of STDs is an important facet of STD control. Reporting not only results in statistical information and disease trends but also provides a method of ensuring that both the patient and his or her sexual contacts have been adequately treated. If there are further specific questions regarding diagnosis and treatment, or response to treatment, a specialist in the field should be consulted.

Special Considerations for Adolescents

As many sexually active adolescents use no birth control and are at risk of becoming pregnant, treatment regimens for STD in pregnancy must be considered.

Street youths and others whose compliance with medical follow up is in doubt should have appropriate laboratory investigations done and receive treatment for gonorrhea and chlamydial infection independent of clinical findings and before culture results are available.

Contact tracing can be more difficult in the adolescent group, and compliance with treatment and follow up is often poor.

Compliance can be a significant problem in the adolescent. Therefore, treatment for outpatients should be as simple as possible without compromising therapeutic principles. Access to facilities, cost of medication, dosage schedule and perception of the severity of illness all affect compliance.

Hospitalization is strongly recommended for all adolescents with pelvic inflammatory disease (PID). As compliance with either medical regimens or appointments may be a problem for many teenagers, optimal treatment cannot be guaranteed on an outpatient basis. Since the sequelae of poorly treated PID are so profound, particularly in terms of increasing risks of infertility, ectopic pregnancies and chronic pelvic pain, aggressive inpatient therapy should always be favoured over outpatient management. If hospitalization is not possible, close outpatient follow up is mandatory. Hospitalization may also be indicated if sexual abuse is suspected.

Educational counselling regarding STD prevention, as well as birth control counselling, should accompany medical treatment of STD in all adolescents, both male and female. It should be adapted to the cognitive and emotional development of the adolescent.

Neonates, Children and Adolescents at High Risk of STD

i) Neonates: mother from a high-risk group (e.g., prostitutes):
  - STD status of mother unknown (i.e., no prenatal care, lack of screening tests).

ii) Children who have been sexually abused.

iii) Individuals with signs or symptoms of infection:
  - adolescents with urethritis, cervicitis, epididymitis or genital warts;
  - male adolescents with pyuria;
  - prepubescent children with urethritis, vaginitis, genital warts or genital herpes;
  - sexually active females with lower abdominal pain.

Individuals who are sexual contacts of proven or suspected STD cases

- individuals with possible exposure;
- adolescents prostitutes, both male and female;
- sexually active adolescents;
- pregnant adolescents;
- adolescents undergoing therapeutic abortion;
- siblings of sexual abuse cases;
- drug abusers.

The specific treatments for most commonly occuring STDs are given in Appendix B, and readers are advised to refer for further details to *Canadian Guidelines for Prevention, Diagnosis, Management and Treatment of Sexually Transmitted Diseases in Neonates, Children, Adolescents and Adults, 1992,*[29] published by Health and Welfare Canada. The provinces may follow national guidelines or may promulgate their own guidelines with minor modifications; these are available through local public health departments.

3.   FOOD-BORNE DISEASE

Food-borne disease contributes significantly to the burden of morbidity from communicable disease in Canada. The Federal Health Protection Branch receives about 5,000 reports of such infections per year. This, however, is likely a gross under-estimate as most infections are unreported; the actual number may likely be 500,000. From 1982 to 1989 in Ontario, 90% of food-borne outbreaks were caused by bacteria, 6% by viruses and 4% by chemicals (domoic acid in molluscs and MSG).[31] The most common foodborne infections were caused by *Salmonella sp.*, *Staph. Aureus.*, *Clostridium perfringens*, and *Campylobacter sp.* Deaths related to food-borne disease have been reported in recent times from botulism (fermented salmon eggs), an *E. Coli* 0157:H7 outbreak in a nursing home, salmonellosis (chicken), staphylococal intoxication (evaporated milk) and sulfites (hamburger loaf). *Giardiasis* is a water-borne disease that has caused outbreaks of gastroenteritis symptoms in Canada from unfiltered water supplies.

4.   SUMMARY

Despite the widespread availability of most vaccines, localized outbreaks of communicable diseases such as measles, meningitis and TB occur in Canada and are associated with significant mortality and morbidity. This chapter focused on two areas of communicable diseases: vaccine preventable diseases and sexually transmitted diseases.

Although vaccine preventable diseases are almost erradicated, sporadic cases and outbreaks of a number of infectious diseases are being reported. These include: *Pertussis*—In 1989 and 1990, there were large numbers of outbreaks of pertussis. The severity of the disease has decreased due to widespread vaccination which affords partial protection. *Measles*—A major resurgence of vaccine-preventable cases of measles occurred in Canada in the late 1980s and early 1990s. The cases have largely been in the 10-14 year age group, most of whom had been previously vaccinated. The resurgence of measles incidence in Canada is largely due to primary vaccine failure. *Rubella*—There was a marked increase in the number of cases of rubella in the late 1980s. The cases of rubella have been occurring in those of high school age and the 20-29 year age group. *Influenza*—It is of special significance in the winter months. The mortality from influenza (particularly in the elderly) and pneumococcal infections (which may arise as a complication of influenza infection) exceeds that of all vaccine-preventable childhood disease. *Meningococcal Meningitis*—Bacterial meningitis is an inflammation of the coverings of the brain and spinal cord. Its incidence was low in the early 1980s, however, it peaked in 1989 and then declined in the 1990s. The disease primarily affects children, especially those up to one year of age. In recent years, the proportion of cases occurring in adolescents and adults has been increasing steadily. *Haemophilus b disease*—Prior to 1987, this disease occurred in one child in 200 under the age of five. However, in the early 1990s the incidence was reduced to 27 from 54 per 100, 000. The decrease was largely due to new conjugate vaccines given to infants under 12 months. *Hepatitis B*—This is one of the most important communicable diseases. From 1982-92, the incidence has almost doubled, with the peak incidence in those aged 25-29. Hepatitis B is a sexually transmitted disease particularly among young adults. *Tuberculosis*—This is a significant chronic infection in a number of at-risk populations (e.g., alcohol dependent people, persons with HIV, immigrants and Aboriginal Peoples).

It is important to realize that the effectiveness of vaccination, in protecting individuals against disease, is dependent on both the efficacy, or performance of the vaccine under ideal conditions, and on the degree of coverage achieved. The primary immunization for infants and children against diphtheria, whooping cough, tetanus, poliomyelitis and hemophilus b starts at the age of two months and is given at four and six months, with booster doses at 18 months and at four to six years of age. Measles, mumps and rubella vaccine is given after the first birthday. The College of Physicians and Surgeons of Ontario published *Immunization: Benefits, Risks, and Reportable Events, A Guide for Ontario Physicians* to inform physicians of their responsibilities relating to immunization. The guide addresses the benefits, adverse reactions, material risks, and reportable events in discussing each vaccine.

Genital chlamydia, gonorrhea and AIDS now account for more than half of the reported cases of all notifiable diseases combined. Infection with genital chlamydia has emerged as the most frequent STD in recent years in Canada. The disease is most prevalent among sexually active young women aged 15-19 years. Despite effective antibiotic therapy, there has been a rise in the incidence of gonorrhea in the past two decades and a persistence of syphilis.

The incidence of AIDS has been on the rise. On June 30, 1993, there was a cumulative total of 9,083 cases of AIDS. Carriers of HIV will develop AIDS within 10-11 years after infection. Most AIDS cases have been reported in Ontario, Quebec, and B. C. AIDS is caused by HIV, which is transmitted by four routes: (a) sexual contact with an infected partner; (b) via infected blood and blood products; (c) from an infected mother to her unborn child and perinatally; and (d) through the use of needles by IV drug abusers. AIDS is becoming one of the major causes of death among males 30-39 years of age in Canada. Strategies to control AIDS have focused on preventing the spread of HIV infection. Strategies to control the sexual transmission of the virus include: promoting behavioural change to limit the number of sexual partners and the use of condoms for safer sex. As well, the Red Cross has initiated a policy of requesting that anyone belonging to a high-risk group refrain from donating blood. This chapter presented general guidelines for the treatment of sexually transmitted diseases and specific treatment schedules for selected diseases are given in Appendix B.

Food-borne disease contributes significantly to the burden of morbidity from communicable disease in Canada. Food-borne disease can be caused by bacteria, viruses, and chemicals.

5. REFERENCES

1. Management of People Exposed to Pertussis and Control of Pertussis Outbreaks. *Can Med Assoc J* 143(8):751-753, 1990.
2. Guidelines for Measles Control in Canada. *Can Dis Wkly Rep 17(7):35-40, 1991.*
3. Arbuckle T and Sherman G. Is Congenital Rubella Syndrome a Vanishing Disease? Health and Welfare Canada, *Chronic Dis Can* 13(2):24-28, 1992.
4. Anonymous. Statement on Influenza Vaccination for the 1992-3 Season. *Can Med Assoc J* 147(5):673-676, 1992.
5. Gilmore A. Ottawa's Meningococcal Outbreak Provided a Lesson in Professional Judgment and Science. *Can Med Assoc J* 147(5):729-732, 1992.
6. Universal Vaccination Against Hepatitis B. *Can Med Assoc J* 146(1):36, 1992.
7. Hepatitis B in Canada: The Case for Universal Vaccination. Position Statement. *Can Med Assoc J* 146(1):25-27, 1992.
8. Statistics Canada. Tuberculosis Incidence in Canada, 1989. *Health Reports* 2(4):303, 1990.
9. *Tuberculosis. Information for Physicians. Preventable, Curable, Yet still a Problem, What is your Role?* The Lung Association. Metropolitan Toronto and York Region. 1992.

10. McIntyre L. Update on Immunization. *Drugs and Therapeutics for Maritime Practitioners* 13(1/2):1-12, 1990.
11. Health and Welfare Canada *Canadian Immunization Guide,* 3rd ed. Ministry of Supply and Services, Canada, Ottawa, 1989, Reprinted 1990.
12. College of Physician and Surgeons of Ontario. *Immunization: Benefits, Risks, and Reportable Events. A Guide for Ontario Physicians.* Toronto: College of Physician and Surgeons of Ontario, November, 1990.
13. Statement on Haemophilus Influenzae Type b Conjugate Vaccines for use in Infants and Children. *Can Med Assoc J* 146(8):1363-1366, 1992.
14. National Advisory Committee on Immunization. The Revised Guidelines for Booster Vaccination Against Hepatitis B. *Canada Communicable Disease Report* 18(16):121-122, 1992.
15. Statement on Influenza Vaccination for the 1992-3 Season. Epidemiologic Report. *Can Med Assoc J* 147(5):673-676, 1992.
16. Guidelines for Controlling Meningococcal Disease. Epidemiologic Report. *Can Med Assoc J* 146(6):939-942, 1992.
17. Chlamydial Infection in Canada. Epidemiological Report. *Can Med Assoc J* 147(6):893-896, 1992.
18. Strike C. AIDS into the 1990's. Statistics Canada, *Canadian Social Trends* Winter:22-24, 1991.
19. AIDS Surveillance in Canada. *Canada Communicable Disease Report 19(15):116-117, 1993.*
20. Hankins C. Women and HIV Infection and AIDS in Canada: Should We Worry? *Can Med Assoc J* 143(11):1171-1173, 1990.
21. Ministry of Health Ontario. *Mandatory Health Programs and Services and Guidelines.* Program Standard. Sexual Health, Toronto, 1989, pp 30-31.
22. Bowie W, Warren WK, Fisher WA, et al. Implications of the Canada Youth and AIDS Study for health care providers. *Can Med Assoc J* 143(8):713-716, 1990.
23. Rafuse J. MD's, Nurses Play Major Role in Success of "Sexuality Clinics" at Ottawa High Schools. *Can Med Assoc J* 146(4):593-596, 1992.
24. *Sexually Transmitted Diseases in Canada, 1985.* Health and Welfare Canada, Ottawa, 1986.
25. *Understanding AIDS and HIV Infection: Information for Hospitals and Health Professionals.* Ministry of Health, Government of Ontario, Toronto, 1988.
26. Stimson G. Editorial Review: Syringe-Exchange Programmes for Injecting Drug Users. *AIDS* 3:253-260, 1989.
27. *Human Immunodeficiency Virus Antibody Testing. Counselling Guidelines from The Canadian Medical Association.* Ottawa: Canadian Medical Assoc, 1990.
28. Nutbeam D and Blakey V. The Concept of Health Promotion and AIDS Prevention. A Comprehensive and Integrated Basis for Action in the 1990's. *Health Promot Int* 5(3):233-242, 1990.
29. *Canadian Guidelines for the Prevention, Diagnosis, Management and Treatment of Sexually Transmitted Diseases in Neonates, Children, Adolescents, and Adults.* Gully P, ed. Laboratory Centre for Disease Control, Health and Welfare Canada, Ottawa, 1992.
30. *STD Treatment Guidelines.* Ministry of Health Ontario. Government of Ontario, Toronto, June, 1992.
31. LeBer C. Reported Food-borne Outbreaks in Ontario, 1982-1989. Ministry of Health Ontario. *Public Health and Epidemiology Reports Ont* 4(26):122-124, 1991.

CHAPTER NINE
Environmental Health

1. GENERAL FRAMEWORK

In recent years, there has been increasing recognition of the interdependence of human health and the health of the global ecosystem, with its many life forms. Much of this awareness has been generated by community-based environmental advocacy groups such as Greenpeace and Pollution Probe, as well as First Nations Peoples, who have all highlighted the importance of the physical environment. Historically, the field of environmental health has usually dealt with food and water safety, and with inspection and investigation of environmental hazards that may arise from inadequate sanitation. In most of Canada (apart from areas such as reservations for First Nations peoples where physical facilities may be grossly inadequate), provision of sanitation, potable water supply and food free from gross contamination have been largely achieved. There is, however, a growing concern over the status of the environment and the consequences of environmental pollution. Chemical contamination is of particular concern. This concern is not only limited to the effects on human health but also to the viability of ecosystems in general and other species in particular.

Public attention has been captured by recent reports detailing the effects of acid rain on forest and aquatic ecosystems, climatic changes resulting from the "greenhouse effect," depletion of the ozone layer and effects of marine pollution on aquatic life. Public interest has also been heightened as a result of numerous reports linking environmental exposure to adverse human health outcomes. There is a growing awareness of possible links between illness and many features of industrialized society. Indoor air quality has been investigated in many modern buildings, following reports of symptoms in employees or residents, resulting in a newly identified illness pattern: the "Sick Building Syndrome." Publicity surrounding emergency response measures following the inadvertent release of hazardous agents has also focused attention on the control aspects of environmental health. The evacuation of the Montreal-area town of Ste. Basile-Le Grande (Quebec) in August 1988, following the fire-related release of polychlorinated biphenyls (PCBs), and the 1990 Hagersville (Ontario) tire fire are examples.

Environmental health may be defined as the study of conditions in the natural and built (physical) environment which can influence human health and well-being. As the impact of environment on human populations is widespread, environmental health is generally categorized as a discipline of public health. While other disciplines assess the impact of environmental agents or hazards on the individual patient, the focus of study in environmental health is the impact of these agents on the health of the population. The environment (as it affects health) can be divided into working and non-working categories. The workplace environment is often associated with high level exposure of a population predominantly of adult age and in good health. In contrast, non-workplace environmental exposures are generally low level and may be chronic. The population at risk consists of: persons at the extremes of age, developing fetuses, and the ill or immunocompromised. Thus, while many of the pathogenic agents are similar, there is an arbitrary distinction between working and non-working environmental health. The specific concerns relating to the working environment (Occupational Health) will be addressed in chapter 10. An overview of environmental health in Canada is given in the publication by Health and Welfare, *A Vital Link: Health and the Environment in Canada,*[1] an excellent source for much of this material.

2.   STUDY OF ENVIRONMENTAL HEALTH

The study of environmental health issues relies on two primary disciplines, toxicology and epidemiology. **Toxicology**, the science of "poisons" (toxins), attempts to identify adverse effects of substances on health and to predict harmful dosages. One of the fundamental tenets of toxicology is that any substance can be a poison if given in a large enough dose. On the other hand, a carcinogen may have no "threshold" dose below which it no longer causes cancer. The other discipline, **epidemiology**, as has been previously defined, is the study of the distribution and determinants of health and disease in human populations. Although these disciplines provide a vast amount of information on specific environmental health hazards, the interpretation of these data and subsequent regulatory decisions is often difficult. This section will address some of these difficulties.

There are a variety of problems in the measurement of a specific toxic agent. The levels are often difficult to determine, both in the human body and in the ambient (surrounding) environment. As technology progresses, the detection of minute quantities of chemicals is enhanced, but the interpretation of their significance to human health may remain difficult. When a level is measurable, it often does not reflect the concentration in the target organ of interest; rather, it represents a crude attempt to assess dose by measuring tissue fluid levels (usually blood). Often the agent itself is not toxic but is metabolized to toxic end-products within the body. When ambient levels can be defined, the dose-response relationship at low levels is often difficult to predict because most toxicological or epidemiological data are obtained from high dose animal experimentation or occupational exposure. Extrapolation to low doses is uncertain, and there are several models to choose from. Often an arbitrary safety factor is applied to the threshold dose to derive an acceptable intake (exposure) level for humans. This safety factor attempts to account for both inter- and intraspecies variation.

The study of other adverse health outcomes, particularly mutagenic or carcinogenic effects, is complicated by the long latency period following exposure. During the latency period for most cancers, exposures to causal agents may be terminated or periodic. Adverse outcomes may manifest only in a small fraction of the exposed population. This again makes epidemiologic analysis difficult. Furthermore, the effects of a specific agent are often masked by the confounding effects of multiple exposures. The relationship between agents grows even more complex when one accounts for synergistic, promoting or attenuating interrelationships of chemical mixtures. Finally, the study of environmental health is also complicated by the fact that many adverse outcomes are nonspecific and subjective. The upper respiratory and conjunctival symptoms of the "Sick Building Syndrome," for example, are difficult to quantify objectively. Analysis becomes more difficult when one considers that such non-specific and ill-defined psychosomatic symptoms have also been induced by fear of ill-effects from the environment. Frank et al. (1988) reviewed the strengths and weaknesses of a number of epidemiologic studies related to environmental concerns and summarized these as: (i) lack of certainty of exposure to putative agents; (ii) large potentially exposed population; and (iii) relatively common adverse health effects.[2]

2.1. ASSESSMENT AND MANAGEMENT OF HEALTH RISKS

Each of us is exposed to a variety of risks, environmental and behavioural, every day. Health Canada, Environment Canada, provincial Ministries of Health and Environment, and municipal Departments of Health and various consumer groups are among the leading authorities responsible for identifying and assessing the risks to human health posed by the environment. Evaluation of the political, economic, societal and technological implications of the risk is undertaken. Options for managing risks are then identified according to the best available evidence. Decisions are then made for the development of policy, regulations and other measures for protection of the public.

Canadians may be exposed to toxic substances through a variety of sources, including food, water, air, soil, and consumer products. A number of methods are used to assess the health risk posed by a specific environmental agent. The method used is often determined by the source and type of the agent or how the problem is perceived.

The process of health risk assessment for chemical contamination of food was briefly described in chapter three in illustrating the derivation of indicators of environmental contamination. This example can be generalized to the overall process of **risk assessment**, the first approach to assessing health risks posed by contaminants.   Two closely associated concepts, **risk management** and **risk communication**, deal with actions taken to reduce risk and to communicate with the public about the environmental hazards which people perceive.   Another method deals with the **investigation of clusters** of non-communicable diseases, such as congenital defects or cancer in the community due to putative environmental agents.

2.1.1. Risk Assessment

There are four major steps in the risk assessment of any environmental contaminant.[3] These are:

Hazard Identification

Does the substance potentially have adverse effects and what are they?   What organ systems do they affect?   Information is obtained from laboratory, genetic, animal and human epidemiological studies.

Exposure Assessment

What are the possible routes of human exposure and how much of the contaminant was there exposure to?   Potentially, chemicals may enter the body following inhalation, skin absorption, or ingestion (directly or in food or drink).

Dose-Response Assessment

What is the dose-response relationship following exposure to the chemical or agent?   Is there a threshold below which no adverse effects occur, or is there some measure of risk from any exposure? This is particularly important for carcinogenic chemicals for which it may be necessary to specify exposures with an acceptable degree of risk: less than one chance in a million for an individual to develop cancer over a lifetime (if exposure cannot be eliminated entirely).

Risk Determination

Given the potential toxicity of the substance, the actual or estimated exposure and the dose-response relationship, what are the likely effects on human health? What is the measure of uncertainty inherent in this calculation? Options for minimizing the risk are then developed and analyzed to complete the "risk assessment cycle."

2.1.2 Risk Management

Risk management is the next series of steps following risk assessment. It involves decision making and implementation of options for management of the identified risk. For example, when considering food contaminants, if a potential daily intake (PDI) exceeds the tolerable daily intake (TDI), certain risk management options are considered (for definitions of these terms, see chapter three). The options include: (i) establishing guidelines or promulgating specific regulations controlling the toxic substance or substances; (ii) restricting the sale or distribution of food produced in an area which may have been identified as the source of the contamination; (iii) recommending changes in dietary habits. Before initiating any specific action, however, the federal Health Protection Branch must assess its advantages and disadvantages. For example, removal of certain foods from the market or recommendations to change dietary habits could deny the people at risk of an essential source of nutrition, which might cause a more serious health problem than that associated with the chemical contaminant.

2.1.3. Risk Communication
The communication of risk in relation to environmental hazards, and public health hazards in general, depends on an important concept: the perception of risk by the lay public often differs from that of "experts." Experts tend to think and express risk in terms of the actual numbers affected and numerical probabilities. The lay public perceive risk according to the degree of "unfamiliarity" of the threat and whether there is a threat of a catastrophe involving serious adverse events (particularly death) for many people at one time. The model for this concept of risk perception is the **Factorial Model:** the two factors being, respectively, "fear of the unknown" and "dread." These factors can be quantified on two-dimensional axes. For example, in Canada, nuclear installations score very highly on both of these factors (both x and y axes), and public reaction to any possibility of an environmental threat is likely to be high. Another principle of risk communication is that the potential risk of an environmental health hazard should be expressed in readily understandable terms. For example, expressing the risk of cancer from a contaminant in drinking water as less than one chance in a million of a lifetime for an individual is more useful than using scientific language. In general, however, the public has difficulty with the expression of risk as a probability; it prefers to know whether the agent does or does not pose a risk to health (the risk dichotomy concept). Since it is usually impossible to dichotomize risk so absolutely, effective risk communication may involve informing citizens that the measured level of the agent is either above or below a certain guideline or regulated safe level.

3. ENVIRONMENTAL HEALTH ISSUES

In the following section, some environmental agents which have been incriminated as causing ill health are described. The sources of the agents, routes of human exposure, adverse effects and approaches to control are included in the discussion.

3.1.   OUTDOOR AND INDOOR ENVIRONMENT

3.1.1. Ionizing Radiation

There are two types of radiation: ionizing and non-ionizing. Ionizing radiation is emitted from radioactive substances and is capable of producing ions in matter, including cellular matter, causing altered cell physiology. More than 80% of the radiation to which humans are exposed are produced from natural sources, whether from the radioactive elements in the earth's crust, cosmic radiation or ingested or inhaled isotopes. With one major exception, non-background radiation exposure is primarily an occupational hazard for certain categories of workers and will be discussed in greater detail in chapter 10.

Radon

Radon is a naturally occurring radioactive gas which forms as a decay product of uranium 238. Uranium is a trace element found in all soils. As part of the radioactive decay process, radon produces four "daughters" that emit alpha radiation. While human skin acts as a barrier, inhaled radon daughters will deposit their alpha particles internally in the localized area of the bronchial epithelium, which eventually leads to lung cancer. Due to its accumulation indoors it is more of a concern for indoor air pollution; however, it is present in the natural environment as well. Radon gas passes from porous soil into buildings through cracks in basement floors and walls. Given the fact that the majority of an individual's time is spent indoors, there is a potential health risk from natural sources of radon. Health Canada has recommended that the Canadian guideline for existing homes for radon should be 20 picocuries per litre, and for newly constructed homes, four picocuries per litre. Studies indicate that less than one per cent of all homes in Canada (i.e., fewer than 8,000 out of a total of eight million) have high levels of radon.[4] When in doubt, houses must be individually tested for radon levels; extrapolation from neighbouring homes is not appropriate.

Estimates of the lung cancer risk following household radon exposure have been extrapolated from studies of lung cancer incidence in uranium miners. The relative risk for exposed households has been estimated to range between 1.1 and 1.5. It has also been estimated that 5%-15% of lung cancer deaths may be attributable to domestic radon exposure. Occupational standards have been set for exposure to radon for uranium miners and for dwellings in uranium mining communities. In dwellings with high levels, measures such as increased basement ventilation and sealing cracks and holes in the foundation are simple and effective methods for decreasing radon concentrations. As smoking increases an individual's chance of getting lung cancer with radon exposure, residents should be discouraged from smoking.

3.1.2. Living Near Nuclear Facilities

Nuclear accidents at Chernobyl and Three Mile Island have raised public anxiety and affected perceptions of the safety of living in close proximity to nuclear facilities. The major issue is better communication between the public and health-care providers and authorities, based on an expanded knowledge base about radiation effects and the realistic potential for exposure (which is minimal).[5] Many factors can influence the health effects of radiation, including the type of radiation, the rate at which energy is deposited in tissues, the dose of radiation administered and received by tissues and the radiation sensitivity of the affected tissue. The total dose is also important. The effects of high-dose radiation are well documented and are described in chapter 10. Less is known about low-dose exposure. A study of the rates of childhood leukemia in the vicinity of nuclear facilities in Ontario (Chalk River, Port Hope, Elliot Lake, Pickering and Bruce) demonstrated only a slightly increased number of observed leukemia deaths. In the United Kingdom, the higher incidence of childhood leukemia has raised the issue of paternal exposure to possible workplace hazards. A study in Ontario has not provided support for this hypothesis.[6]

Electromagnetic Fields
The use of electricity creates two kinds of invisible fields: electric and magnetic. Electric fields are produced by voltage, magnetic fields by current. Together they are referred to as "electromagnetic fields," a form of non-ionizing radiation. In Canada, the strongest electric field normally encountered by the public is about 10 kilovolts per meter and is found under high voltage transmission lines. Other sources of exposure to electric fields are electric blankets, computers, fluorescent lighting, household appliances and wiring. From most of these sources the electric field strength seldom exceeds one kilovolt per meter. The strongest magnetic fields are those produced by hair dryers.

Considerable research has been carried out on the health effects of exposure to electromagnetic fields. The results of this research are conflicting, and therefore it is not clear whether or not a health hazard exists. For example, some studies have linked exposure to electromagnetic fields with increased cancer rates, particularly leukemia and brain cancer.[7] Similar studies have failed to find such a link.

3.1.3. Outdoor Air Pollution, Acid Rain and their Control
Air pollution exists when certain substances are present in the atmosphere in sufficient concentrations to cause adverse affects. Natural sources include volca-noes and forest fires. In Canada, air pollution results primarily from the incom-plete combustion of fossil fuels, particularly by cars, with release into the atmosphere of various oxides of sulfur, nitrogen and carbon. In addition, a variety of toxic trace elements (lead, cadmium, beryllium, asbestos) have also been detected. Air pollution also consists of: aerosols, which reduce visibility; particulate matter such as lead or asbestos particles; and organic and inorganic gases.

Ozone Depletion and Pollution
Ozone (O_3) is a gas in the stratosphere, forming a layer that protects the earth from harmful ultraviolet radiation. Recently there has been growing concern about the

depletion of ozone in the stratosphere causing an increased incidence of skin cancer of all types including melanoma, as well as expected increases in other health effects, such as cataracts and other ophthalmic conditions, and depressed immune function which may increase susceptibility to cancers. The mechanism for the destruction of the ozone layer is that some synthetic chemicals, chlorofluorocarbons (CFCs) and halons are released into the atmosphere during the production, use and disposal of products such as air conditioners, plastic foams and solvents. In the presence of sunlight in the atmosphere, these molecules are split, the chlorine reacts with the ozone, breaking it down. CFCs, along with carbon dioxide, methane and nitrous oxide, also traps heat close to the earth's surface causing **global warming** ("greenhouse effect").

A number of strategies have been introduced to address these concerns. In 1987, a major conference of industrial nations in Montreal agreed to stop production of CFCs by the year 2000 in a document known as the "Montreal Protocol."[8] Canada intends to reach the target by 1997. Other initiatives are the conservation, recovery and recycling of ozone-depleting chemicals. More recently, an awareness raising campaign about the health effects of ozone depletion ("Ozone Watch Program") has been introduced by Environment Canada. A weekly ozone index is published along with the recommendations appropriate to the level. The recommendations are for limitation of time spent in direct sunlight that will cause burning to fairer skin types. In addition, skin protection precautions are being promoted, such as the wearing of hats, sunscreens and protective clothing.

Ozone pollution in the troposphere or ambient air, however, can cause a variety of health problems such as irritation of the upper and lower respiratory tract.[9,10] Ozone is not directly released into the atmosphere in significant amounts, but forms when nitrogen oxides and hydrocarbons react in the presence of sunlight or electrical discharges such as lightning storms. Nitrogen oxides are produced when fossil fuels are burned in motor vehicles, power plants, furnaces and turbines. In Ontario, for example, vehicle emissions account for about 60% of total nitrogen oxide emissions. Hydrocarbon emissions result from incomplete combustion of gasoline and from evaporation of petroleum fuels, industrial solvents, paints and dry cleaning fluids. Ozone in the troposphere may result in decreased functional capacity of the lungs. Ozone may be related to increased hospital admissions[11] for respiratory ailments. Adverse health effects may be exacerbated in those suffering from respiratory diseases and those engaging in heavy exercise when the air quality is poor. Children may also be particularly vulnerable to the effects of ozone.

The Canadian federal government has set the National Ambient Air Quality Objective for ozone at 82 ppb based on a one hour average level. This standard affords a considerably greater margin of safety than the federal ozone standard in the United States, 120 ppb. In Canada, data from 45 sites show a 15% decline in ozone levels from 1979 to 1987 with an average decrease of 1.5 ppb per year.[1] However, the 10-year trend for ozone levels in Ontario has remained relatively constant. At present, ozone pollution in the troposphere is a serious problem.

Although air pollution is thought to be an urban phenomenon, rural ozone concentrations can often be higher. Ozone reflects the long-range transport of air pollution since nitrogen oxides and hydrocarbons can travel long distances from urban areas before reacting. Since control measures are generally expensive and complex (and require cooperation between different sectors of society), ozone will likely continue to be a concern in the future.

Acid Rain
Acid rain refers to the oxidation of the sulfur and nitrogen precursors to acidic compounds. These compounds can remain suspended in the atmosphere (pre-depositional) or can fall to earth as precipitation (depositional). The negative impact on plant and aquatic ecosystems has been widely studied, but only recently have human health hazards been investigated.[12] Increases in mortality and morbidity have been temporally associated with periods of high atmospheric concentrations of pollutants in ecological studies. The Great London Fog of 1952 demonstrated an association between cardiorespiratory mortality and SO_2 concentrations. Analysis of hospital admissions in Ontario has revealed an association between admissions for respiratory illness and levels of atmospheric pollutants. Animal studies have confirmed decreased pulmonary function and impaired clearance mechanisms, although human volunteer studies have yielded conflicting results. An estimated 4,000 deaths per year occur in Canada as a result of atmospheric pollution, primarily in heavily industrialized urban centres.

Control of Outdoor Air Pollution
A number of strategies have been developed to minimize air pollution. The Air Pollution Index implemented in some provinces, based on the continuous measurement of levels of sulfur dioxide and suspended particulate matter, gives warnings of air pollution build-ups; these can then be aborted by closing down polluting industries if necessary. Monitoring air quality (Air Quality Index, see chapter three) is undertaken on a national basis, and recent trends have been encouraging. The establishment of emission standards for all sources has contributed to control of air pollution, including those for cars (for which catalytic converters have been introduced), ferrous foundries and asphalt paving producers. Pollution abatement technology has been developed and adopted, such as tall stacks to disperse pollutants over wider areas (if they cannot be eliminated entirely), and high temperature incinerators. Optimal use of road and transit systems are objectives to be achieved and are being addressed, for example, in Toronto under the Healthy Cities approach to healthy public policy (see chapter one). Healthy public policy in the environmental context has great potential in involving major stakeholders vital to the development and implementation of workable solutions to pollution. Many proposed solutions have enormous cost-implications. Round-table conferences of industry and government, for example, have been held in Ontario on environmental issues and illustrate a collaborative approach. On the other hand, enforcement of legislation has led to penalties for

non-observance of regulations regarding environmental pollution, and although these are not considered severe enough by some interest groups, enforcement could still have a deterrent effect.

3.1.4. Indoor Air Pollution

Indoor air quality has recently been scrutinized, following complaints of adverse health effects and discomfort in occupants of sealed buildings. A variety of non-specific health effects have been identified, including eye and upper respiratory tract irritant symptoms, as well as headache, fatigue and nausea. Other building-associated illnesses include Pontiac fever (an influenza-like illness) and Legionnaire's disease. A variety of indoor pollutants can be measured, originating from building materials, furnishings, heating and human activities. Indoor pollutants also originate from the external environment. The most frequent pollutants include tobacco smoke, volatile organic compounds, formaldehyde and other odours. The degree of ventilation and entry rate of fresh air, as well as the reaction rate between chemicals, determines the concentration of indoor pollutants. Other factors such as temperature and humidity are also important for comfort. Psychological factors also play a role.

There is a correlation between levels of carbon dioxide in indoor air, a measurable surrogate marker, and the prevalence of complaints about indoor air quality. At levels of CO_2 less than 500 parts per million (ppm) there are usually no complaints; from 500 to 1,000 ppm, occasional complaints, and over 1000 ppm, many complaints. Increasing the ventilation should be a first line approach to complaints of poor indoor air quality. There is a tendency to avoid precise measurement of actual contaminants, as these have not proved helpful in reducing adverse health effects to date. The proposed 1995 National Building Code is intended to set standards for residential mechanical ventilation systems and to ensure adequate ventilation.

Associated with indoor air quality is the recent identification of the health hazards of passive smoke exposure. These are discussed in chapter seven. A variety of studies have demonstrated an increased relative risk for lung cancer for nonsmokers exposed to household smokers.[13] These studies have spurred the initiative for non-smoking workplace policies and bylaws regulating smoking in public places across Canada.

3.2.   WATER QUALITY

Ensuring a safe potable water supply has long been a prerequisite for public health. The initial emphasis on water quality is related to its aesthetic and bacteriologic parameters. In Canada, water quality should conform to accepted guidelines, such as the Guidelines for Canadian Drinking Water Quality (see chapter three). For recreational water, assessment of potential sources of contamination and monitoring of the levels of *Eschericia coli*, as markers of fecal contamination, are now recommended. Beaches not complying with the provincial guidelines, or those provided by Health Canada, for example, may be closed by the local Medical Officer of Health pending improvement in these parameters.

Recently, people have become concerned about chemical contamination of water. There are more than 70,000 industrial chemicals, and hundreds of new chemicals are developed each year. Many of these chemicals, including household detergents, fail to biodegrade, resulting in their accumulation in soil and water. The major chemical contaminants in water which have an impact on health are PCBs, dioxins, furans, mercury, lead, and pesticides (these are discussed below). Of the combined pollutants that endanger health in the modern world, experts estimate that only about 6% come from drinking water, about 90% come from food and 1% to 2% from air.[14]

In response to the public's increasing use of bottled water and devices to treat municipal water, the City of Toronto Department of Public Health undertook a risk assessment of drinking water in 1990.[15] Comparing municipal tap water with bottled and device-treated water, the study's results reinforced confidence in tap water. Bacterial contamination was not found in tap water, but was found in both device-treated and bottled water. Trace chemical contaminants were found in all three types of water; however, tap water was considered superior overall due to the variability of the chemical contaminants in the other water sources and the lack of guidelines for acceptable levels. Four groups of chemicals caused some concern in tap water. Lead usually enters drinking water while standing in water pipes and can be avoided if recommendations are followed (see section in this chapter discussing lead). Aluminium levels are largely present as a result of added alum, for which alternative technologies can be adopted (see the section in this chapter on aluminium). Trihalomethanes are produced when chlorine is added to the water for disinfection; alternatives are available such as the use of pre-ozonation for disinfection to reduce the need for chlorine. Finally, a number of other organic, potentially carcinogenic compounds were detected in trace levels for which further investigation is required.

Interest in water quality and its possible human health effects has also been centred, in Canada, on the Great Lakes due to the known persistence of toxic chemicals arising from industrial and commercial production and use. Current knowledge of the level of contamination in open waters and in aquatic biota has come from the findings of a study undertaken by Environment Canada, Health Canada, and the Department of Fisheries and Oceans.[16] In summary, although this is a polluted ecosystem, levels of toxic chemicals in open waters were well below Canadian and international drinking water standards. Sediment studies demonstrated that pollution by synthetic organic chemicals and heavy metals peaked in the 1960s and early 1970s, declining in the 1980s. Levels of contaminants in Great Lakes aquatic birds and fish have decreased since the 1970s; however, sublethal effects on enzyme systems and reproductive effects and congenital defects in a number of species have been attributed to chemical contaminants.

3.3.   TOXIC CHEMICALS

Only a minute fraction of the total number of chemicals in use today have had adequate toxicological testing prior to their introduction. Less than one per cent have an established threshold limit value to regulate occupational exposure. Furthermore, toxicity testing is limited to tests for acute large dose toxicity and mutagenicity. A review of the adverse health outcomes of the differing classes of chemicals is beyond the scope of this chapter. Instead, this section will examine a small number of the most prominent chemical classes in relation to environmental health.

3.3.1. Metals

Many metals are essential human micronutrients. At higher doses, however, these elements can have serious toxic effects (these are discussed in detail in chapter 10). Environmental exposures to metals have also been documented as a cause of disease in human populations. Best known are the neurological and teratogenic consequences following contamination of Minamata Bay in Japan with organic mercury. In Northwestern Ontario, consumption of fish obtained from rivers contaminated by industrial effluent has also led to mercury poisoning in the First Nations population.

Lead

Source Lead is a naturally-occurring metal present throughout the environment in rocks, soil, water and air. While it has been mined, smelted and used in making tools and ornamental objects since prehistoric times, concentrations of lead in the environment have increased steadily since the industrial revolution. The most dramatic increase has occurred since the 1920s following the introduction of lead additives into automobile gasoline to prevent engine knocking. Lead is released into the air through industrial emissions and the combustion of leaded gasoline. While industrial emissions (i.e., from smelters and refineries) can cause high concentrations of lead near the source, most of the lead in air is a by-product of the combustion of leaded gasoline. Concentrations of airborne lead are therefore generally higher in cities than in rural areas. Regardless of their source, lead can be inhaled or ingested by humans and may circulate in the blood and be deposited in bone and other tissues. Either long-term exposure to low levels or short-term exposure to high levels can seriously affect human health. Measures taken in recent years have significantly reduced human exposure to lead.

Concentrations of lead in the air have declined significantly since the introduction of unleaded gasoline in Canada in 1975. In fact, studies indicate that between 1973 and 1985, airborne lead concentrations fell by 76%, a change that matches almost exactly the increased use of unleaded gasoline. The most recent data available (December 1987) show that levels of lead in the air of large cities in eastern Canada and the Maritimes have declined even further and are now close to levels observed in rural areas.

Exposure All Canadians are exposed to lead in the air, dirt, household dust, food, drinking water and various consumer products. For the general population, food is the largest source of exposure to lead, accounting for up to 80% exposure in adults and 90% in children. Lead is in virtually all of the food we eat. In addition to naturally-occurring lead, food can become contaminated from several sources: (i) airborne lead can be deposited directly onto crops and can also seep into soil and be absorbed into plants; (ii) the use of lead soldering in the manufacture of cans results in lead dust which can directly contaminate food. Also, the lead in the solder itself can leach from the container into the food.

Intake of lead from this latter source is declining as the use of cans without lead solder becomes more common in food processing industries. In addition, Canadian food processors have improved quality control in order to reduce lead levels in food. These and other initiatives have contributed to a dramatic decrease in the intake of lead from food.

In most areas of Canada, the concentration of lead in natural water supplies is very low. However, the use of lead solder in plumbing in newer homes, lead service connections to the main water supply, or lead pipes in very old homes, can all contribute to significant levels of lead in domestic water. These problems are more evident in areas with very soft or acidic drinking water (low pH). Lead levels in domestic water increase with the length of time water is left standing in the plumbing system. It is a good idea for people living in areas that have soft water to flush domestic plumbing systems by letting water run through the taps for a few minute prior to first use for drinking each day. As well, only water from the cold tap should be used for drinking, cooking, and in particular for making baby formula.

Airborne lead particles are often deposited in household dust. This source of lead appears to be especially important to young children who ingest a significant amount of soil and dust through their common habit of putting things in their mouths (**pica**). Paint manufactured prior to the current regulations may contain lead, and ingested paint chips can pose a threat to children. Also, stripping or sanding old paint during home renovations can produce lead particles which may be inhaled or ingested by the occupants.

Health effects Lead is absorbed into the bloodstream and deposited in bone and other tissues. Results of long-term exposure to lead may be less noticeable but are nevertheless serious. While the most obvious manifestation is anemia, exposure to lead has also been linked to impairment of mental function, visual-motor performance, memory and attention span, as well as lack of appetite, abdominal pain and constipation, fatigue, sleeplessness, irritability and headache. It has also been determined that chronic exposure to lead may affect kidney function.

In the general population, two groups - the unborn child and children up to six years of age - are at a greater risk of the adverse health effects of lead. During pregnancy, lead can cross the placenta and reach the unborn child. Researchers believe that the last trimester of pregnancy may be the most critical time for this to occur. In the past when workers were exposed to high levels of lead, increased spontaneous abortions and stillbirth rates were noted in female workers in the lead industry. Young children are a high-risk group for several reasons. They take in more lead per unit of body weight than adults, and they are developing at a rapid rate and are more susceptible to the adverse effects of lead. Children also absorb a higher proportion of lead from food sources (about 50% absorption, compared to about 10% by adults). Over the past decade, some researchers have found that exposure to even low levels of lead prior to birth or during infancy and early childhood can cause impaired intellectual development, behavioural disturbances, decreased physical growth and hearing impairment. Although scientific evidence is so far insufficient, the impact of lead on young children is an ongoing concern in Canada.

Control Elevated blood lead levels can be detected by a simple fingerprick blood test. There are guidelines which dictate the safe level of lead for individuals and the community, and these are recommended by a joint Federal/Provincial Advisory Committee on Environmental and Occupational Health. When the recommended levels are exceeded then intervention is appropriate: identification of the source of exposure, control of the source, or removal of individuals from further exposure. The proposed Canadian Guideline for lead in drinking water is a maximum acceptable level (MAC) of 0.01 mg/L, or 10 parts per billion. Municipal water treatment removes lead effectively and the alkalization of water can reduce leaching from corroded pipes. To avoid post-treatment exposure, taps should be flushed for two minutes if water is left standing for more than eight hours, and replacement of lead pipes and lead solder by municipalities and homeowners may be necessary if lead levels at point-of-use exceed recommended levels.

Mercury

Source Elemental mercury is either a vapour or liquid and is used in electrical equipment and the tanning industry. The major source is natural degassing of the earth's crust. Industrial releases may also be deposited in the environment, both close to industry and at great distances (for example, in the far North). Acidic environments favours mercury deposition. Organic mercury (predominantly methyl mercury) is more toxic to humans, and it may be formed by the action of microorganisms on elemental mercury deposited in the flooding of land or by their action in the human body after elemental mercury has been ingested.

Health Effects Methyl mercury is rapidly absorbed when elemental mercury is converted into this organic form. Acute intoxication can cause paraesthesia, ataxia, impairment of vision, hearing, psychosis and kidney damage. This level of poisoning has not been reported in Canada. Chronic low-dose poisoning of up to 300 µg/day results in an asymptomatic period (of some months), during which time the mercury penetrates cell membranes and binds with proteins and sulfhydryl groups. Liver and kidney damage can occur, as can central nervous system impairment of sensory, coordinating and visual functions.

The brain of the developing fetus is particularly at risk if exposed to high levels of circulating maternal organic mercury. Possible effects include retarded physical growth and coordination, cerebral palsy and more subtle effects on coordination, behaviour and IQ.

Exposure Fish bioconcentrate mercury (absorbed as it flows past the gills) in their muscle tissue by a factor of 10 to 100,000 times the ambient (surrounding) levels. Most exposure to mercury today occurs through the eating of fish.

Canadians who are at risk for organic mercury poisoning are those who rely on subsistence fishing and do not heed guidelines. In particular, the fetus of a fish-eating mother is at risk if maternal levels are elevated. Surveys of mercury levels (in hair and blood) undertaken in 350 First Nations communities have indicated a disturbing prevalence of elevated mercury levels in 2.5% of communities.[1] Neurological effects in adults were not detected in these populations.

Control The MAC for mercury, as recommended by the Guidelines for Drinking Water Quality, is two parts per billion (ppb). Advisories are issued if the concentration in fish is greater than 0.05 parts per million (50 ppb). It is recommended in certain areas that white fish be preferred over lake trout for consumption. Pregnant women living in certain areas should not consume large amounts of fish.

Conventional water treatment removes 70%-80% of inorganic mercury in turbid waters and less in clear water. Organic mercury is not affected by conventional water treatment but is effectively removed by activated carbon filtration.

Cadmium

Cadmium is a relatively rare element in the earth's crust; however, as a result of industrial and municipal wastes it is accumulating in the soil at a rate of 1% increase per year. Cadmium is used in the process of electroplating metals, as a stabilizer for plastics, in batteries, and high technology industries (e.g., the manufacture of television tubes and nuclear reactor shields). It is also released in the burning of fossil fuels, incinerator discharges and in cigarette smoke. It is one of the five most common leachates in water near hazardous waste sites.

Plants taking up cadmium from contaminated soil, and the use of sewage sludge as fertilizers for feed crops, result in bioconcentration of cadmium in vegetables, poultry and beef. The settling of incinerator deposits on crops augments the levels found in plants. Fish also bioconcentrate cadmium. Most exposure to cadmium therefore occurs by food intake. Cigarette smokers who smoke a pack a day double their usual intake of cadmium.

Cadmium is a known animal carcinogen and a "probable human carcinogen". Acute high-dose inhalation exposure causes severe lung irritation, nausea, vomiting, diarrhea and chills. Long-term low-dosage exposure in humans leads to kidney damage and multiple system effects including emphysema, liver damage, testicular, immune system and central nervous system damage. Unlike lead and mercury, there does not appear to be transplacental transfer of cadmium.

The WHO has set the provisional tolerable daily intake of cadmium at 1 to 1.2 micrograms per kilogram. The MAC for cadmium in drinking water is 5 ppb. Activated carbon filtration removes cadmium from water. Control measures in the future will likely involve regulation of the use of sewage sludge as a fertilizer and of incinerator discharges. Occupational measures are discussed in chapter 10.

Aluminum
Aluminum is one of the commonest elements in the earth's crust. Food ingestion is responsible for 96% of the usual human aluminum intake, drinking water, 3.5%, and antacids and other consumer products, the remainder. The concentration of aluminum in drinking water varies according to geological factors, soil acidity, and acid rain. It may also be added in the form of alum (aluminum sulphate) during the treatment of municipal water in the coagulation-flocculation stage. This process causes the formation of larger particles which then settle out water impurities.

The potential health effects of aluminum in drinking water are the cause of ongoing controversy, particularly in relation to its putative role in Alzheimer's Disease (AD), the most common cause of dementia.[17] Animal toxicological studies have demonstrated that cats and rabbits whose brains were injected with aluminum developed neurofibrillary tangles similar to those found in patients with AD. A disorder known as dialysis encephalopathy, a rapidly fatal neurologic syndrome, has been observed in dialysis patients, who were also found to have high levels of aluminum in their brains. The characteristic pathological changes of AD, however, were absent. Many researchers have found elevated levels of aluminum in the brains of AD patients who have died, although this evidence is not consistent. At this point the role of aluminum in causation of AD has not been established, according to the criteria described in chapter two.[18]

3.3.2. Polychlorinated Biphenyls and Dioxins

Polychlorinated Biphenyls (PCB's)
Source   PCBs are a class of highly stable, non-corroding and relatively non-flammable chemicals first manufactured on a commercial scale in 1929. For several decades, they were used extensively in a wide range of industrial applications, especially the manufacture of electrical and heat exchange equipment. In the past, PCBs have also been used in such products as ink, oil, sealant, caulking compound and carbonless copy paper. In the 1970s, concerns over health and the environmental impact of PCBs led to their substitution by other compounds and eventually to a North American ban in 1977 on the manufacture, importation and most non-electrical uses of PCBs. Electrical uses of PCBs are now being phased out, with stringent requirements for handling and disposal.

Studies have found trace levels of PCBs everywhere in the environment. This is thought to be due primarily to improper disposal practices and accidental releases from the 1930s to 1970s, followed by long range transport of PCBs by air currents. PCBs do not readily break down in the environment. This persistence, coupled with their tendency to accumulate in the fat of living organisms, means that they are often present and biomagnified in the food chain. Although PCBs are no longer being manufactured, significant amounts remain in certain types of equipment. As well, public concern over how to dispose of PCBs properly has led to stockpiling of these substances at sites across Canada. Despite stringent safeguards on storage of PCBs and PCB-contaminated wastes, releases into the environment remain a potential risk.

Exposure Humans are regularly exposed to minute amounts of PCBs through food, air and water. As a result, all humans have a detectable level of PCBs in their body fat and blood. These levels are not likely to cause adverse health effects. Ingestion is the most common route of entry. The average Canadian intake of PCBs for adults from all routes has been estimated at less than 10 micrograms per day. Uncontrolled fires involving PCBs can pose a significant threat to human health. When PCBs are heated, they are transformed into an array of dangerous chemicals, including furans and occasionally dioxin. Following a fire, particles containing these toxic chemicals may settle on a variety of surfaces, including the ground and water, thereby resulting in a potential for human exposure.

Health Effects Sustained, high-level exposure to PCBs has been associated with adverse health effects. These include a severe form of acne (chloracne), eye discharge, swelling of the upper eyelids, hyperpigmentation of the nails and skin, numbness of limbs, weakness, muscle spasms, chronic bronchitis, and decreased birth weight and head circumference in newborns. These health effects were identified following an incident in Japan in 1968 involving the accidental mixing of PCBs with cooking oil. Scientists generally agree that short-term, low-level exposure to PCBs is unlikely to have a significant health impact. However, there is potential cause for concern over long-term exposure to low concentrations.

The International Agency for Research on Cancer recently concluded that there is some evidence to link long-term, high-level PCB exposure with an increased incidence of cancer, particularly liver cancer. This is based on studies of humans exposed to high concentrations of furan-contaminated PCBs. Laboratory rats exposed for a lifetime to high levels of a PCB mixture also developed liver cancer.

Associations have been found between prenatal exposure to PCBs and slight reductions in mental development in children. Transplacental transfer has been documented and was predictive of low birth weight, smaller dimensions of the infant and cognitive, motor and behavioural development deficits. There is no evidence of any harmful effects from the small amounts of PCBs found in breast milk. Health professionals advise that the known benefits of breast feeding outweigh any potential risks that may be associated with PCBs in human milk.

PCBs bioconcentrate in fish, and those who eat fish on a regular basis are thus at risk of health effects associated with PCBs. First Nations people who survive on subsistence fishing are at risk as they may not heed guidelines. The guideline for avoidance of eating fish is 2 ppm.

Control As mentioned previously, PCBs are being phased out following legislation banning their production. However, transport and storage of existing wastes containing PCBs (>50 ppb) pending destruction are also regulated under the Transportation of Dangerous Goods Act and Canada's Environmental Protection Act, respectively, as well as under provincial legislation. Suitable disposal facilities for the destruction of PCBs are not widely available in Canada but are planned, including mobile facilities for on-site high temperature incineration. Chemical processes for decontaminating PCB contaminated oil are currently used predominantly.

Dioxins and Furans

Source Dioxins are a family of toxic substances called polychlorinated dibenzo-para-dioxin. A second family of closely-related toxic substances known as polychlorinated dibenzofurans is very often present with dioxin. Recent research has indicated that elevated doses of dioxin and furans can significantly damage the health of laboratory animals. The impact of these substances on humans and wildlife is less certain. Dioxin and furans are therefore the subject of considerable controversy, both in the public realm and within the scientific community. Dioxins and furans have never been purposely manufactured, but are rather by-products of the production of certain chemicals (such as some pesticides and wood preservatives), of the chlorine bleaching process used in some pulp and paper mills, and of the incomplete combustion of materials that contain both chlorine atoms and organic matter. Although they are most often man-made, some natural occurrences, such as forest fires, are believed to contribute to the presence of dioxins and furans in the environment.

Dioxins and furans originate from a variety of sources and can be transported in the atmosphere over long distances. As a result, they are found at very minute levels throughout the environment. High concentrations can generally be linked to specific polluting sources, such as chemical dumps, obsolete municipal incinerators or pulp and paper mills using chlorine in the bleaching process. Polychlorinated biphenyls used to be an important source of furans, which are contaminants in commercial PCB mixtures. As indicated above, today most PCBs are contained in secure facilities, and are a source of furan releases to the environment only in the event of accidental leakage or fires.

Exposure People living in industrialized nations are constantly being exposed to minute amounts of dioxins and furans through their presence in food, air, water, soil or some consumer products. Scientists have shown that food is the major source of dioxins and furans for humans.

Health Effects As dioxins and furans are soluble in fat they can accumulate in the bodies of all animals, including humans. No long-term effects have been found in fish, wildlife or domestic animals that can be definitively linked to exposure to the low levels of dioxins and furans typically found in the environment. However, the remarkable loss of reproductive capability in fish-catching birds in the Great

Lakes area in the 1970s may have been associated with dioxins and furans. The toxic effects of dioxins and furans on vegetation are not known.

On the other hand, recent scientific studies do indicate that high levels of dioxins and furans can significantly damage the health of laboratory animals, including: weight loss, skin disorders, effects on their immune system, impaired liver function, induction of liver enzymes, impaired reproduction (including birth defects) and increased numbers of tumors. While dioxin has been shown to have a range of long-term effects on laboratory animals, effects on humans are equivocal. In studies of humans who have been exposed to high levels of dioxins and furans through their work or accidentally, the health effect which has been most consistently observed is a chloracne. This skin condition is not exclusive to dioxins and furans, and usually disappears several months after the affected person ceases to be in contact with the contaminant. Some of the people exposed to chemicals contaminated with dioxins and furans have also displayed other adverse effects on the skin, liver, immune system, sensory organs or behaviour. No conclusive link has been established between human exposure to dioxins and furans and effects such as cancer or abnormal reproduction.

Control   Recent developments in research have enabled scientists to measure dioxins and furans at levels as low as several parts per trillion or even parts per quadrillion (a part per quadrillion is equivalent to one cent in 10 trillion dollars). Establishing levels of exposure to dioxins and furans which might be considered acceptable for the general population is controversial.

Despite the lack of direct evidence that current exposures to dioxins and furans in Canada contribute to health problems in humans, the government of Canada recognizes that these compounds are undesirable environmental contaminants and that, where possible, their unintentional production should be limited. Investigations by both government and industry is continuing on several fronts. These include sampling and analysis of air, sediments, wildlife, fish, industrial effluent and sludge and pulp from pulp and paper mills using chlorine bleaching. The Health Protection Branch of Health Canada monitors dioxin levels in a variety of foods, human breast milk, water, and some paper products. The federal government no longer permits the sale and use of pesticides containing 2,3,7,8-TCDD (a form of dioxin) and has regulated the content of other dioxins in pesticides remaining on the market. Monitoring programs indicate that 2,3,7,8-TCDD is not found in currently marketed pest control products. The government of Canada, in conjunction with the provinces, has also established codes of practice to reduce contamination by the wood preservation industries. These efforts to control sources of dioxins and furans have had a positive impact. One indicator of this is that levels of dioxins and furans in Great Lakes fish-eating birds have declined.

Pesticides

Pesticides are toxic chemicals unique as a class of environmental agents as they are deliberately added to the environment for the express purpose of killing some form of life. They have been categorized as "economic poisons" as they have important beneficial effects on food supply and on health. For example, the use of insecticides has eliminated or controlled vector-borne disease in many parts of the world.

Both acute and chronic human health effects related to pesticide exposure have been identified. The acute effects are primarily occupational in origin. Among the variety of delayed health effects associated with pesticides, none has been more prominent than the carcinogenic effects of "Agent Orange." This compound, containing the herbicide 2,4-D, and contaminated with the potent carcinogen 2,3,7,8-TCDD (a dioxin), was sprayed over many of the Vietnam field camps, jungles and roadways during the Vietnam war. Studies of exposed Vietnam veterans have revealed an excess of soft tissue sarcomas and lymphomas. Studies of the teratogenic consequences of Agent Orange exposure have produced inconclusive results.

In 1980, the International Agency for Research on Cancer (IARC) published a review of the carcinogenicity of compounds.[19] The conclusions were: (i) the following are proven carcinogenic for humans: arsenic and certain arsenic compounds, asbestos, benzene, soot, tars and mineral oils; (ii) the following are probably carcinogenic for humans: amitrole, carbon tetrachloride and ethylene oxide; (iii) the following pesticides could not be classified as to their carcinogenicity, but require further investigation: chlordane-heptachlor, DDT, dieldrin and HCH-lindane.

In general, pesticide residues contaminate food products and can concentrate in the ecological food chain. Every human body is born with measurable pesticide levels, related to their widespread use. The delayed effects of pesticide exposure are difficult to investigate as exposures are universal and not easily measured, a latency period applies to all carcinogenic outcomes, and there are no unexposed control groups. Given these difficulties, the delayed health risks of pesticide exposure are often below the power of detection of epidemiological studies.

4.   CREATING A SAFE ENVIRONMENT

With increasing recognition of the importance of the ecosystem has come respect for the maintenance of the integrity of the environment for its intrinsic value, as well as for human needs. A number of strategies have been developed and are discussed below. They include the broad framework of healthy public policy in relation to the environment, sustainable development, the management of waste, and response to environmental emergencies. Strategies to protect human health in relation to the environment include both direct and indirect approaches. Establishing guidelines for human exposure to toxic substances are direct strategies. It is anticipated that reduction of the production of chlorofluorocarbons to sustain the atmosphere's integrity will also have beneficial effects on human health. This is an example of an indirect environmental health approach. In the restoration and maintenance of a safe environment, the responsibility and role of individual commitment and action, as well as of government, is fundamental to the success of environmental measures.

4.1. HEALTHY PUBLIC POLICY

Healthy public policy aims at mobilizing many segments of the community to reduce the adverse health effects on humans which may result from deleterious environmental exposures. The measures utilized include intersectoral and inter-departmental action, legislation, regulations and guidelines, community organization, education and advocacy (see chapter one). A unifying approach to public policy in environmental protection has developed in the form of the sustainable development concept. Specific strategies are discussed below. First, however, it is instructive to review the population-based theoretical position that provides the rationale for healthy public policy approaches in relation to the environment, as articulated by Rose.[20] He proposed that in a continuous distribution of exposures, large numbers exposed to small risk from environmental exposure generate the bulk of the resulting disease. In comparison, far fewer cases occur in those at high risk due to extreme exposure, as may occur, for example, in an occupational setting. As well as paying attention to those at high risk, Rose recommended mass measures as part of the solution to reducing exposures in the total population which have the potential to generate most of the illness.

4.1.1. Regulations and Guidelines

Federal
Jurisdictional responsibility for environmental issues are shared between the federal and provincial governments and areas of overlap are usually resolved through close co-operation. The Canadian Environmental Protection Act (CEPA, 1988) is the cornerstone of federal environmental legislation, providing the framework for protection from pollution, especially hazardous substances. Under the Act, a list of priority toxic substances is to be developed. Substances identified as toxic are transferred to the toxic substances List and subject to regulations which may be applied to their entire life cycle. Environment Canada enforces the Act, and Health Canada contributes to the development of regulations and guidelines. Other pieces of federal legislation relevant to environment and health are the following: the Food and Drugs Act and Regulations (Health Canada); Pest Control Products Act (Agriculture Canada); and the Hazardous Products Act and Regulations (Consumer and Corporate Affairs Canada).   There is, however, fragmentation at this level of government with the federal government's role in

the control of hazardous substances partitioned between 24 departments administering 58 Acts of Parliament. The federal government is also entirely responsible for setting national policy with regard to environmental pollutants which can travel across provincial or international boundaries. Examples of such pollutants are atmospheric sulfur and nitrogen dioxides which cause acid rain.

A new area of federal legislative development is the Environmental Assessment and Review Process which is intended to be formalized into the Canada Environmental Assessment Act. This process is used to identify and review the implications to multiple sectors, including health, of all projects, with both public and professional input being obtained. The issue of the siting of dams and nuclear facilities is a major one in Canada, and Environmental Assessments are a means of identifying implications for the whole ecosystem as well as for human health. Provinces have also developed environmental assessment processes and regulations.

Federal government departments also make health-based guidelines for air, drinking and recreational water. These are not enforceable but are used by many jurisdictions as guidelines for development of their own regulations. Guidelines have the advantage of a capacity for greater responsiveness in comparison to legislation but the disadvantage of unenforceability.

Provincial
The provinces have primary responsibility for the quality of local air and water, the quantity and types of emissions allowed to industries, the disposal of toxic waste products and the identification and management of environmental health hazards. For example, Ontario's Environmental Protection Act (1971) and Amendments requires control of pollutants below any level known to produce a hazard or discomfort to humans, livestock, damage vegetation, or cause corrosion or soiling of buildings. Provinces are also responsible for setting soil contamination guidelines. Provincial Ministries of the Environment play a primary role in this field, but share responsibilities with Labor, Natural Resources, and Health Ministries among others. Responsibilities in relation to environment and health are fragmented at the provincial level as well as at the federal level as previously indicated.

Municipal
Local municipalities are responsible for garbage disposal. Some municipalities have taken initiatives such as recycling programs and are at the forefront of cleaning up the environment to improve health. Local government can request the province to pass enabling legislation to allow local regulations regarding environmental hazards to be developed and implemented.

Role of Public Health
Public health departments usually have municipal and provincial mandates for the enforcement of regulations regarding safe food and water, sanitation, and other

environmental hazards such as restriction of smoking in public places. In addition, the role of public health in environmental issues is frequently that of an "honest broker"; (getting the stakeholders to the table, providing information on health effects, legitimizing concerns and issues by encouraging expression of these by stakeholders and then negotiation of solutions which address the concerns of all parties to the extent possible). A stakeholder is a party affected in some way, frequently economic, by a decision or issue, or who has a mandate or responsibility for involvement. The community is a major stakeholder. The role of public health is described in more detail in chapter 14.

Intersectoral Initiatives

Recently in Canada there have been a number of initiatives undertaken in relation to the environment which have included many departments of government and other sectors. For example, the Great Lakes Action Plan, a five-year plan initiated in 1989, involves six federal departments; Agriculture Canada, Environment Canada, Fisheries and Oceans, Public Works Canada, Transport Canada, and Health Canada. The three distinct components of the plan are: the Great Lakes Cleanup Fund, the Great Lakes Health Effects Program, and the Preservation Program for environmental quality and assessment. The significant findings of a study on toxic chemicals in the Great Lakes undertaken under the program's auspices were highlighted earlier in this chapter.

Canada's Green Plan, published in 1990, incorporates community involvement and education, legislation, and participation by stakeholders in partnerships to improve the environment. Environment is one of the concerns earmarked to be placed on the agenda of many sectors, both private and government. Canada's Green Plan is an excellent example of healthy public policy related to the environment. The federal government and provinces have made a commitment in this plan (i) to clean the air, water and land, (ii) to eliminate dumping of toxic substances into the environment, (iii) to sustain forestry, agriculture and fisheries development, (iv) to protect 12% of Canada as park space, (v) to preserve the integrity of the Arctic and the global environment, including a reduction of greenhouse gases, (vi) to develop partnerships in environmental literacy, and (vii) to prepare for environmental emergencies.

4.1.3. Sustainable Development

This is the concept of productive economic activity which leaves resources in the natural environment intact. Human development and the achievement of human potential require a form of economic activity that is socially as well as environmentally sustainable, for present and future generations. Certain widely held human values, such as support for growth in populations, need for material production, increasing material expectations and belief in technology, have caused specific ecological phenomena which threaten human health. The major issues are: (i) global warming and climatic change with possible consequent food shortages and change in distribution of vector-borne diseases; (ii) ozone depletion; (iii) ecosystem contamination; and (iv) resource depletion. Sustainable development is a conceptual model incorporating a number of generic approaches to reverse the deterioration of the earth; **prevention of pollution** beyond the point where natural systems cannot cope; **conservation** of natural resources by sparing or reduced use, recycling and reuse, with municipal recycling programs a positive indication of action in this area; and **sustained yield**, whereby renewable resources are utilized at a rate that does not exceed their continued replenishment. The reader is referred to earlier sections in this chapter which described relevant control strategies.

Waste Management

Waste management involves the disposal, destruction or storage of **solid waste** and **sewage** (and industrial discharges and nuclear waste). More recently it has begun to include other waste management practices such as recovery from the waste stream and the adoption of a sustainable environment framework to reduce the volumes of waste produced. Canadians produce over 30 million tons of solid waste per year: (i) garbage and refuse; (ii) sludge from waste treatment plants, water supply treatment plants, or air pollution control facilities; and (iii) other discarded material, including solid, liquid, semi-solid; or contained gaseous material from commercial, mining and agricultural operations and from community activities. Hazardous waste, a major component of this solid waste (comprising eight million tons per year), refers to radioactive or biomedical material, material produced during particular industrial processes, and waste containing one or more particular potentially hazardous substances at certain concentrations or containing corrosive, ignitable or otherwise hazardous material.

There are three main approaches currently to solid waste disposal in Canada. These are: (i) **burial**, ideally in modern sanitary landfills which satisfy criteria relating to aesthetics, health and prevention/monitoring of leaching (diffusion of substances into ground water from the landfill site); (ii) **incineration**, in which controlled combustion is used to stabilize and eliminate hazardous material, convert organic into inorganic matter and kill pathogens; and (iii) **transformation,** for example, anaerobic digestion by microorganism or pyrolysis (chemical decomposition caused by combustion in an oxygen-starved environment), which can reduce waste volume by 91%. **Sewage** (apart from areas where septic tanks are used) is treated in Canada in municipal sewage treatment plants. After a process of screening and settling, the sludge produced is digested and dewatered to form sludge cakes which are then incinerated. Effluent liquids are chlorinated and discharged into bodies of water, causing concerns as to the possible effects of chlorinated organic compounds (such as trihalomethanes and chloramines) on the aquatic life.

Canada's Green Plan 1990 indicates a federal commitment to a 50% reduction of wastes in Canada by the year 2000. Packaging, which accounts for 36% of the waste stream has been targeted in particular. The policy emphasizes reduction, reuse, recycling, and recovery, which are all elements of sustainable development. Special provision is made for disposal of hazardous waste with support for Household Hazardous Waste drop-off programs and location of new hazardous waste destruction facilities (e.g., for PCBs) and supporting technology. The Green Plan acknowledges the need for consultation, discussion and involvement of stakeholders, such as industry, in developing and implementing environmental policies.

4.2. MANAGING ENVIRONMENTAL ACCIDENTS

The management of life-threatening incidents involving exposure to toxic chemicals (Bhopal, India) or radiation exposure (Chernobyl, USSR) is difficult. It requires collaboration from several levels of government and at times from international experts. Most of these incidents are not so dramatic but are nonetheless serious. Guidotti has outlined the necessary steps to evaluate unknown health effects.[21] The first step is to **evaluate the problem**, documenting evidence and obtaining accurate information on the nature and magnitude of the hazard. The second step is to **contain** the problem, co-ordinating efforts with responsible public and private agencies. The third step is to **evaluate health effects**, focusing on specific outcomes, when the exposure is known, and on the primary organ systems of concern (dermal, respiratory, hepatic, neurological and renal) and carcinogenic and fetotoxic effects when the exposure is not known.

5.   SUMMARY

Environmental health may be defined as the study of conditions in the natural and built environment which can influence human health and well-being. The focus of study in environmental health is the impact of environmental or hazardous agents on the health of the population. The environment as it affects health can be divided into workplace and non-workplace categories. The workplace environment (occupational health) is often associated with high-level exposure, with the exposed population being predominantly of adult age and in good health. In contrast, non-workplace environmental exposures are generally low level and often chronic. The population at risk contains the extremes of age, developing fetuses and the ill or immunocompromised persons.

The study of environmental health relies on toxicology and epidemiology. Epidemiology is the study of the distribution and determinants of health and disease in human populations. Toxicology, the science of poisons, attempts to identify adverse effects and predict harmful dosages. One of the fundamental tenets of toxicology is that any substance can be a poison if given in a large enough doses.

Canadians are exposed to toxic substances through a variety of sources, including food, water, air, soil, and consumer products. Risk assessment, management and communication are strategies in dealing with health risks posed by the environmental contaminants. There are four major steps in the risk assessment of any environmental contaminant. These are: hazard identification, exposure determination, dose-response determination and risk determination. Risk management is the next series of steps following risk assessment and involves decision making and implementation of options for management of the risk which have been identified. The communication of risk in relation to environmental hazards is dependent on the perception of risk by the public versus the perception of risk by the "experts."

Environmental health issues are focused around the outdoor and indoor environment, water quality, and toxic chemicals. Factors in the outdoor and indoor environment that affect health consist of: ionizing radiation, electromagnetic fields, air pollution, and acid rain. Ionizing radiation, emitted from radioactive substances and the natural background, leads to altered cell physiology. Due to conflicting research results, it is not clear whether or not electromagnetic fields are a health hazard. The main sources of exposure to these fields are high voltage transmission lines, computers, electric blankets, fluorescent lighting and household appliances. Air pollution results primarily from the incomplete combustion of fossil fuels, particularly by cars. Recently, there has been a depletion of ozone in the stratosphere causing an increased incidence of skin cancer of all types including melanoma, cataracts, and depressed immune function. Acid rain refers to the oxidation of the sulfur and nitrogen precursors to acidic compounds. Increases in mortality and morbidity have been temporarily associated with periods of high atmospheric concentrations of pollutant. With respect to water quality, the major chemical contaminants in water are PCBs, dioxins, furans, mercury, lead and pesticides. Toxic chemicals include metals (such as lead, mercury, aluminum), polychlorinated biphenyls and dioxins. Although metals are essential micronutrients, at higher doses these elements can have serious toxic effects. For example, excessive exposure to lead results in its deposition in bone and other tissues. The most obvious clinical manifestation of lead toxicity is anemia, but impaired mental function, visual-motor performance, memory and attention span have also been cited. PCBs do not readily break down and hence they remain in the environment. This persistence, coupled with their tendency to accumulate in the fat of living organisms, means that PCBs are often present in the food chain. Some of the health effects attributed to PCBs include a severe form of acne, swelling of the upper eye lid, muscle spasm, chronic bronchitis, and decreased birth weight and head circumference in newborns. Thus, the major substances posing environmental threats to human health are ozone pollution, tobacco smoke, acid rain, pesticides, PCBs and lead.

A number of strategies have been proposed in order to create a safer environment. These strategies consists of healthy public policy, waste management and managing environmental accidents. Healthy public policy aims at mobilizing many segments of the community to reduce the adverse health effects on humans which may result from deleterious environmental exposures. The measures utilized include regulations and guidelines, education and advocacy, legislation and community organization. Sustainable development is also a form of healthy public policy. It is the concept of productive economic activity which leaves resources in the natural environment intact. Sustainable development is a conceptual model incorporating a number of generic approaches to reversing the deterioration of the earth: prevention of pollution, conservation and sustained yield. Waste management involves the disposal, destruction or storage of solid waste and sewage. There are three main approaches currently to solid waste disposal in Canada. These are burial, incineration, and transformation. The management of life-threatening exposures to toxic chemicals requires collaboration from several levels of government. The steps in management are: evaluating the problem, containing the problem, and evaluating the health effects.

6. REFERENCES

1. *A Vital Link. Health and the Environment in Canada.* Health and Welfare Canada. Published under the authority of the Minister of National Health and Welfare, Ottawa, 1992.
2. Frank JW, Gibson B and McPherson M. Information Needs in Epidemiology; Detecting the Health Effects of Environmental Chemical Exposure Environment. In: *Information Needs for Risk Management* Monograph No. 8, Fowler CD, Grim AP and Munn RE, eds. Institute of Environmental Studies, University of Toronto. Toronto, 1988, pp 129-144.
3. *Determining the Human Health Risks of Environmental Chemicals. Resource Manual.* Environmental Protection Office. Department of Public Health, Toronto, Ontario, 1991.
4. Radon. *Issues.* Health and Welfare Canada, Ottawa, Sept, 1988.
5. Klich B. Medical Symposium Explores Radiation Risks and Public Concern. *Ontario Medical Review* 59(10):23-30, 1992.
6. McLaughlin J, Anderson T, Clarke EA and King W. *Occupational Exposure of Fathers to Ionizing Radion and the Risk of Leukemia in Offsprings: A Case Control Study.* Atomic Energy Control Board, Ottawa, 1992.
7. Electromagnetic Fields. *Issues.* Health and Welfare Canada, Ottawa, Sept, 1989.
8. Gindi M. Ultraviolet Radiation: A Public Health Perspective. Ontario Ministry of Health. *Public Health and Epidemiology Reports Ont* 3(9):136-140, 1992.
9. Pietrusiak M. Ozone in the Troposphere. *Ontario Disease Surveillance Report* 10(17):305-308, 1989.
10. Lippman M. Health Effects of Ozone, A Critical Review. *J Air Pollut Control Assoc* 39(5):675-695, 1989.
11. Bates D and Sizto R. Relationship Between Air Pollutant Levels and Hospital Admissions in Southern Ontario. *Can J Public Health* 74(2):117-122, 1983.
12. Naus M. Health Effects of Acid Rain Exposure. *Ontario Disease Surveillance Report* 9(17):296-298, 1988.
13. Spitzer W, Lawrence V, Dales R, et al. Links Between Passive Smoking and Disease: A Best-Evidence Synthesis. A Report of the Working Group on Passive Smoking. *Clin Invest Med* 13(1):17-42, 1990.

14. Is Our Drinking Water Safe? University of Toronto. *Health News* 7(4):1-6, 1989.
15. *Summary Report: The Quality of Drinking Water in Toronto: A Review of Tap Water, Bottled Water and Water Treated by a Point-of Use Device.* Department of Public Health, Toronto, Ontario, 1990.
16. T*oxic Chemicals in the Great Lakes and Associated Effects - Synopsis.* Environment Canada, Health and Welfare Canada and Department of Fisheries and Oceans. Ministry of Supply and Services, Canada, Ottawa, 1991.
17. Jaiyeola A. Alzheimer's Disease and Aluminum. Ontario Ministry of Health. *Public Health and Epidemiology Reports Ont* 3(1):68-71, 1991.
18. Jaiyeola A. Alzheimer's Disease and Aluminum: How Strong is the Evidence? Why Drinking Water? Ontario Ministry of Health. *Public Health and Epidemiology Reports Ont* 4(12):112-114, 1991.
19. I.A.R.C. Working Group. An Evaluation of Chemicals and Industrial Processes Associated with Cancer in Humans Based on Human and Animal Data. *Cancer Res* 40(1):1-12, 1980.
20. Rose G. Environmental Factors and Disease: The Man Made Environment. *Br Med J* 294(6577):963-965, 1987.
21. Guidotti T. Managing Incidents Involving Hazardous Substances. *Am J Prev Med* 2(3):148-54, 1986.

CHAPTER TEN
Occupational Health and Disease

This chapter will deal with the work environment and its impact on health. **Occupational Health** may be defined as the maintenance and promotion of health in the working environment. The delivery of occupational health services involves not only physicians, chiropractors, and nurses but also hygienists, engineers and safety officers. The jurisdiction for enforcement of occupational health legislation lies with the provinces. Exceptions to this are federally regulated industries such as the grain industry and the transportation industry. Because of this, variation in legislation and regulations governing occupational health can be observed across Canada. However, the principles of the worker's right to know, the worker's right to refuse dangerous work, and the need for joint safety and health committees exist across most of the country. The joint safety and health committee is an important bipartite forum where employees and employers can manage issues of concern.

1. CANADIAN WORKFORCE AND WORK-RELATED HEALTH INDICES

The distribution of the labour force in Canada has changed over the last few decades. A greater proportion of the population today works in the service industry. In 1989, there were 10 and a half million Canadians in the paid labour force.[1] Seventy-three per cent of these people worked in service industries such as restaurants, trade and commerce, transportation, and public administration. About twenty-four per cent were working in goods-producing industries such as manufacturing, mining and construction and about 2.5% in agriculture, forestry and fishing. In 1987, approximately 57% of the individuals in the total work force were male. In the service industry, 52% of the workers were female while in goods-producing industries, only 23% of workers were female.

The annual incidence of occupational injuries and illnesses is about 12% of the Canadian workforce, with 6.2 % suffering from non-disabling (non-compensated) injuries and illness and 5.5% who suffer from disabling (compensated) injuries and illnesses. The total absolute number of non-fatal injuries rose between 1987

**Table 10.1: Workers' Compensation Board Injury Analysis:
Circumstances Causing Injuries and Parts of the Body
Affected in Order of Frequency**

Parts of the Body Injured	Circumstances Causing Injury
Back, spine, chest, trunk	Over exertion
Hands/fingers	Struck by falling object
Feet, toes, lower limb	Caught in between
Upper limb	Falls
Eyes	Step on / strike object
Multiple sites	Exposure/contact to extreme temp.
Face and head	Electric current

and 1989. However, many factors apart from safety issues may have contributed
to this apparent increase, including the level and nature of economic activity and
the employment rate. Reliable data, from which measures of morbidity from
occupational disease may be calculated, are difficult to obtain; this is in part due
to the multifactorial nature of disease. Most literature publications use Workers'
Compensation Board (WCB) data; these, however, reflect only compensated, not
total cases. A review of Canadian statistics indicates that about 1 in 6,000 deaths
is secondary to work. Approximately 85% of these deaths are attributed to
accidents. The highest fatality rates in 1987-1989 in Canada due to injury were in
the following industries: forestry 12.7 per 10 000 workers, fishing 9.1, mining 5.1,
construction 2.9 and transportation 1.6. The circumstances of injury and body
parts injured are seen in table 10.1.

Injuries account for 97% of all compensated cases by WCB; the remainder are
occupational diseases. The most common kind of occupational injury/illness
from WCB data is back injury. Some 45% of work injuries result in disability.
Five per cent become permanently disabled. The pattern of temporary occupational injuries/diseases causing disability has been described in figure 5.6. The
pattern of occupational injuries/diseases causing permanent disability in Ontario
are hearing loss, diseases affecting joints and tendons, and dermatitis; permanent
disabilities secondary to injuries are related to strains and sprains, contusions,
fracture, cuts, wounds, amputation, and multiple injuries. The economic impact
results in both direct and indirect costs. In 1987 alone, $1.65 billion were paid out
by WCB in Ontario.

2. ORGANIZATION OF OCCUPATIONAL HEALTH RESOURCES

Occupational health resources are based in government, industry, educational institutions, union-based centres, consultants and hospitals. The federal government relies on two ministries to set standards and provide appropriate health services: Labour Canada and Health Canada. At the provincial level, responsibility for regulation lies with one or more departments/ministries (e.g., Ministry of Labour, Ministry of Mining, Ministry of Health) and service provision to the civil service lies with another (Ontario Ministry of Government Services). Major industries have corporate medical departments where company-hired health professionals are responsible for the surveillance and monitoring of workers as prescribed by law and corporate policy. The range of health professionals hired depends on the size and complexity of the industry/corporation and may include a physician, nurse, industrial hygienist, psychologist, and chiropractors. Educational institutions, hospitals, union-based centres and consultants provide some, if not all, occupational health services either on a fee-for-service basis or other payment mechanisms. The occupational health services provide primary, secondary, and tertiary prevention.

2.1. PREVENTION

Primary prevention in occupational health involves **substitution**, e.g., replacement of silica powder with a silica-free inert powder in the moulding trade. If substitution cannot be applied then **segregation** using engineering controls is attempted, including **ventilation. Personal hygiene** and **protective equipment** (e.g., respirators, gloves and goggles) are used if the measures outlined above are not feasible. Education and supervision are also required.

Industrial engineers use several methods for setting standards for the exposure limits to hazardous substances in the work environment. When legislation recognizes these limits they constitute legal standards. Where levels are not defined, the acceptable code of practice is usually set on a 40-hour work week (i.e., eight hours a day). They rely on **Threshold Limit Values** (TLVs), previously described in chapter three. These TLVs are usually known as time weighted averages (TWAs). These values are determined by the American Conference of Governmental Industrial Hygienists (ACGIH), and the assumption is that a small percentage of workers will suffer adverse effects as a result of exposure at the TLV-TWA set. These values are published annually. A revision of the values is undertaken if the scientific literature provides justification. All provinces have lists of **designated substance**s which provide regulations for employers, employees and for joint health and occupational safety committees which cover the control of worker exposure to toxic substances.

Health promotion in the workplace has emerged as an effective approach, enabling access to the substantial numbers of persons in the workplace not only for prevention of work-associated health problems, but for wellness programs incorporating attention to lifestyle and other health determinants.[2,3] These determinants include the broad, systemic work and social conditions or environments which influence employee health. Specific work practices, job design, work process and lifestyle may need change. A comprehensive approach beyond lifestyle and based on community development and healthy public policy strategies discussed in chapter one, is relevant. For example, provision of a day care centre on-site and flexible work hours would facilitate the health of women employees of child-rearing age. Worker empowerment can be enhanced by small group development and community organizing. Joint collaboration of employers and workers, beyond the collective bargaining process, will secure the fulfilment of employee needs as well as organizational goals.

The Federal government has introduced a Corporate Model of a Workplace Health System which has been piloted throughout the country. Employers can request a survey of workers' health and health concerns to determine the health needs of employees. The survey is then analyzed and recommendations made, in conjunction with management, through a Workplace Health Committee for the introduction of prevention programs for prevalent problems or risk factors. Recently the emphasis has moved away from provision of expensive gymnasiums and equipment, which were part of the initial response to health promotion in the workplace by larger companies. Programs now often include dietary advice, including attention to the type of items offered by the cafeteria if one is provided, stress management, and smoking cessation counselling, as well as opportunities for enhancing fitness and broader changes to the work environment as discussed above.[2]

Secondary prevention in occupational health involves the use of pre-placement and periodic examinations. The pre-placement examination findings help in establishing an individual's baseline characteristics. Periodic examinations facilitate early diagnosis and may also serve as an early indicator of the effectiveness of plant hygiene controls. The government of Canada established a Task Force on Health Surveillance of Workers in 1981, which was similar to the Periodic Health Examination Task Force, and readers are advised to refer to it for recommendations on specific surveillance procedures.

Another aspect of secondary prevention in the workplace is the issue of **employee screening for substance abuse.** Mandatory pre-employment and random testing has been introduced in many industries in the US. The Canadian Medical Association (CMA) has issued a statement advising that employee testing for substance abuse is not warranted, except as an adjunct if performance impairment is suspected on other grounds in employees in safety-sensitive jobs.[4] Although a great many drugs can be detected in the urine, the test characteristics, such as sensitivity, specificity and predictive value (see chapter two), are very poor. Nor do the tests indicate when the substance was used, as levels may persist for weeks. There is also little correlation between levels detected and extent of impairment of work performance, which is the most germane issue. The most commonly abused substance, alcohol, is generally not tested for as the emphasis has been on detecting illicit drugs. The issue generates much concern from a civil liberties perspective.

If substance abuse is detected, whether by organized screening or observation of impaired performance, such as may occur with alcoholism, an organizational response, including provision of counselling and cessation programs, is required. Many industries provide employee assistance programs for those with alcohol problems.

Tertiary prevention involves treatment, rehabilitation and retraining under the auspices of Workers' Compensation.

Workers' Compensation Board
Generally speaking, where occupation is the established causative factor in the injury/disease, the Workers' Compensation Board is the funding agency. Workers' compensation falls within the jurisdiction of provincial statutes. The general principles are uniform, however. The main features of workers' compensation include: (i) autonomous Boards; (ii) the employers pay for costs; (iii) the Boards decide benefits; (iv) negligence is not a factor; (v) first aid, medical treatment and rehabilitation are covered; (vi) most workers are covered; (vii) a no-fault insurance system; and (viii) worker abdicates his/her right to sue the employer. An employer under WCB must notify the Board within seven days of an employee becoming injured. The employer is responsible for first aid to the worker and transport to hospital. The treating physician must submit a report to the Board. Work injury is compensable no matter who is at fault. In addition to treatment, the Workers' Compensation Board offers rehabilitation consisting of physiotherapy, occupational therapy, counselling, social work, and chiropractic, services.

3.   COMMON OCCUPATIONAL DISEASES

The balance of this chapter will focus on the clinical aspects of common occupational diseases. More detailed clinical reviews are available in textbooks of occupational medicine. The occupational health history must be a routine component of any health history. When occupational disease is suspected, the history should be suitably detailed. Generally speaking, there are two main parts: (i) a work history including exposure and controls; and (ii) a health history where the review of symptoms is tailored to ascertain a relationship, if any, to work. While this history is being elicited, other significant environmental exposures (such as hobbies) should also be ascertained. Occupational diseases have their origin in the working environment. It should be noted that similar diseases may be caused by non-occupational exposures, the distinction being the location of the exposure.

The agents causing occupational disease may be divided into three broad groups: biological, physical and chemical. It is essential to note that at the time of diagnosis some conditions must be fulfilled before attributing causality to the workplace. These conditions include: (i) adequate concentration and duration of exposure; (ii) absorption by the body; (iii) appropriate temporal sequence; and (iv) consistency of ill health effects with the putative exposure. The list of occupational diseases may be endless. However, this chapter will focus on those deemed significant because of their frequency of occurrence or the severity of the disability produced. Known or highly suspected carcinogens in the workplace are listed in table 10.2.

3.1. BIOLOGICAL AGENTS

These include bacteria, rickettsia, viruses, fungi and protozoa. Diseases caused by such agents may be regarded as occupational in origin when the nature of the work involves exposure to the organism. Thus tuberculosis may be accepted as an occupational disease when it occurs in health-care professionals whose daily work has caused them to be exposed to *M. tuberculosis*. The majority of occupational diseases of infectious origin occur in groups of employees exposed to animals or birds, such as abattoir workers, veternarians and pet shop dealers. An example of this type of biological disease (undulant fever) is given below. Of more recent concern, however, are blood-borne infections such as AIDS and Hepatitis B in the workplace, particularly (but not exclusively), in the health-care setting. Blood is increasingly being recognized as a potentially toxic substance.

Blood-Borne Occupational Disease
The occurrence of occupationally acquired blood-borne infection is dependent on the frequency and types of hazardous exposures, the risk associated with each type of discrete exposure and the prevalence of infection in the patient population. The prevalence of blood-borne infective agents in persons admitted to one Canadian hospital were: Hepatitis B surface antigen, 2.1%; HIV antibodies 0.6%; antibodies to the Hepatitis C virus 0.5%.[5] The generalizability of these results cannot be assumed. The other factors are discussed below.

The risk of a health worker contracting Hepatitis B from an occupational exposure is significant. Risks among US health-care workers (from Occupational Health and Safety Administration, OSHA and the Federal Register) are quoted, as insufficient data is available from Canada.[6] OSHA's risk assessment yields an estimated 20-31 cases of clinical hepatitis per 1000 and risk of death of 2-3/1,000 on the basis of a 45-year working life.

In regard to HIV infection, although the proportion of health-care workers infected is similar to the general population, there is a statistically greater

Table 10.2: Known or Highly Suspected Carcinogens in the Workplace (Adapted)

Substance	Where Encountered	Type of Cancer
Asbestos	Very widespread use, especially in construction, auto repair and ship building, present in many products	Lung cancer, mesothelioma
Coke oven emissions	Steel mills, coke ovens	Lung cancer
3,3'-Dichlorobenzidine	Pigment manufacturing, polyurethane production	---
Radium	Limited use	---
4,4'-Methylenebis[2-chloroaniline]	Plastics manufacturing; elastomer, polyurethane foam, epoxy resins	---
Uranium and radon	Underground mining	Lung cancer
β-Naphthylamine	Chemical, dyestuff, rubber industries	Bladder cancer
Auramine and magenta	Dye manufacturing	---
Carbon tetrachloride	Very widespread use, as fire extinguisher, for cleaning clothing, as solvent	---
Benzidine	Clinical pathology laboratories; chemical, dyestuffs, plastics, rubber, wood products industries	Liver cancer
β-Propiolactone	Plastics, chemical, pharmaceutical industries	---
Vinyl chloride	Petrochemical, plastics, rubber industries	---
Chloromethyl methyl ether	Chemical industry, nuclear reactor fuel processing	Angiosarcoma of liver
Bis(chloromethyl) ether	Chemical industry, nuclear reactor fuel processing	Respiratory tract cancer
Ethylenimine	Chemical, paper, textile industries	---
N-Nitrosodimethylamine	Chemical, rubber, solvent, pesticide industries	---
Chloroprene	Synthetic rubber industry	---
Trichlorethylene	Previously very widespread use as solvent and degrading agent; now withdrawn from use	Animal evidence
Benzene	Very widespread use in industry as solvent and chemical constituent	Leukemias, lymphomas

Substance	Where Encountered	Type of Cancer
Acrylonitrile	Plastics, textile industries	---
Leather dust	Leather goods industry	---
Wood dust	Hardwood industries	---
Chromate (hexavalent)	Electroplating, metal products, photography, textile industries	---
Nickel	Widespread use especially in metal products, chemical, battery industries	Skin cancer
Ionizing radiation	Very widespread use especially medical and industrial X-ray	Cancer of hemopoetic system
Arsenic	Very widespread use	Skin cancer
Cutting oils	Machining, metal working trades	---
Hydrazine	Mechanical applications, pharmaceutical industry	---
Ethylene dibromide	Fumigant, anti-knock gasoline, additive industries	---
Pesticides, specifically aldrin, dieldrin, DBCP (1,2-dibromo-3-chloropropane)	Agriculture and pesticide manufacturing (all but DBCP now withdrawn)	---
Agent Orange	War veterans, hydro workers, forest workers	Skin, lymphoma
Silica	Mining, chemical industry, glassmaking, ceramics, foundries and sandblasting	Silicosis

Source: Guidotti, T.L., Goldsmith, D.F. Occupational Cancer *Amer. Fam. Phys.*, 34:3:148, 1986. Reproduced with the permission of the authors and the publisher.

proportion of infected health-care workers with no known risk factors or an undetermined transmission category. The risk of seroconversion among cohorts of health-care workers with parenteral exposures has been shown to be small, less than 0.5%. In relation to occupational exposure to HIV in Canada, no seroconversions have been documented in the national surveillance program on occupational exposure to HIV among 317 health-care workers with percutaneous, mucous membrane, and skin exposures as of April 5, 1992.[7]

Universal precautions, intended to prevent parenteral, mucous membrane, and non-intact skin exposures of health-care workers to blood-borne pathogens, have been recommended and widely introduced.[8] There is some concern, however, about the effectiveness of universal precautions in preventing occupational spread of HIV. A surveillance study by the Federal Centre for AIDS indicated that health-care workers were exposed to blood despite protection, but seroconversions did not result.[9] The basic tenet of universal precautions is that every specimen should be regarded as hazardous and treated with equal care. The reader is advised to review the recommendations made by the National Committee for Clinical Laboratory Standards. No attempt is made here to reproduce these, but a few salient points from the recommendations are made. Universal precautions include prevention of sharp instrument injuries, use of protective barriers, and immediate washing of hands and surfaces contaminated by blood and other fluids to which universal precautions apply. These measures are intended to supplement existing practices of hand washing and use of gloves to prevent infection. Universal precautions apply to blood and other body fluids containing visible blood and tissues, but do not apply to feces, nasal secretions, sputum, sweat, tears, urine and vomitus, unless they contain visible blood.

A further current issue in relation to occupational spread of HIV is the reciprocity of rights of patients and health-care workers with regard to HIV testing.[10] Attention was drawn to the potential of risk for patients contracting HIV from infected practitioners by reasonable evidence that three patients were infected with HIV by a dentist.[11] This type of transmission is, however, regarded as a rare occurrence. Guidelines for the continuing practice of HIV-positive physicians have been produced in a number of jurisdictions. The Laboratory Centre for Disease Control has advised that mandatory testing of health-care workers and patients for HIV is not currently warranted due to the extremely small risk of HIV transmission in this setting and the impracticality of this measure.

As an adjunctive measure to prevent blood-borne infection, recommendation has been made for pre-exposure Hepatitis B vaccination (see chapter 10) for health-care workers potentially exposed to blood. Compliance among health workers for Hepatitis B vaccination has been high. Protocol for appropriate post-exposure hepatitis B, testing, passive immunization and active vaccination have been developed.[12] Protocols have been designed to reduce the incidence of blood-borne infections in hospitals and other health-care settings.[13]

Undulant Fever (Brucellosis, Malta Fever)

Undulant fever is an acute infectious disease characterized by a prolonged febrile course with irregular remissions and exacerbations. It is caused by a member of the Brucella group of microorganisms. The causative agent is ingested from contaminated food and drink, particularly milk, butter and cheese from infected goats and cows. It is also contracted by those who handle infected meat and meat products. The majority of cases occur in farmers, milkers and abattoir workers. The average incubation period is two weeks, with the onset being gradual. Fever, anorexia, constipation, loss of weight and generalized muscle and joint pains are common characteristics.

3.2.   PHYSICAL AGENTS

Excessive Noise

The effects produced by excessive noise may include fatigue, impaired hearing, increased blood pressure, decreased efficiency and emotional disturbances. Noise can be measured by a sound level metre, which determines the intensity of a sound in the immediate environment in terms of decibels. Ordinary conversation varies from 35 to 65 decibels. The normal threshold of audibility is 0 decibels. Intensities above 80 decibels are annoying and noise levels of 100 to 130 decibels have been found to cause temporary and permanent deafness. Levels above 130 decibels are painful to the ear.

Although industrial noise is usually a combination of sounds at different frequencies, it is still possible to establish the main source of a noise and take appropriate steps to eliminate or reduce it. Initial loss in acuity occurs for sounds with high frequencies, particularly those around 4,000 cycles per second (Hz). Brief exposures to high noise levels results in temporary hearing loss, with recovery occurring over several days to weeks. On the other hand, exposure during the work day to sustained noise levels of 85 decibels or higher for several months may result in permanent partial impairment of hearing. In general, the greater the loss in acuity for conversation, the more seriously the person is handicapped.

In assessing the importance of noise in producing deafness, a careful search must be made for those organic conditions which are recognized as causing deafness. There is considerable individual susceptibility to the effects of noise. Pre-placement and periodic audiograms are essential for employees working in high noise levels. It is necessary also to distinguish between occupational impairment and the normal deterioration in hearing which occurs with advancing age (presbyacusis). Noise may be prevented or eliminated by one or more of the following methods: (i) elimination of noise at its source, (ii) isolation of noisy operations, (iii) reduction of noise by sound insulation, and (iv) use of personal protective devices against noise.

Temperature and Humidity

Excessively high temperature and humidity occur in many industries, principally as a result of the heat and moisture produced by industrial processes. This may be accentuated during the summer months by a high external temperature. Very high temperatures may bring about heat cramps, heat exhaustion or heat stroke.

Heat Cramps Heat cramps may occur in people who sweat profusely as a result of heavy physical work performed in hot environments, and are due to sodium chloride depletion. The characteristic symptoms consist of spasmodic contractions of the muscles of the extremities and abdominal wall. The body temperature is usually normal or slightly elevated, the pulse rate slightly increased, the blood pressure normal and the skin moist. Nausea and vomiting may occur. The cramps disappear completely and rapidly following intravenous injection of physiological saline and can be prevented by oral administration of salt and water.

Heat Exhaustion This usually occurs in hot weather, with the initial symptoms being fatigue, headache and dizziness. These may proceed to a state of unconsciousness or collapse. The body temperature may be low or elevated (though not exceeding 102°F), the skin may be moist, the pulse is rapid and weak, and the blood pressure is usually low. The clinical picture is that of shock.

Heat Stroke This is often called sunstroke when the cause is the radiant heat from the sun. In industrial workers, heat stroke occurs most frequently during prolonged heat waves. The condition is due to failure of the temperature-controlling centre of the hypothalamus. The onset may be sudden, with the outstanding symptom being a high body temperature falling between 107°F and 110°F. The pulse is rapid (except in the late stages) and the blood pressure is elevated. Other characteristics include laboured respiration, hot and dry skin, flushed face, depressed nervous system, incontinence and vomiting. The state of coma may last for hours or days.

Cold Exposure of extremities to the cold can cause chilblains or precipitate attacks of Raynaud's disease. Raynaud's disease is an idiopathic, paroxysmal, bilateral cyanosis of digits, due to arterial or arteriolar contractions, brought on by cold or emotions. Re-warming the affected part reverses the temporary damage. Frostbite is a more severe and largely irreversible form of local cell injury. Upon thawing, hyperanemia and increased capillary permeability cause edema, swelling and thrombosis, followed by ischemia and gangrene in the digits.

Repeated Motion and Vibration

In many industrial processes, certain muscles or groups of muscles are used to a greater extent than in ordinary life, causing new employees to develop muscular stiffness and soreness. Certain occupations subject the skin of the hands, feet, or other parts of the body to excessive friction, producing blisters and abrasions. In these cases, the body must gradually adjust itself to more severe muscular effort, or develop compensatory hardening and thickening of the skin. Occasionally, the employee must be given lighter work during the period of adjustment.

Tenosynovitis, Bursitis In certain trades (such as carpentry and bricklaying), the resumption of work in the spring after the winter layoff requires the use of poorly-conditioned muscles in the repetitive movements of hammering or sawing. At the same time, these muscles must maintain some degree of contraction in gripping the tool and are subject to the effects of repeated shocks or blows. These conditions frequently lead to the development of tenosynovitis, bursitis and myositis, causing pain and swelling in the tendons, joints or muscles subjected to the strains. In the treatment of occupational tenosynovitis and bursitis, transfer to other work, or removal from the job, so that the affected part can be put at rest, is important.

Traumatic Vasospastic Disease (Raynaud's Phenomenon) The clinical effects resulting from prolonged use of piston-operated vibrating tools have been recognized for some years. Portable vibrating tools are of two main types: (i) the piston-operated pneumatic tools, such as road and rock drills, chipping hammers or riveting hammers, and (ii) the newer rotating tools that consist essentially of a handle through the centre, which is a rotating spindle carrying a head, and are driven by an electric motor or compressed air. Both types of tools may be carried in the hands. In either case, the vibrations of the tool are transmitted to the hands and arms of the operator.

The most common effect is a disturbance of the blood vessels of the fingers which is quite similar clinically to Raynaud's disease. The condition may develop after two years of exposure to the vibrations, but usually requires longer exposure. Sometimes the condition first becomes apparent after exposure to vibration has ceased. Exposure to cold is the precipitating factor inducing the vasospastic attacks.

Occupational Cramps These are usually associated with prolonged performance of repeated muscle movements. Cramps or spasm may develop in the muscles involved in the repetitive task. Function is impaired for the performance of other muscular movements. Muscular wasting and signs of paralysis are rarely present.

Abnormalities of Air Pressure

Exposure to abnormally high atmospheric pressures occurs in diving operations and in occupations where compressed air shafts and caissons are used, as in construction of tunnels, bridge piers and building foundations. Workers are exposed to air pressures exceeding the hydrostatic pressure of water at the depths in which they work.

Decompression Sickness Most frequently encountered by industrial workers, symptoms usually appear within the first few hours following too rapid decompression. This rapid decompression leads to the formation of emboli which block off the blood supply to various parts of the body, including the spinal cord. The most common symptom is severe pain in the muscles and joints of the arms and legs. Other symptoms include tetanus, epigastric pain, dyspnea, paralysis of skeletal muscle and shock. Death may occur rapidly or may follow secondary complications. Prevention consists of limiting the lengths of time a worker may stay in compressed air at specified pressures, and requiring adequate periods for decompression after each work period.

Barotrauma Occurs as the result of too sudden increases or decreases in atmospheric pressures. A sudden increase with a blocked eustachian tube may result in otic barotrauma (rupture of the tympanic membrane), whereas a sudden decrease, with blocked nasal sinuses, may cause sinus barotrauma. A similar effect can occur in other gas containing cavities (e.g., intestines), if the external air pressure is suddenly decreased.

Radiation

There are two types of radiation: ionizing and nonionizing. Radioactivity is measured in becquerels (Bq.) which is one disintegration per second within the nucleus of a radionuclide. Ionizing radiation consists of X-rays, gamma rays, alpha particles, beta particles and neutrons.

(i) **X-rays** are streams of photons that have great penetrability and move at high speed. (ii) **Gamma rays** are high energy rays that have great penetrability. (iii) **Beta particles** are electrons which can penetrate several centimetres of body tissue. (iv) **Alpha rays** are positively charged and have poor penetrance. They can be easily impeded. (v) **Neutrons** are uncharged particles which exist only for a fraction of a second.

Exposure from X-rays and gamma radiation is measured in Roentgens; on the other hand, the unit *rem* expresses a dose equivalent. The exposure of radiation workers is limited to five *rems* a year. This exposure limit is determined pursuant to the Atomic Energy Control Board of Canada which is responsible for most regulations in the radiation field.

As a result of these regulations, all atomic radiation workers have to wear dosimeter film badges to measure exposure. These are periodically measured to determine the exposure dose. The effects of alpha and beta particles, neutrons, and X-rays and gamma rays on the body are believed to be due to the process of ionization. Alpha and beta particles are charged particles and produce ionization directly as they pass through atoms in their path. X-rays, gamma rays and neutrons are not charged particles, but when absorbed, the energy liberated can induce ionization. The ultimate effect of ionization is damage to, or death of, the cells. Changes appear in the nucleus, and to a lesser extent, in the cytoplasm. Cell division is retarded, and chromosome damage may result in the production of abnormal cells. The ability of the body to repair the damage will vary with the total energy absorbed (the unit of absorbed energy is the "sievert"), the frequency of exposure and the period of time over which the exposure is spread. Greater doses can be tolerated if fractionated than if given as a single exposure.

The type and severity of the injury depends on the extent of the tissue exposed and on the particular tissue which absorbs the radiation. The lymphoid tissue, including bone marrow, lymphocytes and Peyer's patches, appears to be the most sensitive to radiation, followed, in decreasing order of susceptibility, by polymorphonuclear leukocytes; epithelial cells, including the hair; gonads;

endothelial cells including blood vessels and peritoneum; connective tissue; muscle cells; and finally, the nerve cells.

The relative hazard to the body varies with the type of radioactive particle or radiation. Alpha particles, because of their low penetrating power, are important only when the alpha emitter is taken into the body as by inhalation of radon gas or ingestion of radium paint. Beta particles can exert an effect locally on the skin, as with radioactive materials. X-rays always produce their effects as the result of external exposure, though the deep tissues may be affected. Gamma rays may originate externally (as with a cobalt-60 camera) or internally, following absorption of the radioactive material.

The effects of ionizing radiation may be subdivided into somatic and genetic. The somatic effects, in turn, may be immediate (acute) or delayed (chronic). The acute somatic effects are known as **radiation sickness**; this varies in severity from skin reactions, which result chiefly from beta particles and low energy (soft) X-rays absorbed largely by the skin, to severe illness with death occurring within a week of exposure. The latter follows exposures of 600 rads or more. Nausea and vomiting develop within an hour of such exposures; these may subside for a few days, only to be followed by the return of nausea, vomiting, diarrhea, fever, bleeding and ulceration of the mucous membranes. The blood lymphocyte count declines and secondary infection may occur. Death is usually the result of intestinal or hemopoietic injury. With lower doses, e.g., 300 to 600 rads, the symptom-free period will usually last for several days to two weeks, followed by a return of symptoms and some mortality within two to four weeks of exposure. With doses of 100 to 300 rads there may be only slight initial symptoms, but loss of hair, anorexia, pallor, petechiae and moderate emaciation can occur up to the fourth week. Fatality should be rare. Treatment of acute radiation sickness is so far only palliative.

The delayed somatic effects of ionizing radiation include leukopenia, anemia, sterility, fetal injury, bone necrosis and sarcomata (as occurred among dial painters who ingested radium paint during World War I); lung cancer (reported among uranium miners in Czechoslovakia and the Colorado plateau), chronic atrophic dermatitis, hyperkeratoses, epitheliomata, leukemia, breast and thyroid cancer (reported among survivors of Hiroshima and Nagasaki), and production of cataracts by neutron exposure. Except for leukemia, a long latency period of 15-25 years is characteristic of malignancies secondary to radiation exposure.

With respect to the genetic effects of ionizing radiation, there are little human data. The majority of both natural and radiation mutations is of recessive inheritance, and the probability of their becoming manifest in future generations is small. In follow-up studies on the survivors of the Japanese bombings, so far there has been little evidence of a deleterious effect on succeeding generations.

In order to protect employees working with ionizing radiation the following measures are taken:

- Spacing: The intensity of the exposure to X-rays and gamma rays decreases as the square of the distance from the source. Hence tongs or remote control instruments are used to handle radioactive sources.
- Shielding: e.g., use of lead screens, lead aprons and gloves.
- Exhaust ventilation to remove radioactive dusts and gases.
- Hygienic measures: including fresh overalls and gloves daily, wearing lead aprons in potentially "hot" areas and in clean areas, washing hands. Walls, phones and benches should have smooth impervious surfaces to prevent contamination and facilitate washing.
- Pre-employment examination, with emphasis on the applicant having normal hematology.
- Wearing film badges or pencil-type ionization chambers (dosimeters) by all personnel, changed every two weeks. These provide a record of cumulative dose to date.
- Periodic blood checks, watching particularly for signs of lymphocytopenia, anemia and thrombocytopenia.
- Radon breath samples periodically from workers handling radium. Radon gas can be measured in exhaled air.
- Periodic urinalyses from workers working with uranium and other radioactive materials.
- Monitoring of work areas by trained physicists or radiation technicians.
- Removal of individuals from exposure when cumulative dose exceeds permissible level, until sufficient time has elapsed to bring the average dose once again within the permissible limit.

Non-Ionizing Radiation
Non-ionizing radiation comprises ultraviolet, infrared and ultrahigh frequency radiation.

Ultraviolet Radiation   Exposure to ultraviolet rays occurs chiefly in arc and electro-welding. The intensity of the ultraviolet radiation increases with the temperature of the welding process. Exposure may also occur in the use of ultraviolet rays for inspecting razor blades, blue prints and golf balls and in the examination of bedding for the presence of used materials. Ultraviolet rays are also used in the diagnosis and treatment of skin diseases.

UV radiation primarily affects the eyes, skin and superficial blood vessels. Symptoms appear four to 12 hours after exposure, with skin developing an erythema, followed by freckling and pigmentation. The eyes may react to the UV by developing ophthalmia with acute conjunctivitis, lacrimation, photophobia and burning. In severe cases, corneal ulceration, iritis and cataracts may develop. Harmful effects are not observed when the individual is more than 25 feet from the source.

Infrared Radiation   Infrared radiation (so-called "Heat" rays) are given off in such high temperature processes as welding, glassblowing, foundry work and other occupations where metal and glass are heated to the molten state. In these processes, there may be a concomitant exposure to ultraviolet rays and to excessive light radiation. Infrared rays are utilized in industry in the heating and drying of many materials, e.g., painted and lacquered objects and automobiles.

Infrared radiation causes a vasodilation of the skin and stimulation of cellular activity. In excessive doses, it produces an erythema followed by pigmentation and freckling. The most serious effect of prolonged exposure to infrared radiation is the development of a cortical cataract at the posterior pole. This cataract form is found in workers over 35 years of age who have been exposed for some years to the glare from molten glass or metal or from furnaces.

Ultra-High Frequency Radiation   Currently this is of little importance (as it is not used as frequently in industry); however, its importance may be relevant in the future. The use of high frequency has been reported to cause complaints of tiredness, exhaustion, headache, chills, dizziness and numbness. The complaints disappeared upon removing the source, and no serious effects have been reported.

Video Display Terminals   The Canadian Medical Association indicated the following in a policy statement: "Many reputable scientific surveys have shown that VDTs do not emit ionizing radiation (X-radiation). The health problems experienced by many VDT operators are, according to the best knowledge available, essentially ergonomic, being related the physical characteristics of the work place. VDT users more often have visual, musculoskeletal and stress-related complaints than other workers. Proper ergonomic standards (e.g., appropriately designed work spaces, approved office furniture and machines, adequate lighting and glare reduction, regular rest breaks and suitable environmental conditions) should be encouraged in the work place to maximize comfort of VDT operators."[14]

Electricity

The effects of electrical currents upon the body depend on external and individual conditions. The severity of the damage is proportional to the strength and duration of the current. In general, the higher the voltage, the greater will be the current passing through the body. The strength of the current will be increased if the skin is wet or damp. The current chiefly affects the organs through which it passes. When the current passes through the brain, the patient may be rendered unconscious. Death is caused by ventricular fibrillation, failure of the respiratory centre, or prolonged tetanus of the respiratory muscles resulting in suffocation. Voltages as low as 35 volts have been known to cause death. If the current does not pass through any of the vital organs, other parts of the body may be affected. This may result in functional or structural damage which may be either temporary or permanent. Permanent disability is usually the result of electrical burns in tissues directly affected by the current. A discussion of electromagnetic fields that are generated by electric current and are indirect effects of electricity to which workers may be exposed is given in chapter nine.

3.3.   CHEMICAL AGENTS

Organic Dusts
Organic dusts contain carbon and are largely derived from substances of animal or plant origin. Common examples are dusts and fibres arising from the handling or manufacture of: wood, bone and shell; fur, skins, hides and leather; brooms and straw; flour and grain; tobacco; jute, flax (linen), hemp, cotton, wool (worsted, etc.); felts and carpets; rag and paper; or sweepings.

Though most organic dusts do not cause pneumoconiosis or pulmonary fibrosis of a specific disabling nature, many are irritants to the upper respiratory passages and to the conjunctivae and skin, causing bronchitis, conjunctivitis and dermatitis. Many organic dusts may elicit allergic reactions in sensitized persons, with production of asthma and urticaria. Workers may exhibit no outward symptoms until they are exposed to a dust to which they are sensitized, when they develop an allergic reaction characterized by a decrease in the vital capacity from a normal of about 5 L to 2.5 or 3 L and by decreases in the timed forced expiratory ventilation fractions (FEV_1, FEV_2, FEV_3) indicating bronchiolar spasm, wheezing and dyspnea. Such adverse effects are usually relieved by cessation of the exposure, and tend to recur when the patient returns to the job.

Mineral Dusts
Though it is doubtful whether any dust can be regarded as entirely harmless under conditions of extreme exposure, for practical purposes mineral dusts can be divided into two classes: active and inert. The majority of dusts encountered, industrially or otherwise, are relatively inert, as, for example, are carbon and metal dusts, most of the silicate dusts and emery dust. Some of the inert dusts may cause radiological pulmonary shadowing from the deposition of radio-opaque material in the lungs, without initiating fibrosis or loss of pulmonary function. Their main importance lies in the problem they present in differential diagnosis. Siderosis, which is due to the deposition of iron dust in the lung, is probably the most frequently encountered non-disabling pneumoconiosis.

Among the active dusts, silica, asbestos (a silicate) and the fume from the fusion of bauxite ore are the chief offenders in producing disabling pulmonary disease in this country. It has been conclusively established that the vast majority (over 90%) of the particles which reach the alveoli are less than 3 microns (3/1000 mm) in diameter. Most particles larger than 3 microns either settle out of the air before it is breathed, or are trapped in the secretions of the nose and throat and eliminated or swallowed. As a rule, dusts vary greatly in size, depending to some extent upon the mechanical processes involved in their production, for example, wet versus dry drilling of hard rock.

Silica   From the point of view of numbers of people exposed and cases of disability produced, "free" silica (silicon dioxide, SiO_2) is the chief cause of pulmonary dust disease and in contrast, "combined" silica (silicate, SiO_3) is probably inert. Silica is the main constituent of sand, sandstone, and granite, and is present in iron ore and coal. Exposure to silica occurs in several occupations (such as hard rock mining, sandblasting, granite cutting). The approximate average duration of exposure required for the development of silicosis varies widely for different occupations from five years in unprotected sandblasting to 30 years in molders and granite cutters. The prolonged inhalation of dusts containing free silica may result in the development of a disabling pulmonary fibrosis known as silicosis. The Committee on Pneumoconiosis of the American Public Health Association defines silicosis as "a disease due to the breathing of air containing silica (SiO_2), characterized by generalized fibrotic changes and the development of miliary nodules in both lungs, and clinically by shortness of breath, decreased chest expansion, lessened capacity for work, absence of fever, increased suscepti-bility to tuberculosis (some or all of which symptoms may be present) and characteristic X-ray findings."

An emerging controversy in occupational medicine is the relationship between silicosis and lung cancer. Numerous studies have been reported in the literature. The additive effects of silica and carcinogens such as benzpyrenes have been proven without a doubt. However, whether silica by itself is a carcinogen has not been clearly established.

In making a diagnosis of silicosis, it is essential to ascertain whether the worker was exposed to silica and if so, whether sufficient exposure to cause the disease occurred. The X-ray film, *per se,* is of little value in determining disability and in fact may be misleading.

Asbestos   Canada is one of the principal asbestos-producing countries. There are three forms of asbestos, namely chrysotile, amosite, and crocidolite. Canada produces mainly chrysolite which is chiefly hydrated magnesium silicate, occur-ring as a white fibrous ore. The fibres, when separated, may be spun into yarn and woven in much the same manner as ordinary textiles or they may be ground and mixed with other materials to form insulating boards or sheets. Exposure to the dust occurs in the crushing, carding, spinning and weaving of the material, and in the manufacture of brake linings and insulating products.

The essential lesion in asbestosis is a diffuse fibrosis which probably begins as a "collar" around the terminal bronchioles. Usually, at least four to seven years of exposure are required before a serious degree of fibrosis occurs. Apparently there is less predisposition to tuberculosis than is the case with silicosis. In men with asbestosis who have been autopsied, lung cancer has been reported in 15% to 23%. Thus there is evidence for accepting lung cancer as an occupational disease in those who have asbestos fibrosis of the lungs. The sentinel carcinoma for asbestos is mesothelioma.

Coal   Graphite is a crystalline form of carbon; ash-free anthracite coal is an amorphous form of the same element. In the pure state, these dusts cause no fibrosis of the lung. As they occur in nature, however, graphite and anthracite frequently contain considerable amounts of free silica, and exposed workers may develop a modified form of silicosis, or anthracosilicosis, characterized by diffusely-scattered, small stellate patches of fibrosis, each surrounded by an area of focal emphysema. Like true silicosis, anthracosilicosis may be disabling. The incidence of the disease has been shown to be related to the concentration of silica dust in the air and to length of exposure.

Metallic Dusts and Fumes
The following important metallic dusts and fumes will be outlined: i) lead, ii) mercury, iii) cadmium and iv) nickle.

Lead   Of the metallic dusts and fumes, lead and its components are probably the most important, not only because of their widespread use in industry, but also because of the serious disability which may result from poisoning. The environmental aspects of lead contamination have been described in chapter nine. The occupations which expose workers to the highest levels of lead are the manufacture of storage batteries and the reclamation of scrap metal. Exposure also occurs in soldering operations and lead burning, in the manufacture of paints containing lead and in the sanding of surfaces coated with lead paints. Other exposures to lead occur in the printing trade, in the breaking up of ships coated with lead paints, in the glazing of pottery, in the manufacture and use of certain insecticides and in the blending of tetraethyl gasoline.

The toxicity of the various lead compounds appears to depend upon several factors: (i) the solubility of the compound in the body fluids; (ii) the size of the particles (solubility is greater, of course, in proportion to the smallness of the particles); (iii) conditions under which the compound is being used. Where a lead compound is used as a powder, atmospheric contamination will be much less if the powder is kept damp. Of the various lead compounds, the carbonate, the monoxide and the sulphate are considered to be more toxic than metallic lead or other lead compounds. Lead arsenate is very toxic, due to the presence of the arsenic radical. The toxicity of lead chromate or chrome yellow is less than would be expected due to its low solubility.

To study the effects of lead exposure in workers, two separate entities must be kept in mind: lead absorption and lead poisoning. Lead absorption is that condition in which workers experience absorption but do not have clinical evidence of lead poisoning. They will show an increased lead urinary excretion rate, perhaps an increased blood lead level, a reduced or falling hemoglobin, perhaps an increased basophilic stippling of red blood cells and, on rare occasions, a lead line along the gum margin. Despite this evidence of increased lead absorption, these workers feel well and have no complaints about their health.

Lead poisoning (or lead intoxication) may be acute or chronic.

(i) **Acute lead poisoning** results from a single exposure to a large dose and is rarely encountered in industry. Accidental ingestion of lead acetate or lead subacetate is the main source of lead. Signs and symptoms of acute lead poisoning include metallic taste, vomiting, colic, and constipation or bloody diarrhea. Central nervous system symptoms predominate when exposure is from organic lead compounds (such as tetraethyl or tetramethyl lead).

(ii) **Chronic lead poisoning** is a classic example of a cumulative poison. It occurs from the inhalation or ingestion of small amounts of lead dust, fumes, or vapours over a relatively long period of time. The diagnosis of early lead poisoning is often difficult since the presenting symptoms are very general (such as headache, weakness and pallor; see also chapter nine). To make a diagnosis of occupational lead poisoning, the following criteria must be met: a history of significant exposure to lead at work, clinical signs and symptoms which are compatible with lead poisoning, and supportive laboratory evidence (i.e., increased urinary or blood lead levels, increased erythroprotoporphyrin and low hemoglobin). Ideally, prevention of lead poisoning consists of avoiding exposure to lead. Minimum requirements for examining workers exposed to lead consists of a complete medical examination periodically and periodic inquiry into general health, together with urine or blood lead measurements. If blood lead is above 0.08 mg/100 ml, that individual is at a high risk for developing lead poisoning.

Mercury Mercury and mercury compounds are used widely in many industries. For example, they are used in the manufacture of scientific instruments, industrial chemicals, in the photographic industry, in the pharmaceutical industry, in the manufacture of amalgams with copper, tin, silver and gold, in dentistry and in power generators. The effects of environmental exposure to mercury have been described in chapter nine.

Acute exposure to mercury is fairly rare, particularly in industry. The ingestion of mercury produces severe corrosion of the upper alimentary tract. Chronic exposure to mercury usually results in any or all of the following: erethism (a form of anxiety neurosis), vasomotor disturbances, renal damage, depression, central and peripheral nerve disorders, lesions in the mouth and teeth, and nausea and vomiting.

There are some clinical differences between organic and inorganic mercury poisoning. Erethism, stomatitis and salivation are less marked with organic compounds, whereas motor and sensory disturbances are greater. Urinary excretion of mercury of more than 300 micrograms/day is associated with a chronic condition.

Cadmium Today the largest use of cadmium is the electroplating industry. Almost all industrial exposures are due to the inhalation of fumes emitted in smelting impure zinc, in distilling cadmium sponge, or in welding or burning cadmium plated metal.   The occurrence of cadmium poisoning is increasing due to its increased use.   The effects of acute and chronic cadmium toxicity are described in chapter nine.

Nickel It is used in the manufacture of alloys of iron, chromium and tungsten. Its salts are also used widely. In industry, exposure occurs through the inhalation of the dusts and fumes that are by products of the production of the metal. Nickel and its salts are not considered to cause systemic poisoning. Recently, cases of lung and sinus cancer have been found in greater than normal numbers among men employed in the calcining and sintering operations. However, the most common effect resulting from exposure to nickel compounds is the development of nickel-itch seen most commonly in people doing nickel plating.

Volatile Solvents and Organic Materials
The following important classes of solvents will be outlined: (1) aromatic hydrocarbons, (2) chlorinated hydrocarbons, (3) alcohols, esters, ketones.

Aromatic Hydrocarbons (i) Benzol is perhaps the most dangerous of solvents used commercially. In acute poisoning, the worker becomes confused or dizzy, complains of tightening of the leg muscles and of pressure over the forehead, then passes into a stage of excitement. If the worker continues to be exposed, he/she may lapse into a coma. In non-fatal cases, recovery is usually complete. In chronic poisoning the onset is slow with vague symptoms (e.g., fatigue, headache, and nausea). With continued exposure, aplastic anaemia or leukemia may develop. (ii) Toluene and xylene are closely related chemically to benzol but is less toxic. The same effects of benzol on the body are not seen with exposure to toluene or xylene.

Chlorinated Hydrocarbons Chlorinated hydrocarbons are used widely in oils, greases and waxes. They are generally nonflammable, and their toxicity to the liver and kidney ranges from very high to very low. Carbon tetrachloride is the most toxic of this group. Following exposures to high concentrations, the worker may become unconscious, and if exposure is not terminated, death can follow from respiratory failure. Exposure to lower concentrations, insufficient to produce unconsciousness, usually results in sever gastrointestinal upset and may progress to serious kidney and hepatic damage.

Alcohol, Esters and Ketones Under these categories are included methyl, propyl and butyl alcohol, and methyl and ethyl acetate as well as acetone.

Methyl Alcohol It is used as a solvent in the manufacture of lacquers, varnishes, shellac and cleaning and polishing materials. In industry, exposure occurs mainly through inhalation of the vapour, but also via absorption through the skin. Severe exposure leads to dizziness, unconsciousness, cardiac depression and eventually death.   In mild to moderate exposure, blurring of vision, photophobia and conjunctivitis, followed by blindness may occur. The finding of methyl alcohol in the blood, or of formic acid in the urine in amounts exceeding 150 mg/day indicate absorption of methyl alcohol.

3.4.   GASES

Industrial gases may be divided into two groups: those irritating to the upper respiratory tract (e.g., ammonia, and sulphur dioxide), and those which are not irritating (e.g., carbon monoxide, and arsine).

Sulphur Dioxide This gas occurs widely in industry. Concentrations of 3 to 5 ppm produce a detectable odour. Higher concentrations (20 ppm) produce immediate irritation of the eyes and coughing. Concentrations above this level cannot be tolerated, and continued exposure may result in edema of the larynx and lungs, and bronchopneumonia. Repeated exposure to the gas results in nasopharyngitis, bronchitis, shortness of breath on exertion, increased fatigue and alteration of the sense of taste and smell. Brief exposures, lasting up to 1/2 hour, to concentrations up to 100 ppm do not produce disability, but concentrations of 400 to 500 ppm are dangerous, even for short exposures.

Carbon Monoxide Carbon monoxide is produced by the incomplete combustion of carbon-containing materials and is nearly always present in the gases given off from burning substances. Poisoning is most common from automobile exhaust gas, illuminating gas, and from poorly designed or unvented gas burners in stoves or heaters.

Carbon monoxide combines with hemoglobin in blood to form carboxyhemoglobin. With concentrations up to 10% of carboxyhemoglobin in the blood, there rarely are any symptoms. Concentrations of 20% to 30% cause shortness of breath on moderate exertion and slight headache. Concentrations from 30% to 50% cause severe headache, mental confusion and dizziness, impairment of vision and hearing, and collapse and fainting on exertion. With concentrations of 50% to 60%, unconsciousness results, and death may follow if exposure is long. Concentrations of 80% result in almost immediate death. There is usually no cyanosis; since carboxyhemoglobin is a bright red compound, the lips may take on a "healthy" red appearance. Acute cases of poisoning, resulting from brief exposures to high concentrations, seldom result in any permanent disability if recovery takes place. The possibility of chronic effects as the result of repeated exposure to lower concentrations is controversial.

Hydrogen Sulphide (Sour Gas) This is a colourless gas, having an offensive, rotten-egg odour. However, the gas rapidly paralyzes the olfactory nerve endings, so that heavy exposure may occur without the patient being aware of it. It is not used in industry. It is a hazard in sewers, mines, wells and tunnels. Hydrogen sulfide results in asphyxiation due to paralysis of the respiratory centre. High concentrations may cause rhinitis, bronchitis and occasionally pulmonary edema. Exposure to very high concentrations causes immediate death. Chronic poisoning results in headache, inflammation of the conjunctivae and eyelids, digestive disturbances, loss of weight and general debility.

Silo Filler's Disease Silo filler's disease is due to poisoning by oxides of nitrogen. A silo is an airtight structure in which green crops such as corn and clover are pressed and kept for fodder. The decomposition of organic material produces oxides of nitrogen which can cause pulmonary edema; this may clear or result in the development of a condition known as bronchiolitis fibrosa cystica. There is lung hemorrhage, edema, hypertrophy of alveolar epithelium and the formation of hyaline membranes. X-rays show a diffuse fine nodular infiltrate in the lungs, concentrated in the suprahilar area.

3.5. OCCUPATIONAL DERMATITIS

This section will deal with skin diseases in a general manner. The skin forms a major component of the interface between the work environment and the worker unless the worker is completely protected by barrier clothing. Skin diseases constitute a major portion of compensated occupational disease. Occupational skin disease may be categorized into contact dermatitis, occupational acne, pigmentation disorders, neoplastic disorders and miscellaneous disorders.

Contact dermatitis may be irritant or allergic. Irritant contact dermatitis is a result of direct injury to the skin as with acids, alkalis, metal compounds, detergents and solvents. Immunology does not play a role in the development of irritant contact dermatitis. On the other hand, an allergic contact dermatitis is the result of an immunologic reaction to a chemical agent. The presence of allergic contact dermatitis is usually confirmed by patch testing.

Occupational acne is the result of exposure to various agents which causes a chronic inflammatory process in the pilosebaceous follicles. Agents implicated in the development of occupational acne include oil, fats and tars. Chloracne is the pathognomonic marker of exposure to halogenated aromatic hydrocarbons, including PCBs, dioxins, and organochlorine pesticides. Pigmentation disorders may be staining, hyperpigmentation or hypopigmentation. Examples of exposures that result in staining include aniline dyes, picric acid, nitric acid, coal tar, and silver. Exposure to phytotoxins, ionizing radiation, or ultraviolet light may result in hyperpigmentation. Phenols and hydroquinones, on the other hand, may result in hypopigmentation. Radiation, and ultraviolet light, arsenic and polyaromatic hydrocarbons are some of the agents associated with the development of skin cancer.

Finally, exposure to different extremes of temperature may result in miscellaneous skin disorders, for example, chilblains, immersion foot, and frostbite as a result of exposure to cold, and sunburn and, toasted skin syndrome as a result of exposure to heat.

4.   SUMMARY

Occupational health may be defined as the maintenance and promotion of health in the working environment. The annual incidence of occupational injuries and illnesses in the Canadian workforce is about 12%. Injuries account for 97% of all compensated cases by WCB and the remainder is occupational diseases. In 1987 alone, $1.65 billion were paid out by WCB in Ontario. The most common kind of occupational injury/illness from WCB data is back injuries.

Primary prevention in occupational health first involves substitution, and if this is not possible, then segregation is attempted, including ventilation. Personal hygiene and protective equipment are used if the measures outlined above are not feasible. Secondary prevention in occupational health involves the use of pre-placement and periodic examinations. Another aspect of secondary prevention in the workplace is the issue of employee screening for substance abuse. Tertiary prevention involves treatment, rehabilitation and re-training under the auspices of Workers' Compensation. Health Promotion in the workplace has emerged as an effective approach enabling access to the substantial numbers of persons in the workplace not only for the prevention of work-associated health problems, but for the introduction of wellness programs incorporating attention to lifestyle and other health determinants.

The agents causing occupational disease may be divided into three broad groups: biological, physical, and chemical. In order to establish causality between the workplace and the health problem the following conditions must be met: adequate concentration and duration of exposure, absorption into the body, appropriate temporal sequence, and consistency of ill health effects with the putative exposure.

Biological agents include bacteria, viruses, fungi, protozoa and rickettsia. Disease caused by these organisms may be regarded as occupational in origin when the nature of the work involves exposure to the organism. Since quite a few diseases are spread via blood (e.g., AIDS, Hep B), it is beginning to be recognized as a toxic substance. The occurrence of occupationally acquired blood-borne infection depends on the frequency and types of hazardous exposures, the risk associated with each type of discrete exposure and the prevalence of infection in the patient population.

Physical agents have the potential of creating ill health for the worker. The effects produced by excessive noise may include fatigue, impaired hearing, increased blood pressure, decreased efficiency and emotional disturbances. Industrial noise is a combination of sounds of different frequencies. Very high temperatures may bring about heat cramps, heat exhaustion or heat stroke. Exposure of hands, feet, ears, and nose to the cold can cause chilblains or precipitate attacks of Raynaud's disease. Frostbite is a more severe and largely irreversible form of local cell injury. The most common effect resulting from repeated vibration is a disturbance of the blood vessels of the fingers. Muscular stiffness, soreness, blisters and "occupational cramps" are clinical signs of the adverse effects of repeated motion on certain body parts. Decompression sickness and barotrauma are examples of the body's reaction to abnormalities of air pressure. There are two types of radiation: ionizing and non-ionizing. The ultimate effect of ionization is damage to, or death of, the cells. The type and severity of the injury depends on the extent of the tissue exposed and on the particular tissue that absorbs the radiation. Non-ionizing radiation comprises UV, infrared and ultrahigh frequency radiation. Electrical currents travelling through the body damage tissues through which it passes. Hence, excessive noise, temperature and humidity, repeated motion and vibration, abnormalities of air pressure, radiation, and electricity all pose threats to human health.

Chemical agents consist of: organic dusts, mineral dusts and metallic dusts and fumes. Organic dusts are derived from substances of animal or plant origin (e.g., from wood, flour, bone). These dusts are mainly irritants to the upper respiratory passages and to the conjunctivae and skin, causing bronchitis, conjunctivitis and dermatitis. Mineral dusts include silica, asbestos, and coal. Prolonged inhalation of "free" silica leads to silicosis. The most serious feature of silicosis is that it predisposes one to tuberculosis infection. In asbestosis, the essential lesion is a diffuse fibrosis, which probably begins around the terminal bronchioles. Metallic dusts and fumes incorporate lead, mercury, cadmium and nickel. Lead is perhaps the most important metallic dust because it is the most used and because of the serious disability which may result from poisoning. There are two types of poisoning: acute and chronic. Acute lead poisoning results from a single exposure to a large dose, usually occurring as a result of accidental ingestion of lead salts. Chronic lead poisoning occurs from the inhalation or ingestion of small amounts of lead dust, fumes or vapours over a relatively long period of time.

Volatile solvents and organic materials also affect the health of the worker. The three important classes of solvents are: aromatic hydrocarbons, chlorinated hydrocarbons, and alcohol, esters and ketones. Among the aromatic hydrocarbons, benzol is the most dangerous solvent used commercially. Poisoning can be both acute and chronic. The toxicity of chlorinated hydrocarbons varies from very high to very low, attacking the liver and kidney. Carbon tetrachloride is the most toxic of the group. Methyl alcohol may cause dizziness, unconsciousness, cardiac depression and eventually death. Gases used in industry are either irritating to the upper respiratory tract (e.g., ammonia, chlorine) or are not irritating (e.g., carbon monoxide, hydrocyanic acid).

Skin diseases comprise a major portion of compensated occupational disease. Occupational skin disease may be categorized into contact dermatitis, occupational acne, pigmentation disorders, and neoplastic disorders.

5.   REFERENCES

1. *Occupational Injuries and their Cost in Canada 1987-1989.* Statistics and Analysis Unit. Legislation Development and Liason. Occupational Safety and Health Branch. Ministry of Labour, Canada, 1991.

2. Deroche F. Promoting Health in the Workplace. *Ontario Prevention Clearinghouse News* 3(4):1-2, 1992.

3. Erfurt J, Foote A, Mex A, Heirich M and Gregg W. Improving Participation in Worksite Wellness Programs: Comparing Health Education Classes, a Menu Approach, and Follow-Up Counselling. *Am J Health Promot* 4(4):270-278, 1990.

4. CMA Policy Summary. Drug Testing in the Workplace. *Can Med Assoc J* 146(12):223A-B, 1992.

5. Louie M, Low DE, Feinman SV, McLaughin B and Simor AE. Prevalence of bloodborne infective agents among people admitted to a Canadian Hospital. *Can Med Assoc J* 146(8):1331-1334, 1992.

6. Liss G. *Estimates of the Burden of Illness due to Occupational Exposure to Bloodborne Infections.* Prepared for the Task Force on Universal Precautions. Health Studies Service. Ministry of Labour, Canada, 1990.

7. Wallace E. Update - National Surveillance of Occupational Exposure to the Human Immunodeficiency Virus (HIV) April 15,1992. Ministry of Health, Ontario. *Public Health and Epidemiology Reports Ont* 3(13):210, 1992.

8. Update: Universal Precautions for the Prevention of Human Immunodeficiency Virus, Hepatitis B Virus, and other Blood-Borne Pathogens in Health Care Settings. *Can Dis Wkly Rep* 14(27):117-123, 1988.

9. *National Surveillance of Occupational Exposure to the Human Immunodeficiency Virus.* Federal Centre for AIDS, Ottawa, 1992.

10. McQueen M. Conflicting rights of patients and health care workers exposed to blood-borne infection. *Can Med Assoc J* 147(3):299-302, 1992.

11. Update: Transmission of HIV Infection During Invasive Dental Procedures. *Can Med Assoc J* 146(4):519-521, 1992.

12. Health and Welfare Canada *Canadian Immunization Guide,* 3rd ed. Ministry of Supply and Services, Canada, Ottawa, 1989, reprinted 1990.

13. Ontario Hospital Association and Ontario Medical Association Communicable Disease Surveillance Protocols. Ministry of Health Ontario. *Public Health and Epidimiology Reports* 3(12):187, 1992.

14. Video Display Terminals (Policy Statement). *Can Med Assoc J* 135(6):688A, 1986.

CHAPTER ELEVEN
Periodic
Health Examinations

Since the release of Lalonde's document on "A New Perspective on Health of Canadians" in 1974, an increased emphasis has been placed on disease prevention and health promotion through various strategies such as health education, taxation, regulations and modification of lifestyles. Physicians have also focused their activities on early detection of diseases and/or early interventions. In this chapter, major clinical activities, specifically the periodic health examination, are discussed.

The annual check up was an attempt to integrate preventive activities into clinical practice. The presumed reasons for annual examinations included prevention of specific diseases by risk factor identification and intervention, early identification and treatment of disease, establishment of a baseline examination and development of the patient-doctor relationship. However, their effectiveness was never fully established. The practice of annual examinations could be criticized on many grounds. These include the ritualistic nature, the content and frequency, the low yield, irrelevance to the needs of different age groups and the inclusion of tests and procedures with scanty evidence of effectiveness or efficacy as case-finding manoeuvres. It was in this context that the Canadian Task Force on the Periodic Health Examination was established by the Conference of Deputy Ministers of Health in 1976.

1.   CANADIAN TASK FORCE ON PERIODIC HEALTH EXAMINATION

Terms of Reference
The terms of reference within which the Task Force worked were relatively straightforward.

- To identify the main killing or disabling conditions, unhealthy states and unhealthy behaviours affecting Canadians and to determine which could possibly be prevented according to present knowledge.

- To consider evidence for the benefit of early detection or prevention of killing or disabling conditions, unhealthy states and unhealthy behaviours in the non-complaining individual. (If early detection or prevention were judged to be beneficial, the particular condition would be termed preventable.)
- To define groups in the population at high risk for specific preventable conditions, states and behaviours.
- To design health protection "packages" shown to be effective—or, in special circumstances, desirable on other grounds—that should become part of periodic health examinations at defined ages and for defined population groups.
- To make recommendations on the procedures, content, frequency and appropriate providers of periodic health examinations and preventive interventions at defined ages and for defined population groups.
- To propose specific measures for evaluation of the effectiveness and efficiency of the recommended plan for periodic health examinations that would permit recurring reassessment and improvement.

The Task Force concluded that it would be better to identify preventable conditions of importance to each age group, and to assess the detection manoeuvres and preventive interventions related to each condition. The Task Force's main recommendation is therefore that the routine annual check up be abandoned in favour of a selective approach that is determined by a person's age and sex. The Task Force recommends a specific strategy comprising a lifetime health-care plan based on a set of age- and sex-related health protection packages. This was quite an innovative approach, and other countries have adopted similar approaches. For example, the recent publication by the US Preventive Services Task Force, *Guide to Clinical Preventive Services*, outlines an assessment of the effectiveness of 169 interventions in clinical practice.[1] The other impressive aspect of the Task Force was its recognition that the new scientific information that is constantly emerging could result in the Task Force altering its early recommendations or including new conditions in the health protection packages.

The Task Force received many submissions and had several discussions with different groups. Based on all of these, the Task Force made recommendations in 1979,[2] 1984,[3] 1986,[4] 1988,[5] 1989,[6,7] 1990,[8-11] 1991,[12-17] and 1992.[18-20] As the new information becomes available, the Task Force continually updates its earlier recommendations and adds new ones. These recommendations are published in the Canadian Medical Association Journal, and readers are advised to refer to this publication. A recent publication provides the background papers on which these recommendations by US and Canadian Task Force are based.[21]

2.   DEFINITIONS

The Task Force used certain key words and terms which are defined below.

Beneficial Manoeuvre

An intervention or manoeuvre is considered beneficial when more good than harm accrues to the individual or to the groups of individuals to whom it is applied.

Early Detection

Early detection of a condition or a disorder refers to its identification in an individual before symptoms and signs make the condition apparent to the affected individual, the immediate family or non-professional observer. Early detection is also referred to as presymptomatic detection.

Effectiveness

Effectiveness is the attribute of an intervention or a manoeuvre that results in more good than harm to those to whom it is offered. Effectiveness is determined by both the efficacy of the intervention and the actual compliance. The task force assesses effectiveness of preventive interventions.

Efficacy

Efficacy is the attribute of an intervention or clinical procedure that results in more good than harm to those who accept and comply with the intervention and subsequent treatment.

Efficiency

Efficiency is the attribute of effective intervention or manoeuvre under circumstances when it is made available to those who can benefit from it with optimal use of the resources required.

Groups at High Risk for Preventable Conditions, States and Behaviour

These are groups in which the frequency of such entities is demonstrably higher than in the general Canadian population. For such high-risk groups it may be justified to institute the detection manoeuvres that are not judged necessary or feasible for the general population.

Health Protection Packages

These are sets of procedures that are particularly applicable to the periodic health examination at certain ages and in certain at-risk groups.

Periodic Health Examination

This is a group of tasks designed either to determine the risk of subsequent disease or to identify disease in its early, symptomless stage. Simple interventions, such as injections for immunization, application of laboratory tests for early detection, administration of screening instruments and counselling, are covered by this definition.   The periodic health examination is applied to the patient who is asymptomatic for the preventable condition.

Preventable Condition, State, or Behaviour

This is a condition that has been demonstrated by well-designed clinical investigations to be either completely preventable or detectable at a stage when its progress or the impact of its consequences can be favourably affected by treatment.

Preventive Intervention

This is any intervention that reduces the likelihood of a disease or disorder affecting a person (primary prevention), that interrupts or slows the progress of a disease or the irreversible damage from a disease through early detection and treatment (secondary prevention), or that slows the progress of the disease and reduces resultant disability through treatment of established disease (tertiary condition).

The Task Force used criteria to assess potentially preventable conditions and classify recommendations for inclusion or exclusion of the conditions.   These criteria were the current burden of suffering (impact on the individual and on society), the manoeuvre (risks and benefits; sensitivity, specificity and predictive values; and the safety, simplicity, cost and acceptability) and the effectiveness of the intervention.

Effectiveness of Intervention

The effectiveness of intervention was graded according to the quality of evidence obtained, as follows:

I-1:   Evidence obtained from at least one properly randomized controlled trial.

II-1: Evidence obtained from well-designed controlled trials without randomization.

II-2: Evidence obtained from well-designed cohort or case-control analytic studies, preferably from more than one centre or research group.

II-3: Evidence obtained from comparisons between times or places with or without the interventions. Dramatic results from uncontrolled experiments (such as the results of the introduction of penicillin in the 1940s) could also be regarded as this type of evidence.

III: Opinions of respected authorities, based on clinical experience, descriptive studies or reports of expert committees.

Classification of Recommendations

On the basis of these considerations the Task Force made a clear recommendation for each condition as to whether it should be specifically included in a periodic health examination. Recommendations were classified as follows:

A: There is good evidence to support the recommendation that the condition be specifically considered in a periodic health examination.

B: There is fair evidence to support the recommendation that the condition be specifically considered in a periodic health examination.

C: There is poor evidence regarding the inclusion of the condition in a periodic health examination, but recommendations may be made on other grounds.

D: There is fair evidence to support the recommendation that the condition be excluded from consideration in a periodic health examination.

E: There is good evidence to support the recommendation that the condition be excluded from consideration in a periodic health examination.

Because the effectiveness of treatment or of the preventive measure for a condition was of such importance to the Task Force, the final recommendation for each condition relied heavily on its assessment of the evidence for effectiveness of treatment. Thus a class A recommendation was rarely made in the absence of grade I evidence regarding effectiveness of treatment or prevention. However, an exception to this rule occurred when a clinical intervention was shown, in grade II terms, to save the lives of victims of a previously universally fatal condition. For example, if malignant hypertension is left untreated, all affected patients will die; if treated, most will survive. Thus grade II evidence is sufficient for a class A recommendation. Such examples are rare, however, and grade I evidence was required for the highest recommendation for most conditions.

3.   HEALTH PROTECTION PACKAGES

Appendix C displays 18 health protection packages which have been updated to 1993, for various age groups, and for both sexes. Each package has been given a code. In some instances, the letter representing the recommendation made by the task force is followed by the letter R, which indicates that the recommendation was made only for a designated high-risk group. In some packages, in addition to the conditions that apply to the general population, conditions are listed that should be sought only in defined high-risk situations, which are identified by the letter R within the code.

Other preventive health practices such as fitness to drive vehicles or airplanes[22,23] and the pre-employment examination of workers (see chapter nine) are also important for physicians.

4.   COMPLIANCE

A number of studies of compliance with the Canadian Task Force on the Periodic Health Examination has been undertaken.[24,25] A recent study concluded that most (90%) primary care physicians complied with the recommendations of the task force for; breast examination, mammography, cervical smears and initial counselling against smoking.[26] Most of the physicians stated that they perform preventive manoeuvres in the context of an annual general physical examination rather than integrating them into routine patient care.

5.   SUMMARY

Since 1974, increased emphasis has been placed on disease prevention and health promotion through various strategies.   These strategies include health education, modification of lifestyle and early detection and intervention by physicians.

This chapter discussed the periodic health examination and the Canadian Task Force on the Periodic Health Examination. The Task Force was established to assess the effectiveness of the annual check up, which has been criticized on several grounds. Some of the terms of reference within which the Task Force worked included to design effective health protection packages, define groups in the population at high risk for specific preventable conditions, and consider the benefits of early detection. The Task Force concluded that it would be more efficient to identify preventable conditions of importance to each age group and the appropriate intervention. Hence, the Task Force recommended that routine annual check ups be abandoned in favour of a selective approach that is determined by a person's age and sex. The Task Force also realized that since new scientific information is constantly emerging, which may alter its earlier recommendations, new conditions to the health protection packages may have to be added.

This chapter also examined some of the definitions used by the Task Force. For example, the terms early detection, efficacy, efficiency, peridoic health examination, preventitive intervention were all defined.

Today, there is an increasing emphasis on disease prevention and health promotion in medical practices. The periodic health examination outlines the major initiatives taken by the Canadian Task Force on this subject.

6. REFERENCES

1. Guide to Clinical Preventive Services: An Assessment of the Effectiveness of 169 Interventions. Report of the U.S. Preventive Services Task Force. Baltimore: Williams and Wilkins, 1989.

2. The Canadian Task Force on Periodic Health Examination: The Periodic Health Examination. *Can Med Assoc J* 121(9):1193-1254, 1979.

3. Idem: The Periodic Health Examination: 2, 1984 Update, *Can Med Assoc J* 130(10):1278-1285, 1984.

4. Idem: The Periodic Health Examination: 2, 1985 Update, *Can Med Assoc J* 134(7):724-729, 1986.

5. Idem: The Periodic Health Examination: 2, 1987 Update, *Can Med Assoc J* 138(7):618-626, 1988.

6. Idem: The Periodic Health Examination: 1989 Update, *Can Med Assoc J* 141(3):205-207; 209-216, 1989.

7. Idem: The Periodic Health Examination: 1989 Update: 3. Preschool Examination for Developmental, Visual and Hearing Problems. *Can Med Assoc J* 141(11):1136-1140, 1989.

8. Idem: The Periodic Health Examination: 1990 Update: 1. Early Detection of Hyperthyroidism and Hypothyroidism in Adults and Screening of Newborns for Congenital Hypothyroidism. *Can Med Assoc J* 142(9):955-96, 1990.

9. Idem: The Periodic Health Examination: 1990 Update: 2. Early Identification of Depression and Prevention of Suicide. *Can Med Assoc J* 142(11):1233-1238, 1990.

10. Idem: The Periodic Health Examination: 1990 Update: 3. Investigations to Prevent Lung Cancer other than Smoking Cessation. *Can Med Assoc J* 143(4):269-272, 1990.

11. Idem: The Periodic Health Examination: 1990 Update: 4. Well-Baby Care in the First 2 Years of Life. *Can Med Assoc J* 143(9):867-872, 1990.

12. Idem: The Periodic Health Examination: 1991 Update: 1. Screening for Cognitive Impairment in the Elderly. *Can Med Assoc J* 144(4):425-430, 1991.

13. Idem: The Periodic Health Examination: 1991 Update: 2. Administration of Pneumococcal Vaccine. *Can Med Assoc J* 144(6):665-671, 1991.

14. Idem: The Periodic Health Examination: 1991 Update: 3. Secondary Prevention of Prostate Cancer. *Can Med Assoc J* 145(5):413-428, 1991.

15. Idem: The Periodic Health Examination: 1991 Update: 4. Screening for Cystic Fibrosis. *Can Med Assoc J* 145(6):629-635, 1991.

16. Idem: The Periodic Health Examination: 1991 Update: 5. Screening for Abdominal Aneurysm. *Can Med Assoc J* 145(7):783-789, 1991.

17. Idem: The Periodic Health Examination: 1991 Update: 6. Acetylsalicylic Acid and the Primary Prevention of Cardiovascular Disease. *Can Med Assoc J* 145(9):1091-1095, 1991.

18. Idem: The Periodic Health Examination: 1992 Update: 1. Screening for Gestational Diabetes Mellitus. *Can Med Assoc J* 147(4):435-443, 1992.

19. Idem: The Periodic Health Examination: 1992 Update: 2. Routine Prenatal Ultrasound Screening. *Can Med Assoc J* 147(5):627-633, 1992.
20. Idem: The Periodic Health Examination: 1992 Update: 3. HIV Antibody Screening. *Can Med Assoc J* 147(6):867-876, 1992.
21. Lawrence RS and Goldbloom RB, eds. Preventing Disease: Beyond the Rhetoric. New York: Springer-Verlag, 1990.
22. CMA Council on Health Care's Subcommittee on Emergency Medical Services: Physicians' Guide to Driver Examination, 5th ed. The Canadian Medical Association, Ottawa, 1991.
23. Special subcommittee of Canadian Medical Association. *Fit for Flying? A Guide for Mandatory Medical Reporting.* The Canadian Medical Association, Ottawa, 1986.
24. Battista RN, Palmer CS, Marchand BM et al. Patterns of Preventive Practice in New Brunswick. *Can Med Assoc J* 132:1013-1015, 1985.
25. Battista RN. Adult Cancer Prevention in Primary Care: Patterns of Practice in Quebec. *Am J Public Health* 73:1036-1039, 1983.
26. Smith HE and Herbert CP. Preventive Practice Among Primary Care Physicians in British Columbia: Relation to Recommendations of the Canadian Task Force on the Periodic Health Examination. *Can Med Assoc J* 149(12):1795-1809, 1993.

Part 3

Canada's Health-Care System

CHAPTER TWELVE
Evolution of
National Health Insurance

The most important development in health-care delivery in Canada has been the evolution from a free enterprise system of medicine to a publicly financed health-care system. To understand this, it is essential that we examine the history of the health-care system in Canada.[1-3]

1. HEALTH CARE PRIOR TO 1950

1.1. HEALTH AND THE BRITISH NORTH AMERICA ACT

In 1867, Canada's confederation was proclaimed in the British North America (BNA) Act (now known as the Constitution Act, 1982), our most fundamental constitutional document. At that time, the government's role in the health-care system was minimal. Most of the Canadian population had to rely on its own resources for medical care, and hospital services were provided only by charitable trusts and religious organizations. Naturally, those who drafted the BNA Act and the fathers of Confederation could not predict the volume of industrial and technological growth, and the health-care needs for the coming years. The only references to health matters in the BNA Act are found in Section 91 which enumerates the power of the federal government and Section 92 which enumerates provincial powers:

Section 91 It shall be lawful for the Queen, by and with the Advice and Consent of the Senate and the House of Commons, to make laws for the Peace, Order, and good Government of Canada, in relation to all Matters not coming within the Classes of Subjects by this act assigned exclusively to the Legislature of the Provinces; and for greater certainty, but not so as to restrict the Generality of the foregoing Terms of this Section, it is hereby declared that (notwithstanding anything in this Act) the exclusive legislative Authority of the Parliament of Canada extends to all Matters coming within the Classes of Subjects next hereinafter enumerated; that is to say,

Sub. Sec. 6 The census and statistics.
Sub. Sec. 11 Quarantine and the establishment and maintenance of Marine Hospitals.

Section 92 In each Province the Legislature may exclusively make laws in relation to Matters coming within the Classes of Subjects next hereinafter enumerated; that is to say,

> ***Sub. Sec. 7*** The establishment, maintenance and management of Hospitals, Asylums, Charities and Eleemosynary Institutions in and for the Province, other than Marine Hospitals.

The above sections are quoted in detail because of the frequency of current discussions on the relative responsibilities of the federal and provincial governments in matters concerning the health of our people. Thus, health is primarily a provincial responsibility, but the federal government also has specific responsibilities in health. Areas of federal responsibilities are described in the next chapter. One of the early Indian Treaties had mentioned the provision of a "medicine chest" as a responsibility of the federal government.[4] Over the years, courts have interpreted the "medicine chest" clause as a federal responsibility to provide health-care to Aboriginal Peoples.

1.2. CONFEDERATION TO 1950

The origin of public medical care and hospital insurance can be traced to Saskatchewan. In 1914, the rural municipality of Sarnia, Saskatchewan, experimented with a form of medical care insurance by offering a physician a retainer to practise in the area. The experiment was so successful that, two years later, the provincial government passed the Rural Municipality Act. It permitted any rural municipality in Saskatchewan to levy property taxes to retain doctors providing general practitioner and public health services in the area. The effect of this legislation was to encourage doctors to settle in Saskatchewan, then a province for only 11 years and still emerging from the frontier stage of development. These publicly supported plans continued to operate for some years, numbering about 100 by 1946. Similar but less extensive plans were adopted by Manitoba in 1921 and Alberta in 1926.

In 1916, Saskatchewan took one of the first steps to break down the tradition of municipal responsibility for hospital care by passing the Union Hospital Act, permitting municipalities to combine into hospital districts for building and maintaining hospitals. In the following year, legislation gave municipalities the right to collect taxes to finance hospital care for all or most of their residents. By 1946, many local plans were operating in the province.

The first attempt to develop a national health insurance program was in 1935, when the federal government passed the Employment and Social Insurance Act to collect taxes in order to provide certain social security benefits, including health benefits. However, the provinces challenged this Act, because it encroached on their jurisdiction. Their position was later upheld by the Supreme Court of Canada. After World War II, the world sought 'reconstruction'. This goal brought about certain promising changes which bettered the lives of people in some countries, particularly in the western world. The provision of social services—especially in the area of health, education, and welfare—was influenced by this concept.

At the same time, it was extremely difficult for the provincial governments and major Canadian hospitals to find adequate financial resources to provide health services. Health costs were rising. There were technological advances and the union movement was influencing the hospital work force. The result was a number of legislative acts. Between 1942 and 1944, the Select Committee on Social Security of the House of Commons received reports on Social Security for Canada, the Report of the Advisory Committee on Health Insurance and a draft bill for comprehensive national health insurance. After considering these reports, the Select Committee produced a specific proposal for a broad program of social security, including health insurance on a cost-share and phased-introduction basis. It was presented to the provincial governments in 1945 at the Dominion-Provincial Conference on (Post War) Reconstruction. This proposal was rejected because the provinces and federal government could not reach an agreement on the financial arrangements.

Saskatchewan decided to proceed on its own, and in 1947 it introduced a hospitalization plan for all residents, financed by a combination of premiums and general taxes. This example was followed by other provinces. British Columbia introduced its universal hospital insurance program in 1949, and Alberta a limited plan in 1950. Newfoundland and Labrador joined Confederation in 1949 with their own health insurance plan.

A step towards the development of a national insurance program was the enactment of the National Health Grants of 1948. This Act marked the entry of the federal government into the health field. Under it, grants-in-aid were provided to the provinces for a variety of public health services: hospital construction, laboratory services and professional training for public health. These grants were viewed as "fundamental prerequisites of a nation-wide system of health insurance." Later, other grants were added. All these grants, except for Professional Training Grants and Public Health Research Grants, were gradually abolished after the introduction of the national health insurance program.

2.   THE HEALTH-CARE SYSTEM BETWEEN 1950 AND 1977

Since provinces had jurisdiction over health, the role of federal government was restricted to assistance in paying the bills. However, the federal government could steer the health-care system by imposing conditions whenever it shared the cost of programs. There have been a number of federal acts passed since 1950; one of the first was the Hospital Insurance and Diagnostic Services Act of 1957.

2.1.   THE HOSPITAL INSURANCE AND DIAGNOSTIC SERVICES ACT OF 1957

This Act was passed by Parliament in 1957 and enacted in 1958. Five provinces immediately joined. By 1961, it was operating in all provinces and territories, covering 99% of the population of Canada. The main purpose of this Act was to establish and maintain services and facilities leading to better health and health care for the population as a whole, by providing, as its name implies, hospital care and diagnostic services. It was a service-oriented approach emphasizing quality of care, effective utilization of beds and availability of resources. Although all residents of Canada were eligible for hospital insurance coverage, the federal law excluded services for persons eligible for similar benefits under other federal or provincial legislation. For example, services provided to workers under Workers' Compensation legislation or to veterans under the Pensions Act were excluded from cost-sharing under the Hospital Insurance and Diagnostic Services Act.

A basic principle that influenced the development of hospital insurance legislation was the belief that existing traditions should be maintained as far as possible. Therefore, the pattern of hospital care and ownership that existed before 1957 was retained, and provincial autonomy in health care was not infringed. As a result, even today, 90% of Canadian hospitals (with 94% of the beds) are still owned and governed by voluntary bodies. The policy of provincial autonomy allowed each province to decide upon its own administrative methods, while ensuring a basic uniformity of coverage throughout the country.

Range of Insured Services
The Act stipulated that all of the following must be provided as insured in-patient services:

- accommodation and meals at the standard or public ward level;
- necessary nursing service;
- laboratory, radiology, and other diagnostic procedures;
- drugs, biologicals, and related preparations;
- use of operating room, case room, and anesthetic facilities, including necessary equipment and supplies;
- routine surgical supplies;
- use of radiotherapy facilities, where available;
- use of physiotherapy facilities, where available;
- such other services as are specified in the agreement.

At the option of each province, any of the above could also be provided as insured out-patient services. These varied from province to province, but a fairly comprehensive range is now provided by hospitals in all provinces. Provinces may include additional benefits in their plans without affecting the federal-provincial agreements. Hospital insurance is portable anywhere in the world during periods of temporary absence, although subject to provincially regulated limits. In many cases, elective hospitalization outside the province may require prior approval. This approval may be withheld in some provinces if equivalent services are available within the province.

Methods of Financing
The federal contribution paid to the provinces for insured in-patient and out-patient services amounted to approximately 50% of the costs of these services. Shareable costs under the agreements with the provinces excluded most hospital construction costs but could include the cost of movable equipment and most fixed equipment specifically required by hospitals. Each province was free to determine how its share of the costs would be financed. Most provinces financed their share of costs out of general revenue, but some provinces also imposed premiums and/or certain authorized charges (user fees).

2.2.   THE MEDICAL CARE ACT OF 1966

2.2.1. Events Leading to the Medical Care Act of 1966
Hospital insurance paved the way for medical care insurance. Saskatchewan once again was the first province to experiment with a compulsory, government sponsored medical care insurance program. The program's principles were: prepayment, universal coverage, high quality of service, and acceptability to both providers and receivers of services. The legislation received royal assent in November 1961, and in spite of a strike by physicians, the program was implemented on July 1, 1962. British Columbia, Alberta and Ontario adopted their own medical coverage programs between 1963 and 1966.

In 1965, the federal government's Royal Commission on Health Services (appointed in 1961, its chairman, the Honourable Emmett M. Hall, Justice of the Supreme Court of Canada) completed the most comprehensive assessment of health services undertaken to that date. It found that nearly 60% of Canadians had some form of insurance against the costs of medical care, but approximately 30% of this coverage was inadequate. The Commission recommended strong federal government leadership and financial support for medical care. However, it also recommended that the operating controls of the program be decentralized under the provincial governments. General standards and guidelines were suggested as part of the federal government's conditions, but the Commission felt that each province should be permitted wide latitude in its program. Closely related were recommendations for greatly expanded support for teaching, research, and other facilities for training health personnel. Finally, in the summer of 1965 a new federal proposal, based on the recommendations of the Hall Commission, was introduced at a federal-provincial conference.

2.2.2. Enactment of the Medical Care Act of 1966

After a series of discussions between the federal and provincial governments, the Medical Care Act of 1966 was enacted and it was implemented in 1968. By 1971, all the provinces were participating in its programs. Under the Medical Care Act, the federal government contributed to each province half of the average per capita medical care costs incurred by all provinces, multiplied by the number of insured persons in that province. As the average cost in poorer provinces was lower than in richer provinces, these cost-sharing arrangements gave larger payments to the poorer provinces. Hence, the federal contribution as a proportion of the total cost for medical care varied among provinces. In 1975-76 the proportion ranged from 40.8% in British Columbia and 49.2% in Ontario, to 67.7% in Prince Edward Island and 75.6% in Newfoundland. Under the Act, all physicians' services and some additional services provided by dentists and chiropractors were covered. To be eligible for federal contributions, the provincial medical services plan was required to meet criteria called the "Four Points": comprehensive, universal, portable and publicly administered.

Comprehensive Coverage

At a minimum, the plan was to provide comprehensive coverage for all medically required services rendered by medical practitioners, without dollar limit or exclusions, provided there was medical need, unless coverage was available under other legislation. The plan was to be administered in such a way that nothing financially impeded or precluded an insured person from receiving necessary medical care. Certain surgical-dental procedures by dental surgeons (when rendered in hospital) were included from the beginning and provision was made to add other professional services such as benefits, when the federal government considered this desirable. Each province could provide additional insured benefits.

Universality

The plan was to be uniformly available to all eligible residents (no fewer than 95 per cent of the population). Premium discrimination according to previous health, race, age, or non-membership in a group was not permitted, but partial or complete premium subsidization for low income groups or the elderly was allowed, if all qualifying residents were treated equally. Each province determined whether its residents should be insured on a voluntary or compulsory basis. Utilization charges at the time of service were not precluded by the federal legislation if they did not impede, either by their amount, or by the manner of their application, reasonable access to necessary medical care, particularly for low income groups.

Portability

Benefits were to be portable when the insured was temporarily absent from the province, anywhere in the world and also when the insured was changing jobs, retiring or moving place of residence from one province to another, provided any required premiums were paid.   When an insured resident moved to another province, the first province should provide medical care benefits during any waiting period imposed by the medical insurance plan of the second province. No province could impose a waiting period in excess of three months before a new resident was entitled to obtain coverage. Some provinces required that the patient obtain approval before having elective (i.e., non-emergency) care outside the province. In general, provinces limited the amount payable for medical services received out of province to the amount payable for similar services in the patient's province.

Public Administration

The plan was to be non-profit and administered by a public agency accountable to the provincial government for its financial transactions.

The above criteria left each province with substantial flexibility in determining the administrative arrangements for the operation of its medical care insurance plan and in choosing its financing plan (through premiums, sales tax, other provincial revenues, or a combination thereof). Federal contributions to the provinces under this program totaled $1.7 billion in the fiscal year 1975-76.

3.   1977-1984: NEW FINANCING OF HEALTH-CARE PROGRAMS AND THE CANADA HEALTH ACT

In the 1970s, the shared cost health programs became a critical problem for both the federal and provincial governments. The chief bone of contention between the two levels of government was increasing health-care costs. In 1976, total health expenditures in Canada exceeded $13 billion. Because these programs were "open-ended" (i.e., the federal government paid the provinces about half of the cost for insured hospital and medical care cost), they impeded federal governmental program planning in other fields. The provincial governments were also unhappy because, while the most expensive aspects of health care were cost-shared, other important and innovative aspects (e.g., development of community based services instead of general hospital care) were not shared. To alleviate this, a new agreement on financing arrangements was reached at the Conference of First Ministers in December 1976. The legislation was enacted on March 31, 1977, as the Federal-Provincial Fiscal Arrangements and Established Programs Financing Act [EPF], 1977, and included Extended Health-care Services.

3.1.   ESTABLISHED PROGRAMS FINANCING ACT, 1977

Description of Financing Arrangements

Commencing April 1, 1977, federal contributions to the provinces for the established programs of hospital insurance, medical care and post-secondary education, were no longer directly related to provincial costs but the new arrangements included:

- the transfer to the provinces of tax room and associated equalization, and
- cash payments.

In general terms, the total federal contributions for the above three programs are now based on the current escalated value of the 1975-76 federal contributions for these programs. The tax room vacated by the federal government consisted of a reduction in the federal tax schedule of 13.5 personal and 1.0 corporate income tax points. This permitted the provinces to increase their tax rates to collect additional revenue without necessarily increasing the total tax burden on Canadians. An equalization payment was available to raise the value of the tax points in all provinces up to the national average value of tax points. The yield from the new provincial taxes would normally increase faster than the rate of growth of the Gross National Product (GNP). The yearly cash payments to the provinces had approximately the same value as the tax room transferred. The formula for the cash payments is complex, and interested readers may consult the original act.

These financing arrangements initially provided each province with more money than it would potentially have received under the previous cost-sharing formula, but the increase was tied to the GNP and population growth. There was greater equality among the provinces in what they received from the federal government per capita. At the same time, provinces had greater flexibility in the use of their own funds and federal contributions. The arrangements were more stable for both levels of government. Program administration was simplified because federal auditing of provincial records was no longer required. The terms of the program's financing arrangements are indefinite, but a provision in the legislation permits the federal government to terminate the arrangements with three years' notice.

The federal government had attached broad conditions to its cash payments in order to guarantee adequate standards of health care across the country. The conditions were the same as those used for hospital and medical care insurance since their beginning: comprehensiveness, universal coverage, portability of benefits, and non-profit administration by a public agency.

Extended Health-Care Services

Under the EPF Act of 1977, a financial contribution was made by the federal government for Extended Health-Care Services. The payments began on April 1, 1977. The Extended Health-Care Services Program allowed the federal government to make block-funded contributions to the provinces to assist them in the provision of the following services:

- nursing homes (intermediate care);
- adults' residential care;
- converted mental hospitals;
- home care (health aspects);
- ambulatory health care.

Funding for 1988-89 was approximately $48 per capita of provincial population ($1.27 billion), with escalation on the same basis as that of the EPF (i.e., based on the growth of GNP and the population). Since this program was viewed as complementary to basic hospital and medical care insurance, the only condition of payment was that the province furnish to the federal Minister of Health information reasonably required by the federal government for its international obligations, national planning and standards, and information exchanges with the provinces.
The purposes of this program were:

- to provide the provinces with financial assistance in providing lower-cost forms of health care in conjunction with the insured services of the Hospital Insurance and Diagnostic Services Act and the Medical Care Act;
- to encompass most of the spectrum of health and institutional health services within a similar block-funding financial arrangement;
- to provide the provinces with greater flexibility.

3.2. EVENTS LEADING TO CANADA HEALTH ACT

The EPF no longer tied federal payments to particular forms of health services, which reduced the federal steering effect. During the late 1970s, health-care costs increased faster than the GNP, leading the provinces to bear greater costs. As a result, the provinces introduced measures of cost containment such as a reduction in the number of hospital beds and restraints on increasing physicians fees. An increasing number of physicians responded to this by "extra-billing" their patients.[5] These factors led to charges from the public and interest groups that medicare was being "eroded." The federal government established another commission to review the Canadian health-care system. The Honourable Emmett M. Hall, who had reviewed the health-care system in 1964, was appointed as Commissioner.

In 1980, Mr. Justice Hall published the results of this extensive review.[6] This health services review emphasized the issue of accessibility of services. Hall concluded that billing by physicians above the negotiated fee schedule (extra-billing) was threatening to violate the principle of uniform terms and conditions and preclude access to services for some persons. He therefore recommended that this practice be banned and that fair compensation for physicians' services be determined through negotiation between physicians and governments, with binding arbitration if negotiations failed. Those physicians unwilling to accept the plan as payment in full would be required to practice entirely outside the plan, as was already the case in Quebec. They would bill their patients directly, with their patients responsible for the full cost of the service.

In 1981, the Parliamentary Task Force on Federal-Provincial Fiscal Arrangements, an all-party task force of federal MPs, published a review of the EPF Act of 1977, entitled "Fiscal Federalism in Canada".[7] The portion of this report dealing with the health-care system reviewed problems in the delivery system for health care and in the fulfillment of various program conditions outlined in the original hospital and medical care insurance acts. As well, it addressed the question of whether the national health-care system was underfunded and recommended, as had Mr. Justice Hall, consideration of the formation of a national health council, independent of government and of health-care providers, to act as a coordinating body for defining, planning, and implementing health policy for Canada. Such a council could monitor whether health program conditions were being met.

3.2.1. Enactment of the Canada Health Act, 1984

Following these two major reports, the federal government introduced proposals for a new "Canada Health Act", in May 1982, which was enacted in April 1984. The following are the major features of the Canada Health Act:

1. The Canada Health Act replaced two existing acts, the Hospital Insurance and Diagnostic Services Act and the Medical Care Act.

2. The new Act sets out program criteria and conditions of payment for the cash portion of the federal contributions made to the provinces for insured health services and payments made to the provinces for extended health-care services.

3. The insured health services covered by this legislation are all necessary hospital services, physician services and surgical-dental services performed in a hospital.

4. The extended health-care services covered by this legislation are nursing home intermediate care, adult residential care, home care and ambulatory health care.

5. The criteria that a provincial health program must meet to be eligible for the full cash portion of the contribution are:

   a) Public Administration   The program must be administered by a public authority accountable to the provincial government.
   b) Comprehensiveness   The program must cover all necessary hospital and medical services, and surgical-dental services rendered in hospitals.
   c) Universality   One hundred per cent of the eligible residents must be entitled to insured health services.
   d) Portability   The waiting period for new residents must not exceed three months. Insured health services must be made available to Canadians temporarily out of their own province at no extra charge to patients. Payment for out-of-province services to be paid for by the home province at home province rates. Payment for out-of-country services to be paid for by the home province at home province rates.
   e) Accessibility   Reasonable access to insured health services is not to be precluded or impeded, either directly or indirectly, by charges or other mechanisms.

Reasonable compensation must be made to physicians and dentists for providing insured health services. Adequate payments must be made to hospitals in respect of insured health services. The conditions of payment that provinces must meet to be eligible for the full cash portion of the federal contribution and payment also include: *(i) Provision of Information*: reasonable information on the operation of the program is to be supplied by the provinces to the federal Minister of Health, *(ii) Visibility*: federal contributions to the programs are to be given appropriate visibility.

In addition to these conditions, the Act also states that extra-billing and user charges must not be permitted except as outlined in the regulations attached to this Act.

Where a provincial plan fails to satisfy any of the program criteria, or the province fails to comply with either of the conditions of payment (provision of information and visibility), the Act provides that the cash portion of the federal contribution or payment may be reduced. This reduction is discretionary and must be preceded by consultation with the province. Where a province fails to comply with the condition of payment relating to extra-billing and user charges, the Act provides for a non-discretionary reduction of the cash portion of the federal contribution by the amount charged through extra-billing or user charges. For the first three years after proclamation, funds withheld from provinces because of extra-billing or user charges were to be held in Public Accounts of Canada, and were to be paid to the province if the practices of extra-billing or user charges are eliminated during those three years. The Act came into force on April 1, 1984.

4.   BEYOND THE CANADA HEALTH ACT

As indicated above, one of the conditions of the Canada Health Act was a partial withholding of funds from provinces which allowed extra-billing by physicians and hospital user charges. Provinces such as Ontario, Alberta, Manitoba, Saskatchewan and New Brunswick allowed extra-billing. With the introduction of the Canada Health Act, these provincial governments had to enact legislation which would ban extra-billing, or else they would lose revenue from the federal government. This, in turn, created strained relations between the two levels of governments and also between provincial governments and their respective medical associations. For example, in 1986, when the Government of Ontario introduced legislation banning extra-billing, some physicians in that province went on strike. But by 1987, all provinces had banned extra-billing. The Canadian health-care system appeared to be evolving toward an increased federal role, especially in the areas of formulation, monitoring and enforcement of program conditions.

4.1.   BILLS C-96, C-69 AND C-20

The federal government, however, has been forced into a position of progressive withdrawal of transfer payments for health and post-secondary education to the provinces as a result of budgetary deficit pressure.[8] These transfer payments, which were established under the EPF arrangements previously described, are given to the provinces partly as tax credits and partly as cash. The total grant was to be revised annually according to changes in population and GNP. Subsequent to the Canada Health Act, the Federal Government has stabilized its financial commitment by amending the funding formula in its favour. Bill C-96, introduced in 1986, reduced the annual per capita escalator to 2% below GNP growth. In 1991, Bill C-69, also known as the Government Expenditures Restraint Act, was proclaimed, further reducing the escalator and froze transfer payments for two years (1990-1991 and 1991-1992) and reduced further increases after that to 3% below GNP growth. Bill C-20, passed in 1991, extended the freeze to 1994-5 and allowed the federal government to withold any federal transfer payment for breach of the Canada Health Act. It is anticipated that the cash component of the transfer payments will be non-existent by the year 2000.

The withholding of cash is really the only control the federal government has over implementation by the provinces of the criteria for federal payment for "Medicare" described above. There is concern, therefore, that as federal cash payments diminish and disappear (as predicted), and provinces face increasing financial constraints provincially-implemented universal health insurance as characterized under the Canada Health Act 1984 may be eroded.

5.   OTHER FEDERAL-PROVINCIAL FINANCED HEALTH PROGRAMS

5.1.   CANADA ASSISTANCE PLAN (1966)

Under this plan, the federal government pays 50% of the cost of cash assistance and health and welfare services to persons in need. The program is administered by provincial governments, which are free to make available a wide range of health-care benefits. The range of benefits varies from province to province, but may include such services as eyeglasses, prosthetic appliances, dental services, prescribed drugs, home care services, and nursing home care. The only eligibility requirement specified is that of need, which is determined through an assessment of budgetary requirements, client income and resources. A province cannot demand previous residence as a condition for initial or continued assistance. The eligibility requirements and rates of assistance are set by the provinces and adjusted to local conditions and needs of special groups. The provinces must establish procedures for appeal from decisions relating to the provision of assistance.

The reduction of federal transfer payments previously discussed in relation to health care has also affected the Canada Assistance Plan. Growth in these payments was capped at 5% as part of Bill C-69. Reduction of the financing of social assistance in this manner is likely to have adverse effects on the psychosocial determinants of health.

5.2. VOCATIONAL REHABILITATION OF DISABLED PERSONS (1952)

This program has been administered by Health Canada since April 1, 1973. Under it, the federal government contributes 50% of the costs incurred by all provinces except Quebec in providing a comprehensive range of services for the vocational rehabilitation of physically and mentally disabled persons. Services include social and vocational assessment, counseling, training, maintenance allowances, the provision of tools, books, and other equipment, remedial and restorative treatments, and the provision of prosthetic and orthotic appliances, wheelchairs and other mobility aids.

6. DESCRIPTION OF NATIONAL HEALTH INSURANCE PROGRAMS OF SELECTED COUNTRIES

A comparison cannot easily be made with health insurance programs in other countries, because even the term "medicare" has different meanings from country to country. In most countries, health insurance arrangements have developed to meet particular needs, and are influenced by socioeconomic and political considerations, as well as historic trends in medical practice. In Canada, the Medical Care Act and the Hospital Insurance and Diagnostic Services Act were federal health programs. They achieved their objectives through a series of interlocking provincial plans which qualified for federal support by meeting minimum criteria. The Canadian approach to the development of a national program has been to provide, step by step, major segments of publicly-financed personal health care to virtually the whole population. The programs are designed to ensure that all residents of Canada have access to prepaid medical and hospital care.

6.1. UNITED KINGDOM

The British National Health Service is a comprehensive program of publicly-financed medicine covering not only professional services, but also hospitalization, and other benefits such as drugs, dental care, eyeglasses and hearing aids. It was introduced in 1947 and has recently undergone a transformation as the result of reforms introduced from 1989 to 1991.

Everyone is eligible to receive mostly free medical care through the National Health Service (NHS). Patients register with general practitioners, who provide primary care and referrals to specialists. Until recently, there was a choice of general practitioners; however, with the recent reforms, district health authorities are the one who contract services of general practitioners and hospitals and distribute them to the local population. This may hamper the free choice of the practitioners. Since there were line ups for the acute non-emergency hospital care, elective surgery and specialists physicians services in Britain, the government has allowed the development of small private health insurance to cover these services. Approximately 10% of the population has private insurance. Just over one-third physicians are general practitioners who work as independent contractors to the NHS. Physicians on the hospital staffs are salaried; however, because they are allowed part-time private practice, many of them are engaged in such. During private practice, they bill the private health insurance plans for their services.

Before the reform, hospitals were run by the district health authorities and received the global lump-sum budgets, set ultimately by the central government. Since reform, two mechanisms have developed. The district health authorities still can contract hospital services as they did before and pays the hospital accordingly. The group of general practitioners are also now allowed to contract services from the hospital for their patients. For the patients of these general practitioners, the government reimburses the general practitioners on a capitation basis for the hospital cost. The government directly pays the group as a part of its capitation fee and general practitioners pay the hospitals. The hospitals in the area are allowed to bid for the contracts which has brought an element of competition.

6.2   UNITED STATES

Health care is delivered through private insurance, which covers about three-quarters of the population. Most of those covered by private insurance are covered through employer-based group insurance, and a small proportion are covered by individual policies. Two major government sponsored programs are Medicare and Medicaid. Medicare is a federally subsidized program for those over 65 years of age, for certain disabled people under age 65 and for persons suffering from chronic renal diseases; benefits are not generally available outside the United States. Medicare consists of two parts. Part A is a hospital insurance program for those portions of the population mentioned above, generally requiring contributions by participants for a minimal period of their working lives. Part B is an optional, social security arrangement for medical care insurance, covering part of the costs of services by medical practitioners and certain other benefits. Some of the economically deprived in the United States benefit from a companion Medicaid program. The eligibility for

Medicaid benefits is based on income and means criteria, and it is determined by county welfare boards in states. The benefit covers in-patient and out-patient hospital services, laboratory and radiology, basic physician medical services, and skilled nursing facility coverage for patients over age 21. It is estimated that approximately 36 million people in the United States have inadequate or no health insurance. For this reason the Health Security Act of 1993 is being implemented in the United States. The Clinton administration is hoping to reform the health-care system in the following way: a) universal health-care coverage for all Americans and legal residents that will provide prepaid, flat-fee, and comprehensive services through managed competition between "regional alliances" of consumers and providers' of "health plans" that would merge Medicaid, and subsidize the self-employed and small businesses; b) comprehensive benefits through a standard "core-benefit package"; c) improved Medicare for those over 65; d) new long-term care program for the elderly, disabled, and chronically ill; e) improved service to underserved rural areas and inner cities; f) a single standard claim form and administration for all health plans by January 1, 1995; and g) formation of a National Health Board to oversee it. The alliances are expected to be in place by January 1997.[9,10]

6.3.   AUSTRALIA

A universal system of health insurance known as Medicare came into being in 1984, and a Medicare "levy" on each person who applied for these benefits was introduced to partly finance the cost. All residents in Australia (except diplomats and their families and short-term visitors) are entitled to benefits following application for a Medicare card. The system for medical and hospital care that was introduced is essentially two-tiered and could be regarded as an approach to rationing. All Medicare beneficiaries are entitled to procedures and care requiring hospitalization provided by doctors on roster at hospitals. Additional hospital insurance can be purchased to cover gaps between schedule fees (75% of fee usually paid by Medicare) and the costs of a private attending physician who is paid on a fee-for-service basis and, usually, but not always, has better private amenities. Pensioners and social security beneficiaries are not usually required to pay gaps between schedule fees and Medicare benefits. There is a safety net threshold for "calamities" whereby full schedule fees are reimbursed if the difference between schedule fees and benefits paid exceeds AUS$246 per year. For personal medical services, schedule fees are published and Medicare re-imbursement is paid at 85% of the schedule fee for general practitioners. Although not obliged to abide by the scheduled fees, in 1991-2, 70% of general practitioners direct-billed the government and received 85% of the scheduled fee reimbursement. Usually pensioners and social welfare recipients are charged only the Medicare benefit rate. For specialist fees, 85% of the schedule fee, or the fee less $26.80, whichever is the greater amount, is re-imbursed by Medicare. Ancillary services such as private dentistry, physiotherapy, chiropractic, appliances and some medicines are not covered under Medicare. Insurance can be purchased to cover these. Pharmaceutical benefits are provided for most prescribed items purchased at pharmacies according to a frequently revised list of the benefits attracted. In 1980, about 60% of health-care costs in Australia were paid through public funds. More recently there has been pressure on governments to eliminate private health insurance and institute a completely state-controlled medical insurance system.[11]

6.4.   FRANCE

Coverage in France is provided by a statutory health insurance scheme, which is part of the public social security system. Health insurance in France is financed by contributions from employers and employees, calculated in percentages of wages and salaries up to certain ceilings. The health insurance is comprehensive, including services rendered at home, at a doctor's office, or in a hospital. Included are home care, dental and nursing care, drugs and prostheses, and replacement income during illness. No disease is excluded. One sickness fund covers most employees and their dependents, or about four-fifth of the population. Several smaller funds cover the self-employed, farmers and some special groups of workers (for example miners) and pensioners. The sickness funds are quasi-autonomous non-governmental bodies which are managed by employer associations and trade unions, but they are subject to close central government regulation, particularly with regard to payroll tax rates and fee schedules.[12] The maximum plan benefit is established as a percentage of a ceiling value agreed upon by the medical profession and the government social security personnel in the case of ambulatory and home care, and it is established by the government for hospital care. The patient is generally required to pay a co-charge to the provider of the service, and hence there is a market for supplementary insurance which is provided by several thousand "mutuelles." Old age pensioners, invalids, and veterans are exempt from the co-charge, as are patients undergoing expensive or long-term treatment, major surgery, or hospitalization over 30 days. About two-thirds of physicians are paid on a fee-for-service basis by their patients, who are then (partially) reimbursed by their sickness funds and mutuelles. In some instances (e.g., for hospital and institutional care) it is possible for patients to assign their rights to be reimbursed to a third party, being then responsible only for paying the co-charge to the attending physician. Public hospitals account for about two-third of beds and are staffed largely by full-time and part-time salaried physicians. Private, for-profit hospitals and clinics account for the remainder of the beds, and these are staffed by fee-for-service physicians.

7.   SUMMARY

The BNA Act of 1867 (now known as the Constitution Act of 1982) gave the federal government a minimal role in the health-care system. Section 91 of the Act states that the federal government has power with respect to census, statistics, and quarantine, whereas section 92 of the Act gave provinces the primary responsibility in health matters. The federal government has become involved in health care by sharing the cost of programs and thus having a steering effect on the health-care system. Since 1950, a number of federal acts have been passed. The major ones are: the Hospital Insurance and Diagnostic Services Act of 1957 (which provided for universal hospitalization), and the Medical Care Act of 1966 (which provided universal coverage of necessary medical services provided by physicians). The federal government shared 50% of the cost of these programs with the participating provinces, provided the provinces met four criteria: universality, portability, comprehensiveness and public administration. All provinces participated in these programs. In the 1970s, the shared cost health programs became a critical problem for both the federal and provincial government and this led to the legislation of the Federal-Provincial Fiscal Arrangements and Established Programs Financing Act (EPF) of 1977. In this Act, the federal government, in lieu of 50% cost-sharing, agreed to pay the provinces: (a) through transfer of income tax points and (b) by cash contribution which were tied with an increase in the GNP. The EPF no longer tied federal payments to a particular form of health services, thus reducing the federal steering effect.

During the early 1980s, several critical reviews of the EPF were published, which led to the enactment of the Canada Health Act in 1984. In this Act the federal government amalgamated the Hospital Insurance and Diagnostic Services Act and the Medical Care Act. The Canada Health Act also established five criteria that the provincial health program must meet in order to be eligible for the full cash portion of the federal government contribution. The criteria were public administration, comprehensiveness, universality, portability and accessibility. It banned extra-billing, which had been complied with by all the provinces by 1987. It appeared that the Canadian health-care system was evolving toward an increased federal role, especially in the areas of formulation, monitoring and enforcement of program conditions. However, as a result of budgetary deficit pressure the federal government was forced to reduce transfer payment for health and post-secondary education to the provinces. Bills C-96, C-69 and C-20 were enacted to freeze the cash flow to the provinces. This has resulted in a diminished federal role in health-care policy formation.

It is claimed that Canada has a national Medicare program. This is incorrect, because health care is actually a provincial responsibility. As has been already noted, the involvement of the federal government is through financial contributions, which have made it possible for the federal government to establish national standards. As a result, what we have in Canada are 10 provincial and two territorial health-care systems, which are structured around federal guidelines and which provide mainly sickness care. However, the dichotomy between provincial and federal responsibility in the health sector however has increasingly become a source of tension between the two levels of government.

8. REFERENCES

1. Vayda E and Deber R. The Canadian Health Care System: An Overview. *Soc Sci Med* 18(3):191-197, 1984.
2. *Review of Health Services in Canada 1976.* Department of National Health and Welfare, Canada. Ottawa, 1976.
3. The Health Care System in Canada and its Funding: No Easy Solutions. First Report of the Standing Committee on Health and Welfare, Social Affairs, Seniors and the Status of Women (reconstituted Committee). Government of Canada, Ottawa, June 1991.
4. Young T. *Health Care and Cultural Change: The Indian Experience in the Central Subarctic.* Toronto: University of Toronto Press, 1988, p 82.
5. Heiber S and Deber R. Banning Extra-Billing in Canada: Just What the Doctor Didn't Order. *Can Public Policy* 13:62-74, 1987.
6. *Canada's National-Provincial Health Program for the 1980's. A Commitment for Renewal.* Hall E. Special Commissioner. Health and Welfare Canada, Ottawa, 1980.
7. *Fiscal Federalism in Canada.* Parliamentary Task Force on Federal-Provincial Fiscal Arrangements. Ministry of Supply and Services, Canada, Ottawa, 1981, pp 97-120.
8. Poulin C. The History of Health Care Funding in Canada and the Implications of Bill C-20. *Public Health and Epidemiology Report Ont* 3(10):160-164. And Guest Commentary by Pollett G. same issue pps 164-165, 1992.
9. Angell M. The Begining of Health Care Reform: The Clinton Plan. *N Engl J Med* 329(21):1569-1570, 1993.
10. Nair C and Karim R. An Overview of Health Care Systems: Canada and Selected OECD Countries. *Health Reports* 5(3):259-279, 1993.
11. Australian Institute of Health and Welfare. *Australia's Health 1992: The Third Biennial Report of the Australian Institute of Health and Welfare.* Thompson NJ, ed. Canberra: Australian Government Publishing Service, 1992.
12. *Health Policy Studies No.1: U.S. Health Care at the Cross-Roads.* Paris: Organisation for Economic Co-operation and Development; Washington, DC, OECD Publications, 1992.

CHAPTER THIRTEEN
Federal and Provincial Health Organizations

1. FEDERAL HEALTH ORGANIZATION

At the time of Confederation, the federal government had relatively little jurisdiction over health care. In 1872, the Department of Agriculture had primary responsibility for federal health activities. Gradually, these activities were dispersed among several departments: Agriculture, Inland Revenue, and Marine and Fisheries. In 1919, the Department of Health was established by an act stating that its duties, powers and functions "extend to and include all matters relating to the promotion or preservation of the health, social security and social welfare of the people of Canada over which the Parliament of Canada has jurisdiction." In 1929, the Department of Soldiers' Civil Re-establishment was discontinued and the Department of National Health became the Department of Pensions and National Health. In 1945, that department was split into Health and Welfare Canada and the Department of Veterans' Affairs. At that time, the task was two-fold: to promote, preserve and restore the health of Canadians, and to provide social security and social welfare to Canadians. In June 1993, the department was reorganized and the Welfare part of the Department was moved to what is now called Human Resources Development. The remaining department is now known as Health Canada. The Department responsibilities are focused on the following principal objectives: (i) universal access for all Canadians to quality health services; (ii) protection against disease and environment hazards; (iii) promotion of healthy lifestyles and promotion, encouragement and development of fitness. Health Canada is composed of a number of programs: Health Program and Services, the Medical Services, and Health Protection which are described in detail in the following sections. The other programs consist of: Policy and Consultation; Corporate Services; Strategic Planning and Organizational Renewal; National Pharmaceutical; and Strategy. The federal Minister of Health is responsible for the departments listed above. Under the Minister there are Deputy and Associate Deputy Ministers, a number of Assistant Deputy Ministers, as well as Regional Director Generals who report to the Minister through the Deputy Ministers.

2.   HEALTH PROGRAMS

Health Canada is divided into three main branches, with the Assistant Deputy Ministers heading each branch: (a) Health Programs and Services, (b) Medical Services and (c) Health Protection.

In addition, the Medical Research Council reports to Parliament through the Minister of Health. The functions and activities carried out by each branch are reported briefly in the following sections.[1,2]

2.1.   THE HEALTH PROGRAMS AND SERVICES BRANCH

The Health Programs and Services Branch provides financial and technical support to the provinces and territories for insured health-care services and certain extended health-care services, as well as promoting the adoption and maintenance of healthy lifestyles and fostering public health research. This branch is made up of five directorates: Health Insurance, Extramural Research Programs, Health Services, Health Promotion and Fitness Canada.

Health Insurance
The objective of this program is to ensure that all residents of Canada have reasonable access to insured health-care services on a prepaid basis and to support extended health-care services. The program monitors and enforces the adherence of the provinces and territories to the established criteria and conditions for federal contribution as outlined in the Canada Health Act (as described in the previous chapter). It provides the payments to the provinces and territories in accordance with the Canada Health Act and the Federal-Provincial Fiscal Arrangements and Federal Post-Secondary Education and Health Contributions Act.

The Extramural Research Program
This program is delivered through the National Health Research and Development Program. Through this program, Health Canada obtains information and develops and evaluates innovations pertinent to the achievement of broad departmental objectives. Applications for grants are accepted from any appropriately qualified individual or institution, or in special cases, from provincial and municipal governments. The program supports the formulation and conduct of studies, research, and demonstration projects in areas such as the biology of human populations, environmental health hazards, lifestyles, and the health-care delivery system. The Research Personnel Support Program assists those who wish to pursue a career in research in one of those areas. In 1992-93, the program provided approximately $28 million for research support.

Health Services
The primary focus is to promote the continuing development and maintenance of reasonable standards of health care and parity among provincial health programs. This program includes six separate sub-programs, namely mental health, community health, health assessment, institutional and professional services, health facilities design and health manpower, and the Canadian Blood Committee. In all of these programs, the directorate assists the provinces by assuming leadership and coordinating functions through the Federal/Provincial Advisory Committee structure which was established to assist the Conference of Deputy Ministers in fulfilling its mandate.

Health Promotion
The objective of this program, established in 1978, is to help Canadians achieve healthy lifestyles. The four strategies used by the directorate for health promotion are: (i) equipping the public to deal with lifestyle issues; (ii) promoting a social climate that supports healthy lifestyles; (iii) supporting self help and citizen participation in health promotion; and (iv) social welfare and other established programs. The Health Promotion program is divided into 12 components for the purposes of planning, management and delivery. Of these, five address lifestyle issues, notably nutrition, smoking, alcohol use, drug use, and hypertension. Health Canada has been a major partner in the promotion of Heart Health in Canada by supporting provincial surveys to establish baseline data on the prevalence of cardiovascular risk factors and developing demonstration provincial projects for implementing heart health promotion. Four components address the concerns of particular population groups: namely children and youth, women, the elderly, and the disabled. The Active Living program has focused on health promotion in relation to disability. Three components address functions or methods of delivery central to health promotion, that is, communications, school health and health promotion in the work place.

The work of the Health Promotion Directorate is done in two ways:

- Operational activities performed by the department directly or under contract consist of direct communication with the public through media advertising, promotional activities, and distribution of information. The most prominent advertising programs carried out by the department are: Break Free (anti-smoking), Really Me (anti-drug), Stay Real, and a cannabis information project.
- Help offered to voluntary and professional groups who wish to be active in health promotion include: joint planning ventures; major projects undertaken on a shared cost and time basis; provision of program materials; expert consultation; and contributory funding.

Fitness
Canada's Fitness Branch seeks to raise the fitness level of Canadians and increase participation in physical recreation. The branch activities can be grouped into the following areas: promotion, communications, and resource development.

2.2.   THE MEDICAL SERVICES BRANCH

This branch (MSB) is responsible for health care and public health services for Aboriginal Peoples and all residents of the Yukon, as well as for quarantine and immigration medical services, the health of civil servants, a national prosthetics service, and civil aviation medicine.

Indian and Northern Health Services
The basic objective of this program is to assist Aboriginal Peoples and residents of Yukon to attain a standard of health comparable to that of other Canadians. Insured hospital and medical care programs for Aboriginal Peoples are administered by the Yukon government, whereas the MSB manages other health services including a comprehensive public health program, special arrangements to facilitate communication between health stations and the transportation of patients referred from isolated communities to medical centres. In certain zones, several universities provide medical personnel and students in rotation. As residents of a province or territory, Indians are entitled to the benefits of the cost-shared provincially-operated medical and hospital insurance plans. These insured benefits are supplemented by the Medical Services Branch, which assists Indian bands to arrange transportation and obtain drugs and prostheses. A comprehensive public health program provides dental care for children, immunization, school health services, health education, and prenatal, postnatal and well baby clinics. Direct financial assistance to organizations of native people supports Indian programs directed toward improving the quality of life.

Since Indians are distributed widely throughout Canada, a network of 421 specially designed health facilities has been instituted in all provinces: 55 nursing stations, 109 health centres, six hospitals, and 251 other facilities. The MSB is in the process of transferring control of health services to native people. A number of bands across the country currently have control while other bands are in the process of acquiring control. Also, under the Community Health Representative Program, increasing numbers of Indians are being trained and employed in public health and medical care programs.

Quarantine and Regulatory Service
The MSB is responsible for the inspection of all vessels, aircraft and other conveyances and their crews and passengers arriving in Canada from foreign countries in order to prevent the entry of diseases such as cholera, plague, and yellow fever. Fully equipped quarantine stations are located at all major seaports

and airports. The Branch is also responsible for enforcing standards of hygiene on federal property including ports and terminals, vehicles travelling inter-provincially, and Canadian ships and aircraft.

Immigration Medical Service
The MSB determines the health status of all persons referred to them by Employment and Immigration Canada both in this and other countries. It also provides or arranges for health-care services for certain classes of persons after arrival in Canada, including immigrants who become ill en route to their destination or while seeking employment.

Public Servants' Health
The MSB is responsible for a comprehensive occupational health program for federal employees throughout the country and abroad. This service includes health counselling, surveillance of the occupational environment, pre-employment, periodic and special examinations, first aid and emergency treatment, and a wide range of advisory services and special health programs.

Civil Aviation Medicine
The MSB provides an advisory service to Transport Canada concerning the health and safety of all involved in Canadian civil aviation. Regional and central headquarters aviation medical officers review all medical examinations, participate in aviation safety programs, and assist in air accident investigations. Close liaison with authorities responsible for foreign aviation medicine is maintained, because standards are usually based upon international agreements.

Prosthetic Services
The objectives of the Prosthetic Services are to make available high quality prosthetic and orthotic rehabilitation, under the terms of agreements with most provinces and with the Veterans Affairs Canada, and to provide a centre of expertise in this field.

Disability Assessment
A number of MSB physicians provide an assessment and advisory service to the Unemployment Insurance Commission, in relation to claims for benefits under the Sickness and Maternity Benefit Plan. (The Canada Pension Plan maintains its own disability assessment service.)

Emergency Health Services
Emergency Health Services prepares plans to ensure that the health component of the MSB would be able to operate in the event or threat of nuclear attack, and to advise, assist, and stimulate provincial and municipal health departments in emergency health planning for both peacetime and wartime emergencies.

2.3. HEALTH PROTECTION BRANCH

The Health Protection Branch (HPB) is responsible for protecting the public against unsafe foods, drugs, cosmetics, medical and radiation-emitting devices, harmful microbes, technological and social environments deleterious to health, environmental pollutants and contaminants of all kinds, and fraudulent drugs and devices. This program also monitors the occurrence and causes of communicable and non-communicable diseases, and establishes laboratory medicine standards.

The HPB incorporates five operational directorates: Foods, Drugs, Environmental Health, National Health Surveillance, and Field Operations. It is responsible for enforcing the Food and Drugs Act and Regulations, the Narcotic Control Act and Regulations, the Proprietary or Patent Medicine Act, and the Radiation Emitting Devices Act and Regulations. In addition, under the Hazardous Products Act and Regulations, the HPB has joint responsibility with Consumer and Corporate Affairs Canada for product safety.

Food

Standards of safety and purity of food products are developed through laboratory research and maintained by a regular and widespread inspection program. The inspection of food manufacturing establishments plays a major role in assuring clean, wholesome foods containing ingredients that meet recognized standards. Changing food technology requires the development of laboratory methods to ensure the purity of new ingredients and the quality of packaging material. The Food and Drugs Regulations list chemical additives that may be used in foods, the amounts that may be added to each food, and the underlying reasons for the additives, such as those used as preservatives. Information on a new additive is submitted and reviewed carefully before it can be included in the permitted list. Considerable emphasis is placed on studies to ensure that the levels of pesticide residue in foods are not a health hazard. The effect of new packaging and processing techniques on food spoilage is also of special concern.

Drugs

The Health Protection Branch regulates both the manufacture and distribution of drugs in Canada. The conditions under which drugs are to be manufactured are described in the Manufacturing Facilities and Control Regulations. These relate to facilities, employment of qualified personnel, quality control procedures, maintenance of records, and a system permitting a complete, rapid recall from the market of any batch of drugs. Pharmaceutical plants are visited regularly by inspectors to ensure that the drugs produced meet the standards required for sale in Canada. Plants manufacturing biologicals to be sold in Canada, such as serums and vaccines, must be licensed according to the specifications of the Food and Drugs Act and Regulations, whether they are located in Canada or abroad.

When a new drug is to be placed on the market, the manufacturer is required by law to provide specific information, including a quantitative list of its ingredients, evidence of its safety and effectiveness, the formulation of dosages, and reports of any adverse effects. This information is studied to ensure that the drug is safe and effective for the purposes claimed. Even after a new drug is on the market, its sale can be banned by the HPB if the Drug Adverse Reaction Reporting Program indicates that it is unsafe or injurious.

Another major activity of HPB is the Quality Assessment of Drugs Program which enables the public to purchase high quality drugs at reasonable prices. This program includes inspection of manufacturing facilities, assessment of claims and clinical equivalency of competing brands, and provision of information to professionals and to the general public.

Environmental Health

The Environmental Health directorate is responsible for studying the adverse effects on human health of the chemical and physical environment, and for ensuring the safety, effectiveness and non-fraudulent nature of medical devices. The Directorate has the responsibility of developing health hazard assessments for the work and home environments, household products, and criteria for assessing air and water quality. Research is conducted on radiation hazards, and environmental and occupational exposures are monitored. Health Canada has taken new initiatives and extended programs under the Action Plan for Health and the Environment as part of the Federal Environmental Agenda (Green Plan). The Great Lakes Health Effects Program, which involves health surveillance, human exposure monitoring and toxicological testing, entered its third year in 1992-93.

National Health Surveillance

The objectives of the program are to coordinate the identification, investigation, control, and prevention of diseases in Canadians. These objectives are achieved through the following programs:

Disease Surveillance This program includes (i) developing surveillance programs and analyzing the occurrence of particular diseases; (ii) studying and evaluating data on communicable and non-communicable diseases in hospitals, laboratories, communities and internationally; and (iii) developing policies to control communicable and non-communicable diseases. The Laboratory Centre for Disease Control (LCDC)[3] is responsible for these functions and is similar to the Centers for Disease Control and Prevention (CDC) in the United States. Analyzing provincial and national data, the LCDC produces publications such as the *Canada Communicable Disease Report*, *Chronic Diseases in Canada* and others targeted to a variety of audiences.[4] It also responds to requests from provinces to investigate outbreaks.

Disease Control Services The Disease Control Services of LCDC carry out a range of laboratory work including: (i) providing authoritative identification of infectious diseases in clinical specimens referred by provincial public health or university and teaching hospital laboratories for the diagnosis of individual patients; (ii) developing methods and reagents for the early, rapid and reliable detection of established and emerging infectious diseases; (iii) promoting high levels of quality assurance in laboratory diagnoses through national programs in reagent evaluation and proficiency testing and training of personnel; (iv) characterizing human pathogens and evaluating their role in human infectious diseases from a national perspective for the prevention and control of epidemics; and (v) developing biotechnology for transfer to industry for commercialization of diagnostic commodities.

National AIDS Strategy (NAS) It is operated by the National AIDS Secretariat. The Strategy is involved in the following areas: (i) Prevention and Control - The NAS performs and funds laboratory and epidemiological research to control and contain the spread of HIV infection, to retard the development of AIDS, and to find effective treatments and a vaccine. NAS will also develop improved diagnostic techniques and encourage more seroprevalence surveys to determine the true prevalence of HIV infection in Canada. An AIDS Treatment Information Service (ATIS) was established following the demise of a progenitor program in 1992. (ii) Public Awareness and Education - The NAS promotes education and awareness in the general public to assist in preventing and controlling HIV infection and AIDS.

3.   RELEVENT SOCIAL PROGRAMS

The relevent social welfare programs which have impact on health are described here. They are now located in Ministry of Human Resources Development. The Social Program promotes and strengthens the income security of Canadians; shares in the cost of provincial and territorial social assistance, welfare services and rehabilitation programs; and assists in the development of social services to meet changing social needs. The two important programs are briefly described below.

Income Security Programs
The income security programs have the responsibility to promote and preserve the social security and social welfare of Canadians through the administration of the Old Age Security Act, the Family Allowances Act and Parts II and III of the Canada Pension Plan Act. Through a network of regional offices and client service centres, the Branch provides a full range of services to the public, including provision of general information on all aspects of income security benefits.

Social Service Programs
These programs consist of major federal-provincial cost-sharing programs providing basic assistance for those whose budgetary needs exceed available resources (for

whatever reason), and counselling and consultation on social and welfare related issues, including employability, services to individuals afflicted with physical and mental impairment, child welfare, child abuse and family violence, family and community services, and voluntary action. Contributions are also provided to help seniors maintain and improve their quality of life and independence, as well as to encourage utilization of skills, talents and experience within the community.

4.   OTHER RELEVANT PROGRAMS

Health Canada has a number of other branches dealing with specific areas. There are also individuals with special assignments and advisory councils affiliated with the department. The tasks of relevant branches, individuals, and advisory councils are given below.

The objective of the **Policy and Consultation Branch** is to provide advice to the Minister, Deputy Minister and other branches on trends and issues, policy requirements and communications and information needs relative to departmental objectives, priorities and programs. The Branch has three main roles designed to meet that objective. First, it undertakes research analysis and advises on health policy issues. Secondly, it acts as a resource for policy development and communications activities of other branches. Finally, it provides to the Department, its provincial counterparts and national and international organizations, information on health related matters.

The **Intergovernmental and International Affairs Branch** coordinates Canada's participation in international health and social affairs, and promotes networking between international, intergovernmental and non-governmental organizations. One of its principal responsibilities is coordinating, monitoring and, where required, initiating policies and strategies on issues which affect more than one branch or require interdepartmental consultation. It also maintains a centre for gathering and disseminating information on international trends in health and welfare matters.

The **Senior Advisor, Status of Women** is the key advisory and coordinating position responsible for the development, continuous assessment, implementation and integration of a range of policies and programs to ensure the promotion and preservation of the health, social security and social welfare of Canadian women and their families. She/he chairs the standing Departmental Advisory Committee on the Status of Women Concerns to ensure effective cooperation by all branches in the achievement of departmental and federal goals. The Office has been designated the Canadian focal point for the Pan-American Health Organization's Program on Women, Health and Development.

The **Principal Nursing Officer** advises the Department on matters concerning nursing and health. This includes the professional and ethical responsibilities of nurses; assessing the impact of nursing on the health and well-being of Canadians;

promoting basic, higher and continuing education for nurses; optimizing Canadian nursing skills, encouraging research and development activities in nursing and health-care; and advising, consulting and assisting with the planning and evaluation of nursing and health-care services at local, provincial, national and international levels by invitation.

The National Advisory Council on Aging was created by Order-in-Council on May 1, 1980, to assist and advise the Minister of Health Canada on issues related to the aging of the Canadian population and the quality of life of seniors. The Council has members from all parts of the country as well as a mix of language, ethnic groups and occupational backgrounds. The Council reviews the needs of seniors, recommends remedial action, act as liaison with other groups, encourages public discussion, and disseminates information. In carrying out its responsibilities, the Council works closely with the Minister of State for Seniors.

5. PROVINCIAL HEALTH SYSTEM

Constitutionally, the provincial governments have primary responsibility for all personal health matter such as disease prevention, treatment and maintenance of health. Activities such as preventive health services, hospital services, treatment services for tuberculosis and other chronic diseases, and rehabilitation and care of the chronically ill and disabled, have therefore been chiefly dependent upon this level of government. Provincial administrations must work closely with hospitals and voluntary community health associations, the health professions, and teaching and research institutions. Methods of organizing, financing and administering health ministries vary from province to province. For instance, in some provinces programs such as hospital insurance, medical care insurance, tuberculosis control, cancer control and alcoholism programs are administered directly by the provincial ministry of health. In other provinces the same programs may be the responsibility of separate public agencies directly accountable to a provincial minister of health. In some provinces, the health ministry is amalgamated with the ministry of community and social services, an emerging trend across the country.

Other organizations can also have health responsibilities. For example, in some provinces the ministry of labour is responsible for occupational health, the ministry of community and social services is responsible for the cognitively impaired, and the ministry of education is responsible for the management and treatment of physically challenged children. Voluntary associations such as the Victorian Order of Nurses and the Arthritis Society may provide specialized health services, which in many cases are supported in large part by government financing. This diversity stems from tradition and financial considerations. In many provinces one-third to one-half of the total budget is allocated to health services. To reduce the power of a minister with such a large budget, the functions of the health ministries can be distributed throughout different ministries. However, this has resulted in fragmentation and duplication of services.

5.1. LOCAL AND REGIONAL HEALTH BOARDS/COUNCILS

For general administrative purposes, many provinces are divided into health regions or districts for health planning with health boards established as advisory or administrative bodies. For example, Manitoba is divided into 10 regions for purposes of administration and service delivery. Each region's health service delivery system is managed by a regional director. The director is responsible for the administration and delivery of the field services of Manitoba Health and Manitoba Family Services. Both Quebec and Saskatchewan have regional/district boards for the administration of health and social services. Almost all of the provinces are organized into community health and/or mental health regions.

The regional/district board have wide ranging membership from different constituencies such as hospitals, professional groups, voluntary agencies, elected representatives from local municipalities, and consumers. Most board members are usually appointed, not elected, and hence lack accountability to the community. In Saskatchewan, however, each district board will have a board of eight elected members and up to four appointed members. Government appointments for the board are necessary to allow for inclusion of individuals with certain expertise or cultural backgrounds whose concerns may not already be represented. The functions of the board include regional planning of health services, delivering and managing the services including the formulation of views about the need for new health facilities (e.g., building of hospitals). Many of these boards lack authority because they have no fiscal responsibility. This dissociation of planning and funding has led to tension between the regional and provincial governments. Therefore, most health planning boards are consultative only in nature except in Quebec and Saskatchewan, where the recent legislation has provided fiscal control to the board (see chapter 16). Government funding in Saskatchewan to the district will be based on needs assessment and population count, and each district will be allowed to borrow the money but will not be allowed to tax local communities.

5.2. FUNCTIONAL ORGANIZATION OF PROVINCIAL MINISTRY OF HEALTH

Since there are constant changes in administrative structure of provincial health ministries, no organizational chart of the ministries is included here. However, the functional organization remains stable. Provincial health responsibilities fall into three areas (table 13.1): provision of direct services, provision of services through financial assistance (indirect services) and administrative services.

Table 13.1: Functions of the Provincial Health System

Direct Services	Indirect Services	Administrative Services
Public health services	Financial assistance programs	Health services planning
Home care programs	Hospital and medical care	Health manpower planning, training, and regulation
Mental health services	Dental care	Standard setting for health institutions and public places
Services for tuberculosis and cancer patients	Prescription Drugs	Health research
Health services in remote areas	Services for allied health professionals	Health surveillance (communicable disease control)
Ambulance services	Other services e.g., health appliances and equipment	Emergency health services
Public Health Laboratories	Services for welfare recipients	Vital statistics

5.2.1. Direct Services

Direct services are those services which in a majority of provinces are under the jurisdiction of the Ministry of Health with regards to budget, policies and control. For all these functions, in each health ministry, there are corresponding departments, branches or agencies which provide direction and monitoring. However, while these services are centrally planned and controlled, they are delivered at the local level, and hence they are described in detail in chapter 13 except for those services which are mainly regionally based such as Native and Northern health services, ambulance services and occupational health.

Native and Northern Health Services

In the provinces with sparsely settled northern areas, the provincial health departments provide both treatment and preventive health services. Saskatchewan, Manitoba and Ontario have set up northern health services, and other provinces have similar services.

Alberta has no Native Health branch, but it does have a program for Native Mental Health Services which has made links with traditional native healers to provide service beyond normal psychiatric intervention to native clients. Additionally, more than 20 staff members of the Mental Health Division have participated as co-trainers to native counsellors at the Nechi Institute on Alcohol and Drug Education. There is also a Native Community Development Program in Lac La Biche which provides services geared towards suicide prevention and the improvement of self-esteem and family life in native communities.

British Columbia's Community and Family Health Division administers the Community Native Health program which aims to integrate the needs of Natives for appropriate, accessible health services into the programs of the Ministry of Health. The program assists in policy and program development, the training of Aboriginal counsellors, cross-cultural training for ministry staff, planing and priority development regarding Aboriginal community health issues, and community agency funding through consultation with Aboriginal groups.

The Community Health Services (Operations) Division in Manitoba has a Northern Health branch. Primary care and public health nursing is provided by Manitoba Health to 23 northern and remote areas with limited access to other medical services and facilities. A 1964 Memorandum of Agreement divides responsibility for providing health-care services to northern communities which are distant from major medical centres between Manitoba Health and the Medical Services Division of Health Canada. Clinical and community health services are provided under federal jurisdiction to communities with a majority Status Indian population, and under provincial jurisdiction to communities with a majority Non-Status Indian and Metis population. New initiatives include post-forest fire intervention activity after the 1989 forest fire disaster, and discussions with representatives from the federal government, provincial government and native communities regarding increasing local control of the administration and delivery of health-care services by Indian bands in Manitoba.

Saskatchewan's Community Health Division has a Northern Health Services Branch which provides primary care, public health nursing, mental health services, physician services, children's dental services, home care, public health inspection, nutrition counselling, speech and language pathology and health education to residents of Northern Saskatchewan. Community mental health nurses and mental health social workers maintain regular contact with all northern communities including Indian band offices to ensure that northern residents with mental health problems receive assistance and counselling. As well, community health educators provide interpretive services to people who speak Cree and Dene.

Ontario has three very interesting programs. The first one deals with the provision of financial subsidies either in the form of grants or tax breaks to professionals who settle in designated under-serviced areas. The second one deals with providing travel subsidies to residents of Ontario who live in areas remote from specialized facilities. The third program specifically deals with Aboriginal Peoples and is in the process of developing programs which can be accessed by natives on reserves who are the primary responsibility of the federal government. Similarly, Quebec has transferred health and social service program to some of the northern native groups.

Occupational Health

Services designed to prevent accidents and occupational diseases and to maintain the health of employees are the common concern of provincial health departments, labour departments, Workers' Compensation Boards, industrial management and unions.

Provincial agencies regulate working conditions and offer consultant and educational services to industries. All provinces have legislation (Factories Acts, Shop Acts, Mine Acts, Workers' Compensation Acts) setting standards for health, safety and accident prevention on the job. Most provinces maintain environmental health laboratories that study industrial health problems such as the effects of noise and other exposures on workers.

The nature and extent of occupational health services vary from province to province depending on the type of industry. In provinces with large-scale mining operations, there are usually strong programs which provide experts in dust control, toxicology and industrial diseases. In other provinces there may be a different mix of expertise as in provinces where insecticides or industrial chemicals are problems.

Public Health Laboratories

Public health laboratories assist with the identification and control of epidemic and endemic diseases. All provinces maintain a central public health laboratory and most have branch laboratories to assist local health agencies and the medical profession in the protection of community health and the control of infectious diseases.

5.2.2. Indirect services

As indicated above, all of the services listed here are not directly provided by the provincial government, the total or partial cost of the programs or services are covered through either government-run health insurance programs or subsidies for the cost of services and/or drugs and/or appliances. With these mechanisms, provinces are able to exert pressure on professionals and institutions for setting standards for the services and controlling cost.

Health Insurance Programs

The basic principles of hospital and medical insurance enunciated by the federal government were described in chapter 11. Only the salient features of the provincial insurance programs will be described here. In some provinces, administration of the hospital insurance plan and the medical insurance plan is combined, whereas in others the two plans have separate administrative structures.

Health insurance coverage is automatic and compulsory in most provinces, requiring only some form of registration. Most provinces, except for Alberta and British Columbia, fund their health care either through general revenues and/or a levy on payrolls. Alberta and British Columbia partly recover the costs of health care through premiums. The Canada Health Act Annual Report published yearly by Health Canada is an excellent source of details on the functioning of the health insurance plans in each province.[5] Coverage is available to all Canadian residents on equal terms and conditions and cannot be denied on grounds of age, income or preexisting conditions.

The federal government has established a Health Insurance Supplementary Fund with provincial contributions to provide for payment of claims for health services (hospital or medical) for residents of Canada who have lost coverage through no fault of their own. This might occur, for example, when someone moving from place to place was not recognized as eligible under the rules of any province. It would not apply if coverage was lost through the individual's own fault, as in non-payment of premiums.

Those provinces charging premiums make some provision to cover those unable to pay (such as welfare recipients and those with incomes just above the poverty level) through full and partial subsidies. All provinces also provide additional services for residents receiving public assistance and for those over age 65. These commonly include prescription drugs and may also include dental services, eyeglasses, prostheses, home care services and nursing home care, depending on the province. Many provinces also provide for the services of chiropractors, podiatrists and optometrists. Usually there is a dollar limit on these services above which a person is not covered. For services not covered by the national health insurance programs and not universally available to insured residents in a given province, the Canada Assistance Plan Act provides for the federal government to share the costs of the additional health services to social assistance recipients 50-50 with the province.

The Alberta Health-Care Insurance Plan offers additional health insurance to residents who cannot obtain Alberta Blue Cross coverage through an employer on an individual basis at special rates. Blue Cross coverage is also provided at no charge to registrants aged 65 and older and their dependants, as well as to eligible widows and widowers aged 55 to 64 and their dependants. The Alberta Health-Care Insurance Plan is partially funded by premiums. Medical and non-medical practitioners registered with the Plan are monitored by the Professional Review function.

Recently a number of provinces have introduced unique identifier systems for individuals insured in their health plans. Individuals are given plastic cards with magnetic strips which store information on encounters with the medical care system, diagnoses and treatment. There is a provision for confidentiality of medical information, and access to the relevant information is available only to authorized health professionals. This information system will also help to improve research, program evaluation and planning. To avoid the fraudulent use of cards by non-registrants, the Northwest Territories and Quebec have introduced photo identification cards similar to the driver's license, and other provinces are in process of adopting such a system.

Drug Plans

The provinces of Manitoba, Saskatchewan and British Columbia provide prescription drugs with either small co-payments or a ceiling. However, all provinces have drug plans to cover those eligible for certain drug benefits (e.g., those receiving public assistance and those over 65). Most provinces provide drugs for the treatment of venereal disease, tuberculosis and other infections where a public health hazard exists, and where treatment costs are very high (for example, cystic fibrosis and AIDS). Some of the interprovincial variations are highlighted below.

Saskatchewan's Prescription Drug Plan is administered by the Prescription Drug Services Branch of the Insured Services Division. The Branch provided a program to protect more than 960,000 eligible residents against extreme drug costs in 1990/91, and it provided almost $90 million in benefits to Saskatchewan residents. Permanent residents of British Columbia receive assistance with the purchase of the following: most physician-, dentist-, or podiatrist-prescribed drugs; insulin, needles and syringes for people with diabetes mellitus; glucose strips, where blood sugar level measurement is medically indicated, and for gestational diabetics with valid Certificates of Training in the use of these strips; certain ostomy supplies; and designated permanent prosthetic appliances and orthotic devices, with prior approval. This assistance is provided under the province's Pharmacare Program according to five plans. Plan A, for residents over 65, covers drug costs and 25% of dispensing fees up to $125 per year, and 100% of dispensing fees over that amount. Plan B, for residents of licensed, continuing care/long-term care facilities, provides benefits at no cost. Plan C, for people covered by the Ministry of Social Services and Housing, provides benefits at no cost. Plan D, for individuals under age 65, provides reimbursement for 80% of the costs of eligible purchases which exceed an annual deductible of $325, with a maximum cost per family of $2,000. Lastly, Plan E, for children eligible for the At Home Program, provides benefits at no cost.

Within Manitoba's Communicable Disease Control Branch is the Life Saving Drug Program, which provides medication for life-sustaining purposes to those who cannot afford them. Eligible residents of New Brunswick receive prescription drug benefits under the province's Prescription Drug Plan. There are several individual drug plans; beneficiary groups include New Brunswickers over age 65, nursing home residents registered with Medicare, people with cystic fibrosis, organ transplant recipients requiring cyclosporin, people requiring the Human Growth Hormone drug, AIDS sufferers requiring "Retrovir" (AZT), clients with health cards issued by the Department of Income Assistance, and children in the care of the Minister of Health and Social Services.

Prince Edward Island's Division of Pharmacy Services administers a Drug Cost Assistance Plan for seniors, which requires the senior to pay the total dispensing fee and $4.00 of the total cost of the drug ingredient for approved drug benefits; the plan covers the remaining cost. As well, the Division provides and pays for drugs needed for diabetes, cystic fibrosis, organ transplants, hemolytic disease of newborns, psychosis, rheumatic fever and rheumatic heart disease, mental health aftercare, sexually transmitted diseases, tuberculosis, kidney failure and AIDS.

Appliances and Equipment

Appliances and equipment comprise devices and equipment necessary or complementary to medical treatment. Provinces differ in the benefits provided, and examples are provided below to illustrate inter-provincial variations.

The Alberta Aids to Daily Living (AADL) program is coordinated by the Public Health Division. AADL assists with the provision of program-approved medical equipment and supplies to Albertans living at home with a chronic or terminal illness or disability. Those over age 65 do not cost-share, while those under 65 do, a discrepancy noted in the "Action Plan" of the Premier's Council on the Status of Persons with Disabilities.

B.C.'s Community and Family Health Division has a Medical Supply Services program which provides support to patients receiving specialized home maintenance care. The kidney dialysis service, which supports all home and community dialysis procedures, is the core operation of the program. Medical and nutritional supplies are also coordinated to address hemophilia, parental nutrition and enteral nutrition. All of the program's services are provided with quality assurance and provincial advisory committees in close cooperation with each patient's originating hospital. The Services to the Handicapped Branch has an At Home Program which provides respite support and medical equipment and supplies to families caring for a child with severe disabilities. The Hearing Services Branch operates the British Columbia Hearing Aid Program to provide selection, fitting, repair and sale of hearing devices at competitive prices.

Along with its Continuing Care Branch, Manitoba also has a Medical Equipment and Supplies Branch which provides a support service by acquiring, warehousing, distributing, maintaining and repairing a range of medical supplies and equipment required in order to support the care and independent living of physically disabled individuals within their own communities. The equipment is purchased in bulk and provided on loan to eligible Manitoba residents under the authorization of a health-care professional. Eligible are those who have been physically disabled through disease, traumatic injury or the natural aging process, resulting in the need for medical equipment to support their care and independence in the community. In 1989-90, 24,364 clients were registered with the program.

Within the New Brunswick Public Health and Medical Services Division, Community and Environmental Health Branch, is the Seniors Rehabilitative Equipment Program. Under this program, seniors may borrow (without charge) standard and specialized equipment to assist in the activities of daily living. The equipment is loaned by the Canadian Red Cross Society and the Department of Health and Community Services provides the funding.

Ontario's Assistive Devices Program pays up to 75% of the price of goods such as electric wheelchairs, myoelectric limbs, hearing aids and respiratory equipment. In 1990-91, 125,000 people bought equipment with the help of ADP. In that year, the program also began to provide funding to older Ontarians for the purchase of low-technology visual aids and custom-made braces and splints.

Saskatchewan's Community Health-Treatment Services Branch has a Saskatchewan Aids to Independent Living program which provides equipment and other support to people with disabilities. People referred by designated health professionals are eligible for benefits such as mobility and environmental aids and other special equipment as well as support for the costs of drug and supplies required by certain conditions.

Administrative Services

Administrative Services are those operational functions which government undertakes to plan, forecast and evaluate the necessary government services.

Planning of Health Services

Almost all provincial ministries of health have a group of civil servants who, with the help of outside consultants, do short and long range planning of health services. These groups may be loosely structured or have a defined status within the ministry, for example, the division of strategic planning and research within the Ministry of Health in Ontario.

Often the minister recognizing the deficit in services appoints a special committee composed of outstanding citizens and professionals with some backup from civil servants. The task of these committees is to recommend mechanisms for delivering health services to the population or subgroups of the population. Some examples of these committees' reports are the Rochon Commission Report in Quebec, outlining the blueprint of health and social welfare services, and the Rainbow Report: Our Vision of Health by Premiers Commission on Future Health Care for Albertans.

Planning and Training of Health Human Resources

The Ministry of Health in many provinces is actively involved in assessing the future needs for health human resources. In cases where there is an oversupply of health professionals (for example, doctors and nurses), some of the provinces have taken active steps to reduce the number of students admitted into these professional schools, or discourage immigration of these professionals. In situations where there is a lack of human resources, subsidies have been provided to students entering that profession.

Regulation of Health Professions

The established health professions, like medicine, dentistry and pharmacy, have been regulated by their respective licensing bodies, which are mandated by provincial legislation. The other health professionals and technicians are usually regulated or certified (for details see chapter 17).

Standard Setting for Health Institutions and Public Places

All of the acute, chronic, rehabilitation, extended care and mental health hospitals are governed by specific legislation. Standards are set for nursing homes in many provinces as well. There are definite standards and guidelines for public places like restaurants, food handling places, industries, and factories. Legislation usually emanates from within the civil service or from concerned members of the legislature.

Health Research

Most provinces have intramural health research to help long-range planning of health services. Wealthier provinces (like Alberta, British Columbia, Quebec and Ontario) have funds earmarked for extramural research. These research grants are usually peer-reviewed and span from basic research to demonstration grants for developing newer health-care systems. In some provinces there has been a recent trend for the Ministry of Health to invite tenders for the areas to be researched.

Emergency Health Services

The Emergency Health Services Division, established in 1959 within Health Canada encourages the provinces (with the support of an advisory committee) to develop their own emergency health services divisions. These are organized under a provincial director who is generally assisted by a medical, paramedical and a nursing consultant. Federal Emergency Health Services are represented in the provinces by the Regional Director of the Medical Services Branch.

The fourfold tasks of provincial emergency health services are to ensure that vital health functions are maintained during or reorganized after emergency or disaster, to encourage and assist local planners in the establishment of emergency medical units, to train health professionals and the general public in emergency health procedures, and to place emergency medical units from the national stockpile in strategic locations.

Vital Statistics

Each province has a registrar-general who is responsible for keeping records of vital events such as births, marriages, and deaths. This department usually provides statistical information pertaining to these vital events. The reporting of births, deaths, and marriages are mandatory in all provinces and specific forms are designed to record these events (see chapter two on birth and death certificates). These data are also provided to the federal government which publishes national statistics.

6.   SUMMARY

This chapter dealt with the types of health services provided by the federal and provincial governments.

At the time of Confederation the federal government had relatively little jurisdiction and involvement in the health care of Canadians. In 1919, the Department of Health was established and its responsibilities "...include all matters relating to the promotion or preservation of health, social security and social welfare of the people of Canada over which the Parliament of Canada has jurisdiction." In 1945, Health and Welfare Canada was created with two-fold tasks: to promote, preserve and restore the health of Canadians; and to provide social security and social welfare to Canadians. In 1993, Welfare Department of Health and Welfare Canada was separated. The federal ministry of health is now known as Health Canada and is composed of three programs: the Health Programs and Services Branch, Medical Services Branch and Health Protection Branch.

The *Health Programs and Services Branch* provides financial and technical support to the provinces and territories for insured health-care services and certain extended health-care services, as well as promote the adoption and maintenance of healthy lifestyles and fostering public research. This branch is made up of five units: health insurance, extramural research programs, health services, health promotion and fitness. Secondly, is the *Medical Services Branch* which is responsible for health care and public health services for Aboriginal Peoples and all residents of the Yukon, as well as for quarantine and immigration medical services, the health of civil servants, a national prosthetics service, and civil aviation medicine. Thirdly, is the *Health Protection Branch* which is responsible for protecting the public against unsafe foods, drugs, cosmetics, medical and radiation-emitting devices, harmful microbes, technological and social environments deleterious to health, environmental pollutants and contaminants of all kinds, and fraudulent drugs and devices. This branch also monitors the occurrence and causes of communicable and non-communicable diseases, and establishes laboratory medicine standards.

Health Canada has a number of other branches dealing with specific areas. For example, there is the Policy, Communications and Information Branch, the Intergovernmental and International Affairs Branch, the Senior Advisor and Status of Women.

The social programs in the Ministry of Human Resources Development which influence health are: Income Security and Social Services. They promote and strengthen the income security of Canadians; shares in the cost of provincial and territorial social assistance, welfare services and rehabilitation programs; and assist in the development of social services to meet changing social needs.

As noted in earlier chapters, provincial governments have primary responsibility for all personal health matters such as disease prevention, treatment and maintenance of health. Activities such as preventive health services, hospital services, treatment services for TB and other chronic diseases, and rehabilitation and care of the chronically ill and disabled are all under the jurisdiction of the provincial government.

The services provided by the provincial government can be classified as (i) direct, (ii) indirect and (iii) administrative services. Direct services are those services which in the majority of provinces are under jurisdiction of the Ministry of Health with regards to budget, policies and control. Examples include: home care programs, public health services, and mental health services. Indirect services, on the other hand, are those whose costs are covered either totally or partially by either government-run health insurance programs (for example, hospital and medical services provided by a physician) or by subsidizing the cost for services and/or drugs and/or appliances. With these mechanisms, provinces are able to exert pressure on professionals and institutions for setting standards for the services and controlling costs. Administrative services are those operational functions which government undertakes to plan, forecast and evaluate the necessary government services.

7. REFERENCES

1. *Review of Health Services in Canada,* 1976. Health and Welfare Canada, Ottawa, 1976.
2. Health and Welfare Canada *1993-94 Estimates, Part III, Expenditure Plan*, Minister of Supply and Services Canada. Ottawa, 1993.
3. Health and Welfare Canada. Health Protection Branch. *Laboratory Centre for Disease Control.* Ministry of Supply and Services, Canada, Ottawa, 1992.
4. Health and Welfare Canada. Health Protection Branch. Laboratory Centre for Disease Control. *Bureau of Chronic Disease Epidemiology Program Description:* Fiscal Year 1991-92. Ottawa, 1992.
5. Health and Welfare Canada. *Canada Health Act Annual Report, 1988-89.* Ministry of Supply and Services, Canada, Ottawa, 1989.

CHAPTER FOURTEEN
Local Health Services

1. OVERVIEW OF LOCAL HEALTH SERVICES

If illness, suffering or symptoms occur, an individual usually relies initially, and sometimes for prolonged periods on informal support. Once these are exhausted community-based health services are accessed by clients at the local level. The variety of health services available at the local level include primary care, secondary care, hospital care, home care, public health services and private nursing homes. The funding sources for these services are varied as well, some funded by governments, others by voluntary agencies and still others by individuals, through either private insurance or out-of-pocket expenditure. While in all provinces, basic hospital and medical services are provided under government health insurance plans, there is variability in what is provided either through public or private insurance or personal expenditure. Affluent provinces and provinces with social democratic governments have traditionally provided a larger range of services financed through public revenue. While most of the services listed in this chapter are basic health services, there is a large array of services dealing with health promotion, disease prevention, and health maintenance as well as support services (such as social, educational and vocational services) for those who are chronically or acutely ill. These services may also deal with special groups of people, e.g., Aboriginal Peoples, battered women, and those with Alzheimer's Disease. The larger centres in Canada have directories outlining these services. These directories give a description of the services and contact phone numbers. In rural communities information could also be obtained through the local Health Unit.

1.1. PRIMARY HEALTH-CARE SERVICES

At this point, it is appropriate to define some commonly used terms. Primary health care (or first contact care) includes services provided at the first contact between the patient and the health professional. Primary health care is generally provided by physicians, dentists, chiropractors, pharmacists, nurse-practitioners, optometrists, dietitians and others. These services include treatment, promotion and maintenance of health, follow-up care, and the complete continuing care of the individual (including referral when required).[1] Therefore, primary health-care providers must fulfil three essential functions beyond treating the patients:[2]

Guardian The primary care provider and patient enter into a relationship in which continuity is implicit. As a result of the increasing complexity of our health-care systems, there is an increasing need for someone (perhaps a team) to accept responsibility for the ongoing care of the person or family.

Gatekeeper In performing this function, the primary care provider has a dual role towards the patient: as a guide or information resource and as the appropriate mechanism for referral elsewhere in the health-care system.

Chronicler The primary care provider acts as a chronicler or recorder of the patient's health related interactions with the system and its providers.

1.2. SECONDARY AND TERTIARY HEALTH CARE

Secondary health care is usually delivered by specialized human resources. Patients normally enter secondary care after referral from primary care providers because their health problems require specialized skills and facilities not available in the primary care sector. Problems seen in secondary care includes serious cardiovascular disorders, major accidents, burns, major fractures, cancers, major behavioural disorders, and special pediatric, medical and obstetric problems. These conditions usually require specialized care provided by specialists in community or general hospital. Unusual inherited disorders, certain forms of cancer, complicated pregnancies, rare and complicated cardiovascular disorders, catastrophic trauma and complex immunological disorders need treatment by further referral to tertiary health care centres which have very specialized facilities and professional skills and are usually found only in university teaching hospitals.

2.   PROVISION OF MEDICAL SERVICES

The major component of primary health care in Canada is **primary medical care**. Most of the primary medical care is provided in the community through private practices, by general or family practitioners, and to a lesser extent, by pediatricians, internists, obstetricians and gynecologists. This is not the case in the United States where primary medical care is provided predominantly by specialists. A small proportion of the population seeks their primary medical care through a community health centre, walk-in-clinic or the emergency room of a hospital. More than 90% of the Canadian population can identify their primary medical care provider. The major part of **secondary medical care** is also provided in the community setting, and **tertiary medical care** is mainly provided by physicians practising in the hospital setting.

Canadian physicians receive remuneration for their services in the following manner : (i) fee-for-service, (ii) salary, (iii) sessional payment, and (iv) capitation. The majority of physicians bill for most of their services through provincial health insurance plans (i.e., fee for service). This mode of payment for service is "volume driven." Approximately 30% of physicians are on salary (for example, interns, residents, geographic full-time practitioners and civil servants). Those on sessional payment plans receive lump sum amounts for the time they make their services available. An example of this is a psychiatrist working a half day in a mental health clinic and receiving a flat rate for this service. In the capitation system, physicians receive a fixed amount of payment per patient for all services rendered. It is claimed that capitation or the salary is more conducive to a holistic approach to health care, where a physician is more likely to pay attention to all determinants of health, and practise disease prevention and health promotion. The capitation system for primary care physicians is prevalent in the United Kingdom and is usually found in health services organizations (HSOs) in Canada and the US.

2.1. ORGANIZATION OF MEDICAL PRACTICES

Most physicians in Canada practise medicine either as solo practitioners or in groups. Some groups consist of individuals from the same discipline, (e.g., family practitioners), while others consist of specialists from different disciplines. Most practitioners have their offices in the community. In urban centres with medical schools, practices of full-time teachers are located in the university hospitals. These physicians are called geographic full-time practitioners.

2.1.1. Alternate Delivery Models

Most primary health care is delivered in physicians' offices on a fee-for-service basis. The fee schedule offers physicians the incentive to provide more expensive and less time-consuming services. Many preventive services which incorporate counselling take a longer time, provide less remuneration and are often neglected. With an emerging emphasis on cost containment, disease prevention and health promotion, the government and physicians are attempting to develop alternate models for health-care delivery that will enable them to be less "volume driven" and that will put a cap on the health-care costs. The following are examples of alternative delivery models:

Community Health Centre

A community health centre has a voluntary board comprised of members from the community. It receives an annual budget for specific health programs from the provincial government. It provides a wide range of human services such as medical, dental, social, nursing and others under one roof. All the professionals, including physicians, are on salary. Many of these centres are located in deprived areas or they serve disadvantaged groups such as the poor, the elderly, Aboriginal Peoples and immigrant groups. In Quebec, these centres are called local community service centres (CLSCs) of which there are approximately 146. These centres integrate health and social services emphasizing prevention, health promotion and provision of other personal services at one location. They are also required to provide services for extended hours in the evenings and weekends.

Health Services Organization

Health services organizations (HSOs) are organized by two or more physicians as a form of group practice. Instead of fee-for-service, physicians receive remuneration on a fixed per capita rate. In this form of practice, the patients are committed to receiving services from the group for a defined period and thus they are "locked-in" and must pay if they seek services elsewhere. The physician receives the same payment for these patients irrespective of the patient's rate of service utilization. It is in the physician's interest to keep their patients as healthy as possible, so they will consume fewer health-care resources. It is assumed that the physician will place greater emphasis on disease prevention and health promotion. At present, this form of organization only exists in Ontario and the US.

Comprehensive Health Organization

A comprehensive health organization (CHO) has a voluntary community board comprised of members from the community and CHO users. It provides a wide range of services such as medical, hospital, home care and other support services under a single unified management. It also provides a comprehensive approach to health including disease prevention and health promotion. Institutional care is replaced, where possible, with ambulatory and community-based care. The CHOs are in some ways similar to health maintenance organizations (HMOs) in the United States. CHOs could receive their funding from health insurance plans on a capitation basis. The physicians are paid by the CHO in a manner mutually agreed upon (fee-for-service, capitation or salary). It is anticipated that in large or medium urban communities, CHOs will serve defined populations of 15,000 people and over. At present there are no formal CHOs, but the Ontario Government is in the process of funding a few pilot CHOs.

3.   SERVICES OF OTHER HEALTH PROFESSIONALS

There are many other health professionals who provide primary health care in their speciality and the major ones are described below:

Nurses Some nurses work along with a physician and provide primary health care under the physician's supervision, while others work independently in community health centres, occupational health services or in remote areas where no physicians are available. They are generally paid by salary. In Canada there are few nurse-practitioners (only a few practise in very remote areas).

Dentists Dental services are provided mainly in offices of the dentists with the help of dental hygienists and to some extent by local public health units or government sponsored clinics. Dentists are mainly paid by fee-for-service through private insurance, public insurance (in some provinces) or individual payment.

Chiropractors Chiropractic services are mainly provided in offices and, to a limited extent, in clinics organized by the Workers' Compensation Board. They are usually paid on a fee-for-service basis, through private insurance, government insurance, or by individuals.

Podiatrists They are similar to chiropractors, in that they mainly work through private offices and few work through either public health units or general hospitals. Their payment mechanism is also similar to chiropractors.

Optometrists They mainly work through private offices or with optical dispensing outlets. Their payment mechanism is similar to chiropractors.

Midwifery It is only recently that a few Canadian provinces (Ontario, Quebec, Alberta and British Colombia) recognized midwifery as a discipline. Their main source of income used to be charges to individual users of their services; however, funding mechanisms through government health insurance plans are being worked out in number of provinces.

Pharmacists They mostly provide their services through privately owned and operated drug stores; non-owner and institution-based pharmacists are usually paid by salary.

Others Physiotherapists, occupational therapists, speech pathologists, audiologists, social workers, nutritionist and clinical psychologists are usually employed by hospitals, home care and public health units, but a number of them are in private practice and are paid for by individuals or private health insurance.

As one can see, there is a range of primary health-care services provided by different professionals. The entry point into the primary health-care system depends upon various factors such as the economic status and education of consumers, their health beliefs, type of health insurance, and the availability and accessibility of services and professionals.

4.   HEALTH-CARE INSTITUTIONS

Major institutions include allied special hospitals, chronic care hospitals, and nursing homes.

4.1.   HOSPITALS

4.1.1.   Characteristics and Functions

The first hospital in Canada, Hôtel Dieu de Preçieux Sang, was established in Quebec City in 1639. Prior to 1850, hospitals were perceived as dirty, infested, crowded, and unpleasant places, staffed by heartless and ignorant attendants, to which people would go only as a last resort. In this period, the overall mortality rate was high (20%). Florence Nightingale, Joseph Lister and others revolutionized hospital care by introducing antisepsis, asepsis, good food, and proper nursing. This reduced mortality from 20% to 2%. By the beginning of this century, hospitals became a place where patients went by choice to be cured.

Today, hospitals are the major centre for health-care activities. Hospitals are institutions that primarily take care of sick people by providing inpatient services, services for many ambulatory patients in out-patient clinics and emergency rooms, and rehabilitation services. In certain cases, they also provide limited public health and home care services. Some large hospitals act as teaching resources for the education of physicians, nurses, and other allied health professionals. Many teaching hospitals are engaged in research activities. In recent years, there has been a trend to broaden the hospital's role to include disease prevention and health promotion.

The Federal-Provincial Task Force has classified institutions based on the type of care they provide: (i) Type 1 is residential care; (ii) Type 2 is extended health care; (iii) Type 3 is chronic care; (iv) Type 4 is special rehabilitative care; and (v) Type 5 is acute care. The classification used by Statistics Canada for hospitals is based on the type of service provided and is as follows:[3] i) General hospitals that provide acute care in the community. These hospitals may have units for long-term care and if they are affiliated with the universities they are called teaching hospitals; ii) Allied special hospitals that provide chronic care such as rehabilitation or extended care or deals with special age groups (pediatrics) or specific conditions (cancer); iii) Nursing homes that are organized residential facilities where some residents receive nursing care by full-time registered or licensed practical nurses. The nursing home either supervises medications and/or provides assistance with three or more activities of daily living, for example, bathing, dressing, walking or eating; and iv) Mental institutions that include mental hospitals dealing with chronic long-term mental illness; psychiatric hospitals and psychiatric units in general hospitals dealing with short-term intensive psychiatric treatment and special facilities for emotionally and mentally challenged patients.

4.1.2. Organization of Hospitals

Hospitals, under the Public Hospital Act, are governed by a voluntary board of trustees. There are various forms of hospital boards and they are in constant evolution. Generally speaking, the majority of board members are not professionals in the health-care field and are either elected or appointed. Recently, physicians practising in the hospital and other hospital employees have also been represented on some hospital boards. The most recent development is the presence of some hospital administrators on the board as voting members, sometimes as office holders. Under provincial legislation, the board of trustees is responsible for the governance of the hospital, subject to compliance with the term of the Public Hospitals Act. The board acts as the agent for the public in assuring proper financial operations and quality of care.

Most hospitals are paid by the provincial government. Payment methods include a) **Global budget** - a prepaid sum is given to the institution, which must cover all costs of services provided; b) **Per diem** - a fee is paid for each day the patient receives care in the institution. The average per-diem cost is entirely artificial and the true cost of care for each day is generally unknown and highly variable (expensive at the beginning of the stay, and cheaper at the end); c) **Per case** - a fee is paid for each case (this system is usually based on the diagnosis, such as diagnostic related groupings or case-mix basis) and may or may not be adjusted for severity; and d) **Line-by-line basis** in which payments are allocated on individual items of expenditures.

Almost all hospitals have a Chief Executive Officer (CEO), President, or Administrator in charge of day-to-day operations and executing policies formulated by the board. Working with the CEO is the Administrator, responsible for day-to-day operations and to whom all personnel report. The Administrator may be supported by one or more assistant administrators, each controlling a functional area (e.g., Medical Director, and Directors of Nursing, Plant and Engineering, Finances and Human Resources).

The Public Hospitals Act requires that the board establish a Professional or Medical Advisory Committee (PAC or MAC). In many hospitals, the PAC has the responsibility for advising on capital purchases of medical equipment, regulation of the professional staff, and similar matters. The PAC is usually chaired by the Chief of Staff/Discipline and consists of chiefs of different medical disciplines, chiefs of other health professional services and a member from the Board of Trustees.

The functional organization of a hospital is illustrated in figure 14.1. The organizational chart covers the whole range of services a hospital may provide; however, not all hospitals provide all services listed here. A hospital's size and teaching status determine the complexity of services available. Large teaching hospitals provide the widest range of services.

In recent years, concerns have been raised by communities with regards to the organization, governance, accountability and functions of public hospitals, which are reflected in a recent document published in Ontario.[4] Specific recommendations in this report were: (i) each hospital develops a social contract with the community in the form of a formal, signed document with a five-year term. The document would be a formal and accountable articulation of the informal understanding which currently exists between many hospitals and the communities they serve; (ii) the contract should be negotiated within a planning framework, and be facilitated by the district health council or other designated body. It should stipulate the types of programs and services which the hospital has agreed to provide the community. It is seen as a means of improving the accountability and responsibility of Ontario's hospital system. Changes in the social contract or hospital programs would necessitate approval by the Ministry of Health; (iii) the special status of the medical staff of hospitals in governance should be eliminated, such that they would be responsible to the CEO on an equal basis as other health professionals and not separately represented on the Board; (iv) hospital boards should be constituted to reflect the community, include a broad spectrum of skills, have meetings and decision making more open to the public and exclude health professionals from the board. Boards should develop mission statements and engage in long-term planning. It would be the board's responsibility to monitor the social contract and fiscal policy. A number of advisory committees to the board representing the community, professionals and employees should be constituted.

4.1.3. Organization of Staff in Hospitals
Physicians play pivotal role in terms of hospital utilization. They admit patients, decide what tests and/or treatments are needed, and how long patients stay. In most Canadian hospitals, physicians are not employees but users of hospital facilities for their patients. Physicians are said to have "privileges" at a certain hospital but are not paid by the hospital. However, this is not the case for radiologists, pathologists, and a few other specialists such as emergency room physicians.

Hospital Privileges Typically, a physician requests the privilege of admitting patients to a general hospital, and expects to be responsible not only for their care but also for patients referred by other doctors. The board screens the physician's qualifications and confirms the hospital's need for another physician. Granting of admitting privileges to physicians is based on impact analysis, which considers the following: the potential number of patients physicians would attract to the hospital with their specialized skills, the drain on hospital resources through their activities, the ability of a physician's reputation to enhance the hospital's prestige, and the number of physicians providing the same or similar services. The board may reject the application or grant full or partial privileges, perhaps with some conditions (e.g., a general practitioner may not be allowed to do major surgery). Appointments are usually made for one year. Once physicians become members of the medical staff, in addition to the right and responsibility of looking after any patients they admit, they undertake certain responsibilities to the hospital. Medical staff members may be required to provide service in the emergency room in

Figure 14.1: Functional Organization of a Hospital

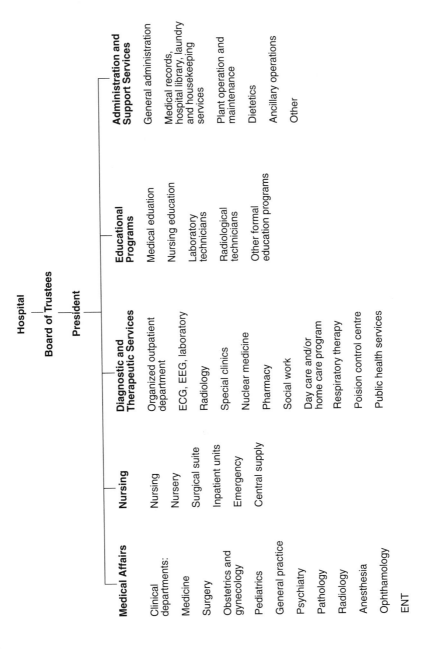

Source: Adapted from Agnew G. Harvey: Canadian Hospitals 1920-1970. University of Toronto Press, 1974.

rotation, serve on committees, maintain and give final approval to hospital medical records, attend staff meetings and abide by any rules and regulations passed by the medical advisory committee or hospital board.

The medical staff is expected to be self-governing and self-disciplining through peer review and a wide variety of devices which have evolved between medical staff and boards, and in some cases, governments. The most common devices are organizational in nature. For example, it is now assumed that every hospital should have a Chief of Staff, who is usually a respected senior doctor, for each medical and surgical discipline. They are responsible for ensuring the quality of care delivered. Formerly, the Chiefs of Staff exercised their influence by example or persuasion. Lately, legislation in some jurisdictions gives the Chief authority to relieve a physician of a case if it is obvious that the physician is not giving adequate or proper care to the patients.

In addition, it is common practice for hospitals to set up a series of committees charged with responsibility for monitoring the hospital's functioning. Some of these are the Admission and Discharge (or Utilization), and Medical Records and Tissue Committees. Recently, quite sophisticated data processors can automatically examine performance in terms of established norms (e.g., How many cases admitted with a diagnosis of pneumonia had appropriate bacteriological work done? How many had antibiotic sensitivity tests?) For most provinces, this type of monitoring is done on a collective basis by the Hospital Medical Records Institute (HMRI).

5.   PUBLIC HEALTH SERVICES

Since 1961, there had been a rapid growth in public health services at the provincial and local levels of government; however, with recent fiscal constraints services are now curtailed. All provincial governments maintain departments responsible for public health matters and divide geographical regions into health units. Since metropolitan areas have a high population density, they have their own health units; some large cities possess several. For example, Metropolitan Toronto has six health units. Health units are semi-autonomous, form liaisons with local hospitals, medical practitioners, and voluntary health agencies, and they have their own buildings and staff, except in Quebec. The Province of Quebec has been divided into 18 Regional Boards of Health and Social Services which have a Director of Public Health who has the following functions: i) assessment of the health needs of the population and development of most effective preventive interventions; ii) surveillance and control of communicable and noncommunicable diseases; iii) dealing with real or perceived public health emergencies and iv) developing an expertise in health promotion and disease prevention. The public health director works closely with the local community services centres and other regional health and social services agencies.

Most health units are directed by health boards; its members are usually appointed by provincial and/or local municipalities. These boards determine the overall direction of programs and policies. The board is assisted by an executive administrator or medical officer of health (MOH) who is responsible for the daily administration of programs. The MOH advises the local board of health and is not only responsible for public health duties but also for evaluating the health status of the community. In order to plan, coordinate and evaluate community health programs and services, they work with a multi-professional health team and collaborate with other health and social agencies, both official and voluntary. Thus, the role of the MOH is usually that of health administrator and coordinator of community health matters. In some parts of the country, however, the medical officer of health is employed as a consultant only for medical matters such as communicable diseases and screening programs. The administration in this case is then carried out by a qualified health administrator.

Despite the rhetoric of increased emphasis on disease prevention and health promotion, less than three per cent of total health-care funding is devoted to local health units. The major portion of funding for local health units comes from the provincial government with some funding from local government, except in Alberta, where total funding is from the provincial government. With these financial arrangements, local governments have retained autonomy in policy and program planning while following provincial guidelines. The lack of uniformity in services provided across the province is compensated by assessment and fulfilment of the local needs.

5.1.   THE FUNCTIONS OF PUBLIC HEALTH UNITS

The mandate of the local health units stem from the Public Health Acts or regulations passed by the provincial legislature. For example the document *Mandatory Health Programs and Services Guidelines in Ontario*[5] outlines standards for public health services in general and lists the goals and objectives for specific programs. Local governments also have some authority to pass bylaws related to health (e.g., bylaws regulating noise levels and smoking in public places). The extent of services actually provided depends on the provincial Public Health Act and the number of qualified personnel employed by each agency in relation to the population. Because of a shortage of some categories of public health personnel, many rural agencies are unable to employ a full complement of staff. In addition to mandated activities, local health authorities, especially in urban areas, have expanded into many new health fields outside their traditional role. Foremost among these are health promotion, mental health, services for the aged and disabled, and issues related to the physical environment.

Communicable Disease Control

The control of communicable disease continues to be a basic function of health units. Their duties include disease surveillance, the provision of consultation services to local physicians and hospitals, the provision of immunizing agents, health education, special epidemiological surveys and studies. The enforcement of acts and regulations give the authority for the control of communicable disease. Health units are responsible for the investigation and management of communicable disease outbreaks such as food poisoning in nursing homes, measles outbreaks in schools, and diarrheal outbreaks in day care centres. Local health units operate sexually transmitted disease (STD) clinics which provide free diagnostic and treatment services at convenient hours. In some areas, these units pay private physicians to give free and anonymous treatment. Local health units are involved in case-finding, follow-up of contacts and health education programs for STDs. They also provide contraception and family planning services.

Maternal and Child Health, and Women's Health

In recent years, traditional maternal and child health divisions in public health units in many provinces have been renamed and expanded in their functions, with more focus on family and women's health. They are called by different names in different provinces, but they have similar functions. Public health nurses employed by local health units carry out preventive health programs such as education and immunization of infants and children in clinics. The maternal and child health services may include classes for expectant parents, postnatal visits to all or high-risk new parents, advice on parenting, and visits to day care centres. Immunization of children is a statutory program in public health units in Alberta and Prince Edward Island, whereas immunization is shared by private physicians and health units in other provinces. Alberta also has comprehensive preschool surveillance programs (screening for growth and development) which cover about 90% of children.

In many provinces, health services for school children are provided by health units; however, in others the local education authority or private practitioners may provide this service. The type of school health services varies considerably across Canada and the provision of services by the larger city departments may differ from that found in a rural health unit. Vision screening tests and immunization programs have become standard practice in most local areas, while audiometric screening is discretionary in urban areas. It is the public health nurse who provides continuity for the health surveillance of school children, and who maintains contact with the parents and family doctor.

Women's health services range from involvement in breast screening programs, genetic services, family violence and health-care needs of immigrant, refugee and racial minority women.

Health Promotion

There has been a shift in emphasis of programs provided by public health units from communicable disease control toward health promotion, community development and health advocacy. Health promotion as a separate discipline has been receiving increasing recognition. Strategies include educational methods to improve knowledge and skills, encouragement of public participation in health practices conducive to healthy living, and the creation of environments supportive of health by public policy. Many local health departments employ health promotion specialists. Their responsibility includes continually assessing the health needs of their community, coordinating local health promotion services and consulting with personnel in the voluntary and civic organizations interested in health. Public health nursing is involved in implementing and planning health promotion strategies. Community development workers may help communities become mobilized against a public health problem. For example, they can provide information on second hand smoke and its effects on health, enabling citizens to bring about the necessary environmental changes through political or legislative processes. Nutrition consultants prepare reference and educational materials for professional health personnel and for the public. Examples of health promotion programs include the Heart Health Programs in most provinces, and the City of Toronto programs aimed specifically at groups such as recent immigrants, refugees, visible minorities, and the homeless. Health promotion programs provide education in schools on smoking, alcohol, drugs, AIDS, sex, and nutrition. The extent of the diffusion of the innovative approach of health promotion in public health units has, however, not been evaluated. Some academic health promotion units, such as the Centre for Health Promotion at the University of Toronto, have developed affiliations with Public Health Units to promote basic research in the discipline of health promotion and its application.

Dental Health

Public health initiatives such as fluoridation of municipal water supplies and improved dental hygiene have successfully reduced dental caries in Canadian children. Public health has now focused on provision of dental treatment to underprivileged groups. Dental health divisions of provincial ministries, in collaboration with local health units, have sponsored the provision of dental care for children in remote areas. Travelling clinics staffed by provincial dental teams are employed in Manitoba, Nova Scotia, Ontario, and Prince Edward Island to visit rural and remote areas. These clinics deliver a considerable amount of emergency care for all age groups. A program subsidizing dental expenses in communities lacking a resident dentist has been developed in British Columbia, while in rural Alberta, dentists who volunteer to supply services on a private practice basis for short periods are provided with dental equipment, office facilities and living accommodation. In some provinces, the Dental Health Division of the Provincial Health Department administers school dental programs. This responsibility may be delegated either to the department of education or to the board of health, particularly in cities.

In all of these models, dentists or dental hygienists are employed to carry out functions such as case-finding, education, prevention and treatment. Such services are generally provided to preschool children or up to grade one or two. Treatment services are offered primarily to children from lower income groups.

Environmental Health

Public health inspectors hired by local health units protect the public from physical, chemical and biological hazards. This is carried out through the inspection of food handling premises such as restaurants, butcher shops and bakeries. Public health inspectors are responsible for community sanitation such as the maintenance of sanitary supplies of potable water, milk and food, disposal of wastes and the quality of recreational water. They also respond to public complaints and emergency situations such as spills of toxic chemicals. In some of the larger cities indoor air pollution monitoring is carried out by public health units. As the environmental agenda widens, a number of health units have hired environmental specialists to do environmental risk assessments and provide consultation for their staff.

6.   HOME CARE

The new trend in health care is community-based rather than hospital-based care. Although currently a small percentage of provincial health budgets is allocated to home care, many believe that it should be expanded as a cost-effective alternative to institutionalized care.

6.1.   HISTORY

Until early in this century, the rich were cared for at home while the poor, homeless or indigent were treated in hospitals.[6] With the emergence of provincial and national health insurance plans and the resulting expansion in the institutional sector, home care functions were transferred to hospitals and nursing homes. However, this pattern has gradually been reversing itself in the past 20 years. In most provinces, provision of home care services began with smaller, urban programs run through agencies such as the Victorian Order of Nurses.[7] With rising hospital costs and pressure on hospital facilities, home care programs were developed, mainly to unload hospital patients who only needed additional nursing services or physiotherapy. Comprehensive, government-oriented home care plans were developed by some provinces in the 1970s. In 1977 the Established Program Financing legislation provided the first concrete financial support for alternative health-care programs. Now all provinces and territories have government home care directorates or divisions, although they lack a common approach to funding and delivery.

6.2.   TYPES OF HOME CARE

Different basic forms of home care are described below:
Maintenance and Preventive Home support services (such as homemaker, transportation and meals-on-wheels programs) provide autonomy and mobility when needed to compensate for assessed functional deficits.   The services are not primarily medical, although they may be provided along with medical treatment. Although most clients can remain at home without the help of these services for some time, early use of the services can prevent health decline and institutionalization.
Long-Term Care Substitution or Chronic Care Services These services are provided to clients with significant functional deficits, usually resulting from one or more medical conditions, who require these services in order to remain in their homes.   Chronic care services are designed to maintain clients with stable conditions, or to delay deterioration and thus institutionalization.
Acute Care Substitution Acute home care is usually provided after an episode of hospitalization to people who are unable to travel to outpatient facilities, and it is provided on a short-term basis according to need.   This form of home care is designed to reduce the length of the patient's stay in the hospital and to assist the recovery process. Clients usually receive acute home care for two or three days to a maximum of 90 days.

One of the most innovative programs exists in New Brunswick and is known as the "Extra-Mural Hospital," or "Hospital Without Walls." This program is administered free of charge to a case load equivalent to that of a 200-bed hospital. Services provided include a range of palliative and acute care services such as nursing, physiotherapy, intravenous medication, nutritional counselling, respiratory care oxygen therapy, and sick room equipment. Meals-on-wheels, homemaking and other support services can be purchased by the client. In order to receive these services, the client must be formally admitted by an attending physician who directs the client's medical care plan and authorizes discharge. The client also must be acutely but not critically ill, and must require one or more professional services such as nursing, occupational therapy or physiotherapy.
Paliative home care This care is provided to terminally ill patients such as those with AIDS and cancer. The care is provided by a multidisciplinary team at home. This is further discussed in chapter 16.

6.3.   FUNDING AND DELIVERY

Most home care programs are characterized by two features: centralization of control of services within the program, and ongoing coordination of services to meet the changing needs of the patient.   In some provinces, the provincial department of health plays an active role in the financing and administration of home care programs, while in other provinces, local agencies, municipalities and hospitals assume the major responsibility for home care.   However, with the Established Program Financing Act of 1977, home care services became associated with local public health units in some provinces.

At present, spending on home care programs accounts for approximately $1 billion, or less than 2% of total expenditures on the Canadian health system.   Most provincial home care programs are funded by the government, but some charge user fees, often based on the ability to pay.   For example, in British Columbia all public home care programs are fully or partially funded by the Continuing Care Division of the Health Ministry.   Home care services such as Case Management, Home Nursing Care and Community Rehabilitation are provided to those who qualify at no charge, while Homemaker Services charges clients using income testing.[8]

7.   SERVICES FOR MENTAL ILLNESS

Among provincially operated health services, mental health activities represent one of the largest administrative areas in terms of expenditure and employees. In every province at least 88% (nationally, 96%) of the revenue towards mental institutions is provided by the provincial government or the provincial insurance plan.   For the past four decades there has been a gradual shift of provision of mental health services from institutions to community-based services.   The mental health services are provided in the following sites depending on the nature and the severity of illness: mental institutions, psychiatric units of general hospitals, special hospitals, private hospitals, clinics, mental health-care centres, private practitioners such as psychiatrists, family physicians, clinical psychologists, social workers, half way houses, and sheltered workshops

Community mental health facilities are being extended beyond mental institutions to provide greater continuity of care, to deal with incipient breakdown, and to rehabilitate patients in the community.   Psychiatric units in general hospitals contribute by integrating psychiatry with other medical care and making it available to patients in their own community.   Hospital psychiatric units admit approximately 48% of total admissions to all kinds of mental institutions.   Inpatient services in psychiatric units are paid for by all provincial hospital insurance plans. Some provinces have small regional psychiatric hospitals to facilitate patient access to treatment and complete integration of medical services. Day-care centres, allowing patients to be hospitalized during the day and return home at night, have been organized across the country. Community mental health clinics (some provincially operated, others municipally) and psychiatric outpatient services have been developed in all provinces. Under the Canada Assistance Plan and Extended Care Program several provinces are arranging for boarding home care, with the federal government sharing the cost of maintaining needy patients in such homes.

Specialized rehabilitation services assist former patients to function optimally and are operated by mental hospitals and community agencies. They include sheltered workshops that pay for work and provide training, and halfway houses in which patients can live and continue to receive treatment while becoming settled in a job. At present, there is a large gap in available community services for mental health patients with a shortage of housing, jobs, recreational facilities and mental health workers.

Facilities for mentally challenged persons include day training schools or classes, summer camps and sheltered workshops as well as residential care in institutions and community group homes. These facilities provide for social, academic and vocational training. Some are able to profit from academic education; some can only attain self care; many are taught manual skills in training school workshops; and some are placed in jobs in the community. Emotionally disturbed children with personality or behaviour disorders are treated at hospital units, community clinics, child guidance clinics and other outpatient facilities.

Addiction to licit and illicit drugs and alcohol afflict at least 2% - 5% of adult Canadians. It is treated in hospitals, outpatient clinics, hostels, long-term residences or special farms and facilities. Official and voluntary agencies conduct public education programs, treatment, rehabilitation and research. Among these agencies are Alcoholics Anonymous, the Alcoholism Foundation of British Columbia, l'Office de la prevention et du treatment de l'alcoolisme et des autres toxicomanies in Quebec, the Alcoholism Foundation of Manitoba and the Nova Scotia Alcoholism Research Foundation. Community treatment programs have been established under the aegis of the Narcotic Addiction Foundation of British Columbia and the Ontario Addiction Research Foundation, supported primarily by provincial funds. Overall there is a lack of available services for addiction.

8. SERVICES FOR CANCER PATIENTS

More than one in three Canadians will get cancer in his/her lifetime; most will be diagnosed in the middle and later years of life. Special provincial agencies for cancer control, usually in the health ministry or a separate cancer institute, carry out cancer detection and treatment, public education and professional training and research, in cooperation with local public health services, physicians and the voluntary Canadian Cancer Society branches. Although the provisions are not uniform, cancer programs in all provinces provide a range of free diagnostic and treatment services to both outpatients and inpatients. Hospital insurance benefits for cancer patients include diagnostic radiology, laboratory tests and radiotherapy. A number of provinces such as British Columbia and Ontario have organized screening programs for breast cancer.

The lack of uniform provision of services, however, results in differences in community cancer services between provinces and between communities. This can result in a lack of coordination of treatment and less than optimal dissemination of cancer treatment knowledge and information from the major centres.[9] The recommendations of the National Conference on Community Cancer Programs called for a survey of existing cancer services in Canada and ongoing evaluation of the efficiency and quality of cancer care.

9.   SERVICES FOR THE PHYSICALLY AND MENTALLY CHALLENGED

Social and support services are available in the community for challenged persons vary depending on the location of the community and the nature and type of disability. Overall, rural communities have sparse services whereas metropolitan areas are endowed with a full range of services. Persons with rare or very severe disability have fewer resources available for their care in the community. Medical and institutional care such as long-term care in hospitals, extended care, rehabilitation care and nursing home care, as well as many assistive devices for daily living, are available through either government insurance or subsidies. Most communities have home care programs available for persons with disability. There are two types of voluntary agencies which deal with the disabled: one exclusively deals with persons with a specific disease or problem (e.g., the Multiple Sclerosis Society); others deal with specific groups with a disability (e.g., the Easter Seal Society, which deals with children with physical disabilities). Depending on the disability, many voluntary agencies also provide a range of services such as meals-on-wheels, visiting homemakers services, travelling clinics, provision of appliances and equipment, and wheelchairs. At the social service level, there are income maintenance programs, recreational programs, vocational rehabilitation services, special transportation services and independent living accommodations available for the disabled.

10. VOLUNTARY AGENCIES

Voluntary organizations have played an important part in shaping our health, welfare and educational systems. These are non-profit organizations operating under boards of volunteers rather than under the direct control of the government. Their primary or major objectives are the promotion of health, the prevention of illness or disability and the identification, treatment or rehabilitation of persons suffering from disease or disability. Voluntary organizations differ in the nature of their membership: some are organized by citizens to provide service to others and are designated as citizen-member organizations. The more recent ones are organized by patients, their relatives or their friends to provide services for themselves, and hence are designated patient-member organizations. The citizen-member organization is the familiar form of philanthropy. Its members are interested in community service and thus are motivated to give time, thought and money to accomplish an objective which will promote the welfare of their community. Patient-member organizations are motivated by mutual aid. Those who suffer from a disease for which there is now no known cure, or from a disability which causes them to be different from, and even shunned, by other people, often become isolated and withdrawn, or seek the company of fellow sufferers. They are faced with anxieties and frustration from which they find some relief by uniting to fight their common enemy, the disease. The patients may be able to help themselves in specific ways (e.g., by organizing better treatment facilities) or they may hope to help other sufferers, including their own families if the disease is hereditary. Support is gained from the knowledge that they are not alone in facing their problems. Recently some have taken an advocacy role, e.g., AIDS groups. Voluntary organizations are financed to a considerable extent, if not wholly, by fundraising. The organization may conduct its own campaign for funds, or be a member of a federated fund. Many of the agencies also receive public grants.

10.1. OBJECTIVES AND ACTIVITIES

Generally, the objectives and activities of many of these organizations are as follows:[10] (a) Education: Public education and dissemination of information to lay and professional people. (b) Advocacy: Social action, sometimes specified, sometimes implied. (c) Research: The collection of statistics, the investigation of reported "cures," surveys of resources and needs, encouragement and support for basic and clinical research. (d) Direct patient services: Volunteer agencies supply diagnostic and treatment clinics, special equipment (e.g., wheelchairs, crutches, colostomy bags, hoists, inhalation tents, prosthetic appliances), transportation and accommodation for patient and family, home treatment, therapies, vocational assessment and workshops. Sometimes voluntary health organizations take on official functions (for example, the Childrens Aid Society). They also provide many services needed by society, including blood transfusion services, eye banks and first aid. (e) Prevention: The prevention and eradication of the disease or disability. (f) Coordination of key players: The coordination of public and private agencies with similar interests (h) Fundraising.

10.2. ROLE IN RELATION TO GOVERNMENT

Voluntary agencies continually identify new areas of need and provide for those needs to the limit of their capacity. This capacity is related directly to their ability to raise money and in some cases the needs are met only in a token fashion. Nevertheless, the organizations often are able to impress upon the public's mind the importance of the services they provide and occasionally change the public's sensitivity to needs (e.g., the Canadian Mental Health Association's exposé of mental hospitals as tawdry, overcrowded and desolate places for patients). With increasing affluence and heightened social conscience, our governments have recognized that many of these initiatives are maintained by fundamental citizen needs and have funded or taken over the responsibilities of many volunteer organizations' services. In practice then, the functions of voluntary organizations and the government in the health field are intermingled to such an extent that little differentiation in function can be discerned.

10.3. SCOPE OF WORK

Examples of our commonly known national voluntary organizations are listed below:

(i) The Canadian Red Cross Society was established to furnish volunteer aid to the sick and wounded of armies in time of war, in accordance with the Treaty of Geneva; in time of peace or war, to carry on and assist in work for the improvement of health, the prevention of disease and the mitigation of suffering throughout the world. Activities include blood transfusion services, veterans' services, international relief, emergency services, water safety services, Red Cross Youth, and Red Cross Corps.

(ii) The Canadian Cancer Society was established in 1938 to coordinate individuals and agencies to reduce the mortality from cancer in Canada; to disseminate information on cancer; and to research activities about cancer.

Local volunteer groups include the local chapters of larger organizations as well as volunteer organizations that meet special needs in the community. These include volunteer groups working in hospitals, nursing homes and crisis centres.

Voluntary agencies have adapted to the changing needs of society. For example, what was once known as the Canadian Tuberculosis Association has changed its name and mandate, with the decreasing incidence of tuberculosis to the Canadian Tuberculosis and Respiratory Disease Association. Its Ontario chapter calls itself the Ontario Lung Association and focuses on all lung diseases. Voluntary health organizations fulfill an important role in shaping our health-care system and will continue to do so.

11. SELF-HELP GROUPS

People join together in groups for companionship, mutual assistance and the exchange of problem-solving skills. The obvious example of the self-help concept is the family, a small group where socialization, identification and support originate. Self-help efforts are also evident in collective enterprises such as food or housing cooperatives, tenants' associations and civil rights groups. But groups also exist for those who have a common personal concern, such as a physical disability or an addiction. Romeder et al[11] defines self-help groups as follows: They are small, autonomous and open groups that meet regularly. Members share common experiences of suffering and meet each other as equals. The primary activity of these groups is personal mutual aid, a form of social support that focuses on the sharing of experiences, information and ways of coping. In addition to personal change, members often engage in activities directed to social change. Group activities are voluntary and essentially free. Alcoholics Anonymous, established in 1935, has been the model for the development of other self-help groups (e.g., Narcotics Anonymous, Schizophrenics Anonymous). In some cases, there is already a national or international body of self-help groups focused on a given concern and this may offer consultative and public relations support to new self-help groups or associations. Self-help groups usually attract members between 30 and 50 years of age, from the middle class or a common educational level or socioeconomic status. For many people with many types of difficulties, such groups can be very effective in coping with personal pressures. The major activities of these groups include group meetings, sponsorship of new members, educational activities for their members and the general public and advocating for change. Apart from these general services, activities are as diverse as the groups themselves. They include home or hospital visits to the sufferer, hot lines, newsletters and brochures, public conferences, fairs, advocacy, recreational activities, and material aid (sitter services, transportation, and exchange of goods).

12. SUMMARY

The delivery of health care at the local level is provided through a spectrum of services. These health services include primary care, secondary care, hospital care, home care, public health services and private nursing homes. The funding sources for these services are varied. Although in every province basic hospital and medical services are provided under the government health insurance plans, there is a variability in what is provided either through public or private insurance.

Primary health care is that service provided at the first contact between the patient and the health professional. Secondary care is usually delivered by specialized manpower using specialized resources. Patients usually enter secondary care after referral from primary care. Tertiary care requires very specialized facilities and professional skills. Primary medical care is provided mainly by general or family practioners in their offices on a fee-for-service basis. The majority of physicians bill for most of their services through provincial health insurance plans. Apart from the physician, there are a number of other groups of health professionals who provide primary health care (dentists, nurses, chiropractors, optometrists, podiatrists, pharmacists and physiotherapists).

Today, hospitals are the major centre for health-care services. They provide in-patient services, services for ambulatory patients in out-patient clinics, emergency rooms and rehabilitation services. Hospitals are classified on the basis of the kind of the service they provide.

Hospitals are governed by a voluntary board of trustees, which is in constant evolution. Non-health care professionals board members now include health administrators and physicians. Most hospitals are paid by the provincial government for the services they render. Most hospitals have a CEO, President, or Administrator who is in charge of day-to-day operations and executes policies formulated by the board. Most physicians are seen as "users" of hospitals via hospital privileges rather than as "employees" of the hospital.

Health units are semi-autonomous in nature and form liaisons with local hospitals, medical practitioners, and voluntary health agencies. The functions of the health units depend on the mandate provided by the provincial public health act and funding. The control of communicable disease continues to be a basic function of local health units. As well, they are involved in maternal and child health services, health promotion, dental health and environmental health.

Recently, there has been an increasing emphasis on home care. The range of services delivered by the home care programs varies from nursing services alone to a complete array of health and social services. There are three basic forms of home care: the maintenance and preventive model, the long-term care substitution model and the acute care substitution model. Most provincial home care programs are funded by the government, but some charge user fees, often based on the ability to pay.

Mental health activities represent one of the largest administrative areas in terms of expenditure and employees. Community mental health facilities are being extended beyond mental institutions to provide greater continuity of care, deal with incipient breakdown and rehabilitate patients in the community. Currently funding is not adequate to meet the needs of de-institutionilized patients.

Social and support services available in the community for persons with disability depends on the location of the community and the nature and type of disability. Most communities have home care programs available for persons with disability.

Voluntary organizations have played and continue to play an important part in shaping our health, welfare and educational systems. These are non-profit organizations operating under boards of volunteers. Their primary or major objectives are the promotion of health, the prevention of illness or disability and the identification, treatment or rehabilitation of persons suffering from disease or disability.

Self-help groups are small autonomous and open groups that meet regularly. As a result of personal crisis or chronic problems, members share common experiences of suffering and meet each others as equals. The primary activity of these groups is personal mutual aid, a form of social support that focuses on the sharing of experiences, information and ways of coping.

13. REFERENCES

1. *Ontario Health Planning Task Force Report.* Government of Ontario, Toronto, 1974.
2. Tonkin R. Primary Health Care. *Can J Public Health* 67(4):289-294, 1976.
3. *Canadian Hospital Directory 1989-1990.* Volume 37. Canadian Hospital Association, 1989.
4. *Into The 21st Century Ontario Public Hospitals* Report of the Steering Committee. Public Hospitals Act Review. Ministry of Health, Government of Ontario, Toronto, 1992.
5. *Mandatory Health Program and Services Guidelines.* Ministry of Health, Government of Ontario, Toronto, 1989.
6. Home-Based Care, the Elderly, the Family, and the Welfare State: An International Comparison. Ottawa: University of Ottawa Press, 1993.
7. Health Services and Promotion Branch, Health and Welfare Canada. *Report on Home Care.* Ministry of Supply and Services, Canada, Ottawa, 1990.
8. Government of Canada. Federal Provincial/Territorial Subcommittee on Continuing Care. *Description of Long-Term Care Services in Provinces and Territories of Canada.* Health Services Directorate, Health Services and Promotion Branch, Health and Welfare Canada, Ottawa, 1991.
9. Osoba D. Recommendations of the National Conference on Community Cancer Programs: A Vision for the Future. *Can Med Assoc J* 144(11):1433-1436, 1991.
10. Govan E, ed. *Royal Commission on Health Services, Voluntary Health Organizations in Canada.* Ottawa: Ontario Queen's Printer, 1966.
11. Canadian Council on Social Development. *The Self-Help Way, Mutual Aid and Health.* Ottawa, Ontario. 1989.

CHAPTER FIFTEEN
Resources and Expenditures

Canadians are spending an increasing amount of their country's gross national product (GNP) on health care. The gross national product is a measure of the market value of all final goods and services produced in a specified period by Canadians. For example, in 1960, Canada spent 5.3% of GNP on health care whereas in 1990, it spent 9.54% of the GNP or $61,753 million. It has been estimated that Canada's health-care system spends $1 million dollars every 7 1/2 minutes or $193 million every day. Provinces are also allocating up to one-third of their total budget to health and this stretches their available resources. It is one of the most expensive publicly financed health systems in the world. In recent years, one of the major concerns of the federal and provincial governments has been how to restrain costs in the health sector. Questions have been raised about the type of health resources, the effectiveness and efficiency of health resources utilization, the amount of health expenditures and the need for an alternative delivery system. To answer these questions, one must know the characteristics, functions and distribution of major health resources and the process and determinants of resource utilization, health expenditures, and the type of services produced. Most experts believe that the fundamental financial problems in the health-care system are neither due to underfunding nor overspending, but rather poorly distributed and misdirected spending and ineffectively managed resources.

This chapter: (i) considers the process and determinants of resource utilization; (ii) describes the institutions and human health resources that account for much of this expenditure; (iii) presents the expenditures on these resources for health care; and (iv) reviews current, and anticipated, initiatives in Canada that are directed towards achieving greater productivity for the enormous investment in the health sector.

1.   DETERMINANTS OF RESOURCE UTILIZATION

The utilization of resources is a very complex subject and only the most salient features will be described here. Resource utilization is dependent on several factors:

Figure 15.1: The Point of Entry in the Health Care System

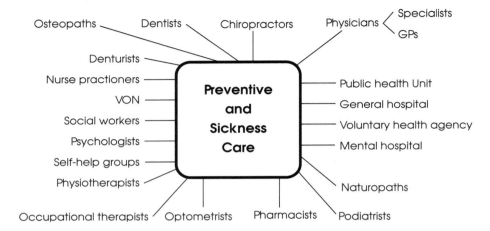

- availability of resources: for example, the ratio of health professionals to population, hours of work per person, the type and nature of health professional mix, and the number and type of hospital beds per 1,000 population;
- general characteristics of the community such as age distribution, housing quality, economic development and level of sanitation which affect the need for services;
- personal factors affecting usage of services such as attitudes, age, sex, family size, marital status, health insurance coverage, education, income, and perceived need for care.
- system characteristics: points of entry in the health-care system, accessibility of resources, cost and barriers to care.

The impact that the points of entry in the health-care system have on the utilization is described below. As described in the previous chapter, there are many entry points to the health-care system (figure 15.1). With provincial and private health insurance plans (dental, drug, and private duty nursing), there are relatively few financial barriers at these entry points. Services of psychologists, social workers, dentists, denturists and nurse practitioners in private practice (except those in northern areas) are less commonly "covered," making these entry points more costly to the consumer, if not to the health-care system. The majority of the population, however, receive their primary care through general/family practitioners and go to specialized resources upon referral by their physicians.

It should be noted that current health-care systems are heavily oriented to the treatment of illness. At present, there is little effective coordination of specialized care within and between hospitals. Arrangements for coordinating services between primary and specialized care are poorly developed in most parts of the

Figure 15.2: Patient Progress Through System

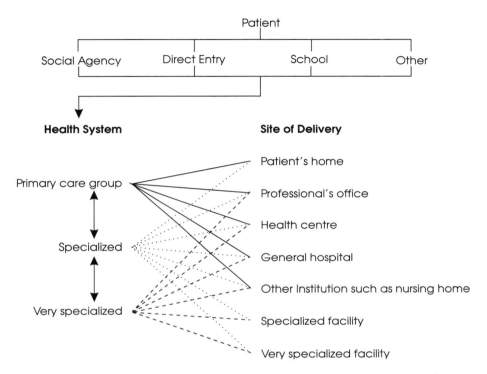

Source: Report of the Health Planning Task Force (Ontario) 1974.

country. Our present system allows patients direct access to primary or secondary care depending on their proximity to, and knowledge about, resources and their attitudes toward the system. The ideal, espoused by many health planners, is a linear progression by the patient from primary to secondary to tertiary care resources as required (figure 15.2). This ideal would be difficult to achieve in the present health-care system unless its organization and payment system are drastically reorganized.

The two major resources needed for the provision of health care are institutions and health personnel. Their distributions and utilization are discussed below.

1.1.   TYPE OF SERVICES PRODUCED BY RESOURCE UTILIZATION

The ultimate aim of the health-care industry is to produce good health. Expenditure on health care is currently minimal for prevention such as immunization against certain diseases. As mentioned earlier, the measurement of health is difficult. Measurement of sickness care has two dimensions.

- Outcome measurement: Improvement, no improvement, deterioration or death all constitute different measurable outcomes of sickness. Except for death, other measures may be subjective. The outcome can also result from factors other than health services. Hence, outcome measurement is not always possible even though it is preferred by many health planners.
- Utilization measurement: It is easier, though ultimately less useful, to measure the type and amount of resources used rather than their effects on the patient. Utilization or process measurements are very commonly used. Utilization measurement assumes that utilization has a positive effect on the outcome.

2.   INSTITUTIONAL RESOURCES

The most expensive health resources are the institutions as they are both technology- and human-resource intensive. The different types of health institutions have been described in the previous chapter.

2.1.   INSTITUTIONAL RESOURCES

In 1990, Canada had approximately 1,239 general, allied, special, private and governmental hospitals with a capacity of roughly 178,541 beds. Public hospitals accounted for 88% of all hospitals and 96% of the beds.[1] Of the public hospitals, 76% of the approved beds were in general hospitals and 11% were in extended care hospitals, with the rest distributed among psychiatric, pediatric and rehabilitation hospitals. There were 51 separate mental institutions with 13,614 beds. The long-term care centres include homes for special care, nursing homes, homes for the aged, and community care facilities. There is a lack of standardization across the country in nomenclature defining the long-term care centre. In 1991, there were 6,068 long-term care centres with a total bed capacity of 237,165.[2] Almost all general and chronic hospitals and the majority of nursing homes are publicly owned. Most mental institutions are owned by provincial governments.

For every 1,000 Canadians in 1989-90, there were 6.8 beds in institutions (3.8 for short-term care, 2.3 for long-term care and 0.7 in mental institutions) and 8.8 beds in homes for special care (including homes for the aged and the mentally retarded). These bed capacities per 1,000 population are among the highest in Western nations. Of course, interprovincial variations exist within each category. This may be explained more by the wide dispersion of the population than by morbidity patterns: the small, scattered nursing stations in remote and rural areas, each having a few beds, results in overall more beds per 1,000 population although the number of actual bed days per patient is less than the Canadian average. Quebec and Ontario have the lowest bed capacity for short-term beds, Saskatchewan the highest. Quebec, Alberta and British Columbia have the highest long-term rated bed capacity, and the Maritime provinces and the Territories the lowest.

For mental institutions, the rated bed capacity in Canada is 0.5 per 1,000 persons; Manitoba, New Brunswick, and Newfoundland are significantly above this, and Saskatchewan, Nova Scotia and Alberta somewhat below. The de-institutionalization of mental patients to return them to community-based living have resulted in a decline in bed capacity.

For special care facilities, the rated bed capacity was 8.8 per 1,000 population in Canada in 1991. These special care facilities include nursing homes, and homes for the aged, mentally or physically handicapped, and others with a minimum of four beds, providing nursing, custodial or counselling services (but not active treatment). There is great disparity among the provinces, from 12.0 beds per 1,000 population in Saskatchewan and 16.9 in Prince Edward Island to 5.4 in Quebec. Newfoundland, Yukon, and Northwest Territories all have rates below the Canadian average, possibly because of their age structures. However, federal-provincial financial arrangements prior to 1977, which did not include extended care, may have contributed to the problem. The newer financing arrangements including a per capita grant for extended care, have led to partial rectification of the problem.

2.2. UTILIZATION MEASUREMENTS FOR INSTITUTIONAL CARE

In the 1988-89 fiscal year, the number of hospitalization days (or patient days as they are commonly called) in Canadian general and allied special hospitals reached about 47 million. This represents a rate of 1.8 days per capita. The average length of hospital stay for 1988-89 was 10.9 days. British Columbia and Quebec stood clearly above the Canadian average of patient days, partly because of their relatively larger number of available short-term beds (empty hospital beds tend to be filled), and also because of the relative isolation of their populations. Prince Edward Island and the Territories had rates considerably below average.

Similarly, one may look at hospital separation rates per 1,000 population, which also were quite variable among the provinces. In 1989-90, the national rate was 133 per 1,000, ranging from 94 in the Northwest Territories to 209 in Saskatchewan. There was a definite downward trend in hospital admissions per 1,000 population from 1974 to 1989 (165 to 133). More than 7.8 million patient days were spent in mental institutions in fiscal 1983-84, but many of these were by patients with a very long duration of stay. Another measurement of utilization is the number of visits to emergency and ambulatory care units. During 1988-89 fiscal year for example, there were about 1.6 million visits to surgical day care units, which amounted to 61.4 visits per 1,000 population in Canada.

3.   HUMAN HEALTH RESOURCES

Human health resources consist of those individuals who provide direct health services (such as nurses, physicians, dentists, chiropractors, and respiratory technicians), and those who provide ancillary and support services (such as maintenance and repair, housekeeping, food services and administration).

3.1.   DISTRIBUTION OF HUMAN HEALTH RESOURCES

The health-care sector is considered the third largest industry in the country, employing approximately 834,000 Canadians. About 60% of these directly provide health services and 40% are in ancillary jobs. About 80% of all health industry employees work in health institutions.

For 1990, 531,664 individuals were listed in *Health Personnel in Canada* as providing direct health services to Canadians.[3] Of these, 58% were nurses and nursing assistants, 11.2% were physicians, 6.1% health technologists, 4.8% worked in dentistry and allied occupations and 3.4% were in pharmacy. Since World War II, the traditional health-care professions of physicians, nurses and dentists have expanded to over 150 categories of health occupations. Most have been developed as extensions of established health professions (e.g., nurses' aids, licensed practical nurses, technicians, nurse practitioners, dental hygienists, and dental technicians). Others have developed from some special body of knowledge (e.g., clinical psychologists). As these new occupations evolved, many of their practitioners tried to achieve independent status as a self-regulatory "profession". Most provincial governments are beginning to regulate and/or license them (chapter 17).

Human health resources are unevenly distributed. The main concentrations are in large urban centres and in traditionally wealthy provinces like Ontario, Quebec and British Columbia. Over the past few decades human health resources have significantly increased in number, thus reducing their ratio to the population in most categories (table 15.1).

Nurses

Registered nurses represent about 50% of all health human resources in Canada. In 1991, of the total 262,288 registered nurses in Canada, 90.7% were employed in nursing.[4] There was one active nurse per 118 population. They were working mainly in hospitals (73%), but 9% worked in community health settings, 7.2% in nursing homes, 3.0% worked in educational institutions and the remainder worked in different settings. Part-time nurses accounted for a growing proportion of the nursing workforce in all health-care sectors. In 1991, part-time nurses accounted for 40% of hospital nurses, 51% of those in nursing homes and 36% of community health nurses. Also, there was one licensed nursing assistant per 321 population.

Table 15.1: Number and Ratio of Active Health Human Resources, 1990

Health Occupations	Total Number	Ratio to Population	(Ratio in 1976)
Audiologists & Speech Therapists	3322	1:8080	1:22119
Chiropractors	3494	1:6849	1:13623
Dentists	14394	1:1865	1:2463
Dental Assistants	1772	1:15147	1:7909
Dental Hygenists	8832	1:3039	1:11962
Dieticians and Nutritionists	6083	1:4418	1:8726
Health Records Administrators	3170	1:8467	1:11269
Health Services Executives	3065	1:8757	1:19331
Health Technologies:			
Electroneurophysio. Technologist	320	1:83878	1:69965
Laboratory	19612	1:1392	1:1415
Radiology	12054	1:2227	1:2890
Respiratory	3637	1:7380	1:17692
Nursing:			
Registered	223965	1:119	1:168
Licensed Nursing Assistant	82281	1:321	1:323
Occupational Therapists	3830	1:7008	1:15388
Opticians	3735	1:7186	1:10056
Optometrists	2702	1:9934	1:13128
Orderlies	18087	1:1443	1:1554
Osteopaths	33	1:813361	1:345648
Pharmacists	18337	1:1464	1:1658
Physicians	59409	1:452	1:557
Physiotherapists	9886	1:2715	1:16449
Public Health Inspectors	1538	1:17446	1:28697

Source: Health Personnel in Canada, 1990, Ottawa. Ministry of Supply and Services, 1992.

Physicians

In 1990, Canada had 59,409 active civilian physicians of which 7,568 (12.7%) were interns and residents, and of the remainder (51,841), 52.7% were general practitioners and 47.3% specialists. In 1990, the physician to population ratio was 1:452; the optimum ratio espoused by the World Health Organization is 1:655. The national average in 1990 was one general practitioner per 982 population and one specialist per 1,095 population: Nova Scotia, Quebec, British Columbia and Ontario were above the average while the Yukon and Northwest Territories, Saskatchewan, and the Atlantic provinces (with the exception of Nova Scotia) possess relatively low ratios primarily due to the small numbers of specialists. On the other hand, Quebec has a relatively high proportion of specialists (50.4%) and is the only province where it exceeds 50%. In 1990, Quebec and Ontario had the largest numbers of interns and residents, and Prince Edward Island and New Brunswick the smallest. Many provinces are expressing concern about this high physician to population ratio and number of measures are being taken to curtail the physician numbers.

3.2.   UTILIZATION MEASUREMENTS FOR PROFESSIONAL SERVICES

The most detailed information is available for physicians because physicians are paid directly through provincial health insurance. For the fiscal year 1983-84, there were approximately 145 million medical consultations and visits in the 10 provinces, an average of about six per person. In Ontario, for example, in 1987-88, payments for professional fees-for-service amounted to $3.6 billion, with an average of 9.95 claims per insured person at a cost of $393 per capita.[5] Of this amount, 90.5% went to physicians and the rest to other private practice professionals including chiropractors, optometrists, physiotherapists, dentists, chiropodists, and osteopaths, as well as some professional services which have special payment arrangements.   Also covered were payments for out-of-province care, health centres and STD clinics. This may be compared with total payments of $541 million in 1972-73, an average of 5.10 claims per insured person, of which 94% were for medical services; and total payments of $742 million in 1975-76, an average of 6.14 claims per insured person, 95% for physician services. Thus there has been a trend of steadily increasing number of services per capita along with the increase in cost of these services. This may be due to either consumer- or provider-initiated factors, or both.

Another measure of utilization of physician services is the number and rate of operations performed. In 1983-84, there were about 4.8 million operations done in Canada, about 65.5% of them on in-patients, for a total rate of surgery of 193 per 1,000 population.   100 minor and 71 major surgical procedures and 22 obstetrical interventions were performed for every 1,000 Canadians.

Table 15.2: Trends in Health Expenditures in Canada, 1960-1990

	1960	1970	1980	1990
Total expenditure (in millions of dollars)	2033	5786	22703	61753
Per captia expenditure (in dollars)	113.5	271	943	2318
Percent of gross national product	5.3	6.8	7.52	9.54

These expenditures include both government and personal expenditures on health related goods and services.

Source: National Health Expenditures in Canada, 1975-1985, Health and Welfare Canada, 1986 and Canadian Hospital Directory, Sept. 1990, Ottawa: Canadian Hospital Association, 1992.

4.   HEALTH EXPENDITURES

In 1990, Canada spent 9.54% of the GNP or $61.7 billion on health care. The GNP is often used to compare trends in health expenditures within a country. Table 15.2 shows that health expenditures in Canada are rising.

Provincial and federal government revenue, generated from general taxes and borrowing, provides about 75% of the money spent on health care and the remainder is paid by the individuals either directly or through private health insurance. For the government's share of health-care spending, the proportion paid by the federal government amounts to 30% compared with 70% by the provincial governments. The federal government contributes to the provinces in the form of transfer payments which are tax credits, and cash as agreed under the Established Programs Financing and Canada Health Acts. As described in chapter 12, these cash transfer payments are diminishing, which has implications for the resources available to the provinces and the types of services they provide. Ottawa's funding cuts have caused the provinces to lose $4 billion of anticipated revenue in 1992 alone. The provinces generate their share of the revenue for the health expenditures in the following manner:

- 72.5% of health-care costs are paid by the public in the form of taxes. Six of the 10 provinces levy special health-care taxes or premiums in addition to general taxes.
- Alberta and British Columbia charge individual premiums to those who request medicare benefits; Alberta earmarks money from the premiums for health care.

• Quebec, Ontario, Manitoba and Newfoundland levy payroll taxes on employers. Quebec charges a flat rate of 3.75% of every employer's payroll. Manitoba charges 2.25%; Newfoundland charges 1.5%, with smaller employers exempted. Ontario has a sliding scale from 0.98% to 1.95% according to payroll size. Payroll taxes tend to be controversial. One advantage is that they do not hit the poor as hard as flat-rate premiums, but they do not spread the net as wide, and the self-employed escape the tax altogether. Ontario's new payroll tax was expected to raise a mere 16% of its $16.5 billion health bill in the 1991-92 fiscal year.

Premiums and payroll taxes have only paid for about one-tenth of health spending in Alberta and British Columbia and one-quarter in Quebec in the past decade. General revenue is the predominant funding resource available for health care.

As indicated in chapter 12, government contributions include payment for physicians' services; institutional services; hospital-based dental surgical services in all provinces and children's and/or welfare recipients' dental services in some provinces; and supply of drugs and certain appliances for certain groups such as those over 65 or welfare recipients. Personal expenditures include dental and other services not covered by government insurance, drugs and appliances, and payments for extra services such as charges for private hospital rooms.

Statistics Canada, the chief source of such information, categorizes the sources of health expenditures as follows:

• **Institutional:** all types of hospitals and nursing homes.
• **Professional:** services of physicians, dentists, chiropractors naturopaths, osteopaths, optometrists, podiatrists, physiotherapists, private duty nurses and Victorian Order Nurses; but excludes professional services paid through institutions (e.g., nursing).
• **Drugs and appliances:** prescribed and over-the-counter drugs (except prescriptions dispensed in institutions), as well as eyeglasses, hearing aids and other prostheses.
• **Other:** health services prepayment, administration of general public health activities, and research and construction of medical facilities.

The per capita total health expenditure in Canada has risen from $271 in 1970 to $2,318 in 1990 (in current dollars). Over the last few years, approximately half of Canadian health expenditures went to institutional care (hospitals 39% and 10% for homes for special care); about a quarter (23%) on professional services (physicians 16.0%, dentists 5.4% and other professionals, 1.4%); and about 14% for drugs and appliances. Thus the major portion (87.0%) was spent on personal health care, and the remainder on public and voluntary health agencies, research and health insurance administration.

4.1.   INSTITUTIONAL EXPENDITURES

Of the $30.5 billion spent on institutional care in 1990, more than three-quarters (79%) was for general and allied special hospitals. On average, the per diem cost in acute hospitals is three to four times that in chronic or long-term care hospitals. The estimated cost of one day's stay in a public hospital was $355 in 1987-88, of which about 75% went to pay salaries and wages (15.5 paid hours per patient day).

Almost all of the funding of Canada's 1,240 hospitals, comes from provincial governments. The cost of running hospitals has risen almost 8% per year over the past five years. Wages, salaries and benefits account for almost three-quarters of public hospitals' operating budgets; 45% goes to nurses. Canada has more than 262,000 working registered nurses, who earn from $27,475 to $52,000 per year. In Canada, several factors have led to increased hospital costs:

* binding arbitration of unsettled labour disputes;
* increases in workers' compensation assessments, payroll health taxes, unemployment insurance and Canada Pension Plan payments;
* new laws on environmental protection, pay equity and occupational health and safety;
* new technology, drugs and methods of treatment (hospital drug costs alone have been rising 10% to 14% per year);
* the cost of other supplies and services, which has risen faster than government financing.

In response to these rising costs, hospitals have tried to treat more people on an out-patient basis. Between 1976 and 1988, out-patient visits rose 61.3% while in-patient days rose just 15.6%. The real cost of an in-patient day rose 16.3% during that time, while the cost of treating the average out-patient fell by 2.3%, creating significant financial advantages for the latter.

4.2.   PROFESSIONAL EXPENDITURES

Expenditure for professional services by physicians, dentists and other specialists amounted to about $14.1 billion (22.8% of total spending) in 1990. This does not include professionals like nurses, physiotherapists, occupational therapists, social workers and a few physicians employed by institutions. Expenditures for physicians' services constituted approximately 70% of all professional services, amounting to $9.8 billion. This includes gross fees for physicians in private practice only. In 1990 the total fee payments to physicians rose to $9.8 billion from $0.6 billion in 1972. Relatively high fee increases in some provinces (especially in British Columbia, Ontario and Alberta in the early 1980s) had caused significant changes in these figures.

Rising expenditures for physicians' services may be attributed to a number of factors. For example, the rise in total physician fees of $3,188.5 million, occurring between 1974-75 and 1983-84, may be allocated as 64.5% due to increase in price of services ($228.4 million) and 35.5% due to increase in utilization ($125.9 million). It can also be reviewed in terms of physician factors with 24.1% of the increase attributable to increase in physician supply, and 75.9% due to increase in fee payments per physician. Breaking it down another way, 64.5% is due to price increase, 9.0% due to population increase, and 26.5% due to increased utilization per insured person: 15.1% because of increase in per capita physician supply and 11.4% due to increase in utilization per physician. One may speculate about the extent to which this increase in utilization is brought about by increased needs or expectations of the consumer versus physician-generated factors such as extra recalls and procedures. Also of great importance is whether better health resulted from this increase.

Doctors get about 15 cents of every health-care dollar in the form of fees. Their decisions regarding the treatment of patients, however, have a major influence on how the rest of the money is spent. It is estimated that every doctor in Ontario costs the system about $500,000, half in direct billings and half in drugs prescribed, lab tests ordered and hospital admissions authorized. In 1990, Canadian doctors' billings alone came to $9.4 billion. In 1990 the 52,000 active civilian doctors in Canada billed an average of $181,000 each. More than 90% of doctors in private practice are paid on a fee-for-service basis. Government employees, community health centre staff and most of Canada's 7,560 hospital interns and residents are salaried doctors.

Seven cents of the health-care dollar is spent on the services of dentists and other health-care professionals such as chiropractors, optometrists and physiotherapists. Almost all of this amount goes to dentists.

4.3.   DRUGS AND APPLIANCES, AND OTHER EXPENDITURES

In 1990, $8.6 billion was expended for drugs and appliances, half for prescription drugs. Drugs and appliances claimed 14 cents of the health dollar in 1990, up from nine cents in 1975. Saskatchewan is the only province that provides prescription drug coverage to all of its residents; the other provinces usually pay for those over 65. Miscellaneous items (such as public-health programs, eyeglasses and the administrative costs of running private health insurance plans) accounted for about 12 cents of the health-care dollar. Prevention of illness, mainly subserved by public health units and voluntary agencies, accounted for about 3.5% of total health expenditures.

Table 15.3: International Comparisons of Total Health Expenditures as a Percentage of Gross Domestic Product

NATION	1960	1970	1980	1990
	Percentage	Percentage	Percentage	Percentage
CANADA	5.50	7.20	7.40	9.00
France	4.20	5.80	7.60	8.90
Sweden	4.70	7.20	9.50	8.70
United Kingdom	3.90	4.50	5.80	6.10
United States	5.20	7.40	9.20	12.40

Sources: *Overview of International Comparisons of Health Care Expenditures.* Geneva: Organization for Economic Cooperation and Development, Health Data Bank, 1989.
Schieber GJ and Poullier J-P, eds.   *Health Care Systems in Transition: The Search for Efficiency.* Geneva: Organization for Economic Cooperation and Development, 1990, p12.

5.   MANAGEMENT ISSUES IN HEALTH-CARE

We have not yet considered the appropriateness of use of our resources or the problems in making decisions on such allocation.   One of the major problems facing the Canadian economy and the health-care system is the amount and type of resources used to produce "health" and "sickness care."

Canada spent 9.54% of the Gross National Product on health care in 1990 which represented a 180% increase from 1960. The first significant rise was in the late 1960s following the introduction of universal insurance. By the early 1970s governments became alarmed by this rapid rise and set up a task force on the cost of health services, which delivered its report in 1970. Attempts to control the level of health expenditure met with temporary success in the 1970s.   The proportion of GNP declined initially and then levelled off from 1973 to 1980 in the range of 7.4 to 7.5%, although the actual dollars and per capita dollars spent had risen. Since 1981, it has been rising again. To put the current figure in an international perspective, trends for Gross Domestic Product (GDP) are given in Table 15.3.   The GDP is a measure of the market value of all final goods and services produced in Canada during a specified period by both Canadians and non-Canadians (GNP considers production by Canadians only and hence these measures differ). The trend for GDP indicates that the percentage spent on health has continued to increase. In 1990, Canada spent 9.0% of its GDP on health care, the United Kingdom spent 6.1% and the United States, 12.4%.

Many factors contribute to the variation in health-care expenditures among these nations. As described in chapter 12, these health-care systems differ widely in their sources of funding, including the balance of private and public funding. They also vary in the degree and form of state planning, the remuneration of health professionals (particularly physicians), and the nature of services provided. Thus international comparisons are of questionable significance since they tell us what nations spent, but little, if anything, about what they spent it on - the mix of services, possible duplication of facilities, doctor to population ratios, health needs or system inefficiencies. There is no evidence that Americans, for example, are healthier because they allocate a higher share of GDP to health care.

One significant difference between the health-care system in the US and in Canada is the administrative costs. In the US with its voluntary medical and hospital insurance systems, 12.5% of spending goes to administrative overhead, whereas in Canada administrative costs are under 3%. Furthermore, there are savings in hospital administrative costs because there is no need to price and itemize every service, bandage and pill on the patient's bill. The savings in accounting, nurses' time and paperwork are large. Moreover, there are savings in the more rational distribution of high technology such as NMR scanners, which hospitals in the US acquire for competitive reasons and then frequently under-utilize. Canada, on the other hand, has "sole source funding." Provincial governments are directly responsible for the overall allocation and coordination of resources to the health services sector. This avoids the fragmentation of decision making and wasteful competition for resources which can occur when independent non-profit or fee-for-service providers seek financing from a variety of private and public sources. The difference is in our philosophy: Canadians endeavour to develop a health-care system directed to health needs, not a competitive entrepreneurial system to serve an illness market. However, spiralling health-care costs are of concern to US and Canadian governments.

5.1.   STRATEGIES FOR INSTITUTIONAL RESOURCES

5.1.1. Rationalization

Rationalization of health services may involve re-structuring, re-alignment, decentralization and some institutional closures. These changes are undertaken to minimize duplication of services, provide appropriate levels and type of care, consolidate strengths, shift towards innovative structures and functional arrangements which may make more effective use of resources and contain costs. Many analysts maintain that the central problem of health services in Canada is that hospitals and other medical institutions have been acting in the interests of the health-care providers instead of the communities they serve.

Rationalization can involve major transformations of the health-care system. An example is Newfoundland's rationalization strategy, undertaken in 1991 as part of a major cost-cutting assault on its health-care system. In anticipation of government budgetary cuts, a small 41 bed acute-care hospital, Springdale Hospital, voluntarily cut its operating costs from $3 million to $2.4 million by transforming itself into an institution for long-term frail elderly and chronically ill patients. Obstetrics, pediatrics and general surgery were eliminated, following reductions in acute-care hospital beds and staff, reorganization of the delivery of medical services and restriction of doctors' incomes. A large regional hospital in Grand Falls, 100 kilometers from Springdale, continues to provide the services which were eliminated. Economic restraints forced the province's hospitals to become more efficient: hospital boards and administrations were merged, duplication reduced, and unneeded beds closed.

The rationalization process was quite extensive elsewhere in the province with a closure of 450 of the province's 3,000 beds along with 850 jobs in this sector. The income freeze for physicians resulted in some doctors threatening to close their offices in protest, and the government eventually agreed to a 3% increase. However, the provincial medical association then voluntarily imposed financial penalties on high-billing doctors, with the proceeds distributed equally among all physicians to compensate for the effects of the wage cap. Despite these major changes in Springdale and elsewhere in Newfoundland, there has not been a major reduction in patients' access to care. The re-organization proceeded on the following premises:

- Primary care (emergency attention, minor procedures usually done in a doctor's office or clinic) should be available to all within one hour.
- Secondary care (general surgery, delivering babies and services provided by specialists) should be no more than two or three hours away, concentrated in regional hospitals.
- Tertiary care (complex procedures, high-technology care for critically ill patients) will be concentrated in a single hospital, the Memorial University Health Sciences Centre in St. John's.

In addition, resources available for long-term care of Newfoundlanders who can no longer manage at home actually increased in the 1992 budget. Some concerns have arisen, however:

- longer waiting lists for some services, crowded hospital wards;
- increased frequency of long waits in emergency rooms before patients are admitted to hospital;
- increased workload and stress among hospital employees due to layoffs;
- changed work practices for nurses involving more menial duties and longer shifts.

5.1.2. Funding of Acute Care Hospitals

Approximately half of all health expenditures are related to hospital care. Global budgeting has had some effectiveness in controlling the costs of acute care hospitals in Canada in the 1970s and 1980s. It has been recommended, however, that hospitals be funded on a "case-mix" basis; that is, by the type and severity of diseases treated at the hospital. This is a similar system to Diagnostic Related Groups (DRGs) which gained prominence in the 1980s in the US. Hospitals were reimbursed for the intensity of care needed according to the severity classification of the patient's illness. However, hospitals tended to classify patients into more severe diagnostic categories to gain more reimbursement (popularly known as DRG "creep"); cost-containment could not be achieved.

5.1.3. Ambulatory/ Day Care/ Extended Care

The original federal-provincial funding arrangements in *The Hospital Insurance and Diagnostic Services Act* of 1957 encouraged expansion and utilization of acute care hospitals for which federal funds were provided. Ambulatory care, medical day care, day surgery, health centres, rehabilitation services, extended care facilities, and home care cost less than acute care hospitals but were not federally funded. These funding biases have been corrected by Established Programs Financing (EPF) in 1977, which included a per capita grant for extended health care, designed to cover nursing homes and ambulatory care. The flexibility in the EPF formula allowed provinces to develop these services in anticipation of growing needs associated with the "aging society" in Canada. Under EPF, there has been a shift in spending in favour of extended health care. Statistics supplied by Health and Welfare Canada indicate that the proportion of total federal health-care cash contributions going towards extended health care has increased from 11.7% in 1976-77 to 19.0% in 1988-89, and for public health services it has remained static at 4.2% over the same period.

5.1.4. Preadmission and Discharge Planning

Hospital stays for surgery, or other elective procedures, can be shortened by out-patient laboratory tests and other work-up prior to admission. After-care in a stepped-down environment, and preparation for discharge care are effective in reducing hospital costs.

5.1.5. Home Care

Home care opens institutional beds for acute care and costs considerably less than hospital care. It is claimed by some researcher that home care of the elderly can result in savings of 50% to 75% of the costs of equivalent care in a hospital.[6] Another benefit of treatment in the home is the psychological benefits experienced by the client and their family. The elderly are better able to adapt to a disability in their own home, and home care patients tend to comply more readily to treatment requirements. Furthermore, patients who receive health-care treatment in hospitals often experience confusion, disorientation, anxiety and personality conflicts, all of which can hinder his or her progress. A home-care program can also be tailored to the client's particular needs taking into account the limitations of the client's home. As well, a client at home remains a consumer, thus benefiting the economy as a whole. Some of the current issues and concerns regarding home care are discussed below.

Cost-Effectiveness In the current climate of increased fiscal restraint, there has been considerable emphasis on home care as a cost-effective alternative to institutionalized health care. However, efforts to determine the cost-effectiveness of home care services are impeded by what has been termed the "paradox of efficiency." One would expect home care to be efficient if it opened up hospital beds and if the treatment cost less than it would in an institution. However, open beds are filled immediately by other patients. As well, some home care clients may not have otherwise sought any other form of medical care, and thus health-care problems may be discovered that would have otherwise gone untreated. As a result of these two consequences, the overall costs to the health system may actually increase with the expansion of home care services, as more people end up being treated. If utilization can be monitored for appropriateness, and the generally higher rates of patient satisfaction maintained, more care in the home remains a desirable goal.

Consumer Choice In institutional settings, the physician is the decision maker, whereas in the home the patient is in his or her own environment and services are rarely delivered by a physician. This has the benefit of encouraging the participation of the patient and family in decision making, and may therefore improve the psychological health of the patient.

Risk and Liability There is an increased risk to the home care patient in emergency situations since emergency services and technology are at a greater distance from the patient. Furthermore, monitoring of the home care patient is often less intensive than in an institutional facility. Thus there is a transition of a significant amount of responsibility from health-care providers to the patient. The Federal/ Provincial/ Territorial Working Group on Home Care pointed out that this is the downside of the power shift mentioned above: "You cannot both empower clients and families, and retain traditional notions of risk and responsibility at the same time."[7]

Turf War Although many would be pleased with the reduced or stabilized rates of institutionalization that increased home care may bring, intersectoral rivalries within the health-care field may result. For example, those pressing for the addition of a new wing for a hospital will resent the argument that no addition is needed because of the home care alternative.

Rights People who would normally be treated in institutions will demand the "right" to receive treatment at home. Thus, whereas home care is currently provided in situations where the treatment would generally be short term and/or low cost, home care may be claimed as a right by high-cost, long-term clients such as young people with disabilities.

Private vs. Public Home Care Every province and one territory have some non-government home care programs, such as the Ontario Association of Visiting Homemaker Services. Most of these programs centre around support services, such as technology, supplies, and professional and para-professional services. There has been increasing concern about the growing privatization in home care. British Columbia, Alberta, Ontario and New Brunswick all have privatization as an explicit objective of public policy. In Ontario, half of the available home support services involve the commercial sector, 17% in Quebec, and almost all home care in British Columbia is provided by the private sector, with public monitoring and case management. There is concern, however, that the private home care sector, especially the for-profit agencies, will provide services that are less accessible, less accountable, and of lower quality than those provided directly by government agencies.[8] It also encourages elitism and a two-tiered system. Concern regarding increased public/private collaboration revolve around the issues of quality control, coordination and accessibility.

Other Issues Issues in the home care field include the growing range of complex services required for clients such as those with AIDS; the increasing demand for palliative care; the high costs both at home and in institutions of Alzheimer and other dementias; the issues involved with training health-care workers in the delivery of home care services; and the high costs of 24-hour, seven days per week coverage.

5.1.6. Risk Management
Risk management is the reduction of an institution's potential for liability by the identification of predictors of either an extended or complicated hospital course or adverse outcome (such as mortality). Monitoring a sample of patient charts for indicator conditions concurrent with their hospitalization can highlight the intervention needed to avert a poor outcome. Complaints about care must also be handled appropriately by the institution's administration.

5.1.7. Strategies for Human Health Resources: Physicians
Another cost control intervention has been control of health human resources, particularly the number of physicians and their remuneration, which, in the early 1990s, emerged as major issues of concern to provincial governments.

Physician Human Resources
A major report commissioned by the Conference of Deputy Ministers of Health which dealt with Canadian physician resource planning appeared in 1992. This was called Barer-Stoddard Report.[9-15] The generation of the report incorporated the input and views of major stakeholders. The assumption was that cost control in the health-care system is intimately linked to the supply, mix and distribution of physician human resources and their remuneration. Physicians generate most health-care costs directly or indirectly but the public interest may not be met by this distribution of health-care resources.[16] The life cycle of physicians has

potential sites of intervention to control supply and maximize attrition through policy decisions. It was also used to explain that decisions made in a physician's daily job may have major impact on the supply of physicians but bear no relationship to the community's need for physician services.

Barer and Stoddard proposed a three-tiered national strategy for physician resource management. The first tier made recommendations concerning the following issues:

(i) *Graduates of Foreign Medical Schools (GOFMS):* These account for 25% of the physician supply in Canada, and comprise Canadians trained elsewhere, "visa" physicians recruited into Canada to meet special needs and visa trainees for postgraduate programs. It was recommended that Canada reduce its reliance on GOFMS and limit immigration of physicians, require compliance of visa physicians with the terms of their contract, and use the non-selected supply of GOFMS creatively, such as for areas poorly supplied with physicians.

(ii) *Overall supply of physicians*: The overriding objective of physician resource policy should satisfy the health needs of the population, given the resources society is prepared to commit. Barer-Stoddart rejected the notion of the ideal physician/ population ratio that has been used as a planning tool. Canada, however, is faced with an oversupply of physicians; since the early 1950s the physician supply has been increasing faster than the population. The report recommended an immediate 10% reduction in the number of medical undergraduate students in Canadian universities.

(iii) *Mix and number of residency training positions*: The current mix of residency positions bears no relation to that which would best meet current and future physician needs. Instead it reflects historical precedent and the prestige of subspecialties. The report called for the development of a reasonable and acceptable approach to rationalizing the mix and location of residency positions. Restructuring the funding of academic centres and replacing institution-specific bargaining for residency positions would be pivotal. Reducing the number of training positions would also redistribute physicians more appropriately toward the primary care sector.

(iv) *The geographic maldistribution of physicians*: Despite the overabundance of Canadian physicians, northern and rural areas are underserviced. Incentives to locate in underserviced areas included student-loan remission programs for residents agreeing to practise in designated rural areas for specific periods, and other financial incentives. The Ontario government has already attempted to redistribute physicians geographically to areas designated as "underserviced," (primarily Northern Ontario), through tax-free grants or guaranteed incomes for the first four years in practice in a designated area. In British Columbia, a so-called "northern differential" exists, giving a higher fee schedule to those in more remote communities, based on a percentage added over and above the standard provincial fee schedule, graded according to degree of remoteness from the lower mainland. The Quebec government has taken a different approach. It pays a much lower fee schedule to new physicians in urban centres than those in outlying areas. Quotas on billing numbers could restrict the number of urban practitioners.

By the end of 1992 a number of provinces had implemented the ceiling on the number of medical students, ensuring compliance of GOFMS with visa requirements was being enforced, and attempting to reduce physician-generated costs by reducing the number of physicians. Responses of organized medicine were, in part, were mixed; however, the Royal College of Physicians and Surgeons of Canada expressed concerns about the reduction in undergraduate medical students and the adjustment of speciality ratios. The College did, however, recommend a moratorium on the recognition of new specialities.

Clearly, some accurate assessment is needed to determine the appropriate number of physicians required to provide "enough" but not excess services. In addition, the problem of inappropriate distribution must be addressed both among specialities and in terms of geography.

Physician Remuneration

In addition to costs related to number of physicians, there is the issue of physician remuneration itself.[17] This has become an increasingly contentious issue in recent years. Physicians want to receive what they regard as fair compensation for their services, which may lead them to practices such as "opting out," "extra-billing" or "balanced-billing." All involve a payment by the patient to the physician above the level paid by the provincial health plan. Under the Canada Health Act of 1984, provinces which allowed extra-billing were to be penalized financially. As a result, by 1987 all provinces had banned extra-billing. However, questions of "fair" compensation will continue. The issue of "extra-billing" may arise again as a result of the diminution of the federal government's transfer payments to the provinces and the consequent lack of federal control over provincial health insurance programs' fulfilment of the requirements of the Canada Health Act.

It has also been argued that the present fee-for-service system fails to adequately compensate preventive services and encourages rapid patient turn-over, excessive patient recalls and the performance of unnecessary procedures. Although a restructuring of fee schedules might be able to correct this problem, those holding this view usually favour salaries for physicians as a better way of aligning services with patient needs. Another alternative is to pay via capitation. Some combination of these mechanisms is also feasible.

Team approach to health care, particularly in ambulatory settings such as community health centres,[18] with the effective utilization of nurses, dietitians, social workers and other professionals is growing in popularity. These professionals might provide primary care in their field of expertise, or work as part of a more comprehensive approach to health care, particularly in its preventive aspects, than is now provided in many primary care settings. Some have recommended alternative models, such as the Health Services Organization or the Health Maintenance Organization. Quality of care might be improved. Clearly, for economic benefit to occur these alternative approaches must reduce the need for, and use of, physicians' services, not simply be "added on" to them. The alternative health-care delivery models should explore the use of health-care professionals other than physicians. Midwives may be utilized for normal home and hospital deliveries.

Caps on Physician Incomes
Other strategies to reduce the open-ended provincial spending on physicians are to "cap" individual doctor's incomes at a certain level (as occurred in Ontario in 1992) or to "cap" or limit overall provincial payments for medical fees. This latter strategy may be accompanied by utilization adjustment, or the deduction from physician payments of an amount for increases in utilization of medical services beyond specified levels for a period. In Ontario, organized medicine collaborated with government to limit billings and to impose penalties. In British Columbia, similar initiatives resulted in protest from organized medicine and a number of doctors opted out of the provincial health insurance scheme.

Other Physician Remuneration-Containment Measures
Restriction of the granting of billing privileges by the health insurance plans and prorated payments for new physicians have also been recommended. Joint management committees of organized medicine and government have emerged in some provinces, principally in Ontario, where the Ontario Medical Association agreed to the limits on physician billing contingent on being recognized as the exclusive bargaining agent for physicians in that province. Confrontation as well as partnership strategies, however, may develop in this contentious arena.

5.1.8. Practice Guidelines
In an environment of an explosion of scientific and clinical information, clinical guidelines have emerged as explicit and structured evidence-based approaches to medical decision making which have the potential to enhance quality of care.[19] They also have the potential for cost containment and more appropriate utilization of resources. They are seen by some as an intrusion into the professionalism of health-care providers. Guidelines are not enforced; rather they are recommendations which may change professional norms. As guidelines are explicit, they can provide standards for optimum care and evaluate the quality of care.

However, the existence of guidelines does not ensure their implementation. Marketing the guidelines to physicians and other health-care providers is necessary to achieve changes in behaviour. Practical assistance in supporting the recommendations of the guidelines, such as the availability of alternative tests or procedures, must also be available. For example, guidelines for the utilization of cesarean sections were developed by the obstetric profession in Canada in response to major variations in rates for cesarean sections in different provinces. In 1989, the rate of cesarean sections in Ontario had tripled since 1970, to 19.5 per 100 hospital deliveries, far higher than that in Manitoba. Forty per cent were performed because the woman had had a previous cesarean section. New standards were promulgated, particularly advocating vaginal birth after cesarean section (VBAC). The promulgation of the standards did not, by themselves result in changes in the rates of cesarean sections. A comparative intervention[20] in the US, however, which involved counselling and education of physicians and a peer-review process to promote the guidelines, did reduce the number of cesarean sections. Cesarean sections became more frequent among women aged over 35, and in dystocia/breech deliveries. Vaginal births after cesarean sections increased considerably. These were considered a more appropriate utilization of surgery and likely contributed to cost containment.

Increasing public interest in the outcome of medical care, the need for cost containment, and the suspicion that some medical care may be unnecessary or inappropriate, will all result in a shift towards the supervision of quality of care and the identification of optimal practice patterns. It is considered that "sensible, flexible guidelines produced by the appropriate panels will help improve practice."[21] Recently, government and organized medicine have become interested in the cost-containment potential of guidelines. For example, in Ontario, the Institute for Clinical Evaluative Sciences was established by the Ontario Ministry of Health and the Ontario Medical Association, partly to undertake research into practice "styles," the individual characteristic approaches of physicians to investigating and managing problems based on other factors besides rational scientific evidence.

5.1.9. Technology Assessment

Technology (some of it very expensive) has proliferated in health care in recent times. Technology assessment has been developed to examine the efficacy and safety of a technology, its appropriate clinical use, the relative risks and benefits, and the ethical and social implications. However, no systematic process for the identification and acquisition of new technology exists in Canada. Interprovincial differences in priorities and disparities in wealth make it difficult to establish uniform approaches to health technology. The Federal Health Protection Branch of Health Canada administers the Food and Drugs Act which regulates a limited number of medical devices, as well as medications. These devices include implantables, condoms, AIDS tests, menstrual tampons and contact lenses. The Act does not cover devices used externally, nor most other technology, which is introduced independently by the provinces. A recent initiative in Canada has been the establishment of a Coordinating Office for Health-Care Technology Assessment which was introduced following proposals by Feeny and Stoddart (1988).[22] The Coordinating Office undertakes technology assessments on request.

A fundamental concept which provides the rationale for technology assessment is the diffusion of technology. As new technology emerges it is usually taken up enthusiastically. A period of some re-assessment then occurs during which limitations of the technology's application or its adverse effects come to light. The technology then becomes incorporated into the practices of health professionals and institutionalized, even if, as usual, the initial glowing promise is not fully realized. Unless some intervention in this cycle occurs, such as assessment of the cost-effectiveness, enormously expensive technology can become the standard of practice without evidence of its efficiency.

The Technology Assessment Iterative Loop[23] provides a model for informed decision making as a result of technology assessment. The seven steps are the following :

- identification of technologies with the greatest potential for reducing the burden of illness by primary, secondary or tertiary prevention or by levels of care;
- efficacy: i.e., therapeutic potential under ideal circumstances;
- screening and diagnosis: i.e., accurate detection of those in need;
- community effectiveness;*
- efficiency;*
- synthesis and implementation;
- monitoring and reassessment.

* The reader is advised to review chapter three for a discussion of community effectiveness and methods for assessing efficiency.

Technology assessment may use cost-utility ratios, whereby the social value of the technology is incorporated into the assessment for comparison of competing technologies. Technologies are compared on the incremental cost to achieve, say, an additional quality-adjusted life year (QALY).[24] It has been recommended that the use of health technology be based on defined population needs.

5.1.10. Quality Assurance and Total Quality Management

Quality assurance (QA) is a management system which assures the quality of health care provided by workers and received by clients. Care should be correctly given, reliable and empathetic. Quality assurance is a method of constantly improving standards and the frequency of attaining them. Quality assurance is defined by the Canadian Council on Health-Care Facilities Accreditation (CCHCFA), the national agency that accredits health-care facilities of all descriptions across Canada, as a five-stage process comprising: (i) the establishment of functional goals; (ii) the implementation of procedures to achieve those goals; (iii) the regular assessment of performance relative to the goals; (iv) the proposal of solutions to close the gap between performance and goal; and, (v) the documentation and reporting of this assessment activity.

For QA to work, the institutions must encourage two related processes: the continuous assessment of quality and the communication of problems and attainments of desired changes through the management structure.[25] A number of approaches have been developed specifically for the hospital sector, such as the Medical Audit Committee which compares care given for a specific disease with the standards of care set for that disease. Another example is the Tissue Committee, reviewing all tissue removed during surgery and comparing it with the preoperative diagnosis. The third example is the Health Record Committee which reviews selected patient records for their completeness. As indicated earlier, the Hospital Medical Record Institute also provides large sets of data for comparisons between similar size institutions.

While institutions have quality assurance programs there are usually no organized review of the community-based practices of health professionals. Licensing or regulating bodies usually have dealt with patient complaints; however, changes in recent legislation, in a number of provinces, require them to monitor quality of care provided by professionals in their offices. Increasingly, health professions and institutions will be required to be accountable to the public and the government for the resources they use and the manner in which they practise.

Total quality management (TQM) is a management philosophy which provides a framework for health care to improve quality while controlling costs. In TQM, management focuses on the system, rather than at the individual level, making decisions that support quality and removing barriers to quality in the bureaucratic, hierarchical system. Participation and teamwork are vital. It is based on a continuous feed-forward process, called continuous quality improvement (CQI), and in this way differs from quality assurance, which tends to depend on retrospective recognition of "outliers" in patterns of care. Total quality management has not been widely implemented in the health-care system in Canada to date. A number of initiatives for implementation, however, have commenced. It is complementary to quality assurance in that it provides the management loop for rectifying difficulties which are identified. This aspect is frequently lacking in quality assurance activities which tended to emphasize data collection. Quality assurance also focuses on individuals, often in relation to their peers, and is thus less powerful than total quality management, which examines issues affecting the performance of the organization as a whole.

5.1.11. Utilization Review and Management

Utilization review is concerned with comparison of the volume and intensity of service utilization. It is of particular interest that there exists large differences between the rates of use of medical services between geographic regions or between practitioners, yet there are no discernible differences in health outcomes. Establishing ideal "rates" is problematic, however. Large differences in the rates of medical or hospital services observed between geographic regions are called small-area variations (SAV). The finding of large differences (SAV), adjusted for age, sex and other variables, questions the assumption that all the services in the regions with higher rates are medically necessary.[26] It is considered likely that the rapid growth of per capita utilization of medical services between 1971 and 1985 of 67.8% in Canada was due to physicians increasing their volume of services to compensate for restrained fee schedules.[11] This assumption of physician-driven utilization can be challenged by a number of alternative explanations, and further research is needed. Other explanations include aging, technology, drugs, expanded medical capability, heightened consumer information and expectations, new government programs, constraints in hospital budgets and expanded medical capabilities.

Utilization review and management[27] monitors the utilization of services, analyzes variations, and assesses interventions to reduce inappropriate use of services and provide feedback and education. This may be hospital based or, less frequently, community based.

5.1.12. Rationing in Health Care
When resources for health care and services are finite and limited, rationing is one option which may result in equitable distribution of health care. An example of explicit rationing in health care is the proposed Oregon Health-Care Plan in the United States.

Oregon's Basic Health-Care Act
In 1989, the Oregon Legislature passed the Basic Health-Care Act[28] which called for the extension of Medicaid coverage to all Oregonians below the poverty level. Seventeen per cent of the state's population was not covered by health-care insurance, but under the new legislation coverage would be provided to the single, childless, poor and working poor. In order to pay the costs of the extended Medicaid coverage, the state legislated the rationalization of health-care services. Based on cost, social value and the effectiveness of procedures, the state ranked 709 condition/treatment pairs. Services were divided into three types:

- *Essential:* includes life preserving services, maternal care, preventive care for children and adults, reproductive services, and comfort care for terminally ill patients. These types of services are considered effective, contribute to the quality of life, give good value for the money, and demonstrate community compassion for the terminally ill.
- *Very important:* includes treatment for non-fatal conditions where full or partial recovery is expected, or where the quality of life is expected to improve through treatment.
- *Valuable to certain individuals:* includes non-fatal conditions which are not responsive to treatment; infertility and conditions in which treatment would not significantly improve the quality of life.

Those services deemed valuable to certain individuals may not be covered under the standard benefit package. Thus the central issue in the proposed Oregon health-care funding has been changed from *who* is covered, to *what* is funded. It must be noted that while the Oregon plan proposed limiting the types of services provided under the standard benefit package, it exceeded the coverage provided by Medicare by providing unlimited hospitalization. The standard package also included prescription drugs, dental services, physical and occupational therapy and other services which the federal guidelines did not cover. The Oregon plan was vetoed by then-President Bush in 1992, claiming violation of the Americans with the Disabilities Act. The current Clinton Administration, however, has approved the Oregon Plan in principle. However, it generated a lively debate in health-care communities throughout North America.

Critics of the Oregon rationing process claim that prioritizing services inevitably means that future budget cuts will cause the line below which services will not be funded to continually move upward. However, proponents argue that rationing already implicitly occurs whenever decisions are made to spend money on one service or set of services, because health-care resources are not infinite. In Canadian provinces such as Ontario and Alberta, moreover, a more explicit kind of health rationing is already occurring in the form of "**de-listing**", whereby certain services are being removed from the list of those covered by their health insurance plans. In these cases, user fees must be paid in order to attain these services. What distinguishes the Oregon system of rationing from others, however, is the process used to arrive at the list of priorities. The communities which would be affected, including both health-care workers and consumers, were surveyed as to what types of services they valued most. The responses from these surveys typically ranked quality of life, prevention and cost-effectiveness high on their list of values. Scientific analyses of the effectiveness and cost of procedures and treatments were combined with the input from the community and the condition/ treatment pairs were ranked accordingly. Unlike the hidden rationing and politically determined procedures for choosing which health-care services receive priority for funding experienced in Canada, Oregon appears to offer its citizens an open, publicly-determined procedure for providing basic health-care coverage.[29]

6.   SUMMARY

Within our Canadian system, rapidly rising costs in health care, particularly in the acute care sector, and expanding high-cost technology are straining our resources. The potential demands for health services are virtually unlimited, so it is clear that they cannot all be met. In a system of universally accessible services, demand alone cannot be allowed to determine provision of services. This raises many difficult issues. Who will make the decisions and on what basis? Will the decision be made by government at whatever level, by health-care providers, local health authorities, consumers, or special interest groups? How will resources be allocated with respect to the needs of the elderly who are growing in number and proportion in our society, or the needs of marginalized groups such as Aboriginal Peoples, some immigrants, remote rural communities, and the disabled? Will costly but potentially life-prolonging measures such as renal transplantation and dialysis, or coronary bypass be rationed and if so, on what basis? Can increased expenditure in the areas of health promotion, prevention and primary care reduce the need for expensive acute care services, and if so, what is the appropriate balance?

Resource utilization depends on several factors: (1) resources ratio, which is the availability of resources; (2) general characteristics of the community or population (such as age distribution, housing quality, level of sanitation, etc.); (3) personal factors affecting usage of services such as attitudes, age, sex, family size, etc.; and (4) system characteristics which include: points of entry in the health-care system, accessibility of resources, cost and barriers to care. Our present system allows patients direct access to primary or secondary care depending on their proximity to and knowledge about resources and their attitudes toward the system. The ideal, however, is a linear progression by the patient from primary to secondary to tertiary care resources as required.

The ultimate aim of the health-care industry is to produce good health. Expenditure on health care is presently focussed on treating sickness rather than prevention. Measurement of sickness care has two dimensions: outcome measurement (e.g., improvement, no improvement, deterioration or death) and utilization measurement.

Institutions are the most expensive element of health care as they are both technology- and human-resource intensive. In 1990 Canada had about 1,239 general, allied, special, private and governmental hospitals. Public hospitals accounted for 88% of all hospitals and 96% of the beds. There were 51 separate mental institutions with 13,614 beds. Utilization of institutional care is measured by hospitalization days, hospital separation rates and the number of visits to emergency and ambulatory care units.

Human health resources consist of individuals who provide direct health services such as nurses, physicians, dentists, chiropractors and respiratory technicians, and those who are indirectly involved in health sectors. The health industry is the third largest industry in the country employing about 834,000 Canadians, of whom 80% work in health institutions. Due to technical advances, over 150 categories of health occupations now exist. They have been developed either as extensions of established health professions or alongside some special body of knowledge. Human health resources are unevenly distributed, in that the main concentration is in large urban centres and traditionally wealthy provinces.

In 1990, Canada spent $61.7 billion on health care (which represents 9.5% of the GNP) and health expenditures are continuing to rise. Revenue generated by the provincial and federal government from general taxes and borrowing provides about 75% (30% of which is federal and 70% provincial) of the money spent on health care, while the remaining 25% is paid by the individuals either directly or via private health insurance. Health expenditures are categorized as institutional, professional, drugs and appliances, and other. Over the last few years, approximately half of Canadian health expenditures was spent for institutional care, about one-quarter on professional services, and about 14% for drugs and appliances. The per capita total health expenditure in Canada has risen from $271 in 1970 to $2,318 in 1990.

The following are current approaches to increasing efficient utilization of resources:

(i) With respect to institutional resources, the following strategies that are employed: (1) Rationalization of health services: this involves restructuring, realignment, some closures and decentralization of institutions; (2) Ambulatory/ day care/ extended care; (3) Preadmission planning/discharge planning: hospital stays can be shortened if preparation is made prior to admission to hospital; (4) Risk management: is the reduction of an institution's potential for liability by the identification of indicators predictive of either an extended or complicated hospital course or adverse outcome. (ii) With respect to human health resources (specifically physicians) the following strategies are employed: (1) Physician human resources: cost control in the health-care system is intimately linked to the supply, mix and distribution of physician human resources and their remuneration. Strategies for physician resource management have been proposed and address areas such as graduate foreign medical schools, oversupply of physicians, mix and number of residency training positions and the geographic maldistribution of physicians; (2) Physician remuneration: important issues with respect to this include the rights of physicians to receive what they regard as fair compensation for their services and team approach to health care; (3) Caps on physician incomes.

(iii) Practice guidelines: clinical guidelines have emerged as approaches to clinical judgment and decision making which have the potential both to enhance the quality of care and for cost containment and appropriate utilization of resources.

(iv) Technology assessment: is a procedure which has been developed to examine the efficacy and safety of a technology, its appropriate clinical use, the relative risks and benefits, and the ethical and social implications.

(v) Quality assurance: is a five stage process comprising: establishment of functional goals, implementation and procedures to achieve these goals, regular assessment of performance relative to the goals, closing the gap between performance and goal, and documentation and reporting of this assessment activity.

(vi) Utilization review and management: monitors the utilization of services, analyses variations, assesses interventions to reduce inappropriate use of services and provides feedback and education. Total quality management: is a management philosophy which provides a framework for health care to improve quality while controlling costs.

(vii) Rationing in health care: when resources for health care and services are finite and limited, rationing is one option which may result in equitable distribution of health care.

7. REFERENCES

1. Mix P and Gagnon M. Annual Hospital Preliminary 1989-90. *Health Reports* 3(3):269-273, 1991.
2. Gagnon M. List of Residential Care Facilities, 1991. *Health Reports* 4(2):198, 1992.
3. Minister of National Health and Welfare. *Health Personnel in Canada 1990.* Ministry of Supply and Services, Canada, Ottawa, 1990.
4. Paton S and Lobin T. Nursing in Canada - 1991. *Health Reports* 4(3):321-329, 1992.
5. Ministry of Health. *Practitioner Care Statistics 1987-88* (Pre-Audit). Toronto: Queen's Printer for Ontario, 1989.

6. Home-Based Care, the Elderly, the Family, and the Welfare State: An International Comparison. Ottawa: University of Ottawa Press, 1993.
7. Health Services and Promotion Branch, Health and Welfare Canada. *Report on Home Care*. Ministry of Supply and Services, Canada, Ottawa, 1990.
8. Nahmiash D and Reis M. *An Exploratory Study of Private Home Care Services in Canada*. Health and Welfare Canada, Ottawa, 1992.
9. Barer M and Stoddard G. Toward Integrated Medical Resource Policies for Canada: 1. Background, Process and Perceived Problems. *Can Med Assoc J* 146(3):347-351, 1992.
10. Stoddard G and Barer, M. Toward Integrated Medical Resource Policies for Canada: 2. Promoting Change - General Themes. *Can Med Assoc J* 146(5):697-700, 1992.
11. Idem: Toward Integrated Medical Resource Policies for Canada: 3. Analytic Framework for Policy Development. *Can Med Assoc J* 146(7):1169-1174, 1992.
12. Barer M and Stoddard G. Toward Integrated Medical Resource Policies for Canada: 4. Graduates of Foreign Medical Schools. *Can Med Assoc J* 146(9):1549-15544, 1992.
13. Barer M and Stoddard G. Toward Integrated Medical Resource Policies for Canada: 5. The Roles and Funding of Academic Medical Centres. *Can Med Assoc J* 146(11):1919-1924, 1992.
14. Idem. Toward Integrated Medical Resource Policies for Canada: 6. Remuneration of Physicians and Global Expenditure Policy. *Can Med Assoc J* 147(1):33-38, 1992.
15. Barer M and Stoddard G. Toward Integrated Medical Resource Policies for Canada: 7. Undergraduate Medical Training. *Can Med Assoc J* 147(3):305-312, 1992.
16. Lomas J and Barer M. And Who Shall Represent the Public Interest? The Legacy of Canadian Health Manpower Policy. In: *Medicare at Maturity*. Evans R and Stoddard G, eds. Calgary: University of Calgary Press, 1986, pp 221-286.
17. *Canada's National-Provincial Health Program for the 1980's: A Commitment for Renewal"*. Hall EM, Special Commissioner. Ottawa, Health and Welfare Canada, 1980.
18. Canada, Parliament, House of Commons, Special Committee on the Federal-Provincial Fiscal Arrangements. *Fiscal Federalism in Canada - Report of the Parliamentary Task Force on Federal-Provincial Fiscal Arrangements*. August 1981, pp 97-120.
19. Health Services Research Group Standards, Guidelines and Clinical Policies. *Can Med Assoc J* 146(6):833-837, 1992.
20. Myers S and Gleicher N. A Successful Program to Lower Cesarean Section Rates. *N Engl J Med* 319(23):1511-1988, 1988.
21. Linton A and Peachy D. Guidelines for Medical Practice: 1. The Reasons Why. *Can Med Assoc J* 143(6):485-490, 1990.
22. Feeney D and Stoddart G. Toward Improved Health Technology Policy in Canada: A Proposal for the National Health Technology Assessment Council. *Can Public Policy* 14(3):254-265, 1988.
23. Feeney D, Guyatt G and Tugwell P, eds. *Health Care Technology: Effectiveness, Efficiency and Public Policy*. Montreal: The Institute for Research on Public Policy, 1986.
24. Goel V, Deber R and Detsky A. Nonionic Contrast Media: Economic Analysis and Health Policy Development. *Can Med Assoc J* 140(4):389-395, 1989.
25. Wilson CRM. *Hospital-Wide Quality Assurance: Models for Implementation and Development*. Toronto: WB Saunders, 1987, p 8.
26. Health Services Research Group Small-Area Variations: What Are They and What Do They Mean? *Can Med Assoc J* 146(4):467-470, 1992.
27. Anderson G, Sheps S and Cardiff K. Hospital-Based Utilization Management: A Cross-Canada Survey. *Can Med Assoc J* 143(10):1025-1030, 1990.
28. McPherson A. The Oregon Plan: Rationing in a Rational Society. *Can Med Assoc J* 145(11):1444-1445, 1991.
29. Emson H. Down the Oregon trail - The Way for Canada? *Can Med Assoc J* 145(11):1441-1443, 1991.

CHAPTER SIXTEEN
Emerging Issues in Health Care Delivery

The present national health-care system in Canada arose as a result of the addition of universal health insurance to a preexisting system of hospitals and medical care. Provinces have an exclusive jurisdiction in most health matters in Canada. Hence, what is generally referred to as the national health-care system in Canada is really 10 different provincial and two territorial government health insurance plans. While these are referred to as health-care systems, their primary focus and funding mechanisms deal mainly with illness rather than health. Increasing costs to look after the sick and infirm, the government monopoly in health care, the rise of consumerism, conflicts between government and professionals, changing demographic patterns, evidence of inequalities in health, awareness of the need for disease prevention and health promotion for achieving health for the population, the emergence of technology and the inappropriate use of resources by patients and providers have led people to question the health-care system, which in turn has led to an extensive study at the federal and provincial levels. In the last decade, most provinces set up task forces, commissions, boards of inquiry and working groups to address the problems identified in the current health-care system.[1-12] Usually, widely respected citizens were appointed by government and major national organizations to perform these studies, with specific terms of reference and necessary resources, and to recommend changes in policy. During this process, other citizens and groups representing different constituencies submitted their views on particular issues. The final policies and programs recommended to the government are shaped by these presentations. All recent task force and Royal Commissions reports from different provinces have been summarized by Mhatre and Deber, (1992)[13] and the Angus Report (1991).[14]

1. EQUITY AND ACCESS

A review of recent provincial commissions concluded that Canada "wants to achieve equitable access to health."[13] The previous objective in Canada of ensuring equal access to medical care has largely been achieved by the universal system of hospital and medical insurance. It is now widely held that the development of medical care has reached its zenith in contributing to improved health status. Due to the current situation in the Canadian political, economic, and social environment, citizens differ in the likelihood that they will achieve health as defined in its broadest sense of a resource for everyday living. These determinants of heath have been described in chapter four and disparities particularly evident in the health status of special groups such as the elderly, children living in poverty, Aboriginal Peoples and the disabled have been reviewed in chapter six. There are also socioeconomic disparities in health status generally distributed through the population, such that life expectancy is five to six years less for those whose incomes fall into the lowest quintile than those in the highest.[15]

Achieving equity in health so that income, geography, age, gender or cultural background are not limitations will involve a re-ordering of priorities. A number of strategies that incorporate increased attention particularly to reducing inequities related to psychosocial determinants have been proposed. Some, such as integration of health and social services would result in transformation of many aspects of the organization of health services if fully implemented. Others, such as cultural and racial sensitivity, would reduce barriers to care for Aboriginal Peoples and other cultures. Attention to literacy in health communications would facilitate the communication of health information to those with the highly prevalent problem in Canada of literacy limitations. These strategies are discussed below. The second section of the chapter then moves on to discuss consumerism which has provided significant pressure on the health system to increase access and reduce inequities. Some of the major service delivery areas, such as long-term care, palliative care and mental health services have been heavily influenced in this way and recent developments are reviewed. Primary care is discussed as an approach to reducing inequities in health care. Finally, the discussion moves to regionalization and decentralization, which have been proposed, and partly implemented in Canada, as strategies that would result in a more rational allocation of resources and services relevant to local needs and which could incorporate community input.

1.1.   CULTURAL AND RACIAL SENSITIVITY

The term "multicultural health" is used to refer to health care which is provided in a culturally and racially sensitive manner. A multicultural health-care facility is one which "reflects the contributions and interests of diverse cultural and social groups in its mission, operations and products or services."[16] In order for health care to become truly multicultural, health-care providers must be aware of the cultural and ethnic determinants of health, the differing beliefs concerning health and medicine among ethnic communities, and the barriers faced by members of ethnic minorities in gaining access to health care.

Determinants of Health in Multicultural Communities

In general, mortality and morbidity rates are higher among members of cultural and racial minority groups.[17] Factors such as assimilation to the culture of the host country in terms of diet and lifestyle, the degree to which the ethnic traditions are maintained, and the extent of support systems in the immigrant community "have a significant bearing on the incidence and prevalence of diseases such as elevated blood pressure and coronary heart disease."[17]

The health problems of Canada's ethnic groups can be categorized as those problems which are particular to people of certain ethnic origins because of biological factors, and those which are due to environmental factors. For example, the incidence of lactose intolerance is as high as 80% - 90% among American Blacks, Bantus and Asians. Of great concern to physicians is the varying response patients of particular ethnic origins may have to certain medications.[18]

Problems arising from environmental factors include the mental health problems experienced by many immigrants and refugees, especially those from visible minorities. Both immigrants and refugees experience stress associated with migration, separation from family members and communities, loss of homes and possessions, an inability to speak either French or English, difficulty in finding suitable employment, negative public attitudes regarding immigrants and refugees, ethnocentrism and/or racism, and pressures of assimilation which affect family relations. These experiences can lead to feelings of alienation, loss of self-esteem and emotional disorders, placing migrants to Canada at considerable risk for mental illness.[19]

Cultural factors can also be included as determinants of health. Alcoholism is more prevalent among the French and Irish than among Jews and Italians, and some cultures consider obesity to be "healthy." Wife abuse is also tolerated in some cultures more than others, leaving the woman faced with the options of living with the abuse or being isolated from her community.[20]

Inaccessibility of Health Care

The factors which contribute to the inaccessibility of health-care services for members of ethnic minorities include their own cultural beliefs concerning health care and health practitioners, language barriers, a fear of racism and/or ethnocentrism, and, on the side of the health-care providers, lack of information regarding ethnic communities and health, lack of cross-cultural training and ethnically representative staffing, and an unwillingness to deliver health services in a culturally sensitive manner. Differing beliefs concerning health issues can significantly affect the approach to health care for members of some ethnic groups. For example, in many cultures birth control and open discussions of sex and sexuality are unacceptable. Although many cultural communities accept Western medicinal practices, there are many which prefer their own forms of treatment and delivery. Awareness of these differences is therefore vital to the implementation of multicultural health-care practices. Many people prefer to discuss their health problems with someone from an ethnic organization or with an immigration services worker rather than with a trained health-care practitioner, particularly when it comes to mental health.[21] This highlights the need not only for cross-cultural training, but for increased ethnic representation in health-care staff.

Language Barriers

Demographic profiles indicate that approximately 1% of Canadians are unable to conduct a conversation in either official language. Without proper translation and interpretation services, this language barrier can affect members of ethnic minorities at every stage of the health-care continuum. Educational materials that are only provided in the official languages fail to inform members of linguistic minorities about health promotion, disease prevention and how to recognize certain health problems. As well, much of the material designed to inform people about what health-care services and resources are available are only provided in English or French, which creates a further barrier to health care for multicultural communities.

Ineffective translation and interpretation services prevent many people from seeking health-care services, and may create problems for those who do. While many health-care facilities make attempts at translation, they often utilize kitchen or janitorial staff who happen to speak the same language as the client but who are not trained interpreters or health-care practitioners. As a result, much vital information gets lost in the translation, particularly when the client does not feel comfortable having her or his health problems translated by someone who may inform the rest of the client's community, and inappropriate assessments and treatment may result. Thus at every stage in the health-care system language barriers are detrimental to the health promotion, assessment and treatment of members of ethnic minorities.

Racism and Ethnocentrism

Members of visible minorities and ethnic groups often experience racist or discriminatory treatment from health-care practitioners. This behaviour may come in the form of negative comments or attitudes concerning immigrants and refugees, a lack of respect for the different health beliefs of ethnic communities, or stereotyping. The effects of this kind of treatment are two-fold: the patient receives improper or inappropriate treatment and may therefore develop further health problems, and as a result of the poor treatment the patient and others from her or his community are discouraged from seeking treatment in the future.

It is important to realize that the real difficulties in accessing health care do not arise from the traditional health beliefs and practices of ethnic communities. Cultural insensitivity on the part of the health-care providers is seen as the main obstacle for many members of ethnic minorities. For example, whereas out of the general population 30% of mental health clinic patients withdraw from their programs after the first interview, 50% of the patients from ethnic minorities do so. The complaint they make most frequently is that the mental health therapists do not provide treatment that is culturally and linguistically appropriate.[21]

Assimilation Versus Accessibility

The reluctance on the part of many in the health-care field to develop multicultural structures and policies may often be based on the belief that ethnic minorities should simply assimilate to the "Canadian" health culture, and that the health-care system should not be considered responsible for ensuring the accessibility of health-care services to members of cultural communities. This view is not only ethnocentric and unrealistic, it ignores the health implications of forced assimilation. Trovato and Jarvis found in 1986 that individuals who identified strongly with their own ethnic communities had lower levels of suicide than those who did not consider themselves to be part of a cohesive ethnic community.[21]

Organizational Barriers

Factors preventing health-care organizations from successfully addressing multicultural health needs include an unwillingness to become culturally sensitive; a tendency to adopt superficial solutions such as translators from the support staff; a lack of demographic and health data on ethnic communities; insufficient financial and human resources; a lack of training and skill development; an absence of monitoring and evaluative mechanisms; rigid, hierarchical and competitive organizational climates which are not conducive to change; and a lack of commitment from senior management.[21]

Human Resources and Education

Once a commitment to multicultural health has been made, significant changes to the organization must occur, starting with the staff. Health-care practitioners have usually had little education concerning the health profiles and needs of ethnic minority groups. Therefore, extensive cross-cultural training must be provided to and made mandatory for health services workers and students.[22] Emphasis should be placed on the fact that what may be seen by the health-care provider as an accessibility or educational problem may often be interpreted by the consumer as evidence of racism and/or ethnocentrism.

The education and training of health services providers must be accompanied by a change in hiring practices. As well as ensuring that properly trained translators and interpreters are provided, health-care facilities should also promote the hiring of health-care providers who are members of ethnic minorities. This kind of affirmative action policy will reduce the need for translators and interpreters and ensure understanding of the particular health problems of the community, as well as making the health-care facility more welcome for members of the ethnic communities.

1.2. LITERACY

Prevalence of Literacy Problems

The high prevalence of problems with reading both simple and more complex sentences in the Canadian population has already been highlighted in chapter four. One out of every four Canadians is "functionally illiterate." This has serious implications in terms of the ability to participate fully in society, especially in terms of obtaining access to information, making use of community services, and in compliance with medication and other health-related instructions. It is unlikely that remediation and upgrading reading programs will reach all those who could benefit, and therefore awareness and strategies to address illiteracy at the level of the patient and at the level of the community, especially in community-based health education and communication are needed.

Readability and Health

The essential component of literacy awareness in health is critical analysis of printed material that is developed or distributed in terms of its readability. It is estimated that 50% of patients cannot read or have difficulty with instructions at the fifth-grade level. A variety of general options exist that can be utilized for making changes to written material to increase its readability for its intended audience. They include: keeping sentences to 20 words or less (though varying the length); using simple concepts; using words that can be pictured; using active verbs; using material related to the patient's experience; and avoiding unnecessary words.[23] Pictorial cues, use of audiovisual media and stories using photographs or drawings can improve communication if there is a literacy problem.[24]

Medication Compliance

It is estimated that 30%-80% of patients do not use their medication properly. It has been shown that compliance can be improved with verbal reinforcement of instructions by a pharmacist, for example, but more effectively by a brochure or written instructions if these are understood. However, one study of patient education aids assessed the average reading level of the material at grade 11.8 ± 1.7, which was far too high for the average patient.[25]

1.3. CONSUMERISM IN HEALTH CARE

Citizens have always been involved in organizing the delivery of health services to their peers. Over the last century, citizens have become more involved in the health-care system, through voluntary health agencies and, lately, through consumer movements. In the context of health care, the word citizen is often interchanged with the word consumer or client. In the provision of human services, citizens and consumers are difficult to differentiate because each citizen "consumes" some health-care services (e.g., public health services: immunization, water purification, sanitation).

Major Concerns of Consumers About Health Care

Citizens of developed countries now regard health as a basic human right, and governments have responded by providing health care through various programs. However, in recent years, consumers have expressed concerns about inconvenience, the availability of health services, difficulties in communication between practitioners and consumers and inadequacy of health care for certain groups in society. Many people feel that the health-care system is designed for the convenience of the health-care practitioner, rather than the client. Many would prefer to take a more active part in decisions regarding their own health care, be better equipped to give informed consent, and to develop a more personal relationship with their practitioners than is allowed by the assembly-line approach.

In Canada, several aspects of women's health care are being questioned (e.g., unnecessary surgery, particularly hysterectomies). Women have expressed concern over the insufficient numbers of female practitioners, the medical monopoly on methods of birth control and abortion, the over-prescription of drugs for female patients and the paucity of home delivery and midwives.

Modes of Consumers Involvement

Clearly, consumers wish to be more involved in health care. The participation of the citizens involvement could be facilitated by:

(i) the sharing of knowledge by health authorities about the causation of diseases as many of these are related to the lifestyle of the population (e.g., smoking and lung cancer, chronic bronchitis and heart disease). Individual citizens can decrease the risk to themselves after gaining health knowledge and modifying their behaviour.

(ii) the participation of citizens in the formulation of health-care policies. Usually policy is planned as a result of both formal and informal discussions involving citizens. Citizen involvement is usually achieved by the establishment of a royal commission, major task force, or working group at the governmental level and by other health-related agencies initiating specific studies.

(iii) the creation of citizens' voluntary groups: citizens have tried to change the system by forming groups and lobbying.

Citizens may also participate in the health-care system through membership on hospital boards or committees and boards that are involved in the regulation of health professions.

Factors Inhibiting Cosumers' Involvement

Health care, and particularly medical care, is dominated by technology and professional super-specialization. It is very difficult for an individual to know whether the care s/he receives is good. The supply is restricted by the professional bodies through their licensing requirements, creating a monopoly. Also, the suppliers of health services can generate the demand for their own services (e.g., a dentist can ask a patient to come back once or 10 times for treatment of a dental disorder). In this context, the patient tends to do what the professional dictates.

Table 16.1: Consumer Rights in Health Care

I. Right to be informed

- about preventive health care including education on nutrition, birth control, drug use, appropriate exercise
- about the health care system including the extent of government insurance coverage for services, supplementary insurance plans, the referral system to auxiliary health and social facilities and services in the community
- about the individual's own diagnosis and specific treatment program including prescribed surgery and medication, options, effects and side effects
- about the specific costs of procedures, services, and professional fees undertaken on behalf of the individual consumer

II. Right to be respected as the individual with the major responsibility for his/her own health care

- right that confidentiality of his/her health records be maintained
- right to refuse experimentation, undue painful prolongation of his/her life or participation in teaching programs
- right of adult to refuse treatment, right to die with dignity

III. Right to participate in decision making affecting his/her health

- through consumer representation at each level of government in planning and evaluating the system of services, the types and qualities of service and the conditions under which health services are delivered
- with the health professionals and personnel involved in his/her direct health care

IV. Right to equal access to health care (health education, prevention, treatment and rehabilitation) regardless of the individual's economic status, sex, age, creed, ethnic origin, and location

- right to access to adequately qualified health personnel
- right to a second medical opinion
- right to prompt response in emergencies

Source: Consumer's Association of Canada

Health care is episodic and crisis-oriented and the consumer is often dissatisfied. However, once the crisis is over, the problems encountered by consumers are forgotten, and hence complaints are rarely made to providers.

Advantages and Disadvantages of Citizens' Involvement
Consumer participation should narrow the disparity in use of services between the rich and the disadvantaged sections of population, (i.e., overuse by the privileged and under-use by the poor, welfare recipients and rural residents). Increased interaction between the consumer and the health-care professional could accelerate lifestyle modification, such as losing excess weight. Consumer participation in health-care policy planning may provide a sense of gratification and accomplishment, as well as aid in changing the traditional attitudes of people towards health care. However, there are certain unavoidable disadvantages in consumer participation. Greater participation will involve, at least initially, increased expenditure as the consumer lacks knowledge about health care. Citizens will also have to be organized, requiring expenditure for public meetings, seminars and circulation of printed materials, and the newly established organizations will also involve operational costs. Another disadvantage of consumer participation is that technological advances make it increasingly difficult for the layperson to understand and evaluate the quality of the care received from the provider and this may lead to tension. Finally, the wide range of consumer interests and needs makes it difficult to satisfy everyone.

The Future of the Consumer Movement in Health Care
As consumers become more vocal and aware of their rights, several trends have developed. One of these is the consumers' bill of rights in health care. This describes explicitly the health-care providers' responsibility towards the consumer (Table 16.1). While not yet accepted by all, it is gaining widespread support. Further consumer movement will probably lead to citizens being elected rather than appointed to public health and hospital boards and regional and district health councils. There will be a trend towards more programs for the elderly, the dying, the handicapped and the socially disadvantaged, which will cater not only to the medical, but also to the psychosocial needs of these groups. Hospitals will be organized not only for the convenience of the providers, but also of the clients. There is evidence of structural and legal changes (see chapter 17, Regulation Health Professionals Act in Ontario) to enable increasing involvement in the regulation of health professionals, and this may extend to the selection of students for admission to professional schools.

2.   STRUCTURAL ISSUES IN HEALTH CARE

2.1.   INTEGRATION OF HEALTH AND SOCIAL SERVICES

There are many groups, for example the elderly and the poor, the disabled and those with multiple diagnoses, whose health problems dictate a need for a spectrum of health and social services. In many instances, the services available or provided are fragmented. Due to lack of correlation between boundaries for health services and social services, there is frequently poor co-ordination of services for the individual. Individuals may have to enter the system at multiple points and try to make their way through a haze of bureaucracy to receive services at a time when they are most vulnerable due to ill health. These difficulties are compounded by the disadvantaged social circumstances of many of these special groups in society.

One of the common themes in the recent provincial reports is that there should be an integration of health and social services. This desire is for a broad policy framework which better integrates the delivery of all human services, i.e., health and social services.[26] Community control of the planning and delivery of these services so that they are more responsive to local needs is a related objective and usually incorporated in integration.

Since 1970 Quebec has had an integrated system of health and social services after re-organization proposed by the Castonguay-Nepveu Commission. It is organized on a regional basis in the form of Regional Councils (CRSS). These have recently been given responsibility for allocating funding according to regional and sub-regional priorities.

Alberta, Nova Scotia, New Brunswick, Ontario and Saskatchewan have proposed models for integration in their recent provincial reports. In these provinces funding and policy direction would be still be centralized at the provincial level. A different model of integration was strongly supported by the Premiers Council on Health, Equity and Social Justice in Ontario. The recommendation was for decentralization of delivery of health and social services and integration of some of the major elements of the Ministries of Health and Social Services. A number of barriers, however, were identified.

At the provincial level these were: lack of strategic planning across health and social services; fragmented program funding and policy development; incompatible structures of the ministries, and lack of consumer input and influence at this level. At a local level it was considered that the different regional boundaries for each ministry; an uneven service distribution across the province and direct government delivery of services were barriers. Finally, each local area would need a mix of services and resources tailored to its needs, and these would differ between areas.

As previously indicated, integration of health and social services can occur at the executive level of both systems and devolve to a greater or less extent peripherally. It may also occur at a local service delivery level without the need for a total restructuring of health and social services. One model for the achievement of this objective is the community health centre (CHC)[27] which has developed in Canada in the last 30 years. Quebec has developed large number of community health centers which are described in more detail in chapter 13. Essentially a Community health centre is a community-oriented multi-disciplinary centre offering a broad range of services on a non fee-for-service basis. Staff, including medical staff, are salaried and the centres are run by their own community boards.

2.2.   REGIONALIZATION AND DECENTRALIZATION

As will be discussed later in this chapter, regionalization emerged as a major theme of the provincial reports. Consensus has not been reached on a definition of regionalization, but in a report on regionalization and health-care policy in Canada, it was defined as embodying:
"..the selective application over time of concepts contained within its *decentralization*, *geographic*, and *rationalization* dimensions by governments, agencies and pressure groups responsible for the planning, financing and delivery of health and related social services."[28]
The first dimension incorporates the decentralization of administrative authority to regional units with a local accountability because of centralization of resources for a geographic area. The geographic dimension relates to the mandated requirement to provide services to those in a defined region with coterminous boundaries for health and social services funding being regarded as highly desirable. Rationalization involves concepts relating to efficient use of scarce resources. The issue of regionalization is complex and involves re-organization of accountability and responsibility for the management and financing of health-care services. Federal government has had contradictory policies in this area, promoting centralization inherent in the concept of universality and uniform standards in health services, and also decentralization of administrative authority in order to meet local needs.

Most provinces had attempted to integrate health and social services at the level of provincial government and nearly half had amalgamated or integrated community-based social and health services at the delivery level. Ontario, Quebec, Saskatchewan and the Northwest Territories had developed regional health and social services councils either with advisory or executive powers.

2.3.   PRIMARY CARE

Primary health care is an issue of growing concern in the international health field.

Definition The ALMA ATA Conference Declaration of 1978[29] described primary health care as "essential health care based on practical, scientifically sound and socially acceptable methods and technology made universally accessible to individuals and their families in the community through their full participation and at a cost that the community and country can afford to maintain at every stage of their development in the spirit of self-reliance and self-determination."
Key to the notion of primary health care is the idea that there is no one system or set of conditions which can describe primary health care. The type of care provided in each community or country must be relevant to that community or country. Thus in order to determine what constitutes proper primary health care in

a particular society one must apply the relevant results of research into the social, biomedical and health sciences aspects of the community as well as results of public health experience. The minimum requirements of a primary health-care system do include, however, education regarding the prevailing health problems of the community and methods to prevent and control them, promotion of a healthy food supply and proper nutrition. Recently number of provinces have started examining the issues related to the delivery of primary health-care services and possible mechanisms to rectify them. Methods of delivery of primary care in Canada and some of the alternative delivery methods have been described in the section on organization of provincial health-care delivery and local services in chapter 13.

3.   REFORMING THE SYSTEM

3.1.   HEALTH GOALS

Many Commissions have pointed out the lack of formalized goals and objectives for the health system. Goals provide broad statements about the general direction of health programs, and objectives specify the desired results of programs. Objectives should be measurable targets for achievement in a certain time period. It was recommended that provincial governments set health goals and implement systems to monitor their achievement.

3.2.   HEALTH PROMOTION/DISEASE PREVENTION

The commission reports all pointed to the need for a greater emphasis on health promotion and illness prevention. Currently less than 3.5% of health-care dollars are spent in activities related to disease prevention and health promotion. A reduction in health-care costs could be achieved through health promotion and disease prevention strategies. It was recommended that a greater proportion of the health dollars should be spent on these programs. The common recommendation was for a shift from curative to preventive health and a corresponding increase in funding for research and development into health promotion and preventive medicine, typically to 1% of the annual health-care expenditures.

3.3. LONG-TERM CARE

There is no identifiable Canadian policy, terminology, information system or set of standards of care for long-term care. Each province has developed its own range of services and policies. Long-term care is required when health deficiencies impede the capacity to function independently and help is required from formal service providers. The people who use long-term care services are usually the elderly, people with disabilities, or people who have a chronic or prolonged illness. Additionally, there are significant numbers of younger people with disabilities who are either in long-term institutions or being supported by family and friends who they may outlive and then become dependent on the publically provided system. It should be recognized that the family provides the bulk, approximately 80%, of long-term care. Changes to the structure and coherence of family units will doubtless be reflected in the ability of family members, particularly women, to provide informal care. Long-term care covers a variety of services in a range of settings both in the community and in long-term care facilities.

The major theme that has emerged in long-term care internationally and in most of the Canadian provinces is an emphasis on community care for the maintenance of independence in the community for as long as possible. For the majority of elderly, this can be achieved through the provision of instrumental support services (such as home maintenance). Personal health-care services (such as bathing), may also be required for the elderly or disabled and these may be provided in the community, although more usually in an institutional setting. A spectrum of care settings is desirable with staged residential care allowing some supervision and support intervening between community independence and institutionalization. The predictors of institutionalization are advanced age, lack of spouse in the household, hospital admission in the previous two years, cognitive impairment and difficulty with taking care of personal care needs. Of these, cognitive impairment will be a determining factor for many elderly. It has been estimated that up to 65% of the very elderly will suffer cognitive impairment and provisions must be met for the necessary care.

In the above list, the issue of referral and access to long-term care has emerged as a major concern that has been addressed by a number of provincial strategies. The issue is whether a medical referral is required to the home care component of services and/or chronic care beds. Personal choice and consumer input in terms of preference would be incorporated. Cultural sensitivity and appropriateness would be stressed. The quality of life of residents of long-term care institutions is of concern. Commissions have recommended a shift away from institutionalization of extended care patients, as well as a reduction in extended or chronic care beds to 10% in short-term hospitals.

In summary, the trend in long-term care is to move towards maximizing independence in the community for the elderly and disabled through the transfer of resources from the institutional sector to the community. There is no national policy, however, and provinces are at different stages in adoption and development of more appropriate models of service delivery. There is need for leadership at top levels of governments of planning and policy for long-term care.

3.4.   MENTAL HEALTH SERVICES

The major trend in mental health services in recent times in Canada has been the de-institutionalization of mental health services that exists in most of the western world. The response has resulted in a concentration of the severely ill in psychiatric hospitals and the development of psychiatric units within general hospitals with the unintended effect of targeting predominantly those with neuroses and mild mental health disorders while neglecting "difficult patients." Concurrently a network of community-based services has evolved but is criticized in relation to lack of coordination and continuity of care as well as lack of availability of some types of supportive services. Most recently there has developed a recognition that the self-perceived needs of those with psychiatric illness are often at variance with the objectives of professionals and indeed families. Families often push for "cure" and further research, professionals for convenient modes of treatment and "containment," whereas consumer advocacy is emphasizing needs for employment, non-discriminatory housing, drop-in centres and a humanization of psychiatric services.

Deinstitutionalization
Commencing in the 1960s, the US depopulated its mental institutions so that by 1975 the number of in-patients had been reduced by two-thirds. The intention was to promote the integration and rehabilitation of in-patients in the community by means of a "community mental health program."[30] In Canada,[31] 0.4% of the population were in mental institutions in 1960 and half had been hospitalized for more than seven years. In 1961, the report of the Canadian Mental Health Association and the 1964 Report of the Royal Commission on Mental Health Services reflected a commitment to the philosophy of de-institutionalization. There was a call for the integration of psychiatric services into the physical and personnel resources of the rest of medicine, regionalization of treatment services and decentralization of management of psychiatric services and close cooperation and coordination between the psychiatric services in hospitals, clinics and community agencies. Between 1960 and 1976, there was a decrease of over 32,000 beds in Canadian mental hospitals. The bed capacity of psychiatric units in general hospitals was increased to almost 6,000 from less than a thousand beds. De-institutionalization occurred in all provinces and each adopted a different approach to the development of new delivery systems for services.

Two-Tiered System

The establishment of the psychiatric units in general hospitals resulted in the finding by psychiatric professionals of a new group of patients with mild psychiatric symptomatology whom they preferred to work with rather than the severely intractable psychiatric patients. This new group included those with mild depression for whom group therapy was appropriate. Those with more severe mental illness were unwelcome in these units. As there were fewer resources in the psychiatric hospital sector, the severely disabled were dislocated and had no sector in the psychiatric services who would respond to their needs. It soon became evident that the experience of the United States in the general ineffective functioning of the new community-based mental health system in caring for discharged patients was being reproduced in Canada. In addition to removal of resources for specialized psychiatric care, there was inadequate follow up in the community and lack of support for the mechanics of everyday living. The plight of the chronically disturbed ex-psychiatric patient frequently became homelessness or "ghetto type living," exacerbation of symptoms, despondency, suicidal tendencies and alienation by the community.

Community Mental Health Program

Most provinces developed community mental health programs. These included case management, rehabilitation, housing programs and other support services. However, in some provinces, by the 1980s there was fragmentation in the system, poor accountability, ineffective case management, high re-admission rates and lack of ability of hospitals to link with care in the community.[32]

Issues in Mental Health Reform

The sorts of issues that have arisen in strategic planning for mental health services in recent times are the following:[33]

(i) *Target population* Whose needs are to be met and what are the priorities? There needs to be a re-affirmation that those with major mental disorders and those who are significantly disabled comprise 1%-2% of the population that are most in need.

(ii) *Role of the general hospital psychiatric unit* The functions of these units must be reviewed and there is a need for greater availability of different types of resources such as holding beds, intensive "care" beds, day hospitals and crisis intervention services. The relationship to the community support system is also a paramount issue.

(iii) *Role of psychiatric hospitals* Justification of the need for the present ratio of beds/population is not apparent especially if community services are developed. It is estimated that there is a prevalence of 15/100,000 of the major psychiatric disorders and conditions which may be accompanied by severe behaviour disorders such as dementia, mental retardation, brain damage, paranoid schizophrenia and schizophrenia with severe regression. In Canada there are 4,000 psychiatric beds, and it is estimated that possibly only half are required.

(iv) *Political will to provide community support services* It has been demonstrated that community support services can prevent re-admission. What is lacking is adequate provision of resources for community care, and this depends to a large extent on political will.

(v) *Continuity of care* For continuity of care, it is necessary to have in place a range of services that are linked, monitored and evaluated for their provision of ongoing coordinated and integrated community support. An example of an approach to continuity of care is case management which is highly individualized in terms of assessment of need, planning and monitoring of services appropriate for a client.[34]

(vi) *Co-morbidity* The presence of another condition such as substance abuse increases the vulnerability of an individual with a psychiatric condition and needs to be addressed.

(vii) *Service integration* There is need for a single system with a coordinated structure that works for people. Mental health authorities are one model of a centralized co-ordinating structure.

(viii) *Consumerism* As previously indicated, a strong consumer movement is developing and challenging the system to incorporate its input into policy development and services. Some psychiatric patients who have had many dealings with the system of psychiatric care, including institutionalization tend to regard themselves as "survivors" of an inhumane and stifling experience which did not meet their needs. Expressed needs of consumers or "survivors" of the system are income maintenance, adequate housing, social support, non-traditional peer services such as peer support and self-help groups and more choices in life. These are not generally the focus of the traditional psychiatric care approach which supports dependency rather than independence.

Future Canadian Initiatives

There has been a significant resurgence in mental health services planning and policy development in Canada in recent times. Federal guidelines for review of policies and programs were developed following consultation with the provinces and released in 1988.[35] The document identified the importance of mental health for Canadians in the achievement of overall health. Mental health was defined in a broad sense as "the capacity of the individual, the group and the environment to interact with one another in ways that promote subjective well-being, the optimal development and use of mental abilities (cognitive, affective and rational), the achievement of individual and collective goals consistent with justice and the attainment and preservation of conditions of fundamental equality."

Nearly all provinces have undertaken strategies to reform the mental health system and existing services are briefly described in chapter 13. A number of provincial policy initiatives in strategic reform of mental health have been proposed giving indications of future directions.[36] The Graham Report[37] in

Ontario, which was released in 1988, recommended the following: that there be a community focus for the mental health system which should be integrated and interconnected with other components to reduce fragmentation, families and patients should participate in planning and allocation of resources, and the system be targeted for the seriously mentally ill and their families.

Quebec has also articulated a social definition of mental health care, largely due to the social advocacy group Regroupment des resources alternatives en santé mentale. Objectives are more centered on the individual, in terms of rights and participation, and in having needs met in an equitable manner, with a shift of emphasis away from those with serious mental illness as the target group.

3.5. PALLIATIVE CARE

The field of medicine can be divided into two categories, curative and palliative. These differ in their philosophy of treatment. Curative medicine is usually considered as traditional medicine whereby the objective is to ensure a patient's health. Palliation is defined as relieving without curing based on an acceptance of the inevitable. Palliative care is a relatively new field in Canada, having emerged in 1974 and the demand for care is increasing.[38] It is directed to those suffering from a terminal illness, whose needs are quite different from those with acute illness. Palliative care focuses on the management of pain and other symptoms and in meeting the psychological, emotional and spiritual needs of patients and family when curative care is no longer appropriate.

Palliative care should address issues such as psychological support, assistance in interpersonal skills, coordinated service delivery, symptom control, bereavement counselling, independent living, legal and financial issues, matters of spirituality, lifestyle, culture and religion.[39,40] Palliative care requires a multidisciplinary team approach often supplemented by volunteers. Palliative care can be given in the home or in an institutional setting. Acute-care facilities which are geared to diagnosis and treatment, however, do not usually provide the environment, skills and flexibility needed to provide support to terminally ill individuals and their families unless specialized facilities are available, such as designated palliative care beds and a palliative care team.[41] This program involves coordination of services by other health professionals, family support and bereavement counselling in addition to symptom management. In 1990, there were 345 palliative care programs identified in Canada and these comprised 767 designated beds. Each province reported operational palliative care beds.

There is a great diversity in the types of palliative care programs available in Canada and national standards for care do not exist. A recent decrease in the total number of palliative care programs prompted the formation of an Expert Panel on Palliative Care which was comprised of 10 health-care professionals from across Canada. In 1991 this panel made recommendations to the Cancer 2000 Task Force and extended their mandate to present a broad national vision for the palliative care community.[42] The Panel called for radical restructuring of resources and a different re-orienting of priorities so that palliative care and the relief of suffering is seen as an essential fourth phase of cancer control and receives equitable resource allocation.

4. SUMMARY

Canada aims to achieve equitable access to health for all Canadians. So far, equal access to medical care has been largely achieved by the universal system of hospital and medical insurance. However, total equality in health so that income, geography, age, gender or cultural background are not limitations will involve a re-ordering of priorities.

In recent years, it has been increasingly evident that the health-care sector must adapt to Canada's cultural diversity. Many health-care facilities today do not respond to the needs of the members of ethnic groups. This lack of responsiveness is due to cultural insensitivity; for example, the failure of many health professionals to recognize and accommodate differences in language, values or diet can discourage members of ethnocultural minorities from seeking effective health services. As well, the lack of responsiveness is due to the insufficient knowledge of the health-care provider with respect to particular health needs of the ethnocultural group. In addition, the cultural beliefs of members of ethnic communities concerning health care and health practitioners, language barriers, and a fear of racism and/or ethnocentrism prevent them from gaining full accessibility to health care.

The term "multicultural health" refers to health care which is provided in a culturally and racially sensitive manner. Health-care providers must become aware of cultural and ethnic determinants of health, the differing beliefs concerning health and medicine among ethnic communities, and the barriers faced by members of ethnic minorities in gaining access to health care. In order to have multicultural health, both community and professionals need education and awareness of the health status and concerns of ethnic communities in Canada.

One out of every four Canadians is functionally illiterate. This has serious consequences in terms of obtaining access to information, making use of community services, and in compliance with medication and other health related instructions. The essential component of literacy awareness in health is critical analysis of printed material that is developed or distributed in terms of readability.

Citizens of developed countries now regard health as a basic human right, and governments have responded by providing health care through various programs. However, in recent years consumers have expressed concerns about inconveniences, the availability of health services, difficulties in communication between practitioners and consumers and inadequacy of health care for certain groups in society. Citizens are also concerned about the availability of physicians in an emergency. Many people feel that their practitioner is too busy, uninterested or aloof to provide adequate information about their illness and treatment.

Consumers wish to be involved in health care, and their participation can be facilitated by: the provision of knowledge by health authorities about disease causation, the participation of citizens in the formulation of health-care policies and the creation of citizens' voluntary groups. Citizens may also participate in the health-care system through membership on hospital boards or committees and boards that are involved in the regulation of health professions.

Integration of health and social services is advocated as many health problems have psychosocial and economic components; health problems also occur as consequences of psychosocial and economic determinants. Through integration some structural impediments to services are removed and a more equitable access to human services can occur. A number of barriers to integration unfortunately exist. They include: lack of strategic planning across health and social services, fragmented program funding and policy development, incompatible structures of the ministries, and lack of consumer input and influence at this level.

Primary health care is an issue of growing concern in the international health field. It is defined as essential health care based on practical, scientifically sound and socially acceptable methods and technology made universally accessible to individuals and their families in the community through their full participation and at a cost that the community and country can afford to maintain at every stage of their development in the spirit of self-reliance and self-determination.

Long-term care is required when health deficiencies impede the capacity to function independently and help is required from formal service providers. Those using the long-term care services include the elderly, people with disabilities, or those with chronic or prolonged illness. The family provides the bulk of long-term care. The major issue that has emerged in long-term care is an emphasis on community care for the maintenance of independence in the community for as long as possible. The trend in long-term care is to move towards maximizing independence in the community for the elderly and disabled through the transfer of resources from the institutional sector to the community.

The major trend in mental health services in recent times has been the de-institutionalization of mental health services. This philosophy called for the integration of psychiatric services into the physical and personnel resources of the rest of medicine, regionalization of treatment services and decentralization of management of psychiatric services in hospitals, clinics and community agencies. Between 1960-1976, there was a decrease of over 32,000 beds in Canadian mental hospitals. De-institutionalization occurred in all provinces and each adopted a different approach to the development of new delivery systems for services. The establishment of psychiatric units in general hospitals resulted in a two-tiered system, and in response most provinces developed community mental health programs. The types of issues that have arisen in strategic planning for mental health services in recent times are the following: target population, role of general hospital psychiatric unit, role of psychiatric hospitals, political will to provide community support services, continuity of care, co-morbidity, service integration and consumerism. Nearly all provinces have undertaken strategies to reform the mental health system.

Palliative care is a newly emerged discipline which is directed to those suffering from a terminal illness, whose needs are quite different from those with acute illness. Palliative care is distinguished from curative care, in that curative medicine has the objective of ensuring a patient's health whereas palliation is defined as relieving without curing based on an acceptance of the inevitable. Palliative care focuses on the management of pain and other symptoms and in meeting the psychological, emotional and spiritual needs of patients and family when curative care is no longer available. Palliative care requires a mutlidisciplinary team approach often supplemented by volunteers. The care can be provided in the home or in an institution.

5.   REFERENCES

1. *Report from the Royal Commission on Hospital and Nursing Home Costs to the Government of Newfoundland and Labrador.* Government of Newfoundland and Labrador, St. John's, 1984.
2. *A Green Paper On Our Health Care System Expenditures and Funding.* Government of Newfoundland and Labrador, St. John's, 1986.
3. *Health for All Ontario.* Report of the Panel on Health Goals for Ontario. Ministry of Health, Government of Ontario, Toronto, 1987.
4. Ontario, Minister's Advisory Group on Health Promotion. *Health Promotion Matters in Ontario. A Report of the Minister's Advisory Group on Health Promotion.* Toronto: Advisory Group, 1987.
5. Ministere de la Santé et des Services Sociaux. 1) *Improving Health and Well-Being in Quebec*, 1989. 2) *A Reform Centered on the Citizen*, 1990. 3) *The Policy of Health and Well-Being*, 1992. Government of Quebec.
6. *Towards a New Strategy.* The Report of the Nova Scotia Royal Commission on Health Care. Government of Nova Scotia, Halifax, 1989.
7. *New Brunswick Report of the Commission on Selected Health Care Programs.* Commission on Selected Health Care Programs. Government of New Brunswick, Fredericton, 1989.
8. *Improving Health and Wellbeing in Quebec, Orientations.* Ministere de la Santé et des Services Socieaux. Government of Quebec, Ste. Foy, 1989.
9. *Manitoba Health Services Commission Annual Report.* Standing Committee on Medical Manpower. Government of Manitoba, Winnipeg, 1988 - 1989.
10. *The Rainbow Report: Our Vision of Health.* Premiers Commission on Future Health Care for Albertans. Government of Alberta, Edmonton, 1989.
11. *From Vision to Action: Report of the Health Care System Committee.* Premier's Council on Health Strategy. Toronto, Ontario, 1989.
12. *Future Directions for Health Care in Saskatchewan.* Saskatchewan Commission on Directions in Health Care. Government of Saskatchewan, Regina, 1990.
13. Mhatre S and Deber R. From Equal Access to Equitable Access to Health: A Review of Canadian Provincial Health Commissions and Reports. *Int J Health Services* 22(4):645-668, 1992.
14. Angus DE. *Review of Significant Health Care Commissions and Task Forces in Canada Since 1983-84.* Ottawa: Canadian Hospital Association, Canadian Medical Association and Canadian Nurses Association, 1991.
15. Wilkins R and Adams O. *Healthfulness of Life: A Unified View of Mortality, Institutionalization, and Non-Institutionalized Disability in Canada.* Montreal: Institute for Research on Public Policy, 1983.

16. Doyle R and Rahi K, eds. *Organizational Change Toward Multiculturalism.* Social Planning Council of Metropolitan Toronto, Toronto, February 1990.

17. Trovato F. Immigrant Mortality Trends and Differentials. In: *Ethnic Demography: Canadian Immigrant, Racial and Cultural Variations.* Halli I, Shiva S, Trovato F and Driedger L, eds. Ottawa: Carleton University Press, 1990.

18. Masi R. Multiculturalism, Medicine and Health, Part IV: Individual Considerations. *Can Fam Phys* 35(1):69-73, 1989.

19. Government of Canada. *After the Door Has Been Opened: Mental Health Issues Affecting Immigrants and Refugees in Canada.* Report of the Canadian Task Force on Mental Health Issues Affecting Immigrants and Refugees. Ministry of Supply and Services, Canada, Ottawa, 1988.

20. Masi R. Multiculturalism, Medicine and Health, Part V: Community Considerations. *Can Fam Phys* 35(2):251-4, 1989.

21. Tator C. Strategy for Fostering Participation and Equity in the Human Services Delivery System. In: *Organizational Change Toward Multiculturalism.* Doyle R and Rahi K, eds. Toronto: Access Action Council, 1990.

22. City of Toronto. *Multicultural Task Force on Access to Services.* Department of Public Health, Health Promotion and Advocacy Section, Toronto, February,1990.

23. Berg A and Hammitt K. Assessing the Psychiatric Patient's Ability to Meet the Literacy Demands of Hospitalization. *Hosp Community Psychiatry* 31(4):266-268, 1980.

24. Dunn M, Buckwalter K, Weistein L and Palti H. Innovations in Family and Community Health. *Fam Community Health* 8(3):76-87, 1985.

25. Mallet L and Spurill WJ. Readability Evaluation of Nine Patient Drug Education Sources. *Am Pharm* NS28(11):33-36, 1988.

26. Report of the Working Group on Regionalization and Decentralization. *The Language of Health System Reform.* Ottawa: Canadian Medical Association, 1993.

27. Sutherland R and Fulton J, eds. Community Health Services. In: *Health Care in Canada: A Description and Analysis of Canadian Health Services.* Ottawa: M. O. M. Printing, 1988, pp 219-227.

28. Carrothers L, Macdonald S, Home J, Fish D and Silver M. *Regionalization and Health Care Policy in Canada: A National Survey and Manitoba Case Study.* Department of Community Health Sciences, Faculty of Medicine, University of Manitoba, Winnipeg, Manitoba, Canada, 1991.

29. World Health Organization. *Primary Health Care.* Report of the International Conference on Primary Health Care, Alma-Ata, USSR, September 1978, pp 6-12.

30. Bassuk E and Gerson S. Deinstitutionalization and Mental Health Services. *Sci Am* 238(2):332-339.

31. Richman A and Harris P. Mental Hospital Deinstitutionalization in Canada. A National Perspective with Some Regional Examples. *Int J Mental Health* 11(4):64-83, 1989.

32. Wasylenki D, Goering P, Lancee W, Fischer L and Freeman S. Psychiatric Aftercare in a Metropolitan Setting. *Can J Psychiatry* 30(5):329-336, 1985.

33. Wasylenki D, Goering P and MacNaughton E. Planning Mental Health Services: 1. Background and Key Issues. *Can J Psychiatry* 37(3):199-205, 1992.

34. Bachrac L. Continuity of Care for Chronic Mental Patients: A Conceptual Analysis. *Am J Psychiatry* 138(11):1449-1456, 1981.

35. Health and Welfare Canada. *Mental Health for Canadians. Striking a Balance.* Ministry of Supply and Services, Canada, Ottawa, 1988.

36. Goering P, Waslenki D and MacNaughton E. Planning Mental Health Services: 2. Current Canadian Initiatives. *Can J Psychiatry* 37(3):259-263, 1992.

37. Provincial Community Mental Health Committee. *Building Community Support for People: A Plan for Mental Health in Ontario.* Ministry of Health, Government of Ontario, Toronto, 1988.

38. Vincent L, Dawson H, Trentowsky S and Muter M. Survey Underscores Challenge of Planning Palliative Care Services for Cancer Patients. *Ontario Medical Review* 57(10):17-22, 1990.

39. *Palliative Care Services Guidelines, Report of the Subcommittee on Institutional Program Guidelines.* Health Services Directorate, Health Services and Promotion Branch, Department of National Health and Welfare, Canada, Ottawa, 1989.

40. Palliative Care Services, The Royal Victoria Hospital. *The R.V.H. Manual on Palliative Hospital Care.* Montreal, PQ: The Royal Victoria Hospital, 1980.

41. Mount B. The Problem of Caring for the Dying in a General Hospital; the Palliative Care Unit as a Possible Solution. *Can Med Assoc J* 115(2):119-121, 1976.
42. Scott J. Palliative Care 2000: What's Stopping Us? *J Palliative Care* 8(1):5-8, 1992.

CHAPTER SEVENTEEN

Regulation of Health Professionals

The purpose of this chapter is to describe the various health professions and allied occupations. First, professionalism is defined and the historical background of the modern medical profession briefly outlined. Then the various health professions, para-professions and allied occupations are listed and briefly described. Their regulation and future trends in regulation are discussed. The 1990 edition of Health Personnel in Canada[1] listed 30 health occupations. The 1990 edition of the Canadian Hospital Directory[2] listed more than 50 health occupations specifically related to hospitals. There are more than 130 separate fields of employment in the health-care system. However, many are in administrative and support services. For purposes of this chapter, discussion is confined to those occupations directly involved with patient care.

1.   PROFESSIONALISM

The concept of "professionalism" is very difficult to define. Most writers list traits or characteristics normally attributed to the established professions. The significance assigned to the various characteristics varies widely depending upon the writer. According to the third edition of Webster's International Dictionary[3] the meaning of the word" profession" is as follows: "a calling requiring specialized knowledge and often long and intensive preparation including instruction in skills and methods as well as in the scientific, historical or scholarly principles underlying such skills and methods, maintaining by force of organization or concerted opinion, high standards of achievement and conduct, and committing its members to continued study and to a kind of work which has for its prime purpose the rendering of a public service." Similar descriptions can be found in various dictionaries and encyclopedias. Most definitions emphasize the public service or altruistic aspect of professionalism. Bohnen[4] states that this type of description is obviously an idealized one, and considering the influence wielded by the established professions, the foregoing definition undoubtedly represents the image projected by the professions themselves. The following is a list of characteristics commonly attributed to an established profession.

Specialized Knowledge and Skill There is a specific body of detailed knowledge and complex skills which is common and generally unique to the members of the profession, and which require a lengthy period of training to acquire. Professionals' extensive education and the importance of their role in society entitle them to the confidence of their clients and to a position of prestige.

Autonomy Professions are self-regulating, that is, they are governed by associations made up of members of the profession. The professional association sets standards for the practice of the profession, determines who is qualified to practice (licensing authority), and enforces uniformity of practice. A code of ethics is defined. Those who fail to meet the prescribed standard or who violate the code of ethics are disciplined by the professional association. Members are free to practice independently in the manner of their choice (within the aforementioned prescribed limits) and are not subject to bureaucratic control. Bucher & Stelling[5] state that even those members who choose to be employed by institutions or corporations rather than practise privately are generally free to create their own roles.

Service orientation Professionals deal directly with their clients, and their prime concern is to provide good service rather than to pursue self-gain. This does not necessarily imply altruism, simply that personal gain is secondary to service. The professional must be free of outside influence so that s/he can make unbiased decisions with only the client's welfare in mind.

Responsibility The professional makes important decisions on behalf of his/her clients. In the case of medicine, decisions may involve life or death. The client, not possessing the appropriate knowledge, cannot make the decision, so this decision making process is surrendered to the professional. The client trusts the professional and divulges confidential and privileged information. Hass & Sheffer[6] indicate that the professional, on the other hand, must be impersonal and objective in approach.

Recognition Members of established professions are recognized by the lay public as being "professional" and are accorded a certain degree of respect. In most cases, this recognition has also been extended by government, so that the established professions are accorded formal status by statute. However, non-professionals sometimes take exception to these" characteristics" of professions. The requirement of a difficult and lengthy period of training is seen as an obstacle for entry into the profession, restricting membership to an elite group. Friedson[6] states that self-regulation, particularly with regard to licensing authority, is a means of establishing a monopoly. Licensed members of a profession practice under a protective cloak of presumed competence whether or not they are actually competent. Incompetence or unethical behaviour is rarely punished, as members of the professions are reluctant to criticize each other. Uniform norms of practice inhibit innovation.

Many would deny that there is any reliable evidence that professionals are more service-oriented than non-professional workers. There is a strong movement, particularly in the field of medical care, towards individuals' accepting greater responsibility for themselves and surrendering less control to the professional.

Finally, many people today question the power and prestige enjoyed by the established professions.

The foregoing depicts quite opposite views of professionalism. The truth obviously lies somewhere in between. There is no question that the established professions occupy positions of power and prestige in our society. But social structure is dynamic. The medical profession in particular, has not always enjoyed the pre-eminence that it does today, as will be discussed in the next section. Furthermore, significant changes in both the status and the regulation of the professions are presently taking place.

2.   EVOLUTION OF THE MEDICAL PROFESSION

The practice of medicine is ancient, as evidenced by the trephined skulls of prehistoric man, and the recorded histories of Babylon, Egypt, India and China. However, the profession of medicine as it exists in the western world today is a relatively recent phenomenon. Western medicine had its beginnings in ancient Greece with Hippocrates and Aristotle, and with the founding of a Greek medical school in Alexandria in 300 B.C., which continued to operate during the heyday of the Roman Empire. After the fall of Rome, although the knowledge of the Greeks was preserved and translated by monks, little progress was made until the late middle ages. The practice of medicine was a trade which was learned by apprenticeship and had much the same status as other trades.

The first medical school in Europe was founded at Salerno, Italy, in the eleventh century. In 1221, the Holy Roman Emperor, Frederick II, decreed that no one would practice medicine unless he had attended the school at Salerno. This seems to have been one of the earliest attempts at regulating the practice of medicine. Later in the middle ages, medical faculties were established at universities in the major cities of western Europe. The first medical faculty at a university in the United Kingdom was founded in Edinburgh in 1726, and the first medical school in the United States opened in Philadelphia in 1766.

With the establishment of medical faculties at the medieval universities of western Europe, medicine joined the more traditional professions of law and theology as one of the "learned professions," and thus achieved some status. Although the mainstream of the medical profession was now formally trained at universities and medical schools, there was still little scientific basis to the art of medicine. The rapid expansion of scientific knowledge and the tremendous growth of universities which occurred in the late 1800s and early 1900s dramatically changed the practice of medicine. The scientific basis of medicine was established by the great discoveries of men such as Pasteur, Lister and Koch. Medicine became ever more closely connected with science, particularly following the Flexner report on medical education in the United States and Canada, which was published in 1910. Professional schools changed from institutions which had no prerequisites for admission to those which required high school graduation and then university training in the basic sciences. Professional courses lengthened from a few months of lectures to years of disciplined study. Concurrently, the effectiveness of treatment dramatically improved.

The physician became someone to be trusted and sought out in time of suffering, rather than one to be feared and avoided. At the same time, the great body of knowledge required to practise medicine increased the educational gulf between practitioners and patients, giving the profession an aura of mystique. All of these factors combined to enhance the prestige of the profession. The mainstream of the profession also achieved considerable influence with governments, so that by the early twentieth century, all developed countries had enacted legislation which made the medical profession self-regulating with powers of licensure and discipline. The fact that legislation was enacted indicates that the state recognized its own responsibility in regard to the regulation of the medical profession, but delegated this responsibility to the profession. Once the statutes were in place, the state tended to adopt a policy of non-interference and, in a sense, abdicated its responsibility. There were no government representatives on the governing councils of the professional associations. The medical profession achieved virtual autonomy.

The last two decades have seen the beginnings of a reversal in the evolution of professionalization described above. The scientific knowledge upon which medicine is based and the effectiveness of medical treatment have both continued to increase. Nevertheless, the authority of the profession, particularly the degree of autonomy enjoyed for the last half century or more, has been increasingly questioned. There are several reasons for this. First, the increasing democratization of western societies has decreased deference to all forms of authority. Secondly, the great increase in the general level of education, particularly among the large numbers of individuals employed in the other scientific disciplines and the social sciences, has removed the mystique once associated with the profession.

In Canada the most important deprofessionalizing factor has undoubtedly been the establishment of government-sponsored universal medical insurance. Now that the state pays for physician services, it has an obligation to its citizens to ensure that they are receiving good value for their tax money. The responsibility for regulating the practice of medicine, once delegated to the profession by the state, is in the process of being taken back. Although the profession still enjoys considerable autonomy, it is becoming increasingly accountable to government and consumers. The extent to which this has occurred and possible future developments are discussed in later sections.

3.   THE EVOLUTION OF OTHER HEALTH PROFESSIONS

An industrializing society has been described as a "professionalizing" society. The rapid proliferation of knowledge in all fields of science and technology has, in recent decades, brought about the establishment of many new professions, some of which are in the health-care field. In seeking professional status, these groups have tended to follow the model set by the older established professions. They have developed complex technologies, established lengthy periods of training, imposed strict registration requirements, developed codes of ethics, and have sought statutory recognition. Although many groups have been accorded professional status, it could be argued that few of them can be described in terms of the definition earlier quoted from Webster's dictionary. The word "profession" seems to have become more narrowly associated with specialized knowledge, and there appears to be less emphasis on the characteristics of autonomy, service orientation, and responsibility.

The evolution of the other health professions will not be discussed in detail here. Most of them have followed the same pattern established by medicine, but only dentistry has achieved a similar degree of autonomy. With the exception of nursing, they all have a much shorter history than medicine. For example, the world's first school of dentistry was established in Baltimore in 1840.

Medicine is the dominant profession in the health field. In achieving professional status, the main stream of medicine either eliminated, absorbed, or controlled competing disciplines. According to Torrance,[7] pharmacy and nursing, for example, achieved professional status only by becoming subordinate to medicine. Osteopathy and naturopathy/homeopathy managed to survive as separate entities, but only on the "fringe" of medicine and, in most communities, in restricted forms of practice. Optometrists and chiropractors also enjoy an autonomous status, but again are subject to many restrictions (e.g., practitioners cannot prescribe drugs or perform surgery). Most of the other health professions and allied technical trades have evolved as auxiliaries to medicine and are a product of the expansion of the scientific basis of medicine and the resultant need for support trades. This is true of physiotherapy, laboratory technology, radiation technology, etc.

Perspectives on Health Occupations[8] provides the educational and licensing requirements, function, future directions and a listing of the national professional associations for approximately 50 health occupations. For each province, the *Catalogue on Health Manpower Legislation*[9] provides the licensing and/or registration requirements for major health-care providers. Recently the legislation in Ontario has changed and this is discussed subsequently in this chapter. Similarly, a federal publication is available for certifying bodies, professional associations and accrediting agencies for various health occupations in Canada.[10] The next section of this chapter provides examples of how some of these professions are regulated in Quebec and Ontario.

4.   THE REGULATION OF HEALTH PROFESSIONS

The *Constitution Act of 1867* gave provincial governments the responsibility for health care. As discussed in earlier chapters, the federal government, in recent years, has acquired considerable influence in health-care matters through various cost-sharing arrangements under which provinces must meet certain conditions before being eligible to receive federal funds. Nevertheless, the legislation which regulates the activities of the various health occupations is provincial. It follows then that there are 10 different groups of legislation. Although generally similar, there are important differences. As stated in the previous section, the medical profession (and some other health professions) in Canada had achieved virtual autonomy prior to the introduction of universal medical insurance. Since then, most provinces have enacted, or intend to enact, legislation which ensures greater public control of the professions. The earliest and most significant of these changes occurred in the provinces of Quebec and Ontario.

4.1.   THE PROFESSIONAL CODE OF QUEBEC

The Professional Code of Quebec, enacted in 1973, places the regulation of all professions under one Act.[11] A total of 38 professions, 22 of them in the health-care field, are included. The Professional Code of Quebec is unique in that it defines what a profession is and establishes formal criteria by which an occupation gains statutory recognition as a profession. Each profession recognized by the act is governed by a professional corporation. The corporation is charged with the traditional functions of a licensing agency. It determines the qualifications necessary to enter practice, maintains a register of members of the profession, defines the scope of practice, regulates specialists' certificates, determines what acts may be delegated, collaborates with educational institutions regarding the training of professionals, and handles disciplinary matters within the profession. In addition, the corporation is charged with the ongoing supervision of the practice of the profession and is given broad powers to supervise the practices of individual members. This is a significant innovation. Traditionally, professional regulatory bodies have only disciplined members whose unethical or improper behaviour or lack of competence has been reported by third parties. The Professional Code of Quebec requires each professional corporation to maintain ongoing surveillance of the quality of individual practices, and it is empowered to take corrective measures such as, for example, to require refresher training. In addition, the Professional Code ensures that the administration of any given profession is not conducted exclusively by the members of that profession. Non-members of the profession are appointed by the Quebec Professions Board and are there to represent the government and to protect the interests of the public.

The Professional Code also establishes two overall supervisory and regulatory bodies. The Quebec Professions Board is a governmental agency composed of five members appointed by the Lieutenant Governor-in-Council (the Cabinet). It is responsible for ensuring that each corporation properly carries out its duty to protect the public. It monitors the performance of each corporation and is empowered to take corrective action when necessary. For example, it may require a corporation to issue a new regulation or revise an old one, and if the corporation fails to do so, the Board may act in its place. The Quebec Professions Board reports directly to the provincial Cabinet. The second new body is the Quebec Interprofessional Council. It is made up of representatives from each of the professions covered by the Code, and its function is to coordinate the activities of the professional corporations. It has no power to regulate, but can, of course, make recommendations to the Quebec Professions Board.

4.2. THE REGULATED HEALTH PROFESSIONS ACT OF ONTARIO (1991)

The Regulated Health Professions Act of Ontario[12] (RHPA, 1991) replaced the Health Disciplines Act of Ontario which was enacted in 1974.[13] One of the major aspects of the new Act is the expansion of the number of professions under its jurisdiction. The Health Disciplines Act was not as broad in scope as the Professional Code of Quebec in that it was restricted to the five health professions, namely those of physicians, dentists, nurses, pharmacists and optometrists, which were required to be licensed in the province (the distinction between licensing and certification will be discussed later). However, it was enacted for the same basic reason: to obtain greater public accountability in the regulation of the health professions. The expansion of the professions covered under the new Act to 24 including seven not previously covered by legislation is a major progressive step in the new legislation in Ontario. There are other features, however, and one reviewer characterized the legislation as a "template from which many future legislative efforts in health care will evolve."[14] The legislation is regarded as increasing equity within the health professions, reducing the role of the physician as the gatekeeper and increasing direct access for the consumer to a wider variety of professionals. It allows for the growth of new health professions, which can be included as they emerge and apply for regulation to increase their status.

The most revolutionary aspect of the legislation is that the professions are not defined by scope of practice but professionals are licensed to perform various procedures, or authorized acts, which are potentially dangerous and for this reason are controlled. Only five of the professions, medicine, chiropractic, optometry, dentistry and psychology are licensed to "diagnose" and the title "doctor" is also limited to these professionals. Other professionals are licensed only to "assess" and not diagnose. Neither diagnosis nor assessment are defined in the legislation, and interpretations are left for courts to determine. The new Regulated Health

Professions Act of Ontario is structured so that individual Acts regarding each profession's scope of practice and licensed acts follow a general section on Legal and Procedural Provisions which pertain to all the health professions included in the Act. This allows for the coordination of legislation regarding the professions as compared to the previous patchwork of legislation. The Regulated Health Professions Act of Ontario gives the Minister of Health broad powers to supervise the regulation of the 24 disciplines included, increasing accountability and protection of the interests of the public. The public good, rather than professional interests, has been cited by the framers of this legislation as its major objective. A Health Professions Regulatory Advisory Council, comprised of five to seven persons appointed by the Lieutenant Governor in Council, and excluding registered health professionals, shall advise the Minister on the inclusion, or exclusion of health professions from the legislation and proposed changes to scope of practice and licensed acts.

Each health profession is required to constitute a College which is responsible for regulating the practice of the health profession and to govern its members in accordance with the HPRA. The College is required to maintain standards of entry, qualification and practice and to establish and maintain standards of competence and ethics among its members. Each College is required to have a Council, which excludes members of health professions, for its governance. The RPAH Act, similarly to the Professional Code of Quebec, provides for public participation in the functioning of each of the colleges. Public members are appointed to the Council of each College by the Lieutenant Governor-in-Council. Meetings of Council, except in prescribed circumstances, are to be open to the public. In addition, a standard system of committees and a uniform method of handling licensing, hearings, and discipline is established for all Colleges.

The statutory committee structure for each of the 24 health professions included in the legislation is essentially identical. The actual membership of each committee and quorums will, however, differ. These are described under the specific profession. The committees are the: (i) executive committee, (ii) registration committee, (iii) complaints committee, (iv) discipline committee, (v) fitness to practise committee, and (vi) continuing competence committee.

The Health Disciplines Board established under the previous Health Disciplines Act continues as the Health Professions Board, which is an appointed body of from 12 to 20 members, none of whom is a health professional. The Board acts as an appeals agency to decisions made by the Complaints Committees and the Registration Committees of each College. It does not, however, hear appeals from the Disciplinary Committees. These are made directly to the Supreme Court of Ontario. The Disciplinary Committee Chairperson can assign a panel of three to five members for a hearing, one of whom must be a member of the public. The various committees which make up each College will be discussed under the individual professions.

The Minister, through Cabinet, may conduct investigations into the operations of institutions or practices, may require reports to be submitted by the professional

Colleges, review proposed changes in College regulations, and request that a College make, amend, or revoke regulations. If the College fails to do so, the Minister may act in the College's place (through Cabinet). Note that in Quebec these functions are carried out by the Quebec Professions Board, rather than directly by Cabinet.

At this point a distinction should be made between what is meant by licensing and certification. Certain health professionals are required to be licensed. That is, they must hold a licence in order to practice their profession, and all others are prohibited from such practice. Other professions and occupations are certified. In some cases, certification is controlled by government regulations, in which case individuals are prohibited from using the relevant title or claiming to be qualified in the occupation, unless they are appropriately certified and registered. They are not necessarily prohibited from performing some functions of the occupation. In some occupations, certification (registration) is done by voluntary organizations. This type of certification has no legal status but employers will frequently hire only those who are certified by their national or provincial associations, for example social workers.

4.3.   THE MAJOR PROFESSIONS

The three major health professions will now be described, as well as their regulatory organizations in Ontario where such exist.

4.3.1. Medicine

Physicians are required to be licensed in all provinces. Although each provincial College has its unique requirements for licensure, a certain standard of uniformity has been established. All provinces require the physician to pass the national examination of the Medical Council of Canada plus examination by the Royal College of Physicians and Surgeons of Canada for specialists, and examination by The College of Family Physicians of Canada, for family practice.

The licensing agency, The College of Physicians and Surgeons of Ontario, is made up of the following bodies, as detailed in the Regulated Health Professions Act:

The Council of the College   This is the overall governing body and board of directors of the College, and is made up of four members appointed by the medical faculties of four universities in Ontario, four to six lay members appointed by the Lieutenant Governor-in-Council, and 12 to 16 members elected by the membership at large. Its most important functions are the preparation of regulations for the profession as authorized by the Act subject to approval by the Minister, and the appointment of members to the following committees: Executive Committee, Registration Committee, Complaints Committee, Discipline Committee, Fitness to Practise Committee, and Continuing Competence Committee. All of these committees, with the exception of the Fitness to Practise Committee, have lay members.

The Executive Committee This is a committee drawn from the Council who act for the Council between Council meetings. Actions taken by the Executive Committee are subject to ratification at the next Council meeting.

Registration Committee This committee determines eligibility for licensure. The Registrar of the College, who is appointed by the Council, performs this function on a day-to-day basis, but s/he will refer any doubtful applications for licensure to the Registration Committee.

Complaints Committee This body investigates complaints made by members of the public or members of the College regarding the conduct of any member of the College. The procedures followed ensure that the member against whom the complaint has been made is given a fair hearing. The Committee may refer its findings to the Discipline Committee, or to the Executive Committee, or may direct that the matter not be referred further.

Discipline Committee The Discipline Committee is composed of 10 members of Council. It will consider allegations of professional misconduct or incompetence referred to it by the Council, the Executive Committee or the Complaints Committee. If it determines that the allegations are correct and that a member of the College is guilty of professional misconduct or incompetence, it may take the following actions: (i) revoke the license of the member; (ii) suspend the license of the member for a stated period; (iii) impose restrictions on the license of the member; (iv) reprimand the member; (v) impose a fine to the maximum of $5,000; (vi) direct that any penalty above be suspended for a period of time; or (vii) any combination of the above.

Fitness to Practise Committee This committee is composed of 12 members of the College. If the Registrar of the College has evidence that a member of the College may be incapacitated, s/he will report this to the Executive Committee, who in turn may appoint a board of inquiry. The board of inquiry will investigate the matter and report back to the Executive Committee. If appropriate, the Executive Committee will then refer the matter to the Fitness to Practise Committee which will hold a formal hearing. If the member is found to be incapacitated, the Fitness to Practice Committee may: (i) revoke the member's licence; (ii) suspend the member's licence for a stated period; or (iii) attach limits to the member's licence.

Continuing Competence Committee This committee is a new statutory committee under the RHPA required for the purpose of maintaining and enhancing the competence and standards of practice of members in the care of patients and in record keeping in relation to members' practices. The program established by the committee may involve written or oral tests of clinical knowledge, skill or judgment, requirement of member participation in continuing education and remediation programs and other modalities.

Medical Review Committee This is a committee which is not established under the RHPA, but rather under the Health Insurance Act.[15] It is, nevertheless, a committee of the College of Physicians and Surgeons composed of six members nominated by the College but appointed by the Minister, and two lay members, also appointed by the Minister. Its function is to review matters referred to it by the General Manager of the provincial health insurance plan with regard to the billing practices of physicians. Such referrals would occur if it appeared that a physician had billed for services not rendered, for services which were not medically necessary, for services which were not provided in accordance with accepted professional standards, or where the nature of services provided is misinterpreted. The Medical Review Committee, after reviewing the matter, may recommend to the General Manager that s/he refuse payment, reduce the amount of the payment, or require reimbursement from the physician. Thus it is apparent that the Medical Review Committee is a potent regulatory agency which functions in addition to the regular committees of the College as established by the RHPA. There is yet another way in which the practice of medicine is regulated, at least that part of the practice which is conducted within hospitals (see chapter 13).

4.3.2. Dentistry
Dentists are required to be licensed in every province. Graduates of approved Canadian dental schools are not required to write a licensing examination. They may obtain the National Dental Examining Board (NDEB) certificate upon application. Other graduates must pass an NDEB examination to obtain the certificate. The NDEB examination is recognized by all provinces. Specialists are certified by provincial licensing agencies. Most dentists are in private practice and are reimbursed on a fee-for-service basis directly by their patients. Some provinces have prepaid dental plans for children, and many corporations have prepaid plans for their employees and their dependents. In Ontario, the dental profession is now regulated in a manner similar to physicians under the RHPA.

4.3.4. Nursing
Nurses perform many functions depending on their location, their employer, and their appointment. Hospital nurses may perform general bedside nursing care, or may be employed in very specialized units such as intensive care, coronary care, renal dialysis, or neurosurgical units. Public health nurses deal with the community in such matters as immunization and health education. Many nurses hold administrative positions within hospitals or other institutions. Nurses who work in frontier communities frequently perform many of the functions normally reserved for physicians. In addition, nurses may be privately employed by physicians, chiropractors, private care institutions, and corporations.

   Registered nurses, and registered nursing assistants in Ontario are required to be certified/licensed by the College. Generally this means that they must have passed an examination prepared by the Canadian Nurses' Association (a national body). Nurses frequently cease employment for several years at a time (especially during the child-bearing years). If they have allowed their certification to expire, they may be required to take refresher training before being re-certified. Even if they have maintained their certification while unemployed, the institution hiring them may require refresher training. Quebec has a distinct and separate regulatory body for nurses. In Ontario, nurses are now regulated by the RHPA as described above. In other provinces, regulation is delegated to the voluntary professional organization.

5.   SEXUAL ABUSE OF PATIENTS

Sexual abuse of patients by members of health professions, in particular, the medical profession emerged as a prominent and distressing concern in some provinces, e.g., Ontario, Alberta and British Columbia in the early 1990s. Sexual abuse represents a transgression of the trust placed in a health professional. Due to the position of power of the health professional in relation to the patient, any suggestive or sexual behaviour or language in a clinical setting can be deemed inappropriate. In Ontario, a task force on the sexual abuse of patients which was an independent body commissioned by the College of Physicians and Surgeons made a series of recommendations following the review of evidence from patients reporting sexual improprieties on the part of medical practitioners. These recommendations were reviewed and released by the Council of the College of Physicians and Surgeons in late 1992.[16] They recommended that the Regulated Health Professions Act be amended to include a new section regarding actions of professional misconduct of a sexual nature with different levels of offence and penalties, such as fines or revocation of licence for the more severe offences. The legislative amendments have included a requirement that any health professional having reasonable grounds to believe a colleague had committed any of the the sexual offences must report this offence. Sexual abuse in the Regulated Health Professional Act is now defined as sexual intercourse or other forms of physical sexual relations between the practitioner and the patient; touching "of sexual nature" of the patient by the practitioner; or behaviour or remarks "of a sexual nature" by the member towards the patient. However, the legislation also states that the words "sexual nature" do not include touching, behaviour or remarks of a clinical nature appropriate to the service provided.

6. CURRENT ISSUES AND TRENDS

Earlier, it was mentioned that a recent process of deprofessionalization has begun. Legislation aimed at obtaining greater public control of the self-regulating professions has been enacted. This process is certain to continue. Some of the issues involved and trends which may be expected are discussed below.

Since governments are now paying most medical bills, they are likely to become more and more interested in the value they receive for the taxpayers' money, not only in terms of quantity, but also of quality. This could mean greater government involvement in the design of medical school curricula, in the licensing procedures of provincial colleges, and in the monitoring of individual practices. Periodic re-examination for re-licensure, enforced continuing education, and similar measures for ensuring the competence of licensed physicians could result.

The medical profession is certain to see increased government regulation as a threat to its freedom and autonomy. Reaction by the profession is likely to take two forms. First, the profession may become more politicized. Lobbying with governments may increase, as may efforts to enlist the aid of the public. Union-like activities (e.g., withholding of services) will probably become more common. Second, the profession may attempt to improve its own regulation. Stricter requirements for re-licensure, continuing education, peer review and evaluation of individual practices, may be imposed to forestall government action in these areas. Some degree of confrontation seems inevitable, but it is to be hoped that the issues described herein will be resolved in a manner which will lead to better health care for the Canadian people and in the long run a stronger, if less autonomous, profession.

The new legislation in Ontario also throws some light on the future direction on the regulation of health professionals.[17] It states that "the sole purpose of professional regulation is to advance and protect the public interest. The public is the intended beneficiary of regulation, not the members of the professions. Thus, the purpose of granting self-regulation to a profession is not to enhance its status or increase the earning power of its members by giving the profession a monopoly over the delivery of particular health services."

The other major change is that an increasing number of health occupations are demanding to be considered as professions and to participate in health insurance programs similar to physicians. This will create tension among the different health-care providers. Definitions of health professions will become restrictive and professionals will be equated with individuals with specialized knowledge and skill but not necessarily those with responsibility, autonomy and/or service orientation. Many more new problems will undoubtedly arise as both governments and consumers seek a greater voice in health care. One thing is certain, the last decade has brought many changes and the next decade will bring more.

7.   SUMMARY

This chapter examined the definition of professionalism, discussed the historical background of the modern medical professions, and listed and described the various health professions, para-professions and allied occupations, and discussed their regulation and future trends in regulation.

The concept of "professionalism" is very difficult to define, and hence most definitions consist of a list of characteristics commonly attributed to an established profession.   These characteristics include: specialized knowledge and skill, autonomy, service orientation, responsibility and external recognition.

Medicine is the dominant profession in the health field.   In achieving this status, the main stream of medicine either eliminated, absorbed, or controlled competing disciplines.   Other health professions have followed the same pattern established by medicine, but only dentistry has achieved a similar degree of autonomy.

Most provinces have enacted, or intend to enact, legislation which ensures greater public control of the professions.   The earliest and most significant changes occurred in the provinces of Quebec and Ontario.

The Professional Code of Quebec defines what a profession is and establishes formal criteria by which an occupation gains statutory recognition as a profession. Furthermore, each profession is governed by a professional corporation.   This corporation maintains ongoing surveillance of the quality of individual practices, and it is empowered to take corrective measures.   The Professional Code also establishes two overall supervisory and regulatory bodies: the Quebec Professions Board and the Quebec Interprofessional Council.

In Ontario, the Regulated Health Professions Act (RHPA) was enacted in 1991. One of the major aspects of the new Act is the expansion of the number of professions under its jurisdiction.   The RHPA was enacted to obtain greater public accountability in the regulation of the health professions.   The expansion of the professions covered under the new Act increased to 24.   The legislation is regarded as increasing equity within the health professions, reducing the role of the physician as the gatekeeper and increasing direct access for the consumer to a wider variety of professionals.   The most revolutionary aspect of the legislation is that the professions are not defined by the scope of practice but professionals are licensed to perform various procedures, or authorized acts, which are potentially dangerous and for this reason are controlled.

The RHPA gives the Minister of Health broad powers to supervise the regulation of the 24 disciplines included, and increasing the accountability and protection of the interests of the public. The public good, rather than professional interests has been cited by the framers of this legislation as its major objective.

Each health profession is required to constitute a College which is responsible for regulating the practice of the health profession and to govern its members in accordance with the HPRA.

The three major health professions are: medicine, dentistry and nursing. Physicians are required to be licensed in all provinces.   The licensing agency is made up of the following bodies: the Council of the College, the Executive Committee, the Registration Committee, the Complaints Committee, and Discipline Committee, the Fitness to Practice Committee, the Continuing Competence Committee, and the Medical Review Committee. Dentists, as are physicians, are required to be licensed in every province.   As well, in Ontario, the dental profession is regulated in a manner similar to physicians under the RHPA. Nurses perform many functions depending on their location, their employer, and their appointment. Registered nurses in Ontario are required to be licensed by the College.

A recent process of deprofessionalization has begun. Legislation aimed at obtaining greater public control of the self-regulating professions has been enacted and this process is certain to continue. The medical profession is certain to see increased government regulation as a threat to its freedom and autonomy. Reaction by the profession is likely to take two forms: the profession may become more politicized and/or the profession may attempt to improve its own regulation.

8.   REFERENCES

1. *Health Personnel in Canada 1988.* Ministry of Supply and Services, Canada, Ottawa, 1990.
2. *Canadian Hospital Directory 89-90.* Volume 37. Ottawa: Canadian Hospital Association, 1989.
3. *Webster's Third New International Dictionary of the English Language.* Springfield, Mass: G and C Marriam Co., 1971.
4. Bohnen L. *The Sociology of the Professions in Canada (Four Aspects of Professionalism in Canada).* Ottawa: Consumer Research Council of Canada, 1977.
5. Bucher R and Stelling J. Characteristics of Professional Organizations. *J Health Soc Behav* 10(1):3-15, 1969.
6. Freidson E. *Profession of Medicine.* New York: Dodds, Mead and Co., 1970.
7. Torrance G. Socio-Historical Overview: The Development of the Canadian Health System. In: *Health and Canadian Society,* Coburn D, D'Arcy C and New P, eds. Toronto: Fitzhenry and Whiteside Ltd, 1981, p 17.
8. *Perspectives on Health Occupations.* Ottawa: Canadian Medical Association, 1986.
9. *Catalogue on Health Manpower Legislation, 1985.* Federal-Provincial Advisory Committee on Health Manpower. Health Human Resources Division, Health and Welfare Canada, Ottawa, 1985.
10. *Directory of National Certification Bodies, National Professional Associations and National Accreditation Agencies for Various Health Occupations in Canada,* 1990. Health Human Resources Division, Health and Welfare Canada, Ottawa, 1990.
11. *Professional Code.* Statutes of Quebec, Chapter 43, 6 July 1973.
12. Regulated Health Professions Act (Ontario) 1993. Government of Ontario, Queen's Park, Toronto, Ontario, 1993.
13. *Health Disciplines Act (Ontario), Revised Statutes of Ontario, 1980, Chapter 196.* Toronto: Alan Gordon, Queen's Printer for Ontario, September 1981.
14. Pooley D. Regulated Health Professions Act, 1991. The New Benchmark for Future Health Care Legislation. *J Can Chiroprac Assoc* 36(3):161-164, 1992.
15. *Health Insurance Act (Ontario), Revised Statutes of Ontario, 1980, Chapter 197.* Toronto: Ministry of the Attorny General, March 1982.
16. College of Physicians and Surgeons of Ontario. *Task Force on Sexual Abuse of Patients. The Final Report, Nov 25, 1991.* McPhedran M. (Chairperson). Toronto:College of Physicians and Surgeons of Ontario, 1991.
17. *Striking a New Balance: A Blueprint for the Regulation of Ontario's Health Professions.* Ministry of Health, Government of Ontario, Toronto, 1989.

Appendices

APPENDIX A
Educational Objectives

1. CRITICAL APPRAISAL

i) Characteristics of Study Design including sources of bias
(a) RCT
(b) Cohort
(c) Case-Control
(d) Cross-Sectional
ii) Measurements
(a) Characteristics of measurement, distributions, error, reliability, terminology
(b) Measurement of central tendency, dispersion, variability
(c) Test validation - sensitivity, specificity, pre/post-test likelihood, predictive value
(d) Measurement of health and disease in a population
specific rates (e.g., age/sex)
• incidence, prevalence
• standardization
• odds ratio
• relative risk
• attributable risk
• case fatality ratio
• primary/secondary attack rates
iii) Sampling, including sources of bias
iv) Analysis
Tests of significance
• statistical vs clinical
• sample size
• p value, confidence intervals
• common tests (e.g., t-test, x^2)
• intro to multivariateanalysis
v) Efficacy, effectiveness, efficiency, compliance

2. CONCEPTS OF DISEASE AND INJURY PREVENTION AND CONTROL

i) Concept of natural history of disease
ii) Models of causation
iii) Approaches & limitations to classification of health, function & disease
iv)Levels of prevention
(a) Primary (e.g., immunization, lifestyle)
(b) Secondary (e.g., screening, periodic health examination)
(c) Tertiary (e.g., disability, rehabilitation)
v) Screening, surveillance, case-finding, contact tracing
vi) Strategies for control
Points of intervention
• host/agent/environment
vii) Prevention in clinical setting
Periodic health examination
• conceptual approach
• protection packages
• updates of protection packages

3. DATABASE, VITAL STATISTICS, DEMOGRAPHY, HEALTH STATUS

i) Uses and limitations of Canadian data sources
(a) Census
(b) Statistics Canada
(c) Registries
(d) Medical examiners-autopsy

---

* Source: Adapted from the Medical Council of Canada, Objectives for the Qualifying Examination, ed. Baumber J.S., 1992.

(e) Health surveys
(f) Birth certificates
(g) Death certificates
(h) Hospital, medical services data
(i) Workers' Compensation data
ii) Demographic characteristics of the population
(a) Age/sex/structure
(b) Compression of morbidity
(c) Mortality
(d) Fertility
(e) Implications to the health care system
iii) Health indices and health status
(a) Direct
• infant mortality rate
• crude mortality rate
• life expectancy
• causes of death
• specific health surveys
• potential years of life lost
• survivorship
• age/sex specific distribution of mortality
• disability days
• activities of daily living
• prevalence of disability
(b) Indirect
• percentage of low birth weight neonates
• percentage of communities with potable water
• risk factor distribution
(c) Correlates
• morbidity and utilization data
• gross national product
• socioeconomic status of individual
(d) Descriptive epidemiology of diseases and injuries in Canada
• motor vehicle injuries
• cardiovascular disease
• major cancers
• respiratory diseases
• common infectious diseases
• substance abuse

4A. HEALTH-CARE SYSTEM

i) Historical development and principles of health services

(a) British North America Act
(b) Hospital Insurance and Diagnostic Services Act
(c) Medicare
(d) principles of b & c
(e) Established Programmes Financing Act
(f) Canada Health Act
(g) international comparisons
(h) trends and issues in the evolving health system
ii) Organization of health services: federal vs. provincial
iii) Self-regulation of professions
(a) Peer review
(b) Audit
iv) Professional organization
v) Methods of physician payment
vi) Distribution and projections of health manpower
vii) Health resource allocation
viii) Institutional organization
(a) structure
(b) accreditation
(c) audit
ix) Role of voluntary organizations
x) Alternate delivery systems
xi) Women's health movement

4B. PUBLIC HEALTH SYSTEM

i) Role of public health system in
(a) Maternal and child health
(b) Home care
(c) School health
(d) Sexually transmitted diseases
(e) Inspection
(f) Disease surveillance
(g) Mental health
(h) Health promotion
(i) Biological
ii) Role of physicians in public health
(a) Medical health officer
(b) Epidemiologist
(c) Occupational health
(d) Role of the practising physician
iii) statutory responsibilities of the

practising physician
Reportable disease notification
iv) Outbreak investigation
v) National and international health
networks as relevant to the public health
system
vi) Product regulation
(a) Biologicals
(b) Drugs and pharmaceuticals
(c) Medical devices

5. OCCUPATIONAL AND ENVIRONMENTAL HEALTH

i) Exposure
(a) Long-term/low dose
(b) Multiple
(c) Mechanisms of toxic action
• cancer
• reproductive hazards
• respiratory diseases
(d) Routes of entry
(e) Types of exposures
ii) Standard setting
(a) Physical
(b) Chemical
(c) Biological
(d) Psychological
iii) Occupational diseases and injuries
iv) Occupational history taking
v) Risk assessment
vi) Ethics and occupational medicine
vii) Workers' Compensation Board functions
viii) environmental health
food, air, water

6. GROUPS WITH SPECIAL HEALTH-CARE NEEDS

i) Characteristics and health status
(a) Canadian Indian/Inuit/Metis
(b) Immigrants
(c) Low income/unemployed
(d) Elderly
(e) Disabled
ii) Service needs and availability

7. PSYCHOSOCIAL ASPECTS OF HEALTH

i) Health and illness behaviour and risk perception
ii) Compliance
(a) Barriers to individual
(b) Environmental & behavioural factors in compliance
iii) Family, social network and peer group alternatives to kinship
iv) Biopsychosocial, culture, gender and age effects on health
(a) Health beliefs
(b) Patients and providers
v) Health education and health promotion
Individual behaviour versus social change
• healthy public policy
vi) Lifestyle and the environment
vii) Modalities of health education
(a) Behavioural diagnosis & modification
(b) Health marketing
viii) Blaming the victim
Stigmatization
ix) Professional vs consumer control of health-related initiatives

APPENDIX B
Treatment of Common Sexually Transmitted Diseases*

1. TREATMENT OF GONOCCOCAL INFECTIONS

All patients treated for gonorrhea should also be treated for chalamydial infection.

FOR ADOLESCENTS, ADULTS AND CHILDREN (UNDER AGE 9)
(except pregnant women and nursing mothers)

Urethral, endocervical, rectal infection: Adolescents and Adults

Preferred (IM):	Alternative (IM):
ceftriaxone 250mg IM in a single dose PLUS doxycycline/tetracylcine (c)	spectinomycin 2 g IM in a single dose PLUS doxycycline/tetracycline (c)
Preferred (oral) (alphabetical order):	*Alternative (oral):*
cefixime 800mg orally in a single dose (d) PLUS doxycycline/tetracycline (c) OR ciprofloxacin 500 mg orally in a single dose PLUS doxycycline/tetracycline (c) OR ofloxacin 400 mg orally in a single dose PLUS doxycycline/tetracycline (c)	should only be used in areas with active monitoring for resistance to penicillin AND if the percentage of penicillin-resistant isoloates is < 3.0% (e) AND if the infection was acquired in the same geographic area

Pharyngeal infection: Adults and Adolescents

Note: ampicillin, amoxicillin and spectinomycin are not effective in pharyngeal infections and ofloxacin or cefiximine are not recommended at the present time due to insufficient data to support inclusion.	
Preferred:	*Alternative:*
ceftriaxone 250 mg IM in a single dose PLUS doxycycline/tetracycline (c)	ciprofloxacin 500 mg orally in a single dose PLUS doxycycline/tetracycline (c)

* Source: *Canadian Guidelines for The Prevention, Diagnosis, Management, and Treatment of Sexually Transmitted Diseases in Neonates, Children, Adolescents and Adults, 1992,* Health and Welfare Canada, 1992. Reproduced with the permission of the Laboratory Centre for Disease Control.

Urethral, vaginal, rectal infection: Children

Preferred:	Alternative:
cefixime 16 mg/kg orally in a single dose (max. 800 mg) (f) PLUS erythromycin (g) OR ceftriaxone 125 mg IM in a single dose PLUS erythromycin (g)	spectinomycin 40 mg/kg IM (max 2 g) in a single dose PLUS erythromycin (g). If isolate known to be susceptible to penicillin: amoxicillin or ampicillin 50 mg/kg orally plus probenecid 25 mg/kg orally (max 1 g) in a single dose PLUS erythromycin (g)

Pharyngeal infection: Children

Preferred:	Alternative:
**ceftriaxone 125 mg IM in a single dose PLUS erythromycin (g)	If isolate known to be susceptible to penicillin: **aqueous procaine penicillin G 100 000 U/kg (60 mg/kg) IM (max 4 800 000 U) PLUS probenecid 25 mg/kg orally ((max 1g) in a single dose PLUS erythromycin (g)

Notes for the previous tables

(a) For pregnant women and nursing mothers the treatment regimens for adults and adolescents should be followed except that ofloxacin and ciprofloxacin are contraindicated and doxycycline/tetracycline should be replaced by erythromycin 2 g/day orally in divided doses for at least 7 days OR if not tolerated erythromycin 1 g/day in divided doses for 14 days may be substituted (erythromycin estolate is contraindicated in pregnancy)

(b) Ceftriaxone, cefixime, amoxicillin and ampicillin should not be given to persons with cephalosporin allergy or a history of immediate and/or anaphylactic reactions to penicillins.

(c) Doxycycline 100 mg orally x 2/day for 7 days OR tetracycline 500 mg orally x 4/day for 7 days as treatment for chlamydial infection should always be included. Tetracycline is less expensive but compliance is better with doxycycline.

(d) Some experts feel that a dose of 400 mg of cefixime is adequate. The consensus of the experts contributing to these guidelines was that, until conclusive data became available, a dose of 800 mg is recommended.

(e) Contact your local public health authority if you are unsure about the situation in your area. If in doubt use Preferred regimen.

(f) Oral therapies are preferred in children. Recommendations for the use of cefixime are based on data showing efficacy in the treatment of infections caused by organisms similar to Neisseria gonorrhoeae. As there is limited experience with the use of cefixime in children with gonococcal infections antimicrobial susceptibility must be ascertained AND follow up culture assured. If follow up cannot be assured, use ceftriaxone 125 mg IM in place of cefixime.

(g) Erythromycin 40 mg/kg/day orally in divided doses (max 500 mg x 4/day) for 7 days as treatment for chlamydial infection, which should always be included.

(h) Neonates born to women with untreated gonococcal infection are at high risk of infection and require ceftriaxone 50 mg/kg IM (max 125 mg) in a single dose PLUS erythromycin syrup in age-appropriate doses for 14 days.

2. TREATMENT OF CHLAMYDIAL INFECTIONS

ADOLESCENTS AND ADULTS
(except pregnant women and nursing mothers)

Urethral, endocervical, rectal infection

Note: ofloxacin is not recommended at the present time due to insufficient data to support inclusion.	
Preferred:	*Alternative:*
doxycycline 100 mg orally x 2/day for 7 days	if tetracycline is tolerated : tetracylcine 500 mg orally x 4/day for 7 days OR for patients for whom tetracyclines are contraindicated or not tolerated erythromycin 2g/day orally in divided doses for 7 days OR if that regimen is not tolerated erythromycin 1g/day orally in divided doses for 14 days OR try another formulation of erythromycin OR sulfamethoxazole 1 g orally x 2/day for 10 days.

PREGNANT WOMEN AND NURSING MOTHERS

Urethral, endocervical , rectal infection

Preferred:	*Alternative in first 2 trimesters:*
erythromycin 2 g/day orally in divided doses (erythromycin estolate is contraindicated) for 7 days OR if that regimen is not tolerated erythromycin 1 g/day orally in divided doses for 14 days OR try another formulation of erythromycin.	sulfamethoxazole 1 g orally x 2/day x 10 days
	Alternative in last trimester:
	amoxicillin 500 mg orally x 3/day for 7 days (limited data exist concerning the efficacy of this regimen)

NEWBORNS, INFANTS, AND CHILDREN

Newborns and Infants	Children	
	under 9 years	9 years or over
During first week of life: Infants < 2000g erythromycin 20 mg/kg/day orally in divided doses. Infants > 2000g erythromycin 30 mg/kg/day orally in divided doses *> 1 week to 1 month:* erythromycin 40 mg/kg/day orally in divided doses. The above regimen should be given for at least 14 days. Note: topical therapy alone for conjunctivitis is not adequate.	*After 1 month of age:* erythromycin 40 mg/kg/day orally in divided doses (max 500 mg x 4/day) for 7 days OR sulfamethoxazole 75 mg/kg/day orally in divided doses (max 1 g x 2/day) for 10 days.	*Preferred:* doxycycline 5 mg/kg/day orally in divided doses (max 100 mg x 2/day) for 7 days OR tetracycline 40 mg/kg/day orally in divided doses (max 500 mg x 4/day) for 7 days. *Alternative:* for patients for whom tetracyclines are contraindicated or not tolerated: erythromycin 40 mg/kg/day orally in divided doses (max 500 mg x 4/day for 7 days or 250 mg x 4/day for 14 days) OR sulfamethoxazole 75 mg/kd/day orally in divided doses (max 1 g x 2/day) for 10 days.

NOTES:
- Erythromycin dosages refer to the use of erythromycin base. Equivalent dosages of other formulations (except the estolate which is contraindicated in pregnancy) may be substituted.
- If erythromycin has been used for treatment repeat testing after completion of therapy is advisable.

APPENDIX C
Health Protection Packages for the Periodic Health Examination

Chapter 11 described the conceptual framework of the health protection packages for different age groups. The recommended packages were updated to 1993 for prenatal to age 65 and over, and are given on the following pages. The letters A,B,C indicate the classification of the recommendations, and the letter R indicates that the recommendation was made only for a designated high risk group (see pages 277-278 for further details).

Health Protection Package (prenatal)

Target Condition and Recommendation	Manoeuvre	Best Current Estimate of Optimal Frequency of Manoeuvre*	Remarks
Postnatal asphyxia (B)	Detection during pregnancy of causative factors suggesting high risk. Fetal monitoring during labour	At first prenatal visit and during follow-up visits	High risk associated with toxemia, renal and heart diseases, diabetes, gynecologic anatomic disorders and previous obstetric problems (e.g., neonatal deaths)
Neural tube defect (B)	Determination of maternal serum alpha-fetoprotein (AFP) level by radio-immunoassay. If AFP value is elevated, supplement with amniocentesis and ultrasonography	At 16 to 18 weeks of pregnancy	Screening should be available to pregnant women on request if parents understand that confirmation of results may require amniocentesis and ultrasonography, and are prepared to accept therapeutic abortion if the fetus is affected
Down's syndrome (B)	Elicit information on patient's history. If positive, perform amniocentesis only if parents are prepared to accept abortion if an affected fetus is detected	At first prenatal visit	Positive history includes: - evidence that a parent carries a translocation of chromosome 21 - history of Down's syndrome in previous children or among close relatives
Rubella (A)	Hemagglutination inhibition test. Administration of gamma globulin to exposed nonimmune women if abortion is not acceptable	At first prenatal visit	- mother older than 35 years Repeat if a nonimmune patient is later exposed to the disease

Condition	Maneuver	Timing	High-risk notes
Toxoplasmosis (A)	Elicit information on exposure. Serologic testing for evidence of Toxoplasma gondii infection and counselling on hygiene for high-risk group	At first prenatal visit, every 3 months thereafter and at the time of delivery	High-risk patients are those keeping a cat at home or eating raw meat
Gonorrhea (A)	Cervical and urethral smears, and cultures of cervical and urethral secretions and of first-voided urine	At first prenatal visit	Repeat at 36 weeks for high-risk patients
Syphilis (A-R)	Serologic tests for syphilis	At first prenatal visit	Repeat tests in last trimester if woman considered at high risk
Malnutrition (C) and low birth weight (B)	Determination of serum protein and hemoglobin concentrations. Counselling on abstinence from smoking and on adequate protein and energy intake; measurement of height and weight	At first prenatal visit; At first prenatal visit and during follow-up visits	Repeat hemoglobin determination between 28 and 32 weeks; prevention of malnutrition may require provision of food supplements to some individuals and population groups.
Parenting problems (C), including child abuse and neglect (C-R)	Appropriate history taking; determine the parents' attitudes towards the coming baby; counselling	At first prenatal visit and as appropriate on the basis of clinical judgment	High and urgent research priority; identification of specific manoeuvres that would be effective in assessing and treating parenting problems
(A)	Home visitation for risk groups	As appropriate	High-risk groups: low SES, single parent, teen parent
Congenital malformations, multiple pregnancy, prematurity (B)	Ultrasound scan for all women	Once in second trimester	

* Although the optimal frequency of follow-up visits has not been established, they are currently scheduled as follows: once a month through the 28th week, twice a month from the 29th to the 36th week and once a week thereafter.

Target Condition and Recommendation	Manoeuvre	Best Current Estimate of Optimal Frequency of Manoeuvre	Remarks
Alcohol consumption (B)	Elicit information; counselling to reduce alcohol intake; abortion, when acceptable, if the risk to the fetus is considered high	At first prenatal visit and as appropriate on the basis of clinical judgment	Complete abstention from alcohol should be considered during pregnancy
Hypertension (A)	Blood pressure measurement	At all visits	Test for proteinuria at all visits
Blood group incompatibility (A)	Determination of blood group (ABO and Rh); screening for antibodies	At first prenatal visit	See Red Cross manual for techniques generally accepted throughout Canada
Rh-negative state	Screening for anti-D antibodies	At 20 weeks and then every month until 28 weeks; every 2 weeks thereafter	
	Administration of Rh hyperimmune globulin	At 28 weeks if no antibodies were detected in the previous 4 weeks. Within 72 hours of delivery if the newborn is Rh-positive and the mother had no anti-Rh antibodies	Other indications: - spontaneous or induced abortion - amniocentesis - administration of mismatched Rh-positive blood - significant uterine bleeding
Rh-positive state	Screening for antibodies	Between 32 and 36 weeks	

Condition	Action	Timing	Notes
Preterm labour (B)	Elicit information on previous history If history positive: - for incompetence of cervix (B): cerclage of cervix - for other causes (C): referral to high-risk pregnancy care centre	At first prenatal visit	Research priority: how to identify women at risk; to establish the effectiveness of current treatments
Recurrent spontaneous abortion (C)	Elicit history; if positive, investigate to detect possible causes of problem	At first prenatal visit	Possible causes: endocrinopathies, uterine anomalies, chromosomal anomalies, infections and corpus luteum defects
Bacteriuria (B)	Microbiologic examination of urine	In first trimester. Repeat each trimester and at 6 weeks post partum	
Breast feeding (A)	Counselling	At regular prenatal visits	
Postpartum depression (C)	Counselling; elicit symptoms	At routine postpartum visit	

Health Protection Package (for infants at birth and during first week of life)

Condition	Action	Timing	Notes
Postnatal asphyxia (B)	Clinical examination	At birth	Risk factors: respiratory metabolic and cardiac anomalies, sepsis and seizures
Hemorrhagic disease of the newborn (B)	Administration of 1 mg vitamin K_1	At birth	
Congenital syphilis (A-R) (B)	Serologic testing of cord blood	At birth	

Target Condition and Recommendation	Manoeuvre	Best Current Estimate of Optimal Frequency of Manoeuvre	Remarks
Ophthalmia neonatorum (gonococcal) (A)	Instillation of 1% silver nitrate solution into each eye or 1% tetracycline ointment or 0.5% erythromycin ointment	At birth	
Neonatal hypothyroidism (A)	Thyroxine testing with filter paper in all neonates; ancillary spot testing for thyroid stimulating hormone if necessary	During first week of life	Repeat serum thyroxine tests may be used as aids when necessary
Phenylketonuria (A)	Microbiologic inhibition assay (Guthrie) and fluorometric tests	Once each before and after 4 days of age	The tests may need repeating and supplementing with study of amino acids in plasma or blood by paper chromatography
Congenital dislocation of hip (A)	Clinical examination (flexion, abduction and Ortolani manoeuvre); confirmation by roentgenography	During first 2 to 3 days of life	
Interventricular septal defect (B)	Clinical examination and history taking	At birth and at discharge from nursery	Unwarranted labelling for benign murmurs may be harmful; additional tests, if necessary, include chest X-ray, echocardiography and cardiac catheterization
Problems of physical growth and development (B); malnutrition (C)	Clinical examination; measurement of length, weight and head circumference	At birth	Record findings on standardized growth chart. Research priority: to determine the optimal frequency of measurements

Condition	Manoeuvre	Timing	Notes / Research priority
Parenting problems (C), including child abuse and neglect (C-R)	Obtain family history; assessment of parent-child interaction; counselling	During regular visits and rooming-in	High and urgent research priority: identification of specific manoeuvres that would be effective in assessing and treating parenting problems
Strabismus (A)	Inspection of the eye; cover-uncover test	During first week of life	Research priority: to determine the optimal frequency of examination
Hearing impairment (A)	Check newborn's startle or turning response to a novel noise outside field of vision	Once before discharge from nursery	Research priority: to determine the value of each detection and of the detection strategies available
Blood group incompatibility (A)	Cord blood: Coombs' test and determination of blood hemoglobin and bilirubin levels. Clinical examination	At birth	
Accidents (home and motor vehicle) (A)	Counselling of parents about car seat restraints and home safety	Once before discharge from nursery	
Cystic fibrosis (B)	Iontophoresis sweat test on at least two occasions; clinical observation	At birth and at discharge from nursery	Siblings of cystic fibrosis patients
Toxoplasmosis (A)	Serologic testing for evidence of Toxoplasma gondii infection	At birth	When the mother was from a high-risk group
Iron-deficiency anemia (C)	Determination of blood hemoglobin concentration	At birth and at discharge from nursery	High-risk group: premature babies and those born of a multiple pregnancy, from iron-deficient woman or parents in low socioeconomic conditions
Hepatitis B (A-R)	Vaccination and Hep B immune globulin with first dose	Three doses of vaccine: first two, one month apart and last one six months later	

Target Condition and Recommendation	Manoeuvre	Best Current Estimate of Optimal Frequency of Manoeuvre	Remarks
HIV/AIDS (B-R)	Voluntary screening with *pcr* or virus isolation for neonates of HIV positive mothers	At birth	
Child maltreatment (A-R)	Home visitations for high-risk families	As appropriate	High-risk groups: low SES, single parent, teen parent

Health Protection Package (for newborns aged 2 to 4 weeks)*

Target Condition and Recommendation	Manoeuvre	Best Current Estimate of Optimal Frequency of Manoeuvre	Remarks
Congenital dislocation of hip (B)	Clinical examination (flexion, abduction and Ortolani manoeuvre); confirmation by roentgenography	Once	
Lower urinary tract anomalies (males) (C)	Ask about force of urinary stream	Once	
Problems of physical growth (B) and nutrition (C)	Clinical examination; measurement of length, weight and head circumference	Once	Record findings on standardized growth chart. Research priority: to determine the optimal frequency of measurements
Parenting problems (C), including child abuse and neglect (C-R)	Assessment of parent-child interaction; counselling	At each contact with the family	High and urgent research priority: identification of specific manoeuvres that would be effecting in assessing and treating parenting problems
Accidents (home and motor vehicle) (C)	Home assessment; counselling of parents about car seat restraints and home safety	Once	Home visit by allied health professional desirable

Congenital syphilis (A)	Serologic testing	If mother was at high risk
Night time crying (A)	Counselling	At each contact with the family	Weekly
Developmental delay (B)	Inquire of parents about achieved milestones	At each visit
Child maltreatment (A-R)	Home visitation for high-risk families	As appropriate	High-risk groups: low SES, single parent, teen parent
Strabismus (A)	Cover, uncover test and light reflex test	At each visit
Hearing impairment (A)	Response to clap test, ask parents about hearing	At each visit

* This package can be provided by a suitably prepared nonmedical health professional. Provision of the package in the home has important benefits, especially for disadvantaged families.

Health Protection Package 21 (for infants aged 2 months)*

| Interventricular septal defect (B) | Clinical examination and history taking | Once | Unwarranted labelling for benign murmurs may be harmful; additional investigations, if necessary, include chest roentgenography, echocardiography and cardiac catheterization |

* This package can be provided by a suitably prepared nonmedical health professional except for auscultation of the heart

Target Condition and Recommendation	Manoeuvre	Best Current Estimate of Optimal Frequency of Manoeuvre	Remarks
Diphtheria, pertussis, tetanus, poliomyelitis and haemophilium influenzae b (A)	Immunization	Once	First doses: - Only persons in good health should be immunized - The vaccine against pertussis is contraindicated in patients with a history of convulsions - In certain circumstances (e.g., for persons with immunodeficiency) it is better to use inactivated poliomyelitis vaccine (Salk) instead of oral vaccine (Sabin) - Poliomyelitis vaccine is contraindicated in certain conditions
Problems of physical growth (B) and nutrition (C)	History taking; measurement of length, weight and head circumference	Once	Record length and weight on standardized growth chart Research priority: to determine the optimal frequency of measurements
Developmental delay (B)	Inquire of parents about achieved milestones	At each visit	May be supplemented by the Denver Development Screening Test on the basis of clinical judgment
Parenting problems (C), including child abuse and neglect (A)	Assessment of parent-child interaction; counselling	During regular visit(s)	High and urgent research priority: identification of specific manoeuvre that would be effective in assessing and treating parenting problems

Strabismus (B)	Inspection of the eyes; cover-uncover test	Once	Research priority: to determine the optimal frequency of examination
Congenital dislocation of hip (A)	Clinical examination (flexion, abduction and Ortolani manoeuvre); confirmation by roentgenography	At each visit	
Hearing impairment (A)	Response to clap test, ask parents about hearing	At each visit	
Night time crying (A)	Counselling	At each contact with the family	
Accidents (home) (A)	Counselling to reduced risk factors in the home	During visits for other reasons	
Cystic Fibrosis (B-R)	Screening sibling of CF patient with sweat test	Once	

Health Protection Package 4I (for infants aged 4 months)*

| Diphtheria, pertussis, tetanus, poliomyelitis and haemophilius influenzae b (A) | Immunization | Once | Second doses:
- Only persons in good health should be immunized
- The vaccine against pertussis is contraindicated in patients with a history of convulsions
- In certain circumstances (e.g., for persons with immunodeficiency) it is better to use inactivated poliomyelitis vaccine (Salk) instead of oral vaccine (Sabin)
- Poliomyelitis vaccine is contraindicated in certain circumstances |

* This package can be provided by a suitably prepared nonmedical health professional; however, the responsible physician should be informed of the child's health status.

Target Condition and Recommendation	Manoeuvre	Best Current Estimate of Optimal Frequency of Manoeuvre	Remarks
Problems of physical growth (B) and nutrition (C)	History taking; measurement of length, weight and head circumference	Once	Record length and weight on standardized growth chart Research priority: to determine the optimal frequency of measurements
Developmental delay (B)	Inquire of parents about achieved milestones	Once	May be supplemented by the Denver Development Screening Test on the basis of clinical judgment
Parenting problems (C), including child abuse and neglect (C-R)	History taking and observation; counselling	During visits for other reasons	High and urgent research priority: identification of specific manoeuvres (continued on the next page) that would be effective in assessing and treating parenting problems
Accidents (home and motor vehicle) and poisoning (C)	Counselling	During visits for other purposes	If warranted by earlier assessment
Strabismus (A)	Cover, uncover test and light relfex test	At each visit	
Hearing impairment (A)	Response to clap test, ask parents about hearing	At each visit	
Congenital dislocation of hip (A)	Clinical examination (flexion, abduction and Ortolani manoeuvre); confirmation by roentgenography	At each visit	

Health Protection Package 6I (for infants aged 6 months)*

Condition	Intervention	Frequency	Notes
Diphtheria, pertussis, tetanus, poliomyelitis and haemophilium influenzae b (A)	Immunization	Once	Third doses: - Only persons in good health should be immunized - The vaccine against pertussis is contraindicated in patients with a history of convulsions - In certain circumstances (e.g., for persons with immunodeficiency) it is better to use inactivated poliomyelitis vaccine (Salk) instead of oral vaccine (Sabin) - Poliomyelitis vaccine is contraindicated in certain conditions
Problems of physical growth (B) and nutrition (C)	History taking; measurement of length, weight and head circumference	Once	Record length and weight on standardized growth chart. Research priority: to determine the optimal frequency of measurements
Developmental delay (B)	Inquire of parents about achieved milestones	Once	May be supplemented by the Denver Developmental Screening Test on the basis of clinical judgment
Parenting problems (C), including child abuse and neglect (C-R)	History taking and observation; counselling	During visits for other reasons	High and urgent research priority: identification of specific manoeuvres that would be effective in assessing and treating parenting problems.
Hearing impairment (B)	Check startle or turning response to a novel noise produced outside field of vision; check for absence of babbling	Once	Research priority: to determine the value of early detection and of the detection strategies available

* This package can be provided by a suitably prepared nonmedical health professional.

Target Condition and Recommendation	Manoeuvre	Best Current Estimate of Optimal Frequency of Manoeuvre	Remarks
Measles (A)	Immunization	Once	In high-risk groups: - Only persons in good health should be immunized - The vaccine is contraindicated in patients with a history of convulsions (no reaction has been reported in persons allergic to egg protein but caution is advised) - Revaccination at 12 to 15 months
Developmental delay (B)	Inquire of parents about achieved milestones	At each visit	
Strabismus (A)	Cover, uncover test and light reflex test	At each visit	
Congenital dislocation of hip (A)	Clinical examination (flexion, abduction and Ortolani manoeuvre); confirmation by roentgenography	At each visit	

Health Protection Package 12I (for infants aged 12 to 15 months)*

Measles (A)	Immunization	Once	The vaccine may be given alone or in combination with mumps and rubella vaccines, but: - Only persons in good health should be immunized - Measles vaccine is contraindicated in patients with a history of convulsions (caution is advised in persons allergic to egg protein)
Mumps (A)	Immunization	Once	Only persons in good health should be immunized. Mumps vaccine is contraindicated in persons allergic to neomycin and those suffering from altered immune states (caution is advised in persons allergic to egg protein)
Rubella (A)	Immunization	Once	Only persons in good health should be immunized
Problems of physical growth (B) and nutrition (C)	History taking; measurement of height, weight and head circumference	Once	Record length and weight on standardized growth chart. Research priority: to determine the optimal frequency of measurements
Parenting problems (C), including child abuse and neglect (C-R)	History taking and observation; counselling	Optional, during visits for other reasons	High and urgent research priority: identification of specific manoeuvres that would be effective in assessing and treating parenting problems

* This package can be provided by a suitably prepared nonmedical health professional, but the responsible primary care physician should be given an opportunity to review the health status of the infant at this stage.

Target Condition and Recommendation	Manoeuvre	Best Current Estimate of Optimal Frequency of Manoeuvre	Remarks
Strabismus (A)	Cover, uncover test and light reflex test	At each visit	
Hearing impairment (A)	Response to clap test, ask parents about hearing	At each visit	
Congenital dislocation of hip (A)	Clinical examination	At each visit	
Developmental delay (B)	Inquire of parents about achieved milestones	At each visit	
Accidents (home) (A)	Counselling to reduced risk factors in the home	During visits for other reasons	
Night time crying (A)	Counselling	At each contact with the family	

Health Protection Package 1C (for infants aged 18 months)*

Diphtheria, pertussis, tetanus, poliomyelitis and haemophilium influenzae b (A)	Immunization	Once	Fourth doses: - Only persons in good health should be immunized - The vaccine against pertussis is contraindicated in patients with a history of convulsions - In certain circumstances (e.g., for persons with immunodeficiency) it is better to use inactivated poliomyelitis vaccine (Salk) instead of oral vaccine (Sabin) - Poliomyelitis vaccine is contraindicated in certain conditions
Problems of physical growth (B)	History taking; measurement of height, weight and head circumference	Once	Record length and weight on standardized growth chart Research priority: to determine the optimal frequency of measurements
Behavioural and developmental problems (C)	Assessment of parent-child interaction; administration of the Preschool Development Questionnaire	Once	May be supplemented by the Denver Developmental Screening Test on the basis of clinical judgment
Developmental delay (B)	Inquire of parents about achieved milestones	At each visit	
Parenting problems (C), including child abuse and neglect (C-R)	History taking and observation; counselling	Optional, during visits for other reasons	

* This package can be provided by a suitably prepared nonmedical health professional.

Target Condition and Recommendation	Manoeuvre	Best Current Estimate of Optimal Frequency of Manoeuvre	Remarks
Accidents (home) (A)	Counselling to reduced risk factors in the home	During visits for other reasons	
Strabismus (A)	Cover, uncover test and light reflex test	At each visit	
Hearing impairment (A)	Response to clap test, ask parents about hearing	At each visit	

Health Protection Package 2C (for infants aged 2 to 3 years)*

Target Condition and Recommendation	Manoeuvre	Best Current Estimate of Optimal Frequency of Manoeuvre	Remarks
Problems of physical growth (B)	Measurement of height, weight and head circumference	Once	Record length and weight on standardized growth chart. Research priority: to determine the optimal frequency of measurements
Behavioural and developmental problems (C)	Assessment of parent-child interaction; administration of the Preschool Development Questionnaire	Once	May be supplemented by the Denver Developmental Screening Test on the basis of clinical judgment
Strabismus (B) and refractive defects (C)	Inspection of the eyes; cover-uncover test and visual chart test	Once	High research priority: to determine the optimal frequency of eye examination for strabismus and the value of presymptomatic detection of refractive defects

Hearing impairment (B)	Elicit history (particularly of retarded or defective speech development) and conduct clinical examination	Once	Research priority: to determine the value of early detection and of the detection strategies available
Dental caries (A)	Oral examination, plus roentgenography if indicated. Fluoride application is recommended for residents of areas without fluoridated water supply	Annually (from 2 years)	Preferably done in dental office. Research priority: particularly to establish the optimal frequency of examination
Pneumoccocal disease (A-R)	Pneumoccal to patient with sickle cell disease or splenectomy	Every 5 years	

Health Protection Package 4C (for infants aged 4 years)*

Problems of physical growth (B)	Measurement of height, weight and head circumference	Once	Record height and weight on standardized growth chart. Research priority: to determine the optimal frequency of measurements
Behavioural problems (C)	Assessment	Optional	As warranted by earlier assessments
Dental caries (A)	Oral examination, plus roentgenography if indicated. Fluoride application is recommended for residents of areas without fluoridated water supply	Annually	Preferably done in dental office. Research priority: particularly to establish the optimal frequency of examination
Pneumoccocal disease (A-R)	Pneumoccal to patient with sickle cell disease or splenectomy	Every 5 years	

* This package can be provided by a suitably prepared nonmedical health professional.

Health Protection Package CSE (for children aged 5 to 6 years, at time of school entry)*

Target Condition and Recommendation	Manoeuvre	Best Current Estimate of Optimal Frequency of Manoeuvre	Remarks
Diphtheria, pertussis, tetanus and poliomyelitis (A)	Immunization	Booster: once	Booster doses: -Only persons in good health should be immunized -The vaccine against pertussis is contraindicated in patients with a history of convulsions -In certain circumstances (e.g., for persons with immunodeficiency) it is better to use inactivated poliomyelitis vaccine (Salk) instead of oral vaccine (Sabin) -Poliomyelitis vaccine is contraindicated in certain conditions
Problems of physical growth (B)	Measurement of height, weight and circumferences of head, chest and arms	Once	Record height and weight on standardized growth chart. Research priority: to determine the optimal frequency of measurements
Behavioural and developmental problems (C)	Assessment of parent-child interaction; enquiry about educational progress	Once	
Strabismus (B) and refractive defects (C)	Inspection of the eyes; cover-uncover test and visual chart test	Once	Research priority: to determine the optimal frequency of examination

Condition	Procedure	Frequency	Remarks
Hearing impairment (B)	Elicit history (particularly of retarded or defective speech development) and conduct clinical examination	Once	Research priority: to determine the value of early detection and of the detection strategies available
Dental caries (A) and orthodontic conditions (B)	Oral examination, plus roentgenography if indicated. Fluoride application is recommended for residents of areas without fluoridated water supply	Annually	Verification that earlier examinations were done. Research priority: particularly to establish the optimal frequency of examination
Accidents (home, motor vehicle and water) (C)	Counselling	During visits for other purposes	Research priority: to establish the effectiveness of counselling
Tuberculosis (A)	Tuberculin sensitivity testing; immunization with bacille Calmette-Guerin vaccine and chemoprophylaxis as necessary	Once	For children in contact with tuberculosis patients or living in communities with a high infection rate

* The task force recommends that school health professionals ensure that all the detection manoeuvres in this package and in the packages recommended from birth on have been performed. This package is considered a very important encounter with the health care system and a mandatory checkpoint for verification.

Health Protection Package 11C (for children aged 10 to 11 years)*

Condition	Procedure	Frequency	Remarks
Rubella (A)	Immunization of girls	Once	If immunization has not been carried out before
Problems of physical growth (B)	Measurement of height, weight and circumference of head, chest and arms	Once	Research priority: to determine the optimal frequency of measurements

* The examination can be done anytime between 10 and 11 years.

Target Condition and Recommendation	Manoeuvre	Best Current Estimate of Optimal Frequency of Manoeuvre	Remarks
Behavioural and developmental problems (C)	Assessment of parent-child interaction; enquiry about educational progress	Optional	If warranted by earlier assessments
Refractive defects (C)	Testing with visual chart	Optional	High research priority: to determine the value of pre-symptomatic detection of defects
Hearing impairment (B)	Elicit history and conduct clinical examination	Once	Research priority: to determine the value of early detection and of the detection strategies available
Dental caries (A) and orthodontic conditions (B)	Oral examination, plus roentgenography if indicated. Fluoride application is recommended for residents of areas without fluoridated water supply	Annually	Preferably done in dental office. Research priority: particularly to establish the optimal frequency of examination
Accidents (home, motor vehicle and water) (C) Use of alcohol (C) Smoking (A) Problems related to sexual development (C)	Counselling Short counsellig & follow-up visits	At each regular visit, on the basis of clinical judgment	Research priority: to establish the effectiveness of counselling and type of training required for physicians

Health Protection Package 15C (for children aged 12 to 15 years)*

Condition	Examination	Frequency	Comments
Problems of physical growth (B)	Measurement of height, weight and circumferences of head, chest and arms	Optional	As warranted on the basis of clinical judgment
Accidents (C) Use of alcohol (C) Smoking (C) Sexual development (C) (unwanted teenage pregnancy) (B)	Counselling; counselling on sexual activity and contraceptive methods; recommendation of appropriate contraception; abortion if acceptable	Optional	As warranted. Research priority: to establish the effectiveness of counselling
Dental caries (A) Orthodontic conditions (B) Periodontal diseases (C)	Oral examination plus roentgenography if indicated; encourage daily oral hygiene. Fluoride application is recommended for residents of areas without fluoridated water supply	Annually	Preferably done in dental office. Research priority: particularly to establish the optimal frequency of examination
Malnutrition (B-R) (C)	Determination of serum protein concentration; history taking; measurement of height, weight and circumferences of head, chest and arms	At appropriate intervals on the basis of clinical judgment	Adolescent girls
Muscular dystrophy (B)	Determination of serum creatine phosphokinase concentration	Frequent testing may be required since there may be an overlap between values in carriers and in unaffected women	Female relatives of muscular dystrophy patients

* The examination can be done anytime between 12 and 15 years.

Target Condition and Recommendation	Manoeuvre	Best Current Estimate of Optimal Frequency of Manoeuvre	Remarks
Cancer of the cervix (B)	Papanicolaou smear	When first sexually active; recheck within 1 year	Girls should be tested as soon as they become sexually active

Health Protection Package 44WM (for women and men aged 16 to 44 years)*

Target Condition and Recommendation	Manoeuvre	Best Current Estimate of Optimal Frequency of Manoeuvre	Remarks
Poliomyelitis (A)	Immunization	Booster at age 16	Only persons in good health should be immunized. In certain circumstances (e.g., for persons with immuno-deficiency) it is better to use inactivated poliomyelitis vaccine (Salk) instead of oral vaccine (Sabin). The vaccine is contraindicated in certain conditions. Immunization of pregnant women is not contraindicated if protection is required
Tetanus and diphtheria (A)	Immunization	Booster every 10 years (optional for diphtheria)	Only persons in good health should be immunized
Alcoholism (C) Smoking (A) Motor vehicle accidents (C)	Elicit information on patient's history; counselling; provide effective contraceptive services to alcoholic sexually active women; control of underlying medical conditions	At first encounter and at regular and appropriate intervals thereafter	Research priority: to establish the effectiveness of counselling
Family dysfunction; marital and sexual problems (C)	Elicit history; counselling	Appropriate intervals based upon clinical judgment	Research priority: to determine the effectiveness of preventive manoeuvres

Condition	Method	Frequency	Notes
Hearing impairment (A)	Elicit history for high risk and conduct clinical examination. Noise control programs: hearing protectors	During visits for other reasons	Research priority: to determine the value of early detection and of the detection strategies available
Hypertension (A)	Blood pressure measurement	At least every 5 years	At every visit made for other reasons
Dental caries (A) Periodontal diseases (C) Oral cancer (C)	Oral examination, plus roentgenography if indicated; encourage daily oral hygiene	Annually	Research priority: particularly to establish the optimal frequency of examination
Rubella (A) (females)	Immunization of women at risk	Once	If immunization has not been carried out before, and provided the woman is not pregnant and will avoid becoming pregnant for the next 3 months
Cancer of the cervix (B) (females)	Papanicolaou smear	When first sexually active, but recheck within a year, then every 3 years to age 35 and every 5 years thereafter	For subjects at high risk: annual smears, particularly when early age of onset of sexual activity and multiplicity of sexual partners. Research priority: to determine the optimal age and frequency of taking smears
Muscular dystrophy (B) (females)	Determination of serum creatine phosphokinase concentration	Frequent testing may be required since there may be an overlap between values in carriers and in unaffected women	For female relatives of muscular dystrophy patients
Immunizable conditions related to international travel (A)	Immunization; prophylaxis	Varies with different conditions	

Target Condition and Recommendation	Manoeuvre	Best Current Estimate of Optimal Frequency of Manoeuvre	Remarks
Tuberculosis (A)	Tuberculin sensitivity testing; immunization with bacille Calmette-Guerin vaccine and chemoprophylaxis as necessary	On the basis of clinical judgment	For persons exposed to the disease through their work, in contact with infected people or living in communities with a high infection rate
Gonorrhea (A)	Smears of cervix and/or urethra; cultures of cervical and/or urethral secretions and of first-voided urine	At appropriate intervals on the basis of clinical judgment	Pregnant women should be tested; incidence higher in persons with a history of multiple sexual partners
Syphilis (A)	Serologic testing	At appropriate intervals on the basis of clinical judgment	Pregnant women should be tested; incidence higher in persons with a history of multiple sexual partners
Thalassemia (B)	Elicit history; laboratory screening; counselling	Once	For Asian, African and Mediterranean persons of parenting age who, having first been informed that no assistance is available to the carrier, still want to be screened. Research priority: to determine the effectiveness of preventive manoeuvres
Iron-deficiency anemia (C) and malnutrition (B)	History taking; determination of serum protein and hemoglobin concentrations; measurement of height and weight	At appropriate intervals on the basis of clinical judgment	Women in low socioeconomic circumstances; Indians and Inuit; food faddists
Cancer of the skin (B)	Inspection; counselling	At appropriate intervals on the basis of clinical judgment	High-risk groups: persons who work outdoors or are in contact with polycyclic aromatic hydrocarbons

Condition	Procedure	Frequency	High-risk groups
Tay-Sachs disease (B)	Measurement of resistance of serum hexosaminidase to heat inactivation	As part of premarital screening	High-risk groups: Ashkenazi Jews; amniocentesis can confirm the diagnosis if expectant parents are known carriers
Cancer of the bladder (B)	Cytologic analysis of urine	On the basis of clinical judgment	High-risk groups: workers occupationally exposed to bladder carcinogens, and smokers
HIV/AIDS (C-R)	Obtain history of sexual practices and injection drug use to identify high-risk people. For high risk: voluntary screening with ELISA and confirmatory test; repeat after 6 months for seronegative people	At appropriate intervals on clinical judgment At appropriate intervals on clinical judgment	High-risk groups: gay/bisexual men, injection drug users, prostitutes, sexual contact with people with HIV infection, multiple partners and people from countries with high prevalence of HIV infection
Pneumococcal disease (A-R)	Pneumococcal vaccine to patients with sickle cell disease or spleenectomy	Every 5 years	
Prostatic cancer (C)	Digital rectal examination	Annually for males over 40 years	
Coronary Heart Disease (B)	General dietary advice to decrease intake of total and saturated fat and cholesterol for men 30-69 years of age. Stepped fat modified diet (to which cholesterol-lowering drug is added if response is inadequate) for men 30-59 years with mean total cholesterol level greater than 6.85 mmol/L or LDL-C more than 4.90 mmol/L	On the basis of clinical judgment	High-risk groups: severly obese, premature CAD in first degree relative, smokers, hypertension, diabetes, previous history of stroke or peripheral vascular diseases

Target Condition and Recommendation	Manoeuvre	Best Current Estimate of Optimal Frequency of Manoeuvre	Remarks
Suicide (C-R)	Routine evaluation of suicide risk if there is evidence of psychiatric disorder (especially psychosis, depression or substance abuse), recent suicide attempt or death of family member through suicide	At each regular visit, on the basis of clinical judgment	Counselling and follow-up visit should be encouraged, also referral to a psychiatrist should be considerd. Research priorities include (i) evaluating identificaion of psychiatric disorders by family physicians; (ii) evaluating the effectiveness of preventive programs
Cystic Fibrosis (B-R)	DNA analysis for carrier states of CF genetic mutation	As part of premarital screening	High-risk groups: first degree relative of CF individuals
Unwanted Pregnancy	Identification of sexually active adolescents; counselling on sexual activity and contraceptive methods; recommendation of appropriate contraception	At appropriate intervals on basis of clinical judgment	Adolescent females
Hepatitis B (A-R)	Vaccination	Three doses of vaccine: first two, one month apart and last one six months later	Vaccination of special groups: patients on dialysis or blood products, health-care personel exposed to blood or blood products, patients in institutions for the developmentally handicapped and individuals with alternative lifestyles (e.g., drug addicts, gay men)

Health Protection Package 64WM (for women and men aged 45 to 64 years)*

Cancer of the colon and rectum (C-R)	Sigmoidoscopy or colonoscopy	Discretionary	High-risk individuals are first degree relatives of patients with colorectal cancer and women with a history of endometrial, ovarian or breast cancer
Retirement distress (C)	Final counselling examination before retirement as part of a series of periodic health examinations	Once	
Cancer of the breast (A) (female) High risk female: woman with a first degree relative with pre-menopausal breast cancer	Mammography plus physical examination of the breast Mammography plus physical examination of the breast	Annually for women aged 50-64 years Annually for women aged 35-49 years (discretionary)	Research priority: to determine - the separate benefits of mammography and clinical examination - the optimal frequency of these manoeuvres - the benefits in age groups other than the sixth decade, especially the fifth decade - the risk of harm from irradiation using current techniques - compliance in a non-selected population - the specific benefit of breast self-examination - the advantages of employing allied health professionals in screening programs
Hypothyroidism (C) (female)	Clinical examination in post-menopausal women	Every second year	High research priority: to determine if treatment of sub-clinical hypothyroidism alters the clinical course

* Same as package 44WM minus Rubella, Thalassemia, and Tay-Sachs disease plus the above four items.

Target Condition and Recommendation	Manoeuvre	Best Current Estimate of Optimal Frequency of Manoeuvre	Remarks
Pneumococcal disease (A-R)	Pneumococcal vaccine to patients with sickle cell disease or spleenectomy and adults age 55 and over living in an institution	Every 5 years	
Prostatic Cancer (C)	Digital rectal examination	Annually for males over 40 years	
Coronary Heart Disease (B)	General dietary advice to decrease intake of total and saturated fat and cholesterol for men 30-69 years of age. Stepped fat modified diet (to which cholesterol-lowering drug is added if response is inadequate) for men 30-59 years with mean total cholesterol level greater than 6.85 mmol/L or LDL-C more than 4.90	On the basis of clinical judgment	High-risk groups: severly obese, premature CAD in first degree relative, smokers, hypertension, diabetes, previous history of stroke or peripheral vascular diseases
Suicide (C-R)	Routine evaluation of suicide risk if there is evidence of psychiatric disorder (especially psychosis, depression or substance abuse), recent suicide attempt or death of family member through suicide	At each regular visit, on the basis of clinical judgment	Counselling and follow-up visit should be encouraged, also referral to a psychiatrist should be considerd. Research priorities include (i) evaluating identificiation of psychiatric disorders by family physicians; (ii) evaluating the effectiveness of preventive programs

Health Protection Package 65+WM (for women and men aged 65 and over)

Condition	Intervention	Frequency	Notes
Tetanus and diphtheria (A)	Immunization	Booster every 10 years (optional for diphtheria)	Only persons in good health should be immunized
Influenza (A)	Immunization	Annually	Health professionals should be alert to antigenic shifts of organisms in any given year. Contraindications: allergy to egg protein
Hearing impairment (B)	Elicit history and conduct clinical examination	During visits for other reasons	Research priority: to determine the value of early detection and of the detection strategies available
Hypertension (A)	Blood pressure measurement	At least every 2 years	At every visit made for other reasons
Dental caries (A) Periodontal diseases (C) Oral cancer (C)	Oral examination plus roentgenography if indicated; encourage daily oral hygiene	Annually	Research priority: particularly to establish the optimal frequency of examination
Cancer of the colon and rectum (C-R)	Sigmoidoscopy or colonoscopy	Discretionary	High-risk individuals are first degree relatives of patients with colorectal cancer and women with a history of endometrial, ovarian or breast cancer
Malnutrition (C) (B-R) Progressive incapacity with aging (B)	Assessment of physical, social and psychologic function	Every 2 years for ages 65-74. Annually for ages 75 and over	Home visiting is a useful detection procedure. Diagnosis should be de-emphasized; protection of abilities should be emphasized. Research priority: to establish the optimal content and frequency of assessment
Hypothyroidism (C) (female)	Clinical examination	Every 2 years	High research priority: to determine if treatment of sub-clinical hypothyroidism alters the clinical course

Target Condition and Recommendation	Manoeuvre	Best Current Estimate of Optimal Frequency of Manoeuvre	Remarks
Immunizable conditions related to international travel (A)	Immunization; prophylaxis	Varies with different conditions	
Tuberculosis (A)	Tuberculin sensitivity testing; immunization with bacille Calmette-Guerin vaccine and chemoprophylaxis as necessary	On the basis of clinical judgment	For persons exposed to the disease through their work, in contact with infected people or living in communities with a high infection rate
Cancer of the skin (B)	Inspection; counselling	At appropriate intervals on the basis of clinical judgment	
Cancer of the bladder (B)	Cytologic analysis of urine	On basis of clincial judgment	High-risk groups: workers occupationally exposed to bladder carcinogens, and smokers
Cancer of the cervix (B) (female)	Papanicolaou smear	Every 5 years or at appropriate intervals on the basis of clinical judgment	If prior smears have been abnormal. Research priority: to determine the optimal age and frequency of examination
Pneumococcal disease (A-R)	Pneumococcal vaccine to patients with sickle cell disease or spleenectomy and adults living in an institution	Every 5 years	
Prostatic Cancer (C)	Digital rectal examination	Annually for males over 40 years	

| Suicide (C-R) | Routine evaluation of suicide risk if there is evidence of psychiatric disorder (especially psychosis, depression, or substance abuse), recent suicide attempt or death of family member through suicide | At each regular visit, on the basis of clinical judgment | Counselling and follow-up visit should be encouraged, also referral to a psychiatrist should be considered. Research priorities include (i) evaluating identification of psychiatric disorders by family physicians; (ii) evaluating the effectiveness of preventive programs |

INDEX